HANDBOOKS

W9-AVS-395

ONTARIO

CAROLYN B. HELLER

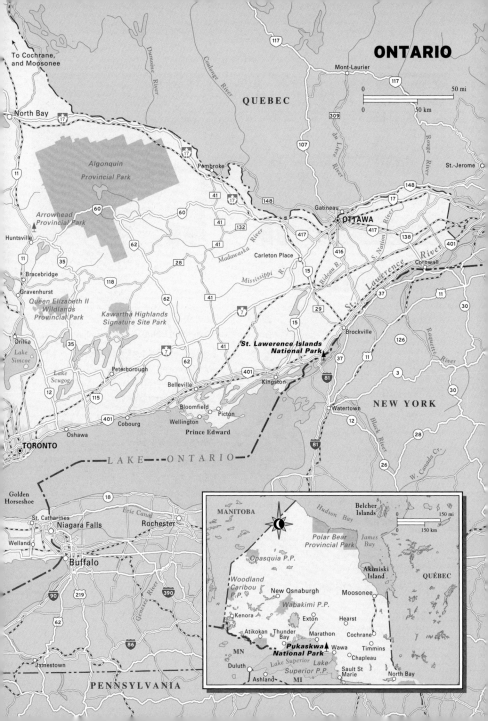

Contents

Discover Ontario

Buzzing urban centers with hip nightspots and eclectic shops. Creative chefs, ethnic eateries, and plenty of local food. Historic sites and modern museums. A relaxing get-away with outdoor adventures and activities for the kids. And all at a good value, too?

That's Ontario.

Toronto is Canada's most multicultural city. Then there's Niagara Falls, Canada's most-visited tourist attraction; Ottawa, the grand national capital; and theater festivals at Stratford and Niagara-on-the-Lake.

Beyond these well-known attractions, Ontario offers much more. Bordering four of the five Great Lakes as well as Hudson Bay, Ontario has more than 3,000 kilometers (2,300 miles) of shoreline. This vast forested province stretches from the southernmost point in Canada nearly to the Arctic.

With all that space, Ontario has countless options for outdoor adventures. You can skate along the world's longest ice rink, hike Canada's longest hiking route, or swim in the country's largest "swimming hole." You can go cycling, canoeing, whitewater rafting, cross-country skiing, even dogsledding. And while you may not think of Canada as a diving destination, you can even scuba-dive among shipwrecks on the floor of the Great Lakes.

Yet Ontario – home to Canada's most diverse population – delivers

plenty of cultural adventures, as well. More than half of Toronto's residents were born outside Canada, giving the city a vibrant multicultural buzz. You could breakfast on French croissants, lunch on Japanese *okonomiyaki,* and end your day with Italian, Greek, or Caribbean fare.

In central Ontario, Old Order Mennonites still travel by horse and buggy and sell homemade preserves at local farmers' markets. Roughly 25 percent of Canada's aboriginal population lives in Ontario, where you can hike through the wilderness with an aboriginal guide or watch a performance at a native-run theater. You can also follow the Underground Railroad, which sheltered fleeing slaves during the U.S. Civil War.

Ontario has laid-back college towns, Canada's first oil well, and scores of wineries, maple syrup makers, and apple orchards. You can take in a hockey game or take the train to an eco-lodge in a remote aboriginal community. You'll find the Thousand Islands and far more than a thousand things to do.

Planning Your Trip

▶ WHERE TO GO

Toronto

Canada's largest city is home to one of the most multicultural populations on the planet. The country's cultural hub, Toronto is a major center for film and theater, with a wide range of museums, eclectic boutiques, and ethnic neighborhoods. The reclaimed waterfront along Lake Ontario has performance spaces and art galleries, along with a lakeside walking and cycling trail. This diversity has made Toronto one of North America's most exciting cities for eating, shopping, and simply exploring.

The Niagara Region

Niagara Falls is a must-see attraction, and whether it's your first visit or your 50th, feeling the spray and watching the cascading curtains crash into the river below is still a thrill. Yet Niagara is more than just the falls. Here in Ontario's major wine-producing region, you can sip new vintages or sample local produce, while the well-preserved town of Niagara-on-the-Lake stages the Shaw Festival, one of North America's premier summer theaters.

Lake Erie to Lake Huron

West of Toronto, sprawling suburbs give way to university towns with nascent arts scenes, wide-open farm country, and sandy beaches. Theater fans flock to the Stratford Shakespeare Festival, while in St. Jacobs, Mennonite communities preserve their traditional customs. You can tour Ontario's newest wine district, visit Canada's southernmost point, or explore the region's dramatic

IF YOU HAVE . . .

ONE WEEKEND: Visit Toronto and Niagara Falls.

FIVE DAYS: Add a Stratford day trip or tour Algonquin Provincial Park.

ONE WEEK: Add Ottawa or Killarney Provincial Park.

TWO WEEKS: Add the Bruce Peninsula and Georgian Bay region, Manitoulin Island, and Sault Ste. Marie, including Lake Superior Provincial Park.

a Mennonite produce vendor, St. Jacobs

history as the terminus of the Underground Railroad. Finally, you reach Lake Huron, where you can sit by the shore and watch the sun go down.

Ottawa

Canada's national capital combines history, culture, and outdoor activities. You can tour Parliament and numerous grand museums, then skate on the Rideau Canal (the world's longest rink), or hike through sprawling Gatineau Park. For foodies, Ottawa has a branch of Le Cordon Bleu culinary school, a variety of food tours, and a growing number of innovative restaurants. This bilingual city knows how to party, too, hosting the nation's biggest Canada Day celebrations and dozens of festivals year-round.

Eastern Ontario

Water, water, everywhere—that's what you'll find in eastern Ontario. Along Lake Ontario (home to the Prince Edward County wine and local food hotbed), in the Kawartha Lakes region around the city of Peterborough, among the Thousand Islands in the St. Lawrence River, and along the Rideau Canal between Kingston and Ottawa, lakes, rivers, and inland waterways mean beaches, boats, or just relaxing by the water. Yet this region has plenty for the history buff, too, from aboriginal culture to Canada's early development.

Georgian Bay and Cottage Country

Getting away to "the cottage" is a long-standing Ontario summer tradition, and even without a cottage of your own, you can escape to

Beavertails, a fried dough snack named for Canada's official animal, originated in Ottawa.

the Caribbean-blue water at Indian Head Cove on the Bruce Peninsula

this lake district. The highlight is Algonquin Provincial Park, one of the province's largest protected green spaces.

Spectacular scenery surrounds Georgian Bay, where more than 30,000 islands dot the waters. Besides three national parks, several beautifully remote provincial parks, and sections of the Bruce Trail (Canada's longest hiking route), you'll find dramatic rock formations, Caribbean-blue water, and a network of lighthouses standing guard along the coast.

The North

Craving eco-adventure? Then northern Ontario is your place. Dotted with lakes and forests, it's prime canoe trip territory. Hiking trails crisscross rocky cliffs, while spectacular beaches line Lake Superior's shores. Yet the north is ripe for cultural explorations, too. Manitoulin Island's "Great Spirit Circle Trail" is a leader in aboriginal tourism, and you can ride the Polar Bear Express Train north to James Bay to experience the culture of Canada's largest aboriginal groups.

▶ WHEN TO GO

Summer is Ontario's busiest season, especially in the lake regions, the wine country, and around Niagara Falls. The weather is warm—often hot—and everything is open. Many summer theaters, beach destinations, and parks operate only between May and October.

If you don't need to travel in July and August, though, you'll often find better weather (sunny skies, moderate temperatures, and lower humidity) in early autumn. October is the peak of the foliage season, when weekend leaf peepers flock to the Ontario countryside. Fall visitors can avoid the crowds by staying in the cities on weekends and heading for the country during the week.

Late spring, from May to early June, is also a good time to travel in Ontario. Although you'll need to be prepared for some rainy days, it's relatively quiet, with fewer tourists and moderate shoulder-season lodging prices. Avoid late spring in the north or if you're planning to hike, canoe, or camp; it's black fly season, and the mosquitoes can be fierce, too. You'll encounter fewer pests in late summer or fall.

Ontario's winter, which begins in November and can continue into April, is cold and snowy—the season for skiing, snowshoeing, and skating. It's not a bad time for a city break, either; in Toronto or Ottawa the cultural calendars are full, and you can often find excellent lodging deals.

▶ BEFORE YOU GO

Passports and Visas

United States citizens need a valid passport, passport card, or Enhanced Driver's License for travel to Canada.

All other visitors need a valid passport and may need a visa. Visas are not required for citizens of the United States, United Kingdom, Australia, New Zealand, Mexico, Singapore, Japan, Republic of Korea, Israel, and most western European countries for stays in Canada of less than six months.

Vaccinations

No special immunizations or vaccinations are required to visit Canada, but it's always smart to ensure that your routine immunizations are up-to-date, particularly if you're traveling with children.

Transportation

Ontario's largest airport is Toronto's Pearson International, with flights from across Canada, the United States, Europe, the Caribbean, Latin America, and Asia. Ottawa is another air gateway, with flights from major Canadian cities, along with several U.S. and some European destinations.

VIA Rail, Canada's national rail carrier, can bring you to Ontario from across the country, whether you're starting from Vancouver, Jasper, Edmonton, Saskatoon, Winnipeg, Montreal, or Halifax. From the United States, Amtrak has train service from New York City to Niagara Falls and Toronto. Bus travel is a reasonable option, too, from the northeastern United States or eastern Canada.

Toronto's comprehensive public transportation system makes a car unnecessary if you'll be staying in the city. Ottawa and Niagara Falls, too, are easy to navigate without a car. Otherwise, outside the province's urban areas, you'll have more flexibility if you drive or rent a car.

Toronto's Union Station is a hub for VIA Rail, Canada's national rail service.

Explore Ontario

► THE BEST OF ONTARIO

This itinerary takes you through southern Ontario's highlights, from Niagara Falls to Toronto, the Muskoka Lakes, Algonquin Provincial Park, Ottawa, the Thousand Islands, and Prince Edward County. It's easiest to do if you have a car, or pick up a rental car when you leave Toronto (you won't need it in the city).

Day 1

Fly in to Toronto. Visit the CN Tower, the city's tallest building, with great views across the metro area, Lake Ontario, and the Toronto Islands. If you dare, take the Edgewalk, a thrilling walk suspended outside the tower, 116 stories above the ground. Back on earth, head west along Queen Street West to browse in the galleries, have dinner at one of the eclectic restaurants, and stop for a night-cap in one of the clubs.

Day 2

Rent a car and drive from Toronto to Niagara-on-the-Lake, about a two-hour trip. Start your visit in the historic downtown district, exploring the Niagara Historical Society Museum and the Fort George National Historic Site. Later in the day, you can tour the wineries; the area has more than two dozen. Have an early dinner, so you can see an evening play at the Shaw Festival.

Day 3

From Niagara-on-the-Lake, it's only a half-hour drive to Niagara Falls. Don't miss a ride on the *Maid of the Mist,* a deservedly popular boat tour that takes you under the falls. Niagara Falls has plenty of other attractions to choose from, including the White Water

Sharp Centre for Design, Toronto

TORONTO FOR CULTURE VULTURES

A long weekend in Toronto will give you time to enjoy the city's museums, galleries, and theaters. Base yourself at the arty **Drake** or **Gladstone** hotels, or choose a lodging in the Entertainment District, like the **Hotel Le Germain** or the **Thompson Toronto.** Plan a day trip to see a show in either Stratford or Niagara-on-the-Lake.

MUSEUM MEANDERING

Don't miss the **Art Gallery of Ontario,** which has an extensive collection of Canadian and International art in a striking building designed by Frank Gehry. Next door, you can't help notice the **Sharp Centre for Design** – it's the checkered box floating in the sky supported by yellow, blue, and purple "pencils."

For world culture, head to the massive **Royal Ontario Museum.** Nearby is the eclectic (and fun) **Bata Shoe Museum,** which houses more than 10,000 shoes – from doll-like slippers worn by Chinese women with bound feet to singer Elton John's sky-high platforms.

GALLERY GAMBOLS

Catch the streetcar to **Queen Street West** to see what's on at the small **Museum of Canadian Contemporary Art.** Wander into whichever galleries and boutiques catch your eye. Detour along Ossington Avenue for the newest galleries, shops, and restaurants.

Head east to **The Distillery District** to browse more galleries, including the **Artscape Building,** which houses more than 30 artist studios. Back downtown, see what's happening at the always-bustling **Harbourfront Centre.** Check out the **Power Plant Gallery** and the **Museum of Inuit Art,** and watch the artists at work in **The Craft Studio.**

ON STAGE AND SCREEN

Catch a concert at **Roy Thompson Hall** or the **Glenn Gould Studio,** a performance of the **National Ballet of Canada,** or a play at one of the Entertainment District theatres. A tour of the **Elgin and Winter Garden Theatre Centre** takes you through Toronto stage history in Canada's only "double-decker" theatre. If you're a movie buff, see what's screening at the **TIFF Bell Lightbox.**

THE PLAY'S THE THING

From Toronto, it's an easy day trip to either the **Shaw Festival** in Niagara-on-the-Lake or the **Stratford Shakespeare Festival** in Stratford. Take a behind-the-scenes tour of the theater before lunch, then see an afternoon matinee. You'll be back in Toronto in time for a nightcap to top off your weekend of art and culture.

Art Gallery of Ontario, Toronto

Horseshoe Falls' distinctive shape is especially visible from the air.

Walk and the Whirlpool Aero Car. Rent a bike to cycle the Niagara River Recreation Trail (if you're energetic, you can ride all the way to Old Fort Erie), or take a hike at the Niagara Glen Nature Reserve. Wrap up your day with Niagara Helicopters' Flightseeing Tour, a dramatic 12-minute flight over the Falls.

Day 4

The Twenty Valley is just a quick drive from Niagara Falls. Tour the wineries and enjoy a leisurely lunch at the elegant Inn on the Twenty. Then return north to Toronto.

Catch the ferry to the Toronto Islands for a late-afternoon walk or bike ride. Back on the mainland, wrap up your day with a light bite downtown or in the Entertainment District.

Day 5

Spend today exploring Toronto. Visit the massive Royal Ontario Museum in the morning; the smaller—and fun—Bata Shoe Museum is right nearby. Then either head north to Casa Loma, Toronto's "castle on the hill," or go downtown, stopping for a peameal bacon sandwich at the St. Lawrence Market on your way to the galleries and shops in the The Distillery District. If the timing is right, take a tour of the Elgin and Winter Garden Theatre Centre. Have dinner in Little India, in Koreatown, or The Danforth, Toronto's Greektown.

Day 6

After breakfast, tour the Frank Gehry–designed Art Gallery of Ontario (and notice the funky Sharp Centre for Design, one of Toronto's most distinctive buildings, next door). Try to time your gallery visit so you can take a guided tour of the collections. Later, walk around Chinatown and Kensington Market, stopping to eat along the way. If you're not too tired, see a play at one of the downtown theaters.

Day 7

Today you'll drive about three hours northeast to the Muskoka Cottage Country. Stop off along the way in Gravenhurst and visit Muskoka Wharf, where you can take a cruise on a restored steamship, tour a heritage boat museum. Continue on to Bracebridge and browse the shops in the cute downtown; be sure to sample a butter tart at one of the cafés. Continue on to Huntsville, where you'll have dinner and spend the night.

Muskoka Wharf in Gravenhurst

Day 8

Coming from Huntsville, you'll enter Algonquin Provincial Park through the West Gate. Algonquin Park measures over 7,500 square kilometers (nearly 3,000 square miles), so there's plenty to explore. Try to schedule one of your Algonquin days for a Thursday, so you can join in the evening Wolf Howl. Stop and see the exhibits at the Algonquin Visitor Centre; there's usually an interesting nature program happening, as well. Spend the night in the park or return to Huntsville for the evening.

Day 9

Return to Algonquin Provincial Park and choose a hiking trail, or visit the Portage Store to rent a canoe or arrange a half-day canoe trip. Another worthwhile stop is the Algonquin Logging Museum. Either stay in the park or return to your Huntsville accommodations.

Day 10

Drive out the park's East Gate, following Highway 60 east for 3.5–4 hours toward Ottawa. After checking in to your Ottawa hotel, take a stroll along the Rideau Canal (and pay a quick visit to the ByWard Museum to get an introduction to the city's early days). Then have dinner at Zen Kitchen; even if you're not a vegetarian, the creative vegan fare is delicious.

Day 11

Cross to the Gatineau side of the Ottawa River to visit the fascinating Canadian Museum of Civilization, where you can learn almost anything you want to know about Canadian history and culture. If you're not museumed out, return to the Ottawa side and visit either the National Gallery of Canada or the Canadian War Museum. Stop for an afternoon tea at the elegant Fairmont Château Laurier, then browse the shops and galleries around the ByWard Market. Stay for dinner and catch some live music at one of the clubs.

Day 12

Get to the Parliament Buildings first thing in the morning to take a tour (it's less crowded early in the day). If you're visiting in July or August, watch the Changing of the Guard, complete with red-coated, fur-hat-wearing guards. Visit any of the museums you missed yesterday, or take a food tour of ByWard Market. If you're feeling energetic, go for an afternoon hike in Gatineau Park. Have dinner in Chinatown or in the Wellington West neighborhood, then see a concert or play at the National Arts Centre or the Great Canadian Theatre Company.

Day 13

Check out of your Ottawa hotel and drive south along the Rideau Canal, stopping in the town of Smiths Falls to tour the Rideau Canal Museum and the adjacent lock station. Continue south to Gananoque, where you'll spend the night. If you've arrived before sunset, take an early-evening Thousand Islands cruise.

Day 14

If you didn't get to cruise the Thousand Islands last night, take a boat tour first thing this morning, or go kayaking among the Islands. Drive to Kingston in time for lunch. Visit the Bellevue House National Historic Site (the former home of Sir John A. Macdonald, Canada's first prime minister), stop into the quirky Penitentiary Museum, and then tour Fort Henry. If you're visiting in July or August, try to attend

the Changing of the Guard, Ottawa

the Sunset Ceremonies at the fort, with military music, gun salutes, and fireworks over the harbor. Otherwise, take a walk along the waterfront or browse the shops on Princess Street before having dinner in a downtown bistro.

The next morning, pick up some snacks at the Kingston Public Market or the Pan Chancho Bakery for your drive back to Toronto.

▶ GEORGIAN BAY CIRCLE TOUR

The best time for this tour, which takes in the striking natural scenery around Georgian Bay, is late summer or early fall. The autumn is especially lovely, as the leaves put on their vibrant color show. Just wrap up the trip before Canadian Thanksgiving (the second weekend in October), when the ferry to Manitoulin Island stops running and many of the region's parks and attractions close for the season.

Day 1

The Bruce Peninsula is about a four-hour drive from Toronto. Check into a hotel in Tobermory or set up camp in Bruce Peninsula National Park, then stop into the National Park Visitor Centre to learn more about the region. Climb the Lookout Tower to take in the views, then hike to the Grotto and the beautiful Indian Head Cove, with its turquoise waters and intricate rock formations. Back in town, have dinner in a café on Little Tub Harbour.

Day 2

Pack a picnic and take the boat to Flowerpot Island to explore Fathom Five National Marine Park, one of only three national marine conservation areas in Canada. It's just a short hike from the ferry dock to the

ONTARIO SIPPING AND SUPPING

Attention, food lovers! Ontario has plenty of gourmet getaways and scrumptious side trips for culinary tourists. From cooking classes and wine tastings to market excursions, food tours, and more, here are some of the province's food- and wine-touring highlights.

WHERE TO WIELD YOUR WHISK

Impress a special someone with some serious short-term culinary training. Spend a day in Ottawa at **Le Cordon Bleu** (www.lcbottawa.com), or in Stratford at the **Stratford Chef School** (www.stratfordchef.com), where you'll work alongside aspiring professional chefs. Self-described "fat guy" Stefan Schuster has a more irreverent approach to food, offering **"Trust the Fat Guy"** cooking workshops at the Hillcrest House B&B (www.hillcresthouse.ca) that he runs with his wife Wendy in Waterloo. Another B&B cooking school is **Mt. Pleasant Country B&B and Culinary Retreat** (www.gourmetsafari.com), near Peterborough, where owner and world traveler Jackie DeKnock specializes in international cuisines.

A popular destination for a learn-to-cook holiday is Prince Edward County, where **From the Farm Cooking School** (www.fromthefarm.ca), the **Waring House Cookery School** (www.waringhouse.com), and **Chef Michael Hoy** (www.chefmichaelhoy.com), all offer courses based on the region's bounty.

RAISE A GLASS

Ontario has three major wine-producing regions: the Niagara Peninsula, Prince Edward County, and the north shore of Lake Erie. The Niagara region is further subdivided into the **Niagara-on-the-Lake** and the **Twenty Valley** wine districts. These wine-making regions are great eating destinations, too. Restaurants both at the wineries and in the nearby towns pair local wines with creative dishes. During your wine tour, sample some **ice wine,** Ontario's signature dessert wine.

Ontario isn't all about the grape though. The province has numerous microbreweries that welcome visitors, including Toronto's **Mill Street Brewery** (www.millstreetbrewery.com); the **Niagara College Teaching Brewery** (www.niagaracollegebeer.ca), Canada's first "teach-

ing brewery;" and **Creemore Springs Brewery** (www.creemoresprings.com) in the Blue Mountains. Toronto's first sake brewery, the **Ontario Spring Water Sake Company** (www.ontariosake.com), has a tasting bar at its shop in The Distillery District.

TO MARKET, TO MARKET

Many Ontario cities and towns have regular farmer's markets, where you can purchase local fruits and vegetables, cheeses, jams, honey, and baked goods directly from the producers. Some of the largest are in Toronto (at the **St. Lawrence Market** and at **Evergreen Brick Works**); in **St. Jacobs** west of Toronto, which has Canada's largest year-round farmer's market; and in Ottawa at the **ByWard Market** and the farmer's market in Lansdowne Park. **Farmers Market Ontario** (www.farmersmarketsontario.com) lists farmer's markets around the province.

Toronto also has several market districts with a multiethnic flavor. Spend an afternoon exploring the **Kensington Market, Chinatown, Greektown,** or **Koreatown. Urban Adventures** (www.urbanadventures.com) leads tours of the Kensington Market, while **A Taste of the World** (www.torontowalksbikes.com) explores Chinatown and other neighborhoods. In Ottawa, **C'est Bon Cooking** (www.cestboncooking.ca) leads ByWard Market tours.

Le Cordon Bleu Cooking School, Ottawa

distinctive "flowerpot" rock formations. When you return to the mainland, take a lighthouse tour, then hike along the Bruce Trail or go kayaking. Walk along the broad, sandy Singing Sands Beach and watch the sun set over Lake Huron.

Day 3

Take the morning ferry to Manitoulin Island. Enjoy a leisurely lunch at Garden's Gate Restaurant, then spend the afternoon at Providence Bay Beach or take a hike to Bridal Veil Falls. Spend the night on the Aundeck Omni Kaning First Nations Reserve at Endaa-aang "Our Place," where you can rent a comfortable cottage or sleep in a teepee.

Day 4

Today you're exploring Manitoulin's aboriginal heritage with the Great Spirit Circle Tour. Start at the Ojibwe Cultural Foundation and Museum to see the exhibits and arrange a workshop on traditional First Nations dance, drumming, or crafts. You can also take their Mother Earth Nature Hike, where an aboriginal guide will help you identify local plants and understand how they're used in aboriginal medicine and cooking. In the evening, see a production by the aboriginal Debajehmujig Theatre Group on the Wikwemikong First Nations Reserve.

Day 5

Get an early start today. It's a three-hour drive to Killarney Provincial Park, a vast and dramatic provincial park with rugged white dolomite ridges, pink granite cliffs, pine forests, and crystal-clear lakes. You'll want to reach Killarney in time for a swim at George Lake and an afternoon of hiking or canoeing. You can camp in the park or stay in one of the lodges in town. Enjoy a fish 'n chips dinner at Herbert Fisheries while you watch the sunset over the harbor.

Day 6

In the morning, take another hike or paddle before driving south toward Parry Sound, stopping for a late lunch at the Little Britt Inn along the way. Once you arrive in Parry Sound, arrange a flight-seeing tour, the most thrilling way to take in Georgian Bay's 30,000 islands; if you're with a special someone, schedule a romantic sunset

Killarney Provincial Park

flight—complete with champagne. If you'd rather stay close to the ground, explore the islands with a sightseeing cruise on the *Island Queen*. In the evening, see a play, concert, or lecture at the Charles W. Stockey Centre for the Performing Arts.

Day 7

Your first stop today is Killbear Provincial Park, an hour's drive from Parry Sound. While it's lesser known than Ontario's larger "destination" parks, its dramatic granite cliffs and quiet sandy beaches are well worth exploring. Later in the day, drive south to Honey Harbour or Port Severn, where you'll spend the night.

Day 8

Of the thousands of islands that dot Georgian Bay, 63 are protected in the Georgian Bay Islands National Park. Your destination today is Beausoleil Island for a full day of hiking, swimming, picnicking, and exploring. Back on the mainland, drive an hour south to Midland for dinner and check in to a hotel, where you'll stay for the next two nights.

Day 9

Travel back in time to the 1600s at Sainte-Marie Among the Hurons, a historic village that "re-imagines" the first European settlement in Ontario, where French Jesuits lived and worked with the native Wendat (Huron) people. In the afternoon, go canoeing at Wye Marsh Wildlife Centre, take a cruise around the offshore islands on the M.S. *Georgian Queen* from nearby Penetanguishene Harbor, or go for a hike or swim at Awenda Provincial Park.

Day 10

As you begin your drive south, stop for a stroll along Wasaga Beach, the world's longest freshwater beach. Another worthwhile detour is the small town of Creemore, where the main street is lined with art galleries, cafes, and shops. After you've had your fill of browsing, have a bite to eat before making your way back to Toronto.

▶ NORTHERN EXPOSURE

An excellent way to see the highlights of Ontario's near-north is by train. In fact, as you travel toward James Bay, you can't go by car even if you want to—no roads run this far north. This itinerary combines several train journeys, beginning in Toronto and traveling to the Cree First Nations communities of Moosonee and Moose Factory Island, with a stopover for canoeing and hiking in the Temagami lakelands along the way. The best time to make this trip is in July or August, when the weather is warm, and the *Polar Bear Express Train* to Moosonee runs daily (except Saturdays).

Day 1

Take Ontario Northland's *Northlander* train from Toronto to Temagami. If you stay at the Smoothwater Wilderness Lodge, staff can meet you at the station. You'll arrive in time for a late afternoon paddle on the property's lake and a leisurely family-style dinner at the lodge; it's the best place to eat in the area, and a bonus is the travel tips you'll get from the other guests.

Days 2-3

Spend the day outdoors around Temagami. Ask the staff at Smoothwater Wilderness Lodge to organize a canoe, kayak, or hiking trip in Lady Evelyn Smoothwater Provincial Park. Return to the lodge for dinner and spend the evening relaxing in the "Gathering Hall."

COOL SLEEPS

Is a bed too boring? If you're looking for an unusual place to lay your head, check out these unique Ontario accommodations.

- You can bed down in a tepee on a First Nations reserve, when you stay at **Endaa-aang "Our Place"** on Manitoulin Island.

- At the **HI-Ottawa Jail Hostel,** in the nation's capital, some of the beds are in cells of the 19th-century former Carleton County Gaol. Ditto for the weirdly fun **King George Inn and Spa,** with rooms behind bars in the former Cobourg Jail, east of Toronto.

- Stay in a lighthouse. For a hands-on lighthouse experience, apply to be an assistant lightkeeper for a week at the **Cabot Head Lighthouse** on the Bruce Peninsula.

- Want to know what it was like to be a soldier in the 1800s? You won't be issued a musket or army rations, but you can spend the night in Kingston's **Fort Henry.**

- The **Walper Terrace Hotel** in Kitchener donates $1 for every guest's stay to the Walper Education Project, which is funding schools and scholarship programs in rural Uganda.

- The **Sugar Ridge Retreat Centre,** with 10 cabins surrounding a contemporary, Zen-style lodge, near Midland, may be one of the quietest places you'll ever stay, whether you come for a yoga retreat or simply a peaceful escape.

- Outside the town of Tobermory on the Bruce Peninsula, **E'Terra** is the ultimate hideaway: the phone number is unlisted, the property has no sign, and the owners won't divulge the address until you make a reservation.

Cabot Head Lighthouse, Bruce Peninsula

You'll have time the next day for another morning hike or canoe excursion in Temagami before catching the late-afternoon *Northlander* train to Cochrane where you'll spend the night.

Day 4

Today you're going where no roads go—north toward James Bay on Ontario Northland's *Polar Bear Express Train* to Moosonee. You'll arrive in Moosonee by mid-afternoon; take a walk around town before catching the water taxi over to Moose Factory Island. Spend the night at the Cree Village Ecolodge, run by the Cree First Nation, and have dinner (with traditional aboriginal ingredients) in the lodge's lovely dining room.

Day 5

You'll spend most of the day on Moose Factory Island. Visit the Cree Culture Interpretive Centre to learn more about Cree culture, language, traditional medicine, and food. Walk over to the Moose Cree Complex; part shopping mall, part community center, it's the hub of the First Nations reserve, so you can glimpse what local life is like on this remote island. After lunch, take a boat tour to James Bay.

The *Polar Bear Express* heads south in the early evening and will take you as far as Cochrane, where you'll need to spend the night. In the morning, board the *Northlander* for the full-day train trip back to Toronto.

TORONTO

Canadians may typically be modest about their country's attractions, but Toronto has plenty to boast about. With more than 5.8 million people living in the metropolitan area, it's the country's largest city and Ontario's provincial capital. As Canada's cultural hub, it's home to one of the most multicultural populations on the planet.

About half of metropolitan Toronto's residents were born outside of Canada, hailing from China, India, Italy, the Caribbean, the Philippines, the Middle East, Portugal—name a country and Toronto probably has residents who used to call it home. This diversity has made Toronto one of North America's most exciting cities for eating, shopping, and simply exploring. You can wander through Little India, Koreatown, Greektown, and at least five Chinatowns.

Toronto is often called "Hollywood North" for the number of movies made here; every September the city hosts the Toronto International Film Festival, one of North America's major film fests. Toronto is also a major center for English-language theater, with dozens of theaters and repertory companies in the metropolitan region. A major event on the city's calendar is the annual Pride Week, one of the world's largest gay–lesbian pride celebrations.

Set on the shore of Lake Ontario, Toronto is reclaiming its waterfront, which now houses performance spaces and art galleries, along with a lakeside walking and cycling trail. Skyscrapers stand side by side with Victorian-era buildings downtown, while farther afield a wide range of museums and eclectic shops satisfy culture- and couture-seekers alike. Whether you want to wrap up your day with

© CAROLYN B. HELLER

HIGHLIGHTS

LOOK FOR ◖ TO FIND RECOMMENDED SIGHTS, ACTIVITIES, DINING, AND LODGING.

◖ **CN Tower:** Toronto's tallest building has two observation levels, as well as a revolving restaurant, all with great views across the city and the lake. Daredevils can even take the "Edgewalk," a thrilling walk suspended *outside* (yes, outside!) the tower, 116 stories above the ground (page 26).

◖ **Harbourfront Centre:** There's always something happening in this waterfront arts complex. You can watch artists at work in their studios, browse gallery exhibits, take in a play or a lecture, go canoeing or ice skating, or just stroll the walkways along the lake (page 28).

◖ **The Toronto Islands:** Only a 10-minute ferry ride from downtown, these small islands in Lake Ontario are the city's backyard, where you can lounge at the beach, ride a bike, or have a picnic. The awesome views of the city skyline are a bonus (page 30).

◖ **The Distillery District:** Where whiskey was once king, the Victorian-era brick buildings that housed the world's largest distillery have been converted into a cool arts district, full of galleries, artist studios, shops, cafés, and theatres (page 39).

◖ **Royal Ontario Museum:** Inside this massive museum of natural history and world cultures, you'll find everything from Egyptian mummies to British neoclassical dining rooms, Buddha statues from China and India, armor from medieval Europe, and scads of kid-pleasing dinosaur skeletons (page 41).

◖ **Bata Shoe Museum:** This quirky – and fun – gallery of footwear traces the history and culture of a wide swath of humanity by showcasing what people wore on their feet (page 43).

◖ **Art Gallery of Ontario:** In a striking Frank Gehry–designed building, Toronto's art museum

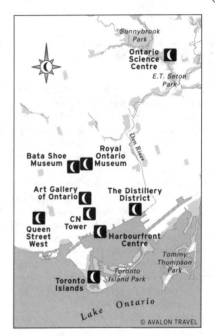

© AVALON TRAVEL

is one of the largest in North America, with significant collections of Canadian, Inuit, African, and Oceanic art. Exploring the building alone is worth the price of admission (page 45).

◖ **Queen Street West:** Lined with art galleries, funky shops, eclectic eateries, and happening bars, the west end of Queen Street is one of the city's "in" arts districts (page 48).

◖ **Ontario Science Centre:** If you're traveling with kids, it's worth the trek to this excellent science museum, which has loads of hands-on activities. Even jaded teens can have fun here (page 50).

a contemporary dinner from one of the city's hottest chefs or unwind over a drink in a neighborhood club, you'll find it all in Toronto.

PLANNING YOUR TIME

Toronto is a year-round destination. Summer is one of the most popular times to visit, particularly if you're traveling with kids. Everything is open, and you'll find plenty of festivals and special events. Just be prepared for hot, humid weather. Although Toronto is northwest of Buffalo, New York, Torontonians are quick to point out that the "lake effect" that dumps piles of snow on their New York State neighbors has a different result in their city. Toronto's position on Lake Ontario's northern shore moderates the winter weather, and the city averages 115 centimeters (45 inches) of snow per year—less than Buffalo can get on a single day. Sure, it's cold in the winter, but Toronto has lots of great museums and indoor attractions, the cultural season will be in full swing, and accommodations are often less expensive than during other times of the year.

The best seasons to visit, though, are the spring and fall. The weather should be temperate, especially in autumn, and the cultural calendar will be full. Just note that if you'll be in town in September during the Toronto International Film Festival, you should book your accommodations well in advance. The film festival is a major event on the city's cultural agenda, and hotels fill up early.

How much time do you need to explore Toronto? You could visit for a weekend and catch the city's highlights or stick around for weeks and still have plenty of things to do. Start with a visit to the **CN Tower** to get an overview of what's where, and then catch the streetcar east to the **St. Lawrence Market** and the **Distillery District.** Browse the shops, have lunch, and then head back downtown for one (or more) of the museums: the **Royal Ontario Museum** if you're into world cultures and natural history; the **Art Gallery of Ontario** for contemporary art (and a striking Frank Gehry–designed gallery building); or the **Bata Shoe Museum** for, well, shoes—but shoes as you've never seen before. Have dinner in the Entertainment District or in the West End, take in a concert or a film, or see what's happening in the clubs.

The next day, visit the lavish **Casa Loma** (the city's "castle on the hill"), have lunch in **Chinatown,** and then either poke around in the **Kensington Market** or spend the afternoon browsing the galleries and shops along **West Queen Street West.**

Alternatively, if the weather is fine, you could catch the ferry to the **Toronto Islands,** or just walk or cycle along the Harbourfront, stopping into the galleries at **Harbourfront Centre.** If you're traveling with kids, you might want to add the **Ontario Science Centre** to your itinerary. Toronto is also close enough to **Niagara Falls** that you can take a day trip there and still be back in town for a late supper.

Sights

Toronto's downtown core is just inland from the Lake Ontario waterfront. Downtown and the Harbourfront include the city's oldest neighborhoods and its newest developments, where narrow streets laid out in the city's early days are just a short walk from the skyscraping waterfront towers. The city's landmark CN Tower is here, and you can also catch a ferry to the Toronto Islands, a waterfront green space just a quick cruise from downtown.

Like most major cities, Toronto has several major museums—of art, science, and natural and cultural history. The city also has some less typical museums, including galleries of textiles and ceramics, a hockey museum, even a museum devoted to shoes. You can tour the city halls—old and new—and visit the provincial legislature, the fort where the city was first settled, or the only "double-decker" theater in Canada.

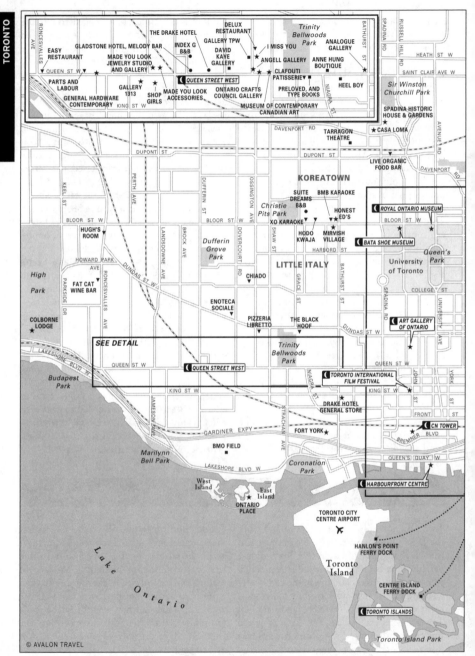

© AVALON TRAVEL

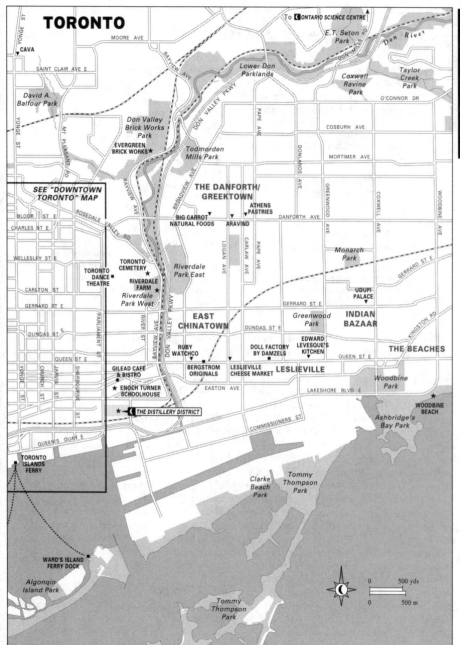

TORONTO

CAVA

MOORE AVE

To **C** *ONTARIO SCIENCE CENTRE*

E.T. Seton Park

Don River

SAINT CLAIR AVE E

Lower Don Parklands

Coxwell Ravine Park

Taylor Creek Park

O'CONNOR DR

David A. Balfour Park

Don Valley Brick Works Park

EVERGREEN BRICK WORKS★

PAPE AVE

COSBURN AVE

DONLANDS AVE

MORTIMER AVE

COXWELL AVE

WOODBINE AVE

Todmorden Mills Park

BAYVIEW AVE

DON VALLEY PKWY

THE DANFORTH/ GREEKTOWN

ATHENS PASTRIES

BIG CARROT NATURAL FOODS ▼   ▼ **★**

ARAVIND

DANFORTH AVE

SEE "DOWNTOWN TORONTO" MAP

ROSEDALE VALLEY RD

BLOOR ST E

CHARLES ST E

WELLESLEY ST E

TORONTO DANCE THEATRE ■

CARLTON ST

GERRARD ST E

DUNDAS ST E

QUEEN ST E

YONGE ST

CHURCH ST

JARVIS ST

SHERBOURNE ST

PARLIAMENT ST

RIVER ST

BAYVIEW AVE

DON VALLEY PKWY

TORONTO CEMETERY ★

RIVERDALE FARM ★

Riverdale Park West

Riverdale Park East

LOGAN AVE

CARLAW AVE

PAPE AVE

GREENWOOD AVE

Monarch Park

GERRARD ST E

GERRARD ST E

KINGSTON RD

UDUPI PALACE ▼

EAST CHINATOWN

DUNDAS ST E

Greenwood Park

INDIAN BAZAAR

RUBY WATCHCO ▼

DOLL FACTORY BY DAMZELS ▼

EDWARD LEVESQUE'S KITCHEN

THE BEACHES

GILEAD CAFÉ & BISTRO ●

ENOCH TURNER SCHOOLHOUSE ★

BERGSTROM ORIGINALS

LESLIEVILLE CHEESE MARKET

LESLIEVILLE

QUEEN ST E

EASTON AVE

LAKESHORE BLVD E

Woodbine Park

WOODBINE BEACH ★

★ C *THE DISTILLERY DISTRICT*

COMMISSIONERS ST

Ashbridge's Bay Park

QUEEN'S QUAY E

TORONTO ISLANDS FERRY

Clarke Beach Park

Tommy Thompson Park

WARD'S ISLAND FERRY DOCK ■

Algonquin Island Park

Tommy Thompson Park

MT PLEASANT RD

YONGE ST

GENOA ST

BROADVIEW AVE

0   500 yds

0   500 m

TORONTO FOR A TOONIE (OR LESS)

On a budget? Don't worry: Toronto has plenty of free and low-cost attractions. Here's how to stretch your dollars while exploring Toronto.

- There's no charge to wander the **St. Lawrence Market, the Distillery District, Kensington Market,** or any of the city's multicultural neighborhoods – although you may want to budget for snacks along the way.

- Walk along the Harbourfront or browse the galleries and shops along **Queen Street West,** all for free.

- Tours of the **Ontario Legislative Assembly** are free, and there's no charge to explore the grounds at the **Evergreen Brick Works.**

- A trip to the **Toronto Islands** will cost a small ferry fare, but once you're there, you can stroll, picnic, and lounge on the sand without spending a penny.

- Many of Toronto's museums offer free or discounted admission at certain times. The **Royal Ontario Museum** is free on Wednesdays 4:30–5:30 P.M. and reduced on Fridays 4:30–9:30 P.M. The **Art Gallery of Ontario** is free on Wednesdays 6–8:30 P.M. The **Bata Shoe Museum** offers a "pay what you can" admission on Thursdays 5–8 P.M. Admission to the **Gardiner Museum** is half-price on Fridays 4–9 P.M.

- Take one of the city's free walking tours. Locals lead free guided walks of their neighborhoods or other favorite places around town on the **Toronto Greeter** tours. The **Heritage Toronto Walks,** highlighting a neighborhood's architectural, cultural, or natural history, are free, as well.

Beyond the museums and other "sights," Toronto's lure is its diverse neighborhoods. There's the bohemian, multicultural Kensington Market, with its cheap eateries and offbeat shops, and Cabbagetown, with its well-manicured Victorian homes. You can explore the galleries and artsy boutiques in the restored Distillery District, on Queen Street West, and in Leslieville to the east. There are the city's many ethnic communities, as well, including several Chinatowns, an Indian district, and neighborhoods that still have their Greek, Korean, and Portuguese roots. And then there's the Harbourfront, with its galleries, gardens, and green spaces to enjoy on a sunny city day.

If you're planning to visit several of Toronto's major attractions, consider purchasing a **CityPass** (www.citypass.com, adults $68, children 5–12 $41), which includes admission to the CN Tower, Royal Ontario Museum, Casa Loma, Ontario Science Centre, and Toronto Zoo. A main benefit of the pass, in addition to discounted admission, is that you can bypass the ticket lines or enter through an "express" line at most of the attractions. You can buy a CityPass online or at any of the included attractions. The pass is good for nine days beginning with the first day that you use it.

THE HARBOURFRONT

In mild weather, the Lake Ontario shore is one of Toronto's loveliest areas, with walking paths along the waterfront, parks, and lots of things to see and do. While the lakeshore is only a short walk from downtown, the Gardiner Expressway, the elevated highway that bisects the city, cuts off the Harbourfront from the rest of the city. Several streets, including Bay, York, and Lower Simcoe Streets, pass underneath the expressway, so you can walk from downtown.

◖ CN Tower

If you've ever seen photos of the Toronto skyline, you've seen the iconic **CN Tower** (301 Front St. W., at John St., 416/868-6937, www.cntower.ca, 9 A.M.–11 P.M. daily in summer;

9 A.M.–10 P.M. Sun.–Thurs., 9 A.M.–10:30 P.M. Fri.–Sat. fall–spring). At 5,533 meters (1,815 feet) high, the tower, which opened in 1976 to provide telecommunications capabilities for the city, held the record for the world's tallest building for many years. Even if loftier skyscrapers have taken away its title, this is still one tall building.

At ground level, you'll find several touristy attractions, including a 3D movie, a surround-sound theater, and a game arcade, but the real reason to visit the tower is to go up. Once you've gone through the security check, boarded the glass elevators, and rocketed 113 stories to the Look Out level (the elevator ride takes only 58 seconds), the views stretch out over the city and Lake Ontario.

The next thrill is a walk across the **Glass Floor,** glass panels that you can look through, stand on, or jump on, depending on your tolerance for heights. It's 346 meters (1,136 feet) straight down. If you want to get even higher, you can go up to the **Sky Pod,** the next observation level at 447 meters (1,465 feet), 34 stories above the Look Out. There's an additional fee for Sky Pod access.

For extreme thrill-seekers, there's the **Edgewalk** (www.edgewalkcntower.ca, May–Oct., call for seasonal hours, $175), where you walk outside (yes, outside!) around the roof of the tower restaurant, 116 stories (356 meters, or 1,168 feet) above the ground. You're harnessed to a safety rail, but you can lean out over the edge, if you dare. When you're suspended outside the building, it's probably not the time to tell you that lighting strikes the tower an average of 75 times per year, but don't worry: the Edgewalk closes during high winds and electrical storms.

The Edgewalk itself lasts 20–30 minutes, although the entire experience, including a safety briefing and other preparation, takes 1.5 hours. The rate includes admission to all the other tower attractions, as well as a video and photos of your experience. To participate in the Edgewalk, you must weigh between 34 and 140 kilograms (75 to 310 pounds). Kids who are at least 13 are allowed, but a parent or

© CAROLYN B. HELLER

The landmark CN Tower rises over the downtown skyscrapers.

guardian must accompany anyone between the ages of 13 and 17 to provide written consent.

There are also three on-site restaurants. The revolving **360 Restaurant at the CN Tower** (416/362-5411, 11 A.M.–2 P.M. and 4:30–10:30 P.M. Mon.–Thurs., 11 A.M.–2 P.M. and 4:30–11 P.M. Fri.–Sat., 10:30 A.M.–2 P.M. and 4:30–10:30 P.M. Sun., Mar.–Dec.; 5–10 P.M. Sun.–Thurs., 5–11 P.M. Fri.–Sat. Jan.–Feb.) makes a complete revolution every 72 minutes, giving you great views over the city. While the prices are high, diners don't have to pay the tower admission and can bypass the ticket line; the price of your meal includes access to the Look Out level and the Glass Floor. On the Look Out level is an upscale bistro, **Horizons Restaurant** (11 A.M.–9 P.M. daily), and at the base of the tower is the casual **Far Coast Café** (8:30 A.M.–6 P.M. daily).

The basic tower ticket, called the "Observation Experience" (adults $23.99, seniors $21.99, kids 4–12 $15.99), includes the Look Out and the Glass Floor. The "Observation Plus" ticket (adults $29.99, seniors $27.99, kids 4–12 $21.99) adds access to one additional attraction, either the Sky Pod, the 3D film, or the motion-theater ride. If you want to do it all, the "Total Tower Experience" (all ages $34.99) includes the Look Out, Glass Floor, Sky Pod, movie, and motion-theater ride.

With two million people visiting the tower in an average year, ticket lines can be long, and all visitors must pass through airport-style security checkpoints. Try to avoid arriving between 11 A.M. and 3 P.M., when the tower is busiest. Between November and April, lines are generally shorter than they are the rest of the year. You can save time by buying your tickets online in advance or by purchasing a City Pass, which includes CN Tower admission; you'll enter through a separate "ticketholders" line rather than wait at the box office.

From Union Station, which is the nearest subway stop, you can walk through the enclosed **SkyBridge** walkway or along Front Street to the tower.

Rogers Centre

Toronto's professional baseball team (the Blue Jays) and Canadian Football League team (the Argonauts) play in the Rogers Centre (1 Blue Jays Way, 416/341-1000, www.rogerscentre. com), formerly known as the SkyDome. The massive arena also hosts mega-concerts, performances, and other events by luminaries ranging from U2 to the Harlem Globetrotters to the Dalai Lama. Opened in 1989, the building's claim to fame is its roof; it's the world's first fully retractable roof, which will open or close in 20 minutes.

If you're a sports fan, consider the **Rogers Centre Tour Experience** (416/341-2771, adults $16, seniors and students 12–17 $12, kids 5–11 $10), a one-hour guided tour of the facility. Tour times vary.

You can buy tickets for all Rogers Centre events at the box office (Gate 9, Bremmer Blvd., 8 A.M.–8 P.M. Mon.–Fri., 10 A.M.–6 P.M. Sat.–Sun.). The Rogers Centre is adjacent to the CN Tower. From Union Station, follow the covered SkyWalk or walk west on Front Street.

You can also take the #504 King streetcar to Peter or John Street, then walk south, or take the #510 Spadina Avenue streetcar to Bremner Boulevard and walk east.

Air Canada Centre

A must-see for hockey fans is the Air Canada Centre (40 Bay St., 416/815-5400, www. theaircanadacentre.com), where the Toronto Maple Leafs play. If you want to wander through the visiting team's dressing room, you can take the **Air Canada Centre Tour** (416/222-8687, tours 10 A.M.–5 P.M. daily, adults $20, seniors and students 13–17 $18, kids 5–12 $10, families $45), a one-hour guided walk through the complex.

The Toronto Raptors basketball team also plays here, and the center hosts major concerts and other events. You can buy event tickets at the Air Canada Centre ticket window (9:30 A.M.–6 P.M. Mon.–Fri., 9:30 A.M.–5 P.M. Sat.).

Part of the Maple Leaf Square complex (www.mapleleafsquare.com), the Air Canada Centre is connected to Union Station via the PATH walkway.

◀ Harbourfront Centre

This complex of buildings on Lake Ontario known as Harbourfront Centre (235 Queens Quay W., 416/973-4000, www.harbourfront-centre.com, hours vary) is activity central, both for arts and literary events and for enjoying the outdoors. There are art galleries and artist studios, theaters, shops, even a skating rink in winter. A waterfront walkway wends behind the center, too. Stop at one of the information desks around the complex to find out what's on the current schedule, or check their comprehensive website for event listings.

On the east side of the complex is **Queen's Quay Terminal** (207 Queens Quay W.), which houses a grocery store, a food court, and some souvenir shops. In summer, **Queen's Quay Terminal Farmers' Market** (3–7 P.M. Wed. June–mid-Oct.) sets up outside, on the southwest corner of the complex, and out front is a ticket and information booth for **boat**

tours. But the main reason to visit is to see the **Museum of Inuit Art** (207 Queens Quay W., 416/640-1571, www.miamuseum.ca, 10 A.M.–6 P.M. daily, adults $6). It's not large, but the galleries are packed with artwork created by artists from all across the arctic regions. Look for profiles of many of the artists with maps showing where they came from.

Look for the smokestack to find the **Power Plant Gallery** (231 Queens Quay W., 416/973-4949, www.thepowerplant.org, noon–6 P.M. Tues.–Fri., noon–8 P.M. Sat., noon–6 P.M. Sun., admission varies), a contemporary art gallery in a former 1920s power station. The eclectic exhibits change regularly, so there's always something new to see.

Inside **York Centre Quay** are other small art galleries, including an architecture gallery on the second floor. You can watch artists at work as you walk through the hallway housing **The Craft Studio. The Centre Shop** (416/973-4993, 11 A.M.–6 P.M. Sat.–Wed., 11 A.M.–8 P.M. Thurs.–Fri.) sells cool, arty stuff—from jewelry to craft supplies to housewares. If you need to get online, the York Quay Centre building has free public Wi-Fi (though you have to register to use it).

The easiest way to get to Harbourfront Centre is to take the subway to Union Station, then catch the #509 Exhibition or #510 Spadina streetcar west three stops to Lower Simcoe Street.

Toronto Music Garden

What do a cellist and a garden designer have in common? In Toronto, they have a garden: the Toronto Music Garden (475 Queens Quay W., www.toronto.ca/parks, dawn–dusk daily year-round, free). Renowned cellist Yo-Yo Ma collaborated with garden designer Julie Moir Messervy to create this waterfront green space inspired by J. S. Bach's "First Suite for Unaccompanied Cello." In Messervy's design, each dance movement within the piece corresponds to a different section of the garden. The music theme may not be entirely obvious as you stroll the pathways, but it's still a pretty oasis along the lake.

Perhaps the best way to appreciate the music garden is to come for the music. **Summer Music in the Garden** (416/973-4000, www.harbourfrontcentre.com, late June–mid-Sept.) is a series of free, one-hour classical and world music concerts. Performances are held at 7 P.M. Thursdays and 4 P.M. Sundays (weather permitting).

The garden is on the Harbourfront, between Spadina Avenue and Bathurst Street. From Union Station, take the #509 Exhibition or #510 Spadina streetcar west to Spadina Avenue.

Fort York National Historic Site

As you stand next to the restored 19th-century barracks, surrounded by condo and office towers, with the hum of traffic along the Gardiner Expressway buzzing in the background, it's hard to imagine that this urban pocket was once the first significant settlement in the Toronto area. In 1793, the lieutenant governor of Upper Canada, John Graves Simcoe, and his troops began building a garrison on the site of what is now Fort York (250 Fort York Blvd., 416/392-6907, www.fortyork.ca, 10 A.M.–5 P.M. daily mid-May–early Sept; 10 A.M.–4 P.M. Mon.–Fri., 10 A.M.–5 P.M. Sat.–Sun. early Sept.–mid-Dec.; 10 A.M.–4:30 P.M. Mon.–Fri., 10 A.M.–5 P.M. Sat.–Sun. early Jan.–mid-May; adults $8.61, seniors $4.31, youth 13–18 $4.31, kids 6–12 $3.23). The original capital of Upper Canada had been in Niagara, closer to the American border, and Simcoe felt it would be safer to move it farther north.

Moving the capital didn't keep it safe, though. During the War of 1812, American troops attacked the fort. As the British forces retreated, they blew up the fort's gunpowder magazine, causing significant American casualties. Two months later, the U.S. troops burned most of what remained of the fort. The British quickly began to rebuild, and many of the fort buildings now standing—including two blockhouses, several barracks, and two powder magazines—date to this period of reconstruction between 1813 and 1815. In the basement of the

Officers' Mess are the remains of Toronto's oldest surviving kitchen.

The best time to visit the fort is during July and August, when you can take a guided tour, watch a demonstration of open-hearth cooking, or participate in other special programs, although at any time, staff are on hand to tell you about the fort and its history. At the time of this writing, a new visitors center was in the works.

Fort York is west of downtown, north of Fleet Street, just west of Bathurst Street. If you're coming from Union Station or the Harbourfront, take the #509 Exhibition streetcar to Fort York Boulevard, and follow the signs to the fort. You can also take the subway to Bathurst station (Bloor-Danforth line), then catch the #511 Bathurst streetcar southbound; it stops opposite the fort's eastern gate.

Ontario Place

A popular summer destination for waterfront fun, the entertainment complex known as Ontario Place (955 Lake Shore Blvd. W., 416/314-9900 or 866/663-4386, www.ontarioplace.com, late May–late Sept.) opened in 1971 on three manufactured islands along Lake Ontario. A major attraction was (and still is) the **Cinesphere,** which was the first permanent IMAX theater in the world; it's now been updated to show 3-D IMAX films.

Canada's first waterslide opened here in 1978 and subsequently developed into a full-blown **Froster Soak City waterpark.** There are carnival-style rides, beaches, a lounge pool, play areas for the kids, and all kinds of special events.

The 16,000-seat **Molson Canadian Amphitheatre** (www.livenation.com) stages big-name concerts. An eclectic lineup takes to the outdoor stage at **Echo Beach** (www.echobeach.ca), where many of the concerts are free (and yes, there's a real sand beach).

From July through Labour Day in early September, the grounds and most attractions are open 10 A.M.–8 P.M. daily, and the waterpark is open 11 A.M.–7 P.M. Opening hours are limited late May through June and from

early September through late September. You can buy individual tickets to the various rides (most are $5–10), or purchase a **Play All Day pass** ($22–80), which includes unlimited admission to most attractions. Note that the all-day pass is required to access the waterpark.

From Union Station or the Harbourfront, take the #509 Exhibition streetcar to Exhibition Place or catch the GO train to Exhibition station. You can also take the subway to Bathurst station, then board the #511 Bathurst streetcar southbound to Exhibition Place. Either way, when you get off the streetcar or train, walk south through the Exhibition Place grounds, over the Lake Shore bridge, and into Ontario Place.

◖ THE TORONTO ISLANDS

Just a short ferry ride across the harbor from downtown, the Toronto Islands (415/397-2628, www.toronto.ca) in Lake Ontario are the city's backyard, where both residents and visitors escape the urban bustle to lounge at the beach, cruise around by bike or kayak, or have a picnic. The awesome views of the city skyline, from the ferries and from the islands themselves, are a bonus; this is the place to take those picture-postcard city snapshots.

The "Toronto Islands" actually consist of several small islands, most of which are connected to each other by bridges. Ferries from Toronto dock at three points: Centre Island, Ward's Island to the east, and Hanlan's Point to the west.

Bring a picnic from the mainland, so you can eat on the beach or as you're exploring. If you'd rather sit down to a restaurant meal, you can choose from several eateries, including the year-round **Rectory Cafe** (Ward's Island, 416/203-2152, www.therectorycafe.com) or the more touristy, seasonal **Shopsy's Island Deli Bar and Grill** (www.centreisland.ca), right next to the Centre Island docks. Washrooms and drinking water are available on the islands.

Centre Island

Centre Island is the entertainment hub, with an amusement park, gardens, bike and boat

© CAROLYN B. HELLER

The Toronto Islands are only a 10-minute ferry ride from downtown.

rentals, and beaches. If you have young kids, head for the **Franklin Children's Garden,** with play structures, a tree house, and a theater that hosts summer storytelling events. There's a beach by the pier on Centre Island, but if you walk or cycle either direction from there, you'll find prettier, less populated sand.

Bike rentals ($7/hour, tandems $14/hour) are available near the Centre Island pier, on the opposite side of the island from the ferry dock; it's 0.75 kilometer, or about a 0.5-mile walk. You can also rent fun "quadricycles," four-wheeled pedal bikes that can seat two ($16/hour) or four ($30/hour) people. On a bike, it takes about an hour to make a leisurely but complete loop of the islands, if you don't stop much to look around. You can take bicycles over from the mainland, although bikes aren't allowed on the Centre Island ferry on busy summer weekends.

In the summer, you can rent **canoes, kayaks,** and **pedal boats** at the Boat House on Centre Island. To find the boat rentals from the Centre Island docks, follow the main path past the amusement park. When you cross the bridge near the fountains, bear left (east) toward the Boat House.

While many come to the islands for their more natural charms, a big attraction for the kids is the **Centreville Amusement Park** (604/203-0405, www.centreisland.ca, 10:30 A.M.–close daily early June–early Sept.; 10:30 A.M.–close Sat.–Sun. May and mid-to-late Sept.), with a 1907 carousel, a Ferris wheel, bumper boats, a roller coaster, antique car rides, and a whole host of other old-time carnival attractions. If you arrive on the Centre Island ferry, it's hard to sneak past the amusements without the kids noticing, since the park is just a short walk from the ferry dock.

Admission to the amusement park itself is free, but you'll pay to ride the rides. A sheet of 50 ride tickets costs $42.48, or you can buy an all-day pass. Passes for individuals are based on height; one-day passes for adults and children who are more than four feet tall are $30.97, less than four feet tall $21.90. Family all-day passes are $96. You can get a small discount on both individual and family passes by buying them online before your visit.

Ward's Island

Ward's Island looks like an urban cottage colony, with the islands' only community of permanent residents, a beach, and a playground. The mostly sandy **Ward's Island Beach** can be a little less crowded than some of the others. Wander past the lakeside homes and imagine living here yourself.

Hanlan's Point

If you see airplanes coming in over the harbor, so low that you think they're going to land on your ferry, it's because they're headed to the Toronto Island Airport, near Hanlan's Point, which also has parks and beaches. On this side of the island is the stone **Gibraltar Point Lighthouse,** built 1808–1809. It's the oldest surviving lighthouse on the Great Lakes and the second-oldest in Canada. The **Gibraltar Beach,** west of the pier, is nice and there's a clothing-optional beach at Hanlan's Point.

Getting There and Around

Catch the **ferry** (9 Queens Quay West, at Bay St., 416/397-2628, round-trip adults $6.50, seniors and students $4, kids 3–14 $3) to the islands from the docks just west of the Westin Harbour Castle Hotel. Both the #509 Harbourfront and #510 Spadina streetcars stop at Bay Street/Queen's Quay.

From downtown, ferries run to three different island docks: Centre Island, Hanlan's Point, and Ward's Island. You can disembark at one and return from another. The schedules for the three ferries are different, though, so be sure to check. While schedules vary seasonally and by time of day, the Centre Island boats run most frequently (mid-Apr.–mid-Oct.), with departures every 15 to 30 minutes in the summer. Boats to Hanlan's Point (mid-Apr.–mid-Oct.) and Ward's Island (year-round) typically operate every 30 to 60 minutes in summer. Only the Ward's Island ferry runs year-round.

Cars are not allowed on the islands, so you'll need to get around on foot or by bicycle.

Bicycling is a good way to tour these flat islands, which are crisscrossed with pathways. In summer, 35-minute **tram tours** leave from Centre Island, a short walk south of the ferry docks.

DOWNTOWN AND THE FINANCIAL DISTRICT
Canadian Broadcasting Corporation Studios and Museum

If you're interested in the history of radio and TV, or if you're nostalgic for the programs of your childhood (do you remember *Mr. Dressup?*), stop into the CBC Museum (250 Front St. W., 416/205-5574 or 866/306-4636, www.cbc.ca, 9 A.M.–5 P.M. Mon.–Fri., free) in the network's Toronto headquarters. Even if you're not Canadian, you can still learn about the Canadian counterpart to the long-running children's show *Sesame Street* (it was called *Sesame Park*) and other interesting tidbits about TV and radio in Canada.

To watch tapings of CBC programs, request tickets by email well in advance of your visit. Check the CBC website (www.cbc.radio-canada.ca) to see what shows are available and how to apply for tickets. The CBC building is a short walk west of Union Station.

Hockey Hall of Fame

If you're a hockey fan, you'll want to make the obligatory pilgrimage to the Hockey Hall of Fame (Brookfield Place, 30 Yonge St., 416/360-7735, www.hhof.com, 9:30 A.M.–6 P.M. Mon.–Sat., 10 A.M.–6 P.M. Sun. late June–early Sept.; 10 A.M.–5 P.M. Mon.–Fri., 9:30 A.M.–6 P.M. Sat., 10:30 A.M.–5 P.M. Sun. early Sept.–late Jun; extended hours during Christmas and March school vacation weeks; adults $17.50, seniors $13, kids 4–13 $11), a museum devoted to the sport and its star players. In addition to all manner of hockey memorabilia, two theaters show archival footage of hockey game highlights and a "be a player" zone lets you wield your own stick.

The hall of fame is on the lower level of the Brookfield Place office tower, a short walk from both the Union and King subway stations.

Design Exchange

The former Toronto Stock Exchange, a 1937 art deco building with a limestone and pink granite facade, now houses the Design Exchange (234 Bay St., 416/363-6121, www. dx.org, 10 A.M.–5 P.M. Mon.–Fri. noon–5 P.M. Sat.–Sun., adults $10, seniors and students $8), a gallery space devoted to Canadian design. The small exhibit area on the main floor is free, but you need to pay admission for the larger gallery upstairs. Ask the staff if you can take a peek at the well-preserved former trading floor on the second level.

Elgin and Winter Garden Theatre Centre

The only "double-decker" theater in Canada, and one of less than a dozen ever built worldwide, the Elgin and Winter Garden Theatres (189 Yonge St., 416/314-2901) are two full-sized theaters—stacked one on top of the other. Constructed as a vaudeville house, the Elgin (originally called Lowe's Young Street Theatre) opened in December 1913 on the main level; the Winter Garden upstairs opened two months later. While the Elgin was (and still is) traditional in style, with red upholstered seats and detailed gold plasterwork on the ceilings and walls, the Winter Garden was designed to resemble a garden. Its walls are painted with floral murals, and real leaves hang from the ceiling, like a garden arbor.

As the vaudeville era ended, the lower-level theater became a movie house that was extremely popular during the 1930s and '40s, but by the 1970s, it had become a porn theater. The Winter Garden, shuttered in 1928, was all but abandoned. In 1981, the Ontario Heritage Foundation purchased the building and launched a multiyear restoration project.

While the Elgin had been renovated repeatedly over the years (the lobby had been painted 27 times), the Winter Garden was essentially preserved from the 1920s, hidden under decades of grime. The restoration team couldn't use water or other liquids to clean the wall murals, which had been created with water-soluble paint. Instead, they used more than 385 kilograms (850 pounds) of raw bread dough, rolling it over the murals to lift off the dirt. The team also harvested more than 5,000 beech branches to replace the crumbling leafy ceiling.

The restored theaters reopened in 1989. Since then, they've been used primarily for touring productions—dramas, musicals, ballets, and operas—as well as various special events. For an event calendar and tickets, contact Ticketmaster (855/622-2787, www.ticketmaster.ca) or phone the theater directly.

Fascinating 90-minute **tours** (5 P.M. Thurs. and 11 A.M. Sat., adults $12, seniors and students $10) of the theater complex are offered year-round. Tours tell you more about the history and restoration of the building, visit both theaters, and tour backstage. Reservations aren't required; just arrive at the theater 15 minutes before the scheduled tour time. For more information about the tours, contact the **Ontario Heritage Trust** (www.heritagetrust.on.ca).

The theater center is just outside the Queen subway station. You can also take the #501 Queen streetcar to Yonge Street.

Old City Hall

Toronto architect Edward James Lennox (1854–1933), who later designed the even more ornate Casa Loma and the nearby King Edward Hotel, crafted the intricately carved Romanesque Revival stone building now known as Toronto's Old City Hall (60 Queen St. W., www.toronto.ca, 8:30 A.M.–4:30 P.M. Mon.–Fri.). When it opened in 1899, it was the largest municipal building in North America.

On the building's exterior, Lennox included stone caricatures that apparently represented politicians of his era. At the main entrance on Queen Street, marked by three stone archways, look closely at the top of the columns on the west side of the center arch and you might spot a face with a handlebar mustache—that's Lennox himself.

Old City Hall was actually the Toronto's third city hall building. The first, which burned down in 1849, was on the current site

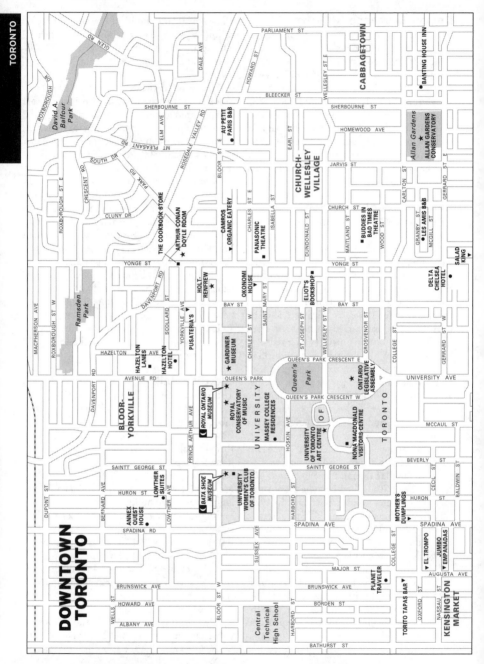

DOWNTOWN TORONTO

TORONTO

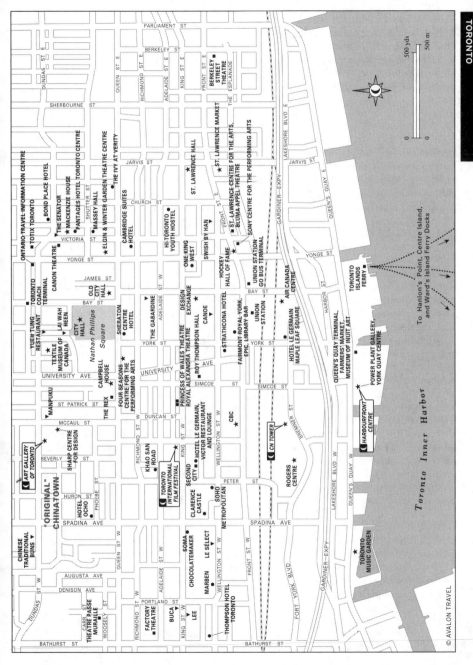

© AVALON TRAVEL

Toronto Inner Harbor

To Hanlon's Point, Centre Island, and Ward's Island Ferry Docks

500 yds
500 m

of the St. Lawrence Market. The St. Lawrence Market building was the second city hall from 1845 to 1899.

Surrounding skyscrapers now dwarf the landmark 103-meter (300-foot) clock tower adorning the structure that housed city offices and council chambers until the mid-1960s. Today, Old City Hall is used as a court building. Visitors can walk around inside (after you clear the security check), taking in the finely detailed mosaic floors and marble walls, but no interior photos are allowed.

Old City Hall is one block west of the Queen subway station and opposite the Bay Street stop on the #501 Queen streetcar.

Toronto City Hall

Two curved towers flanking a spaceship-style pod? Finnish architect Viljo Revell designed the distinctive complex of buildings that is the Toronto City Hall (100 Queen St. W., www.toronto.ca), which opened in 1965. (Sadly, the architect passed away 10 months before the building's opening ceremony.)

When you enter City Hall from the plaza, you can't miss the massive white column in the center of the rotunda; it's the support structure for the **city council chambers** that sit above it. Council meetings, which are open to the public, begin on the fourth Tuesday of every month and usually last for three days; sessions run from 9:30 A.M. until around 6 P.M. You can see a detailed schedule, including topics that will be discussed, on the city website (www.toronto.ca).

To the right of the main entrance (on the east wall) is the **"nail mural,"** a wall sculpture called *Metropolis* that artist David Partridge (1919–2006) crafted from 100,000 nails. Other artwork is on view around the building's first and second floors; feel free to browse.

To the left of the entrance, there's a **scale model of the city.** The buildings in the model that are colored pink are those are designated as historically or architecturally significant.

There are no public tours of City Hall, but ask at the lobby reception desk for a free **self-guided tour booklet,** which points out many

of the building's noteworthy features. The tour booklet is also available online on the city website.

Free concerts and festivals frequently take place on **Nathan Phillips Square,** the plaza in front of City Hall, which is named for the former Toronto mayor who was in office from 1955 to 1962. The plaza's reflecting pool, a pleasant spot for a rest or picnic in summer, becomes a **skating rink** in winter. The arches that span the pool are the **Freedom Arches,** dedicated in 1991 "to the millions who struggled, including Canadians, to gain and defend freedom and to the tens of millions who suffered and died for the lack of it."

City Hall is a short walk from either Queen or Osgoode subway station. You can also take the #501 Queen streetcar to either Bay Street or York Street.

Four Seasons Centre for the Performing Arts

Both the National Ballet of Canada and the Canadian Opera Company perform at the Four Seasons Centre for the Performing Arts (145 Queen St. W., www.fourseasonscentre.ca), where the main auditorium seats more than 2,000 people. To learn more about the building and its resident companies, take a 90-minute **Four Seasons Centre tour** (adults $20, seniors and students $15), which takes you backstage, into the dressing rooms, the wardrobe and wig rooms, the orchestra pit, and the ballet rehearsal studio. You'll get some theater trivia, too, like the fact that the 2006 building houses the world's longest free-spanning glass staircase, or that the center has 103 bathrooms, two-thirds of which are for women!

Call or check the website for tour schedules. You can buy tickets online in advance or simply arrive early on the day of your tour and purchase tickets at the welcome desk in the main lobby. The nearest subway is Osgoode.

Campbell House Museum

Built in 1822 when the Toronto area was still a frontier outpost, the Georgian-style Campbell House (160 Queen St. W., at University,

416/597-0227, www.campbellhousemuseum. ca, 9:30 A.M.–4:30 P.M. Tues.–Fri., noon–4:30 P.M. Sat., also noon–4:30 P.M. Sun. late May–late Sept.; closed Dec. 25–Jan., adults $6, seniors and youth 13–18 $4, kids 5–12 $3) is the oldest remaining house from the original Town of York. On the 30- to 45-minute guided tours, you'll learn about early Toronto history and about the lives of Judge William Campbell—the sixth chief justice of Upper Canada—and his wife Hannah, who built and resided in the house. Although few original furnishings remain, the house is outfitted with elegant period pieces that reflect the Campbells' well-to-do status.

Campbell House was originally located 1.5 kilometers (0.9 mile) to the southeast. After being threatened with destruction in 1972, it was moved to its current location, one block west of City Hall near the Osgoode subway station.

MacKenzie House

Illegitimate children, mental illness, political intrigue, sibling rivalry, even suicide are all part of the history of William Lyon MacKenzie (1795–1861) and his family, who moved to this Georgian rowhouse in 1859, just two years before his death. Yes, when you tour MacKenzie House (82 Bond St., 416/392-6915, www.toronto.ca, noon–5 P.M. Sat.–Sun. Jan.–Apr.; noon–5 P.M. Tues.–Sun. May–early Sept.; noon–4 P.M. Tues.–Fri., noon 5 P.M. Sat.–Sun. early Sept.–Dec.; adults $5.71, seniors and students 13–18 $2.62, kids 5–12 $2.38), you'll learn more about MacKenzie's official biography, as a journalist, political reformer, and politician who became the first mayor of the city of Toronto. Yet the guides also share personal details about his life that make a visit here more than just a historic house tour.

Born in Scotland, MacKenzie immigrated to Canada in 1820. He began publishing a reform-minded newspaper, the *Colonial Advocate,* in 1924 in Queenston, near Niagara Falls, before relocating to Toronto (then called York). One section of MacKenzie House is now a working 1850s replica of MacKenzie's Toronto print shop, with an original 19th-century printing press where you can learn more about MacKenzie's newspaper work and about the printing technology of the time. The rest of the house that you see on the 45-minute tour is restored to the 1860s, although most of the furnishings aren't original to the home.

MacKenzie House is two blocks east of the Dundas subway station. You can also take the #505 Dundas streetcar to Bond Street.

Textile Museum of Canada

Quilts, clothing, fabrics, carpets, kimonos, pillow covers, and hats—you'll find all these and more at the Textile Museum (55 Centre Ave., www.textilemuseum.ca, 11 A.M.–5 P.M. Thurs.–Tues., 11 A.M.–8 P.M. Wed.; adults $15, seniors $10, students and kids 5 and older $6, families $30). The museum's permanent collection includes more than 12,000 objects that come from 200 regions around the world and span almost 2,000 years. They're shown in rotating exhibits, along with changing exhibitions of contemporary and historical textiles from Canada and abroad.

Before or after your museum visit, check out the cool "social fabric" feature on the museum website, which enables you to examine various textiles, ask questions about them, or share comments. To learn more about the exhibits, come on Sunday when you can take a **guided tour** (2 P.M., free with museum admission) of the galleries. On Wednesdays from 5 to 8 P.M., admission is "pay what you can."

The museum is located off Dundas Street West, just east of University Avenue. The closest subway station is St. Patrick; you can also take the #505 Dundas streetcar to Chestnut Street.

St. Lawrence Market

From the Town of York's earliest days, the area bounded by Front, Jarvis, King, and Church Streets was a market district. In 1845, the town built a city hall nearby on Front Street, which housed the mayor's office, the council chambers, the police station, and the jail, as well as a produce and poultry market. When the city again

© CAROLYN B. HELLER

Browse the St. Lawrence Market for produce, cheese, or lunch.

outgrew these quarters and constructed a new municipal building on Queen Street (the structure now known as "Old City Hall") in 1899, the market began to take over the former city offices, evolving into the St. Lawrence Market (Front St. E., between Market and Jarvis Sts., 416/392-7219, www.stlawrencemarket.com).

The St. Lawrence Market is four blocks east of Union Station. You can also take the #504 King streetcar to Jarvis Street.

SOUTH MARKET
The main St. Lawrence Market building, the South Market (93 Front St. E., 8 A.M.–6 P.M. Tues.–Thurs., 8 A.M.–7 P.M. Fri., 5 A.M.–5 P.M. Sat.), is packed with market stalls, selling cheeses, meats, and produce, as well as prepared foods. Not all of it is locally produced, but some is, so look hard if you're into local goodies.

To get an overview of the market and learn more about its history, come for the one-hour **Food Tasting and History Show** (9 A.M. Sat., free). Every Saturday, a vendor showcases a food or product sold at the market and usually offers tastings, too.

If you want a more detailed history of the market district, book a two-hour **St. Lawrence Market History Walking Tour** (647/393-8687, www.brucebelltours.ca, 10 A.M. Tues.–Sat., adults $25) with guide Bruce Bell. Reservations are required; book by phone or in person at the Souvenir Market, just inside the main entrance to the South Market.

The **Market Kitchen,** on the mezzanine level of the South Market, offers cooking classes on topics ranging from easy weeknight suppers to raw food to a seafood workshop that combines a shopping tour of the market's fish vendors paired with a cooking lesson. Most classes are two to three hours long and cost between $50 and $85 per person. You must book in advance by phone or email (416/860-0727, kitchen@stlawrencemarket.com).

On the second floor of the South Market building, the city-run **Market Gallery** (10 A.M.–4 P.M. Tues.–Fri., 9 A.M.–4 P.M. Sat., free) mounts changing exhibitions that in some way reflect the city's art, culture, or history. The gallery space was formerly the Toronto City Council Chamber, when the St. Lawrence Market building housed Toronto's municipal offices in the late 1800s.

NORTH MARKET

Across Front Street from the South Market building, the North Market has been a place for area farmers to sell their wares since 1803. It is still a year-round Saturday **farmers market** (5 A.M.–5 P.M.). On Sundays, an **antiques market** (dawn–5 P.M.) sets up in the North Market.

ST. LAWRENCE HALL

The stately cupola-topped building at the corner of King and Jarvis Streets near the North Market is St. Lawrence Hall (157 King St. E., www.stlawrencemarket.com/hall). Built in 1850, the hall for many years was one of the city's social hubs, hosting concerts, lectures, and balls. The hall also played a role in the abolitionist movement. The North American Convention

of Coloured Freemen, an abolitionist group, met here in 1851 to discuss the issue of former slaves fleeing the United States. After debating whether to encourage these refugees to start new lives in Canada, the Caribbean, or Africa, the 53 delegates concluded that Canada was the best destination for these former slaves.

St. Lawrence Hall is now primarily a city office building, but visitors can go up to the **East Room,** on the third floor, to see the small exhibit about the notables who lectured, performed, or visited here, from Canadian politician and journalist William Lyon Mackenzie to abolitionist leader Frederick Douglass to circus impresario P. T. Barnum.

◖ The Distillery District

Toronto was once home to the world's largest distillery, the Gooderham and Worts Distillery, founded in 1832. Though the stills have long since been stilled, the 13-acre site east of downtown has been redeveloped into The Distillery Historic District (55 Mill St., 416/364-1177, www.thedistillerydistrict.com), where the

© CAROLYN B. HELLER

This former whiskey distillery is now a cool arts district.

Victorian-era brick industrial buildings now house art galleries, shops, cafés, and theaters, as well as high-end condominiums.

The Distillery Historic District is bounded by Parliament, Mill, and Cherry Streets. The easiest way to get here from downtown is to hop on the #504 King streetcar. Get off at Parliament St., then walk two blocks south. You can also follow a **walking path** between the St. Lawrence Market and the Distillery District. It's along the Esplanade bordering David Crombie Park, between Lower Jarvis and Parliament Streets.

GALLERIES AND ARTIST STUDIOS

The **Artscape Building** (55 Mill St., Bldg. 74, www.torontoartscape.on.ca) houses more than 30 artist studios, many of which are open for browsing, and you may be able to watch the artists at work. The best time to visit is on weekends between mid-April and mid-October, when many of the artisans open their studios during the **Distillery Art Market** (11 A.M.–6 P.M. Fri.–Sun.). Other artists and food vendors set up an outdoor market, as well. You can also take a free tour of **Artscape Distillery Studios** (noon, 2 P.M., and 4 P.M. Fri.–Sun. mid-Apr.–mid-Oct.); tours depart from the information booth in Case Goods Lane.

The **Corkin Gallery** (55 Mill St, Bldg. 61, 416.979.1980, www.corkingallery.com, 10 A.M.–6 P.M. Tues.–Sat., noon–5 Sun.) has one of the coolest art spaces in the Distillery District, displaying contemporary works amid the brick columns, steel girders, and soaring ceilings of the building's original structure.

The **Monte Clark Gallery** (55 Mill St., Bldg. 2, 416/703-1700, www.monteclarkgallery.com, 10 A.M.–6 P.M. Tues.–Sat., noon–5:30 P.M. Sun.) shows artworks by well-regarded Canadian and international contemporary artists.

While you may think about multicultural Toronto only in terms of its various ethnic populations, you can learn about a different sort of community at the **Deaf Culture Centre** (55 Mill St., Bldg. 5, Suite 101, 416/203-0343, www.deafculturecentre.ca, 11 A.M.–6 P.M. Tues.–Sat., noon–5 P.M. Sun., free). The center

has a small museum about the deaf community and about technological innovations and communications tools for the deaf. It also offers resources for deaf individuals and their families and friends.

BREWERIES

Toronto's first sake brewery has set up shop in the Distillery District. The **Ontario Spring Water Sake Company** (55 Mill St., Bldg. 4, 416/365-7253, www.ontariosake.com, 11 A.M.–7 P.M. Mon.–Sat., noon–6 P.M. Sun.) has a retail store and tasting bar.

The **Mill Street Brewery** (55 Mill St., Bldg. 63, 416/681-0338, www.millstreetbrewery.com, store 11 A.M.–8 P.M. Mon.–Thurs., 11 A.M.–10 P.M. Fri.–Sat., 11 A.M.–6 P.M. Sun.; brewpub 11 A.M.–midnight Mon.–Tues., 11 A.M.–1 A.M. Wed.–Thurs., 11 A.M.–2 A.M. Fri., 9:30 A.M.–2 A.M. Sat., 9:30 A.M.–midnight Sun.) produces a dozen varieties of beer in their Distillery District microbrewery. Free brewery tours are offered daily (4 P.M. Mon.–Fri., 3 and 5 P.M. Sat.–Sun.); check in at their store 15 minutes before the tour time.

Enoch Turner Schoolhouse

Near the Distillery District, the Enoch Turner Schoolhouse (106 Trinity St., 416/863-0010, www.heritagetrust.on.ca, 10 A.M.–5 P.M. Mon.–Fri., suggested donation adults $5, seniors and students $3) housed Toronto's first free school. Funded by a well-to-do local brewer, Enoch Turner, the school opened in 1849. Its pupils were the children of the immigrants, most of whom were Irish, who settled the surrounding Corktown neighborhood. You can look inside the one-room school to learn more about life and learning in mid-19th-century Toronto.

You can walk to the school from the Distillery District, or take the #504 King streetcar to Trinity Street. The schoolhouse is located behind the Little Trinity Anglican Church.

BLOOR-YORKVILLE AND THE ANNEX

Bloor Street bisects the city from west to east, and its central section, between Avenue Road and Yonge Street, is the Bloor-Yorkville (www.bloor-yorkville.com) neighborhood, known primarily as an upscale shopping destination. Just to the west, along Bloor Street between Bathurst Street and Avenue Road, The Annex (www.bloorannexbia.com) is both more residential and more bohemian, with a mix of cafés, shops, eateries, and bed-and-breakfasts. Many of its businesses cater to students and staff at the nearby University of Toronto.

These centrally located neighborhoods also house several of the city's top cultural attractions, including the Royal Ontario Museum and the Bata Show Museum.

University of Toronto

With more than 75,000 students and over 15,000 faculty and staff, the University of Toronto (www.utoronto.ca) is Canada's largest university. The main St. George campus is roughly bounded by Bloor, Bay, and College Streets and Spadina Avenue. The St. George and Museum subway stops are both near the campus.

Prospective students and visitors can take a 90-minute general campus tour (11 A.M., 2 P.M. Mon.–Fri., free) to learn more about the university. If your interest is primarily in history and architecture, take a campus historical tour (2:30 P.M. Mon.–Fri. June–Aug., free). All tours depart from the **Nona Macdonald Visitors Centre** (25 King's College Circle, 416/978-5000).

As you're wandering around the leafy grounds, see what's on at the **University of Toronto Art Centre** (15 King's College Circle, 416/978-1838, www.utac.utoronto.ca, noon–5 P.M. Tues.–Fri., noon–4 P.M. Sat. Sept.–June; free), which shows wide-ranging exhibits in a Romanesque Revival building. The gallery is off Hoskin Avenue, between St. George Street and Queen's Park Crescent.

Ontario Legislative Assembly

Although Toronto is Canada's largest city, it's not the national capital (Ottawa has that distinction). But it is the capital of the province of Ontario, which, like all Canadian provinces, has its own provincial government.

Ontario's seat of government is the august Legislative Assembly building (111 Wellesley St. W., 416/325-7500, www.ontla.on.ca, tours daily 9 A.M.–4 P.M. late May–early Oct.; 9 A.M.–4 P.M. Mon.–Fri. early Oct.–late May; free) in Queen's Park.

On the free 30-minute **tours** of the building, which opened in 1893, you'll get a brief history of the building and the structure of Ontario's government. Guides also share interesting tidbits about members of the provincial parliament (though they're more historical than scandalous). Reservations aren't required, but the tour schedules can vary depending on what's happening in the building, so it's a good idea to phone ahead.

Visitors are also welcome to observe the provincial parliament in action, which during the legislative session is typically between 9 A.M. and 5:45 P.M. Monday through Thursday. The staff at the information desk in the main lobby can also answer questions about tours and parliament sessions.

To reach the legislative assembly, take the subway or the #506 Carlton streetcar to Queen's Park. The building is a short walk north of the station.

◖ Royal Ontario Museum

A visit to the venerable Royal Ontario Museum (ROM; 100 Queen's Park, 416/586-8000, www.rom.on.ca, 10 A.M.–5:30 P.M. Sat.–Thurs., Fri. 10 A.M.–8:30 P.M., adults $15, seniors and students $13.50, kids 4–14 $12; Wed. discounted admission 4:30 P.M.–closing Fri.) is like a stroll through the history of the world. In this massive museum of natural history and world cultures, you'll find everything from Egyptian mummies to British neoclassical dining rooms, Buddha statues from China and India, armor from medieval Europe, and, of course, lots and lots of kid-pleasing dinosaur skeletons.

Approach the museum building on the Queen's Park side and you'll see an imposing stone face with arched windows that dates back to the early 1900s. But when you come around to Bloor Street, it looks like

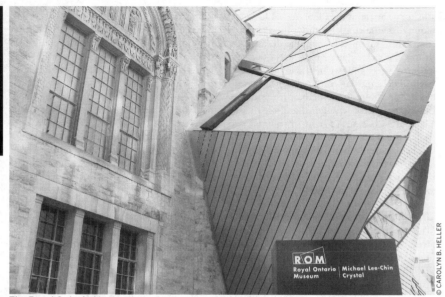

©CAROLYN B. HELLER

The Royal Ontario Museum's contemporary addition appears to hang off the building's facade.

an altogether different structure. Architect Daniel Libeskind designed this contemporary addition, the **Michael Lee-Chin Crystal,** a series of five interlocking glass and steel prisms that appear to hang off the building's Bloor Street facade.

Take a free 45-minute **tour** to get your bearings—either an introduction to the museum's highlights or a more in-depth look at a particular aspect of the collection. Tours are offered daily, but times and topics vary. The ROM also offers lots of lectures, children's programs, and other special events, such as "Mix Mingle Think," a periodic evening event that combines a speaker with a cocktail hour. The museum can get quite crowded, particularly on rainy weekends, during school vacations, over the summer, or whenever there's a blockbuster exhibition on view. Avoid lines at the ticket counter by buying your tickets online in advance ($2 service fee).

Nothing like a typically museum cafeteria, the chic **c5 Restaurant Lounge** (416/586-7928, www.c5restaurant.ca,

11:30 A.M.–2:30 P.M. Tues.–Wed. and Sun., 11:30 A.M.–2:30 P.M. and 5:30–10 P.M. Thurs.–Sat., $15–42), located inside the Michael Lee-Chin Crystal, serves creative contemporary fare. For more casual fuel, there's the **Food Studio** (416/586-7926, 11 A.M.–4:30 P.M. Sat.–Thurs., 11 A.M.–7:30 P.M. Fri.) on the lower level. You don't need a museum ticket to eat at either restaurant.

Both Museum station (Yonge-University-Spadina line) and St. George station (Bloor-Danforth line) are a block from the ROM.

Gardiner Museum

Exhibiting ceramics from ancient times to the present, this art museum (111 Queen's Park, 416/586-8080, www.gardinermuseum.on.ca, 10 A.M.–6 P.M. Mon.–Thurs., 10 A.M.–9 P.M. Fri., 10 A.M.–5 P.M. Sat.–Sun.; adults $12, seniors $8, students $6, kids under 13 free; half-price admission 4–9 P.M. Fri.) shows pieces like a Zapotec funerary urn (created A.D. 500–700), porcelain from Japan and China, and English delftware from the 17th and 18th centuries. To learn more about the museum's exhibits and collections, take a free guided **tour** (2 P.M. Tues., Thurs., Sun.).

If ogling all these fine ceramics pieces inspires you to get your own hands dirty, try a two-hour drop-in **clay class** (6 P.M. Wed. and Fri., 1 P.M. Sun., adults $15, seniors and students $15, kids 12 and under $5). Sign up at the museum's front desk 30 minutes before each session.

Many people visit the museum just to eat in the café, run by a local celebrity chef. **Jamie Kennedy at the Gardiner** (416/362-1957, www.jamiekennedy.ca, 11 A.M.–3 P.M. Sun.–Thurs., 11 A.M.–9 P.M. Fri., $8–11), an airy top-floor space, serves salads, sandwiches, and charcuterie.

The Gardiner is located just opposite Museum station (on the Yonge-University-Spadina line) and a short walk from either St. George or Bay station on the Bloor-Danforth line.

◖ Bata Shoe Museum

If you think that a museum devoted to shoes would appeal only to foot fetishists or footwear-fixated fashionistas, think again. This quirky museum (327 Bloor St. W., 416/979-7799, www.batashoemuseum.ca, 10 A.M.–5 P.M. Mon.–Wed., 10 A.M.–8 P.M. Thurs., 10 A.M.–5 P.M. Fri.–Sat., noon–5 P.M. Sun.; adults $14, seniors $12, students $8, kids 5–17 $5, families $24–35) traces the history and culture of a wide swath of humanity by showcasing what people wore on their feet.

Inside the asymmetrical building, designed by architect Raymond Moriyama to resemble a shoebox with its lid askew, the museum's collections include more than 10,000 shoes—from doll-like slippers worn by Chinese women with bound feet (there's even an overshoe version for wearing while working in the fields), to celebrities' footwear, such as singer Elton John's sky-high platform shoes. They even have British Queen Victoria's silk stocking and a pair of socks that Napoleon wore at Elba. Exhibits include captions with fascinating snippets about the people who wore them.

Elton John's platform shoes are among the thousands on display at the Bata Shoe Museum.

© CAROLYN B. HELLER

On Thursdays from 5 to 8 P.M., admission is pay-what-you-can (suggested donation $5). Free 30-minute guided tours are offered periodically; the schedule is irregular, so check the museum website or phone for dates and times. The nearest subway is St. George.

Arthur Conan Doyle Room

Are you a fan of Sherlock Holmes? On the fifth floor of the Toronto Reference Library, the Arthur Conan Doyle Room (789 Yonge St., 416/395-5577, www.torontopubliclibrary.ca, 2–4 pm Tues., Thurs., Sat., and by appointment.; free), modeled after the study at 221B Baker Street (the mythical sleuth's residence), is full of books by and about the author of the Sherlock Holmes mysteries. Also on display is a variety of Holmes memorabilia, from his trademark pipe to comic books based on Holmes' (fictional) life, as well as Doyle's letters and papers. The collection doesn't circulate, but visitors are welcome to browse, and the helpful staff can tell you about the materials. The library is one block north of the Bloor-Yonge subway station.

Casa Loma

You don't have to travel to Europe to tour a castle; Toronto has Casa Loma (1 Austin Terrace, at Spadina Rd., 416/923-1171, www.casaloma.org, house 9:30 A.M.–5 P.M. daily year-round, last admission at 4 P.M.; gardens 9:30 A.M.–4 P.M. daily May–Oct.; adults $18.19, seniors and youth 14–17 $12.95, kids 4–13 $10; parking $3/hour or $9/day). This opulent "House on the Hill" overlooking the city took three years (1911–1914) to build and contains enough grand salons, towers, and elaborate gardens to satisfy most castle buffs. While kids may not care about the architecture or plush furnishings, they might enjoy climbing the twisty spiral staircase to the turret, finding secret passageways, or following the creepy underground tunnels to the horse stables (where mahogany paneling lines the deluxe stalls).

The ticket price includes a self-guided audio tour with all sorts of details about the house, its owners, and its various furnishings, as well as admission to a documentary film about Canadian financier Sir Henry Pellatt, who built the castle.

From downtown, the most direct route to the castle is to take the subway to Dupont station (Spadina-University line). Exit the subway, walk north two blocks on Spadina Road, and climb the Baldwin Steps (a 110-step staircase) to the castle.

Spadina Historic House and Gardens

Across the road from Casa Loma, the large but decidedly more modest Spadina House (285 Spadina Rd., 416/392-6910, www.toronto.ca, noon–5 P.M. Sat.–Sun. Jan.–Mar.; noon–5 P.M. Tues.–Sun. Apr.–early Sept.; noon–4 P.M. Tues.–Fri., noon–5 P.M. Sat.–Sun. early Sept.–Dec.; adults $7.62, seniors and students 13–18 $4.76, kids 6–12 $3.81) is more typical of an upper-class family home from the first half of the 20th century. Built

© CAROLYN B. HELLER

Casa Loma, the "House on the Hill"

in 1886, the house belonged to the well-to-do Austin family, and nearly all the furnishings, from the ornate art deco wallpaper to the billiards table, are original to the home. Visits to the house are by guided tour only. Watch a 10-minute video about the Austins and their life in Toronto, then follow your guide through their home and history.

Like Casa Loma, Spadina House is at the top of the Baldwin Steps, a short walk (but a steep climb up) from Dupont station.

THE WEST END

West of downtown, Toronto's diverse neighborhoods include some of the city's hippest districts, filled with galleries, restaurants, and funky boutiques, as well as several ethnic neighborhoods—fun to explore when you're hungry.

Kensington Market

Kensington Market isn't a market building. Rather, it's a market neighborhood, filled with vendors' stalls and ethnic eateries that span the globe. There's a Chilean empanada place near a Mexican taco joint, an Indian spice vendor opposite a Latino meat market, and a plethora of fruit sellers, bakeries, nut vendors, cheese shops, and inexpensive clothing outlets. On a mild evening, sidewalk cafés are packed, and people spill out of restaurants and bars onto the streets. Most of the action takes place along Augusta Avenue, Baldwin Street, and Nassau Street, west of Spadina Avenue between Dundas and College Streets.

Generations of immigrants have settled in the Kensington Market area, which gives it its multicultural vibe. In the second half of the 19th century, working-class immigrants from England and Ireland made the neighborhood their home. Then, between 1905 and 1930, Jews fleeing persecution in Europe settled here, many opening up the small shops that resemble those still lining the narrow streets today. After World War II, Caribbean, Chinese, South Asian, and Latin American immigrants joined the European settlers in the market district.

To get to Kensington Market, take the #506 Carlton streetcar to Major Street or Augusta

Avenue, or take the #510 Spadina streetcar and get off anywhere between Dundas and College.

"Original" Chinatown

Toronto's first Chinatown, settled in the early 1900s, was originally located along Elizabeth Street, near Dundas Street, behind the current Toronto City Hall. When the city began appropriating land in the neighborhood during the late 1940s and early 1950s, with a plan to build a new city hall and public square, many Chinatown businesses closed, but many others moved west into the district now known as Toronto's original Chinatown. Chinese groceries, herbalists, and moderately priced restaurants now line Spadina Avenue and Dundas Street, extending north to College and south toward Queen. The neighborhood has grown increasingly multiethnic, too, with Vietnamese and other Southeast Asian businesses joining the Chinese vendors. It's a fun place to browse and, of course, eat.

To get to Chinatown, take either the #505 Dundas or #506 Carlton streetcar to Spadina Avenue. You could also take the #510 Spadina streetcar and get off anywhere between Dundas and College.

◖ Art Gallery of Ontario

Born Frank Owen Goldberg in Toronto in 1929, the internationally acclaimed architect now known as Frank Gehry grew up not far from the Art Gallery of Ontario (AGO; 317 Dundas St. W., 416/979-6648 or 877/225-4246, www.artmatters.ca or www.ago.net, 10 A.M.–5:30 P.M. Tues., 10 A.M.–8:30 P.M. Wed., 10 A.M.–5:30 P.M. Thurs.–Sun., adults $19.50, seniors $16, students and kids 6–17 $11, families $49; free admission 6–8:30 P.M. Wed.). The Art Gallery is now one of North America's largest museums, with more than 80,000 works, so perhaps it's fitting that Gehry designed the gallery's dramatic new building, which opened in 2008. While Gehry has constructed buildings all over the world—from the Guggenheim Museum Bilbao in Spain and the Experience Music Project in Seattle to the Walt Disney Concert

AROUND THE WORLD IN A TORONTO DAY

In this city there are Bulgarian mechanics, there are Eritrean accountants, Colombian café owners, Latvian book publishers, Welsh roofers, Afghani dancers, Iranian mathematicians, Tamil cooks in Thai restaurants, Calabrese boys with Jamaican accents, Fushen deejays, Filipina-Saudi beauticians, Russian doctors changing tires; there are Romanian bill collectors, Cape Croker fishmongers, Japanese grocery clerks, French gas meter readers, German bakers, Haitian and Bengali taxi drivers with Irish dispatchers.

Toronto writer Dionne Brand in her novel *What We Long For*

Although Brand included this description of Toronto in a work of fiction, there's nothing fictional about the city's multicultural makeup. About half of metropolitan Toronto's residents were born outside of Canada, hailing from nearly every part of the globe. And throughout the city, you'll find ethnic enclaves where you can explore the food and culture of Toronto's various communities.

Perhaps the most visible of these neighborhoods are Toronto's Chinatowns – and Toronto has several of these predominantly Chinese districts, not surprisingly, since the Chinese are one of Toronto's largest "visible minority"

groups. Downtown, the **"original" Chinatown,** extending outward from the intersection of Spadina Avenue and Dundas Street, is a traditional immigrant neighborhood, where you'll find Chinese groceries, herbalists, and plenty of modest – and tasty – restaurants. On the east side of the city is the smaller **East Chinatown,** around Broadview Avenue and Gerrard Street, although this neighborhood now has a significant Vietnamese population, as well.

Toronto also has several large Chinese communities in the suburbs of Scarborough east of downtown, Mississauga to the west, and Richmond Hill and Markham to the north. The northern suburbs, in particular, are wealthier communities than the central-city Chinatowns, with higher-end restaurants and shops, many concentrated in malls, catering to this more upscale demographic. The **Pacific Mall** (4300 Steeles Ave. E., Markham) is one of the largest Asian malls in Canada.

Like the Chinese, the South Asian community is a significant "visible minority." Many early South Asian immigrants made their homes in Toronto's **Little India** neighborhood, also known as the "Indian Bazaar," in the city's East End along Gerrard Street East. While Indian residents – and restaurants – have now moved throughout Toronto, you'll still find a concentration of eateries, jewelers, and clothing shops here that cater to the Indian community.

Many of Toronto's Greek immigrants settled

Hall in Los Angeles—the AGO was his first project in Canada.

Among the highlights of the museum's collection, beyond the building itself, are its Canadian collections, which include significant works by Tom Thomson and the Group of Seven (early 20th-century landscape artists), as well as significant contemporary Inuit art holdings. The AGO has the largest collection of African and Oceanic art in a Canadian art museum, the largest public collection of work by the British sculptor Henry Moore (1898–1986),

and a major European "Old Master" collection that's particularly strong in Italian and Dutch painting from the 1600s, and French impressionist works from the 1800s.

The best way to get an overview of the museum's extensive collection and learn about the building's architecture is to take the 60-minute **AGO Highlights Tour** (1 P.M. daily, free). You can also take one of the **Collection Mini Tours** (11:30 A.M. and 2:30 P.M. daily, 7 P.M. Wed., free), a 25-minute walk through a specific area along Danforth Avenue, particularly between Chester and Pape Streets, in the district called "The Danforth," or **Greektown.** The neighborhood has gentrified (and lost some of its Greek character) as younger families and trendier shops have moved in, but Toronto's Greek community, one of the largest outside of Greece, still shops in the markets and traditional bakeries, lingers over coffee and pastry in the cafés, and dines on classic dishes like dolmades (grape leaves) and souvlaki.

Although Toronto's Korean community isn't as concentrated in one neighborhood as some other ethnic groups, the city does have a **Koreatown,** on Bloor Street West, around Christie Street. Markets, restaurants, and karaoke bars cater both to Koreans and others who enjoy the lively district's vibe.

In the early 20th century, many European immigrants settled on the west side of Toronto, including large numbers of Italian and Portuguese. **Little Italy,** primarily along College Street, west of Bathurst, and **Little Portugal,** on Dundas Street, near Ossington, today seem to have a lot of overlap, with Italian restaurants on the "Portuguese" streets and Portuguese bakeries on the "Italian" ones. And increasingly, hip contemporary eateries are moving in alongside the more traditional businesses. No matter, there's still good eating in these districts.

The streets on and around Roncesvalles Avenue, in the city's West End, were settled by Polish immigrants, giving the community the nickname **Little Poland.** This neighborhood still has Polish businesses, primarily bakeries, delis, restaurants, and travel agencies, although the district no longer has a predominantly Polish population. In a recent census, Polish was the second most widely spoken language in the neighborhood. The first? Chinese.

© CAROLYN B. HELLER

shopping for Greek pastries in "The Danforth," Toronto's Greektown

of the AGO's collection, such as its Canadian, contemporary, or African works.

If you need to refuel, you can get coffee and pastries in the fifth-floor espresso bar. For sandwiches, salads, and light meals, there's **caféAGO.** The museum's flagship dining room is **FRANK** (11:30 A.M.–2:30 P.M. and 5:30–10:30 P.M. Tues.–Fri., 11 A.M.–3 P.M. and 5:30–10:30 P.M. Sat., 11 A.M.–3 P.M. Sun., lunch $12–24, dinner $22–31), which serves contemporary fare.

To reach the museum by subway, take the Yonge–University–Spadina line to St. Patrick station. Then walk west on Dundas Street three blocks to the museum. Or take the #505 Dundas streetcar to McCaul or Beverly Streets; both stops are in front of the AGO.

Ontario College of Art & Design

If you can imagine a black-and-white-checkered box floating in the sky, supported only by yellow, blue, and purple pencils, then you can begin to envision one of Toronto's most distinctive buildings, the **Sharp Centre for**

Design at the Ontario College of Art & Design (OCAD, 100 McCaul St., 416/977-6000, www.ocad.ca).

The floating box, or tabletop, section of the building is 9 meters (29.5 feet) tall, 31 meters (102 feet) wide, and 84 meters (275 feet) long and houses studios and classrooms. Twelve colorful hollow steel legs, each measuring 30 meters (100 feet)—or roughly the equivalent of a 10-story building—support the "tabletop." British architect Will Alsop, in partnership with the Toronto-based Robbie/Young + Wright Architects, designed this unusual structure, which opened in 2004.

The building is most remarkable from the exterior. There are no public tours of the interior, but you can go inside to view exhibitions at **Onsite [at] OCAD U** (100 McCaul St., 2nd fl., 416/977-6000 ext. 265, www.ocad.ca/onsite, 11 A.M.–7 P.M. Tues.–Fri., noon–6 P.M. Sat.–Sun., free), a small contemporary gallery space.

C Queen Street West

Head west from downtown through the Entertainment District to the neighborhood known as Queen Street West. The shops and eateries begin to change from chains and mainstream brands to smaller, independent businesses. As you continue west, the neighborhood gets funkier and gets a mouthful of a moniker: West Queen Street West. Though it still has a grunge feel in parts, this "in" arts district is packed with eclectic shops, galleries, arty hotels, and hip bars. To explore the Queen Street West art galleries, plan to wander here in the afternoon; most don't open till noon.

The small **Ontario Crafts Council Gallery** (990 Queen St. W., 416/925-4222, www.craft. on.ca, 10 A.M.–5 P.M. Tues.–Fri., 11 A.M.–6 P.M. Sat., noon–5 P.M. Sun.) shows work by Ontario craftspeople. Check their website or call for a current exhibition schedule.

At the **David Kaye Gallery** (1092 Queen St. W., at Dovercourt Rd., 416/532-9075, www.davidkayegallery.com, 11 A.M.–6 P.M. Wed.–Fri., 11 A.M.–5 P.M. Sat.–Sun.), you'll find paintings, objects, and jewelry by a mix of up-and-coming as well as more established artists.

Housed in a former police station, **Gallery 1313** (1313 Queen St. W., 416/536-6778, www. g1313.org, 1–6 P.M. Wed.–Sat.) is an artist-run space that shows contemporary Canadian art.

General Hardware Contemporary (1520 Queen St. W., 416/516-6876, www.generalhardware.ca, 11 A.M.–6 P.M. Wed.–Sat.) opened in 2010 in a former hardware store west of Lansdowne Avenue to exhibit contemporary art by Canadian and international artists.

On Ossington Avenue, just north of Queen Street West, there's another emerging gallery district. Look for the **Angell Gallery** (12 Ossington Ave., at W. Queen St. W., 416/530-0444, www. angellgallery.com, noon–5 P.M. Wed.–Sat.), which shows contemporary art, and **Gallery TPW** (56 Ossington Ave., at W. Queen St. W., 416/645-1066, www.gallerytpw.ca, noon–5 P.M. Tues.–Sat.), which exhibits photography.

401 Richmond

Just south of Queen Street at Spadina Avenue is 401 Richmond (401 Richmond St. W., 416/595-5900, www.401richmond.net), a rehabbed brick heritage building that is home to artists, galleries, art shops, and other cultural businesses. Poke around and see what's happening, or check out some of these art spaces: **Musideum** (416/599-7323, www. musideum.com, noon–6 P.M. Tues.–Fri., noon–5 P.M. Sat.) carries musical instruments from around the world and also hosts performances; **Open Studio** (416/504-8238; www. openstudio.on.ca, noon–5 P.M. Tues.–Sun.) is an artist-run printmaking center; and **Swipe Design|Books+Objects** (416/363-1332, www.swipe.com, 10 A.M.–7 P.M. Mon.–Fri., 11 A.M.–6 P.M. Sat.) sells design books and lots of cool design stuff.

Museum of Canadian Contemporary Art

The small Museum of Canadian Contemporary Art (952 Queen St. W., 416/395-0067, www. mocca.ca, 11 A.M.–6 P.M. Tues.–Sun., admission by donation) shows cutting-edge creations by Canadian, and some international, artists, working in many different media. The museum is just east of Ossington Avenue.

High Park

On the far west side of the city, Toronto's largest public park (1873 Bloor St. W., 416/397-2628, www.toronto.ca/parks, dawn–dusk daily, free) has Grenadier Pond, hiking trails, playgrounds, gardens, and even a small **zoo** (Deer Pen Rd., 7 A.M.–dusk daily) with cows, sheep, bison, llamas, peacocks, and deer.

Another park attraction is the 1837 **Colborne Lodge** (11 Colborne Lodge Dr., 416/392-6916, www.toronto.ca, noon–5 P.M. Tues.–Sun. May–Aug., call for off-season hours; adults $5.71, seniors and students 13–18 $2.62, kids 4–12 $2.38), the former home of John and Jemima Howard, who founded High Park.

To see what's where in the park, you can catch the "trackless train" (10:30 A.M.–dusk Sat.–Sun. Apr. and Sept.–Oct.; 10:30 A.M.–dusk daily May–Aug; adults $4.50, seniors and kids $3.50), which makes a 30-minute tour of the park grounds.

The Bloor subway runs along the northern border of High Park. Get off at the High Park station. If you're going to Colbourne Lodge, which is on the south side of the park, it's easier to take the #501 Humber/Long Branch streetcar to Colborne Lodge Dr.; from there, it's a short walk up the road. If you've come by subway, you need to walk all the way across the park from north to south to get to Colborne Lodge Drive.

THE EAST END

Exploring Toronto's east side is less about seeing "sights" and more about exploring different neighborhoods and communities.

The area surrounding Church and Wellesley Streets may officially be **Church-Wellesley Village** (www.churchwellesleyvillage.ca), but as the hub of Toronto's large gay and lesbian community, its unofficial name is the "Gay Village."

East of Parliament Street, between Gerrard and Wellesley Streets, lies **Cabbagetown** (www.oldcabbagetown.com). According to

legend, the immigrants who settled here in the 1800s could afford to eat only the cabbage they grew themselves—giving rise to the Cabbagetown name. Nowadays, the cost of the meticulously preserved Victorian homes in this chic corner of town is so high that—to pay their mortgages—the owners might have to eat cabbage themselves! This urban district has several outdoor attractions (all accessible via the #306 Carleton streetcar), including **Allan Gardens Conservatory** (19 Horticultural Ave., 416/392-1111, www.toronto.ca, 10 A.M.–5 P.M. daily, free), greenhouses with more than 1,500 square meters (16,000 square feet) of plants; **Riverdale Farm** (201 Winchester St., 416/392-6794, www.toronto.ca or www.friendsofriverdalefarm.com, 9 A.M.–5 P.M. daily, free), a kid-friendly farm and gardens; and the 1850 **Toronto Necropolis** (200 Winchester St., 416/923-7911, 8 A.M.–8 P.M. Apr.–Sept., 8 A.M.–dusk Oct.–Mar.), a leafy, park-like cemetery where a number of notable Torontonians are interred.

Stretching east along Danforth Avenue between Chester and Pape, is The Danforth, the neighborhood also known as **Greektown** (www.greektowntoronto.com), since it was historically the center of Toronto's Greek community. You'll still find souvlaki shops, traditional cafés, and baklava-filled bakeries, but the Danforth is becoming a trendy district popular with hip young families who shop in the organic market and frequent the local yoga studio.

Around Broadview Avenue and Gerrard Street is one of Toronto's smaller "Chinatowns." This **East Chinatown** actually has a significant Vietnamese population, which means lots of *pho* and *bahn mi* shops line the streets. The #506 Carlton streetcar will take you to this community.

Farther east along Gerrard are the sari shops and curry-scented dining rooms of Little India, in the neighborhood called the **Indian Bazaar** (www.gerrardindiabazaar.com). Take the #506 Carlton streetcar and get off when you begin to see Indian shops.

Ride the #501 Queen Street streetcar east from downtown, and you'll reach the gentrifying neighborhood of **Leslieville,** which is drawing the artistically inclined to its galleries, cafés, and increasingly hip restaurants and shops. Continuing east is the residential neighborhood known as **The Beaches** (www. beachesbia.com). It borders Lake Ontario, with lakefront walkways and, yes, beaches, making it a pleasant spot for a day's excursion.

GREATER TORONTO
Evergreen Brick Works

For more than 100 years, the Don Valley Brick Works made many of the bricks that built Toronto, including notable buildings like Old City Hall and Massey Hall. When the brick works ceased operations in 1986, this complex of buildings northeast of downtown fell into disrepair. Graffiti artists began using its huge brick walls as their canvases, and performance artists held underground raves in the abandoned factory.

Then, in 1991, the site took on a new identity with the launch of Evergreen Brick Works (550 Bayview Ave., 416/596-7670, http://ebw. evergreen.ca), whose mission was to restore the 16 buildings and create a new environmental design and education center. The goal? Bring nature into the city.

Since then, Evergreen Brick Works has launched a variety of "green" programs. If you're interested in green design, local food, cycling and alternative transportation, or a host of environmental issues, pay a visit here.

To get your bearings in this sprawling complex, stop into the **Young Welcome Centre** (9 A.M.–5 P.M. Mon.–Fri., 8 A.M.–4 P.M. Sat., 11 A.M.–4 P.M. Sun.) and see what's on for the day or learn more about the various offerings. Free one-hour tours leave from the Welcome Centre at 1:30 P.M. on Saturdays and Sundays. As you wander through the former factory buildings, notice that much of the graffiti—artistic and otherwise—still adorns the walls.

Hiking trails wend through the property, and in summer, you can get your bike tuned up at the **Bike Works,** or take a workshop to learn do-it-yourself bike repair. In winter, there's free **ice skating** (4–9 P.M. Thurs., 11 A.M.–4 P.M.

Fri.–Sun.). Workshops, exhibits, and other special events take place throughout the year; a calendar is posted on their website.

On Saturdays, a large **Farmers Market** (8 A.M.–1 P.M. late May–early Sept., 9 A.M.–1 P.M. early Sept.–late May) sets up shop here, with vendors selling local produce, cheeses, honey, apple syrup, jam, baked goods, and a variety of prepared foods. In mild weather, it's in the outdoor pavilion; in winter, it moves into the Welcome Centre. You can also pick up a snack at **Café Belong,** which emphasizes local foods.

To get here, take the subway (Bloor-Danforth line) to Broadview station, where you can catch a free shuttle to the Brick Works. The shuttle stop is next to the park on Erindale Avenue, on the east side of Broadview Avenue, just north of the station. The shuttles run every 30–45 minutes.

◖ Ontario Science Centre

"Please touch" exhibits are common at science museums these days, but at the well-designed Ontario Science Centre (770 Don Mills Rd., at Eglinton Ave. E., www.ontariosciencecentre. ca, 10 A.M.–5 P.M. daily, Science Centre: adults $20, seniors $16, youth 13–17 and students $16, kids 4–12 $13; Science Centre and IMAX film: adults $28, seniors $22, youth 13–17 and students $22, kids 4–12 $19, parking $10), the exhibits go beyond button pushing and computer-based games to promote real explorations of the material. Besides the expected displays about space, the human body, and the Earth, you can investigate prejudice, stereotyping, and racism in the thought-provoking exhibit called "A Question of Truth"; you'll meet prejudice straight on after you're arbitrarily stereotyped before you've even entered the exhibit hall. While a play area will entertain the little ones, the museum is especially interesting to older children, and even jaded teens can find cool stuff here. In the Innovation Centre, older kids and teens can choose from activities ranging from creating and testing their own paper airplane designs to constructing a pair of shoes.

Located northeast of downtown Toronto,

© CAROLYN B. HELLER

Toronto's science museum is great fun for kids of all ages.

this sprawling museum is built into a hillside in the Don Valley, so floor numbers go up as you descend into the exhibit halls (1 is the top floor, 6 is the bottom). From downtown, take the subway (Yonge line) to Eglinton Station. Then take the #34 Eglinton East bus to Don Mills Road. The museum is a short walk south on Don Mills Road.

Alternatively, you can take the Bloor-Danforth line to Pape Station, in the Danforth (Greektown) neighborhood. From there, catch the #25 Don Mills bus north to St. Dennis Drive; it stops directly in front of the Science Centre.

Entertainment and Events

Toronto is not only Canada's largest city; it's the country's cultural capital, home to many of Canada's premier cultural institutions. The Toronto Symphony Orchestra, the National Ballet of Canada, the Canadian Opera Company, and the Canadian Stage Company. But the city has a more contemporary side, too. Toronto hosts an annual fringe festival in July and an international writers' fest in October. Among the liveliest summer events are a popular carnival celebrating Caribbean culture and annual Pride Week, one of the world's largest gay and lesbian pride celebrations.

The acclaimed Second City comedy company has a Toronto branch, and the city has a range of professional and local theater groups. Don't forget the nightclubs, the jazz bars, and the sports pubs broadcasting all hockey all the time.

If you're looking for theaters, concert halls, and clubs, you'll find some near Dundas Square while others cluster in the Entertainment District, on and around King Street West just west of the downtown core.

FAMILY-FRIENDLY TORONTO

Toronto has plenty of activities to engage children of all ages.

- Ride to the top of the **CN Tower** and let your little daredevils jump on the Glass Floor (112 stories above the ground).

- The dinosaurs and mummies at the **Royal Ontario Museum** have lots of kid appeal, as do the hands-on exhibits at the **Ontario Science Centre** and the animals at **Riverdale Farm.**

- Young hockey fans won't want to miss the **Hockey Hall of Fame,** and adventurous kids would enjoy poking around the shops and having lunch in the Chinatown or Little India neighborhoods.

- If it's a nice day, take the ferry to the **Toronto Islands** – what youngster doesn't love an amusement park? You can also rent bikes and go exploring.

- Older kids might enjoy a family version of an **Urban Quest** walking tour, where you follow a series of clues through a section of the city. Or you could take a **Toronto Hippo Tour,** to splash into the harbor on an amphibious vehicle.

- When it's time to eat, wander the **St. Lawrence Market** and let everyone pick out their favorite bites. In Chinatown, have dim sum or watch the dumpling makers at work at **Mother's Dumplings.**

- The city's most family-friendly hotel is the **Delta Chelsea Hotel,** a mega-sized property (it's Canada's largest lodging) with an indoor pool with a 40-meter (130-foot) water slide, a "Kid Centre" for games, arts, and crafts, and a regular roster of family activities.

To find out what's going on, the best sources are the free arts and entertainment weeklies: **Now** (www.nowtoronto.com) and **The Grid** (www.thegridto.com) are both available online and at cafés, bookstores, and newspaper boxes around the city. **Xtra!** (www.xtra.ca), another free weekly, covers gay and lesbian events. The **City of Toronto** website (www.toronto.com) also includes an event calendar.

NIGHTLIFE

The neighborhood known as the Entertainment District (on and around King Street West from St. Andrew station west to Bathurst Street) has lots of clubs and bars, as does West Queen West (along Queen Street from Ossington to Gladstone). For hotel bars and lounges, you'll find plenty of options both in the Entertainment District and around downtown.

The Gay Village (around Church and Wellesley Sts., www.churchwellesleyvillage.ca) has long been the center of the city's gay and lesbian scene, although there's an up-and-coming west-side district, dubbed "Queer West"

(along Ossington Ave. and Queen Street West, www.queerwest.org).

Since bars and clubs go in and out of fashion, it's always best to check locally to see what's going on.

Rock, Jazz, and Blues

Jazz club **The Rex** (194 Queen St. W., 416/598-2475, subway: Osgoode, www.therex.ca) hosts 1,000 gigs a year. Two bands play nightly Monday through Thursday, there are three shows on Friday, and at least four groups take the stage on Saturday and Sunday, beginning most weekends at noon.

A range of live music acts perform at **Hugh's Room** (2261 Dundas St. W., 416/531-6604, www.hughsroom.com), with the emphasis on folk and blues artists. Take the subway to Dundas West station; the club is one block south of Bloor Street.

Bands from Willie Nelson to the Talking Heads to the Tragically Hip have all taken the stage at the **Horseshoe Tavern** (370 Queen St. W., 416/598-4753, www.horseshoetavern.

com) since the club first opened in 1947. These days, they're going for an indie vibe, booking up-and-coming new music acts. Take the #501 Queen streetcar to Spadina Avenue, or the #510 Spadina streetcar to Queen Street.

All kinds of events happen at **The Underground at the Drake Hotel** (1150 Queen St. W., 416/531-5042 or 866/372-5386, www.the-drakehotel.ca), from DJ dance parties and indie band concerts, to film screenings and comedy shows. Get there on the #501 Queen streetcar.

Also on West Queen Street West, "Thursday Night Confidential" at the Gladstone Hotel's **Melody Bar** (1214 Queen St. W., 416/531-4635, www.gladstonehotel.com) is a free indie music night showcasing local bands starting at 10 P.M. There's also a world music series on Friday nights (7–10 P.M.), a country music series on Saturdays (7–10 P.M.), and bluegrass nights on Sundays (6–9 P.M.).

Big-name rock and pop concerts perform at the city's two combination sports and entertainment arenas: the **Air Canada Centre** (40 Bay St., 416/815-5400, www.theaircanadacentre.com, box office 9:30 A.M.–6 P.M. Mon.–Fri., 9:30 A.M.–5 P.M. Sat.) and **Rogers Centre** (1 Blue Jays Way, 416/341-1000, www.rogerscentre.com, box office 8 A.M.–8 P.M. Mon.–Fri., 10 A.M.–6 P.M. Sat.–Sun.). For online or phone sales for events at either venue, contact **Ticketmaster** (416/870-8000, www.ticketmaster.ca).

Bars, Pubs, and Lounges

The classic dark wood-paneled **Library Bar** (100 Front St. W., 416/368-2511, www.fairmont.com, noon–1 A.M. Mon.–Fri., 5 P.M.–1 A.M. Sat.) at the venerable Fairmont Royal York Hotel feels ever so sophisticated. Enjoy a confidential chat with a special someone while savoring one of their famous martinis. It's even more atmospheric on Saturday evening when they turn out the lights for "Lounging in the Dark." Afternoon tea is served here on weekends (12:30–4 P.M. Sat.–Sun.).

A chic spot for a drink is the Thompson Toronto Hotel's **Lobby Bar** (550 Wellington St. W., 416/640-7778, www.thompsonhotels.com, 5 P.M.–2 A.M. Tues.–Sat.), where the bar glows with white light and the wall mural is a whimsical interpretation of the Toronto skyline. On the lower level, the **1812 Lounge** (550 Wellington St. W., 416/640-7778, 10 P.M.–2 A.M. Mon. and Fri.–Sat.) is a more secluded drinking den.

In the Entertainment District, meet for a pre- or post-theater libation at the **Victor Restaurant and Lounge** (30 Mercer St., 416/883-3431, www.victorrestaurant.com, 5 P.M.–midnight Sun.–Wed., 5 P.M.–1 A.M. Thurs.–Sat., $14–16), a stylish lounge in the lobby of Hotel Le Germain.

If you're looking for serious karaoke, head for Koreatown along Bloor Street West where crooners take the mike at spots like **XO Karaoke** (693 Bloor St. W., 416/535-3734, www.xokaraoke.com) and **BMB Karaoke** (593 Bloor St. W., 416/533-8786). The **Gladstone Hotel's Melody Bar** (1214 Queen St. W., 416/531-4635, www.gladstonehotel.com) also has popular karaoke nights (10 P.M.–2:30 A.M. Fri.–Sat.).

Comedy

The Toronto branch of the Chicago-based sketch comedy club **Second City** (51 Mercer St., 416/343-0011 or 800/263-4485, www.secondcity.com, shows at 8 P.M. Mon.–Thurs., 8 and 10:30 P.M. Fri.–Sat., 7 P.M. on Sun.) has cabaret-style shows every night. Monday-night performances are a great value at just $12 per ticket. Tickets for Tuesday through Thursday and Sunday shows are $24; Friday and Saturday performances are $29.

THE ARTS

For discounted day-of-show tickets to theater, music, and other cultural events (as well as regular-price advance tickets), visit the **TOtix Toronto** ticket booth (Dundas St. W. at Yonge, www.totix.ca, noon–6:30 P.M. Tues.–Sat.) in Dundas Square.

Theater

Toronto is one of the world's hubs of English-language theater, with more than 90 theater venues in the metropolitan area. A number of professional repertory companies are based here, many of which focus on Canadian plays. The city's large theaters also host major musicals and other touring productions.

The **Canadian Stage Company** (416/368-3110, www.canadianstage.com), one of Canada's largest not-for-profit theater companies, produces contemporary Canadian and international plays. Their main stage is the **Bluma Appel Theatre** (St. Lawrence Centre for the Arts, 27 Front St. E., 416/366-7723 or 800/708-6754, www.stlc.com), two blocks east of Union Station. They also perform at the smaller **Berkeley Street Theatre** (26 Berkeley St.); from downtown, take the #504 King streetcar east to Ontario Street. In the summer, the company goes outdoors for the **Canadian Stage Dream in High Park** (High Park Amphitheatre, late June–early Sept.), a pay-what-you-can outdoor production; bring a picnic.

The **Factory Theatre** (125 Bathurst St., 416/504-9971, www.factorytheatre.ca) produces a full season of all-Canadian plays, including many world premieres. Founded in 1970, the Factory was the first company to present only Canadian works. The #511 Bathurst streetcar stops at Adelaide Street, right near the theater. You can also take either the #501 Queen or #504 King streetcars to Bathurst Street.

Another long-standing local company, the **Tarragon Theatre** (30 Bridgman Ave., at Howland, 416/531-1827, www.tarragontheatre.com) has been producing a mix of new plays, Canadian works, and classic and contemporary international theater since 1970.

Since 1969, the **Theatre Passe Muraille** (16 Ryerson Ave., 416/504-7529) has produced edgy contemporary works. The small Queen West theater space is two blocks from the #501 Queen streetcar's Bathurst Street stop.

The professional **Soulpepper Theatre Company** (www.soulpepper.ca) stages the classics, from Tolstoy, to Tennessee Williams, to David Mamet. The company performs in the Distillery District, at the **Young Centre for the Performing Arts** (55 Mill St., Bldg. 49, 416/866-8666, www.youngcentre.ca).

Buddies in Bad Times Theatre (12 Alexander St., 416/975-8555, www.buddiesinbadtimes.com) is a not-for-profit professional company that has been producing queer theater since 1979. Its plays focus primarily on gay, lesbian, bisexual, and transgendered identity issues. The theater is one block east of Yonge Street, near the Church-Wellesley (Gay Village) neighborhood; the closest subway station is Wellesley.

You never know quite what you'll find on the **World Stage at Harbourfront Centre** (235 Queens Quay W., 416/973-4000, www.harbourfrontcentre.com), but expect creative contemporary Canadian and international performances.

Canada's oldest continuously operating legitimate theater (it was built in 1907), the beaux arts **Royal Alexandra Theatre** (260 King St. W., between Simcoe and Duncan Sts., 416/872-1212 or 800/461-3333, www.mirvish.com) hosts a variety of plays and musicals. The Royal Alex is a short walk from St. Andrew station; you can also take the #504 King streetcar to Simcoe Street.

The 2,000-seat **Princess of Wales Theatre** (300 King St. W., at John St., 416/872-1212 or 800/461-3333, www.mirvish.com), which opened in the Entertainment District in 1993, is one of Toronto's newer stages. Large-scale musicals, from *Miss Saigon* to *The Lion King* to *The Sound of Music,* are a mainstay at the theater. Walk from St. Andrew station or take the #504 King streetcar to John Street.

Opened in 1920 as a vaudeville house, the **Canon Theatre** (244 Victoria St., 416/872-1212 or 800/461-3333, www.mirvish.com, subway: Dundas) was once Canada's largest movie theater; it originally had 3,373 seats. These days, it stages major musicals, like *Billy Elliot,* as well as other theater and dance productions.

The **Elgin and Winter Garden Theatre Centre** (189 Yonge St., 416/314-2901, subway: Queen), the only "double-decker" theater in Canada, houses two full-sized theaters. Drama, musicals, ballet, and opera, as well as various special events go on stage here. For an event calendar and tickets, contact **Ticketmaster** (855/622-2787, www.ticketmaster.ca) or phone the theater directly.

Only the facade of the **Panasonic Theatre** (651 Yonge St., 416/872-1212 or 800/461-3333, www.mirvish.com) was saved when the building, which began life in 1911 as a private residence, was rebuilt in 2005. Located three blocks south of the Bloor-Yonge subway station, it's now a venue for live theater and concerts.

Live Music

The **Toronto Symphony Orchestra** (416/593-4828, www.tso.ca), one of Canada's major orchestras, performs at **Roy Thompson Hall** (60 Simcoe St., 416/872-4255, www.roythomson.com), the 2,600-seat concert hall with a distinctive curved facade designed by noted Canadian contemporary architect Arthur Erickson (1924–2009). You can purchase symphony tickets at the Roy Thompson box office, by phone, or online at the TSO website; you'll pay a service charge for both phone and online orders. The theater, which opened in 1982 and hosts other concerts as well as the TSO events, is in the Entertainment District. Take the subway to St. Andrew station, or ride the #504 King streetcar to Simcoe Street.

Built in 1894, the venerable **Massey Hall** (178 Victoria St., at Shuter St., 416/872-4255, www.masseyhall.com) was once Toronto's most important venue for classical concerts, opera, jazz, and other events, hosting appearances by Enrico Caruso, George Gershwin, Glenn Gould, Oscar Peterson, Bob Dylan, Gordon Lightfoot, and the Dalai Lama. These days, in addition to big-name popular concerts, the theater also stages the annual **Jazz @ Massey Hall** concert series, as well as the **Sing-Along Messiah,** an audience participation version of the Handel classic that's become a Toronto December tradition. Massey Hall is located downtown, between the Dundas and Queen subway stations, one block east of Yonge Street. The Massey Hall Box Office is

© CAROLYN B. HELLER

Groups from the Bolshoi Ballet to the Soweto Gospel Choir perform at the Sony Centre for the Performing Arts.

open on performance days only, between noon and showtime; otherwise, you can buy tickets for Massey Hall events online or at the Roy Thompson Theatre Box Office (60 Simcoe St., 416/872-4255, www.roythomson.com).

Located on the main floor of the Canadian Broadcasting Centre, the 341-seat **Glenn Gould Studio** (250 Front St. W., information 416/205-5000, tickets 416/872-4255, www.cbc.ca/glenngould) is part concert hall and part recording studio, hosting classical and contemporary music concerts. It's named for Toronto pianist Glenn Gould (1932–1982), who performed and recorded extensively until his sudden death from a stroke at age 50. To reach the CBC building, either walk west from Union Station, or take the #504 King streetcar to John Street. The Roy Thompson Theatre box office (60 Simcoe St., 416/872-4255, www.roythomson.com) sells tickets for events at the Glenn Gould Studio.

Canada's largest opera troupe is the Toronto-based **Canadian Opera Company** (416/363-8231 or 800/250-4653, www.coc.ca). They perform at the **Four Seasons Centre for the Performing Arts** (145 Queen St. W., www.fourseasonscentre.ca). You can buy tickets by phone or in person from the Four Seasons Centre box office, or online at the opera website. Subway: Osgoode.

From the Bolshoi Ballet to the Soweto Gospel Choir, the 3,191-seat **Sony Centre for the Performing Arts** (1 Front St. E., 855/872-7669, www.sonycentre.ca) presents international dance, music, and theatrical productions. Tickets are available online through Ticketmaster (www.ticketmaster.ca) or at the theater box office. The theater is two blocks east of Union Station.

The **St. Lawrence Centre for the Arts** (27 Front St. E., 416/366-7723 or 800/708-6754, www.stlc.com), two blocks east of Union Station, has four music organizations in residence. **Music TORONTO** (www.music-toronto.com) presents traditional and modern chamber music, while **Opera in Concert** (www.operainconcert.com) produces operas that are rarely seen in Canada. The professional **Toronto**

Operetta Theatre (www.torontooperetta.com) presents operetta, light opera, and musical theater featuring Canadian performers. The **Hannaford Street Silver Band** (www.hssb.ca), a professional brass band, performs several concerts throughout the year. Visiting musicians and other performers also take to the stage at the St. Lawrence Centre. Contact the St. Lawrence box office for tickets, or order online.

At the **Royal Conservatory of Music** (273 Bloor St. W., 416/408-0208, www.rcmusic.ca, subway: St. George) in the Bloor-Yorkville neighborhood, notable Canadian and international musical acts, including classical, chamber groups, early music performers, and world music, perform at the 1,135-seat **Koerner Hall.**

Dance

The **National Ballet of Canada** (416/345-9595 or 866/345-9595, www.national.ballet.ca), one of the world's top dance companies, works its artistic magic at the **Four Seasons Centre for the Performing Arts** (145 Queen St. W., www.fourseasonscentre.ca). Tickets are available online from the ballet company website, or from the Four Seasons Centre box office in person or by phone. From the Osgoode subway station, you can walk directly into the Four Seasons Centre.

One of Canada's leading contemporary dance companies, the **Toronto Dance Theatre** (416/967-1365, www.tdt.org), established in 1968, performs several Toronto shows a year, either at Harbourfront Centre or at their own Winchester Street Theatre (80 Winchester St.) in Cabbagetown, a short walk from the Parliament Street stop on the #506 Carlton streetcar.

On the upper level of the Queen's Quay Terminal at Harbourfront Centre, the **Fleck Dance Theatre** (207 Queens Quay W., 416/973-4000, www.harbourfrontcentre.com) plays host to a variety of local, national, and international dance performers.

Cinema

If you're interested in film, don't miss visiting the **TIFF Bell Lightbox** (350 King St. W., 416/599-8433 or 888/599-8433, www.tiff.net/

tiffbelllightbox). The distinctive contemporary glass building is not only headquarters for the annual Toronto International Film Festival, it's also home to the **TIFF Cinematheque,** which screens a wide range of movies throughout the year, and to a **gallery** (noon–9 P.M. Tues.–Thurs., noon–10 P.M. Fri.–Sat., noon–6 P.M.) that shows film-related exhibits.

The lazy days of summer mean outdoor movies, right? The **Free Flicks** series (Harbourfront Centre, 235 Queens Quay W., 416/973-4000, www.harbourfrontcentre.com, July–Aug., free) screens films on some summer Tuesday nights; call or check the website for the schedule.

Literary Events
The weekly **Authors at Harbourfront Centre** (235 Queens Quay W., 416/973-4760 or 416/973-4000, www.readings.org) hosts readings and other literary events from September to June. **Pages Books and Magazines** (www.pagesbooks.ca) runs a series of literary evenings called "This Is Not a Reading Series" (TINARS, www.tinars.ca, Sept.–June). Most events take place at the **Gladstone Hotel** (1214 Queen St. W., 416/531-4635, www.gladstonehotel.com).

FESTIVALS AND EVENTS
Spring
Photography buffs should schedule a Toronto visit during the **Scotiabank CONTACT Photography Festival** (416/539-9595, www.scotiabankcontactphoto.com, May), which showcases the work of more than 1,000 local, national and international artists at more than 200 venues around town.

During the last weekend in May, more than 150 museums, historic buildings, art spaces, condos, and religious institutions—including many that aren't usually open to the public—welcome visitors during **Doors Open Toronto** (www.toronto.ca/doorsopen, May, free).

The **Toronto Jewish Film Festival** (416/324-9121, www.tjff.com, May) typically screens 90–100 movies from many different countries, some by Jewish filmmakers, others with themes of Jewish interest.

Luminato (416/368-3100, www.luminato.com, June) is a 10-day arts fest, featuring theater, dance, music, literature, food, visual arts, film, and even magic. Many events are free, although others require a ticket; the website has a schedule and ticketing information.

Summer
Though it may not be as well known as the similarly named SXSW (the South by Southwest festival that takes place in Austin), Toronto's **North by Northeast Music Festival** (NXNE, 416/863-6963, www.nxne.com, June) presents Canadian and international new and indie music, as well as avant-garde film and digital media.

One of the world's largest gay–lesbian pride celebrations, **Toronto Pride Week** (416/927-7433, www.pridetoronto.com, June–July) features 10 days of marches, parades, and entertainment, as well as a street fair and family activities. The annual Pride Parade is a highlight.

Jazz aficionados converge on the city for the annual **Toronto Jazz Fest** (416/928-2033, www.torontojazz.com, June–July), featuring more than 350 performances at locations around the city. The Beaches neighborhood gets into the jazz act, too, with the long-running **Beaches Jazz Fest** (www.beachesjazz.com, 416/698-2152, July). All events are free.

You never quite know what you'll see at the **Toronto Fringe Festival** (416/966-1062, www.fringetoronto.com, July), an eclectic lineup of more than 150 plays and other theatrical performances. Some of the most popular events continue at the end of the festival during the "Best of the Fringe."

The **Scotiabank Caribbean Carnival Toronto** (416/391-5608, www.torontocaribbeancarnival.com, July), formerly known as CariBana, is a three-week celebration of all things Caribbean, with music, dance, street parties, food, and a whopper of a parade.

Toronto's Greek community welcomes visitors to Danforth Avenue during the annual **Taste of the Danforth** (416/469-5634, www.

tasteofthedanforth.com, August), a weekend of food, music, kids' activities, and more that make this one of Canada's largest street festivals.

For many Torontonians, it's not summer till you've been to the **Canadian National Exhibition** (416/393-6300, www.theex.com, August–September), a waterfront fair, with carnival rides, a sand sculpture contest, a dog show, farm animals, a garden show, and all sorts of concerts and special events.

Fall

The city's premier cultural event is the **Toronto International Film Festival** (www.tiff.net, September), which screens more than 300 movies from around the world and draws celebrities from across the globe. Advance ticket sales generally begin in July, although the detailed festival lineup isn't announced until about two weeks before opening night. Contact the **TIFF Bell Lightbox** (350 King St. W., 416/599-8433 or 888/599-8433) to find out when tickets go on sale.

Stay up all night for Toronto's annual **Nuit Blanche** (www.scotiabanknuitblanche.ca, October), a sundown-to-sunrise celebration of the contemporary arts.

A major literary festival, the **Toronto International Festival of Authors** (www.readings.org, October) is 11 days of readings, discussions, and interviews with authors from across Canada and abroad. Most events take place at **Harbourfront Centre** (235 Queens Quay W., information 416/973-4760, tickets 416/973-4000, www.harbourfrontcentre.com).

Winter

Get your holiday shopping done, or pick up a unique souvenir, at the **One of a Kind Show and Sale** (416/960-3680, www.oneofakindshow.com, November–December), an annual arts and crafts market.

During the **Cavalcade of Lights** (www.toronto.com) the city lights its official Christmas tree in Nathan Phillips Square, outside of City Hall. The tree-lighting ceremony, complete with concerts and outdoor ice-skating, takes place the last weekend of November; the Square remains illuminated through December.

The smaller, winter sibling of the Toronto Fringe Festival, the **Next Stage Theatre Festival** (www.fringetoronto.com, January) presents a lineup of new plays.

Shopping

Toronto is a Canadian art center with a good mix of galleries, craft shops, and arts-oriented shops. The city also has a growing cohort of homegrown fashion designers, so it's worth browsing the boutiques. You'll also find many of the same chain stores that populate the malls across North America.

SHOPPING DISTRICTS

The largest mall in the downtown area, **Eaton Centre** (220 Yonge St., 416/598-8560, www.torontoeatoncentre.com, subway: Dundas or Queen, 10 A.M.–9 P.M. Mon.–Fri., 9:30 A.M.–7 P.M. Sat., 11 A.M.–6 P.M. Sun) has more than 230 stores extending along Yonge Street from Queen to Dundas Streets. Most are Canadian or international chains, including

Abercrombie & Fitch, H&M, Lululemon Athletica, Roots, and Sears.

In the **Bloor-Yorkville** neighborhood (near the Bloor-Yonge, Bay, and St. George subway stations), Bloor Street is lined with a mix of midprice and upscale chain stores, from the Gap to Gucci; on some of the side streets, you'll find independent boutiques. Elsewhere in Yorkville, **Hazelton Lanes** (87 Avenue Rd., at Yorkville, 416/968-8680, www.hazeltonlanes.com) houses a collection of high-end boutiques, including Jacadi, Marina Renaldi, and Petra Karthaus; it's about four blocks from either St. George or Bay subway stations.

Galleries, clothing shops, and design studios populate the restored industrial buildings in the **Distillery District** (www.thedistillerydistrict.

© CAROLYN B. HELLER

Love a bargain? Then you'll love Honest Ed's.

com), east of downtown. If you continue east into funky **Leslieville,** along Queen Street East, you'll find more independent designers and vintage furniture shops.

Along **Queen Street West,** there's a mix of chains and independent shops, with the more creative independents winning out as you continue west to the district known as **West Queen West** (from Bathurst Street to Gladstone Avenue and continuing west to Roncesvalles Avenue). Just off Queen Street, Ossington Avenue is becoming a mini-hub for cool shops and restaurants.

DEPARTMENT STORES

Founded in 1670 as a fur-trading company, the **Hudson Bay Company**—Canada's oldest corporation—has grown to become the country's largest retailer. Its flagship chain of department stores, with locations across Canada, is known as The Bay. Among the many Toronto branches, there's one downtown near City Hall (176 Yonge St., 416/861-9111, www.hbc.com, Subway: Queen, 10 A.M.–9 P.M. Mon.–Fri.,

9:30 A.M.–7 P.M. Sat., 11 A.M.–6 P.M. Sun.) and another in the Bloor-Yorkville neighborhood (44 Bloor St. E., 416/972-3333, 10 A.M.–7 P.M. Mon.–Wed., 10 A.M.–9 P.M. Thurs.–Fri., 9 A.M.–7 P.M. Sat., noon–6 P.M. Sun.).

If you're anywhere near the corner of Bloor and Bathurst Streets, you can't miss the screaming neon facade of **Honest Ed's** (581 Bloor St. W., 416/537-1574, 10 A.M.–9 P.M. Mon.–Fri., 10 A.M.–6 P.M. Sat., 11 A.M.–6 P.M. Sun.), a sprawling bargain outlet that sells everything from T-shirts to toiletries to toasters (groceries, too). Ed Mirvish, who founded Toronto's Mirvish theater empire (the Mirvish company currently owns the Royal Alexandra, Princess of Wales, Canon, and Panasonic Theatres), established this store in 1948. The merchandise is nothing special, but there's a lot of it, and as one of their slogans proclaims, "Honest Ed's is for the birds, CHEAP, CHEAP, CHEAP!"

Around Honest Ed's is an emerging shopping district called **Mirvish Village** (www.mirvishvillagebia.com). The most interesting shops and galleries are along Markham Street, just south of Bloor.

If Honest Ed's brags that its lack of service translates into rock-bottom prices, the upscale fashion emporium **Holt-Renfrew** (50 Bloor St. W., 416/922-2333, www.holtrenfrew.com, subway: Bloor-Yonge, 10 A.M.–7 P.M. Mon.–Wed., 10 A.M.–8 P.M. Thurs.–Fri., 10 A.M.–7 P.M. Sat., noon–6 P.M. Sun.) is Ed's polar opposite, boasting top international designers and personal service. And the prices? Well, as the saying goes, if you have to ask, you can't afford it.

BOOKS AND MAGAZINES

Eliot's Bookshop (584 Yonge St., at Wellesley, 416/925-0268, subway: Wellesley, 11 A.M.–8 P.M. Mon.–Sat., noon–8 P.M. Sun.) has three floors crammed full of good-quality used books—a browser's delight.

As you'd expect from the name, **The Cookbook Store** (850 Yonge St., at Yorkville, 416/920-2665 or 800/268-6018, www.cookbook.com, subway: Bloor-Yonge, 10 A.M.–7 P.M. Mon.–Fri., 10 A.M.–6 P.M. Sat., noon–5 P.M. Sun.) sells a wide range of cookbooks and food magazines. They also host cooking events and food-related talks.

The independently owned **Type Books** (883 Queen St. W., 416/366-8973, www.typebooks.ca, 10 A.M.–6 P.M. Mon.–Sat., 11 A.M.–6 P.M. Sun.) not only has a good selection of all types of books, they also sponsor readings and literary events. Take the #501 Queen streetcar to Strachan Avenue.

CLOTHING, SHOES, AND ACCESSORIES
Queen Street West

Local designer Anne Hung sells pretty party frocks at her **Anne Hung Boutique** (829 Queen St. W., 416/364-7251, 12:30–7 P.M. Tues.–Fri., 12:30–6:30 P.M. Sat., noon–5 P.M. Sun.).

Preloved (881 Queen St. W., 416/504-8704, 11 A.M.–6 P.M. Mon.–Wed., 11 A.M.–7 P.M. Thurs.–Fri., 11 A.M.–6 P.M. Sat., noon–6 P.M. Sun.) doesn't sell secondhand duds; instead,

they create one-of-a-kind clothing from reclaimed vintage fabrics.

Work by more than 100 local jewelry designers is on view at the **Made You Look Jewelry Studio and Gallery** (1338 Queen St. W., 416/463-2136, www.madeyoulook.ca). They'll also custom-design special pieces. Across the street, you'll find trendy accessories and more jewelry at **Made You Look Accessories** (1273 Queen St. W., 416/516-9595). Both shops are open 10 A.M.–6 P.M. Monday to Wednesday and Saturday, 10 A.M.–9 P.M. Thursday and Friday, and noon–5 P.M. Sunday.

Part boutique and part art gallery, **Shop Girls** (1342 Queen St. W., 416/534-7467, www.shopgirls.ca, 11 A.M.–7 P.M. Mon.–Fri., 11 A.M.–6 P.M. Sat., noon–5 P.M. Sun.) is a collective that sells clothing, jewelry, and artwork by Canadian designers.

Just north of Queen Street, **I Miss You** (63 Ossington Ave., 416/916-7021, noon–6 P.M. Tues.–Wed., noon–7 P.M. Thurs.–Sat., noon–6 P.M. Sun.) stocks good-quality vintage designer labels and other clothing and accessories, including lots of 1960s cocktail dresses.

Distillery District

For beautifully crafted jewelry, handbags, and other accessories, peruse the wares—many by Toronto-based artisans—at **Corktown Designs** (55 Mill St., Bldg. 59, 416/861-3020, www.corktowndesigns.com, 11 A.M.–6 P.M. Sun.–Wed., 11 A.M.–7 P.M. Thurs.–Sat.).

More than 100 emerging Canadian designers created the distinctive clothing, jewelry, ceramics, glass, and other works at the **Distill Gallery** (55 Mill St., Bldg. 47, 416/304-0033, www.distillgallery.com, call for hours), for both browsing and buying.

Leslieville

Designer Christina Bergstrom creates the unique, vibrantly colored women's clothes she sells in her Leslieville shop, **Bergstrom Originals** (781 Queen St. E., 416/595-7320, www.bergstromoriginals.com, 11 A.M.–7 P.M. Tues.–Wed., 11 A.M.–8 P.M. Thurs.–Fri., 11 A.M.–7 P.M. Sat., noon–6 P.M. Sun.). Bergstrom complements her own pieces with shoes and accessories by other designers near and far. To get here from downtown, take the #501 Queen streetcar eastbound to Saulter Street.

Playful contemporary and vintage-inspired dresses are ready to rock 'n' roll at **Doll Factory by Damzels** (1122 Queen St. E., www.damzels.com). Designers Kelly Freeman and Rory Lindo sell their own line, *Damzels in This Dress,* along with other clothing, gifts, and accessories. Take the #501 Queen streetcar to Caroline Avenue.

GIFTS AND NOVELTIES

Design geeks could lose themselves for hours at **Bergo Designs** (55 Mill St., Bldg. 47A, 416/861-1821, www.bergo.ca, 10 A.M.–8 P.M. Mon.–Wed., 10 A.M.–9 P.M. Thurs.–Sat., 11 A.M.–6 P.M. Sun.), a cool shop that bills itself a "gallery of industrial design." Many international designers are represented, including Alvar Aalto and Philippe Starck, but you'll also find stuff by up-and-coming craftspeople, including quirky jewelry, toys, gadgets, and gift ideas for your artsy friends.

Pawing through the assortment of quirky stuff in the **Drake Hotel General Store** (1144 Queen St. W., 416/531-5042 ext. 101, http://drakegeneralstore.ca, 11 A.M.–7 P.M. Mon.–Wed., 11 A.M.–9 P.M. Thurs.–Fri., 10 A.M.–9 P.M. Sat., 11 A.M.–6 P.M. Sun.) is like visiting a cool friend who has a collection of weird and wonderful things. Need a stick-on mustache? Check. A classic CBC radio bag? Check. Croissant-shaped earrings, Canadian Mountie cocktail napkins, or same-sex cake toppers? Check, check, and check. In addition to the Queen West location, which is just east of the Drake Hotel, they have stores in the Entertainment District (82A Bathurst St., at King St. W., 416/703-6518, noon–8 P.M. Mon.–Fri., 11 A.M.–7 P.M. Sat., noon–6 P.M. Sun.) and in Rosedale (1011 Yonge St., 416/966-0553, 11 A.M.–7 P.M. Mon.–Fri., 11 A.M.–6 P.M. Sat., noon–5 P.M. Sun.).

OUTDOOR GEAR

For clothing, boots, or camping supplies, visit **Mountain Equipment Co-Op** (400 King St. W., 416/340-2667, www.mec.ca, 10 A.M.–7 P.M. Mon.–Wed., 10 A.M.–9 P.M. Thurs.–Fri., 9 A.M.–6 P.M. Sat., 11 A.M.–5 P.M. Sun.), the Toronto branch of Canada's largest outdoor retailer. The store rent tents, sleeping bags, canoes, kayaks, cross-country skis, and snowshoes. You must become a co-op member to make a purchase; anyone can join by paying a lifetime membership fee of just $5.

Sports and Recreation

Whenever the sun shines, residents flock to the lakefront, the Toronto Islands, or the city's many parks, and there are numerous paths for walking and cycling. When winter comes, ice skating keeps Toronto folks busy (unless they head north to the downhill ski and snowboard resorts). And year round, Toronto is Canada's hub for professional sports, especially hockey, baseball, and basketball.

PARKS AND BEACHES

The city's best beaches are on the **Toronto Islands** (ferry: 9 Queens Quay West at Bay St., 416/397-2628, www.toronto.ca, round-trip adults $6.50, seniors and students $4, kids 3–14 $3). The south shore has several narrow but sandy stretches on Lake Ontario. There's also Ward's Island Beach, Gibraltar Beach, even a clothing-optional beach at Hanlan's Point.

The city's most beautiful parkland is **High Park** (1873 Bloor St. W., 416/397-2628, www.toronto.ca/parks, subway: High Park, dawn–dusk daily, free). The park is in the city's west end, south of Bloor Street, with a large pond, playgrounds, hiking trails, and even a small zoo.

Note that the Lake Ontario waters are not always clean enough for safe swimming, so check on the water quality before you dive in.

Phone the city's **Beach Water Quality Hotline** (416/392-7161) or check the Beach Water Quality website (http://app.toronto.ca). City staff will also post signs at the beach if bacteria levels are too high for healthy swimming.

BICYCLING

Toronto has hundreds of kilometers of bike lanes on city streets. However, if you're not an experienced urban cyclist, you may want to stick to one of the off-road cycling trails. The 56-kilometer (35-mile) **Martin Goodman Trail** runs along the Toronto lakeshore. It's part of the 900-kilometer (560-mile) **Waterfront Trail,** which follows the Lake Ontario shore from the Niagara Peninsula to the Quebec border. The **Toronto Islands** (ferry: 9 Queens Quay West at Bay St., 416/397-2628, www.toronto.ca, round-trip adults $6.50, seniors and students $4, kids 3–14 $3) are another popular cycling spot. Bike rentals ($7/hour, tandems $14/hour) are available near the Centre Island pier. You can also rent four-wheeled pedal bikes ("quadricycles") that seat two ($16/hour) or four ($30/hour) people.

Need a bike? Rent a Bixi.

© CAROLYN B. HELLER

To figure out the best cycling routes around Toronto, try the useful **Ride the City** (www.ridethecity.com/toronto) mapping tool, which plots the safest route between two points. You can get more information about cycling in Toronto, as well as a bike-route map, at www.toronto.ca/cycling.

BIXI Toronto (www.toronto.bixi.com), a public bike-sharing system, lets you pick up a bike from one of 80 rental stations around the city, ride it to your destination, and return it to the nearest station when you arrive. The basic rental fee is $5 for 24 hours (or $12 for 72 hours); if you keep your rides short (up to 30 minutes per trip), that's all you pay. Since the service is designed for short hops, there are additional fees for each extra half-hour if you keep a bike for more than 30 minutes per trip. Bikes are located throughout the downtown area (look for rental stations near the subway stops) and around the University of Toronto; if you enter your location on their website, it will display a map of the nearest bike locations.

In the Distillery District, you can rent both regular and electric bikes from **Segway of Ontario** (37 Mill St., Bldg. 37, Unit 106, 416/642-0008 or 866/405-8687, www.segwayofontario.com). The standard bike rentals are $10 for the first hour, $5 for each additional hour, or $35 for the day; the e-bikes are $20 for the first hour, $10 for each additional hour, or $50 for the day.

HIKING

The **Toronto Islands** (ferry: 9 Queens Quay West at Bay St., 416/397-2628, www.toronto.ca, round-trip adults $6.50, seniors and students $4, kids 3–14 $3) and **High Park** (1873 Bloor St. W., 416/397-2628, www.toronto.ca/parks, subway: High Park, dawn–dusk daily, free) are popular hiking destinations. You can also hike the trails that wend around the property at the **Evergreen Brick Works** (550 Bayview Ave., 416/596-7670, http://ebw.evergreen.ca).

ICE SKATING

When temperatures drop, popular places to ice-skate are on the pond in front of City Hall, which becomes the seasonal **Nathan Phillips Square** rink (100 Queen St. W., 416/304-1400, www.toronto.ca, 10 A.M.–10 P.M. daily Nov.–Mar., skate rentals adults $10, kids $5), and at Harbourfront Centre, where the lakeside pond freezes to become the **Pond Rink** (Queen's Quay West, 416/973-4000, www.harbourfrontcentre.com, skate rentals adults $7, seniors and kids 12 and under $6). Skating season is weather-dependent but typically begins in late November or early December and continues until sometime in March.

KAYAKING AND CANOEING

If you want to introduce your kids to canoeing or try it yourself for the first time, head to the **Natrel Pond at Harbourfront Centre** (235 Queens Quay W., 416/973-4000, www.harbourfrontcentre.com, hours vary, $4) for a 15-minute paddle around the petite pond. Nearby, at the **Harbourfront Canoe and Kayak Centre** (283A Queens Quay W. at Rees St., 416/203-2277 or 800/960-8886, www.paddletoronto.com), you can rent canoes ($30/hour, $60/day), kayaks (single $30/hour, $70/day; double $40/hour, $85/day), and stand-up paddleboards ($30/hour, $10/each additional hour). You can also rent canoes, kayaks, and pedal boats on the **Toronto Islands** (ferry: 9 Queens Quay West at Bay St., 416/397-2628, www.toronto.ca, round-trip adults $6.50, seniors and students $4, kids 3–14 $3) during the summer. The rental shop is in the Boat House on Centre Island.

SPECTATOR SPORTS

As in most Canadian cities, hockey is Toronto's major sport, and the team to root for is the National Hockey League's **Toronto Maple Leafs** (http://mapleleafs.nhl.com). They take to the ice at the Air Canada Centre (40 Bay St., 416/815-5400, www.theaircanadacentre.com).

The **Toronto Blue Jays** (416/341-1234 or 888/654-6529, www.bluejays.com), in Major League Baseball's American League, play their home games at the Rogers Centre (1 Blue Jays Way, 416/341-1000, www.rogerscentre.com). The season runs from spring through fall. You

In winter, you can skate at Nathan Phillips Square.

© CAROLYN B. HELLER

can buy tickets online at Ticketmaster (www.ticketmaster.ca) or in person at the Rogers Centre box office (Gate 9, Bremner Blvd., 8 A.M.–8 P.M. Mon.–Fri., 10 A.M.–6 P.M. Sat.–Sun.).

The **Air Canada Centre** (40 Bay St., 416/815-5400, www.theaircanadacentre.com) is also the home court for the **Toronto Raptors** (www.nba.com/raptors), in the National Basketball Association.

The city's Canadian Football League team, the **Toronto Argonauts** (416/341-2746, www.argonauts.ca), plays at the Rogers Centre.

Toronto has a professional men's soccer team, **Toronto FC** (416/360-4625, www.torontofc.ca). They play at BMO Field (170 Princes' Blvd.) on the Exhibition Place grounds, west of downtown. Tickets are available through Ticketmaster (www.ticketmaster.ca). To get to BMO field, take the #509 Harbourfront streetcar west from Union Station to Exhibition, or catch the #511 Bathurst streetcar south from Bathurst station (Bloor-Danforth line) to Exhibition. You can also catch the GO train from Union Station to Exhibition.

Accommodations

Like most metropolitan areas, Toronto offers a range of lodgings from major international hotels to boutique properties to homey B&Bs. Accommodations are concentrated in the downtown area, in the Bloor-Yorkville district, and in the Annex neighborhood around the University of Toronto, but anything within walking distance of the subway or streetcar can be convenient. If you like funky and modern, look for one of the city's newer "art" hotels or B&Bs.

If you're on a tight budget, and you're visiting in summer, check out the residence halls on the University of Toronto campus, which offer basic but good-value rooms. Otherwise, for accommodations under $100 a night, you're generally looking at hostels; most of Toronto's hostels have private rooms, as well as dormitory beds. If you can spend a bit more ($100–150 per night for a double room) you'll have your choice of many B&Bs and, depending on the season you visit, some of the hotels, as well. Outside of the Christmas/New Year's holiday period, rates are typically lowest in winter.

Beware that most Toronto hotels, particularly those downtown, charge for parking, which can range from $10 to $30 and up, and that many large hotels also add a charge for Internet access.

DOWNTOWN AND THE FINANCIAL DISTRICT
Under $100

There's always something going on at the **HI-Toronto Youth Hostel** (76 Church St., 416/971-4440 or 877/848-8737, www.hostellingtoronto.com, $20–45 dorm, $69–89 d), whether it's a pub crawl, karaoke night, or just hanging out in the lounge, listening to music, or playing pool. In summer, the action is on the fifth-floor patio for drinks or barbecues. The hostel has more than 140 beds across nine floors, in all sorts of hostel-basic room configurations: six-, eight-, and 10-bed dorms (male only, female only, and mixed); quad rooms with bunk beds; more spacious "deluxe" rooms

with two or three single beds and a private bath; and private doubles with en suite bath. A basement café serves breakfast and dinner, but many guests prep their own meals in the common kitchen. Wi-Fi is free throughout the building, or you can use their computers for $3 per hour. The hostel is four blocks east of the King subway station. The #504 King streetcar stops a block away at Church Street.

$100-150

One block east of Yonge Street's bustle, **Les Amis B&B** (31 Granby St., 416/591-0635, www.bbtoronto.com, $95–105 s, $125–145 d) has a handy central location on a surprisingly quiet residential street. Set in a narrow 1870s townhouse, five cozy guest rooms have wideboard floors, down duvets, and simple furnishings. On the second floor, one room has a private bath, while the other two share a washroom; the two third-floor rooms share an adjacent bath, as well. Owners Paul-Antoine and Michelle Buer are both vegetarians, and their breakfasts—crepes, waffles, or omelets—are entirely meat-free. They can also accommodate vegans; just let them know if that's your preference. Paul-Antoine is a photographer, and photos of his travels adorn the walls. Granby Street is one block south of College/Carlton streets, one block north of Gerrard. It's a two-block walk from the College subway station. The same owners also run the Au Petit Paris B&B in the Bloor-Yorkville neighborhood.

Like a lowly caterpillar transforming into a colorful butterfly, the 18-story **Bond Place Hotel** (65 Dundas St. E., at Bond St., 416/362-6061, www.bondplace.ca, $119–169 d) has reemerged after a 2011 renovation as a moderately priced urban boutique hotel. Don't expect luxury; do expect comfort and style. The cool lobby, decorated with dark woods and creamy leather chairs, has an espresso bar/café, and the building has a small fitness room. Among the 285 guest rooms, the least expensive standard rooms are small, but they've been updated with

© CAROLYN B. HELLER

"Meet me at the clock," a landmark at the Fairmont Royal York.

blond wood furniture and teal accents, white duvets, flat-screen TVs, and either one queen or two twin beds. The slightly larger "deluxe" rooms are similarly appointed with either one queen and one double bed, or one queen with two twins; many of these rooms have two separate sleeping areas—not separate rooms, but at least somewhat more private. Parking is available for $15 per night; there's also a charge for Wi-Fi. From the Dundas subway station, the hotel is three blocks east; the #505 Dundas streetcar stops at Bond Street, right out front.

Built in the early 20th century and named for the British queen, the 56-room **Hotel Victoria** (56 Yonge St., 416/363-1666 or 800/363-8228, www.hotelvictoria-toronto. com, subway: King, $134–164 d) had a facelift in 2011, emerging as a petite but pretty boutique inn. The style starts in the art deco lobby with a black granite fireplace and marble columns, and continues upstairs, where guest rooms have black furniture, white duvets, and gold accents, along with iPod docks, coffeemakers, and free Wi-Fi. The standard

rooms, with one queen bed or two twins, are cozy; for more space (plus a mini-fridge), opt for a deluxe king or deluxe queen. Breakfast isn't included, but there's a coffee shop on-site, and the location is convenient to most everything downtown.

If you don't need a lot of space and you want a central downtown location at a moderate price, consider the **Strathcona Hotel** (60 York St., at Wellington St. W., 416/363-3321, www.thestrathconahotel.com, $115–165 s, $135–210 d). The rooms in this 12-story building, decorated with white duvets and red accents, cover the basics—decent beds, coffeemakers, TVs—with no extraneous frills. The street-facing rooms are noisier but bright; the interior rooms are quieter and darker. Wi-Fi is available (for a fee), and guests can purchase a discounted pass to the Wellington Fitness Club next door. The Strathcona is across the street from the Fairmont Royal York Hotel, two blocks from Union Station.

The **Cambridge Suites Hotel** (15 Richmond St. E., at Yonge St., 416/368-1990 or 800/463-1990, www.cambridgesuitestoronto.com, $130–205 d) may not be as stylish as some trendier boutique properties, but it's an excellent value. The 229 modern units are all two-room suites, with separate living and sleeping areas (with a flat-screen TV in each room), as well as kitchenettes stocked with refrigerators, microwaves, coffeemakers, dishes, and cutlery. Wi-Fi ($12/day) is available throughout the hotel. The top floor of the 22-story building has a small workout room, hot tub, and sauna.

$150-200

Canada's largest hotel, the 1,595-room **Delta Chelsea Hotel** (33 Gerrard St. W., 416/595-1975 or 800/243-5732, www.deltahotels. com, $150–199 d, $249–299 suite), feels like a small city—one that could be dubbed "Family Town," since it's especially welcoming to families. The indoor pool in the "Family Fun Zone" has a 40-meter (130-foot) water slide, and families can stop into the "Kid Centre" for games, arts, and crafts. In summer, during school vacations, and on weekends year-round, there's even more family entertainment, from bingo to movie nights, and Camp Chelsea offers half- or full-day activities for five- to 12-year-olds. Teens aren't neglected, either; they have their own lounge, with video games, foosball, and movies. If you've left the kids at home, you might prefer the top-floor adults-only pool, hot tub, sauna, and fitness room. The guest rooms range from the 25-square-meter (275-square-foot) standard rooms (with a king, queen, or two double beds) to slightly larger units with kitchenettes to the two-bedroom "Family Fun" suites, equipped with bunk beds, kids' bathrobes, and a play area. Wi-Fi is free in the lobby and lounges, and in the more expensive "Signature Club" rooms; otherwise there's a $14 charge for (wired) Internet access. Parking is $28–33 per night. The hotel is two blocks south of the College subway station.

New in 2011, the **Hotel Ocho** (195 Spadina Ave., 416/593-0885, www.hotelocho.com, $165–258 d) is a trendy 12-room inn in a re-habbed 1902 industrial building. The Ocho has kept many of its original features—exposed brick, stocky wood beams—while adding flat-screen TVs and contemporary art. Even if you don't stay here, you might stop in to the espresso bar (with free Wi-Fi), the lounge, or the eclectic restaurant (lunch $8–14, dinner $12–18), which serves bar snacks like "Dutch Fries" (hand-cut potatoes tossed in Gouda cheese), along with burgers, grilled calamari, and tandoori chicken. The Ocho is two blocks north of Queen Street West; take the #501 Queen streetcar to Spadina or the #510 Spadina streetcar to Queen.

With its colored neon lighting and sleek martini lounge, the lobby at the **Pantages Hotel Toronto Centre** (200 Victoria St., 416/362-1777 or 866/852-1777, www.pantageshotel.com, subway: Queen, $169–289 d) has a space-age air. Upstairs, in the 115 Zen-style suites, with hardwood floors and king or queen beds topped with white duvets, you'll feel more like a Buddha than a sky walker. The larger suites have fully equipped kitchens, some with washer-dryers. If you want more activity than

yoga in your room (the suites come with yoga mats), head for the well-equipped 24-hour fitness room. The hotel is convenient to Massey Hall, too; it's one block south of Dundas Square and one block west of Yonge Street, between Queen and Shutter Streets.

One King West (1 King St. West, 416/548-8100 or 866/470-5464, www.onekingwest.com, $170–390 d), a deluxe condominium-hotel, rents sleekly modern apartments for short or extended stays. The building combines the elegance of a former 1880s bank headquarters, with a new tower that soars above the original structure. Although the hotel caters to business travelers and couples, families (with older kids) who want central downtown lodging will be comfortable here; even the smallest rooms are larger than typical hotel rooms, and they have kitchens with dishwashers and laundry facilities. Parking (valet only) is $30 per day; fortunately, you can leave the car at home, since you can walk directly from the hotel into the underground PATH network and the King subway station.

Centrally located opposite City Hall, just east of the Osgoode subway station, the **Sheraton Centre Hotel** (123 Queen St. W., 416/361-1000, www.sheratontoronto.com, $189–399 d) has 1,377 guest rooms in two towers; the taller soars 43 stories above downtown. The higher-priced club rooms on floors 36–42 have the best city views and give you access to the top-floor lounge, with complimentary breakfast, evening hors d'oeuvres, and Internet access (which normally costs $15/day for in-room access or $20/day for wired access in your room and Wi-Fi in the lobby and other public spaces). The rooms feel "business casual," with white duvets, large desks, and leather arm chairs; the hotel is packed with road warriors during the week, catering to vacationers on weekends. There's an indoor–outdoor pool and a spacious health club. Parking at the hotel is valet-only ($45/day). Check their website for sales and packages.

Built in 1929, the ◖ **Fairmont Royal York** (100 Front St. W., 416/368-2511 or 866/540-4489, www.fairmont.com, $189–409 d) was once the tallest building in the British Empire. While more modern towers dwarf this downtown landmark these days, few have its classic polish. Sure, there are cooler, trendier places to stay, but both the solicitous staff and 1,365 rooms are gracious and welcoming, whether you're the Queen of England (yes, she's stayed here) or a regular Joe. Have a drink in the dark-paneled Library Bar or dinner in the contemporary Epic restaurant. On summer weekends, hotel chefs lead free 30-minute tours of the property's herb gardens and rooftop apiary. Room rates vary significantly; in summer, surprisingly, promotional rates can dip below $150 night. Before you book, sign up for the complimentary President's Club, Fairmont's frequent-stay program, and you'll get free Internet access during your stay. The hotel is across the street from Union Station, with access through the underground PATH network.

They don't build hotels like this anymore, do they? Retaining the elegance of a bygone era, the majestic ambience of **Le Méridien King Edward** (37 King St. E., 416/863-9700, www.starwoodhotels.com/lemeridien, subway: King, $199–314 d) begins in the lobby, with its ornate columns and plasterwork, soaring ceiling, and marble floors. Most of the 289 rooms aren't quite as grand, but they're comfortable, traditionally furnished retreats from the bustle of the surrounding Financial District. You can get online in the guest rooms ($13.95/day), but Wi-Fi is available only in the lobby.

$200-300

As skinny as a guru, the 27-story tower that houses the **Cosmopolitan Hotel and Residences** (8 Colborne St., 416/350-2000 or 800/958-3488, www.cosmotoronto.com, $225–300) has a Zen feel. The rooms are sleek and modern, with wood floors and kitchenettes; there are only five on each floor, adding to the tranquility, and they even come with yoga mats. The larger "Lotus Suites" are configured either as a studio with sleeping and sitting areas or as a one-bedroom unit with a separate living room; they also have in-suite washer-dryers. If you're not sufficiently

blissed out, head for the fitness room or book a treatment in the small spa. The lobby wine bar divides its light bites into those requiring forks and those for fingers only. Tip: For the best views, ask for a room on the 20th floor or above.

Over $300

As a subtle nod to its location adjacent to the Air Canada Centre, larger-than-life photos of hockey, basketball, and soccer stars adorn the guest room walls of the deluxe and intimate **ℭ Hotel Le Germain Maple Leaf Square** (75 Bremner Blvd., at York St., 416/649-7575 or 888/940-7575, www.germainmapleleaf-square.com, $304–374 d). From Frette linens and down duvets to espresso machines, alarm clock/iPod dock combinations, and 40-inch flat-screen TVs, the 167 contemporary rooms have all the expected luxuries, and some unexpected ones, too: if the muscular wall murals aren't sexy enough, many of the glass-walled showers open to the bedrooms (you can pull the shades if you're feeling modest). The athletic artwork may inspire you to work out in the well-equipped fitness room, and the expanded continental breakfast, with fresh fruits, cheeses, charcuterie, and pastries will fuel your activities, energetic or otherwise. Rates include Wi-Fi; parking (valet only) is $35 per night. You can walk from Union Station through the Maple Leaf Square complex to the hotel.

The Ivy at Verity (111d Queen St. E., 416/368-6006 ext 300, www.theivyatverity.ca, $329–349 d) feels like a private club, and it is; this discreetly posh inn is set inside a members-only club for high-powered, professional women. The inn is open to both men and women (as long as you can afford the tab), though the fitness facilities, including the indoor pool (decorated like a Roman grotto, complete with an underwater treadmill), well-equipped fitness room, and spa, are for women only. The four deluxe guest rooms are decorated differently, but they all feel airy and open, with eclectic light fixtures, bamboo floors, and balconies overlooking the pocket courtyard; the marble baths have rainshowers and heated floors. You can request your preferred type of pillow and have your room stocked with your favorite teas. If you need anything else, just call on the 24-hour concierge service. Mornings bring a continental breakfast, and guests have access to the members' lounge for drinks or light meals. **George Restaurant** (416/863-6006, www.georgeonqueen.ca, lunch $18–24, dinner $19–25) shares the building (which once housed a chocolate factory) and provides room service for the Ivy's guests. The hotel is four blocks east of Yonge Street (and the Queen subway station); take the #501 Queen streetcar to Church Street.

More than 450 original artworks decorate the deluxe, subtly Canadian-themed **Ritz-Carlton Toronto** (181 Wellington St. W., 416/585-2500 or 800/542-8680, www.ritzcarlton.com, subway: St. Andrew, $395–635 d), the only Canadian outpost of the Ritz-Carlton chain. The 267 guest rooms are on floors 6 though 20 (the upper 30 stories are condominiums); choose a south-facing, high-floor room for views of the lake, or splurge on a spacious corner suite with bamboo floors and a separate living area. You can see the CN Tower from the indoor pool (and from some of the rooms), and the large fitness center has all the expected equipment. At the spa, book a massage or a facial, or take a yoga class. The restaurant **ToCa** (for "Toronto, Canada") serves dishes from Ontario and across the country.

THE ENTERTAINMENT DISTRICT
$100-200
One of the city's most fashionable lodgings is the chic **Thompson Toronto** (550 Wellington St. W., at Bathurst St., 416/640-7778 or 888/550-8368, www.thompsonhotels.com, $180–275 d). From the expansive lobby bar with its cartoon-style mural of the Toronto skyline, to the 102 guest rooms with sleek dark wood cabinetry, white linens, and whimsical orange chairs, to the rooftop infinity pool overlooking the city, this is one stylish spot. The third-floor yoga studio offers more than 30 classes a week (to guests and the public),

and with three restaurants to choose from, you won't go hungry here, either: The Counter (416/601-3533, www.thecounter.ca, $7–15) is an upscale 24-hour diner; Scarpetta (416/601-3590, www.scottconant.com, 6–11 P.M. Sun.–Thurs., 6 P.M.–midnight Fri.–Sat., $22–28) is the Toronto outpost of celebrity chef Scott Conant; and Wabora (416/777-9901, www.waborasushi.com, $18–42) is an eclectic fusion sushi spot imported from Bracebridge in Cottage Country. The #504 King streetcar stops one block away at Bathurst Street.

Compared to many of Toronto's larger hotels, the **Soho Metropolitan** (318 Wellington St. W., at Blue Jays Way, 416/599-8800 or 866/764-6638, www.soho.metropolitan.com, $199–289 d), with 72 rooms and 19 suites, feels quiet and intimate. With floor-to-ceiling windows, the guest rooms are bright and airy, although there are no views; the hotel occupies the first four floors of a condominium tower. Contemporary maple furniture, Frette linens, large walk-in closets, and marble baths with heated floors are standard; in-room safes have an outlet inside, so you can recharge your laptop while storing it securely. Weekdays are busy with business travelers, and the hotel attracts many longer-term guests, perhaps because the majority of the rooms have kitchen facilities. You may want to set aside time for a workout in the health club or the indoor lap pool, since the hotel's Senses Bakery is known for its breakfast pastries. By public transit, take the #504 King streetcar to Peter Street, then walk two blocks south (Peter Street becomes Blue Jays Way). Taking the #510 Spadina streetcar to Front Street will put you about three blocks from the hotel, across Clarence Square.

Over $200
Like its sister property at Maple Leaf Square, **Hotel Le Germain** (30 Mercer St., 416/345-9500 or 866/345-9501, www.germaintoronto.com, $295–415 d) is run by a hip and helpful crew, offering au courant accommodations with Egyptian cotton bedding, down duvets, and large bathrooms, many with glass showers that look out into the bedroom. Have a

complimentary cappuccino in front of the fireplace in the "library" (a lobby lounge), or head for the rooftop terrace (there's a putting green on the roof, too). The stylish **Victor Restaurant** (5 P.M.–midnight Sun.–Wed., 5 P.M.–1 A.M. Thurs.–Sat., $14–16) serves sharing plates that work before theater or after a evening out. Wi-Fi is free; parking (valet only) is $35/night.

The 11-story brick hotel is located on a quiet side street one block south of King Street West, between John and Peter/Blue Jay Way.

BLOOR-YORKVILLE AND THE ANNEX
Under $100

Sometimes it's the little touches that make a even a budget lodging stand out. At **Planet Traveler** (357 College St., at Brunswick, 647/352-8747, www.theplanettraveler.com, $30 dorm, $75 d), a privately run hostel near Kensington Market and the University of Toronto, those little touches include "phone booths" with Wi-Fi where you can make skype calls and electrical outlets in the lockers to keep your electronic gear safe while you recharge. The main lounge area is bright and cheerful, with lime green accents. Other facilities include a communal kitchen, a coin-op laundry, and a rooftop deck with views across downtown.

Planet Traveler's dorms (either all male or all female) have six beds and a bathroom; they're not large, but large windows make them feel more spacious. Private rooms have a bed (either a double or a double with a single bunk above) and not much else; guests share the bath with four other rooms, and there's an additional common washroom down the hall. Rates include continental breakfast and Wi-Fi. Take the #506 Carlton streetcar to Augusta Avenue, which stops within a block of the house. You could also take the #510 Spadina streetcar to College Street; the hostel is three blocks west of the Spadina/College intersection.

$100-150

On the University of Toronto campus, the **University Women's Club of Toronto** (162 St. George St., 416/979-2000, www.uwconbloor. com, subway: St. George, $89 s, $115 d) runs a small bed-and-breakfast on the upper floors of the club building; it's open to the public, males and females alike. The Victorian-style guest rooms have been nicely updated, although the six rooms share three baths. It feels a bit like lodging with your proper aunt, but if you don't need a private bath or other hotel services, it's a good value for this central location. Rates include breakfast and Wi-Fi; parking is available for $10 per night.

Annex Quest House (83 Spadina Rd., 416/922-1934, www.annexquesthouse.com, $105–120 d) is an ascetic yet serene 18-room guesthouse, decorated with Indian-print cotton bedspreads, rag rugs on the wide-plank floors, and copper wash basins in the private bathrooms; free Wi-Fi, too. There's no breakfast, but the rooms have fridges and coffeemakers, so you can do it yourself, or head for one of the cafés on nearby Bloor Street. The inn is two blocks north of the Spadina subway station; note that north of Bloor Street, Spadina Avenue becomes Spadina Road.

The owners of Les Amis B&B run a sister property, **Au Petit Paris B&B** (3 Selby St., 416/928-1348, www.bbtoronto.com/aupetitparis, $95–105 s, $130–145 d). This homey bed-and-breakfast has four guest rooms in a narrow townhouse; rooms are decorated in bright, warm colors with new wood floors, and all have private baths. There's no living room or lounge area for guests, but there is a top-floor deck, which is a lovely spot for an evening glass of wine. A vegetarian breakfast is served, and there's free Wi-Fi. The closest subway station is Sherbourne (Bloor-Danforth line), two blocks away. You can also walk from Bloor-Yonge station in about 10 minutes.

In the residential Annex neighborhood, **Lowther Suites** (88 Lowther Ave., 416/925-4600, www.lowthersuites.com, $110–225 d) has five spacious one- or two-bedroom apartments with full kitchens and washer-dryers in a renovated brick mansion. Rates include Internet access and parking. The property caters to independent travelers—there's no common area, food service, or other hotel-style services (although a caretaker is always on call). It's particularly well suited to longer-term stays. Lowther Suites is a three-block walk to either the St. George or Spadina subway station.

Over $150

Toronto has plenty of luxurious lodgings, but one of the most deluxe has to be the intimate **Hazelton Hotel** (118 Yorkville Ave., 416.963.6300 or 866.473.6301, www.thehazeltonhotel.com, $395–550 d). The 77 sizable rooms and suites have extra insulation to keep your business private, and amenities like 42-inch flat-screen TVs, roomy rainshowers (plus heated bathroom floors), and plush pillowtop mattresses, as well as a spa, health club, and indoor lap pool, to keep your business fun. The solicitous concierge service will arrange whatever you need. The hotel even has a private screening room in case you're hosting a film premiere or a posh playoffs party. If you're not traveling by chauffeured limousine, Bay is the most convenient subway station.

THE WEST END
$100-150

Fancy a stay in an art gallery? The main floor of the **Index G B&B** (50 Gladstone Ave., 416/535-6957, www.indexgbb.com, $90 s, $100–120 d) is a contemporary gallery space. Upstairs are five spare but arty guest rooms with original artwork on the walls. In the morning, help yourself to a simple continental breakfast (cereal, fruit, yogurt, coffee, tea) in the gallery. There's also free Wi-Fi. The #501 Queen streetcar stops at Gladstone Avenue, one block away, and you're just a short stroll from the West Queen West action.

Personable proprietor Albert Tan welcomes guests to the **Suite Dreams Toronto B&B** (390 Clinton St., 416/538-0417, www.suitedreamstoronto.com, subway: Christie, $109 s, $139–169 d) in his home on a residential street in Koreatown. This 2003 townhouse has four guest rooms and a grand piano in the living room; it's comfortable without being either

The Drake Hotel is a hub of activity along Queen Street West.

© CAROLYN B. HELLER

trendy or fussy. The high-ceilinged top-floor unit runs the length of the house and has all the closet space you could want. The rear-facing room on the second floor has a sleigh bed and a small fridge; the sunny front rooms are smaller but still spacious. All rooms have private baths, except for the basement-level garden room, which is gloomier but has direct access to the patio out back. Albert is happy to dispense tips and chat with guests; he cooks up a full hot breakfast, including a deliciously nutty granola made from his own secret recipe. The B&B is one block east of Christie Street, a half-block north of Bloor.

Over $150

The funky **[Gladstone Hotel** (1214 Queen St. W., 416/531-4635, www.gladstonehotel.com, $165–275) is a combination art gallery and hotel in a restored 1889 building. The 37 rooms are all unique, designed by different artists. In the "Teen Queen," the walls are plastered with photos of teen idols, while the "Offset" resembles a sleek urban loft. Most rooms aren't large, but they are way cool, with small flat-screen TVs, iPod docks, and Wi-Fi.

As much a place to lounge, drink, and eat as to sleep, the **(Drake Hotel** (1150 Queen St. W., 416/531-5042 or 866/372-5386, www. thedrakehotel.ca, $189–259 d) pioneered the city's "art hotel" concept when West Queen West was in its fledgling days as an arts district. Now, along with the nearby Gladstone Hotel, it's a neighborhood cultural hub. Guest rooms range from the cozy "Crash Pad" (big enough to crash, but not much else) to the progressively larger "Dens," "Salons," and "Suite," with hardwood floors, exposed brick walls, TVs, iPod docks, and original artwork. If you're staying with a special someone, you might inquire about the hotel's "Pleasure Packs," which range from "Some cheeky suggestions to get your night started" ($39) to the "Feather + flog + vibrate + velvet + oil" ($160). Not that I've tried them personally. . . .

THE EAST END
$100-150

Laid-back and comfortable best describes the vibe at the **Banting House Inn** (73 Homewood Ave., 416/924-1458 or 800/823-8856, www.bantinghouse.com, $89–125 s, $104–140 d), a seven-room B&B in Cabbagetown. Named for Frederick Banting, the discover of insulin, who once lived here, the brick Victorian was built at the turn of the 20th century and retains period details like the original woodwork and stained glass, but the guest rooms are simple; one has an en suite bath, but the rest share bath facilities. The house has a homey parlor with a fireplace and comfy chairs, as well as a lovely garden out back. Rates include a full breakfast; parking is available for $10/day. The inn is three blocks from the Jarvis Street stop on the #506 Carlton streetcar or four blocks from the Wellesley subway station.

Food

In multicultural Toronto, eating out can be a major cultural event, with choices ranging from Vietnamese, Thai, Japanese, Korean, and all manner of regional Chinese restaurants to Indian, Latino, Portuguese, Italian, Polish, Ukrainian, Caribbean, and more. You can find everything from simple noodle shops to roti stands to Indian buffets, often within a single neighborhood. And it's not all mom-and-pop ethnic-joints, either. Toronto has some of Canada's top restaurants, a roster of celebrity chefs, and innovative dining rooms serving creative cuisine for every budget.

DOWNTOWN AND THE FINANCIAL DISTRICT

The **St. Lawrence Market** (93 Front St. E., 416/392-7219, www.stlawrencemarket.com, 8 A.M.–6 P.M. Tues.–Thurs., 8 A.M.–7 P.M. Fri., 5 A.M.–5 P.M. Sat.) is a fun place to browse, whether you're looking for produce, cheeses, or a more substantial lunch. Most stalls and

eateries are open during the regular market hours, but some open later or close earlier; call to confirm if you have your heart set on visiting a particular vendor.

The **Nathan Phillips Square Farmers' Market** (100 Queen St. W., 8 A.M.–2:30 P.M. Wed. June–mid-Oct.) takes over the plaza in front of City Hall on summer and fall Wednesdays.

Asian

Despite the name, **Salad King** (340 Yonge St., 2nd Fl., 416/593-0333, www.saladking. com, 11 A.M.–10 P.M. Mon.–Thurs., 11 A.M.–11 P.M. Fri., noon–11 P.M. Sat., noon–9 P.M. Sun., $6–10) doesn't specialize in salads. It's a cheap and cheerful Thai eatery that's convenient for a quick bite downtown. They serve curries, noodles, and several choices for vegetarians. If you do want a salad, try their green papaya version.

A long-standing favorite for high-end

Cantonese fare, the formal ◖ **Lai Wah Heen** (Metropolitan Hotel, 108 Chestnut St., at Dundas, 416/977-9899, www.laiwahheen. com, 11 A.M.–3 P.M. and 5:30–10:30 P.M. Sun.–Thurs., 11 A.M.–3 P.M. and 5:30–11 P.M. Fri.–Sat., $16–48) is particularly popular for midday dim sum. Not only are the classics, like *char siu bao* (puffy white buns filled with barbecued pork) or *siu mai* (steamed pork, shrimp, and scallop dumplings), impeccably executed, the chefs create new interpretations of tea lunch treats, such as wontons stuffed with cumin-scented lamb, jumbo siu mai wrapped with glutinous rice and foie gras, or steamed dumplings made of Wagyu beef. Located near the Textile Museum, the restaurant is a three-block walk from the St. Patrick subway station. You can also take the #505 Dundas streetcar to Chestnut Street.

With exposed brick walls, original wideboard floors, and mix of traditional chandeliers and industrial lighting, **Swish by Han** (38 Wellington St. E., 647/343-0268, http:// swishbyhan.wordpress.com, lunch noon–2 P.M.

Mon.–Fri., 5–10:30 P.M. Mon.–Wed., 5 P.M.–2 A.M. Thurs.–Sat., small plates $7–17, larger plates $18–34) could be any trendy warehouse eatery. Yet what sets it apart are the contemporary interpretations of classic Korean fare. Brothers Leemo and Leeto Han, executive chef and general manager respectively, offer a range of Korean small plates designed to share, including the addictive spicy pork buns (barbecued pork piled on an onion roll with a chili-sesame relish), a zesty-sweet wild mushroom salad, and the *kimchi guksoo* (cold noodles with a kimchi vinaigrette); among the larger dishes are *ssäm* sets (grilled meats with lettuce wraps) and do-it-yourself tabletop barbecue. To drink, try *soju* (a Korean vodka) or *makkoli* (an unfiltered rice wine). Located just west of the St. Lawrence Market, the restaurant is a four-block walk from the King subway station, or two blocks from the Church Street stop on the #504 King streetcar.

Bakeries and Cafés

Chef Marc Thuet and his wife and business

Stop for a peameal bacon sandwich while exploring the St. Lawrence Market

© CAROLYN B. HELLER

partner Biana Zorich starred in *Conviction Kitchen,* a TV reality show that followed their efforts to staff restaurants in Toronto and Vancouver with convicted criminals. There's no such drama at **Petite Thuet** (1 King St. W., at Yonge St., 416/867-7977, www.petitethuet. com, subway: King, 7 A.M.–7 P.M. Mon.–Fri., 8 A.M.–5 P.M. Sat.–Sun., $5–14), their French bakery-café in the Financial District. Pastries are a highlight, from the croissants and beignets for *petit déjeuner,* to the decadent and delicious chocolate *macarons.* They also serve salads, pizzas, and panini, though they're known for their seasonal lobster sandwich, which sells out early.

If you've never sampled the Canadian bacon known as "peameal" (or even if you have), a good place to try it is at the St. Lawrence Market's **Carousel Bakery** (416/363-4247), which sells the "world famous peameal bacon on a bun." The sandwich may not be quite as famous as their sign proclaims, but it's still a tasty, meaty lunch. Not a meat eater? The market's **Cruda Cafe** (647/919-5721, www. crudacafe.com, 9 A.M.–5:30 P.M. Tues.–Fri., 9 A.M.–5:30 P.M. Sat.) sells fresh juices, smoothies, raw wraps, and other vegetarian fare. If you like condiments and want a Toronto-made foodie souvenir, visit **Kozlik's Mustard** (416/361-9788), which has been making tasty mustards in the city since 1948.

A handy spot to fuel up while you're browsing in the Distillery District is the **Brick Street Bakery** (55 Mill St., Bldg. 45a, 416/214-4949, www. brickstreetbakery. ca, 8:30 A.M.–4 P.M. Mon., 8:30 A.M.–7 P.M., Tues.–Sat., 8:30 A.M.–6 P.M. Sun., $5–9). Croissants, brioche, and scones pair with your morning coffee; later in the day, popular sandwiches include lamb *kofta* (a lamb burger with fennel slaw in a tortilla wrap), the straightforward chicken and bacon club, or a vegetarian combo of portobello mushrooms, zucchini, red peppers, and basil puree. Revive your flagging energy with a cookie, date square, or mini-tart.

Stop into **SOMA Chocolatemaker** (55 Mill St., Bldg. 48, 416/815-7662, www.soma

The Senator is Toronto's oldest restaurant.

© CAROLYN B. HELLER

chocolate.com, generally open 10 A.M.–8 P.M. Mon.–Sat., 11 A.M.–6 P.M. Sun., call to confirm hours, especially in winter) just to sniff the chocolatey goodness. This Distillery District chocolate and gelato shop is also a mini-factory where you can watch the chocolate makers at work. Come hungry—it's not easy to choose between the beautifully crafted bonbons and pastries, freshly made gelatos and sorbets, and a variety of hot chocolate drinks, including the Mayan hot chocolate spiced with ginger, orange peel, vanilla, and chili. As their tagline says, it's "a place to eat, drink, and worship chocolate." Amen.

Contemporary

With sturdy pine tables and walls decorated with old photos, **The Gabardine** (372 Bay St., at Richmond, 647/352-3211, www.thegabardine.com, 8 A.M.–10 P.M. Mon.–Fri., $12–23) looks like it's always been in the Financial District—surprisingly, it opened in 2011. In the morning, stop in for pastries, oatmeal, or a breakfast sandwich; later in the day, it's upscale pub fare. Sandwiches include pulled pork with aioli and spicy pickled cabbage or a tuna panino with olive tapenade, while the larger plates run from beet risotto with goat cheese to roast chicken with mashed potatoes to beef stroganoff served over buttered noodles. Because they cater to the office crowd, Gabardine is closed on weekends. The Queen streetcars stop at Bay Street, one block north of the restaurant, or it's a two-block walk from the Queen subway station.

Whether you're dining with a client, a special someone, or your great-aunt Tillie, the gracious staff at **Epic** (100 Front St. W., 419/860-6949, www.epicrestaurant.ca, subway: Union, 7 A.M.–10 A.M., noon–2 P.M., and 5:30–10 P.M. Mon.–Fri., 5:30–10 P.M. Sat.–Sun., lunch $14–29, dinner $24–44), the flagship restaurant at the Fairmont Royal York Hotel, will ensure you're well cared for. Tables are discreetly spaced, and the menu includes just enough contemporary touches—a bit of foam here, a *sous vide* there—to keep things interesting while still offering options for more conservative palates. Order whatever is local and in season—whether it's baby arugula or Prince Edward County goat cheese in your salad, colorful beets garnishing the seared scallops with puy lentils, or a simple bowl of fresh strawberries to end your meal. At breakfast, choose à la carte items or explore the ample buffet ($23–29). You can also opt for a three-course prix fixe at lunch ($25) or dinner ($45).

One of Toronto's long-standing "special occasion" restaurants is **Canoe** (66 Wellington St. W., 416/364-0054, www.oliverbonacini.com, 11:45 A.M.–2:30 P.M. and 5–10:30 P.M. Mon.–Fri., lunch $21–28, dinner $37–47), which looks out across the city from its perch on the 54th floor of the Toronto Dominion Bank Tower. Canadian ingredients predominate in the inventive dishes, whether at lunch in the classic *tourtière* (Quebecois meat pie) or braised rabbit over pappardelle, or in the evenings with the sea bass sauced with wild leeks, venison from the prairies, or Ontario rib eye with tortellini stuffed with beef tongue and marrow. You can assemble an all-Canadian cheese plate, or sample sweets

like Niagara apple cake or Canoe's interpretation of Ontario's popular butter tart. Although you'll find bottles from around the world, the voluminous wine list has a strong Canadian focus, too. Reservations are recommended, and you'll feel most comfortable among the suits if your attire is somewhat dressed up. Note that Canoe is closed on Saturdays and Sundays. The restaurant is a short walk from the King, St. Andrews, or Union subway stations.

Although you no longer get two fried eggs for $0.45 or a hot "hamburg" plate for $0.60, as the old menu up front proclaims, you can still tuck into good old-fashioned diner fare at **The Senator** (249 Victoria St., 416/364-7517, www.thesenator.com, subway: Dundas, 7:30 A.M.–2:30 P.M. Mon., 7:30 A.M.–2:30 P.M. and 5–9 P.M. Tues.–Fri., 8 A.M.–2:30 P.M. and 5–9 P.M. Sat., 8 A.M.–2:30 P.M. Sun., lunch $9–15, dinner $16–22), reportedly Toronto's oldest restaurant. It certainly looks the part, with burgundy vinyl booths, a checkerboard floor, and the 1920s-style lunch counter. While the menu does make concessions to modern tastes—breakfast choices include homemade granola alongside the omelets and pancakes, and the beef for the burgers is naturally raised—it's the classics like bacon and eggs, roast turkey sandwiches, and homemade meat loaf that have been bringing in the customers for decades.

THE ENTERTAINMENT DISTRICT

Centered along King Street West from University to Bathurst, this downtown neighborhood is home to many of the city's theaters and concert venues. It's also an increasingly hip dining district. The **Metro Hall Farmers' Market** (55 John St., near King St, 8 A.M.–2:30 P.M. Thurs. late May–early Oct.) sets up in David Pecaut Square, near Roy Thompson Hall.

Asian

Chef Nuit Regular, who owns **Khao San Road** (326 Adelaide St. W., 647/352-5773, www.khaosanroad.ca, 11:30 A.M.–2:30 P.M. and 5–10 P.M. Mon.–Sat., $8–16) with her husband Jeff, hails from Chiang Mai in northern Thailand, and her big, bold dishes taste like they're imported directly from her homeland. The *tom yum* soup perfectly balances sour, salt, and chili fire, and even that old standby, pad Thai (in a version called "Sam Roas style"), is flavorful, packed with peanuts, and not excessively sweet. In another popular dish, *khao soi,* chicken or beef and egg noodles swim in a rich, lime-scented coconut milk curry broth. The casually hip Entertainment District space, with a long bar and sturdy wood tables, isn't large, and it can get packed; make reservations, particularly if you're trying to eat before a show. Take either the #501 Queen or #504 King streetcar to Peter Street; the restaurant is one block east of Peter.

From his start as a Hong Kong kitchen apprentice to his rise to Food Network stardom, chef Susur Lee has been wowing the food world. His latest Toronto venture, **Lee** (603 King St. W., at Portland St., 416/603-2205, www.susur.com, 5:30–11:30 P.M. Mon.–Sat., $16–28), in a coolly dark loungey space, starts with signature "Susur Bites," like spicy Hunan chicken wings, Peking duck roll with foie gras mousse, and cross-cultural cheeseburger spring roll. His main plates draw from Asia, too, but continue adding western twists: spice-crusted diver scallops come with sweet bean pesto and orange brûlée, and fried bananas, green lentil curry, and coconut chutney gussy up the rack of lamb. Whatever you might think about celebrity chefs and their antics, Lee's food is never boring. The #504 King streetcar stops at Portland Street, right by the restaurant.

Bakeries and Cafés

SOMA Chocolatemaker (443 King St. W., at Spadina, 416/599-7662, www.somachocolate.com, 9 A.M.–8 P.M. Mon.–Wed., 9 A.M.–9:30 P.M. Thurs.–Fri., noon–9:30 P.M. Sat.), an artisan chocolate and gelato café with an original location in the Distillery District, now has an Entertainment District outpost. Besides the hot chocolate, truffles, pastries, and ice cream, this branch also serves savory snacks, from pizza to sandwiches.

Contemporary

The Oliver and Bonacini Restaurants group, which operates the high-end Canoe, among others, runs two eateries in the TIFF Bell Lightbox Theatre, headquarters of the Toronto International Film Festival. Head for the café-style **O&B Canteen** (330 King St. W., 416/288-4710, www.oliverbonacini.com, 11 A.M.–close Mon.–Fri., 10 A.M.–close Sat.–Sun., $7–22) in a window-lined see-and-be-seen street-level room. It's perfect for a quick bite before or after a show, with audience favorites like sandwiches, pastas, roast chicken, and either steak or salmon with frites. Their "grab and go" counter offers light meals to take out starting at 8 A.M.

The more expensive seats—and more innovative menus—are upstairs in the upscale **Luma Restaurant** (416/288-4715, www.oliverbonacini.com, 11:45 A.M.–3 P.M. and 5–11 P.M. Mon.–Fri., 5–11 P.M. Sat., 11 A.M.–3 P.M. Sun., lunch $9–26, dinner $16–36), where you can lunch on a duck confit omelet, Asian-spiced red snapper poached in coconut milk, or grilled veal steak with arugula salad. In the evening, start with a movie-themed cocktail (like Fellini's Bellini or the Beetlejuiced, which mixes gin, cucumber, lime, pink peppercorns, and soda) before digging into equally Oscar-worthy mains that might include seared pork loin with kohlrabi, arctic char with salsa verde, or a lamb sirloin and sweetbreads combination.

Though **Marben** (488 Wellington St. W., between Spadina and Portland, 416/979-1990, www.marbenrestaurant.com, 11 A.M.–11 P.M. Tues.–Thurs., 11 A.M.–2 A.M. Fri., 10 A.M.–2 A.M. Sat., 10 A.M.–11 P.M. Sun., $7–18) is wildly popular for brunch, it's at lunch and dinner that the creative Ontario comfort food really shines. The kitchen transforms humble dishes like egg salad or fritters into "Carl's Crispy Egg Salad" with celery remoulade and caramelized onion vinaigrette or "Alex's Pork Rib and Duck Confit Fritters" with chipotle aioli. They're open late, too, so you can fuel up after a show. Take the #510 Spadina streetcar to Wellington, or the #504 King streetcar west to Spadina or Portland.

French

Ask Torontonians to recommend a classic French bistro and the name you'll keep hearing is **Le Select Bistro** (432 Wellington St. W., btw. Spadina and Portland, 416/596-6405, www.leselect.com, 11:30 A.M.–10 P.M. Mon.–Wed., 11:30 A.M.–10:30 P.M. Thurs.–Fri., 11 A.M.–3:30 P.M. and 5–10:30 P.M. Sat., 10:30 A.M.–3:30 P.M. and 5–9:30 P.M.Sun., $13–30). This old favorite serves traditional bistro dishes, including steak frites, *choucroute garnie* (pork with sauerkraut), and cassoulet. It's convenient for a bite after a show, since they offer a late-night menu after the theater curtain time. Take the #504 King streetcar to Spadina or Portland, or the #510 Spadina to Wellington.

Italian

If you can, bring the gang to **Buca** (604 King St. W., at Portland, 416/865-1600, www.buca. ca, 11 A.M.–3 P.M. and 5–10 P.M. Mon.–Wed., 11 A.M.–3 P.M. and 5–11 P.M. Thurs.–Fri., 5–11 P.M. Sat., 5–10 P.M. Sun., $19–32), a stylish yet unintimidating Italian eatery in a brick warehouse building. Lounge at the long communal tables and sample a range of shared plates like house-cured meats and "fritti," from smelts to crispy pig ears. The pastas are tasty, too (try the eggplant ravioli). If you're planning a tête-à-tête, head for the cavelike wine room, where you can sit at the wine bar or in front of the glass-fronted wine cellar. Take the #504 King streetcar to Portland Street; the restaurant entrance is down a narrow lane.

BLOOR-YORKVILLE AND THE ANNEX

Gourmet grocer **Pusateri's** (57 Yorkville Ave., at Bay St., 416/785-9100, www.pusateris.com, Subway: Bay, 8 A.M.–8 P.M. Mon.–Wed., 8 A.M.–9 P.M. Thurs.–Fri., 8 A.M.–7 P.M. Sat.–Sun.) is like a miniature Whole Foods Market, selling produce, cheeses, breads, and prepared foods. The prices are high, but so is the quality.

Speaking of **Whole Foods Market** (87 Avenue Rd., 416/944-0500, www.wholefoodsmarket. com, subway: St. George or Bay, 9 A.M.–10 P.M. Mon.–Fri., 9 A.M.–9 P.M. Sat.–Sun.), the large natural foods retailer has a Yorkville outpost, around the corner from Pusateri's.

Asian

With its cartoon logo, red lanterns, and fast-food ambience, **Okonomi House** (23 Charles St. W., 416/925-6176, 11 A.M.–10 P.M. Mon.–Fri., noon–10 P.M. Sat.–Sun., $6–7) looks like a Japanese Denny's. But no matter—you're here for the *okonomiyaki,* a pancake that resembles a cross between an omelet and a crepe. They're fried up fast, filled with cabbage, onions, and your choice of beef, pork, bacon, vegetables, squid, or shrimp, for a quick, filling meal. It's worth the extra $0.50 to add salty bonito (fish flakes) and seaweed to punch up the flavor. The restaurant is two blocks south of the Bloor-Yonge subway, between Yonge and Bay streets.

Vegetarian

Camros Organic Eatery (25 Hayden St., 416/960-0723, www.camroseatery.com, 11:30 A.M.–7:30 P.M. Mon.–Fri.) is a cheery cafeteria serving Persian-influenced vegetarian stews, rice dishes, and salads. The selection rotates, but you might find *gheyme* (a yellow lentil and potato stew flavored with limes and plums), cabbage rolls with a minty brown rice stuffing, or *adas polo* (brown rice with lentils, saffron, cinnamon, and raisins). Try the fresh kale salad with slivers of beets and a lemony dressing. Prices depend on the number of dishes you select (2-dish combination $7.99, 3-dish $10.79, 4-dish $11.99). The restaurant is one block south of Bloor Street and a half-block east of Yonge; from the Bloor subway station, exit toward Hayden Street.

Recover from the excesses of Casa Loma at the **Live Organic Food Bar** (264 Dupont St., at Spadina, 416/515-2002, www.livefoodbar.com, 11:30 A.M.–9:30 P.M. Mon.–Thurs., 11:30 A.M.–10 P.M. Fri., 11 A.M.–3 P.M. and 4–10 P.M. Sat.–Sun., $12–16), a vegan and raw café at the foot of the hill leading up to the mansion. This chipper orange and green space looks rather like a colorful composed

© CAROLYN B. HELLER

Hankering for Chinese dumplings? Head for Mother's....

salad, and you can try one of several out-of-the-ordinary salad options, including the "detox" (kale, parsley, kelp noodles, seaweed, quinoa, and avocado, in a lemon and hemp tamari dressing). Among the many raw choices are raw pizza (the crust is made of walnuts) and a beet "burger," a patty made of beets, nuts, and sunflower seeds, served with housemade pickles and veggie chips. "Health-conscious" doesn't mean "ascetic" here; you can pair your meal with a cocktail, like the "purple rain," a mix of organic blueberries, strawberries, sparkling water, and vodka. The restaurant is one block east of the Dupont subway station (Yonge-University-Spadina line).

THE WEST END

Some of Toronto's most interesting eateries are along West Queen West, Ossington Avenue, and Dundas Street West—a hotbed of casually contemporary bistros, tapas joints, and fun and funky dining rooms.

Inexpensive eateries abound around Kensington Market and in Toronto's original Chinatown. Although no longer exclusively Old World Italian, Toronto's **Little Italy** (www.littleitalyintoronto.ca) district, along College Street west of Bathurst, is still a lively with sidewalk cafés and trattorias. You may still hear Portuguese in the bakeries and cafés along Dundas Street, heading west from Ossington Avenue, in the neighborhood known as **Little Portugal** (www.littleportugal.ca). Look for traditional Portuguese breads and the sweet custard tarts known as *pasteis de nata*. Roncesvalles Avenue, between Queen and Bloor Streets, is the heart of the community known as **"Little Poland."** If you want to sample pierogis or stuffed cabbage rolls, this is the place. **Koreatown** (www.koreatownbia.com) is centered along Bloor Street West, between Bathurst and Christie Streets. In addition to restaurants serving traditional dishes like pork bone soup, spicy fried chicken, or grill-it-yourself barbecued meats, also look for bakeries that prepare authentic Korean sweets.

Asian

West Queen West isn't only about hip cafés and funky diners. If you're craving a comforting bowl of noodle soup, head for **Pho Tien Thanh** (57 Ossington Ave., 416/588-6997), a Vietnamese spot that specializes in the traditional noodle soup called *pho*. Take the #501 Queen streetcar to Ossington, then walk two blocks north.

Watch the deft dumpling makers at work at ◖ **Mother's Dumplings** (421 Spadina Ave., 416/217-2008, www.mothersdumplings.com, 11 A.M.–10 P.M. daily, $5–8), which specializes in *jiaozi*, the steamed or boiled dumplings native to northeastern China. Order a steamer, or two, or more—filled with shrimp, egg, and chive; cabbage, mushroom, and tofu; or pork with pickled cabbage (in an unusual whole wheat wrapper)—to pair with their excellent northern-style side dishes; try the "tofu strip salad" (bean curd dressed with peppers and fragrant cilantro), the garlicky smashed cucumbers, or the spicy kimchi. Cash only. They're located at the north end of Chinatown, one block south of College Street. Take the #510 Spadina streetcar to either College or Nassau Streets, or the #506 Carlton streetcar to Spadina Avenue.

A dingy basement room with about as much ambience as, well, a dingy basement room, **Chinese Traditional Buns** (536 Dundas St. W., 416/299-9011, 10 A.M.–10 P.M. daily, $3–10) nonetheless cooks up simple and scrumptious specialties of China's Shanxi province and other western regions. Try the Xi'an cured pork sandwich (like a Chinese pork slider), or any of the hand-pulled noodles, including the ground meat–topped *dan dan mien* or the super-spicy Shanxi-style noodles sauced with chili oil and vinegar. It's located in Chinatown, just west of Spadina Avenue; take the #505 Dundas streetcar to Spadina, or the #510 Spadina streetcar to Dundas.

Sheltered from the hubbub of the food court in the Village by the Grange building, **Manpuku** (105 McCaul St., 416/979-6763, www.manpuku.ca, 11:30 A.M.–8 P.M. Mon.–Wed., 11:30 A.M.–11 P.M. Thurs.–Fri.,

noon–11 P.M. Sat., $4–7), a surprisingly serene Japanese eatery, is a good choice for a quick, inexpensive meal near the Art Gallery of Ontario (it's just across the street). Choose from several simple udon noodle soups, rice plates, and curries. The #505 Dundas streetcar to McCaul stops right out front.

Bakeries and Cafés

Craving croissants, brioche, or pain au chocolat? **Clafouti Patisserie** (915 Queen St. West, 416/603-1935), a cozy French café, is your place. Take the #501 Queen streetcar to Strachan Avenue. It's not so easy to get into the **Easy Restaurant** (1645 Queen St. W., 416/537-4893, www.easyrestaurant.ca, 9 A.M.–5 P.M. daily, $9–19), at least on the weekends. This funky diner serves breakfast all day and is a long-standing brunch favorite, so expect lines. The only problem with ordering their signature *huevos divorciados* (poached eggs with black beans, tortillas, salsa, guacamole, and ancho-chile jam) is that you'll be hungry again in about three days. Take the #501 Queen or the #504 King streetcar to Roncesvalles Avenue.

The specialty at Korean bakery **Hodo Kwaja** (656 Bloor St. W., 416/538-1208, 9 A.M.–10 P.M. daily) is walnut cake, a walnut-shaped pastry that's filled with red bean paste or a slightly sweet potato mixture. Even better are the brown sugar pancakes with peanuts; eat them while they're hot, though, because they don't keep. An excellent and unusual snack! The bakery is about two blocks east of the Christie subway station.

Contemporary

From duck heart tartare, to pig's head tacos, to tongue on brioche, the menu at **The Black Hoof** (928 Dundas St. W., at Bellwoods Ave., www.theblackhoof.com, 6 P.M.–1 A.M. Thurs.–Sat., 6–11:30 P.M. Sun.–Mon.; small plates $9–24) reads like a challenge—at least if you don't normally nibble the "nasty bits." But if you're eager to embrace nose-to-tail eating, join the hordes at this mod meatery for tapas and a cocktail or glass of wine. They don't take reservations, so prepare to wait, and they don't accept credit cards, either. The #505 Dundas streetcar will get you here.

At neighborhood bistro **Delux** (92 Ossington Ave., at Queen W., 416/537-0134, www.deluxrestaurant.ca, 11:30 A.M.–3 P.M. and 6–10:30 P.M. Tues.–Thurs., 11:30 A.M.–3 P.M. and 6–11 P.M. Fri.–Sat., 10:30 A.M.–3 P.M. and 6–10 P.M. Sun., lunch $6–14, dinner $15–24), chef Corinna Mozo cooks Cuban cuisine at lunch, when you can tuck into sandwiches like achiote and lime chicken with avocado or a traditional *cubano*. For Sunday brunch, the menu includes conch fritters, French toast with bananas in dulce de leche, and duck confit hash with fried plantains. In the evenings, the fare is French-inspired with some Latin accents— the steak frites come with salsa verde, and the pan-roasted pickerel is paired with house-made chorizo. If you don't fancy a mojito or a cuba libre (rum, lime, and coke), the wine list includes labels from Ontario, France, and elsewhere. Take the #501 Queen streetcar to Ossington, then walk three blocks north.

Crowds of carnivores are cruising into **Parts and Labour** (1566 Queen St. W., at Dowling Ave., 416/588-7750, www.partsandlabour. ca, dinner 6 P.M.–2 A.M. Tues.–Sat., brunch 11 A.M.–3 P.M. Sun., mains $17–34), where shattered windshields and recycled lights decorate the garage-like space. The modern meat-centric menu rumbles from beef tartare with a fried quail egg and pickled peppers, to roasted and smoked chicken with Brussels sprouts and pork belly, to a whole branzino (fish) grilled and paired with rapini. In "The Shop," on the lower level, you can listen to live music most weekends. If your own wheels are in the shop, hop on the #501 Queen streetcar; it stops in front of the restaurant.

Nibbles like gorgonzola crostini with kale and raisins, pork belly confit paired with apple slaw, and shrimp baked in a piri piri–garlic butter sauce bring the neighbors (and visitors from farther afield) to the **Fat Cat Wine Bar** (331 Roncesvalles Ave., 416/535-4064, www.fatcat. ca, 5–10 P.M. Mon.–Thurs., 5–11 P.M. Fri.–Sat.;

small plates $6–13). This is a relaxed place to unwind over a glass of wine and inventive small plates. You can order many of their wines, including a number of Ontario labels, in three- and six-ounce pours—the better to sample different varieties. The #506 Carlton streetcar toward High Park stops at Roncesvalles Avenue, a few blocks north of the restaurant.

Italian

Every neighborhood needs a sociable wine bar and Italian eatery like **C Enoteca Sociale** (1288 Dundas St. W., 416/534-1200, www. sociale.ca, 5–11 P.M. daily, $13–18). Whether you bring the family, a pal or two, or a special someone, the welcoming staff will look after you, offering a large selection of wines and a carefully curated choice of Roman-style plates. There are always several homemade pastas, like pappardelle with rabbit ragu or the simple spaghetti *cacio e pepe* (with pecorino cheese and black pepper), a savory grilled octopus served with potatoes, and heartier plates like Ontario lake trout with caponata. Book ahead—the restaurant is small and always busy. Fortunately, they set aside half their seats for walk-ins, so if you can't reserve, don't despair; just expect to wait. To get here, take the #505 Dundas streetcar to Dovercourt, just west of Ossington.

The same owners run the always-packed **Pizzeria Libretto** (221 Ossington Ave., at Dundas, 416/532-8000, www. pizzerialibretto.com, noon–11 P.M. Mon.–Sat., 4–11 P.M. Sun., pizzas $10–17) around the corner. Libretto tames the hungry hordes with Neapolitan-style pizza, paired with interesting salads like arugula with pears, walnuts, and Piave cheese, or antipasto platters laden with cured meats and regionally made cheeses. Take the #505 Dundas streetcar to Ossington Avenue.

Mexican and Latin American

The only thing "jumbo" about this tiny Kensington Market shop may be the appetites of the patrons who flock here for their signature stuffed pastry. **Jumbo Empanadas** (245 Augusta Ave., at Nassau, 416/977-0056,

9 A.M.–8 P.M. Mon.–Sat., 11 A.M.–8 P.M. Sun., $5–6) serves tasty Chilean empanadas filled (more traditionally) with beef or chicken with olives and hard-boiled egg, or (more Toronto) with vegetables, including a spinach–mushroom–pepper mélange. Take the #510 Spadina streetcar to Nassau Street, or the #506 Carlton streetcar to Major or Augusta.

Tacos are the specialty at **El Trompo** (277 Augusta Ave., between Oxford and College Sts., 416/260-0097, www.eltrompo.ca, 11 A.M.–8 P.M. Tues.–Thurs., 11 A.M.–9 P.M. Fri.–Sat., 11 A.M.–6 P.M. Sun., $6–13), a lively Mexican café. They come in plates of four or five (don't worry, they're small); ask for a combination, so you can sample different varieties. A favorite is the pork *al pastor,* with pineapple and cilantro (add a scoop or two of tomatillo salsa); other good choices include chorizo (slightly spicy sausage), grilled beef with onions, or chipotle-sauced chicken. Beyond tacos, they have *queso fundido* (like a Mexican cheese fondue) and several types of *quesadillas.* If you're not drinking beer or a margarita, try the milky, cinnamon-scented *horchata* or fruity *jamaica.* It can get a bit noisy in the colorful but cramped dining room, so in mild weather, try to nab a sidewalk seat. El Trompo stays open a little later in the summer; call to confirm their current hours. Get off the #506 Carlton streetcar at Major or Augusta, and walk one block south.

A notch more upscale than many other Kensington Market spots, **Torito Tapas Bar** (276 Augusta Ave., at College St., 416/961-7373, www.toritorestaurant.com, 5–11 P.M. daily, tapas $7–12) is a narrow slice of a space serving Spanish-style small plates. Nibble on Serrano ham, pan-fried sardines, a Spanish "tortilla" (omelet), or piquillo peppers stuffed with salt cod, sip some sherry or Rioja, and relax—you're in Spain. Both the #506 Carlton and #510 Spadina streetcars stop nearby.

Portuguese

When you tire of grunge waitstaff, warehouse-bare rooms, and hipper-than-thou pig ear–filled menus, retreat to the Old World **Chiado** (864 College St., 416/538-1910, www.chiadorestaurant.com, noon–2:30 P.M. and 5–10 P.M. Mon.–Fri., 5–10 P.M. Sat.–Sun., lunch $16–20, dinner $30–48), where the dignified waiters wear crisp white aprons and the candlelit tables are dressed in starched white cloths. The menu is "progressive Portuguese"; the salt cod is grilled, then roasted with olive oil and garlic, and traditional piri piri sauce glazes the pan-seared monkfish. If the prices seem rich, either come for lunch or sup on a selection of tapas ($5–12). Chiado is in the Little Italy neighborhood; take the #506 Carlton streetcar west to Ossington Avenue.

THE EAST END

What to eat in Toronto's East End? Head to the Danforth, also known as Greektown, for Greek food, "Little India" (the Indian Bazaar) for food from South Asia, and to Leslieville for more contemporary fare.

Big Carrot Natural Foods (348 Danforth Ave., 416/466-2129, www.thebigcarrot.ca, subway: Chester, 9 A.M.–9 P.M. Mon.–Fri., 9 A.M.–8 P.M. Sat., 11 A.M.–6 P.M. Sun.) is a well-stocked natural foods market in the Danforth neighborhood.

Contemporary

One of the pioneers of Leslieville's foodie renaissance, **Edward Levesque's Kitchen** (1290 Queen St. E., 416/465-3600, www.edwardlevesque.ca, lunch 11:30 A.M.–2:30 P.M. Fri., dinner from 5:30 P.M. Tues.–Sat., brunch 9 A.M.–3 P.M. Sat.–Sun., lunch $8–15, dinner $18–25) is perpetually packed for their just-creative-enough weekend brunch. But with mains like thick-cut pork chops with homemade plum sauce, roasted scallops with celeriac puree, and haddock cakes served with a green tomato and corn relish, this laid-back French-influenced bistro is a worthy choice for dinner, too. Take the #501 Queen east to Leslie, then walk two blocks farther east.

Imagine a dinner party at the home of a friend who's a wildly creative first-rate chef. Chef/co-owner Lynn Crawford is that host, when you dine at **Ruby Watchco** (730

© CAROLYN B. HELLER

Udupi Palace

laptop toters hang here for coffee and pastries in the morning (Wi-Fi is free), while all types stroll in later in the day for soups, salads, and an ever-changing array of substantial mains like pork schnitzel with anchovy mignonette or a Moroccan-spiced chickpea and vegetable stew. The café is open Monday through Saturday from 8 A.M. to 5:30 P.M., with lunch served from 11 A.M. to 2:30 P.M. In the evenings (from 5:30 P.M. Tues.–Sat.) and for Sunday brunch (10 A.M.–3 P.M.), the space morphs into a somewhat more upscale "bistro." Reservations are accepted for evenings only.

Greek

The menu is simple at **Athens Pastries** (509 Danforth Ave. at Logan Ave., 416/463-5144, $5), a Greek café in the Danforth neighborhood. Spinach-, cheese-, or meat-filled pies wrapped in a flaky phyllo dough, as well as a few sweets including *loukoumades* (honey donuts), pair beautifully with a strong cup of coffee. It's cash only, but nothing on the menu is more than $5. Take the Bloor-Danforth subway to Chester or Pape; it's between the two stations.

Indian

A long-established restaurant in the Little India neighborhood, **Udupi Palace** (1460 Gerrard St. E., 416/405-8189, www.udupipalace.ca, noon–10 P.M. Sun.–Thurs., noon–11 P.M. Fri.–Sat., $6–10) specializes in south Indian vegetarian and vegan dishes, including a lengthy list of *dosas,* crisp pancakes that come stuffed with potatoes, onions, vegetables, *paneer* (cheese), or a combination. Don't expect much in the way of ambience in the cavernous space; it's all about the food. Take the #506 Carlton streetcar to Ashdale Avenue, or take the subway (Bloor-Danforth line) to Coxwell station and then transfer to the #22 bus, which runs south along Coxwell Avenue to Gerrard.

Queen St. E., 416/465-0100, www.rubywatchco.ca, dinner Tues.–Sat., $49 prix-fixe), a neighborhood bistro serving a single four-course prix fixe menu that changes nightly. Examples of Crawford's wow-worthy spreads include cantaloupe salad with pickled onion and ricotta salata; seared trout with arugula sauce, quinoa with roasted grapes, and grilled chili-scented zucchini; a "ciel de charleroix" cheese paired with roasted plums; and lemon-vanilla panna cotta. Peruse the weekly dishes on the restaurant's website, but phone for reservations. From downtown, take the #501 Queen streetcar east to Broadview.

Down a lane off King Street East, two blocks east of Parliament Street and a short walk from the Distillery District, ◖ **Gilead Café and Bistro** (4 Gilead Pl, at King St. E., 647/288-0680, www.jamiekennedy.ca, $12–18) is a casual contemporary space run by celebrity chef Jamie Kennedy. Arty types and

Practicalities

INFORMATION AND SERVICES
Tourist Information

Tourism Toronto (416/203-2500 or 800/499-2514, www.seetorontonow.com), the city's convention and visitors association, has loads of information on their website to help you plan a Toronto visit, including a detailed calendar of events around town.

The provincial **Ontario Travel Information Centre** (20 Dundas St. W., 416/314-5899 or 800/668-2746, www.ontariotravel.net, 10 A.M.–6 P.M. Mon.–Sat., noon–5 P.M. Sun.), just west of Dundas Square, can provide information about travel around Toronto and elsewhere in the province.

Media and Communications

Canada's two national newspapers, the *Globe and Mail* (www.theglobeandmail.com) and the *National Post* (www.nationalpost.com), are headquartered in Toronto, and the city has two other daily newspapers: the *Toronto Star* (www.thestar.com) and the *Toronto Sun* (www.torontosun.com).

Toronto's two arts-and-entertainment weeklies, *Now* (www.nowtoronto.com) and *The Grid* (www.thegridto.com), have extensive listings of things going on around town. *Toronto Life Magazine* (www.torontolife.com), published monthly in print and available online, also covers the arts, restaurants, and things to do, as does *Where Toronto* (www.where.ca) and *Post City News* (www.postcity.com).

GETTING THERE

As Canada's largest city, Toronto has flights from all over the world, as well as train and bus connections from across Ontario, from all major Canadian cities, and from many U.S. points, as well.

By Air
TORONTO'S PEARSON AIRPORT

Toronto's Pearson International Airport (YYZ, 416/247-7678 or 866/207-1690, www.torontopearson.com) is Canada's largest, with flights from basically everywhere—across Canada, the United States, Europe, and Asia. The airport is 24 kilometers (15 miles) northwest of downtown, in the suburb of Mississauga. Most major Canadian and U.S. carriers, and many international airlines, fly into Toronto.

Pearson Airport has two terminals: Terminal 1 and Terminal 3. Air Canada uses Terminal 1, as do Lufthansa, United, US Airways, and Air New Zealand; WestJet, along with Aeromexico, Air France, American Airlines, British Airways, Cathay Pacific, Delta, and Qantas, uses Terminal 3. Check with your airline or the airport website to confirm which terminal you need.

The Toronto subway doesn't run all the way to Pearson airport, but you can travel between downtown and the airport by public transit, at least if you don't have piles of luggage. Neither the buses nor the subways have luggage racks.

From the airport, the **#192 Airport Rocket bus** ($3) will take you to the subway. It runs to Kipling station, on the Bloor-Danforth line, which goes from west to east across the city. Make sure you get a transfer on the bus, so you don't have to pay another fare when you board the subway. The first #192 bus leaves the airport at 5:40 A.M. Monday through Saturday and at 8 A.M. Sunday; the last departure from the airport is at 2 A.M. Service runs every 10 to 20 minutes.

You need exact change to pay your fare on the bus. You can also purchase a single-fare ticket from a **TTC ticket machine** inside Terminal 1. There are two ticket vending machines on the Ground Transportation level, just inside from where the TTC buses stop. The machines accept cash or credit cards.

Once you're on the subway, you'll need to transfer again from the Bloor-Danforth line if you're headed to the Union Station area, the Harbourfront, or other points downtown. Get off at St. George Station, and change to the Yonge-University-Spadina line heading southbound.

Between 2 A.M. and 5 A.M., when the #192 Airport Rocket isn't running, you can instead take the **#300A Bloor-Danforth bus** ($3), which operates from the airport into the city along Bloor Street and Danforth Avenue, essentially following the route of the Bloor-Danforth subway line. Buses run about every 30 minutes.

A convenient but more expensive way to get from the airport to the central city is to take the **Toronto Airport Express** (905/564-3232 or 800/387-6787, www.torontoairportexpress.com, one-way/round-trip adults $23.95/39.95; one-way seniors and students $21.55), a shuttle bus that runs between the airport and a number of downtown hotels. It also stops at the Toronto Coach Terminal (the long-distance bus station) and across the street from Union Station (at the Fairmont Royal York Hotel). Reservations aren't required, but you save 5 percent if you book online in advance. Kids under 12 travel free if they're with a paying adult. The buses also have free Wi-Fi.

A taxi from Pearson airport to downtown Toronto will cost $45–60 and generally takes 30–45 minutes, depending on traffic conditions and the destination.

TORONTO'S CITY CENTRE AIRPORT

Toronto has a second airport on the Toronto Islands, the City Centre Airport (YTZ, www.torontoport.com). While the number of flights to the Islands airport is more limited, it's easier to get between this airport and downtown than it is to get to or from Pearson.

Porter Airlines (416/619-8622 or 888/619-8622, www.flyporter.com) is the main carrier serving the Islands airport. Within Ontario, Porter flies between Toronto and Ottawa, Windsor, Sudbury, Sault Ste. Marie, and Thunder Bay. They also fly to Montreal, Quebec City, Halifax, Moncton, and St. John's (NL) in Canada and

to Boston, Chicago, and New York/Newark in the United States. **Air Canada** (514/393-3333 or 888/247-2262, www.aircanada.com) flies between the City Centre Airport and Montreal.

For an airport on an island, the City Centre Airport is surprisingly easy to get to, in part because it's so close to the downtown core. A **free ferry** (5:30 A.M.–midnight daily) runs between the airport and the foot of Bathurst Street, about every 15 minutes. The crossing takes just a few minutes.

From there, you can catch the #509 streetcar to Union Station or the #511 streetcar up Bathurst Street to the Bathurst subway station. Porter Airlines also operates a free **shuttle bus** between the airport ferry dock and the Fairmont Royal York Hotel (100 Front St. W.), opposite Union Station, with departures approximately every 15 minutes.

BUFFALO-NIAGARA INTERNATIONAL AIRPORT

If you're traveling to Toronto from the United States, check prices for flights to Buffalo-Niagara International Airport (4200 Genesee St., Cheektowaga, NY, 716/630-6000 or 877/359-2642, www.buffaloairport.com), instead of Pearson; you may find lower fares. Flying via Buffalo can also be convenient if you're planning to visit the Niagara region as part of your trip, since you can stop off in Niagara between Toronto and Buffalo.

Megabus (705/748-6411 or 800/461-7661, www.megabus.com, 3–3.5 hours, $17–23) offers the cheapest way to travel between Toronto and the Buffalo airport. They run two buses a day in each direction. Several other shuttle and limo services operate between Toronto and Buffalo-Niagara International; check the airport website for a complete list.

By Train

Toronto's rail depot is **Union Station** (65 Front St. W., www.toronto.ca/union_station) downtown. VIA Rail, Amtrak, Ontario Northland, and GO Transit trains all run to Union Station, which is also a stop on the Toronto subway (Yonge-University-Spadina line).

VIA RAIL CANADA SERVICE

Toronto is a hub for VIA Rail (888/842-7245, www.viarail.ca) trains that travel across Canada. Trains from the east travel to Toronto from Ottawa, Kingston, and Montreal; you can connect in Montreal for Quebec City, Moncton, and Halifax. Trains traveling west go to Winnipeg, Saskatoon, Edmonton, Jasper, and (eventually) Vancouver. Shorter routes within Ontario operate between Windsor, London, and Toronto; between Sarnia, London, and Toronto; and between Niagara Falls and Toronto.

From Montreal to Toronto (5–6 hours, one-way economy adults $78–157, seniors $78–141, students $78–109, kids 2–11 $54–79), VIA Rail runs six trains a day in each direction Monday through Friday, four on Saturday, and five on Sunday.

From Ottawa to Toronto (4.5–5 hours, one-way economy adults $72–144, children 2–11 $36–72), five trains run in each direction Monday through Friday, three on Saturday, and four on Sunday. Both the Montreal and Ottawa trains stop in Kingston en route to Toronto.

VIA's flagship route, **The Canadian,** crosses Canada from Vancouver to Toronto, via Jasper, Edmonton, Saskatoon, and Winnipeg. If you do the trip nonstop, it takes 3.5 days. There are departures three times a week in each direction. Fares vary by class of service; choose from options that include a seat, a bunk, or a private cabin. Within Ontario, you can catch *The Canadian* to Toronto from Sudbury or Parry Sound, although the train stops in both those communities in the middle of the night.

There are several daily trains between Windsor and Toronto (4–4.5 hours, one-way economy adults $61–118, seniors $61–106, students $61–82, kids 2–11 $40–59) and two a day between Sarnia and Toronto (4.5 hours, one-way economy adults $59–99, seniors $59–89, students $59–70, kids 2–11

$37–50). Both the Windsor and Sarnia trains travel via London.

VIA Rail runs two trains daily in each direction between Toronto and Niagara Falls (two hours, one-way adults $23–43, seniors $23–39, students $23–31, kids 2–11 $16–22), one in the early morning and one in the late afternoon.

AMTRAK (U.S. SERVICE)

The Amtrak **Maple Leaf** (800/872-7245, www.amtrak.com) travels from New York City's Penn Station to Toronto's Union Station (65 Front St. W., 311/392-2489, www.toronto.ca/union_station, 12.5 hours, adults $112–139, kids 2–15 $56–69). The train runs once a day, with major stops at Poughkeepsie, Albany, Syracuse, Rochester, Buffalo, Niagara Falls (N.Y.), Niagara Falls (ON), St. Catharines, Grimsby, Aldershot (Burlington), and Oakville en route to Toronto. Amtrak's American staff operate the train from New York to Niagara Falls (ON), and Canadian crews take over between Niagara Falls and Toronto.

If you're coming from Detroit, you can cross the border to Windsor and catch the VIA Rail train from there.

From Chicago and U.S. points farther west, there's no direct rail service to Toronto. You can either take the Amtrak **Wolverine** train from Chicago to Detroit (6.5 hours), where you can cross the border and transfer to VIA Rail; or take the Amtrak **Lake Shore Limited** train from Chicago to Buffalo (10.5 hours). From Buffalo, change to the **Maple Leaf** or catch a bus on to Toronto leg. On any of these routings, be prepared for long layovers.

ONTARIO NORTHLAND

If you're traveling between Toronto and the Muskoka Lakes or other points in northeastern Ontario, consider the **Northlander** train, run by Ontario Northland (800/461-8558, www.ontarionorthland.ca). You can catch the train to Union Station from Gravenhurst, Bracebridge, or Huntsville in the Muskoka

"Cottage Country" or from North Bay, Temagami, Cochrane, or other towns farther north. Check the website for detailed service information.

GO TRAINS

GO Transit (416/869-3200 or 888/438-6646, www.gotransit.com) operates a network of trains and buses that travel between the suburbs or surrounding communities and the city center. It's primarily a commuter option, so most schedules are optimized for business days, with lots of service into Toronto in the mornings and out of the city in the evenings, and less frequent service on weekend.

Seven GO Train lines link Toronto with nearby towns, including Oakville, Burlington, Hamilton, Milton, Brampton, Georgetown, Barrie, Richmond Hill, Markham, Lincolnville, and Oshawa. GO also provides seasonal service to Niagara Falls, running weekends and holidays from late May through mid-October.

By Bus

The **Toronto Coach Terminal** (610 Bay St., 416/393-7911, www.torontocoachterminal. com) is the city's main long-distance bus depot, located one block north of the corner of Dundas and Bay. The closest subway station is Dundas (two blocks to the east); or walk from St. Patrick (four blocks to the west). You can also take the #505 Dundas streetcar to Bay Street.

GREYHOUND

Greyhound (www.greyhound.ca) reaches Toronto from many Canadian and U.S. cities, although many routes involve a change of buses along the way. Greyhound runs frequent buses between Toronto and Ottawa (5–6 hours, one-way adults $47–92, kids 2–11 $47–70); from Montreal (8–9 hours), change buses in Ottawa; from Quebec City, Halifax, and points farther east, transfer in both Montreal and Ottawa.

From the west, Greyhound reaches Toronto from Calgary (52 hours) and Winnipeg

(31–32 hours), stopping in Thunder Bay, Sault Ste. Marie, and Sudbury en route. From Vancouver, change buses in Calgary; from Edmonton, transfer in either Calgary or Winnipeg.

From the United States, Greyhound runs buses to Toronto from New York City (10–11.5 hours, one-way adults $45–85, kids 2–11 $45–64), with stops in Syracuse and Buffalo. To Toronto from Boston (13.5–17.5 hours), transfer in New York City, Syracuse, or Springfield (MA); from Philadelphia (14–17.5 hours) and Washington, D.C. (15–19 hours), change buses in New York City.

Greyhound has several daily buses to Toronto from Detroit (5.5–6 hours), with stops in Windsor and London. From Chicago, the fastest route (12 hours) has a transfer in Detroit.

ONTARIO NORTHLAND

Ontario Northland (800/461-8558, www. ontarionorthland.ca) runs buses between Toronto and northeastern Ontario, including the Muskoka Lakes, Parry Sound, Sudbury, Timmins, and Temagami, and Cochrane.

MEGABUS

Megabus (705/748-6411 or 800/461-7661, www.megabus.com) has some of the best fares to Toronto from Niagara Falls (2 hours, one-way $10–23), Kingston (3 hours, one-way $10–37), Montreal (6 hours, one-way $10–49), New York City (10–11 hours, one-way $12–85), Syracuse (5.25–5.75 hours, one-way $14–55) Washington, D.C. (11–11.5 hours, one-way $12–45), Baltimore (10–10.5 hours, one-way $33–45), Philadelphia (10–10.5 hours, one-way $15–45), and Pittsburgh (7 hours, one-way $15–42). On some routes, some one-way sale fares may be as low as $1.50. It's definitely worth checking the website to try to snag a deal, particularly if you have flexible travel dates.

GO BUSES

In addition to a commuter train network, **GO Transit** (416/869-3200 or 888/438-6646, www.gotransit.com) runs buses between surrounding communities and downtown Toronto. GO Transit buses arrive and depart from the **Union Station GO Bus Terminal** (141 Bay St., at Front St. W.), not from the Toronto Coach Terminal.

Among the main GO bus routes to and from Toronto, there's service from Niagara Falls, St. Catharines, Hamilton, Kitchener, Waterloo, Cambridge, Guelph, Orangeville, Barrie, and Peterborough.

By Car

Toronto is 450 kilometers (280 miles) from Ottawa, 558 kilometers (349 miles) from Montreal, 2,115 kilometers (1,322 miles) from Winnipeg, 1,926 kilometers (1,204 miles) from Halifax, and a long-haul 4,550 kilometers (2,844 miles) from Vancouver.

Several major highways run in and around the Toronto area. The **Gardiner Expressway** follows the lakeshore into downtown Toronto. West of the city it connects with Queen Elizabeth Way (known as the QEW), which despite its rather noble-sounding name is actually a traffic-clogged multilane highway that continues around Lake Ontario to Hamilton and the Niagara Region. East of downtown, the Gardiner meets the Don Valley Parkway, a main route from the eastern and northeastern suburbs.

Highway 401 crosses the region north of Toronto proper. It's the main east–west route across southern Ontario, extending east to the Quebec border and west to Windsor.

Highway 407 (www.407etr.com), an electronic tollway, parallels the 401 farther north. There are no tollbooths; highway technology records your use of the road by taking a picture of your license plate or, for regular highway users, through a transponder (an electronic device that you lease and attach to the windshield). Tolls are charged by distance and time of travel; the end-to-end charge is $21–25. Even if you've driven from out of the province, or from the United States, your license plate information will be recorded and you'll be sent a bill.

FROM THE UNITED STATES

From the United States, Toronto is 160 kilometers (100 miles) from Buffalo, New York; 808 kilometers (505 miles) from New York City; 906 kilometers (566 miles) from Boston; 378 kilometers (236 miles) from Detroit; and 854 kilometers (534 miles) from Chicago.

The nearest highway border crossings from the United States are at the Peace, Rainbow, Whirlpool, and Queenston-Lewiston Bridges near Niagara Falls; the Blue Water Bridge on Highway 402 and I-69/94 at Sarnia/Port Huron on the Michigan border; the Ambassador Bridge or the Detroit-Windsor Tunnel between Detroit and Windsor; or via the Thousand Islands Bridge east of Gananoque.

GETTING AROUND

Toronto is built on the shores of Lake Ontario. Beginning at the lake and heading north, downtown Toronto includes the Harbourfront, the Financial District, and a mix of residential and commercial neighborhoods. "Downtown" extends north to Bloor Street, a main east–west street that borders the University of Toronto (U of T) campus. North of Bloor is Midtown, where you'll find many of Toronto's residential neighborhoods alternating with commercial developments.

Yonge Street, Toronto's main north–south artery, bisects the city, beginning at the lakeshore and continuing north well beyond the city limits. "East" addresses are east of Yonge; "west" addresses are west of Yonge. Pay careful attention to the "east" and "west" designators, since 1200 Queen Street East would be in Leslieville in the city's far east end, while 1200 Queen Street West is eight kilometers (five miles) away on the city's west side.

Toronto has a comprehensive public transit system, including a subway, streetcars, and buses, so it's easy to get around the city without a car, particularly if you choose a lodging that's within walking distance of a subway or streetcar stop. The **Toronto Transit Commission** (TTC, 416/393-4636, www.ttc.ca) runs the transit network within the city. Use the on-line Trip Planner (www.ttc.ca) to figure out the best way to get from one point to another. The TTC website also has detailed maps of the streetcar and bus routes.

TRANSIT FARES AND PASSES

The fare structure is the same for the TTC subways, streetcars, and buses. The most expensive way to ride any of these public transit options is to pay cash for a single ride (adults $3, seniors and students 13–19 $2, and kids 2–12 $0.75). In the subway stations, pay your fare at the ticket collector's booth; they'll make change if you need it, but they don't accept credit or debit cards. On buses or streetcars, pay your fare when you board; you will need exact change.

Cheaper than the individual cash fares are **tickets** or **tokens** (adults $12.50 for five/$25 for 10, senior/students $8.25 for five/$16.50 for 10, children $5.50 for 10 only), available in sets of five or 10 and good for the subway, streetcars, and buses. Buy tickets or tokens (cash only) from the fare collectors when you enter any of the subway stations, or purchase them from grocery stores, convenience stores, and drugstores around the city. The TTC website (www.ttc.ca) lists sales outlets, or contact TTC Customer Service (416/393-4636) for the nearest location.

If you expect to ride public transit frequently, consider purchasing a pass. The TTC **Day Pass** (adults $10) offers unlimited rides on subways, streetcars, and buses during a single day. Purchase the day pass from the fare collectors in the subway stations, then simply show the pass to the fare collector when you board the subway (enter next to the collector booth, not through the regular turnstiles), or to the driver when you board a streetcar or bus. On Saturdays, Sundays, and holidays, the day pass is an even better deal, particularly for families. One pass is good for unlimited one-day travel for up to six people, including up to two adults and up to four children age 19 and under.

For a longer stay, consider purchasing a

Weekly Pass (adults $36, seniors and students $28). Weekly passes are good for seven days, beginning on Monday and continuing through the following Sunday. However, if you arrive in Toronto on Wednesday and plan to stay a week, a weekly pass doesn't make sense, since you could use it for only three days (Mon.–Wed.). The fare collectors in the subway stations sell weekly passes, as do a variety of grocery and other stores. You can buy a weekly pass between the previous Thursday until the Tuesday of the week in which you'll travel.

To transfer between the subway, bus, or streetcar, get a "transfer" (a paper ticket) that allows you to connect without paying an additional fare. Transfers are valid only for the next available bus or streetcar and only at locations where the two routes intersect. In the subway stations, get a transfer from the automated transfer machine, located after passing through the turnstiles. On the bus or streetcar, ask the driver.

If you're using a daily or weekly pass, you don't need a transfer. Simply show your pass each time you board.

Subway

The Toronto subway has four lines: two main lines that are most useful to visitors and two shorter "spur" lines that extend service into the suburbs. The two main lines are the **Bloor-Danforth line,** which runs east–west across the city, following Bloor Street and Danforth Avenue, and the **Yonge-University-Spadina line,** which runs on a roughly U-shaped route. From its southernmost point at Union Station, a section of the Yonge-University-Spadina route runs north along Yonge Street to Finch station in North Toronto. The other section follows University Avenue in the downtown area, and then continues northwest to Downsview station, also in North Toronto. You can transfer free of charge between the two lines at Spadina, St. George, and Bloor-Yonge station.

The subway operates from 6 A.M. to 1:30 A.M. Monday through Saturday and from 9 A.M. to 1:30 A.M. Sunday. Trains generally run every

© CAROLYN B. HELLER

The Toronto subway is a convenient way to get around.

few minutes, slightly less often late at night and on Sundays.

Streetcar

The TTC operates a network of streetcars that run along major streets downtown and beyond. Most streetcars run 6 A.M.–1 A.M. Monday through Saturday and 9 A.M.–1 A.M. Sunday. Between 1:30 and 5 A.M., the **Blue Night Network,** an overnight bus service, operates along some streetcar routes. Stops are marked with a blue band, and service runs at least every 30 minutes. Blue Night service runs along the Queen and Carlton streetcar routes as the #301 Queen and #306 Carlton.

Among the more useful routes for visitors are:

- #501 Queen: The system's longest route travels along Queen Street from the West End through downtown to Leslieville and the Beaches.
- #504 King: Operates from Roncesvalles Avenue in the West End along King Street

through downtown, continuing east past the Distillery District, then turning north along Broadview Avenue, and connecting to the Bloor-Danforth subway at Broadview station.

- #505 Dundas: Travels west-to-east along Dundas Street.
- #506 Carlton: From High Park in the West End, runs along College Street, Carlton Street, and Gerrard Street, and connects to Main Street station on the Bloor-Danforth subway line.
- #509 Harbourfront: Travels between Union Station and Exhibition Place, passing Harbourfront Centre and Fort York en route.
- #510 Spadina: Runs between Spadina station (on both the Bloor-Danforth and Yonge-University-Spadina subway lines) and Union Station, via Spadina Avenue and Queen's Quay along the harbor.

Bus

In downtown Toronto, you can reach most

places by subway or streetcar. As you venture further from the city center, buses become more convenient.

To figure out if buses travel to your destination, enter your starting and ending point into the TTC's online Trip Planner (www.ttc.ca). The website also maps all the bus routes in the city.

Buses typically run from 6 A.M.–1 A.M. Monday through Saturday and from 9 A.M.–1 A.M. Sunday. After 9 P.M., women traveling alone on Toronto city buses can ask to be let off between stops, so you don't have to walk as far to your destination.

From 1:30 A.M. to 5 A.M., the overnight **Blue Night Network** runs buses along the Bloor-Danforth and Yonge subway routes. The #300 Bloor-Danforth bus operates along Bloor Street and Danforth Avenue between Pearson Airport to Victoria Park Avenue, while the #320 Yonge bus follows Yonge Street from Union Station north to Steeles Avenue.

Blue Night buses also run along many regular bus routes. Stops are marked with a blue band, and service runs at least every 30 minutes. The TTC website (www.ttc.ca) has maps and schedules of all Blue Night buses.

The PATH Network

Underneath downtown Toronto, the PATH is a 27-kilometer (16-mile) network of interconnected underground walkways. You can walk from building to building, protected from the weather. The walkways are lined with shops, and in some areas, you'll find more stores and services underground than you will at street level!

The PATH extends from Union Station north to City Hall, Eaton Centre, and the Toronto Coach Terminal, bounded roughly by Yonge Street to the east and University Avenue to the west, with a couple of spurs continuing west into the Entertainment District. The walkways are marked by multicolored directional signs to help you find your way.

Following the PATH can be somewhat confusing for newcomers, because you don't have the landmarks you see at street level. Many of the signs direct you to particular buildings,

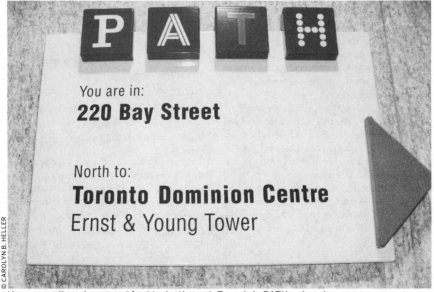

© CAROLYN B. HELLER

You can walk underground for blocks through Toronto's PATH network.

and you may not know whether you want to go, for example, toward the Canadian Pacific Tower or First Canadian Place. You can always come up to the street if you can't figure out where you are. Tourism Toronto (www.seetorontonow.com) has a useful PATH map on their website, and you can often find copies at hotels, museums, and other attractions around the city.

Taxi

Toronto taxis are metered, so make sure the driver uses the meter. Rates include an initial charge of $4.25, with an additional charge of $1.75 for every kilometer traveled. Short trips around the downtown area can cost $8–15.

You can hail taxis on the street, although it's often easy to find them in front of hotels, train or bus stations, shopping centers, and tourist attractions, such as museums.

Call **416-Taxicab** (416/829-4222) from anywhere in Toronto and you'll be connected to taxi services in your area. Visit their website (www.416-taxicab.com) for more information about this handy service.

Car

Unless you plan to explore the suburbs or take day trips out of town, it's easier to get around Toronto without a car. Traffic can be quite heavy, with morning and evening rush hours extending from at least 7–9 A.M. and 4–6 P.M. Monday through Friday.

Many of the downtown streets are one-way, and turns, both left and right, are often restricted from major arteries. While right turns are allowed at red lights in Ontario, they're often prohibited in downtown Toronto; look for signs at the intersection.

Drivers must also yield to streetcars. When a streetcar stops, the cars behind it must also stop at least two meters (six feet) behind and wait for passengers to board or unload.

PARKING

There's metered on-street parking throughout Toronto, but the rate varies by location ($1.50–3.50/hour), so be sure to check the meter or ticket dispenser. Some streets have single-space meters that take coins only. Other streets have ticket dispensers that cover a block or section of a block; these meters take either coins or credit cards and give you a ticket to put on the dashboard of your car.

The city also operates 160 parking lots containing about 20,000 spaces. The **Toronto Parking Authority** (www.greenp.com) has a useful parking lot finder that shows the location and rates at all municipal parking lots.

When booking a hotel reservation, ask about the cost and availability of parking if you're planning to bring a car. Daily parking charges can add significantly to your costs, particularly at the major downtown hotels.

CAR RENTALS

All the major North American car rental companies have outlets at Toronto's Pearson Airport (YYZ, 416/247-7678 or 866/207-1690, www.torontopearson.com), and most have offices downtown, as well:

- Alamo (877/222-9075, www.alamo.ca)
- Avis (800/879-2847, www.avis.ca)
- Budget (800/268-8900, www.budget.ca)
- Dollar (800/848-8268, www.dollarcanada.ca)
- Enterprise (800/261-7331, www.enterprise rentacar.ca)
- Hertz (800/654-3131, www.hertz.ca)
- National (877/222-9058, www.nationalcar .ca)
- Thrifty (800/847-4389, www.thrifty.com)

A number of smaller car rental agencies also have offices near the Toronto airport, and they provide a shuttle from the terminal to their locations. It's worth checking to see if their rates are lower than other major companies.

- Advantage Car Rentals (905/672-2063 or 866/672-0123, reservations 866/398-2933, www.advantagecarrentals.com)
- Discount Car Rentals (416/249-5554 or 800/263-2355, www.discountcar.com)

- Fox Rent-A-Car (800/225 4369, www. foxrentacar.com)
- Payless Car Rental (416/675-2000 or 800/729-5377, www.paylesscar.com)
- Zoom Rent-A-Car (905/670-7368 or 888/317-9666, www.zoomrentals.com)

It's often cheaper to rent a car at an in-town location than at the airport. If you're flying into or out of Pearson, however, you'll need to factor in the additional time and cost of getting to/from the airport.

Note that most rental-car companies do not allow you to drive on Highway 407, or they'll charge you a premium over the basic toll charges. If you're renting a car, save yourself the hassle and avoid the 407.

Tours
WALKING TOURS

One of the best ways to get to know a city is to meet local residents. If you don't know anyone in Toronto, here's a program that can help. The **Toronto Greeter** (aka TAP into TO!, 416/338-2786, www.toronto.ca/tapto, free) offers a free tour of a Toronto neighborhood led by a local "greeter," an enthusiastic resident and volunteer tour guide. Choose which neighborhood to visit, or let the greeter select a favorite area. If you have a particular interest, you can request a guide who's knowledgeable in that subject. Tours typically lasts two or three hours and are available year-round. Request a greeter at least a week in advance; sign up or get more information on the program website.

Heritage Toronto Walks (416/338-3886, www.heritagetoronto.org, May–Oct.) are free walking tours that highlight a neighborhood's history, whether architectural, cultural, archaeological or natural. Check their online schedule or phone the information line for walk times and locations. Reservations aren't required; just show up a few minutes before the walk's departure.

The guides for **Urban Adventures** (www. urbanadventures.com) walking tours know and love Toronto, and they want you to know and love it, too. They offer several different tours, including "Toronto Highs and Lows" (3 hours, $37), a downtown walking tour highlighting good and bad times in the city's history; a food-focused tour of Kensington Market and Chinatown (2 hours, $25), and a "Beer Makes History Better" tour (3.5 hours, $37) that combines a walking tour through the St. Lawrence Market and Distillery District with stops at several pubs for a brew.

The Urban Adventures guides also run walking tours as **The Tour Guys** (647/230-7891, www.tourguys.ca), including a 90-minute pay-what-you-can tour (10 A.M., 1 P.M., and 4 P.M. Tues.–Sun. mid-May–early Sept.; 1 P.M. Fri.–Sat. early Sept.–mid-May) that includes the Old and New City Halls, Nathan Phillips Square, Eaton Centre, the Bay, and surrounding landmarks. The tours are offered free, but you're encouraged to tip your guide.

On an **Urban Quest** (www.urbanquest.com, year-round, $20/team), you solve a series of clues that lead you from place to place around town. You can do a quest with any number of people, but most are designed for two to four, just right for vacationing pals or families. Typically lasting around 1.5 hours, the quests end at a mystery restaurant where you can have lunch or dinner (not included in the quest fee).

The **West Queen West Art + Design Tour** (www.artinsite.net, noon–2:30 P.M. Sat.; $15/person, $25 for two) gives an insider's look at the artists, galleries, and various denizens of this arty neighborhood. Tours begin in the Gladstone Hotel lobby (1214 Queen St. W.) and end at the Drake Hotel.

The Royal Ontario Museum runs **ROM Walks** (416/586-8000, www.rom.on.ca/programs, 2 P.M. Sun. and 6 P.M. Wed. May–Sept.; free), guided walks that highlight the history and architecture of particular neighborhoods. Check their website for the weekly schedule.

BOAT TOURS

On a **Toronto Hippo Tour** (416/703-4476 or 877/635-5510, www.torontohippotours.com, May–Oct., adults $39, seniors and students $34, kids 3–12 $25), ride through downtown, then splash into Lake Ontario on an amphibious vehicle. The tours run 90 minutes: 60 minutes on land and 30 minutes on the water. There is a 10 percent discount if you book online.

Take a two-hour sail around Toronto Harbour on a traditional 165-foot three-masted schooner with the **Toronto Tall Ship Boat Cruises** (416/260-6355 or 800/267-3866, www.tallshipcruisestoronto.com, May–Sept., adults $21.95, seniors $19.95, kids 5–15 $11.95).

Want to see Toronto from a traditional Voyageur canoe? **Canoe Toronto** (416/993-4224, www.canoetoronto.com, May–Sept.) runs a 30-minute paddling tour around Toronto Harbour ($10), a 90-minute paddle around the Toronto Islands ($20), and a 2.5-hour Islands paddle with a stop on Centre Island. Canoes can accommodate 10–18 paddlers each.

FOOD TOURS

A Taste of the World (416/923-6813, www .torontowalksbikes.com, adults $45, seniors and students $40, kids 12 and under $30) leads foodcentric walking tours in Chinatown, Kensington Market, and other neighborhoods. Tours run 3.5 hours and include snacks along the way. Some tours run year-round, but there are more frequent tours in the warmer months; check their website for a tour schedule.

On the **ChowBella** (647/403-8030, www. chowbellaconcierge.com) "West Queen West Tasting Tour" (11:30 a.m. Sun., $49), sample the eclectic flavors of Toronto's west side, from tea to olive oil to poutine.

THE NIAGARA REGION

Niagara Falls, an easy drive south of Toronto or across the border from New York State, is one of the most-visited destinations in all of Canada. Families, honeymooners, tour groups, and everyone in between make their way to this iconic, must-see attraction. Whether it's your first falls visit or your 50th, feeling the spray on your face, watching the cascading curtains tumble and crash into the river below, or glimpsing a rainbow arching over the torrents is still a thrill.

Yet Niagara is more than just the falls. Beyond the town of Niagara Falls, with its quirky mix of stunning natural beauty and honky-tonk tourist lures, the Niagara region offers plenty of attractions.

The Niagara Peninsula is Ontario's major wine-producing region, and a prime destination for a wine country getaway. Wine-tasting and -touring lures visitors to Niagara-on-the-Lake, home to more than two dozen wineries. Many more are clustered in the Twenty Valley area, in the towns of Beamsville, Vineland, and Jordan—a popular day trip from Niagara Falls. Niagara-on-the-Lake is also home to one of North America's premier theater festivals—the annual Shaw Festival, which produces works by noted Irish playwright George Bernard Shaw.

The towns along the Welland Canal, from St. Catharines south to Port Colborne, attract boat enthusiasts as well as vacationers seeking a quiet getaway that's still convenient to the peninsula's other attractions. Built back in the 1820s, the canal provides a shipping route between the Great Lakes. Freighters, barges, and

© CAROLYN B. HELLER

THE NIAGARA REGION

HIGHLIGHTS

LOOK FOR 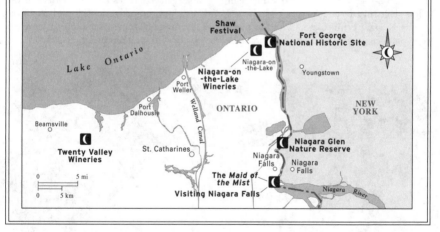 TO FIND RECOMMENDED
SIGHTS, ACTIVITIES, DINING, AND LODGING.

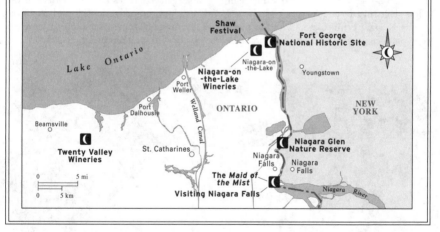 Visiting Niagara Falls: No matter how many times you've seen these thundering waterfalls – the Horseshoe Falls on the Ontario side of the Niagara River and the American Falls on the New York banks – they're still spectacular (page 98).

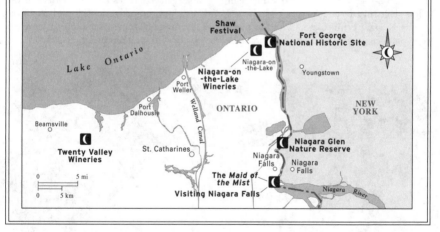 The *Maid of the Mist*: Since the 1840s, these ferry boats have taken visitors to the base of the falls, so put on your rain poncho and climb aboard. A cruise aboard the *Maid* is still the best way to hear the crashing waters and feel the spray (page 99).

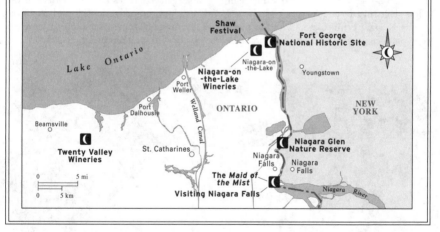 Niagara Glen Nature Reserve: The window-lined Nature Centre at this park north of the falls has great views of the Niagara River Gorge. Take a guided hike through the reserve, or hit the trails on your own (page 102).

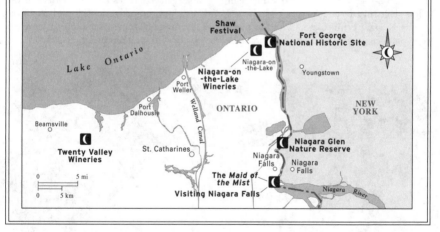 Shaw Festival: From April through October, the town of Niagara-on-the-Lake hosts one of North America's major theater festivals, devoted to the works of Irish playwright George Bernard Shaw, along with more contemporary plays (page 119).

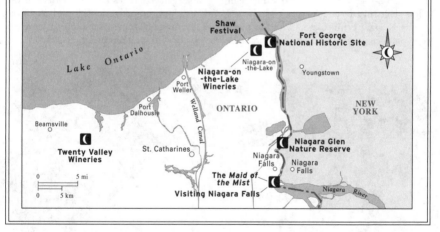 Niagara-on-the-Lake Wineries: With more than two dozen wineries clustered in this small region, you can easily stop at many producers – and sample many varieties – in a short visit (page 122).

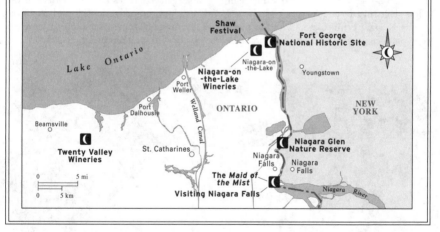 Fort George National Historic Site: An important battleground during the War of 1812, this restored fort overlooking the Niagara River is now a national historic site. Learn about the Niagara region's early history and watch staff demonstrate traditional weaponry, cook on an open hearth, and perform fife and drum music (page 124).

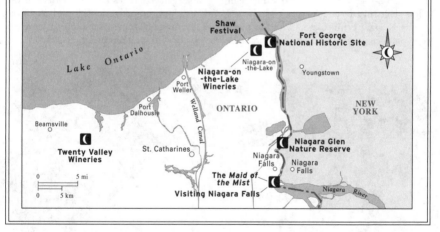 Twenty Valley Wineries: Ontario's major wine-producing region includes the towns of Beamsville, Vineland, and Jordan. You can sample ice wine, Ontario's distinctive dessert wine, as well as other varietals (page 130).

THE NIAGARA REGION

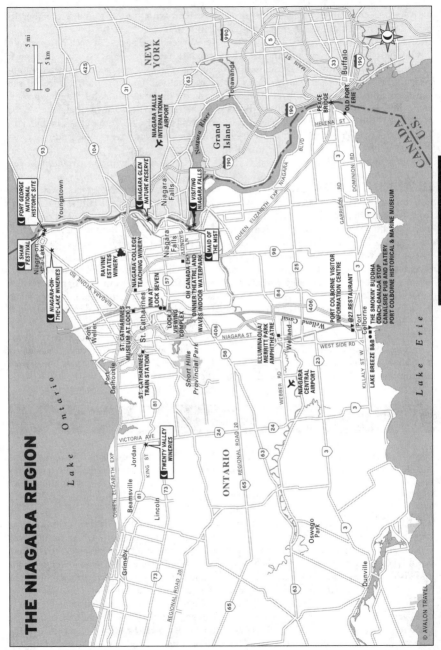

© AVALON TRAVEL

pleasure craft continue to navigate the canal's eight locks, and you can watch mega-ships up close as they lock through.

Outdoors lovers can explore an extensive network of cycling paths that crisscrosses the Niagara Peninsula, or set out on the Bruce Trail, an 800-kilometer (500-mile) hiking route that extends to the tip of the Bruce Peninsula. History lovers will find numerous historic sites that date to the War of 1812.

From wine-tastings to places to unwind, Niagara is much more than just the falls.

PLANNING YOUR TIME

You can easily visit Niagara Falls on a day trip from Toronto or upstate New York, but there's plenty to do around the Niagara Peninsula to occupy a long weekend. Plan at least a day or two at **Niagara Falls,** another day in **Niagara-on-the-Lake,** and a third touring either the **Twenty Valley Wine Country** or the **Welland Canal.**

Summer is peak season in the Niagara region. From late June through early September, everything is open, and most attractions keep long hours, from 9 A.M. until at least 7–8 P.M. The **Shaw Festival** begins with preview productions in April, and shows run through

October, with June through September its prime time.

Weekends are busiest in both Niagara Falls and Niagara-on-the-Lake, especially in summer and early fall, so you'll find more accommodation options (and often lower prices) if you can visit midweek. Look for lodging in some of the less-touristed towns along the nearby Welland Canal—St. Catharines, Thorold, Port Colborne—if you have trouble finding a room in your price range.

At Niagara Falls, many attractions open for the season in April or May and close in late October or early November. Visiting the falls during the spring or fall "shoulder" periods outside the June–August peak can mean fewer crowds. September and October are harvest season for the region's vineyards, making it a popular wine-touring time.

The falls themselves are, obviously, still there year-round, and you can save significantly on accommodations by visiting midwinter, when far fewer tourists are around. Just prepare for snow and cold temperatures.

Whenever you visit, check attractions' opening hours before you set out, since many Niagara-area sights change their hours with the seasons.

Niagara Falls

The city of Niagara Falls is home to about 82,000 people and hosts more than 10 million visitors every year—all because of the spectacular torrents of water that cascade down the Niagara River. Long popular as a honeymoon destination, Niagara Falls has plenty of appeal for everyone from kids to seniors.

The Niagara River connects two of the Great Lakes—Lake Ontario and Lake Erie—and also separates Canada from the United States. That means that there are actually two cities of "Niagara Falls"—one in Ontario, the other across the river in New York State—and two main waterfalls, as well, the Horseshoe Falls on the Canadian side and the American

Falls on the New York shore. The Ontario side of the river is more developed, with numerous attractions in addition to the falls, mixing history, green space, and (unfortunately) plenty of tacky tourist traps.

The area along the Niagara River closest to the Horseshoe Falls is known as **Table Rock,** where a large visitor center houses several attractions. The **Fallsview** area, with lots of skyscraping hotels, is atop the Niagara Escarpment, a steep climb up the hill above Table Rock.

To the north of Table Rock along the river is **Queen Victoria Park** and the departure point for the *Maid of the Mist,* a deservedly popular boat ride that takes you under the falls. Up

THE NIAGARA REGION

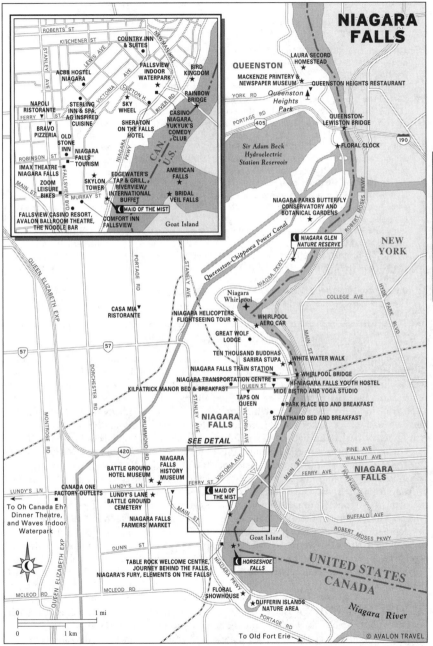

NIAGARA FALLS

ROBERTS ST
KITCHENER ST
LEWIS AVE
COUNTRY INN & SUITES
ACBB HOSTEL NIAGARA
FALLSVIEW INDOOR WATERPARK
BIRD KINGDOM
NAPOLI RISTORANTE
STERLING INN & SPA, AG INSPIRED CUISINE
SKY WHEEL
RAINBOW BRIDGE
FERRY
BRAVO PIZZERIA
OLD STONE INN
CASINO NIAGARA, YUKYUK'S COMEDY CLUB
SHERATON ON THE FALLS HOTEL
ROBINSON ST
NIAGARA FALLS TOURISM
IMAX THEATRE NIAGARA FALLS
ZOOM LEISURE BIKES
SKYLON TOWER
EDGEWATER'S TAP & GRILL, RIVERVIEW INTERNATIONAL BUFFET
AMERICAN FALLS
MURRAY ST
BRIDAL VEIL FALLS
FALLSVIEW CASINO RESORT, AVALON BALLROOM THEATRE, THE NOODLE BAR
COMFORT INN FALLSVIEW
MAID OF THE MIST
Goat Island

QUEENSTON
LAURA SECORD HOMESTEAD
MACKENZIE PRINTERY & NEWSPAPER MUSEUM
QUEENSTON HEIGHTS RESTAURANT
YORK RD
Queenston Heights Park
PORTAGE RD
QUEENSTON-LEWISTON BRIDGE
190
FLORAL CLOCK
Sir Adam Beck Hydroelectric Station Reservoir

NEW YORK

NIAGARA PARKS BUTTERFLY CONSERVATORY AND BOTANICAL GARDENS

Queenston-Chippawa Power Canal
NIAGARA GLEN NATURE RESERVE

COLLEGE AVE

Niagara Whirlpool
WHIRLPOOL AERO CAR

CASA MIA RISTORANTE
NIAGARA HELICOPTERS FLIGHTSEEING TOUR
GREAT WOLF LODGE
TEN THOUSAND BUDDHAS SARIRA STUPA
WHITE WATER WALK
NIAGARA FALLS TRAIN STATION
NIAGARA TRANSPORTATION CENTRE
WHIRLPOOL BRIDGE
KILPATRICK MANOR BED & BREAKFAST
QUEEN ST
HI-NIAGARA FALLS YOUTH HOSTEL
MIDE BISTRO AND YOGA STUDIO
TAPS ON QUEEN
PARK PLACE BED AND BREAKFAST
STRATHAIRD BED AND BREAKFAST

NIAGARA FALLS

PINE AVE
WALNUT AVE
SEE DETAIL
NIAGARA FALLS HISTORY MUSEUM
FERRY AVE
NIAGARA FALLS
CANADA ONE FACTORY OUTLETS
BATTLE GROUND HOTEL MUSEUM
LUNDY'S LN
LUNDY'S LANE BATTLE GROUND CEMETERY
FERRY ST
MAID OF THE MIST
BUFFALO AVE
To Oh Canada Eh? Dinner Theatre, and Waves Indoor Waterpark
NIAGARA FALLS FARMERS' MARKET
ROBERT MOSES PKWY
DUNN ST
Goat Island

TABLE ROCK WELCOME CENTRE, JOURNEY BEHIND THE FALLS, NIAGARA'S FURY, ELEMENTS ON THE FALLS
HORSESHOE FALLS
UNITED STATES
CANADA
MCLEOD RD
FLORAL SHOWHOUSE
DUFFERIN ISLANDS NATURE AREA
Niagara River
PORTAGE RD
To Old Fort Erie
© AVALON TRAVEL

0   1 mi
0   1 km

THE AMERICAN SIDE OF THE FALLS

There are two cities of "Niagara Falls" – one on the Ontario side of the Niagara River and another on the opposite bank in New York State. On the New York side, the Falls area is part of the **Niagara Reservation State Park** (716/278-1796, www.niagarafallsstatepark. com). You'll find the best views of the Falls at **Prospect Point,** right next to the American Falls. The overall views of the American Falls are more majestic from the Canadian shore, but you're closer to the spray on the U.S. side. The *Maid of the Mist* tour boats also operate from Prospect Point, giving you essentially the same ride as you would get departing from the Canadian docks.

If you want to feel the spray full in your face, head for **Goat Island,** where you can descend alongside Bridal Veil Falls on the **Cave of the Winds** (716/278-1730, 9 A.M.-5 P.M. Sun.-Thurs., 9 A.M.-9 P.M. Fri.-Sat. May-late June; 9 A.M.-9 P.M. Sun.-Thurs., 9 A.M.-10 P.M. Fri.-Sat. late June-early Sept.; 9 A.M.-7 P.M. Sun.-Thurs.,

9 A.M.-9 P.M. Fri.-Sat. early Sept.-mid-Oct.; 9 A.M.-5 P.M. daily mid-late Oct.; adults US$11, kids 6-12 US$8) that follows a wooden walkway to a platform just six meters (20 feet) from the Falls. You'll receive a rain poncho, but should still expect to get wet.

The **Visitor Center** (8 A.M.-6 P.M. Sun.-Thurs., 8 A.M.-9 P.M. Fri.-Sat. May-late June and early Sept.-mid-Oct; 8 A.M.-9 P.M. Sun.-Thurs., 8 A.M.-10 P.M. Fri.-Sat. late June-early Sept.; 8 A.M.-6 P.M. daily Oct.-Apr.; free) has exhibits about the Falls, as well as coffee, ice cream, and snacks.

The **Rainbow Bridge** connects Niagara Falls, Ontario, with Niagara Falls, New York. You can cross the bridge by car, on foot, or by bike, but remember: Even if you're just strolling across for the afternoon, this is an international border and you need to *bring your passport.*

For more information, contact **Niagara USA** (10 Rainbow Blvd., Niagara Falls, NY, 716/282-8992 or 877/325-5787, www.niagara-usa.com).

---

the slope just north of the *Maid of the Mist* is **Clifton Hill,** with numerous places to stay, as well as the flashing neon of arcades, wax museums, and other kitschy attractions.

North along the river is the **Whirlpool** area, where the river makes a 90-degree turn. A number of parks and natural attractions are clustered between the Whirlpool and **Queenston,** a historic district 12 kilometers (7.5 miles) north of the falls.

Away from the river, Queen Street is the main business route through "downtown" Niagara Falls, although there's actually more development along Ferry Street and Lundy's Lane, which run east–west from the river across the city to the QEW (Queen Elizabeth Way), the highway that connects Toronto with the Niagara region.

◗ VISITING THE FALLS

Niagara's Falls aren't the world's tallest or widest falls, but they certainly rank among

the most spectacular. The Niagara Falls began forming during the last ice age, more than 12,000 years ago, and they have actually moved 11 kilometers (7 miles) during that period. They originally began to the north of their present location, near the Niagara Glen.

The best (free) vantage point for viewing the falls is near the **Table Rock Visitor Centre** (6650 Niagara Parkway, www.niagaraparks. com), adjacent to the Horseshoe Falls. Be prepared for some spray to mist around you, even as you walk or stand nearby.

The larger **Horseshoe Falls,** often called the Canadian Falls (on the Ontario side of the Niagara River), are 670 meters (2,200 feet) wide and curve in a semicircular "horseshoe" from bank to bank. While the Horseshoe Falls measure only 57 meters (188 feet) from top to bottom, more than 168,000 cubic meters (44 million gallons) of water crash over the falls every minute during daylight hours.

On the New York shore, the **American Falls**

have a gentler curve. In fact, unless you see them from above, they look like a straight curtain of water stretching 260 meters (850 feet) wide and between 21 and 34 meters (70–110 feet) tall, depending on where you measure.

A third narrow waterfall, known as **Bridal Veil Falls,** almost looks like part of the American Falls, since it's just beside it, separated from the American Falls by Luna Island. The Bridal Veil Falls measure 17 meters (56 feet) across.

◖ The *Maid of the Mist*

Since the 1840s, these tour boats (Queen Victoria Park, 5920 Niagara Parkway, 905/358-5781, www.maidofthemist.com, daily Apr.– late Oct., check website for seasonal schedules; adults $16.50, kids 6–12 $10.10) have been ferrying visitors to the base of the falls, and they're still the best way to hear the thundering waters and feel the spray. The first *Maid* was a steamboat ferry that launched back in 1846, initially to transport people and cargo across the Niagara River, but it soon took on a new role as a sightseeing boat. Notable passengers have included Princess Diana and her sons, U.S. presidents Theodore Roosevelt and Jimmy Carter, Soviet president Mikhail Gorbachev, and the actress Marilyn Monroe.

Departing every 15 minutes, the *Maid* first cruises to the American Falls, then ferries into the Horseshoe Falls basin. The ride lasts about 30 minutes, and yes, you will get wet!

The *Maid* also runs from the American side of the falls, leaving from Prospect Point in the Niagara Reservation State Park (716/284-8897, adults US$13.50, kids 6–12 $7.85).

Journey Behind the Falls

This walk behind the falls (Table Rock Welcome Centre, 6650 Niagara Parkway, www.niagaraparks.com, daily year-round, check website for seasonal schedules; adults $14.60, children 6–12 $8.95 mid-Apr.–mid-Dec.; adults $11.25, children $6.95, mid-Dec.–mid-Apr.) lets you see the waterfalls from a different perspective.

You start your "journey" in an elevator

© CAROLYN B. HELLER

The *Maid of the Mist* has been ferrying visitors to the base of the Falls since the 1840s.

that descends 45 meters (150 feet) through the rock beside the Horseshoe Falls. Then you walk through underground tunnels to two observation decks, where the falls crash just beside you. The spray on the observation platforms can be drenching, so protect your camera gear, your guidebook, and anything else that you don't want waterlogged. You explore at your own pace; allow about 30 minutes, longer if you're with kids who relish the falls' chilly shower.

Save this attraction for a warm day if you can; the spray can feel frigid. From mid-December through mid-April, the lower observation deck, which gives you the best falls view, is closed (it's too icy), so admission prices are reduced.

Niagara's Fury

A two-part multimedia show, *Niagara's Fury* (Table Rock Welcome Centre, 6650 Niagara Parkway, www.niagarasfury.com, shows daily year-round, check website for seasonal schedules; adults and students 13 and older $15, kids 6–12 $9.75) tries to explain how the falls were created. It starts with a short cartoon, told from the perspective of a friendly little beaver who is struggling with a school report about the ice age and how the falls emerged. Then you move into a circular theater, where lightning flashes, the earth shakes, and water pours from the ceiling as you "experience" the birth of the falls.

Older kids may think *Niagara's Fury* is cool, but young children may be frightened by the crashing thunder and shaking floor. Although the entire show lasts less than 20 minutes, give this one a miss if you're short on time; the real falls are far more dramatic.

White Water Walk

As you go north of Horseshoe Falls, the Niagara River bucks and churns through a section known as the whirlpool rapids. Rated as Class 6 whitewater—defined as "extremely difficult to successfully maneuver...usually considered unrunnable"—the rushing rapids slicing through the deep gorge are impressive, even from the shore, where the White Water Walk (4330 Niagara Pkwy., www.

niagaraparks.com, daily early Apr.–late Oct., call for seasonal hours; adults and students 13 and older $9.50, kids 6–12 $6.25) gives you an up-close look.

After taking an elevator 70 meters (230 feet) into the gorge and walking through a tunnel to the riverbank, you follow a 300-meter (0.25-mile) boardwalk along the Niagara River rapids. Stairs lead to two observation areas at the river's edge.

A small exhibit area near the elevators profiles some of the daredevils who attempted various stunts on the Niagara River or over the falls—just don't try these tricks yourself. Not only is stunting extremely dangerous (few of the adventurers survived), it's now illegal, and trespassers can face hefty fines.

The White Water Walk is four kilometers (2.5 miles) north of Horseshoe Falls, on the Peoplemover route. You can follow the walk at your own pace, but most people find that 30–45 minutes should be enough time.

Whirlpool Aero Car

Over thousands of years, the Niagara River slowly eroded a path through the Niagara Escarpment, creating a deep canyon, called the Great Gorge. North of the falls, as the river wends through the gorge, it makes a sharp right-angle turn, which forces the water into a counterclockwise spin. This unusual churning water formation, the Niagara River Whirlpool, is difficult to see from shore (at least without a long, steep hike), but it's easily visible from above, aboard the Whirlpool Aero Car (3850 Niagara Parkway, www.niagaraparks.com, daily early Apr.–early Nov., call for seasonal hours; adults and students older than 13 $12.25, kids 6–12 $7.95).

The unusual-looking Aero Car, which Spanish engineer Leonardo Torres Quevedo designed, has been transporting passengers over the whirlpool since 1916. You stand in the red cable car, which is attached to the overhead cables by a sunshine yellow contraption that looks like half of a giant bicycle wheel. As you ride across the gorge and back, the views extend up and down the river.

The Aero Car is 4.5 kilometers (3 miles) north of Horseshoe Falls, on the Peoplemover route. Although the ride itself takes just 10 minutes round-trip, the Aero Car accommodates only 35 people and tickets are issued for specific times, so be prepared to wait.

Skylon Tower and Sky Wheel

For an aerial view of the falls, take the "yellow bug" elevators—they do resemble yellow beetles—that scoot up the outside of the Skylon Tower (5200 Robinson St., 905/356-2651 or 877/475-9566, www.skylon.com, 8 A.M.–midnight daily in summer, 11 A.M.–9 P.M. daily in winter, adults $13.91, kids 2–12 $8.11) to the observation deck 236 meters (775 feet) in the sky. You can also buy a combination ticket that includes a show in the 3D/4D theater (adults $25.50, kids 2–12 $15.06). Tickets are discounted if you buy them online in advance.

Yet another vantage point for viewing the falls is the 10-minute whirl on the Sky Wheel (4950 Clifton Hill, 905/358-4793, www.skywheel.ca, call for seasonal hours, adults $10, kids under 13 $7), a 53-meter (175-foot) Ferris wheel.

SIGHTS
Museums

Lundy's Lane, which runs east–west across the city of Niagara Falls, was the site of a major battle between American and British troops in the War of 1812. Both sides suffered some of the heaviest casualties of the war during the Battle of Lundy's Lane on

THE WAR OF 1812

The **War of 1812 Bicentennial** runs from 2012 to 2015, with numerous special events around the Niagara region that will commemorate the period when the United States declared war on Britain and battles raged across the Niagara Peninsula. Bicentennial events will include battle reenactments, walking tours, parades, lectures, concerts, dinners, and more. For details, check with the following organizations:

• **Niagara 1812 Bicentennial Legacy Council** (www.discover1812.com)

• **Niagara Parks Commission** (www.niagara-parks.com)

• **Town of Niagara-on-the-Lake's Bicentennial Committee** (www.1812niagaraonthelake.ca)

Many individual attractions around the Niagara region are also hosting War of 1812 events:

• **Fort George** (www.pc.gc.ca)

• **Laura Secord Homestead** (www.niagara-parks.com)

• **Niagara Falls History Museum** (www.niagarafallshistorymuseum.ca)

• **Niagara Historical Society Museum** (www.niagarahistorical.museum)

• **Old Fort Erie** (www.niagaraparks.com)

© CAROLYN B. HELLER

A drummer beats out traditional tunes at Fort George National Historic Site.

July 25, 1814. Neither side "won" the battle, but American troops withdrew south to Fort Erie, setting the scene for the Battle of Fort Erie later that summer.

Along Ferry Street and Lundy's Lane (Ferry changes its name west of Main Street), several sights help you learn more about Lundy's Lane and Niagara's 19th-century history.

In an 1874 stone building, with a modern glass-walled addition, the **Niagara Falls History Museum** (5810 Ferry St., www.niagarafallshistorymuseum.ca) houses more than 25,000 artifacts about the region's history, with featured exhibits about the War of 1812. As this book went to press, the museum was under renovation; check their website for an update and for current hours of operation.

A short walk farther west, the **Lundy's Lane Battle Ground Cemetery,** also known as the Drummond Hill Cemetery, is on the site where the Lundy's Lane Battle was fought. The cemetery has a mix of historic and more recent graves, including a monument honoring Laura Secord, a Canadian heroine during the War of 1812, who is buried here.

On the 30-minute guided tours of the **Battle Ground Hotel Museum** (6151 Lundy's Ln., 905/357-9866, www.niagarafallshistorymuseum.ca, noon–4 P.M. Fri.–Sun. May–mid-Oct., admission by donation), a restored wood-frame tavern, you'll learn about life in Niagara Falls from the 1830s to the 1850s, when the falls were already a tourist attraction and travelers gathered in taverns such as this one. The museum also houses some artifacts from the War of 1812.

Ten Thousand Buddhas Sarira Stupa

One of Niagara's most incongruous sights might be this peaceful Buddhist temple (4303 River Rd., 905/371-2679), also called the Cham Shan Buddhist Temple, built in the 1990s, which looks as if it were transported directly from a city in China. The seven-story pagoda houses Buddhist arts and artifacts (Sat.–Sun., June–mid-Oct.), while a smaller Buddhist temple (9 A.M.–5 P.M. daily) is in an

© CAROLYN B. HELLER

Escape from the frenzy of Niagara Falls at the peaceful Ten Thousand Buddhas Sarira Stupa.

adjacent building. A walk around the property may help you recover your Zen state after Niagara's tourist frenzy.

🌀 Niagara Glen Nature Reserve

Some of the best views of the Niagara River and gorge are from the window-lined Nature Centre at the Niagara Glen Nature Reserve (Niagara Parkway, 905/354-6678, www.niagaraparks.com, call for seasonal hours, free)—and those views, which include glimpses of the Niagara River Whirlpool, are entirely free. Inside the **Nature Centre,** a small exhibit area includes a "touch table" to explore rocks, fossils, and animal skulls found in the gorge, as well as displays about the area's flora and fauna.

The Glen has about six kilometers (3.8 miles) of hiking trails that descend into the Niagara Gorge. The **River Path** is a particularly scenic route that follows along the Niagara River all the way to the Whirlpool. This trail has lots of steep climbs and descents, so Parks staff recommend allowing at least three hours round-trip, even for experienced hikers. You can pick up a trail map at the Nature Centre or get one online at the Niagara Parks website.

Park naturalists lead one-hour guided hikes (11 A.M. and 2 P.M. daily in summer, $6), where you learn more about the area's history, geology, plants, and wildlife as you explore the walking paths. Because some of the terrain is quite steep, these guided walks are best suited for adults and older children.

You can also rent bicycles (half-/full-day $20/30) at the Nature Centre. The Niagara River Recreation Trail, which extends from Niagara-on-the-Lake south to Fort Erie, runs right past Niagara Glen. Niagara Glen is open year-round, although hours vary with the seasons and with the weather conditions. Niagara Glen is eight kilometers (five miles) north of Horseshoe Falls, on the Peoplemover route.

Floral Clock

As you're traveling along the Niagara Parkway between the falls and Queenston, stop to check the time at this 12.2-meter-wide (40-foot-wide) working clock (14004 Niagara Parkway, www.niagaraparks.com, dawn–dusk daily, free), inlaid with more than 15,000 plants. Ontario Hydro, the regional power company, originally created this floral attraction back in 1950. Its hour hand measures 4.5 meters (14.5 feet); the minute hand is 5.3 meters (17.5 feet). Niagara Parks staff change the clock's botanical design twice a year, as the seasons change.

The Floral Clock is 11.5 kilometers (7 miles) north of Horseshoe Falls, on the Peoplemover route.

Bird Kingdom

Housed in a former corset factory, the world's largest free-flying indoor aviary (5651 River Rd., 905/356-8888 or 866/994-0090, www.birdkingdom.ca, 10 A.M.–5 P.M. daily, adults $16.95, seniors $14.95, kids 4–15 $11.95) is fun for children, especially on a bad-weather day. In the "small aviary," more than 40 species of tiny birds flit about, while in the main glass-walled sanctuary, nearly 400 birds representing approximately 80 species, from the brilliant

orange-red scarlet ibis to the African royal starling to multicolored macaws, fly all around you as you wander the paths.

Animal encounters and activities, from bat feeding to snake handling, are held throughout the day; check the schedule on the website (or at the admission desk) to time your visit to the activities that most interest you and your family. Inside the main aviary is a surprise: a traditional **Javanese tea house.** This intricately hand-carved teak structure houses a snack bar, though unfortunately it serves pizza, hot dogs, and coffee, rather than more exotic Indonesian fare.

The Bird Kingdom is 2.5 kilometers (1.5 miles) north of the Horseshoe Falls, just north of the Rainbow Bridge.

ENTERTAINMENT AND SHOPPING
Nightlife

Jay Leno, Aretha Franklin, Olivia Newton-John, Sean Penn, and Ringo Starr have all

Hiking trails at the Niagara Glen Nature Reserve descend into the Niagara Gorge.

arcades, virtual reality, and other ways to spend money on Clifton Hill

© CAROLYN B. HELLER

performed at the 1,500-seat **Avalon Ballroom Theatre** (6380 Fallsview Blvd., 888/325-5788, www.fallsviewcasinoresort.com), in the Fallsview Casino Resort, which has a regular lineup of concerts, Broadway-style musicals, comedians, and other shows. Children under 19 are not permitted in the theater. You can buy tickets through the theater box office or from Ticketmaster (www.ticketmaster.ca).

As long as you don't mind a few corny jokes about Mounties and beavers, the *Oh Canada Eh?* dinner theater (8585 Lundy's Ln., 905/374-1995 or 800/467-2071, www.ohcanadaeh.com, 6:15 P.M. Mon.–Sat. mid-Apr.–mid-Oct., adults $57–70, kids 3–16 $29–35) is an evening of rollicking good fun that's been entertaining Niagara visitors since 1994. As you tuck into a hearty multicourse meal featuring dishes from across Canada, enthusiastic performers take you on a cross-country journey of Canadian music, from Newfoundland sea shanties to songs by Joni Mitchell, Neil Young, and Leonard Cohen.

Among the many places where Niagara Falls can separate you from your money are its two casinos: **Casino Niagara** (5705 Falls Ave., 905/374-3598 or 888/325-5788, www.casinoniagara.com) and the **Fallsview Casino** (6380 Fallsview Blvd., 888/325-5788, www.fallsviewcasinoresort.com). At Casino Niagara, **YukYuk's Comedy Club** (5705 Falls Ave., 877/968-5233, www.casinoniagara.com, $12–17) has four stand-up comedy shows every week (Thurs.–Sat.). Both casinos are open 24 hours daily seven days a week; guests must be at least 19 years old to enter either casino.

Cinema

The **IMAX Theatre Niagara Falls** (6170 Fallsview Blvd., 905/358-3611 or 866/405-4629, www.imaxniagara.com, shows on the hour 10 A.M.–9 P.M. June–early Sept.; call or check the website for off-season hours; adults $14.50, kids $10.50) screens "you are there" films about the falls and the daredevils who've tried to plummet over the rushing water. Also onsite is the **Daredevil Gallery**

©CAROLYN B. HELLER

a mountie and friend at the *Oh Canada Eh?* dinner theater

(adults $9.30, kids $7.50), which tells the stories of the falls-plunging thrill seekers. Combination tickets for the IMAX movie and gallery (adults $24, kids $18) are available, as are packages that include the movie, the gallery, and admission to the nearby Skylon Tower (adults $38, kids $27). You get discounts ranging from 20 to 45 percent if you buy your tickets online.

Festivals and Events

The **Fireworks over the Falls** (www.niagaraparks.com) illuminate the night sky on Fridays, Sundays, and holidays (10 P.M. June–early Sept.) and on Fridays only (9 P.M. early Sept.–early Oct.) in the fall. Before the summer fireworks shows, there are free concerts in Queen Victoria Park (8 P.M. Fri., Sun., and holidays, June–early Sept.).

During the **Winter Festival of Lights** (www.wfol.com, Nov.–Jan., free), the falls are illuminated nightly, and fireworks over the falls continue weekly. Additional light displays are at the Dufferin Islands Nature Area.

Shopping

What would a mega tourist attraction be without an outlet mall? Just off the QEW, west of the falls, the 40 stores at the **Canada One Factory Outlets** (7500 Lundy's Ln., 905/356-8989 or 866/284-5781, www.canadaoneoutlets.com, 10 A.M.–9 P.M. Mon.–Sat., 10 A.M.–6 P.M. Sun. May–Dec.; 10 A.M.–6 P.M. daily Jan.–Apr.) carry a variety of North American brands, from Levi's, Guess, and MEXX to Coach, Reebok, Nike, and Ecco.

SPORTS AND RECREATION
Parks

Escape from the hubbub around the falls with a walk though the **Floral Showhouse** (7145 Niagara Parkway, 905/354-1721, www.niagaraparks.com, 9:30 A.M.–8 P.M. daily late May–early Sept.; 9:30 A.M.–5 P.M. daily early Sept.–late May, free). Eight different floral shows change with the seasons, including geraniums in June, begonias in the early autumn, and poinsettias, cyclamen, and azaleas in December. In summer, you can also stroll through the gardens surrounding the showhouse, which is 500 meters (0.5 mile) south of Horseshoe Falls, on the Peoplemover route.

Dufferin Islands Nature Area (Niagara Parkway, www.niagaraparks.com, dawn–dusk daily, free) is crisscrossed with walking trails to explore the region's natural side. You can follow the paths and bridges that connect several small islands. From November to January, lighting displays illuminate the islands as part of the annual **Winter Festival of Lights** (www.wfol.com). The nature area is 750 meters (0.5 mile) south of the falls, between the Floral Showhouse and the Rapidsview Parking Lot.

More than 2,000 butterflies flit around the **Butterfly Conservatory** (2405 Niagara Parkway, 905/356-8119, www.niagaraparks.com, open daily year-round; call or check the website for seasonal hours; adults $12.25, kids 6–12 $7.95), alighting on the tropical flowers and on visitors' arms and heads. You start your visit with a six-minute video about butterflies and their habits, from which you learn, among other things, that butterflies smell with their antennae and taste with their feet. The conservatory is a good choice for a winter day, since the climate inside is tropical year-round, and for families with kids; not only are many little ones fascinated by the butterflies, but children under six are admitted free.

The Butterfly Conservatory is on the grounds of the **Niagara Parks Botanical Gardens** (2565 Niagara Parkway, 905/356-8554, www.niagaraparks.com, dawn–dusk daily year-round, free), a 40-hectare (100-acre) expanse of manicured grounds, ornamental flowers, and herb gardens, crisscrossed with walking paths. Among the flowering highlights are rhododendrons and irises, which typically peak during the month of June, and roses that bloom from mid-June into September; check the parks' website or call for a more detailed bloom schedule. Admission to the Botanical Gardens is free; however, you must pay admission to the Butterfly Conservatory.

The Gardens and Butterfly Conservatory are nine kilometers (six miles) north of Horseshoe Falls, on the Peoplemover route, opposite the Niagara Glen Nature Reserve.

Biking

Zoom Leisure Bikes (6289 Fallsview Blvd., 866/811-6993, www.zoomleisure.com, half-/full-day $20/30) rents bikes from their locations at the Best Western Fallsview Hotel and at the Niagara Glen Nature Centre (Niagara Parkway, www.niagaraparks.com). If you rent for a full day, they'll deliver your bike free, as long as you're within eight kilometers (five miles) of their Fallsview store.

Zoom also offers cycling tours, including a 5.5-hour **pub lunch and winery tour** ($119), where you ride from Niagara Falls to Niagara-on-the-Lake, stopping for lunch at the Taps on Queen microbrewery and for samples at several local wineries; they'll shuttle you back to Niagara Falls at the end of the tour.

Hiking

Ontario's premier hiking route, the 800-kilometer (500-mile) **Bruce Trail** (www.

niagarabrucetrail.org), which runs all the way to the northern tip of the Bruce Peninsula, begins in Queenston. Throughout the year, the **Niagara Bruce Trail Club** offers frequent hikes of varying lengths and levels of difficulty around the Niagara region; guests are welcome. If you'd like to participate in more than one or two hikes, the club will ask you to become a member ($50/year).

The **Greater Niagara Circle Route** (www.niagararegion.ca) includes more than 140 kilometers (87 miles) of paved walking or cycling trails. It loops around the Niagara Peninsula, following the Niagara River south from Niagara-on-the-Lake, to Niagara Falls, to Fort Erie, turning west to Port Colborne, north along the Welland Canal to St. Catharines, and east to return to Niagara-on-the-Lake.

Ice Skating

At the open-air **Rink at the Brink** (www.wfol.com, noon–9 P.M. Sun.–Thurs., noon–midnight Fri., 10 A.M.–midnight Sat., Dec.–Feb.), near the Table Rock Centre, you can skate in view of the falls. Skate rentals are available.

Waterparks

Sixteen waterslides, a huge wave pool, and a water play area keep families splashing at the **Fallsview Indoor Waterpark** (5685 Falls Ave., 888/234-8408, www.fallsviewwaterpark.com, call or check their website for seasonal hours, day pass $45). The park offers accommodations packages with several nearby hotels, including the Sheraton on the Falls, Crowne Plaza Niagara Falls–Fallsview Hotel, Skyline Inn, and Hampton Inn at the Falls.

The **Waves Indoor Waterpark** (8444 Lundy's Lane, www.americananiagara.com, 10 A.M.–9 P.M. daily July–Aug.; 10 A.M.–8 P.M. Sun.–Thurs., 10 A.M.–9 P.M. Fri.–Sat. Sept.–June), located at the Americana Resort on the west end of Lundy's Lane, also has a wave pool, water slides, a kiddy play structure, and whirlpools. Prices for waterpark passes, which are good for four hours, vary by day ($19.95 Mon.–Thurs., $24.95 Fri.–Sun., $29.95 Sat.).

ACCOMMODATIONS

Niagara Falls has thousands of rooms, in everything from barebones motels to homey B&Bs to glitzy hotel towers. In general, the closer you are to the falls, the higher the price, and any room with even a partial falls view will cost more than a viewless lodging.

Accommodations are clustered in several main areas. The Fallsview area, on the Niagara Escarpment above the Horseshoe Falls, has predominantly high-end hotel towers and some of the best falls views. A mix of basic chain hotels and more upscale properties lines the streets surrounding Clifton Hill. North of the falls, along River Road and the surrounding residential streets, are numerous bed-and-breakfasts. Along Ferry Street and Lundy's Lane west of the falls, you'll find a mix of old-fashioned roadside motels and more modern chains. Some of the cheapest rooms are on the west end of Lundy's Lane (which, despite its picturesque name, is a busy multilane boulevard), near the entrance to the QEW; just budget for parking near the falls or plan to take the bus, since it's too far to walk.

Rates are generally highest in July and August and during any holiday weekends. Fall weekends, when the leaves are in full color, are also busy. Room rates can fluctuate wildly, even within the same month, depending on occupancy, the weather, and whether any special events are on the calendar, so check different travel dates if you have some flexibility in your plans. Outside of the July–August peak season, you can often find great deals, with the budget-price to mid-range chain properties around the falls advertising rooms in the $59–99 range. Winter rates can drop even lower.

Under $100

Around the corner from the bus and train stations, a short walk from the Queen Street downtown district, **HI-Niagara Falls Youth Hostel** (4549 Cataract Ave., 905/357-0770 or 888/749-0058, www.hostellingniagara. com, $29–35 dorm, $89 d) provides cheap beds, space to hang out, and plenty of

To find the Sterling Inn & Spa, look for its distinctive "milk bottle."

opportunities to meet other travelers with activities ranging from barbecues to pub crawls. The four-bed dorms are cramped, the six-bed rooms slightly less so, and both come in male-only or female-only options. There are also two-bed "deluxe" dorms ($45)—basically a shared twin room—and tiny double-bedded private rooms; all rooms and dorms share baths. Linens and towels are included, as is a light continental breakfast, with fruit, toast, cereal, coffee, or tea. You can prep your own meals in the communal kitchen or play pool or foosball in the basement lounge. Free Wi-Fi.

The privately owned **ACBB Hostel Niagara** (5741 McGrail Ave., 905/359-4815, www.hostelniagara.ca, $30–35 dorm, $68–72 d) is on a rather barren-looking street, but it's more centrally located than the HI property, just behind the upscale Sterling Inn, a short stroll from the Clifton Hill action. Their six-bed dorms are female-only or mixed, and they have private twins and doubles, as well; all share baths. Linens and towels are provided. The coffee pot is always on, and in the morning you can start your day with a breakfast "snack"—fruit, oatmeal, muffins, or granola bars. Free parking is an added benefit, as is free Wi-Fi. The same owners run another hostel, ACBB Accommodations, in London (ON).

A stay at the **Strathaird Bed & Breakfast** (4372 Simcoe St., 905/358-3421, www.strathairdinn.com, May–Oct., $70–95 s, $80–105 d) is like a visit with a favorite aunt and uncle. Owners Tom and Val Jackson offer guests a warm Scottish welcome to their modest but comfortable home, encouraging you to have a cup of tea or relax on the porch. The three guest rooms upstairs cover the basics: queen-sized beds, en suite baths, air-conditioning, and free Wi-Fi, and in the morning, you'll fuel up with a full Scottish breakfast of eggs, bacon, beans, tomatoes, fruit, and coffee or tea. Rates include parking, or if you phone ahead, they'll pick you up at the train or bus station. The Peoplemover bus stops on River Road, one block away.

$100-200

Owners Carolyn and Gary Burke have lived in their 1886 heritage home—complete with its own turret—for more than 30 years, and they share their knowledge of the area with their guests at the **Park Place B&B** (4851 River Rd., 905/358-0279, www.parkplaceniagara.com, $150–175 d). You can sit on the wraparound porch facing the river; if River Road gets too noisy, as it can in summer, you can retreat to the sunroom overlooking the garden. Upstairs, each of the two guest rooms has a king-sized bed, a fireplace, and a large bathroom with a whirlpool tub; one has a sauna and private balcony, as well. You can choose between breakfast delivered to your room or served by candlelight in the Victorian-style dining room. The Peoplemover shuttle stops one block away.

The 1891 brick Victorian home that is now the **Kilpatrick Manor B&B** (4601 Second Ave., 905/321-8581, www.kilpatrickmanor.com, $149–209 d) was the first house in its neighborhood, a residential district a short walk from Queen Street. Owners Nance and Kevin Kilpatrick completely renovated the interior, creating several upscale guest rooms with rich brocade linens, fireplaces, antique furnishings, and modern en suite baths. Kevin, a professional chef, whips up elaborate morning meals that might include breakfast ravioli (stuffed with bacon, eggs, and cheese) or peach-stuffed French toast. You're not within walking distance of the falls, but the peace and quiet is worth it.

Among the many family-friendly midrange chain properties around Clifton Hill, a good choice is the **Country Inn & Suites** (5525 Victoria Ave., 905/374-6040, www.countryinns.com, $140–170 d). Though there's nothing especially country-like about this seven-story motel, it's got what families need, including standard rooms with two queen beds, an indoor pool, a games room, a complimentary buffet breakfast, and Internet access; kids under 18 stay free. Parking is available for $6 per day. Room rates drop significantly outside the July–August high season; look for additional discounts on stays of three nights or more.

Across the street from the Fallsview Casino, the **Comfort Inn-Fallsview** (6645 Fallsview Blvd., 905/358-9353 or 800/463-1938, www.comfortinnfallsview.ca, $135–190 d) gives you a Fallsview location for moderate rates. The rooms are standard chain-motel style, but the kids will appreciate the indoor and outdoor pools, and if you need more space, ask about the slightly larger "family rooms" with two queen beds and a sleep sofa or the two-bedroom family suites. Free Wi-Fi.

Look for the milk bottle to find the ◖ **Sterling Inn & Spa** (5195 Magdalen St., 289/292-0000 or 877/783-7772, www.sterlingniagara.com, $160–240 d). Occupying the 1928 former home of a dairy and ice cream producer, this boutique hotel has a three-story milk bottle above its entrance. Inside, the 41 contemporary guest rooms are spare but spacious, with couple-courting features like king-sized beds, fireplaces, and large steam showers or whirlpool baths for two; some retain the building's original bones, from exposed brick walls to wood rafters. Overall, the feel is upscale if not deluxe, but there are pampering touches: rates include a breakfast tray delivered to your room each morning. Wi-Fi and parking are complimentary, too.

The **Old Stone Inn** (5425 Robinson St., 905/357-1234 or 800/263-6208, www.oldstoneinn.on.ca, $129–244 d) is a "don't judge a book by its cover" kind of place. Originally built as a flour mill in the early 1900s, the exterior looks like a run-of-the-mill motel. Go inside, though, and you'll find an upscale boutique-style inn. The dining room (lunch $10–19, dinner $18–36), with its soaring ceiling and stone walls, is in the original part of the building, while in the newer guest wings, the 69 traditional rooms, furnished with period pieces, range from units with two double beds to two-room suites; some have fireplaces and whirlpool tubs. There's also an indoor pool. Rates, which in summer are generally much lower midweek than on weekends, include Wi-Fi and parking.

Over $200

The prime rooms at the contemporary **Sheraton on the Falls Hotel** (5875 Falls Ave., 905/374-4445 or 800/325-3535, www.starwoodhotels.com, $200–370 d), a mirrored tower opposite the American Falls, are those overlooking the waterfalls, of course. You'll pay a significant premium for falls view rooms on summer weekends, but the upcharge is smaller midweek and at other times of the year, when the falls are just as grand. Other facilities include indoor and outdoor pools, a fitness center, and a spa where treatment rooms overlook the falls; Casino Niagara is right nearby. Note that there are additional charges for Internet access ($15/day) and parking (from $19/day).

Your kids may not care about seeing the falls once they're splashing and sliding in the water park at the **Great Wolf Lodge** (950 Victoria Ave., 905/354-4888 or 800/605-9653, www.greatwolf.com, $250–350 d), a resort that features a wave pool, several water slides, a water "roller coaster," even a four-story tree house that gets drenched with spray. Several eateries and snack bars keep the hunger wolf at bay, and not only is there a spa for adults, the Scooops Kid Spa pampers preteens, too, with manicures, pedicures, and kiddy facials. Every night, the little ones can put on their PJs for the lodge's story hour. Once the kids are totally worn out, settle them into a standard family suite with two queen beds or one queen plus a sleep sofa, or choose one of the fun themed suites; the Wolf Den has a bunk bed for the kids in a cave-themed room, the KidKamp puts the bunks inside a tentlike nook, and the KidCabin includes a mini–log cabin right in your room. The rooms all have microwaves and mini-fridges, in case the cubs need a snack. Waterpark access, which is limited to hotel guests, is included in the room rates. The lodge is seven kilometers (4.5 miles) north of the Horseshoe Falls.

A 30-story tower, the **Fallsview Casino Resort** (6380 Fallsview Blvd., 888/325-5788, www.fallsviewcasinoresort.com, $269–349 d) feels like a small city. The lobby, with its art deco–style ceiling, checkerboard floor, and

Doric columns, channels the French Belle Époque, while the 374 guest rooms are more spare, perhaps to avoid competing with the views of the falls that you have from the majority of the rooms. There's an indoor pool, a spa, a collection of shops and boutiques, 18 restaurants and fast-food outlets, and of course the casino itself, which is the largest gaming facility in Canada. The 1,500-seat theater hosts concerts, comedy shows, and other big-name entertainment. Note to those who need to be online all the time: Internet service starts at $6 for 15 minutes.

FOOD

If you're right at home in chain restaurants, then you'll be happy eating in Niagara Falls. The chains are cheek-to-jowl on the streets surrounding the falls, particularly in the Clifton Hill area. However, if you're looking for decent quality or independent eateries, you'll have to look a little harder. Queen Street, the still-reviving downtown district, is worth checking out, as is the area on Ferry Street near Stanley Avenue. It's also a short drive to Niagara-on-the-Lake, where you'll find more dining options.

The Niagara Parks agency runs restaurants and snack bars at several of the visitor centers around Niagara Falls, which are convenient when you're touring the area. Meals range from basic sandwiches to high-end fare; expect crowd-pleasing dishes, rather than spectacular cuisine.

Elements on the Falls (6650 Niagara Parkway, 905/354-3631, 11:30 A.M.–4 P.M. and 4:30 P.M.–close daily, lunch $15–27, dinner $28–50) has great views of the Horseshoe Falls. Other Parks restaurants include the **Queenston Heights Restaurant** (14184 Niagara Parkway, Queenston, 905/262-4274, mains lunch $11–21, dinner $28–36), and two dining options at Queen Victoria Place: **Edgewaters Tap and Grill** (6345 Niagara Parkway, 905/262-4274, $11–26) and **Riverview International Buffet** (6345 Niagara Parkway, 905/262-4274).

The small **Niagara Falls Farmers' Market** (5943 Sylvia Pl., 905/356-7521 ext. 4701, www.niagarafalls.ca/farmersmarket, 6 A.M.–noon

Sat.) operates year-round near the intersection of Main and Ferry Streets.

Fallsview

Want to eat above it all? In the Skylon Tower's **Revolving Dining Room** (11:30 A.M.–3 P.M. and 4:30 P.M.–close daily, lunch $25–33, dinner $40–75), which makes a complete rotation every hour, even a hamburger will set you back 25 bucks, but tower admission is free when you ride up for a meal. For families, the **Summit Suite Buffet Dining Room** (11:30 A.M.–3 P.M. and 5–10 P.M. Mon.–Sat., 10:30 A.M.–2:30 P.M. and 5–10 P.M. Sun., adults/kids lunch $27.50/12.50, dinner $40/15), which also includes tower admission, is a better value.

Looking for a late-night bite in the Fallview area? Look hard and you'll find **the Noodle Bar** (6380 Fallsview Blvd., 888/325-5788, www.fallsviewcasinoresort.com, 1 P.M.–5 A.M. Mon.–Thurs., noon–5 A.M. Fri.–Sun., $9–19), hidden inside the Fallsview Casino. Most people turn up in this red, black, and gold room for a restorative bowl of noodle soup. You choose your type of noodles, then select your soup from nearly 20 varieties, ranging from *shui kow* (silky dumplings stuffed with shrimp and wood ear mushrooms) to the slightly spicy oxtail with lemongrass. While the flavors may not entirely hit the jackpot, for 10 bucks, it outscores the food court. Because you have to enter through the casino, no one under 19 is admitted; follow the signs for 17 Noir Restaurant (the Noodle Bar shares its space).

You'd be unlikely to stumble into ◖ **AG Cuisine** (Sterling Inn, 5195 Magdalen Ave., 289/292-0005, www.agcuisine.com, 5:30–9:30 P.M. Tues.–Sun., $23–25), but this stylish restaurant on the lower level of the Sterling Inn is earning kudos for some of the most creative cuisine around the falls. With its retro white banquettes, red drapes, and twinkling chandeliers, the dining room channels the Rat Pack, while the food is ever so *au courant*. Executive chef Cory Linkson favors regional ingredients in his artfully plated dishes, and the well-constructed wine list emphasizes Niagara producers. You can put yourself entirely in the chef's hands

THE NIAGARA REGION

with the five-course tasting menu ($65), with optional wine pairings for an additional $40.

Ferry Street

Say you want good food, moderate prices, and a family-friendly feel, with a bonus for being walking distance from Clifton Hill. The **Bravo Pizzeria** (5438 Ferry St., 905/354-3354, www.bravopizzeriagrill.com, 11:30 A.M.–midnight daily, $11–21) is your place. Pizzas cooked in the wood-fired oven are the specialty, ranging from simple tomato and basil, to Greek-style with feta, olives, and spinach, to the arrabbiatta, loaded with spicy sausage, hot Calabrese salami, and peppers. The generous overstuffed sandwiches include Italian options, like chicken parmigiana or locally cured prosciutto with fresh mozzarella, as well as Montreal smoked meat and other deli favorites. Soups, salads, and pastas round out the multipage menu. The beer selection may be even more international than the visitors to the falls, featuring brews from 70 countries. Free parking.

Italian classics done well have kept the family-run **Napoli Ristorante** (5485 Ferry St., 905/356-3345, www.napoliristorante.ca, 4 P.M.–close daily, $12–26) in business since 1962. At this traditional trattoria, you might start with the *aranchini* (rice balls stuffed with prosciutto and arugula), fried calamari, or a freshly made Caesar salad. Then share a pizza; tuck into a pasta, such as the orechiette abruzzese (shaped like "little ears" and tossed with rapini and homemade sausage) or the handmade ricotta and parmigiano gnocchi; or fuel up with the grilled veal chop or the chicken stuffed with butternut squash. The wines include both Niagara and Italian labels. Free parking is a bonus.

Queen Street and North

Simple, fresh fare dominates the menu at the peaceful **Midé Bistro and Yoga Studio** (4337 Queen St., 289/296-5632, www.midebistro.com, 11 A.M.–3 P.M. Tues.–Thurs., 11 A.M.–9 P.M. Fri.–Sat., $8–14) on Queen Street downtown. Among the several salad options, try the "ancient grains," with quinoa, spinach, dried fruit, and nuts, or choose a sandwich like the grilled eggplant, roasted red pepper, and goat cheese. Cool retro-modern white stools line the long bar in this stylish space, and in mild weather, a garage door opens the front of the restaurant to the street. If you're not mellow enough by the time you've finished your meal, you can take a hit from their oxygen bar, sign up for a class in their adjacent yoga space, or book a treatment in the on-site spa.

The full-bodied Red Cream Ale, lighter Charleston Lager, and creamy Vanilla Wheat are among the brews on tap at **Taps on Queen** (4680 Queen St., 289/477-1010, www.tapsbeer.ca, noon–10 P.M. Sun.–Tues. and Thurs., noon–midnight Wed. and Fri.–Sat., $10–17), a local microbrewery and pub. To go with your beer, choose pizza, sandwiches like the giant meatball sub or the barbecued pulled pork, or comfort fare like macaroni and cheese or fish 'n' chips. In mild weather, their sidewalk patio is a popular place.

Gracious, Old World **Casa Mia Ristorante** (3518 Portage Rd., 905/356-5410, www.casamiaristorante.com, lunch 11:30 A.M.–2:30 P.M. Mon.–Fri., dinner 5–10 P.M. daily, $20–58) feels light-years away from the frenzy of the falls—just the place to celebrate an anniversary, a business deal, or just a special "date night." The courtly staff circulate through the serene dining room with its white tablecloths and terrazzo floors, offering traditional Italian dishes. The larger plates range from classics like cannelloni fiorentina (delicate sheets of pasta stuffed with ground veal and spinach) to more contemporary beet gnocchi with gorgonzola cream sauce or handmade linguini topped with duck confit. Choose among 30 wines by the glass and hundreds more by the bottle. At lunch, the menu is a bit simpler, with pizzas and sandwiches (like the veal, mozzarella, and tomato sauce on ciabatta) joining the pastas and more substantial mains, including lemon chicken and a catch of the day.

Casa Mia is about a 15-minute drive north of Horseshoe Falls, but you don't have to worry about finding your way; the restaurant offers free transportation to and from area hotels.

THE NIAGARA REGION

INFORMATION AND SERVICES
Tourist Information

A good source for guidance about things to do and places to stay in Niagara Falls is **Niagara Falls Tourism** (5400 Robinson St., 905/356-6061 or 800/563-2557, www.niagarafallstourism.com), the city's Visitor and Convention Bureau.

The **Niagara Parks Commission** (877/642-7275, www.niagaraparks.com) operates several seasonal information offices around Niagara Falls that can help you out once you're in town. Their objective is to encourage you to visit Niagara Parks attractions (and sell you tickets), but they can provide information, as well. They all operate from June through August, opening at 9 A.M. daily:

- **Maid of the Mist Welcome Centre** (outside the *Maid of the Mist* ticket booths)
- **Clifton Hill Welcome Centre** (Clifton Hill at Falls Avenue)
- **Murray Street Welcome Centre** (near Queen Victoria Place)
- **Table Rock Welcome Centre** (6650 Niagara Parkway, near Horseshoe Falls)

Discounts and Passes

Niagara Parks sells the **Niagara Falls Adventure Pass** (www.niagaraparks.com, mid-Apr.–late Oct., adults $44.95, kids 6–12 $32.95), which includes admission to four attractions—the *Maid of the Mist,* Journey Behind the Falls, *Niagara's Fury,* and the White Water Walk. It includes two days' transportation on the Peoplemover buses and on the Incline Railway, as well as small discounts at the Butterfly Conservatory, the Whirlpool Aero Car, and other attractions. You'll save at least 30 percent off the individual ticket prices if you plan to see all or most of these attractions. The Adventure Pass is available online, at any of the Niagara Parks Welcome Centres, or at any of the attractions included in the pass.

GETTING THERE

The main commercial airports serving the Niagara region are in Toronto and in Buffalo,

New York. Niagara Falls has train service from Toronto and Buffalo, with connections to other Canadian and U.S. cities, and you can get there by bus from a variety of destinations, as well. By car, it's about a two-hour drive from Toronto and less than an hour from Buffalo (traffic and border crossings permitting).

If you're traveling between Niagara and Buffalo or other U.S. points, remember that you must cross an international border. Allow extra time for border formalities, and make sure you have your passport.

By Air
TORONTO

Toronto's **Pearson International Airport** (416/247-7678 or 866/207-1690, www.torontopearson.com) has flights from across Canada, the United States, and overseas. All the major car rental agencies, and several local rental companies, have offices at Pearson airport.

The most direct way to travel from Pearson to Niagara Falls is to take the **Niagara Air Bus** (905/374-8111 or 800/206-7222, www.niagaraairbus.com, 1.5 hours, one-way $73), a door-to-door airport shuttle. If you book the shuttle online at least three days in advance, fares are discounted 10 percent.

A cheaper but more roundabout way to travel from Pearson is to go to the **Toronto Coach Terminal** (610 Bay St.) in downtown Toronto, where you can catch the inexpensive Megabus to Niagara Falls. This route might be worth the extra time if you can book a low Megabus fare or if you want to stop off in Toronto along the way.

From the airport you can take the **Toronto Airport Express** bus (905/564-3232 or 800/387-6787, www.torontoairportexpress.com, one-way adults $23.95, seniors and students $21.55) to the Toronto bus terminal, which takes about an hour and stops right at the coach terminal.

BUFFALO, NEW YORK

If flying from the United States, you may find

BRIDGES TO NIAGARA

To travel between the United States and Canada in the Niagara region, you have to cross the Niagara River on one of four bridges. All are toll bridges; you pay the toll when you're *entering* Canada.

The bridges can get clogged with traffic, and the wait time can vary, so before you choose your route, check the border lineups online or by phone through the **Niagara Falls Bridge Commission** (800/715-6722, www.niagarafallsbridges.com). You can also get border crossing updates from the **U.S. Customs and Border Protection** (http://apps.cbp.gov/bwt) and the **Canadian Border Services Agency** (www.cbsa-asfc.gc.ca).

The **Peace Bridge** (www.peacebridge.com, 24 hours, $3) is the southernmost crossing, linking I-190 from the Buffalo area with the QEW in Fort Erie.

The **Rainbow Bridge** (www.niagarafallsbridges.com, 24 hours, $3.25) directly connects Niagara Falls, Ontario, with Niagara Falls, New York. The main highway routes to this bridge are the QEW on the Canadian side and I-190 on the U.S. side.

You must have a NEXUS card to cross the **Whirlpool Bridge** (www.niagarafallsbridges.com, 7 A.M.-11 P.M., $3.25), north of the Rainbow Bridge. NEXUS is a "pre-screened" traveler program designed to expedite border crossings for frequent travelers between the United States and Canada. To get more information about the NEXUS program, contact the **U.S. Customs and Border Protection** (www.cbp.gov) or the **Canadian Border Services Agency** (www.cbsa-asfc.gc.ca).

North of the falls, the **Queenston-Lewiston Bridge** (www.niagarafallsbridges.com, 24 hours, $3.25) connects Queenston, Ontario, and Lewiston, New York. This is the closest bridge to Niagara-on-the-Lake. Choose another crossing if you have a NEXUS card, though, since there's no NEXUS lane on this bridge.

cheaper flights into the **Buffalo-Niagara International Airport** (4200 Genesee St., Cheektowaga, NY, 716/630-6000 or 877/359-2642, www.buffaloairport.com). All the major North American car rental agencies have locations in the Buffalo airport.

The cheapest way to reach Niagara Falls from the Buffalo airport is by bus. Both **Coach Canada** (705/748-6411 or 800/461-7661, www.coachcanada.com, 1.5–1.75 hours, one-way adults $10.30, seniors and students $9.30, kids $5.15) and **Greyhound** (800/661-8747, www.greyhound.ca, 1.25–1.5 hours, one-way adults $9.20–13.20, seniors $8.20–11.20, kids 2–11 $6.90–9.65) run two daily buses in each direction between the Buffalo airport and the **Niagara Transportation Centre** (4555 Erie Ave., Niagara Falls).

Several taxi, shuttle, and limo services offer much more frequent, but more expensive, service between Buffalo airport and Niagara Falls. Note that pricing varies, so the most economical carrier will depend on the number of people in your party. Check the Buffalo airport website (www.buffaloairport.com) for additional transportation information.

- **Buffalo Airport Express** (716/472-8580 or 800/604-1570, www.buffaloairportexpress.com): Scheduled shuttle service to/from major Niagara Falls hotels.

- **Buffalo Airport Shuttle** (716/685-2550, www.buffaloairportshuttle.com): Scheduled shuttle service to/from major Niagara Falls hotels.

- **Buffalo Airport Taxi** (716/633-8294, www.buffaloairporttaxi.com, 7 A.M.–9 P.M., one-way $55 per person): Scheduled shuttle service to/from major Niagara Falls hotels.

- **Gray Line Niagara Falls** (716/285-2113 or 877/285-2113, one-way $80 per car, for up to three people): Private car service to/from any Niagara Falls address.

- **Jewel of Niagara** (905/351-3996, www.jewelofniagara.com, one-way $80 per car, for up to three people): Private car service to/from any Niagara Falls address.
- **Niagara Air Bus** (905/374-8111 or 800/206-7222, www.niagaraairbus.com, one-way $83 per person, 10 percent discount for three-day advance online bookings): Door-to-door service to/from any Niagara Falls address.

By Train

VIA Rail, GO Trains, and Amtrak all provide service to the **Niagara Falls Train Station** (4267 Bridge St.), which is north of the falls, one block from the Queen Street downtown district.

VIA Rail (888/842-7245, www.viarail.ca, two hours; one-way adults $23–43, seniors $23–39, students $23–31, kids 2–11 $16–22) runs two trains daily—one in the early morning and one in the late afternoon—in each direction between Toronto's Union Station (65 Front St. W., 311/392-2489, www.toronto.ca/union_station) and Niagara Falls.

From late May through mid-October, **GO Transit** (416/869-3200 or 888/438-6646, www.gotransit.com, Fri.–Sun., one-way adults $19.15, seniors and kids 6–12 $9.60) runs weekend and holiday train service from Toronto's Union Station. For the two-hour trip, there's one train in each direction on Friday and three daily trains on Saturdays, Sundays, and holidays.

On Saturdays, Sundays, and holidays, these seasonal GO trains also run as the **bike train** (www.gotransit.com), with two coaches specifically designed to carry bicycles.

The **Amtrak *Maple Leaf*** (800/872-7245, www.amtrak.com) travels from New York City's Penn Station to Toronto's Union Station, stopping in Niagara Falls. The train runs once daily, with major stops at Poughkeepsie, Albany, Syracuse, Rochester, Buffalo, and Niagara Falls, New York, before crossing into Canada. The New York City–Niagara trip (one-way adults $59–84, kids 2–15 $30–42) takes 9.5 hours.

By Bus

Long-distance buses, including those from Toronto and New York City, arrive at and depart from the **Niagara Transportation Centre** (4555 Erie Ave., 905/357-2133), across the street from the Niagara Falls Train Station.

Megabus (www.megabus.com) has frequent service between Toronto's Central Bus Station (610 Bay St.) and Niagara Falls. The trip takes about two hours, and fares can be as low as $1.50 each way (yes, really!), although more typical one-way fares are $10–15.

GO Transit (416/869-3200 or 888/438-6646, www.gotransit.com, 2–2.75 hours, one-way adults $16.15, seniors and kids 6–12 $8.10) operates several daily buses from Toronto's Union Station to Niagara Falls, but note that you have to change buses at Burlington en route.

Coach Canada (www.coachcanada.com) travels to Niagara Falls from Hamilton (1.5–1.75 hours, one-way adults $21.10, seniors and students $19, kids 2–11 $10.55), with connections to Kitchener and Cambridge. They also run buses between the falls and the Twenty Valley, with stops in Jordan (0.75 hour, one-way adults $8.65, seniors and students $7.80, kids 2–11 $4.35), Vineland (0.75–1 hour, one-way adults $9.55, seniors and students $8.60, kids 2–11 $4.80), and Beamsville (1 hour, one-way adults $11.40, seniors and students $10.30, kids 2–11 $5.70).

From the United States, **Megabus** (www.megabus.com) operates a daily bus between New York City's Port Authority Terminal and Niagara Falls (9 hours, one-way $45–51). **Greyhound** (www.greyhound.ca) has several daily buses from New York City to Niagara Falls, but they're slower than Megabus (10.5–11 hours, one-way $46–71).

By Car

Niagara Falls is 130 kilometers (80 miles) southeast of Toronto. From downtown Toronto, you can take the Gardiner Expressway west to the QEW. Follow the QEW south as it skirts the Lake Ontario shore, then passes Hamilton and St. Catharines. Exit onto Highway 420 east, which will take you into Niagara Falls.

Coming from the United States, Niagara Falls is 40 kilometers (25 miles) from Buffalo, New York. Interstate 190 from Buffalo goes north to the four bridges over the Niagara River, which separates New York from Ontario.

Tours from Toronto

Many tour companies offer one-day excursions from Toronto to Niagara Falls. Prices and services vary widely, from barebones backpacker trips to deluxe limousine tours. In general, you'll save money exploring on your own, but the convenience of a tour may be worth the extra money.

Toronto hotels can offer recommendations, or contact the following companies:

- **Chariots of Fire** (www.chariots-of-fire .com, $60) runs good-value Niagara Falls day tours that include either the *Maid of the Mist* boat tour or the Skylon Tower, a winery stop, and round-trip transportation. They have three pickup /drop-off points in the Toronto area: one near Pearson Airport, one at 33 Yonge Street near Front Street downtown, and one at 279 Yonge Street near Eaton Centre.

- **Greyline Tours** (www.grayline.ca, adults $132, seniors $119, kids 5–11 $87, family $381) runs daily trips from Toronto that include a buffet lunch, a *Maid of the Mist* boat tour, and stops at the Whirlpool Rapids, the Floral Clock, and a winery. Their "Freedom Tour" (adults $106, seniors $91, kids 5–11 $70, family $306) includes the same stops but without meals. Both include return transportation from many Toronto hotels.

- **HI-Toronto Youth Hostel** (416/971-4440 or 877/848-8737, www.hostellingtoronto. com) sells a "Discovery Package" ($70) that includes a Niagara Falls day tour, admission to the CN Tower, and a free Toronto city tour; you must be a Hostelling International member to qualify for this package rate.

- **Toronto Tours** (www.niagaratours.com, adults $159, seniors and students $149, kids

$109) includes a ride on the *Maid of the Mist,* a winery stop, a meal, and round-trip transportation from your Toronto hotel.

GETTING AROUND

You can easily walk along the river near the falls, between Table Rock and the *Maid of the Mist,* and up to Clifton Hill, where many hotels are located. You can also walk between the Horseshoe Falls and the Fallsview hotel district, although it's a fairly steep climb up the hill. To reach other attractions, from the Whirlpool north to Queenston or south to Fort Erie, travel by bus or car. Cycling is another good option; you can pedal the 56-kilometer (35-mile) Niagara River Recreation Trail between Niagara-on-the-Lake and Fort Erie.

By Bus

The **Niagara Parks Peoplemover** (www.niagaraparks.com, 10 A.M.–close daily mid-Apr.– late Oct., check the website for seasonal hours; adults $8.85, kids 6–12 $5.35) is a convenient shuttle bus that runs every 20 minutes along the Niagara Parkway, stopping at all the major attractions. Regular service starts at Table Rock near Horseshoe Falls and runs north to the Floral Clock, 11.5 kilometers (seven miles) north of the falls. The **Niagara Falls Adventure Pass** from Niagara Parks includes two free days of Peoplemover rides.

On weekends from late May through late June, and daily from late June to early September, the Peoplemovers continue north from the Floral Clock to Queenstown Heights Park, 12 kilometers (7.5 miles) north of the falls. During this same period, there's also a free shuttle bus from the Rapidsview parking area, 1.5 kilometers (one mile) south of Horseshoe Falls, to Table Rock. If you've driven to the falls area, you can park your car for the day in the Rapidsview lot ($10) and ride the Peoplemover from place to place.

Niagara Falls Transit (www.niagarafalls.ca) operates the **Falls Shuttle** (late May–mid-Oct., adults $3.50, kids 6–12 $1), which has three routes originating from the base of Clifton Hill.

NIAGARA ON TWO WHEELS

The Niagara region is one of Ontario's most bike-friendly areas, crisscrossed with a network of bike routes and cycling paths. To first get yourself and your bike to Niagara, take the **Bike Train** (www.biketrain.ca). From late May through mid-October, **GO Transit** (416/869-3200 or 888/438-6646, www.gotransit.com) trains running between Toronto's Union Station and Niagara Falls on Saturdays, Sundays, and holidays have two coaches specifically designed to carry bicycles. While many accommodations will provide places for you to store your bike, **Cycle and Stay Niagara** (www.cycleandstayniagara.com) is a network of B&Bs located on or near a bike route that are particularly cyclist-friendly.

For more information about bicycling in the Niagara region, check the website for **Cycle Niagara** (www.cycleniagara.com), which has a directory of regional cycling resources. The Niagara Region website (www.niagararegion.ca, click on "Maps and Trails") has a great resource for cyclists: an online regional cycling route planner that allows you to specify your starting point, the approximate distance you want to ride, the level of difficulty, and types of sights you might like to see along the way.

They also have a bike map app that you can download to a mobile device.

If your Niagara cycling adventures whet your appetite for seeing more of Ontario by bike, explore the **Welcome Cyclists Network** (www.welcomecyclists.ca), which can help you plan cycling trips across the province.

THE GREATER NIAGARA CIRCLE ROUTE

The Greater Niagara Circle Route (www.niagararegion.ca) includes more than 140 kilometers (87 miles) of mostly paved cycling trails, which lets you cycle to many of the area's highlights. The trail loops around the Niagara Peninsula, following the Niagara River south from Niagara-on-the-Lake to Niagara Falls and on to Fort Erie. It then turns inland between Fort Erie and Port Colborne, running along the Welland Canal from Port Colborne to St. Catharines before returning to Niagara-on-the-Lake.

The circle route is actually made up of a number of shorter trails, so if you don't want to cycle the whole loop, you can choose one or more of the following routes:

- The **Niagara River Recreational Trail** (56 kilometers, 35 miles, www.niagaraparks.

The downtown route goes north, stopping at the VIA Rail station, along Queen Street downtown, Victoria Avenue, and River Road as far north as the Whirlpool area. The Lundy's Lane route goes west, to the Fallsview area, Ferry Street, and out Lundy's Lane past the QEW; this route would be handy if you're staying at a Lundy's Lane hotel. The Chippewa/Marineland route travels south along the Niagara Parkway, then loops north through the Fallsview district. In summer (late June–early Sept.), the Falls Shuttle runs every 30 minutes (9 A.M.–1 A.M.); in spring and fall, service is hourly. A 24-hour pass costs $10 per adult and includes free travel for two kids under 17; purchase the pass on the bus, at the **Niagara Transportation Centre**

(4555 Erie Ave., opposite the train station), or at many hotels.

If you're just traveling between Niagara Parks attractions along the Niagara Parkway, the Peoplemover shuttle is more convenient, but the Falls Shuttle can take you to more destinations around the city of Niagara Falls.

Daunted by the steep hill between the Fallsview district and the falls themselves? The **Falls Incline Railway** (www.niagaraparks.com, late May–early Nov., one-way $2.50, kids under 5 free) transports passengers up and down the 30-meter (100-foot) embankment between the Table Rock Visitor Centre and Fallsview Boulevard, near the Fallsview Casino and the Skylon Tower. The ride on one

com) follows the Niagara River from Fort George in Niagara-on-the-Lake past Niagara Falls to Fort Erie. The section of the trail between Niagara-on-the-Lake and the falls is one of the region's most popular.

- Crossing the southern end of the Niagara Peninsula, parallel to the Lake Erie shore, the paved **Friendship Trail** (www.friendshiptrail.forterie.ca) runs 16 kilometers (10 miles) from Seaway Park in Port Colborne to Fort Erie, where it joins the Niagara River Recreational Trail.

- The **Welland Canals Trail** (www.welland.ca) is a 42-kilometer (27-mile) north-south cycling path that connects St. Catharines and Port Colborne, running along the Welland Canal.

LAKE ONTARIO WATERFRONT TRAIL

The Niagara region is at the western end of the Lake Ontario Waterfront Trail (www.waterfronttrail.org), which follows the shores of Lake Ontario and the St. Lawrence River from Niagara-on-the-Lake all the way to the Quebec border. Extending for roughly 900 kilometers (560 miles), the trail includes a mix of dedicated off-road cycling paths and on-road routes, typically on less trafficked residential streets, although some sections do run along the shoulder of more major roads.

On the Niagara Peninsula, the waterfront trail connects the towns of Niagara-on-the-Lake, St. Catharines, Lincoln, and Grimsby, continuing on to Hamilton and then north to Toronto.

NEW YORK TO NIAGARA

If you want to ride your bike from New York State to the Niagara region – you can. Cyclists are allowed to cross the Peace Bridge between the Buffalo area and Fort Erie. You don't have to pay the toll, but you do need the same documents (including your passport) as you do if you're coming by other means of transportation. You can pick up the Niagara River Recreation Trail or the Friendship Trail on the Ontario side of the bridge.

Cyclists can also cross the Rainbow Bridge ($0.50). If you're in Niagara Falls – either Ontario or New York – and you want to cross over to the other Niagara Falls, the Rainbow Bridge is the most direct route. Again, passports are required.

Cyclists and pedestrians are not allowed on the Queenston-Lewiston Bridge.

of the two 40-passenger cars is quick—about one minute.

By Car

Parking near the falls is quite limited. If you can leave the car at home, you'll save yourself some parking hassles.

The least expensive long-term parking near the falls is at the **Rapidsview Parking Lot** ($10/day), on the Niagara Parkway 1.5 kilometers (one mile) south of the falls. From here, you can hop on a free shuttle to Table Rock and Horseshoe Falls. The parking area is open Saturdays and Sundays from mid-May through late June, and daily from late July through early September.

Other parking lots include the **Falls Lot,** directly behind the Horseshoe Falls, which has daily parking rates; the **Floral Showhouse Lot,** with parking by the hour; and **Queen Victoria Place,** which also has hourly parking. You can park for free at Niagara Parks' locations outside the central falls area, including the White Water Walk, Whirlpool Aero Car, Botanical Gardens and Butterfly Conservatory, Niagara Glen, and Old Fort Erie.

When driving around the falls, watch out for pedestrians. Many become captivated by the waterfalls and thus completely oblivious to traffic.

Tours

It lasts only 12 minutes, but **Niagara**

Helicopters Flightseeing Tour (3731 Victoria Ave., 905/357-5672, www.niagara-helicopters.com, 9 A.M.–sunset daily, adults $132, couples $252, kids $85) is an exciting way to see the falls from a different perspective. Aboard a six-passenger Bell 407 helicopter, your flight path takes you along the Niagara River, over the Whirlpool, past the American Falls, and around the Canadian Horseshoe Falls; their semicircular horseshoe shape is most apparent from the air. You don headphones to listen to narration about the sights along the way (and block out some of the chopper noise).

VICINITY OF NIAGARA FALLS
Queenston
Located 13 kilometers (eight miles) north of Niagara Falls and 11 kilometers (6.8 miles) south of downtown Niagara-on-the-Lake, the quiet village of Queenston houses several historic sites.

QUEENSTON HEIGHTS NATIONAL HISTORIC SITE
British and Canadian troops clashed with the American invaders in the Battle of Queenston Heights, one of the early skirmishes of the War of 1812 fought on Niagara soil. Through the British won the battle, the British commander, Major General Isaac Brock, was killed.

The battle site is now the **Queenston Heights Park** (www.niagaraparks.com), with gardens, picnic tables, and a bandshell, where the **Queenston Summer Concert Series** (free) entertains visitors on summer Sunday afternoons.

Also in the park is **Brock's Monument,** a national historic site honoring the fallen British military leader. Parks Canada runs interpretive programs at the monument (905/262-4759, www.pc.gc.ca, 10 A.M.–5 P.M. daily May–early Sept.), or you can follow a self-guided tour.

MACKENZIE PRINTERY AND NEWSPAPER MUSEUM
In 1824, political reformer and journalist William Lyon Mackenzie (1795–1861) began publishing a newspaper, the *Colonial Advocate,* in this Queenston house. This ivy-covered stone building, which dates to the late 1700s, is now a museum (1 Queenston St., 905/262-5676, www.niagaraparks.com or www.mackenzieprintery.org, 10 A.M.–4 P.M. daily May–early Sept., adults $5, kids 6–12 $3.75) devoted to Mackenzie's life and work, the early history of the Niagara–York (now Toronto) region, and the development of printing technology from the 18th century to the present. The museum also houses Canada's oldest printing press, a wooden device built in Britain in 1760, which was used to print Ontario's first newspaper, the *Upper Canada Gazette,* in 1793.

Guided tours run 30–45 minutes and include plenty of hands-on activities. You can set your name in movable type—and learn how hard it was to be a printer's apprentice!

The Printery is 13.3 kilometers (8.3 miles) north of Horseshoe Falls.

LAURA SECORD HOMESTEAD
During the War of 1812, Laura Ingersoll Secord and her husband James were ordered to billet several American soldiers in their Queenston home. One night in 1813, they overheard the American officers planning an attack on British forces at nearby Beaverdams. Since James had been injured several months earlier during the Battle of Queenston Heights, Laura decided that she would go warn the British commander of the impending American assault. The commander was based near Thorold, 32 kilometers (20 miles) away, and her journey on foot through the dense woods took 18 hours. As a result of Secord's information, the British set up an ambush and defeated the Americans in the Battle of Beaverdams on June 24, 1813.

Today, Secord is often called Canada's "Paul Revere," after the American who made a similar journey during the American Revolutionary War to warn that British troops were arriving in Boston. The home where she and her husband lived, the Laura Secord Homestead (29

Queenston St., 905/262-4851, www.niagara-parks.com, 11 A.M.–5 P.M. daily May–early Sept., 11 A.M.–4 P.M. Wed.–Sun. early Sept.–mid-Oct., adults $9.50, kids 6–12 $6.25) is now a museum, with information about her life and times, and furnishings from the early 1800s.

Also on the property is the gothic-style **Queenston Chapel,** a Methodist church built in the 1860s and subsequently moved to the Secord Homestead site.

The Homestead is 13.3 kilometers (8.3 miles) north of Horseshoe Falls, a short walk from the Mackenzie Printery.

Old Fort Erie

At the southeastern point on the Niagara Peninsula, a short hop across the river to the New York shore, the British built their first fort in Ontario back in 1764. The fort became a base for an alliance of British, Loyalist, and Iroquois soldiers during the American Revolution (1775–1783), but it took its place in history later, during the War of 1812, when it became Canada's bloodiest battlefield. During the six-week Siege of Fort Erie in 1814, more than 3,000 troops were killed or wounded. Later that year, as American troops were withdrawing to Buffalo, they destroyed what remained of the fort.

It wasn't until the 1930s that Old Fort Erie (350 Lakeshore Rd., Fort Erie, www.niagara-parks.com, 10 A.M.–4 P.M. daily May–mid-Oct., adults $12.25, kids 6–12 $7.95) was restored and opened to the public. You can tour the rebuilt fort, wandering into the soldiers' barracks, officers' quarters, kitchens, and other buildings, where costumed staff tell you about the history of the fort and the region.

Old Fort Erie is 19 kilometers (12 miles) south of Niagara Falls. It's a pretty drive along the Niagara Parkway, although it's a bit faster to take the QEW.

THE NIAGARA REGION

Niagara-on-the-Lake

Although it's just 20 kilometers (12.5 miles) up the road from Niagara Falls, the small town of Niagara-on-the-Lake (NOTL) feels like it's on a different planet. While the city of Niagara Falls teeters between brash, honky-tonk, and naturally spectacular, NOTL is more reserved, with a cute (perhaps excessively so) main street, historic attractions that date primarily from the War of 1812, a peaceful lakeshore, and hundreds of B&Bs.

The town's main attraction is theatre; it's home to the highly regarded Shaw Festival, which runs from April through October. Wine touring is the other major draw; you can visit more than two dozen wineries.

The town of Niagara-on-the-Lake is divided into several different sections. The "historic downtown" is centered along Queen Street, bounded by Lake Ontario and the Niagara River. The village of Virgil, along Niagara Stone Road (Highway 55), is the area's commercial hub, while the village of St. Davids to the south is more rural, home to several of the area's wineries.

◖ SHAW FESTIVAL

"You see things; and you say 'Why?' But I dream things that never were; and I say 'Why not?'"

Perhaps Shaw Festival founder Brian Doherty had these words from George Bernard Shaw's 1921 play *Back to Methuselah* in mind when he conceived the idea of a summer festival devoted to Shaw's work. Whatever his inspiration, Doherty, a lawyer, playwright, and Shaw fan, launched the Shaw Festival (10 Queen's Parade, 905/468-2172 or 800/511-7429, www.shawfest.com, Apr.–Oct.) in the summer of 1962, when he produced eight performances of Shaw's *Don Juan in Hell* and *Candida*.

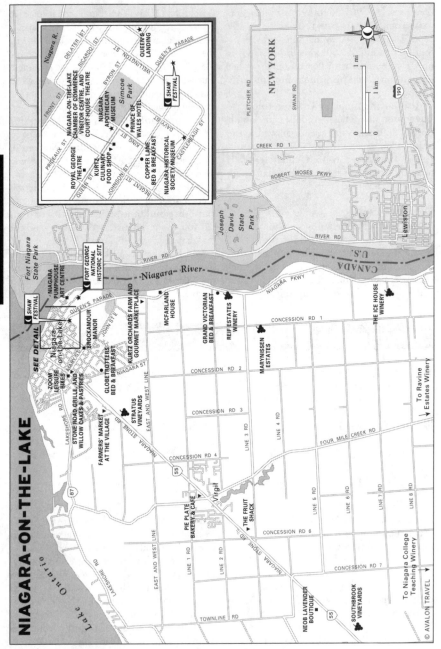

THE NIAGARA REGION

NIAGARA-ON-THE-LAKE

Inset: Niagara-on-the-Lake town detail

- QUEEN'S LANDING
- NIAGARA-ON-THE-LAKE CHAMBER OF COMMERCE VISITOR CENTRE, AND COURT HOUSE THEATRE
- NIAGARA APOTHECARY MUSEUM
- SHAW FESTIVAL
- PRINCE OF WALES HOTEL
- ROYAL GEORGE THEATRE
- KURTZ CULINARY FOOD SHOP
- COPPER LANE BED & BREAKFAST
- NIAGARA HISTORICAL SOCIETY MUSEUM
- Simcoe Park

Niagara R.
DELATER 1ST
FRONT ST.
BICARDOS ST.
PRIDEAUX ST.
WELLINGTON ST.
BYRON ST.
QUEEN'S PARADE
DAVY ST.
CASTLEREAGH ST.
KING ST.
QUEEN'S ST.
JOHNSON ST.
REGENT ST.

NEW YORK
- PLETCHER RD
- SWAN RD
- 190
- CREEK RD 1
- ROBERT MOSES PKWY
- RIVER RD
- Lewiston
- Joseph Davis State Park

Main map
- Lake Ontario
- Fort Niagara State Park
- Niagara Pumphouse Art Centre
- FORT GEORGE NATIONAL HISTORIC SITE
- SHAW FESTIVAL
- SEE DETAIL
- Niagara-on-the-Lake
- BROCKAMOUR MANOR
- Queen's Parade
- JOHN ST E
- KURTZ ORCHARDS FARM AND GOURMET MARKETPLACE
- McFARLAND HOUSE
- GRAND VICTORIAN BED & BREAKFAST
- REIF ESTATES WINERY
- MARYNISSEN ESTATES
- THE ICE HOUSE WINERY
- Niagara River
- CANADA
- U.S.
- NIAGARA PKWY
- CONCESSION RD 1
- ZOOM LEISURE BIKES
- STONE ROAD GRILLE AND WILLOW CAKES & PASTRIES
- GLOBETROTTERS BED & BREAKFAST
- STRATUS VINEYARDS
- FARMERS' MARKET AT THE VILLAGE
- NIAGARA STONE RD
- EAST AND WEST LINE
- NIAGARA ST
- MARY'S
- JOHN ST E
- LAKESHORE RD
- CONCESSION RD 2
- CONCESSION RD 3
- LINE 3 RD
- LINE 4 RD
- FOUR MILE CREEK RD
- To Ravine Estates Winery
- CONCESSION RD 4
- 55
- Virgil
- PIE PLATE BAKERY & CAFÉ
- THE FRUIT SHACK
- LINE 1 RD
- LINE 2 RD
- LINE 5 RD
- LINE 6 RD
- LINE 7 RD
- LINE 8 RD
- CONCESSION RD 6
- CONCESSION RD 7
- 87
- LAKESHORE RD
- EAST AND WEST LINE
- NEOB LAVENDER BOUTIQUE
- 55
- SOUTHBROOK VINEYARDS
- TOWNLINE RD
- To Niagara College Teaching Winery

1 mi
1 km
0

the Shaw Festival's Royal George Theatre, Niagara-on-the-Lake

for its upcoming season at the end of the previous summer. You can order tickets (adults $32–106) online, by phone, by fax (905/468-3804), by mail (Box 774, Niagara-on-the-Lake, ON L0S 1J0), or in person at any of the festival theatres.

You can save money on tickets by attending preview performances; before a play's official "opening," tickets are discounted up to 30 percent. Throughout the season, Sunday-evening performances are typically less expensive than other evening shows. Discounted tickets are also available for students ($24–29) at certain performances, patrons under age 30 ($30), and families; for each regular adult ticket you buy, you can purchase one or two youth tickets (for ages 18 and under) for $30.

Theaters

The Shaw Festival stages its productions at four theaters in Niagara-on-the-Lake. Its flagship venue is the 856-seat **Festival Theatre** (10 Queen's Parade), built in 1972 on the east end of downtown. The building also houses the 202-seat **Studio Theatre.** Parking in the Festival Theatre lot costs $8 during performances.

The festival's other two stages are on NOTL's main downtown street: the 327-seat **Court House Theatre** (26 Queen St.) and the similarly sized **Royal George Theatre** (85 Queen St.), a former vaudeville house with 328 seats. There's a metered parking lot near the Court House Theatre (Market St., at Regent St.); for the Royal George, the closest parking is on the surrounding streets.

Tours

For a fascinating behind-the-scenes look at the festival, take the hourlong **backstage tour** (11 A.M. Sat.–Sun., May; 11 A.M. Tues., Wed., Sat., Sun. June–Oct.; $5) of the Festival Theatre. You'll learn about the festival's history; visit the rehearsal hall (staff estimate that actors rehearse one hour for each minute they spend on stage!); tour the dressing rooms; walk through the wardrobe shop (nearly three-quarters of the costumes used on stage are new every

Shaw himself had no connection to Niagara-on-the-Lake. Born in Dublin, Ireland, in 1856, author George Bernard Shaw (1856–1950) wrote 63 plays, five novels, numerous essays, and more than 250,000 letters during his 94-year life, most of which he lived in England.

The festival's original mandate was to perform plays by Shaw and his contemporaries, who range from Chekhov to Tennessee Williams. More recently, directors have expanded this mission to include plays about the time period when Shaw lived, as well as works by contemporary playwrights who are controversial or political in the same way that Shaw was during his lifetime.

The Shaw Festival operates as a repertory theatre, with plays running simultaneously on four stages around town. The festival company typically includes 65–70 actors per season, many of whom return year after year—as do many of its patrons.

Tickets

The festival typically announces the lineup

year), which occupies a staff of 40; and find out more about set design and construction.

Lectures and Workshops

Before many evening performances, a company member hosts a free **pre-show chat** (Festival Theatre, 7:30 P.M. late May–mid-Sept.), giving an introduction to the evening's play. Call or check the festival website for a schedule.

Want to learn about set design or costume construction? Practice your acting skills or hone your British accent? Take one of the **theatre workshops** (905/468-2172 or 800/511-7429, www.shawfest.com) offered throughout the season. Most run two or three days and include tickets to at least one performance.

⚑ WINERIES

Niagara-on-the Lake has more than two dozen wineries. You'll find them along Highway 55/Niagara Stone Road; on York Road in St. Davids, running east toward Queenston; along the Niagara River Parkway and the concessions (rural roads) parallel to the parkway; and on Lakeshore Road skirting Lake Ontario.

Most NOTL wineries are open year-round and charge a small fee ($2–5) for tastings; if you purchase wine, you may get credit for your tasting fee. Larger wineries offer regularly scheduled tours, but smaller facilities may offer tours only by appointment or not at all.

The Niagara College Teaching Winery

The Niagara College Teaching Winery (www.niagaracollegewine.ca) is Canada's only licensed "teaching winery," where students study wine making, viticulture, and marketing, and staff a working winery on 38 acres of vineyards. Even if you're not ready to sign up for a wine-degree program, stop into the college-run **Wine Visitor and Education Centre** (135 Taylor Rd., 905/641-2252, www.niagaracollegewine.ca, 10 A.M.–6 P.M. daily May–Oct.; 11 A.M.–5 P.M. Sun.–Fri., 10 A.M.–5 P.M. Sat. Nov.–Apr.) to start your wine explorations in the region. They can provide you with information about area wineries and offer tastings of

© CAROLYN B. HELLER

one of the many wineries that make Ontario's signature "ice wine"

the college's wines, including the reserve wines known as the "Dean's List."

The college doesn't neglect beer, either: the **Niagara College Teaching Brewery** (www.niagaracollegebeer.ca) is Canada's first "teaching brewery"—a two-year program where students learn all aspects of the beer business. Sample the students' brews in the retail shop (10 A.M.–6 P.M. daily, $2). You can tour the brewing facility, too; call ahead for an appointment.

Ravine Estates Winery

The tasting room at the small, family-owned Ravine Estates Winery (1366 York Rd., St. Davids, 905/262-8463, www.ravinevineyard.com, 11 A.M.–5 P.M. Sun.–Fri., 11 A.M.–6 P.M. Sat.) is in a historic clapboard home built in the early 1800s. They make merlot, cabernet franc, chardonnay, and sauvignon blanc. Stop here if you're hungry, too; there's a French-inspired bistro, bakery, and deli on-site.

Southbrook Vineyards

You can't miss the striking azure wall—200

FOOD AND WINE EVENTS

With so many wineries and local food producers around the Niagara Peninsula, it's no surprise that several festivals and events showcase the area's wine and food.

The Niagara region's more than 100 wineries kick off the summer tasting season at the **Niagara New Vintage Festival** (www.niagarawinefestival.com, June) with two weeks of food and wine events.

Wouldn't running be more fun if you could stop for chocolate along the way? That's the philosophy behind **The Chocolate Race** (905/932-6356, www.thechocolaterace.com, Aug.), a 5- and 10-kilometer walk and run, with a chocolate-dipping stop en route and more chocolate treats at the finish line. Though there are prizes for the top contestants, it's a charity event, rather than a hard-core race.

In the fall, the **Niagara Wine Festival** (www.niagarawinefestival.com, Sept.) celebrates the harvest with tastings, concerts, and other special events, while the **Niagara Food Festival** (www.niagarafoodfestival.com, Sept.) in Welland serves up tastes of local food.

It's worth braving the winter weather for the **Niagara Ice Wine Festival** (www.icewinefestival.com, Jan.), where the tastings, winery tours, gala party, and other festivities highlight the region's distinctive dessert wines. And because the Niagara Peninsula is not only about ice wines, there's the **Twenty Valley Winter WineFest** (www.twentyvalley.ca, Jan.), which calls itself the "not just ice wine festival."

---

meters (650 feet) long and three meters (10 feet) high—that slices across the fields at Southbrook Vineyards (581 Niagara Stone Rd., 905/641-2548 or 888/581-1581, www.southbrook.com, tastings 10 A.M.–5 P.M. Mon.–Sat., 11 A.M.–5 P.M. Sun.), marking the entrance to Canada's first certified biodynamic winery. Inside, you can sample their wines in the sleek glass-walled tasting pavilion; they're known for their chardonnays and their cabernet–merlot blends. Tours of the vineyards and winery are offered on Saturdays and Sundays; call for schedule. The farm-to-table **Vineyard Bistro** (11 A.M.–4 P.M. Wed.–Sun. late May–mid-Oct., $8–16) serves pizzas and salads outside on the patio.

Stratus Vineyards

With a marble bar, library-style shelves lined with wines, and views across the fields, the tasting room at Stratus Vineyards (2059 Niagara Stone Rd., 905/468-1806, www.stratuswines.com, 10 A.M.–5 P.M. daily May–Dec., noon–5 P.M. Wed.–Sun. Jan.–Apr.) feels like a luxurious lounge, rather than a muddy-boots winery. Tasting flights of four wines ($10) are served in crystal stemware, and special events, from cheese tastings to concerts to posh picnics, take place throughout the season. Their signature wines are blends, labeled simply "Stratus White" and "Status Red." It's also the first winery in the world to receive LEED (Leadership in Energy and Environmental Design) certification, a "green" building stamp of approval.

Reif Estates Winery

Opened in 1982, the German-style Reif Estates Winery (15608 Niagara Parkway, 905/468-7738, www.reifwinery.com, tastings 10 A.M.–6 P.M. daily Apr.–Oct., 10 A.M.–5 P.M. daily Nov.–Mar.; tours 11:30 A.M. and 1:30 P.M. daily Apr.–Oct., $5) specializes in Gewürztraminer and Rieslings, but they also make chardonnay, pinot noir, cabernet merlot, cabernet franc, and other wines. In addition to the standard tastings, you can book a variety of special options, including a blind tasting of either a red or white flight ($15). They also make their own raisins from cabernet franc grapes, dried in a former tobacco kiln; ask for a taste, or buy a package to nibble.

Marynissen Estates

The family-owned Marynissen Estates (1209

Concession 1 Rd., 905/468-7270, www. marynissen.com, 10 A.M.–5 P.M. daily) is known for big, bold, old-world reds, particularly cabernets. Tours (hourly, Sat.–Sun. in summer) not only visit the production facilities, but also take you out into the vineyards, which include the oldest cabernet sauvignon vines in Canada.

The Ice House

On a hot summer afternoon, the sign for "ice wine slushies" may lure you down the lane to The Ice House (14778 Niagara Parkway, 905/262-6161, www.theicehouse.ca, 11 A.M.–dusk daily), a small producer of, yes, ice wine. They make two ice wine varieties: the white vidal, and a more unusual cabernet sauvignon. Sample both in their tasting room as you learn more about how ice wine is made. If only every slushie shop could make their chilled treats with ice wine!

SIGHTS

Stop into the **Niagara Historical Society Museum** (43 Castlereagh St., 905/468-3912, www.niagarahistorical.museum, 10 A.M.–5 P.M. daily May–Oct., 1–5 P.M. daily Nov.–Apr.; adults $5, seniors $3, students $2, kids $1) to learn more about the history of the Niagara region. Housed in the first building in Ontario built specifically as a museum (the original structure dates to 1907), the museum today has more than 40,000 historical artifacts, and its exhibits trace Niagara's history from the early aboriginal communities, to the founding of Upper Canada, through the War of 1812 and into the present day.

A pharmacy that operated on the town's main street for more than 140 years, the **Niagara Apothecary Museum** (5 Queen St., 905/468-3845, www.niagaraapothecary. ca, noon–6 P.M. daily mid-May–early Sept., noon–6 P.M. Sat.–Sun. early Sept.–mid-Oct., admission by donation) is still filled with many of its original drug jars and bottles.

One of the oldest buildings in Niagara-on-the-Lake, **McFarland House** (15927 Niagara Parkway, www.niagaraparks.com, noon–5 P.M.

daily, early May–early Sept., noon–5 P.M. Sat.–Sun. early Sept.–mid-Oct.; adults $5, kids 6–12 $3.75) is also one of the town's few structures to have survived the War of 1812. Scottish immigrant John McFarland settled in NOTL, which was then known as Newark, when the British Crown granted him 608 acres of land to reward his services as a boat builder to King George III. McFarland and his descendents lived in the Georgian-style house, which he built on the property in 1800, for more than 140 years. As you tour the restored home, you can learn more about life in the area from 1800 to 1830. Afternoon tea is served in the garden in summer.

The small gallery in the **Niagara Pumphouse Art Centre** (247 Ricardo St., 905/468-5455, www.niagarapumphouse.ca, 9 A.M.–4 P.M. Mon.–Fri., 1–4 P.M. Sat.–Sun. June–Aug.; noon–4 P.M. Mon.–Fri., 1–4 P.M. Sat.–Sun., Sept.–May; free) shows work by local artists. It's worth a look at the building itself, a Victorian structure overlooking the Niagara River that supplied the town's water from 1891 to 1983.

⬛ Fort George National Historic Site

Between 1796 and 1799, British troops built a fort on the banks of the Niagara River to protect the river—an important supply route to the Great Lakes—as well as the growing town of Newark (the present-day Niagara-on-the-Lake). When the Americans attacked the Niagara region during the War of 1812, U.S. troops bombed Fort George and forced the British to withdraw in May 1813, during the fight that became known as the Battle of Fort George. The Americans occupied Fort George until December 1813, when the British forced them to retreat to Fort Niagara, on what is now the New York side of the river. British troops once again took control of Fort George and held it through the duration of the war. By the 1820s, however, the British had built a new stronghold nearby at Fort Mississauga (on the grounds of what is now the Niagara-on-the-Lake Golf Club), and Fort George was abandoned.

Today, at the Fort George National Historic Site (51 Queens Parade, 905/468-6614, www. pc.gc.ca or www.friendsoffortgeorge.ca, 10 A.M.–5 P.M. daily May–Oct., 10 A.M.–5 P.M. Sat.–Sun. Apr. and Nov., adults $11.70, seniors $10.05, kids 6–16 $5.80, family $29.40, parking $5.90), visitors can tour the restored fort's buildings and grounds, including two blockhouses that served as soldiers' quarters, a guardhouse, the 1796 powder magazine (the only structure to survive the War of 1812), the officers' quarters, and the kitchen, where costumed guides are often baking or cooking snacks for visitors on the open hearth. Guides staff many of the fort buildings and can tell you about the history of the period. Fife and drum corps periodically perform, and staff demonstrate how to operate muskets like those used during the War of 1812.

ENTERTAINMENT AND SHOPPING

The Shaw Festival (10 Queen's Parade, 905/468-2172 or 800/511-7429, www.shaw-fest.com, Apr.–Oct.) is obviously the main "entertainment" in town, but beyond the theaters, you'll find other arts events, as well. **Music Niagara** (905/468-5566 or 800/511-7429, www.musicniagara.org, mid-July to mid-Aug., $15–45) is a summer festival of classical, jazz, blues, and choral music concerts at venues around town, including wineries, churches, parks, and restaurants.

Queen Street is the main downtown shopping street, lined with boutiques, galleries, cafés, and restaurants. Most seem designed for tourists, so browse away. For Shaw books, T-shirts, and other memorabilia, visit **Bernard's** (10 Queen's Parade, 905/468-2172 or 800/511-7429), the gift shop in the Festival Theatre lobby. Outside of downtown, Niagara Stone Road (Highway 55) is the region's commercial hub, particularly around the village of Virgil, midway between the QEW and the historic district.

Husband-and-wife team Robert and Melissa Achal founded the **NEOB Lavender Boutique** (758 Niagara Stone Rd., 905/682-0171, www. neoblavender.com, 10 A.M.–6 P.M. Mon.–Sat.,

10 A.M.–5 P.M. Sun.) and they readily share their passion for their 8,000 lavender plants and other flowers and herbs. Their shop is stocked with oils, lotions, and other bath and body products, as well as lavender cookies and even lavender-scented coffee. Take a free five-minute tour of their greenhouse to learn more about the plants and their uses, or request a more in-depth tour (45 minutes, $2) of the fields and greenhouse.

Another crop grown in the Niagara area is ginseng, which many Asian cultures use to make tea or herbal remedies. You can find out more about ginseng's uses at **Great Mountain Ginseng** (758 Niagara Stone Rd., 905/685-7328 or 866/900-0527, www.greatmoun-tainginseng.com), which also sells a variety of ginseng products.

Part farmstand and part gourmet food market, **Kurtz Orchards Farm and Gourmet Marketplace** (16006 Niagara Parkway, 905/468-2937, www.kurtzorchards.com) sells fresh produce, cheeses, baked goods, and sandwiches. You can also take an **Orchard and Vineyard Tour** with lunch on the grounds ($22–26); call for schedules. They're well known for their line of jams, jellies, and salsas, which they also sell at the **Kurtz Culinary Food Shop** (38–40 Queen St, 905/468-3815) downtown.

SPORTS AND RECREATION

Both walkers and cyclists enjoy the 56-kilometer (35-mile) **Niagara River Recreation Trail**, which begins in Niagara-on-the-Lake and follows the Niagara River south to Niagara Falls; it continues on all the way to Fort Erie.

You can rent bicycles from **Zoom Leisure Bikes** (431 Mississauga St./Hwy. 55, 905/468-2366 or 866/811-6993, www.zoomleisure.com, half-/full-day $20/30). If you rent for a full day, they'll deliver your bike to you free, as long as you're within eight kilometers (five miles) of their store. They also offer cycling tours, including a 3.5-hour winery tour ($69), which visits several local wineries.

ACCOMMODATIONS

The **Niagara-on-the-Lake Chamber of Commerce** (www.niagaraonthelake.com)

can book rooms for you at more than 200 area lodgings. You can also search for lodging availability and prices on their website. For bed-and-breakfast listings and bookings, contact the **Niagara-on-the-Lake Bed and Breakfast Association** (905/468-0123, www.niagarabedandbreakfasts.com).

$100-150

Owners Donna and Fernando Vieira are avid travelers (and Donna edits *Dreamscapes,* a glossy travel magazine), so it's no surprise that the **Globetrotters Bed & Breakfast** (642 Simcoe St., 905/468-4021 or 866/835-4446, www.globetrottersbb.ca, $125–145), the whimsically furnished guesthouse they run in their home on a suburban cul-de-sac, is filled with original art and mementos from their journeys. In the Moulin Rouge room, gold, orange, and red silk saris cocoon the wrought-iron bed and walls. The peach and burgundy Sultan's Tent suite, draped with colorful sheer curtains, feels seductive, too, although its attached twin-bedded room could accommodate a family or friends traveling together. The smallest room, on the main floor, has bright blue walls and a hand-painted headboard. Browse the travel books in the guest library to consider your next adventure. Rates include a full breakfast, Wi-Fi, and parking.

$150-250

Just a short walk from Queen Street and the theatres, the **Copper Lane Bed & Breakfast** (28 Johnson St., 905/468-7097, www.copper-lanebb.com, $155–220 d) was originally built in the 1870s to house military officers and their families. You won't feel confined to your quarters here; you can relax in the book-lined parlor, out in the garden, or on the front porch. There's nothing spartan about the three updated guest rooms, either. They each have a queen bed, fireplace, and modern bath, and the largest, the caramel-hued Nutmeg Room, has a whirlpool tub. A three-course breakfast, Wi-Fi, and parking are included in the rates. Ask about coupons for complimentary tours and tastings at area wineries.

The wraparound porch at the **⟨⟨ Grand Victorian Bed & Breakfast** (15618 Niagara Parkway, 905/468-0997, www.grandvictorian.ca, $170–225 d), furnished with wicker chairs and porch swings, may not be the world's largest, but it's definitely in the running. Built in the 1870s as a summer "cottage," this stately Victorian mansion blends regal architectural details—lofty 12-foot ceilings, original woodwork, stained-glass windows, and numerous fireplaces (there are four on the main floor alone)—with the breezy, laid-back ambience you'd want in a summer getaway. The six guest rooms have period details, including four-poster or canopy beds, antique wardrobes, and oriental rugs atop original wood floors; one has a private sun deck. Owner Eva Kessel serves a hearty buffet breakfast, and rates include a complimentary tour and tasting at the Reif Estates Winery next door. You can swim in the pool or play a round of tennis on the courts out back—at least if you can rouse yourself from that fantastic porch.

You'll want to wake up for the elaborate four-course breakfasts, served promptly at 9 A.M., at the majestic **⟨⟨ Brockamour Manor** (433 King St., 905/468-5527, www.brockamour.com, $179–250 d). Seasonal fruit, freshly baked pastries, a hearty hot dish, even a dessert will start your day right, as you trade travel tips and theatre reviews with your fellow guests. Wander into the billiards room, where you can work off your meal with a round of pool (or lounge around over the newspaper or a game of cards). The six rooms are all spacious, with simple, classic furnishings and modern touches like gas fireplaces, DVD players, and Wi-Fi. Welcoming owners Colleen and Rick aren't NOTL natives, but they've embraced their adopted community and enjoy sharing it with their guests.

Over $250

Queen's Landing (155 Byron St., 905/468-2195 or 888/669-5566, www.vintage-hotels.com, $259–518 d), a majestic Georgian-style brick inn that looks like it's been on the lakeshore for generations, was actually built in 1990. While the furnishings are classic, it doesn't have the creakiness of an old-fashioned hotel. Some of the 142 rooms, decorated in blues and golds, have fireplaces or jetted tubs; the best have views over Lake Ontario. On the lower level is the "Internet library," a combination reading room, lounge, and work center, with overstuffed leather sofas, book-filled shelves, and computers for guest use. There's also an indoor pool. The hotel hosts lots of conferences and business events, but you won't be out of place if you're here for a weekend escape.

Built in 1864, the refined ◖ **Prince of Wales Hotel** (6 Picton St., 905/468-3246 or 888/669-5566, www.vintage-hotels.com, $279–523 d) wows with its elaborately decorated public spaces, from the lobby, with its ornate inlaid wood floor, to the classic drawing room, where afternoon tea is served daily, complete with silver teapots and petite finger sandwiches. Even the indoor pool feels posh, its walls lined with royal portraits, and the "Secret Garden" spa lives up to its name with tucked-away treatment rooms. The decor is somewhat different in each of the 110 traditionally appointed guest rooms; some have antique four-poster beds, Tiffany lamps, or fireplaces, but all have modern amenities ranging from rain showers to heated towel racks. The location couldn't be better, right in the center of town.

FOOD

Queen Street downtown is lined with places to eat, although you'll find more interesting choices and better value if you're willing to explore other parts of town. Several area wineries have good restaurants, too.

Bakeries and Cafés

Amid the scones and croissants that lure morning lingerers, and the gorgeous-looking cakes and tarts (including mini ones, just right for a picnic), **Willow Cakes and Pastries** (242 Mary St., 905/468-2745, www.willowcakes. ca, 8 A.M.–6 P.M. Mon.–Thurs., 8 A.M.–7 P.M. Fri.–Sun., late May–mid-Oct.; 8 A.M.–6 P.M. daily mid.–Oct.–late May), a petite café just outside downtown, also bakes up quiche, pork

pies, and other savory dishes. Pop in for a light lunch or for some treats to go.

You could visit the country-style **Pie Plate Bakery and Café** (1516 Niagara Stone Rd., Virgil, 905/468-9743, www.thepieplate.com) for soup, salad, a sandwich, or a creative pizza. They're all fine choices, but remember, you're here for the pie. The choices vary with the seasons: strawberry in June and July, blueberry from June through September, peach from July through September, and pumpkin in the fall. You can buy whole pies if you're feeding the family, or individual mini-pies to eat right now.

It looks like a strip mall fast-food joint, with its bright red sign and a couple of red picnic tables out front, but **Rest to Go-Go** (Garrison Plaza, Mary St. at Mississauga St., 11 A.M.–9 P.M. Sun.–Thurs., 11 A.M.–10 P.M. Fri.–Sat., $4.50–13), under the same ownership as the upscale Stone Road Grille next door, turns out seriously tasty pizzas, sandwiches, and salads. You can concoct your own sandwich, choosing your protein, cheese, and a variety of fixings, or select from options like Thai chicken salad with peanut sauce or slow-roasted pulled pork. The pizzas range from traditional to innovative, too; the "quacky" is topped with duck confit and caramelized onions, while the "ringo" includes bacon, cheddar cheese, and potatoes.

Contemporary

Benchmark (135 Taylor Rd., 905/641-2252 ext. 4619, www.niagaracollege.ca, lunch 11:30 A.M.–2 P.M. Tues.–Sun., dinner 5–9 P.M. Wed.–Fri., 5–9 P.M. Sat., lunch $10–13, dinner $17–24), the student-run restaurant room at the Niagara College, is teaching its students about local, seasonal cuisine, and that's good news for you. Your chilled asparagus appetizer might come with an ice wine vinaigrette, the eggplant for your eggplant parmesan might have been grown in nearby St. Davids, and the roast chicken might be stuffed with a mix of wild mushrooms and Niagara-made cheese. The wine list includes the college's own labels, as well as those from other Niagara producers. For a lighter bite, stop into **Bench to Go**

(Tues.–Fri.), which sells soups, salads, sandwiches, pastries, and coffee.

Set amid the vines at the Ravine Vineyard Estate Winery, the casual-chic **Ravine Vineyard Bistro** (1366 York Rd., St. Davids, 905/262-8463, www.ravinevineyard.com, 11 A.M.–3:30 P.M. and 4:30–8:30 P.M., $11–27) serves French bistro fare with Niagara ingredients. On the lighter side, the menu includes a simple omelet, salads like a traditional *salade niçoise,* and *moules frites* (mussels with French fries). In the mood for something heartier? There's *coq au vin,* gnocchi with peas and locally made ricotta, or braised veal cheeks served with hand-cut noodles and a salad of fresh herbs.

Despite its nondescript strip-mall setting, the ◖ **Stone Road Grille** (Garrison Plaza, 238 Mary St., www.stoneroadgrille.com, lunch 11:30 A.M.–2 P.M. Tues.–Sun., dinner 5–9 P.M. Sun. and Tues.–Thurs., 5–10 P.M. Fri.–Sat., lunch $12–22, dinner $28–30) serves some of the most interesting fare in town. At midday, you might find a sandwich like the *croque madame,* with slow-roasted ham, locally made cheese, and a fried egg; mussels and French fries; or a duck confit salad. In the evening, the kitchen might create braised oxtail risotto, a chicken sauté with warm potato-bacon salad and fiddleheads, or a "surf and turf" combo of albacore tuna, crispy pork belly, and arugula. If you're more of a grazer, or you just want to taste more dishes, you can order any of the dinner mains in half-size portions.

One of the prettiest spots in town, **Tiara** (Queen's Landing Hotel, 155 Byron St., 905/468-2195 or 888/669-5566, www.vintage-hotels.com, 11 A.M.–2 P.M. and 6–9 P.M. Mon.–Thurs., 11 A.M.–2 P.M. and 5–9:30 P.M. Fri.–Sat., 11 A.M.–2:30 P.M. and 6–9 P.M. Sun., brunch prix-fixe $32, lunch $12–27, dinner $32–42) overlooks Lake Ontario, with tables out on the terrace and inside the grand dining room, where tall windows face the water. At lunch, the menu includes salads and interesting sandwiches, like the pita stuffed with bourbon-glazed shrimp or the grilled panini with ham and Gruyére cheese. Dinner is more formal,

with mains like sweet potato gnocchi served with sweet onion relish and rapini, veal tenderloin cooked *sous vide,* or fire-roasted lamb paired with pico de gallo and tabouleh salad. Save room for dessert, perhaps the lemon curd mousse cake with raspberry coulis or the decadent chocolate peanut butter brownie tower. A five-course tasting menu ($85) is available, and Tiara is also popular for a refined Sunday brunch.

Groceries and Markets

Produce, prepared foods, and baked goods are available at the **Farmers' Market at the Village** (111 Garrison Village Dr., www.farmersmarketatthevillage.ca, 8 A.M.–1 P.M. Sat. late May–mid-Oct.), located just off Niagara Stone Road (Highway 55) at Niven Road.

The Fruit Shack (1267 Niagara Stone Rd., Virgil, 905/468-9821, www.thefruitshack.com, 9 A.M.–6 P.M. daily mid-June–mid-Oct.; call for off-season hours) sells local produce, meats, and homemade baked goods. Their butter tarts are particularly delicious.

INFORMATION AND SERVICES

The **Niagara-on-the-Lake Chamber of Commerce** (26 Queen St., 905/468-1950, www.niagaraonthelake.com, 8:30 A.M.–7:30 P.M. daily May–Oct., 8:30 A.M.–5 P.M. daily Nov.–Apr.) runs a visitors center downtown; it's on the lower level of the courthouse. They can also help you find a place to stay.

GETTING THERE

Niagara-on-the-Lake is on the northeast tip of the Niagara Peninsula, bordering both Lake Ontario and the Niagara River. It's 135 kilometers (85 miles) southeast of Toronto and 20 kilometers (12.5 miles) north of Niagara Falls.

Niagara-on-the-Lake does not have train service, and it has no long-distance bus service, either. The nearest stations with VIA Rail (888/842-7245, www.viarail.ca) service from Toronto or Amtrak (800/872-7245, www.amtrak.com) service from New York are in St. Catharines (5 Great Western St.) or

Niagara Falls (4267 Bridge St.). To get from St. Catharines to NOTL, you either need to take a taxi or rent a car.

By Air

Toronto **Pearson International Airport** (www.torontopearson.com) and **Buffalo-Niagara International Airport** (www.buffaloairport.com) are the commercial airports closest to Niagara-on-the-Lake. The **Niagara Air Bus** (905/374-8111 or 800/206-7222, www.niagaraairbus.com), a door-to-door airport shuttle, can take you from either Pearson (one-way $83) or Buffalo (one-way $79) to Niagara-on-the-Lake. If you book the shuttle online at least three days in advance, fares are discounted 10 percent.

By Car

From Toronto to Niagara-on-the-Lake, take the QEW south, passing Hamilton and St. Catharines. At exit 38B, follow the Niagara-on-the-Lake signs to Highway 55, which is also Niagara Stone Road. Go northeast on Highway 55 for 12 kilometers (7 miles) until it ends at Queen Street. Turn right toward the downtown business district and the Shaw Festival Theatre.

From Buffalo, and points south in the United States, take I-190 north to the Queenston–Lewiston Bridge. Once you've crossed to the Ontario side, the most scenic route is to follow the Niagara River Parkway into Niagara-on-the-Lake.

By Shuttle from Niagara Falls

From Niagara Falls to Niagara-on-the-Lake, you can catch the **5-0 Transportation shuttle** (905/358-3232 in Niagara Falls, 905/685-5464 in NOTL, or 800/268-7429, www.5-0taxi.com, one-way adults $10, kids $5). It leaves three times daily from the Niagara Falls Bus Terminal (4555 Erie Ave., 10:15 A.M., 1:15 P.M., 4 P.M.) and drops passengers at Fort George in NOTL. The first two shuttles also pick up passengers at the Marriott Gateway on the Falls Hotel (6755 Fallsview Blvd.; 9:45 A.M. and 12:45 P.M.), Fallsview Plaza Hotel (6455 Fallsview Blvd.; 9:50 A.M. and 12:50 P.M.),

and the Sheraton on the Falls (5875 Falls Ave.; 10:10 A.M. and 1:10 P.M.). Return shuttles leave Fort George for the Falls at 11 A.M., 2:15 P.M., and 5 P.M.

In the winter, there's only one shuttle a day in each direction, leaving Niagara Falls at 11 A.M. and returning from Niagara-on-the-Lake at 4 P.M.

GETTING AROUND

You can easily walk around the downtown heritage district, between the theatres, the shops, and the lake, and many accommodations are also within walking distance. Few of the wineries are within an easy walk of downtown, though, so you'll need to have a car or bicycle—or book a wine tour—to get out to the tasting rooms. Niagara-on-the-Lake has no public transit.

Niagara-on-the-Lake has plenty of pleasant cycling routes. Follow the Niagara River Recreation Trail south toward Niagara Falls and you can reach many of the wineries by bicycle—at least if you don't drink too much en route.

Parking around town is somewhat limited, particularly on Queen Street and around the theatres. Pick up a copy of the Chamber of Commerce's "Where to Park in NOTL" map, which shows parking lots, meter rates and durations, and free parking locations; you can get the map at the chamber office or on their website.

To find free or less expensive parking, try the side streets away from Queen Street. Beware: town staff won't hesitate to give tickets to visitors who overstay the time on their parking meters. The Chamber of Commerce even has a "Pay Parking Ticket" form on its website!

Walking Tours

The **Niagara Historical Society** offers one-hour walking tours of Niagara-on-the-Lake (10 A.M. Thurs.–Sat. and 2 P.M. Sun. June–Aug., $5). The price includes admission to the Niagara Historical Society Museum, which makes the tour essentially free if you're going to the museum anyway.

Old Town Tours (289/292-3532 or 888/492-3532, www.oldtowntours.ca, 10:30 A.M. and 4 P.M. daily June–Oct., adults $20, kids 7–12

$10) runs 90-minute walking tours through the town's historic district. This tour also includes admission to the Niagara Historical Society Museum, as well as an ice wine tasting.

Winery Tours

If you want to leave the driving to someone else (a good idea if you're drinking), you can choose from a number of winery day tours. Or you can combine cycling and wine touring. Look into the following tour options:

- **Crush on Niagara Wine Tours** (905/562-3373 or 866/408-9463, www.crushtours.com, $69–99)
- **Grape Escape Wine Tours** (905/468-9959 or 866/935-4445, www.tourniagarawineries.com, $59–129)
- **Niagara Getaway Wine Tours** (905/933-4384, www.niagaragetaways.com, $59–129)
- **Niagara Wine Tours International** (800/680-7006, www.niagaraworldwine-tours.com, $65–120)

The Twenty Valley

The Twenty Valley lies in the north-central section of the Niagara Peninsula, west of Niagara Falls and Niagara-on-the-Lake. This wine region is centered around the towns of Beamsville, Vineland, and Jordan, yet it is close enough to Toronto, Niagara Falls, and Niagara-on-the-Lake for a day trip of wine touring. Alternatively, you could make the valley your destination for a getaway weekend.

◖ TWENTY VALLEY WINERIES

At last count, the Twenty Valley had close to 40 wineries, and new ones crop up regularly. The peak season for wine touring is during the fall harvest, generally mid-September through early October. If you're interested in seeing wine production at its full capacity, be sure to visit during this busy time. Summer (particularly July and August) is popular, too, with the vineyards full

The Good Earth Food and Wine Co. also runs a cooking school.

© CAROLYN B. HELLER

and lush and the weather hot. Most wineries remain open year-round, though many reduce their hours from November through April.

Most wineries charge a small fee ($2–5) for tastings, which may be credited toward any wine purchases. Larger wineries typically offer regular tours, while smaller facilities may offer them only by appointment or not at all.

Beamsville

Owner Nicolette Novak grew up on the property that now houses **The Good Earth Food and Wine Co.** (4556 Lincoln Ave., 905/563-6333, www.goodearthfoodandwine.com, winery 11 A.M.–5:30 P.M. daily, restaurant 11 A.M.–3:30 P.M. daily). She and her staff run a small winery, making Riesling, rosé, cabernet franc, and pinot noir, which Novak describes as "good for food"; you can sample these for yourself in their tasting room. Stop into the seasonal "pantry shed" to buy snacks, jams, house-smoked bacon, and other gourmet goodies, or sit down for lunch in their dining room. They also run a recreational **cooking school,** offering three-hour cooking classes ($135) that might focus on local ingredients like summer peaches or techniques like how to grill.

The striking wood-and-stone building that houses the family-owned **Fielding Estate Winery** (4020 Locust Ln., 905/563-0668 or 888/778-7758, www.fieldingwines.com, tastings 10:30 A.M.–6 P.M. daily May–Oct., 10:30 A.M.–5:30 P.M. Nov.–Apr.; tours daily 10:30 A.M., 1:30 P.M., and 3:30 P.M. May–Oct.) overlooks the fields and vineyards, a particularly lovely setting for wine-tasting. The winery is known for aromatic whites, especially Riesling and pinot gris, all made in small batches.

THE NIAGARA REGION

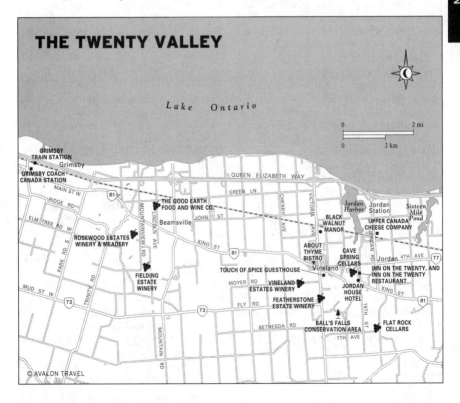

The beehives out back behind the **Rosewood Estates Winery and Meadery** (4352 Mountainview Rd., 905/563-4383 or 866/633-3248, www.rosewoodwine.com, tastings daily 11 A.M.–5:30 P.M. June–Oct., 11 A.M.–5 P.M. Thurs.–Mon. Oct.–May) provide raw materials for Niagara's first mead (honey wine), as well as several varieties of honey. They make wine, too, including pinot noir and Riesling. You can drop in for tastings, but to take a tour, call or email (rosewoodestateswinery@yahoo.com) in advance.

Vineland

Vineland Estates (3620 Moyer Rd., 905/562-7088 or 888/846-3526, www.vineland.com, 10 A.M.–6 P.M. daily May–Oct., 11 A.M.–5 P.M. daily Nov.–Apr.) released their first vintage back in 1983, which makes them an old-timer in these parts. Their signature wines are cabernet franc and Riesling, and they make a distinctive drink called "Vice," a blend of their Vidal ice wine and vodka; it's a one-pour ice wine martini.

You can sample their wines, ice wines, and Vice in their spacious tasting room. A small market upstairs sells cheeses and offers cheese tastings. Tours ($9) generally run daily at 11 A.M. and 3 P.M., but schedules can vary seasonally, so call to confirm. The Vineland Estates Winery Restaurant serves lunch and dinner, and the property has two guesthouses.

Not only are the grapes used at the **Featherstone Estate Winery** (3678 Victoria Ave., 905/562-1949, www.featherstonewinery.ca, 11 A.M.–5 P.M. Thurs.–Mon. Apr.–Dec.) grown without pesticides, the winery relies on sheep to graze in vineyards, as a natural way to prune the vines. The fleecy animals give their name to the Black Sheep Riesling; the winery also produces merlot, pinot noir, and cabernet franc, among others. You can sit on the veranda (11 A.M.–4 P.M. Thurs.–Mon. late May–early Sept., $10–14) for a light lunch, perhaps a cup of soup, a cheese platter, or a turkey sandwich, and a glass of wine, of course.

Jordan

Think wine-tasting can be staid, even snooty?

Then stop into laid-back **Flat Rock Cellars** (2727 Seventh Ave., 905/562-8994, www.flatrockcellars.com, 10 A.M.–6 P.M. Mon.–Sat., 11 A.M.–6 P.M. Sun. Apr.–Dec.; 10 A.M.–5 P.M. Mon.–Fri., 10 A.M.–6 P.M. Sat., 11 A.M.–6 P.M. Sun. Jan.–Mar.) where you can tour the vineyards and cellars, learn about their "gravity flow" production process, and sample their wines, which include Riesling, chardonnay, and pinot noir. If you ever dream of making your own wine, take a walk **In the Winemaker's Boots,** a series of hands-on workshops where you might study tasting, wine blending, or old-fashioned grape stomping. Sessions range from two hours to a full day.

The winery building at **Cave Spring Cellars** (3836 Main St., Jordan, www.cavespringcellars.com, 905/562-3581 or 888/806-9910, tastings daily 10 A.M.–6 P.M. June; 10 A.M.–6 P.M. Mon.–Fri., 10 A.M.–7 P.M. Sat.–Sun. July–Aug.; daily 10 A.M.–6 P.M. Sept.–Oct.; 10 A.M.–5 P.M. Sun.–Thurs., 10 A.M.–6 P.M. Fri.–Sat. Oct.–May; tours daily 3 P.M. June–Sept., 3 P.M. Fri.–Sun. Oct.–May), in Jordan Village, was built in 1871 and houses Ontario's oldest functioning wine cellar. The current winery, founded in 1986, specializes in Riesling, including ice wines, and also makes well-regarded pinot noir.

BALL'S FALLS CONSERVATION AREA

The Twenty Valley isn't entirely about wine touring. Beyond the wineries are several conservation areas where you can go hiking, and the rolling hills make pleasant cycling.

Billing itself as "Niagara's Other Falls," the Ball's Falls Conservation Area (3292 Sixth Ave., Jordan, 905/562-5235, www.npca.ca, grounds daily 8 A.M.–8 P.M. May–Oct., 8 A.M.–4:30 P.M. Nov.–Apr., adults $5.75, seniors and students $4.25) has 10 kilometers (6.2 miles) of hiking trails, including routes that lead to two waterfalls: the 27-meter-tall (90-foot) Lower Falls, and the 11-meter-tall (35-foot) Upper Falls. The falls run strongest in the spring, and the grounds are a pretty spot for a picnic.

In a modern, environmentally sensitive building, the **Ball's Falls Centre for**

Conservation (9 A.M.–4 P.M. daily) has exhibits about the plants and animals that live in the region. Also on the site is a collection of **heritage buildings** (10 A.M.–4 P.M. daily late May–early Sept., 10 A.M.–4 P.M. Sun.–Thurs. early Sept.–Oct.), including a flour mill, church, and blacksmith shop, as well as the home that belonged to the Ball family, who settled here in 1807. Guides take you around the buildings and demonstrate milling, weaving, and other 19th-century skills.

SHOPPING

Jordan Village (www.jordanvillage.com) has a small collection of boutiques and galleries, clustered near the Inn on the Twenty and the Cave Spring Winery. **Ninavik Native Arts** (3845 Main St., Jordan, 905/562-8888 or 800/646-2848, www.ninavik.com, 10 A.M.–6 P.M. daily) shows works by Canadian aboriginal artists, while the **Jordan Art Gallery** (3845 Main St., Jordan, 905/562-6680, www.jordanartgallery.com, 10 A.M.–5 P.M. Sun.–Thurs., 10 A.M.–6 P.M. Fri.–Sat. late May–mid-Oct.; call for off-season hours) exhibits contemporary works, including paintings, prints, sculpture, drawings, and photography, primarily by Niagara artists.

ACCOMMODATIONS
Vineland

Though the home that houses the **Black Walnut Manor** (4255 Victoria Ave., 905/562-8675 or 800/859-4786, www.blackwalnut-manor.com, $175–210 d) was built in 1911, this smart-casual B&B is as far from Victorian kitsch as chardonnay is from Coca-Cola. The three second-floor bedrooms have polished oak floors, soothing pastel walls, and modern furnishings—no knickknacks here—while the airy attic loft suite (available May–Nov. only) has lots of sunny nooks under the sloped ceilings. Guests settle into the leather chairs around the glass-topped table for family-style breakfasts, and they can lounge by the living room fireplace or out by the pool. A bit of daytime traffic noise—the house is set back from a busy road—is the only minor blemish on the otherwise smooth Black Walnut.

From the outside, it's your basic ranch house. Inside the **Touch of Spice Guesthouse** (3849 Victoria Ave., 905/562-0319, www.touchofspiceguesthouse.com, mid-Mar.–mid-Jan., $199 d), things get decidedly spicier. Owners Jason and Gord have redone their suburban pad into a stylish sanctuary that starts with a wine and cheese welcome for their guests, continues out in the hot tub overlooking the garden, and wraps up over the breakfast table with poached eggs with fresh asparagus or homemade scones. When you're ready to settle down for the night, choose either the Zinfandel room, with lime green linens and black painted furniture, overlooking the back garden, or the Cabernet Sauvignon room, with an ornately carved bed frame and deep brown and red bedding; you can blend the cab sauv with the adjacent mocha-toned Merlot room (for an additional $135) to make a two-room suite that shares the bath.

At the entrance to the **Vineland Estates Winery** (3620 Moyer Rd., 905/562-7088 or 888/846-3526, www.vineland.com) are two self-contained lodgings. The cozy one-bedroom B&B Cottage ($175 d) is designed for an escape à deux. The staff provide a complimentary bottle of wine and provisions for a make-your-own breakfast, but you might not see another soul during your stay. The larger Estate Guesthouse ($295/night) looks like a suburban home and can accommodate a family or group of friends. It has three bedrooms, a living room, and kitchen facilities; breakfast provisions and a bottle of wine are included here, too.

Jordan

Owned by the proprietors of Cave Spring Cellars and the more posh Inn on the Twenty, the **Jordan House Hotel** (3751 Main St., 905/562-9591 or 800/701-8074, www.jordan-house.ca, $129–199) is an excellent choice for moderately priced wine-country accommodations. It's an upscale two-story motel attached to a historic tavern, with contemporary chocolate brown and royal blue linens, flat-screen TVs, coffeemakers, and simple but functional bathrooms. Expect no frills, done well.

Looking for a romantic wine-country escape? The **❤ Inn on the Twenty** (3845 Main St., 905/562-5336 or 800/701-8074, www.innonthetwenty.com, $239–369 d) has the region's most deluxe accommodations, staffed by an attentive team. The 27 spacious rooms (the smallest measure more than 500 square feet) are all different, furnished with a mix of antiques and contemporary pieces; some have a separate sitting area and sleeping alcove, some have private terraces, while others are two-level lofts, with a living room and upstairs bedroom. Most have fireplaces and whirlpool tubs. The spa, in an adjacent 1840s building, offers massage, facials, reflexology, and other services.

FOOD
Beamsville

A salad of local vegetables. A cheese platter with Canadian cheeses, fresh-baked breads, and house-made jams. A charcuterie board with locally cured meats. And a sandwich of the day. That's the simple, fresh fare on offer at the **Good Earth Food and Wine Company** (4556 Lincoln Ave., 905/563-6333, www.goodearthfoodandwine.com, 11 A.M.–3:30 P.M. daily, $14–15), where you can lunch on the patio overlooking the vineyards (or inside the dining room during the colder months). If you prefer lunch to go, order a "Moveable Feast" picnic hamper for two (available Wed.–Sun. late May–early Sept. and Fri.–Sun. early Sept.–mid-Oct., $80), with your choice of main dish, along with cheeses, bread, grilled vegetables, salad, fresh fruit, dessert, and a bottle of wine. Place your order online at least 48 hours in advance.

Vineland

You can buy a bottle of wine from a local winery to enjoy with your meal at the **About Thyme Bistro** (3457 King St., 905/562-3457, www.aboutthymebistro.com, 11 A.M.–3 P.M. and 5–9 P.M. Wed.–Sat., 5–9 P.M. Sun., lunch $12–19, dinner $30–39), or choose a Niagara wine from their extensive local list. Either way, pair your vino with a midday choice that might range from an asparagus omelet to a pulled pork sandwich to a confit duck leg with spiced

blueberry ketchup, while in the evening, the fixed-price menu starts with a soup or salad, moves on to mains like grilled Cornish hen with herb spaetzle, fresh trout with sautéed lentils, or a New York strip steak with mushroom poutine, before wrapping up with a crème brulée or a mixed-berry crumble.

Set in a former farmhouse overlooking the vineyards, **Vineland Estates Winery Restaurant** (3620 Moyer Rd., 905/562-7088 or 888/846-3526, www.vineland.com, 11:30 A.M.–2:30 P.M. and 5 P.M.–close daily May–Dec.; 11:30 A.M.–2:30 P.M. and 5 P.M.–close Wed.–Sun. Jan.–Apr., lunch $16–24, dinner $22–34) serves contemporary wine-country fare, including local products where possible, at both lunch and dinner. At midday, you might choose from a "Vintner's Platter" of pâté, cured meats, smoked salmon, cheeses, and pickled vegetables; a hearty bouillabaisse; or a roasted pork loin sandwich with tomato chutney. For dinner? Perhaps rainbow trout with wilted greens and warm bacon vinaigrette, venison with foie gras–infused potato hash, or prosciutto-crusted chicken paired with fiddleheads in brown butter. You could also opt for a five-course tasting menu ($75), with several wine pairing options starting at $35.

Jordan

Need some cheese for your wine-country picnic? Visit the **Upper Canada Cheese Company** (4159 Jordan Rd., 905/562-9730, www.uppercanadacheesecompany.com, 10 A.M.–5 P.M. Sun.–Thurs., 10 A.M.–6 P.M. Fri.–Sat.), which produces several cheeses, including the Camembert-style Comfort Cream and the semi-soft Niagara Gold, from the milk of local Guernsey cows.

The Flat Rock Cellars winery doesn't have a restaurant, but on weekends, **el gastrónomo vagabundo** (www.elgastro.com, 3–6 P.M. Fri., noon–7 P.M. Sat., noon–6 P.M. Sun., $5.50–6), a mobile food truck, ensures you won't go hungry. The eclectic, changing menu includes gourmet tacos, salads, and dishes with Southeast Asian flavors; the roving gastronomes might dish up barbecued pork buns, green papaya salad, or tacos piled high with sweet potato tempura. The truck also pulls into St. Catharines (Market Square, 91 King St., 10 A.M.–2 P.M. Thurs.) once a week.

After a hard day of wine touring, maybe you just want to kick back with a burger and a beer. Then the **Jordan House Tavern** (3751 Main St., 905/562-9591, www.jordanhouse.ca, 11:30 A.M.–9:30 P.M. Sun.–Thurs., 11:30 A.M.–10:30 P.M. Fri.–Sat., $8–15) is your joint. In the homey, high-ceilinged room with a stone fireplace and timbers from the original 1840s saloon that stood on this site, the unfussy but well-executed menu includes straightforward sandwiches, salads, and bar snacks, like the "train wreck fries" layered with ground beef, jack cheese, jalapeños, salsa, and sour cream. The star attractions are the hearty burgers; for a flavorful variation on the patty theme, try the curried lamb burger with green tomato chutney.

The formal, white-tablecloth **Inn on the Twenty Restaurant** (3836 Main St., 905/562-7313, www.innonthetwenty.com, 11:30 A.M.–3 P.M. and 5–9 P.M. daily, lunch $14–21, dinner $24–38), with a wall of windows looking across the forests and fields, is a special-occasion spot. An early adopter of the Niagara regional food movement, the kitchen creates contemporary cuisine that draws on local products. At lunch, you might try the pissaladière (a puff-pastry tart topped with goat cheese, tomato, olives, and caramelized onions), linguini with mushroom ragout, or veal scaloppine. In the evening, starters might include caramelized black cod with asparagus tempura or grilled quail served with foie gras and ginger-rhubarb confit, while mains could range from wild trout paired with sautéed fiddleheads or a pork platter with roast loin, braised shoulder, and a fried pork-filled dumpling. The wine list includes labels from Cave Springs Cellars (under the same ownership), as well as other Ontario producers.

INFORMATION AND SERVICES

For information about the Twenty Valley region, contact the **Twenty Valley Tourism Association** (3720 19th St., Unit 1, Jordan, 905/562-3636, www.twentyvalley.ca). The **Wine Council of Ontario** (4890 Victoria Ave. N., Vineland, 905/562-8070 ext. 221, www.wines ofontario.org) can provide more details about the area wineries.

GETTING THERE AND AROUND

To explore the Twenty Valley, you'll either need to have a car or arrange for a tour. Cycling is another option, although it's hilly terrain.

By Train or Bus

For rail service to the Twenty Valley, the closest **VIA Rail** (888/842-7245, www.viarail.ca) stations are in Grimsby (99 Ontario St.) or St. Catharines (5 Great Western St.).

Coach Canada (www.coachcanada.com) runs frequent buses from Toronto to Grimsby (36 Main St. W., 1 hour, one-way adults $15, seniors $8.50, students $10.50, kids 2–11 $7.50) and St. Catharines (70 Carlisle St., 1.25–1.5 hours, one-way adults $19.80, seniors $10, students $12.90, kids 2–11 $9.90).

By Car

Highway 81 is the main east–west route across the Twenty Valley. It runs between Grimsby and St. Catharines. From Toronto, take the QEW south toward the Niagara Peninsula. It's 95 kilometers (59 miles) to Beamsville (exit 64, Ontario St.), 100 kilometers (62 miles) to Vineland (exit 57, Victoria Ave.), and 102 kilometers (64 miles) to Jordan (exit 55, Jordan Rd./Hwy. 26).

From Niagara Falls, the simplest route is to take the QEW north. To Jordan it's 34 kilometers (21 miles), to Vineland 36 kilometers (22 miles), and to Beamsville 41 kilometers (25 miles).

Winery Tours

For tours that stop at several Twenty Valley wineries, or for cycling tours through wine country, contact the following tour operators:

• **Crush on Niagara Wine Tours** (905/562-3373 or 866/408-9463, www.crushtours.com, $69–99)

- **Grape Escape Wine Tours** (905/468-9959 or 866/935-4445, www.tourniagarawineries. com, $134–159)
- **Niagara Wine Tours International** (800/680-7006, www.niagaraworldwine-tours.com, $75–120)

If you'd like to relax with a yoga class before setting out on a wine tour, check out **Yoga in the Vineyard** (647/454-9642, www.yogainthevine-yard.ca), which offers packages in partnership with several area wineries that include yoga, tastings, winery tours, and an optional meal.

St. Catharines and the Welland Canal

The Great Lakes are part of an extensive shipping route that extends from Lake Superior all the way to the Atlantic Ocean. But until the 1800s, a significant natural obstruction—Niagara Falls—blocked the passage between Lake Ontario and Lake Erie. William Hamilton Merritt (1793–1862), a St. Catharines entrepreneur, proposed the idea of a canal across the Niagara Peninsula, connecting the two lakes. He began raising money, and in 1824, construction began on the first Welland Canal.

Building the canal involved finding a way for ships to "climb the mountain," otherwise known as the Niagara Escarpment, since Lake Erie is roughly 100 meters (326 feet) higher in elevation than Lake Ontario. The solution was a series of locks that lift up ships traveling south through the canal and let them descend the same distance when they journey from Lake Erie to Lake Ontario.

After the first Welland Canal opened in 1829, it was rebuilt three times, refining the route and improving the lock technology. The current, fourth canal opened in 1932.

At 43.5 kilometers (27 miles), the Welland Canal is about half the length of the Panama Canal. On the Lake Ontario side, the canal starts in St. Catharines, the peninsula's largest city. It heads south through Thorold and Welland before reaching the town of Port Colborne, where it meets Lake Erie on the Niagara Peninsula's south shore. Ships transit the canal between April and December. It takes roughly 9–10 hours for a boat to make the journey between the two lakes.

SIGHTS

You can bicycle the entire length of the Welland Canal if you follow the **Welland Canals Trail** (www.welland.ca), a 42-kilometer (27-mile) cycling path that runs from St. Catharines to Port Colborne.

St. Catharines Museum at Lock 3

The exhibits in the well-designed St. Catharines Museum at Lock 3 (1932 Welland Canals Pkwy., St. Catharines, 905/984-8880 or 800/305-5134, www.stcatharines.ca, 9 A.M.–5 P.M. daily May–Nov.; 9 A.M.–5 P.M. Mon.–Fri., 10 A.M.–5 P.M. Sat.–Sun. Dec.–Apr., suggested donation $4) illustrate the history of the Welland Canal and the St. Catharines area. One section of the museum houses the **Ontario Lacrosse Hall of Fame,** devoted to Canada's official summer sport (the official winter sport is hockey). Behind the museum, you can climb up to the **viewing platform** to watch the massive ships pass through the locks.

Port Colborne Historical and Marine Museum

The Port Colborne Historical and Marine Museum (280 King St., 905/834-7604, www. portcolborne.ca, noon–5 P.M. daily May–Dec., free) is a complex of several historic buildings, including an 1835 log schoolhouse (one of the region's oldest), an 1880s blacksmith shop, and a Victorian-era home that now houses **Arabella's Tea Room** (2–4 P.M.), which serves homemade biscuits and jam to visitors. Also on the property is the 1901 **Neff Steam Buggy,**

© CAROLYN B. HELLER

a ship passing through the locks on the Welland Canal, Port Colborne

thought to be the oldest surviving Ontario-made automobile.

ACCOMMODATIONS

Sit on your balcony at the **Inn at Lock Seven** (24 Chapel St. S., Thorold, 905/227-6177 or 877/465-6257, www.innatlock7.com, mid-Mar.–mid-Dec., $105–125 d) and watch the ships travel through the Welland Canal; if you were any closer, you'd be in the canal yourself. Though this modest motel looks right out of the 1960s, with floral bedspreads and pink bathroom tiles, owners Ed and Patty will give you a warm welcome and lots of tips about the canal and the region overall. They've done updates where it counts, too; the building is well maintained, the beds are firm, and there's free Wi-Fi. The location is convenient for cyclists, just off the Welland Canals Trail.

Owner Gloria Simon, an interior decorator who relocated to Port Colborne from Toronto, has done extensive renovations on the 1904 farmhouse that now serves as the comfortable **Lakebreeze B&B** (234 Steele St., Port Colborne, 905/834-1233 or 877/834-1233, www.lakebreezeniagara.com, $120–140 d, $200 2-br suite). She's created three large, eclectically furnished suites, each with their own keyless private entrance, Wi-Fi, and central air-conditioning. An enthusiastic booster for Niagara's south shore, she's happy to suggest things to see and do nearby (and she cooks a fine breakfast, too). The house is a short walk to the Lake Erie shore, the town center, or the Welland Canal.

FOOD

Searching for enlightenment, or at least dinner, from the far corners of the globe, **The Smokin' Buddha** (265 King St., Port Colborne, 905/834-6000, www.thesmokinbuddha.com, 11:30 A.M.–10 P.M. Wed.–Sat., $9–15) cooks up round-the-world small plates, curries, and noodles that take inspiration from Asia, Latin America, India, and the Middle East. Try the Japanese-style "sobo pockets," sweet tofu stuffed with smoked salmon, sprouts, rice, and wasabi mayo, or go global with Korean beef noodles, Thai curries, or chicken enchiladas. The location in the town's old train station, with exposed brick walls and wooden benches, puts you in the mood for your journey.

Stop in for a beer or a bite at the friendly **Canalside Pub and Eatery** (232 West St., Port Colborne, 905/834-6090, www.canalside. ca, lunch and dinner daily, $8–22) facing the Welland Canal. They carry a long list of brews from Canada and abroad, including their own "Lock 8 Lager," and the crowd-pleasing menu runs from burgers and sandwiches to pastas, seafood, and steaks. Save room for a hefty slab of freshly baked carrot cake. There's live music most Friday nights.

@27 Restaurant (27 Main St., Port Colborne, 905/835-2700, www.attwentyseven. com, lunch Tues.–Fri., dinner Tues.–Sat., lunch $10–16, dinner $18–29), the area's most upscale dining room, occupies a bright yellow house near Lock 8. The updated surf 'n' turf fare includes steaks, ribs, grilled fish, and pastas. Try the rack of lamb with a pistachio crust and a date-honey dipping sauce. For lighter bites, order tapas ($7–12) in the lounge.

INFORMATION AND SERVICES

The **St. Catharines Tourism Information Centre** (1932 Welland Canals Pkwy., St. Catharines, 800/305-5134, www.tourism stcatharines.ca), inside the St. Catharines

Museum at Lock 3, has information about the Welland Canal and surrounding region. **Thorold Tourism** (50 Chapel St., Thorold, 905/680-9477 or 888/680-9477, www.thorold-tourism.ca) has a year-round information office inside the Lock 7 Viewing Complex.

For information about Port Colborne and the Niagara Peninsula's south shore, contact the **Port Colborne Visitor Information Centre** (76 Main St. W., Humberstone Hall, Port Colborne, 905/834-5722 or 888/767-8386, www.experienceportcolborne.com, mid-May–mid-Oct.). You can also get visitor information year-round at the **Port Colborne City Hall** (66 Charlotte St., 905/834-1668 or 888/767-8386, www.portcolborne.ca, 8:30 A.M.–4:30 P.M. Mon.–Fri.).

GETTING THERE AND AROUND

Unless you're planning to bicycle around the Welland Canal region, you really need a car, as public transit is limited. **VIA Rail** (888/842-7245, www.viarail.ca) trains run to St. Catharines (5 Great Western St.), where you could rent a car to continue your explorations, or head off on your bike.

If you're going only to Port Colborne, taking the bus is an option. **Coach Canada** (www.coachcanada.com) runs two daily buses from Toronto to Port Colborne (King St., at Clarence St., 800/461-7661, 2.25–2.5 hours, one-way adults $26, seniors $15, students $19, kids 2–11 $13). Once you're in Port Colborne, you can easily walk around town.

LAKE ERIE TO LAKE HURON

Bounded by two of the Great Lakes, the triangle of Ontario stretching west from Toronto includes arty university towns, great theater, traditional Mennonite communities, African-Canadian historical sights, a wine district, and plenty of lakeside beaches and parks. Most are close enough to Toronto for a weekend getaway.

Midway between Toronto and Niagara Falls, the gritty steel town of Hamilton has gradually reinvented itself, and its cool arts and shopping districts and worthwhile museums can easily occupy a day or more.

Farther west are the twin towns of Kitchener-Waterloo, where high tech is rebuilding this formerly industrial region and launching a fledgling arts scene. As Kitchener-Waterloo embraces technology, nearby St. Jacobs and the surrounding farm country are home to Mennonite communities that hold fast to their traditional ways.

Theatergoers make regular pilgrimages to Stratford for the Shakespeare Festival with doses of both the Bard, as well as more contemporary playwrights. Like its British namesake (yes, it's on the River Avon), the town also has a large collection of high-end restaurants and browse-worthy shops.

Southwest of Stratford, the city of London is considerably smaller than its UK counterpart. However, it is Canada's 10th largest metropolitan area, and its large student population has given rise to culture, shops, and pubs.

Many towns in Southwestern Ontario were the last stop on the Underground Railroad, the network of safe houses that sheltered slaves

HIGHLIGHTS

LOOK FOR ◖ TO FIND RECOMMENDED
SIGHTS, ACTIVITIES, DINING, AND LODGING.

◖ **St. Jacobs:** This small town outside Kitchener-Waterloo is a base for learning more about the region's traditional Mennonite community. You'll see farmers driving horse-drawn buggies, and you can purchase homemade jams, produce, quilts, and other hand-crafted items from Mennonite families (page 153).

◖ **Stratford Shakespeare Festival:** North America's largest classical repertory theater has been producing plays by the Bard and other, more contemporary playwrights since 1953. The festival runs annually from April through October (page 158).

◖ **Buxton National Historic Site and Museum:** This museum and its adjacent historic buildings recount the fascinating story of the Buxton Settlement which became the largest 19th-century African-Canadian community in Canada (page 175).

◖ **Point Pelee National Park:** On a spit of land jutting into Lake Erie, the most southern tip of Canada's mainland is a major stopover point for migrating birds, particularly in spring. In autumn, monarch butterflies pass through the area (page 176).

◖ **Pelee Island:** A peaceful getaway for a day, a week, or more, this rocky island in Lake Erie is the southernmost point in Canada. Bring your bike (or rent one on the island); it's a good spot for cycling (page 178).

◖ **John Freeman Walls Historic Site and Underground Railroad Museum:** Built and operated by the descendents of fu-

gitive slaves, this open-air museum illustrates the arduous journey north on the Underground Railroad to freedom in Canada (page 186).

◖ **The Pinery Provincial Park:** The 10-kilometer (six-mile) powdery sand beach at this popular park is one of the loveliest on the Lake Huron shore (page 190).

escaping plantations in the American South. Sights from that era stretch from Windsor, Sandwich, Amherstburg, Chatham, Dresden, and Buxton, and a tour here can dramatically illustrate this history.

Along Lake Erie's shores you can tour an emerging wine district, visit the southernmost point on the Canadian mainland, or hop the ferry to laid-back Pelee Island. On the other side of this region, the Lake Huron shoreline

is lined with beachfront vacation towns and plenty of places to unwind, sit by the shore, and watch the sun set.

PLANNING YOUR TIME

Hamilton, Kitchener-Waterloo, and Stratford are all an easy day trip from Toronto. For a weekend getaway, tour the historic sites and wineries of Southwestern Ontario, or hang out in one of the Lake Huron beach towns.

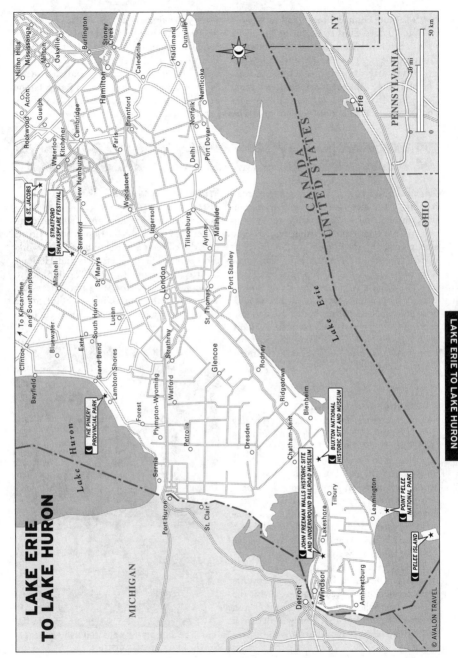

LAKE ERIE
TO LAKE HURON

LAKE ERIE TO LAKE HURON

© AVALON TRAVEL

For a more complete tour, plan to spend a week to 10 days. Start by exploring the museums in Kitchener-Waterloo and the Mennonite communities around **St. Jacobs.** Allow another day to visit Stratford and see at least one play at the **Shakespeare Festival.** From Stratford, drive to Lake Huron and spend a couple of days relaxing in **Bayfield** or at **The Pinery Provincial Park.** Stop off in London or St. Marys as you make your way southwest toward Chatham and Windsor. Visit the African-Canadian heritage sights around Chatham, wine-tour in Amherstburg, and sightsee in Windsor. You can head over to **Pelee Island** for a day, but it's a nice place to cycle, walk, or just unwind if you have more time.

Hamilton and Vicinity

Canada's ninth-largest city, Hamilton hitched its star to the steel industry, and when you pass through town along certain routes, you can still see the smoke-belching legacy of the steel plants. Yet gritty Hamilton, midway between Toronto and Niagara Falls, has a new arty, edgy side. Artists are opening studios in its brick storefronts, young families are finding the city more affordable than nearby Toronto, and funky shops are luring both locals and visitors. In fact, the motto of one local art store is "Art is the New Steel." Hamilton may not have the world's prettiest face, but it's definitely worth a second look.

SIGHTS
Art Gallery of Hamilton

Surprise: Ontario's third-largest public art gallery is in Hamilton. The Art Gallery of Hamilton (123 King St. W., 905/527-6610, www.artgalleryofhamilton.com, noon–7 P.M. Tues.–Wed., noon–9 P.M. Thurs.–Fri., noon–5 P.M. Sat.–Sun.) has a wide-ranging collection, emphasizing 19th-century European and Canadian historical works, African sculpture, and contemporary art from Canada and abroad. Every Sunday at 2 P.M. you can take a free tour of some aspect of the gallery's collection.

The art gallery has an unusual admission structure. The "Level Two Gallery" upstairs is always free, but there's a charge to visit the "Level One Gallery" (adults $10, seniors and students $8, kids 6–17 $4, family $25); on the first Friday of every month, admission is free 5–9 P.M.

Workers Arts and Heritage Centre

Since industry was such an important component of Hamilton's development, it's fitting that the city has a museum devoted to working people. The Workers Arts and Heritage Centre (51 Stuart St., 905/522-3003, www.wahc-museum.ca, 10 A.M.–4 P.M. Tues.–Sat., admission by donation), in the 1860 Custom House, has changing exhibits that might focus

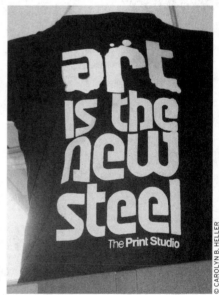

Hamilton's formerly industrial James Street North is now an arts district.

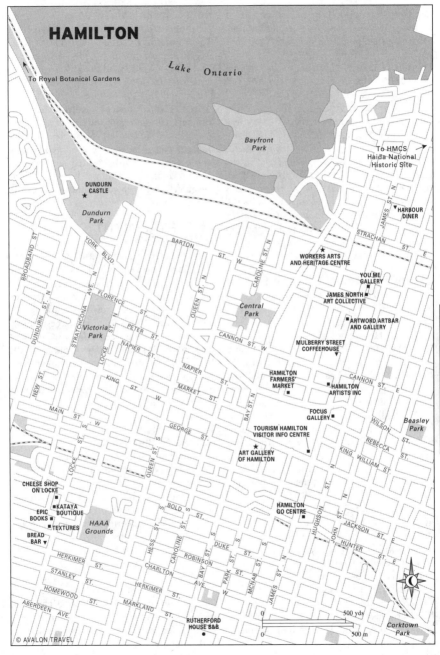

HAMILTON

Lake Ontario

To Royal Botanical Gardens

Bayfront Park

DUNDURN CASTLE ★

Dundurn Park

To HMCS Haida National Historic Site

HARBOUR DINER ▼

BROADBAND ST.

YORK BLVD.

BARTON ST. W

CAROLINE ST. N

JAMES ST. N

STRACHAN ST.

STRACHAN ST. E

WORKERS ARTS AND HERITAGE CENTRE ★

YOU ME GALLERY ■

JAMES NORTH ART COLLECTIVE ■

ARTWORD ARTBAR AND GALLERY ■

MULBERRY STREET COFFEEHOUSE ▼

Central Park

CANNON ST. W

CANNON ST. E

FLORENCE ST.

STRATHCONA AVE. N

DUNDURN ST. N

Victoria Park

LOCKE ST.

PETER ST.

NAPIER ST.

NAPIER ST.

QUEEN ST. N

BAY ST. N

HAMILTON FARMERS' MARKET ■

HAMILTON ARTISTS INC ■

FOCUS GALLERY ■

NEW ST.

KING ST.

MARKET ST.

WILSON ST.

Beasley Park

REBECCA ST.

MAIN ST. S

GEORGE ST.

KING WILLIAM ST.

TOURISM HAMILTON VISITOR INFO CENTRE

LOCKE ST. S

QUEEN ST. S

ART GALLERY OF HAMILTON ★

CHEESE SHOP ON LOCKE ■

KATAYA BOUTIQUE ■

EPIC BOOKS ■

TEXTURES ■

BREAD BAR ▼

HAAA Grounds

BOLD ST.

HESS ST. S

CAROLINE ST. S

DUKE ST.

BAY ST. S

PARK ST. S

HAMILTON GO CENTRE ■

HUGHSON ST. N

JOHN ST. N

JACKSON ST. E

HUNTER ST. E

HERKIMER ST.

STANLEY ST.

CHARLTON AVE.

ROBINSON ST.

HERKIMER ST.

MCNAB ST. W

JAMES ST.

HOMEWOOD ST.

ABERDEEN AVE.

MARKLAND ST.

RUTHERFORD HOUSE B&B ●

Corktown Park

0   500 yds

0   500 m

© AVALON TRAVEL

on Hamilton's steel industry, labor protests, or a history of office work. And yes, it's far more absorbing than punching the clock.

HMCS *Haida* National Historic Site

The HMCS *Haida* (Pier 9, 658 Catharine St., 905/526-6742, www.pc.gc.ca, 10 A.M.–5 P.M. daily mid-May–June, 10 A.M.–7 P.M. July–early Sept., 10 A.M.–5 P.M. Wed.–Sun. early Sept.–mid-Oct., adults $3.90, seniors $3.40, kids 6–16 $1.90, family $9.80) served in the Canadian navy from World War II until 1963. It was one of 27 "Tribal Class" destroyers built for Britain, Australia, and Canada, and it's the only one that remains (13 were sunk, and 13 more were scrapped). Clamber around the ship and learn something about its operation, the Canadian navy, and history in the process.

Dundurn National Historic Site

Hamilton's **Dundurn Castle** (610 York Blvd., 905/546-2872, www.hamilton.ca, 10 A.M.–4 P.M. daily July–early Sept., noon–4 P.M. Tues.–Sun. early Sept.–June; adults $11, seniors and students 13–17 $9, kids 6–12 $5.50, family $27) has a connection to the contemporary British royals. Camilla, Duchess of Cornwall (the second wife of Charles, Prince of Wales), is the great-great-great-granddaughter of Sir Allan Napier MacNab (1798–1862) and his wife Mary, who built and lived in this stately mansion with their daughters, Sophia and Minnie. A lawyer, entrepreneur, and politician, MacNab served as premier of the United Province of Canada (the pre-Confederation union of what would become the provinces of Ontario and Quebec).

Completed in 1835, the home has more than 40 rooms restored to the Victorian era, from the grand public spaces to the modest servants quarters (the family had eight live-in servants). Visits to the house are by guided tour only; tours run about one hour.

To learn more about life in the castle, read *The Diary of Sophia MacNab,* which the older MacNab daughter wrote when she was 13 (the year her mother passed away). It's available in the gift shop.

Royal Botanical Gardens

An antidote to Hamilton's industrial side, the Royal Botanical Gardens (680 Plains Road W., Burlington, 905/527-1158, www.rbg.ca, 10 A.M.–8 P.M. daily, adults $13, seniors and students $10, kids 5–12 $7.50, family $33.50) has more than 1,100 hectares (2,700 acres) of flowers, plants, and trees, and more than 30 kilometers (19 miles) of walking trails. There are roses and magnolia, cherry trees and tulips, and one of the most extensive collections of lilacs in the world. Located northwest of downtown on the Hamilton–Burlington line, the gardens are open year-round; some exhibits are indoors.

ENTERTAINMENT AND EVENTS

The **Artword Artbar and Gallery** (15 Colbourne St., at James St. N., www.artword.net, from 6 P.M. Tues.–Sat. with events from 7:30 or 8 P.M.) is part art gallery and part club, with live blues, jazz, and roots music several nights a week. North America's largest aboriginal arts event, the weekend-long **Canadian Aboriginal Festival** (Copps Coliseum, 101 York Blvd., 519/751-0040, www.canab.com, Nov.) includes a powwow, music and dance performances, an arts and crafts market, and traditional foods.

SHOPPING
James Street North

Just north of downtown, the area now known as the James Street North Gallery District (www.jamesstreetnorth.ca) is an emerging arts community. It's still a bit rough around the edges, but that's what gives it a pleasantly edgy feel. Most galleries keep somewhat limited hours—they're generally open afternoons Wednesday through Saturday—but you can easily spend a couple of hours wandering and browsing.

The liveliest time to explore James Street North is during the monthly **ArtCrawl,** the second Friday of every month, when most of the galleries are open and more people are out and about.

Some galleries to look for include: **Focus Gallery** (66 James St. N., 905/218-9557, www.thefocusgallery.ca, noon–5 P.M. Wed.–Sat.), **Hamilton Artists Inc.** (161 James St. N., 905/529-3355, www.hamiltonartistsinc.on.ca), **James North Art Collective** (328 James St. N., 905/528-6437, www.jamesnorthartcollective.com, noon–5 P.M. Wed.–Sat., noon–4 P.M. Sun.), and **You Me Gallery** (330 James St. N., 905/523-7754, noon–5 P.M. Wed.–Sun.).

Locke Street

Hamilton's other up-and-coming shopping district is on Locke Street (www.lockestreet.com), with trendy boutiques, bookstores, and food shops. Check out **Kataya Boutique** (218 Locke St., 289/389-8264, www.kataya.ca, 10 A.M.–6 P.M. Mon.–Sat., 11 A.M.–5 P.M. Sun.) for locally designed clothing, **Epic Books** (226 Locke St. S., 905/525-6538, 10 A.M.–6 P.M. Tues.–Thurs., 10 A.M.–9 P.M. Fri., 10 A.M.–6 P.M. Sat., noon–4 P.M. Sun.), an independent bookstore, and **Textures** (236 Locke St. S., 905/523-0636, 11 A.M.–5 P.M. daily), a local artists' cooperative.

Nearly three-quarters of the products at the **Cheese Shop on Locke** (190 Locke St. S., 289/389-7000, www.cheeseshoppeonlocke.com, 10 A.M.–6 P.M. Mon.–Wed. and Sat., 10 A.M.–7 P.M. Thurs.–Fri. 11 A.M.–5 P.M. Sun.) are Canadian, so it's a good place to look for cheeses from Ontario and nearby Quebec, as well as other local gourmet products. They host regular wine and cheese pairings, cheese tastings, and other special events.

ACCOMMODATIONS

At **Rutherford House B&B** (293 Park St. S., 905/525-2422, www.rutherfordbb.com, $115 s, $120–140 d), owners David and Janis Topp have two well-decorated rooms for guests on the second floor of their 1880s brick home, conveniently located just a few blocks from downtown. The furnishings, in keeping with the period, are Victorian-influenced without feeling fussy, a mix of antiques and other pieces that Janis (an interior designer) has collected. Rates include a full breakfast served in the formal dining room, Wi-Fi, and parking.

The grand **◖ Osler House B&B** (30 South St. W., Dundas, 289/238-9278, www.oslerhouse.com, $150–175 d), well hidden in the trees in a residential neighborhood, feels like the sort of place you might have inherited— if your relations were at least minor royalty. Yet owners Gary Fincham (an industrial designer) and Sara Burnet-Smith (a physiotherapist) bought, designed, and furnished this 1848 Georgian-style home without the benefit of obvious royal relatives. The house clearly had good bones, with high ceilings, a grand staircase, and spacious rooms, but the owners added the oriental rugs, antiques, silver tea service, and capacious bathrooms with heated floors. Guests can settle in to the gracious parlor or the more casual billiards room, and the three upstairs guest rooms are all large, posh, and quiet. Breakfast is served in the formal dining room, with its Asian-style black and gold furnishings, and here, presentation matters: Gary might serve a cup of beautifully carved fresh fruit, a perfectly formed apricot scone with homemade jam, and a carefully rolled omelet. If you're worried that all this formality seems, well, too formal, don't be; your royal relations might have posh digs, but they'll be happy for you to put your feet up or even shoot some pool.

FOOD

More than 70 vendors sell produce, meat, and prepared foods at the year-round indoor **Hamilton Farmers' Market** (35 York Blvd., 905/546-2096, www.hamilton.ca, 7 A.M.–6 P.M. Tues. and Thurs., 8 A.M.–6 P.M. Fri., 6 A.M.–6 P.M. Sat.). Note the historic "Birks' Clock" in the center of the market that's more than five meters (17 feet) high.

When browsing the galleries on James Street North, stop for a coffee or a bite to eat at the hip **Mulberry Street Coffeehouse** (193 James St. N., 905/963-1365, 7 A.M.–10 P.M. Mon.–Sat., 8 A.M.–10 P.M. Sun.). Plenty of people park here with their laptops (there's free Wi-Fi), and the sandwiches and pastries are tasty.

© CAROLYN B. HELLER

one of the food trucks at the Hamilton Farmers' Market

Before James Street began to get trendy, there was the **Harbour Diner** (486 James St. N., 905/523-7373, www.harbourdiner.com, 8 A.M.–8 P.M. Tues.–Thurs., 8 A.M.–10 P.M. Fri.–Sat., 8 A.M.–3 P.M. Sun., lunch $6–9, dinner $8–22), a café that's both down-home and hip. It's popular for weekend brunch; besides your basic eggs and bacon, the comfort-food menu includes soups, sandwiches, and hearty dinners. If you're missing Thanksgiving, try the turkey dinner sandwich: turkey, mashed potatoes, and stuffing, all smushed onto an overflowing bun.

The guiding principle at **Bread Bar** (258 Locke St. S., 905/522-2999, www.breadbar.ca, 11:30 A.M.–4:30 P.M. and 5 P.M.–close Mon.–Fri., 8 A.M.–4:30 P.M. and 5 P.M.–close Sat.–Sun., $7–15), neighborhood bakery by day and pizzeria by night, is that "good ingredients matter." And those good ingredients make mighty fine pizzas, whether topped with fresh greens, goat cheese, and olives; roasted squash, fried sage, and pancetta; or other flavorful combinations. Wheel in your stroller, bring in your

date, or roll in with your pals, and you'll feel equally at home in this mellow room.

ⓒ Quatrefoil Restaurant (16 Sydenham St., Dundas, 905/628-7800, www.quatrefoil-restaurant.com, noon–3 P.M. and 5 P.M.–close Tues.–Sat., lunch $14–22, dinner $31–44), west of downtown, has put Hamilton on the fine-dining map, serving inventive contemporary fare on white tablecloths. At lunch, try the pan-seared rainbow trout with pickled beets and potato confit, or the more traditional eggs Benedict. In the evening, salmon might be paired with fennel "choucroute" and scallop ravioli, while the locally raised beef might be served with creamed leeks and wild mushrooms. Straightforward, stylish, and scrumptious.

INFORMATION AND SERVICES

The **Tourism Hamilton Visitor Information Centre** (Jackson Square, 2 King St. W., Unit 274, 905/546-2666 or 800/263-8590, www.tourismhamilton.com) can provide information about things to see and events happening around the region.

GETTING THERE AND AROUND

You can explore downtown Hamilton without a car. It's a short walk from the train/bus station to the Art Gallery and the Farmer's Market, and the James Street North Gallery District is also within walking distance.

Hamilton International Airport (YHM, 9300 Airport Rd., 905/679-1999, www.flyhi.ca) is 14 kilometers (nine miles) south of downtown. WestJet (800/538-5696, www.westjet.com) is the airport's main carrier, with nonstop flights to Calgary, Edmonton, Winnipeg, Halifax, and Moncton. Toronto's Pearson International Airport (www.torontopearson.com), just over an hour away, has many more flight options.

Buses and trains arrive and depart from the **Hamilton GO Centre** (36 Hunter St. E., 416/869-3200, www.gotransit.com), an art deco–style building downtown. There's frequent service to Toronto's Union Station

(1–1.25 hours, one-way adults $9.50, seniors and kids $4.75). **Coach Canada** (www.coach-canada.com) can take you to Niagara Falls (1.5–1.75 hours, one-way adults $21.10, seniors and students $19, kids 2–11 $10.55) and to Kitchener (1.5 hours, one-way adults $16.70, seniors and students $15.05, kids 2–11 $8.35). To visit some of the city's other attractions or explore other neighborhoods, you can get around on the city's bus system, the **Hamilton Street Railway** (905/527-4441, www.hamilton.ca, one-way adults $2.55).

Hamilton is midway between Toronto and Niagara Falls. It's 65 kilometers (40 miles) southwest of Toronto, a straight shot down the Queen Elizabeth Way (QEW). To Niagara Falls, continue south on the QEW south for another 70 kilometers (44 miles).

Kitchener-Waterloo and Vicinity

Billing itself as "Canada's technology triangle," the formerly industrial communities of Kitchener-Waterloo (aka K-W) and nearby Cambridge are reinventing themselves as a high-tech and educational powerhouse. Much of the area's rebirth was due to Research in Motion (RIM), the company that put Waterloo firmly on the innovation map after launching the BlackBerry smart phone back in 1999. Other high-tech companies, from Google to Open Text to Christie, have offices in K-W, and the University of Waterloo's well-regarded computer science, mathematics, and engineering programs in turn lead to more technology start-ups launching in the region.

For visitors and residents alike, this high-tech development is slowly triggering a renaissance in other areas, notably the arts. The region has several excellent small museums and galleries, clustered in downtown Kitchener or uptown Waterloo (the city's central core), as well as an increasingly robust calendar of arts events. Like many gentrifying communities, K-W still has its ragged patches, with pawnshops next to hipster coffeehouses, but there's a feeling of excitement here that makes it worth exploring.

Well before the high-tech boom, many early settlers to the region came from Germany, and a wildly popular event remains the annual Oktoberfest, the largest such festival outside of Germany. The most visible day-to-day legacy of this Germanic heritage is in the countryside around K-W, particularly in the village of St. Jacobs, where many residents are traditional Old Order Mennonites, whose simple buggy-driving, technology-shunning lifestyle contrasts sharply with the smart-phone-toting, online-obsessed, high-tech world of their more urban neighbors. See it while you still can.

SIGHTS

The weeklong Kitchener-Waterloo **Oktoberfest** (519/570-4267, www.oktoberfest.ca, Oct.), which claims to be the largest Bavarian festival outside of Munich, celebrates the region's German heritage with beer, music, beer, food, and more beer.

THEMUSEUM

Formerly Kitchener's children's museum, THEMUSEUM (10 King St. W., Kitchener, 519/749-9387, www.themuseum.ca, 10 A.M.–4 P.M. Wed.–Fri., 10 A.M.–5 P.M. Sat.–Sun., kids ages 3 and older $10) has become a "museum of ideas." Kids still have things to see and do, but as you climb to the higher floors in the open, multi-tiered space, exhibits become more sophisticated, like the recent "Rethinking Art and Machine," which showcased artists working with the interaction of art and technology.

Waterloo Region Museum

Starting with its striking, multicolored glass exterior, the Waterloo Region Museum (10 Huron Rd., Kitchener, 519/748-1914, www.waterlooregionmuseum.com, 9:30 A.M.–5 P.M. daily May–early Sept., 9:30 A.M.–5 P.M.

LAKE ERIE TO LAKE HURON

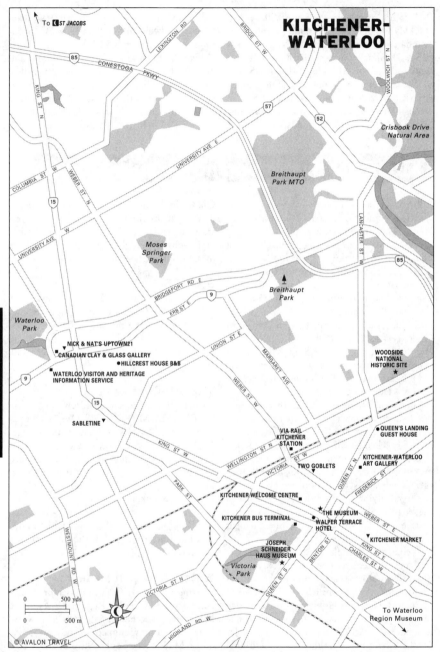

Mon.–Sat., 11 A.M.–5 P.M. Sun. early Sept.–Apr.; adults $10, seniors and students $8, kids 5–12 $5, families $25) isn't your ordinary historical museum. Permanent exhibits trace the region's roots from the original aboriginal inhabitants to the high-tech community of today; one shows the world through the eyes of a teenager, from the 1920s to the present day. Behind the museum, travel back to 1914 in the **Doon Heritage Village** (9:30 A.M.–5 P.M. daily May–early Sept.; 9:30 A.M.–4 P.M. Mon.–Sat., 11 A.M.–4 P.M. Sun. early Sept.–mid-Oct.; 9:30 A.M.–5 P.M. Mon.–Fri. mid-Oct.–late Dec.), a collection of historic homes and buildings where costumed staff help re-create early 20th-century life.

The museum and heritage village are nine kilometers (six miles) southeast of downtown Kitchener, about a 15-minute drive.

Woodside National Historic Site

The Woodside National Historic Site (528 Wellington St. N., Kitchener, 519/571-5684 or 888/773-8888, www.pc.gc.ca, 1–5 P.M. daily mid-May–mid-Dec., adults $3.90, senior $3.40, kids 6–16 $1.90) is the boyhood home of William Lyon Mackenzie King (1874–1950), Canada's longest-serving prime minister. The house has been restored to its appearance in 1891, when Mackenzie King was a teenager, and includes some furnishings that belonged to the King family. Interpreters in period costume are on hand to tell you about the home and its history, or take you on a guided tour. To get here by public transit, take bus #6 (Bridgeport) from the Kitchener bus station to the corner of Lancaster and Wellington, then walk east on Wellington to the site entrance.

Joseph Schneider Haus Museum

The oldest home in Kitchener, the 1816 Joseph Schneider Haus Museum (466 Queen St. S., 519/742-7752, www.region.waterloo.on.ca, 10 A.M.–5 P.M. Wed.–Sat., 1–5 P.M. Sun., mid-Feb.–mid-Dec., adults $2.25, seniors and students $1.50, kids $1.25, family $5) belonged to a Pennsylvania German Mennonite farm family. Although the house today is just a few blocks from the city's urban core, it once sat on a 448-acre farm, and within the restored home it's still the 1800s. Costumed staff do chores appropriate to the season, whether it's cooking, pickling, or spinning, and explain about farm life and Mennonite customs in the 19th century. One room was known as the "Beggar's Room," since families would often house an itinerant traveler who'd work in exchange for a bed. Another section of the building, the "Doddy Haus," common in traditional Mennonite homes even today, would house the older generation after their children were grown and assumed day-to-day management of the farm.

Art Galleries

Compact yet cool, the **Kitchener-Waterloo Art Gallery** (101 Queen St. N., Kitchener, 519/579-5860, www.kwag.on.ca, 9:30 A.M.–5 P.M. Mon.–Wed., 9:30 A.M.–9 P.M. Thurs., 9:30 A.M.–5 P.M. Fri., 10 A.M.–5 P.M. Sat., 1–5 P.M. Sun., free) shows contemporary works by Canadian and international artists, from their 4,000-piece permanent collection and through changing exhibits. The gallery is located in the Centre in the Square theater building and stays open late before performances.

Canadian Clay and Glass Gallery (25 Caroline St. N., Waterloo, 519/746-1882, www.theclayandglass.ca, 11 A.M.–6 P.M. Tues.–Fri., 10 A.M.–5 P.M. Sat., 1–5 P.M. Sun., free) changes its exhibits four times a year, exhibiting contemporary clay and glass works, often in conjunction with multimedia, painting, and other genres, by artisans from Canada and farther afield. Do your gift shopping in the museum's boutique, which sells distinctive jewelry, stained-glass pieces, ceramics, and glass sculptures by more than 140 Canadian craftspeople.

ACCOMMODATIONS

The Kitchener-Waterloo area has a mix of Victorian-style B&Bs, historic inns, and run-of-the-mill chain hotels. Prices rise and availability plummets during university graduations

© CAROLYN B. HELLER

the grand Langdon Hall Country House, outside Kitchener-Waterloo

and other special events, but otherwise, you shouldn't have trouble finding a room.

Built in the 1920s as a private home, the **Queen's Landing Guest House** (187 Queen St. N., Kitchener, 519/576-9297, www.queenslandingguesthouse.com, $90–100 s, $100–110 d) has retained many of its original features, from the dark walnut woodwork to the Art Nouveau stained glass. The large front room has a four-poster bed, a fireplace, and black, white, and gold linens. A second room, overlooking the garden, has a secret nook—a petite sitting area hidden behind the bathroom. Only the smallest room lacks an en suite bath, but its large private bathroom, with a colorful stained-glass window, is just across the hall. Owners Wilma and Brian Skipper have lived in the house for more than 30 years and can tell you all about things to do in the area. You won't go hungry, either; Wilma cooks hearty breakfasts that might include delicious oatmeal pancakes or apricot scones with homemade jam. Wi-Fi and parking are included.

Do you "Trust the Fat Guy"? At the **Hillcrest** House B&B (73 George St., Waterloo, 519/744-3534 or 866/624-3534, www.hillcresthouse.ca, $125–135 d), self-described "fat guy" Stefan Schuster runs this lovely B&B in an 1882 hilltop home in Uptown Waterloo with his wife Wendy. Schuster not only cooks up gourmet breakfasts—his take on eggs Benedict might include poached eggs served on a potato "rosti" and topped with smoked salmon—he also offers "Trust the Fat Guy" cooking workshops for couples or small groups, where he'll show you how to prepare a variety of dishes while keeping your wine glasses and dinner plates filled. The three Victorian-style guest rooms on the second floor are all quite large; two are two-room suites with separate sleeping and sitting areas. Rates include Wi-Fi and parking.

Eleanor Roosevelt, Bob Hope, Elton John, and Lady Gaga have all stayed at the **Walper Terrace Hotel** (1 King St. W., Kitchener, 519/745-4321 or 800/265-8749, www.walper.com, $115–149 d), built in 1893 in Kitchener's downtown. The floors are a bit creaky, but the 85 guest rooms have been upgraded with a mix of old and new furnishings and decorated gallery-style with original artworks. You can sleep here with a good conscience, too: the hotel donates $1 for every guest's stay to the Walper Education Project, which funds schools and scholarship programs in rural Uganda.

Play croquet on the lawn, lounge by the pool, or harness your energy for a game of tennis at the posh **Langdon Hall Country House Hotel and Spa** (1 Langdon Dr., Cambridge, 519/740-2100, www.langdonhall.ca, $259–629 d). Whether enjoying afternoon tea in the window-lined conservatory overlooking the gardens, or strolling through the Carolinian forest at the property's edge, you'll feel like a guest in a formal summer home, and in fact, you are; the grand 1902 brick manor at the center of the property was the summer house of New York–born Eugene Langdon Wilks, a great-grandson of American mogul John Jacob Astor. Twelve of the 52 guest rooms are in the main house, while the rest are in two separate wings; all feel cleanly elegant, with feather beds topped with down duvets, overstuffed chairs that nearly swallow you, fireplaces (in most), and luxurious bathrooms with soaker tubs. Linger over the lavish buffet breakfast, abundant with fresh berries, chocolate croissants, homemade granola, cured meats and fish, and vegetable tarts; voracious eaters can add a hot entrée, like pumpkin pancakes or prawn ragout topped with poached eggs.

FOOD

For a quick bite, stop into the **Kitchener Market** (300 King St. E., Kitchener, 519/741-2287, www.kitchenermarket.ca), where an array of vendors sells Croatian, Caribbean, and other international food to go on the market's upper floor (9 A.M.–5 P.M. Tues.–Fri., 7 A.M.–2 P.M. Sat.–Sun.). On Saturday, the lower level houses a large **Farmers' Market** (7 A.M.–2 P.M.).

It's easy to pass right by **Sabletine** (203 King St. S., Waterloo, 519/568-7373, www.sabletine.com, 9 A.M.–5:30 P.M. Tues., 9 A.M.–6 P.M. Wed.–Fri., 9 A.M.–5 P.M. Sat., 10:30 A.M.–3:30 P.M. Sun., $5–8), but don't miss this petite café. Not only do they serve

chocolate croissants and other excellent French pastries (mmm, lemon tarts), but they also cook up daily soups, sandwiches, and interesting salads, like a hearty wheatberry Waldorf, with apples, cranberries, and nuts. The menu at **Two Goblets** (85 Weber St. W., Kitchener, 519/749-1829, www.twogoblets.com, lunch 11:30 A.M.–2 P.M. Mon.–Sat., dinner 5–9 P.M. Mon.–Sat., $14–20) has more than a dozen variations on the schnitzel theme, as well as goulash, cabbage rolls, and other hearty dishes that show off K-W's Central European roots. On the walls are rustic scenes of peasants making wine; you can fill your own goblets with wine from Germany, Canada, and farther afield. Come hungry if you hope to polish off the ample (and scrumptious) schnitzel and pierogi platter.

The hottest seats at the casually hip bistro **Nick and Nat's Uptown21** (21 King St. N., Waterloo, 519/883-1100, www.uptown21.ca, dinner 5 P.M.–close Tues.–Sat., $20–25) are at the "kitchen counter"—a bar facing the action in the kitchen. The most interesting dishes aren't on the regular menu either: they're part of the daily three- ($35) or four-course ($45) prix fixe, incorporating whatever is in season. You might find a simple salad of baby arugula with sheep's-milk feta and fresh tomatoes, followed by local trout with vegetable fritters, asparagus, greens, and ramps, and a rhubarb honey tart. You can add free bacon to any dish, because… well, because the kitchen loves bacon.

Meals in Langdon Hall's **Dining Room** (1 Langdon Dr., Cambridge, 519/740-2100, www.langdonhall.ca, 7 A.M.–10:30 A.M., noon–2:30 P.M., and 5:30–9 P.M. Mon.–Fri., 7:30 A.M.–10:30 A.M., noon–2:30 P.M., and 5:30–9 P.M. Sat., 7:30 A.M.–10:30 A.M. and 5:30–9 P.M. Sun., brunch $42, lunch $27–34, dinner $29–52) are open to both guests and nonguests. Using local ingredients whenever possible, including vegetables from the hotel's garden, the chefs might concoct slow-roasted pickerel with black salsify and bluefoot chanterelles, grilled lamb paired with fennel hearts and pine aioli, or a vegetarian cassoulet of golden beets, lentils, kale, and salted ricotta cheese. With dinner tabs that can easily top $100 per person (before tax, tips, and drinks), many guests are celebrating special occasions, and the gracious staff do their best to make the experience exceptional. Reservations are required for weekend meals and recommended at other times. You can also dine in the more casual but still luxe **Wilkes Bar** (lunch and dinner daily, $24–32), where menu choices range from fish 'n' chips to seared veal steak with snap peas.

INFORMATION AND SERVICES

The **Waterloo Regional Tourism Marketing Corporation** (519/585-7517 or 877/585-7517, www.explorewaterlooregion.com) can provide information about sights, activities, events, and accommodations in Kitchener, Waterloo, Cambridge, St. Jacobs, and the surrounding towns. Both Kitchener and Waterloo have their own city offices that dispense visitor information: the **Kitchener Welcome Centre** (200 King St. W., 519/745-3536, www. kitchener.ca) and the **Waterloo Visitor and Heritage Information Service** (10 Father David Bauer Dr., Waterloo, 519/885-2297, www.waterloo.ca).

GETTING THERE
By Air
The **Region of Waterloo International Airport** (YFK, 4881 Fountain St., Breslau, 519/648-2256 or 866/648-2256, www.waterlooairport.ca) is located east of K-W. WestJet (www.westjet.com) has a direct daily flight from Calgary with connections to Vancouver, Victoria, Edmonton, and several other Western Canadian cities. Bearskin Airlines (www.bearskinairlines.com) flies nonstop to Ottawa and Montreal.

Alternatively, fly into Toronto's Pearson International Airport (www.torontopearson. com), which has many more flight options, and either rent a car or catch the bus to K-W. Airways Transit's **Toronto Airporter Bus Service** (519/886-2121, www.airwaystransit. com, 1.5–2 hours, one-way adults $56, children 2–21 $33) runs buses four times a day

between Pearson airport and several points in Kitchener-Waterloo.

By Train
VIA Rail (www.viarail.ca) runs trains between Toronto's Union Station and **Kitchener Station** (126 Weber St. W., 888/842-7245, 1.75 hours, one-way adults $26–35, kids 2–11 $13–18). **GO Transit** (416/869-3200 or 888/438-664, www.gotransit.com) also runs regular trains between Toronto and Waterloo in 2012; call or check their website for service updates and schedules.

By Bus
GO Transit buses (416/869-3200 or 888/438-664, www.gotransit.com, one-way adults $14.60, seniors and children $7.30) travel from Toronto to the downtown Kitchener Bus Terminal (15 Charles St. W., 1.5 hours) or to the University of Waterloo (Student Life Center, 200 University Ave. W., 2 hours). Though priced slightly higher than the GO service, **Greyhound** (www.greyhound.ca) also operates numerous daily buses from Toronto to Kitchener (1.5–2 hours, one-way adults $20–29, kids 2–12 $16–22), as well as several buses a day from Toronto to the University of Waterloo (1.75–2.5 hours, one-way adults $20–30, children 2–11 $16–23).

Coach Canada (www.coachcanada.com) runs buses from Kitchener to Hamilton (1.5 hours, one-way adults $16.70, kids 2–11 $8.35) and Niagara Falls (3–3.75 hours, one-way adults $37.80, kids 2–11 $18.90).

By Car
Downtown Kitchener is 105 kilometers (65 miles) southwest of central Toronto; take Highway 401 west to exit 278, where you'll pick up Highway 8 west. Exit onto King Street East if you're heading to central Kitchener. If driving from Toronto, allow about 90 minutes to the Kitchener-Waterloo region, or more if you're traveling during the morning or afternoon rush hours. Uptown Waterloo is about five kilometers (three miles) northwest of downtown Kitchener. From Highway 8, you can either take King

Street East and continue through Kitchener and into Waterloo, or take Highway 85 north to Erb Street East and go west.

GETTING AROUND

With a little effort, you can explore K-W car-free, particularly if you're mainly interested in attractions near downtown Kitchener or Uptown Waterloo. **Grand River Transit** (GRT, 519/585-7555, www.grt.ca) runs a comprehensive network of buses around the region. Out-of-town buses arrive at the Kitchener Bus Terminal (15 Charles St. W.), a hub for GRT buses; from there, buses travel along King Street, connecting downtown Kitchener with Uptown Waterloo. Use the EasyGO trip planner (www.grt.ca) to plot your route.

It's much easier to explore farther afield with a car. Car rental agencies with offices in Kitchener-Waterloo include **Enterprise** (www.enterpriserentacar.ca) and **National** (www.nationalcar.ca). Whether you're getting around on foot, by bus, or by car, pay particular attention to the directional and city designations in street addresses: 10 King Street East in Kitchener is not near 10 King Street North in Waterloo!

◖ ST. JACOBS

This small town just north of Waterloo is a base for learning more about the region's Mennonite community, who settled here in the 1800s. The Mennonites continue to observe traditional customs, traveling in horse-drawn buggies, wearing unadorned clothing, and farming, canning, and quilting as they have for generations.

St. Jacobs' attractions are in two separate areas. The Market District, where you'll find the year-round Farmers' Market, as well as a collection of outlet stores, is three kilometers (1.9 miles) south of St. Jacobs Village, which houses the Visitor Centre and several smaller attractions. While both the market and village are worth a visit, they're undeniably touristy, so make time to explore the surrounding countryside for a clearer glimpse of Mennonite life.

The Market District

Canada's largest year-round farmers market, the **St. Jacobs Farmers' Market** (878 Weber St. N., 519/747-1830, www.stjacobs.com, 7 A.M.–3:30 P.M. Thurs. and Sat. year-round, 8 A.M.–3 P.M. Tues. mid-June–Aug., free) is like the Wal-Mart of farmers markets. You can buy everything from toenail clippers to T-shirts to treadmills. On a busy day, the aisles both inside the market buildings and outside among rows of vendors' booths are as packed as a carnival midway on a hot summer's night. The market sprawls across multiple buildings and what seems like acres of parking lots.

Many of the shopkeepers, particularly those selling fruits and vegetables, homemade jams and pickles, or locally produced maple syrup, are Mennonites—the men in traditional black jackets and straw hats, the women in long dresses and bonnets, with their buggies parked behind their stalls. You can find fresh seasonal produce, lots of homemade baked goods, and locally made crafts, but you'll also see fruits shipped in from Mexico and Chile and trinkets made in China; shop carefully.

One of the market's most popular snack stalls is the **Fritter Company,** which turns apple slices into crispy, batter-fried apple fritters. Prepare for long lineups if you want a fritter fix.

St. Jacobs Village

Stop into the St. Jacobs Visitor Information Centre, not just for information about the region (which they have plenty of), but to see **The Mennonite Story** (1406 King St. N., 519/664-3518, 11 A.M.–5 P.M. Mon.–Sat., 1:30–5 P.M. Sun. Apr.–Dec.; 11 A.M.–4:30 P.M. Mon.–Sat., 2–4:30 P.M. Sun. Jan.–Mar.; suggested donation $4) on the lower level. This informative exhibit includes a video about the Old Order Mennonites in the St. Jacobs region, a history of the Mennonites' European roots (including a replica of a cave where their Swiss ancestors hid from their persecutors), a reproduction

THE OLD ORDER MENNONITES

Most of the roughly 4,000 Mennonites who live in and around St. Jacobs are known as "Old Order Mennonites." The Old Order Community is what many people envision when they think of "Mennonites": men and women wear traditional clothing (the men in dark suits and black or straw hats, the women in simple, long dresses and bonnets), and all reject contemporary conveniences, like cars and computers. In this patriarchal society, women may work before they are married, but once they tie the knot, their responsibilities lie at home. Large families, with an average of seven children, are common. Women don't wear makeup or jewelry and typically sew the long, plain dresses that they and their daughters wear.

Old Order Mennonites settled in Ontario in the 1800s and can trace their roots to Switzerland in the 1500s. While many of the Old Order now have electricity and telephones in their homes, they shun other technologies, from automobiles and clothes driers to radios and TVs. Most speak a German dialect, although all learn English at school. The Old Order communities run their own schools, which children typically attend through grade 8 or age 14.

The Old Order Mennonites are private people, but you can learn more about their communities and customs if you're respectful of their beliefs and traditions. Drive along the back roads just outside the town of St. Jacobs and you'll likely see horse-drawn buggies trotting alongside your car, or black-hatted men pedaling along on their bicycles. On Sundays, you may see lines of buggies heading to the meetinghouse.

Many Mennonite families sell produce, eggs, homemade jams, and quilts from their farms in the countryside around St. Jacobs. They'll post a sign at the end of their driveway if they're open for business. You're welcome to chat while you're browsing their wares or making a purchase, but remember that they're running a business, not opening their homes to gawking tourists. Also, Mennonites frown on picture taking (they believe it can lead to the sin of pride), so don't snap photos of people, and ask permission before photographing their buggies or the products they're selling.

You can also stop into the Mennonite-run **Wallenstein General Store** (7278 Hwy. 86, at Hwy. 10, 519/669-2231), about 12 kilometers (7.5 miles) northwest of St. Jacobs, which sells the traditional hats, religious books, fabrics, and farm supplies used in the Old Order community. Their homemade morning glory muffins ($1) are tasty, too.

Northeast of St. Jacobs, the **Lost Acres Variety Store** (12 Covered Bridge Dr., West Montrose, 519/669-5689) is also Mennonite-run (note the extra-large packages of Jell-O for sale). It's adjacent to Ontario's only remaining covered bridge, the **West Montrose Covered Bridge**, built in 1881; it's also known as the "Kissing Bridge," since it offered a secluded spot to smooch for couple traveling by horse and buggy.

To find other Mennonite-owned businesses, you can simply drive the country lanes – if the sign says "No Sundays Sales," it's likely run by a Mennonite family. You can also purchase the *Map Directory of Local Country Shops in Waterloo and Wellington County* ($4) at the St. Jacobs Visitor Information Centre (1406 King St. N., 519/664-1133 or 800/265-3353, www.

stjacobs.com). Some of the listed businesses, such as those repairing buggies or shoeing horses, don't cater to outsiders, but others welcome your trade. In additional to produce vendors and quilters, look for furniture makers and other artisans.

Some of the area's Mennonite meeting-houses welcome visitors to their Sunday services, but others won't proceed with a service if visitors are present, so don't just drop in. The **St. Jacobs Visitor Information Centre** (1406 King St. N., 519/664-1133 or 800/265-3353, www.stjacobs.com) can direct you to particu-lar churches and brief you on what to expect. Both men and women should dress modestly, covering their shoulders, arms, and legs. Services are typically held in German, although the songs may feel universal. At the Visitor Centre, pick up the helpful free booklet *The Plain and Simple Facts: Inside the Old Order Mennonite Community of the St. Jacobs Area*, which explains more about the community's beliefs and traditions, courtship and marriage customs, schools, and child-rearing practices. They also sell other books about Mennonite culture and traditions.

© CAROLYN B. HELLER

traditional Mennonite hats for sale at the Wallenstein General Store

LAKE ERIE TO LAKE HURON

© CAROLYN B. HELLER

telling the Mennonite Story in St. Jacobs

of a Mennonite meetinghouse, and another video that explains about life in modern Mennonite communities from Brazil to Mexico to Zimbabwe.

Pop into **Hamel Brooms** (1411 King St. N.) to watch the staff make straw brooms as they've done since the early 1900s. The **Country Mill** (1441 King St. N.) is primarily a collection of shops, but the building also houses the modest **Maple Syrup Museum of Ontario** (519/664-3626, free) and the **St. Jacobs Quilt Gallery** (519/664-2728, free), with changing displays of regionally crafted quilts.

Entertainment and Events

Located near the Farmers' Market, the year-round **St. Jacobs Country Playhouse** (40 Benjamin Rd. E., 519/747-7788, www.draytonentertainment.com) stages musicals and other lighter fare. At the more intimate **St. Jacobs Schoolhouse Theatre** (11 Albert St., 519/638-5555, www.draytonentertainment.com), in a stone former school dating to 1867 in St. Jacobs Village, you can watch

professional theater productions with cabaret-style seating.

The annual **Quilt and Fibre Art Festival** (www.stjacobs.com, 800/265-3353), typically held over several days in late May, showcases quilt work by regional artisans. Quilts are displayed in several locations in St. Jacobs, Kitchener-Waterloo, and surrounding towns. As part of the festival, quilts are auctioned off at the **New Hamburg Mennonite Relief Sale** (www.nhmrs.com), one of Canada's largest quilt auctions.

Accommodations and Food

St. Jacobs has a comfortable inn and a couple of B&Bs. You won't go hungry at the **St. Jacobs Farmers' Market** (878 Weber St. N., 519/747-1830, www.stjacobs.com, 7 A.M.–3:30 P.M. Thurs. and Sat. year-round, 8 A.M.–3 P.M. Tues. mid-June–Aug., free), with plenty of stalls selling snacks and more substantial meals. In St. Jacobs Village, the dining options include a bakery and a few sit-down restaurants.

One block off the main street in St. Jacobs Village, **Baumann House Bed & Breakfast** (25 Spring St., 519/664-1515, www.bbcanada.com/3205.html, $85 d) is a welcoming respite from the village hubbub. Owner Claire Bowman keeps three neat second-floor guest rooms, and she can tell you everything about touring St. Jacobs. One room has twig furniture, another has a spool bed topped with a red velvet coverlet, and a third, with twin beds, is done all in lavender; rooms share one bath upstairs and a half-bath on the main level. Breakfast specialties include herb and cheese omelets and pancakes with locally made maple syrup.

Originally a stagecoach stop, **Benjamin's Restaurant & Inn** (1430 King St. N., 519/664-3731, $100–145 d), in a restored 1852 building, is once again catering to weary travelers. The nine country-style guest rooms upstairs are decorated with quilt-topped beds and sturdy oak furniture; free Wi-Fi brings them into the 21st century. The downstairs restaurant (11:30 A.M.–9 P.M. daily, lunch $10–15, dinner $25–36) serves a light breakfast to inn guests and is open to the public for lunch and dinner. At midday, expect salads, sandwiches, and heartier mains like pork schnitzel or bacon-wrapped filet mignon; in the evenings, the fare is "Continental"—stuffed sole, chicken supreme, rack of lamb.

Pick up a Dutch apple square, butter tart, or other sweet from the **Stone Crock Bakery** (1402 King St. N., 519/664-3612, 6:30 A.M.–6 P.M. Mon.–Sat., 11 A.M.–5:30 P.M. Sun.). Next door, you can sit down to a full meal at the family-style **Stone Crock Restaurant** (1396 King St. N., 519/664-2286 or 886/664 2286, 7 A.M.–8 P.M. Mon.–Sat., 11 A.M.–8 P.M. Sun., $17) with bacon and eggs, sandwiches, and solid dishes like roast turkey, meatloaf, or liver and onions. **Jacob's Grill** (1398 King St. N., 519/664-2575, noon–9 P.M. Tues.–Wed., noon–10 P.M. Thurs.–Sat., noon–5 P.M. Sun., $15–19) tries to bridge the gap between traditional and contemporary with a menu that includes everything from macaroni and cheese, fish 'n' chips, and steak frites to lamb curry and Thai sesame noodles. Benjamin's, the Stone Crock, and Jacob's are all under the same ownership.

Information and Services

The knowledgeable staff at the **St. Jacobs Visitor Information Centre** (1406 King St. N., 519/664-1133 or 800/265-3353, www.stjacobs.com, 11 A.M.–5 P.M. Mon.–Sat., 1:30–5 P.M. Sun. Apr.–Dec.; 11 A.M.–4:30 P.M. Mon.–Sat., 2–4:30 P.M. Sun. Jan.–Mar.) can offer directions, point out things to do, and answer questions about the area's Mennonite community.

There's a seasonal **Visitor Information Centre** (855 Weber St., 519/883-3953, 9 A.M.–5 P.M. Mon.–Fri., 8 A.M.–4 P.M. Sat., 11 A.M.–5 P.M. Sun., May–Oct.) opposite the Farmer's Market.

Getting There and Around

St. Jacobs is eight kilometers (five miles) north of Waterloo, via Highway 85. King Street, the village's main street, runs between the village and the market district.

A fun way to get to St. Jacobs is aboard the heritage **Waterloo Central Railway** (www.waterloocentralrailway.com, one-way/round-trip adults $10/15, seniors and students $8/12, kids $7/10), which runs from Uptown Waterloo (Waterloo Station, 10 Father David Bauer Dr., off Erb St. W., 519/885-2297) to St. Jacobs Market and St. Jacobs Village (50 Isabella St.). The train operates three trips in each direction on Tuesdays (mid-June–Aug.), Thursdays (mid-May–late Oct.), and Saturdays (early Apr.–late Oct.). It's a 25-minute ride from Waterloo to the market, and another 20 minutes to the village.

Grand River Transit (519/585-7555, www.grt.ca) bus #21 runs from the Conestoga Mall (550 King St. N., Waterloo) and St. Jacobs, and also connects the Market District and St. Jacobs Village. Buses run about every 30 minutes; there's no service after 7 P.M. or on Sunday. You can make connections to the mall from downtown Kitchener.

LAKE ERIE TO LAKE HURON

Stratford and Vicinity

The main attraction in this town of 30,000 is the Stratford Shakespeare Festival, North America's largest classical repertory theater. While the Bard does account for many of the festival productions, it's not only Shakespeare on the stage; the festival also includes works by many other classical and more contemporary playwrights.

Even if theater isn't your thing, Stratford makes a good getaway, just two hours from Toronto. Due to the presence of the Stratford Chef School, the town has a large number of high-end restaurants, and you can entertain yourself with music, shopping, and a variety of special events throughout the year. If you're not coming for theater, visit Sunday, Monday, or Tuesday, when fewer productions are staged, or outside the festival season, when accommodations are easier to find; prices and crowds both peak from July through September.

If you have teens in tow, they might be hip to another Stratford native: pop singer and teen idol Justin Bieber. The Stratford Tourism Alliance publishes a **"Bieberific"** map to Justin's Stratford (www.visitstratford.ca/Justin), highlighting the schools he attended, the skate park where he hung out, and his favorite ice cream shop (Scoopers, 28 Erie St., 519/272-0133).

SIGHTS

Located in an 1880s pumphouse, **Gallery Stratford** (54 Romeo St., 519/271-5271, www.gallerystratford.on.ca, 10 A.M.–5 P.M. Tues.–Sat. May–Sept., 11 A.M.–3 P.M. Tues.–Sat. Oct.–Apr., adults $5, seniors and students $4) mounts eight to 10 exhibits every year, showcasing Canadian contemporary art. Kids of all ages can create their own art in the gallery's Community Studio, stocked with art supplies. The gallery is east of downtown, a 10–15-minute walk from the Festival Theatre.

Since 1968, local artists have been showing their work along the Avon River at **Art in the Park** (Lakeside Dr., www.

artintheparkstratford.com, Wed. and Sat.–Sun., June–Sept.).

Karen Hartwick, who owns the **Tea Leaves Tasting Bar** (433 Erie St., 519/273-1201 or 800/733-0376, www.stratfordtealeaves.com, 11 A.M.–5 P.M. Wed.–Sat. and by appointment), is a certified tea sommelier who can teach you all about blacks, greens, herbals, and more. She carries 150 different varieties in her petite shop, including her own unique blends, and offers complimentary tastings, so you can try before you buy. You can also book a more in-depth one-hour sampling seminar ($25) or a tea and chocolate tasting ($30). At the **Monforte Dairy Company** (49 Griffith Rd. E., 519/814-7920, www.monfortedairy.com, 10 A.M.–6 P.M. Tues.–Sun.) you can watch the cheese makers at work or take a cheese-making workshop.

Buy a pass to the **Stratford Chocolate Trail** ($20) and you can sample eight chocolate offerings—from truffles, teas, and candy bars to cookies, ice cream, even chocolate martinis—at any of 21 locations around town. Get your pass at the Stratford Tourism Alliance (47 Downie St., 800/561-7926, www.welcometostratford.com).

☑ STRATFORD SHAKESPEARE FESTIVAL

Stratford-born journalist Tom Patterson hatched the idea for a hometown festival devoted to William Shakespeare's works. He then convinced British actor and director Tyrone Guthrie to become its first artistic director. The inaugural production—*Richard III,* with Alec Guinness playing the lead—took to the stage in July 1953 in a giant canvas tent.

Today, the Stratford Shakespeare Festival (519/273-1600 or 800/567-1600, www.stratfordfestival.ca) has produced thousands of plays, many by Shakespeare, but many also by other classical and more contemporary playwrights. The festival typically opens with preview performances in late April and early May

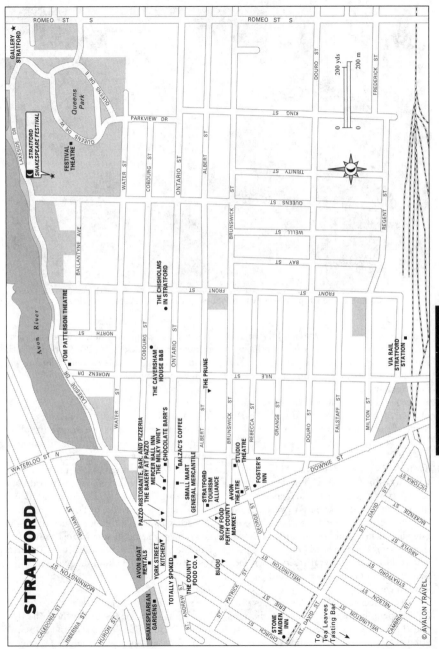

STRATFORD

LAKE ERIE TO LAKE HURON

ROMEO ST S

GALLERY STRATFORD ★

Queens Park

QUEENS DR E

PARKVIEW DR

QUEENS DR W

STRATFORD SHAKESPEARE FESTIVAL

FESTIVAL THEATRE ★

LAKESIDE DR

Avon River

WATER ST

COBOURG ST

ONTARIO ST

ALBERT ST

KING ST

DOURO ST

FREDERICK ST

TRINITY ST

QUEENS ST

WELL ST

BRUNSWICK ST

BAY ST

REGENT ST

ROMEO ST S

0   200 yds
0   200 m

BALLANTYNE AVE

TOM PATTERSON THEATRE

NORTH ST

MORENZ DR

THE CHISHOLMS IN STRATFORD

COBOURG ST

ONTARIO ST

FRONT ST

FRONT ST

THE CAVERSHAM HOUSE B&B

THE PRUNE

NILE ST

NILE ST

BRUNSWICK ST

REBECCA ST

GRANGE ST

DOURO ST

FALSTAFF ST

MILTON ST

VIA RAIL STRATFORD STATION

WATERLOO ST N

WATER ST

PAZZO RISTORANTE, BAR, AND PIZZERIA
THE BAKERY AT PAZZO
MERCER HALL INN
THE MILKY WHEY
CHOCOLATE BARR'S
BALZAC'S COFFEE

SMALL MART GENERAL MERCANTILE

STRATFORD TOURISM ALLIANCE

ALBERT ST

AVON THEATRE

STUDIO THEATRE

FOSTER'S INN

DOWNIE ST

WILLIAM ST

AVON BOAT RENTALS

YORK STREET KITCHEN

TOTALLY SPOKED

SHAKESPEAREAN GARDENS

THE COUNTY FOOD CO.

SLOW FOOD PERTH COUNTY MARKET

BIJOU

GEORGE ST

WELLINGTON ST

VICTORIA ST

DAVID ST

MCKENZIE ST

ARGYLE ST

STRATFORD ST

NELSON ST

CAMBRIA ST

MORNINGTON ST

CALEDONIA ST

HIBERNIA ST

HURON ST

ANDREW ST

PATRICK ST

CHURCH ST

ERIE ST

DAVID ST

STONE MAIDEN INN

To Tea Leaves Tasting Bar

© AVALON TRAVEL

© CAROLYN B. HELLER

inside the Costume and Props Warehouse at the Stratford Shakespeare Festival

and continues through October. July, August, and September are the busiest months, with multiple plays running in repertory and both afternoon and evening performances every day but Monday.

Beyond the plays, the festival offers a variety of theater tours, lectures, and special events. Some of the major events are listed below.

Tickets

Ticket sales (519/273-1600 or 800/567-1600, www.stratfordfestival.ca) for the upcoming season typically open to the general public in January. If you're hoping to visit during a July or August weekend or any holiday period, buy your tickets and book your accommodations as soon as you can. Many regular patrons who return year after year reserve their lodgings for the following season before they even leave town.

Ticket prices range from $50 to more than $110, depending on the type of play, the dates, and the seat location. Seniors, students, and families can purchase discounted tickets, and

when shows aren't sold out, you can buy last-minute "rush" tickets for 20–50 percent off. Rush tickets go on sale two hours before the performance by phone or at the box office, but not online.

Theaters

The Stratford Festival performs its plays at four venues. The largest, the 1,826-seat **Festival Theatre** (55 Queen St.), which was built in 1957, is located east of the town center in Upper Queen's Park. The 480-seat **Tom Patterson Theatre** (111 Lakeside Dr.) is near Lake Victoria, just east of downtown, while the other two performance spaces are right downtown: the 1,090-seat **Avon Theatre** (99 Downie St.) and the 260-seat **Studio Theatre** (34 George St. E.), behind the Avon.

Tours

For a behind-the-scenes look at the Stratford Festival, take the one-hour **Festival Theatre Tour** (55 Queen St., tours at 9 and 9:15 A.M. Wed.–Sun. mid-June–Oct., adults $8, seniors and students $6). You'll also learn more about the current season and past productions.

On the one-hour **Costume and Props Warehouse Tour** (350 Douro St., 9:30, 10, 10:30 and 11 A.M. Wed.–Sat. mid-May–Oct., adults $8, seniors and students $6), you can visit the Stratford Festival's massive costume and props warehouse, one of the largest in North America; it houses over 55,000 costumes and 10,000 pairs of boots and shoes. Amid the racks of gowns, pantaloons, capes, crowns, swords, and all manner of stage paraphernalia, you learn how staff create props from ordinary household objects (a foam pool "noodle" might become the foundation for an archway), how designers make a thin actor achieve the proper abdominal "jiggle" when playing a portly character, and how to remove body odor from elaborate costumes that can't be washed. Wrap up the tour by trying on costumes.

Part of the costume-warehouse building houses the festival's archives, the world's largest performing-arts archives devoted to a single theater. If you're interested in festival history, take the **Archives Tour** (350 Douro St., 10 A.M. and 10:30 A.M. Wed. June–Sept., adults $8, seniors and students $6).

Reservations (www.stratfordfestival.ca) are recommended for all tours (they do sell out).

Lectures

One way to learn more about the Shakespeare festival is to attend the informal **Meet the Festival** (9:30 A.M. Wed. and Fri. July–early Sept., 9:30 A.M. Sat. early–late Sept., free), a question-and-answer session with actors and artistic staff. Talks last about an hour, and they're held at the Tom Patterson and Studio Theatres. After some Friday-evening performances, stick around for a 30-minute **post-performance discussion** (July–Aug., free) with the cast.

Before selected weekday matinees, you can come early for a **Table Talk** (Paul D. Fleck Marquee, Festival Theatre, 11:30 A.M.–1:15 P.M. on certain dates, July–Aug., $35), which includes a buffet lunch and a lecture about one of the season's plays (theater tickets are extra). The lecture schedule is posted on the festival website, where you can also reserve your lunch spot.

ENTERTAINMENT AND SHOPPING

Though Stratford may be better known for its classical theater productions, **SpringWorks** (www.SpringWorksFestival.ca, May), the town's "Indie Theatre and Arts Festival," showcases more avant garde music, dance, and theater performances.

More than 100 concerts, from jazz to Mozart to organ recitals, take place during the month-long **Stratford Summer Music** (www.stratfordsummermusic.ca, mid-May–mid-Aug.).

The town's big foodie fest is the annual **Savour Stratford Autumn Culinary Festival** (www.welcometostratford.com/culinaryfestival, Sept.), which includes a pork roast, local food samplings, barbecues, an outdoor farmers and artisans market, and wine and beer tastings, as well as concerts in the park and activities for kids.

Ontario Street is downtown Stratford's main shopping street, with boutiques, galleries, pubs, and cafés. **Small Mart General Mercantile** (121 Ontario St., 519/271-6283, www.small-mart.ca, 10 A.M.–6 P.M. Tues.–Sat., 11 A.M.–5 P.M. Sun.) sells a quirky mix of clothing with classic Canadian logos, T-shirts, retro candies, watches, and miscellaneous cool stuff.

The Milky Whey (118 Ontario St., 519/814-9439, www.themilkywhey.ca, 10 A.M.–5 P.M. Tues.–Wed., 10 A.M.–6 P.M. Thurs.–Fri., 9:30 A.M.–5 P.M. Sat., 11 A.M.–3 P.M. Sun.) is the place for cheese, with lots of regionally produced varieties. In the fall and winter, they host periodic tastings, pairing cheeses with wines or beers.

Given their last name, Derek and Jacqueline Barr may have been destined to open a chocolate shop: theirs, which sells rich handmade truffles, as well as caramels and other candies, is called **Chocolate Barr's** (136 Ontario St., 519/272-2828, www.chocolatebarrs.com, 9 A.M.–6 P.M. Mon.–Thurs., 9 A.M.–8 P.M. Fri., 9 A.M.–6 P.M. Sat., 11 A.M.–5 P.M. Sunday), of course.

SPORTS AND RECREATION

The 104-kilometer (65-mile) **Avon Trail** (www.avontrail.ca) runs from St. Marys northwest to Conestogo, passing through the Stratford area. The Avon Trail Association organizes regular volunteer-led day hikes. Visitors are welcome; check the website for schedule and contact information.

Stratford is compact enough for exploring by bike. Rent your wheels from **Totally Spoked** (29 Ontario St., 519/273-2001, www.totally-spoked.ca, half-/full-day $20/$35). **Avon Boat Rentals** (40 York St., 519/271-7739, 10 A.M.– dusk May–Oct.) rents canoes, kayaks, and paddle boats alongside the Avon River. You can also take a 30-minute river cruise aboard the *Juliet III* pontoon boat.

Many of the flowers in the **Shakespearean Gardens** (Huron St., at York St.), near the Avon River and the Perth County Court House, are mentioned in Shakespeare's plays. Free garden tours are offered in July and August, Mondays at 2 P.M. and Thursdays at 9:30 A.M.

Stratford has a large population of swans that live along the Avon River. The Stratford Tourism Alliance (47 Downie St., 800/561-7926, www.welcometostratford.com) occasionally offers free guided **Swan Walk** tours where you can learn more about the swans' habits and habitat.

ACCOMMODATIONS

For a fairly small community, Stratford has a large number of lodgings, including motels, inns, and many B&Bs. What you won't find are inexpensive accommodations, at least during the summer theater season. If you're on a tight budget, and you have a car, you might consider driving in from Kitchener-Waterloo or London; you could also come from Toronto for the day without staying overnight.

The **Stratford Tourism Alliance** (47 Downie St., 800/561-7926, www.welcometostratford.com) has a lodging search function on its website, where you can search for available lodgings by date, location, and various features. The Stratford festival also runs an accommodations booking service

(800/567-1600, www.stratfordaccommodations.com).

If you're looking for more B&B options, try the **Stratford and Area Bed & Breakfast Association** (www.sabba.ca).

Under $100

One of Stratford's only budget accommodations is the **SGH Residence** (130 Youngs St., 519/271-5084, www.sgh.stratford.on.ca/residence, $67 s, $78 d), a residence hall with shared baths on the grounds of the Stratford Hospital.

$100-150

In this price range, you'll find some well-maintained motels—not fancy, but comfortable. The trade-off is that you're not within easy walking distance from downtown.

The star of the show at the old-fashioned, family-run **Swan Motel** (960 Downie St., 519/271-6376, www.swanmotel.ca, May–Oct., $108–127 d), two kilometers (1.25 miles) south of the town center, is the pretty manicured grounds, with gardens, picnic tables, and outdoor pool. You get a warm welcome from longtime owners Peter and Colleen Pola before settling into one of 24 simple rooms with mini-fridges, coffeemakers, and free Wi-Fi. Though there's no restaurant, you can stop into the lobby for complimentary morning muffins, coffee, and tea.

Ask for one of the updated units at the 18-room **As You Like It Motel** (379 Romeo St. N., 519/271-2951, www.asyoulikeit.on.ca, May–Oct., $114–160 d); it may be a basic motel, but the updated linens and carpets, mixed with the old-time furniture, give the spaces a cool, almost midcentury-modern vibe. All the rooms have mini-fridges and free Wi-Fi (but no coffeemakers); you can have a light continental breakfast in the dining area behind the front desk. The motel, which also has a pool out back, is 3.5 kilometers (2.2 miles) northeast of the town center.

$150-200

You can choose from 150 varieties of tea when staying at the **Rosewood Manor B&B** (433 Erie St., 519/273-1201 or 800/733-0376, www.bbcanada.com/rosewoodmanor, $160–175 d), located above the Tea Leaves Tasting Bar. The four simple second-floor guest rooms mix Victorian and Asian influences (the nicest is the serene, airy room #2 at the front of the house). Besides offering all the tea you can drink, owner Karen Hartwick cooks a full breakfast, and you can choose from macrobiotic, Japanese, or more typical North American fare. You're not right downtown, but parking is free.

Owners Kent and Dianne Chisholm of **The Chisholms in Stratford** (310 Ontario St., 519/273-6813 or 877/373-6813, www.thechisholmsinstratford.com, $159–179 d), a three-room B&B in an 1881 yellow-brick Victorian, give guests name cards at breakfast, to encourage chatting and swapping travel tips. They also keep a database of what every guest had for breakfast, which is served around the antique dining room table under the chandelier, so return visitors can try something new or come back to old favorites. Guests can make themselves a cappuccino in the parlor or settle into a wicker chair on the expansive front porch. Upstairs, the guest rooms have traditional four-poster beds and wingback chairs, as well as iPod docks, CD players, and free Wi-Fi.

Banana coconut bread, butter tart muffins, and French toast with rhubarb fool are among the breakfast specialties at **The Caversham House B&B** (155 Cobourg St., 519/271-7882 or 866/998-7882, www.thecavershamhouse.com, $155–185 d), a friendly lodging in a 1917 Edwardian house on a residential street close to downtown. The three guest rooms aren't large, but they're well designed, with original oak floors, air-conditioning, and free Wi-Fi; the Henley suite has a private balcony overlooking the garden. Owners Mary Lou and John Middleton want to make you feel at home; you can read in the book-lined living room and help yourself to pop or juice from the guest fridge.

Stratford has several small inns on the upper floors of downtown historic buildings. A well-run choice is **Foster's Inn** (111 Downie St., 519/271-1119 or 888/728-5555, www.fostersinn.com, $142–199 d), with nine unfussy, loft-style guest rooms on the second and third floors. There's free Wi-Fi (just check the signal strength if you're on the top floor), and you can hang out downstairs in the friendly bar or have meals in the brightly painted restaurant; the hearty "B.E.L.T."—a peameal-bacon, egg, lettuce, and tomato sandwich, served with a big pile of home fries—will fuel you up for the day. They don't have parking, but a free lot is two blocks away.

Also above a downtown restaurant, the 14 rooms at the **Mercer Hall Inn** (108 Ontario St., 519/271-1888 or 888/816-4011, www.mercerhallinn.com, $145–210 d) are all decorated differently. They're not deluxe, but they're modern; some have whirlpool tubs, some have fireplaces, and room 209 has a river view. Rates include a voucher for breakfast in the diner-style **Tango Café and Grill** on the main floor, as well as parking and Wi-Fi. Just note that the building has lots of stairs and no elevator.

Over $200

New owners took over the Victorian-style **Stone Maiden Inn** (123 Church St., 519/271-7129 or 866/612-3385, www.stonemaideninn.com, $150–260 d) in 2010, and they're gradually updating the rambling 13-room brick manor house, built in 1873. The first step was hiring a young graduate of the Stratford Chefs School to revamp the breakfast menu; creations include waffles with cinnamon ice cream, granola studded with cocoa nibs, and homemade juices like sparkling apple-juniper or pear, blueberry, and kefir lime. They also offer cooking workshops and forager's weekends (forage for ingredients, then learn to prepare a meal). The well-kept guest rooms are still rather old-fashioned, with floral wallpapers and period furnishings; the nicest one is the high-ceilinged "Romeo and Juliet" room with a hand-carved four-poster bed.

FOOD

With the professional Stratford Chefs School in town, as well as an audience of hungry, well-heeled theatergoers, Stratford serves up plenty of high-end meals; it's a great spot for a gourmet splurge. Reservations are highly recommended during the summer, and they're essential if you're trying to have dinner before

STRATFORD CHEF SCHOOL

Every autumn, three Stratford restaurants are reborn. **The Prune** (151 Albert St., www.old-prune.on.ca), **Rundle's** (9 Cobourg St., www.rundlesrestaurant.com), and **Pazzo** (70 Ontario St., www.pazzo.ca) close their doors to reopen with completely new staffs and menus as the restaurants of the Stratford Chef School (68 Nile St., 519/271-1414, www.stratfordchef.com). This professional culinary institute trains 35 aspiring chefs every year, but the students spend very little time in the lecture hall. Instead, they're running the kitchens and dining rooms of these three transformed restaurants.

Every year, the school brings in international guest chefs who work with the students and oversee diners' meals. You may not have the chance to visit Siena, Italy, or Oxfordshire, England, to eat in the restaurants that chefs Paolo Lopriore (Restaurant Il Canto) or Emily

Lampson (The Kingham Plough) run, but you can dine on their dishes in Stratford. Diners not only get a fine-dining experience for a moderate cost (prices go up slightly through the season as students' experience grows), but can also provide feedback that will assist in the chefs' training.

The chef-school restaurants typically open in late October and run through February each year. Check the school's website for a calendar of regular meals and guest chef appearances. If you want to don your own chef's whites, you can "buy a day" at the Stratford chef school ($200). Sit in on the day's lessons and work beside the students and guest chefs in the restaurant kitchen.

And who knows? The student who's prepping your salad today may be the Fernand Adria or Thomas Keller of the future.

going to the theater. If you're watching your budget, Stratford still offers good eating, with several bakeries, cafés, and locally focused bistros.

While most of Stratford's restaurants are open daily from June through August or September, many reduce their hours, or close altogether, outside of the summer high season. Notable exceptions are the Stratford Chef School restaurants (Oct.–Feb.).

Bakeries and Cafés

Named for the French playwright Honoré de Balzac, **Balzac's Coffee** (149 Ontario St., 519/273-7909, www.balzacscoffee.com) would be right at home in Paris, with its high ceilings, embossed wallpaper, and excellent coffees. You can nibble pastries or sandwiches, or just linger over a cup of joe.

The Bakery at Pazzo (76 Ontario St., 519/508-2244, 8 A.M.–7 P.M. Tues.–Sat.) sells breads, focaccia, pastries, and other finely crafted baked snacks.

You can create your own salad plate from the salad bar at **The County Food Co.** (38 Erie St., 519/275-2665, www.countyfoodco.com, 11 A.M.–7 P.M. Tues.–Fri., 11 A.M.–5 P.M. Sat., 10 A.M.–2 P.M. Sun.; call for off-season hours; $5–12), a café and takeout shop that emphasizes local ingredients. Don't expect a bland assortment of lettuce and shredded carrots: you might find roasted asparagus, Dijon mustard–dressed chickpeas, or celery root and apples with lemon mayonnaise. They make an assortment of sandwiches, too, including the signature stuffed pork schnitzel, a local cheddar/apple/Amish red pepper jelly combo, and chicken salad with pecans and dried cranberries. Try the oversized oatmeal cookies.

Contemporary

Cheerful and unpretentious **York St. Kitchen** (41 York St., 519/273-7041, www.yorkstreetkitchen.com, 8:30 A.M.–4 P.M. Mon.–Thurs., 8 A.M.–4 P.M. Fri.–Sat. 8 A.M.–3 P.M. Sun., closed Sun. Jan.–Apr., lunch $5–7, dinner $14–16), with brightly painted walls and colorful mismatched tablecloths, has been serving interesting yet inexpensive eats since the mid-1990s. Hugely popular for breakfast—their signature morning dish is the hearty "Canadiana" (a BLT with peameal bacon, lettuce, and tomatoes, and an optional fried egg)—they serve sandwiches midday and stews, pastas, and pot pies come evening. Order from their takeout window if you fancy a picnic; they're near the river just behind the main square.

Run by a husband-and-wife team who met as students at the Stratford Chef School, **(Bijou** (105 Erie St., www.bijourestaurant.com, lunch 11:30 A.M.–1:30 P.M. Fri.–Sun., dinner 5–9 P.M. Tues.–Sun. May–Oct.; dinner 5–9 P.M. Fri.–Sat. Nov.–Apr., $25–60) is a small jewel-box bistro that pairs casual—refurbished wood floors and benches, a chalkboard menu—with white tablecloths, well-informed service, and a serious kitchen committed to sourcing locally. The daily-changing menu claims French roots, Asian and Italian influences, and Ontario ingredients; you might start with Jerusalem artichoke soup topped with butter chicken mousse, or pickerel cheeks, steamed and sauced with scallion, ginger, and sesame oil, before moving on to a wild leek and sheep cheese strudel served with green garlic puree and rhubarb juice or a crispy duck leg paired with beluga lentils, baby bok choy, and oyster mushrooms. Don't neglect the desserts: a tasting of Perth County strawberries offers the fruit baked, poached, fried, and made into ice cream, while the peach tarte tatin (with Ontario peaches, of course) might be served with black pepper ice cream and organic basil syrup.

One of Stratford's original fine-dining restaurants, formerly known as "The Old Prune," **The Prune** (151 Albert St., 519/271-5052, www.oldprune.on.ca, lunch 11:30 A.M.–2 P.M. Fri.–Sat., dinner 5–9 P.M. Tues.–Sat. mid-May–mid-Oct., $30–42) is still a favorite theatergoers' dining destination. Pairing classical French techniques and local ingredients, the kitchen creates dishes like cider-glazed duck served with chive pancakes; seared tuna with spring radishes, fava beans, and preserved lemons; or risotto with wild leek pesto.

Italian

Pazzo Ristorante, Bar, and Pizzeria (70 Ontario St., 519/273-6666 or 877/440-9666, www.pazzo.ca, pizzeria: 11:30 A.M.–midnight Tues.–Sat.; ristorante: lunch 11:30 A.M.–2 P.M., dinner 5–8:30 P.M. Tues.–Sat., $11–20) is two restaurants in one. On the lower level is a more casual pizzeria, which also serves salads, pastas, and panini; the excellent pies range from classic combos like "quattro formaggi" (topped with parmesan, mozzarella, provolone, and asiago cheeses), to "the Medici'" (hot peppers, fresh tomatoes, pesto, and black olives), to the carnivore-friendly "Italian stallion" (loaded with prosciutto, Italian bacon, and spicy Calabrese sausage). On the main floor is a more upscale restaurant, with sleek white chairs and oversized windows, where the contemporary Italian creations might include pork-hock ravioli with pea puree; grilled octopus with fingerling potatoes and fava beans; or roasted guinea hen with blue corn polenta cake and candied fennel. In winter, the pizzeria remains open, while the main floor becomes one of the restaurants run by the Stratford Chef School.

Groceries and Markets

Stratford has two farmers markets: the **Stratford Farmers' Market** (Stratford Rotary Complex, 353 McCarthy Rd., 519/271- 5130, www.stratfordfairgrounds.com, 7 A.M.–noon Sat. year-round, also 3–7 P.M. Wed. June–Sept.) and the **Slow Food Perth County Market** (Market Sq., behind Stratford City Hall, 10 A.M.–2 P.M. Sun. June–Oct.).

INFORMATION AND SERVICES

The **Stratford Tourism Alliance** (47 Downie St., 800/561-7926, www.welcometostratford.com, 8:30 A.M.–4:30 P.M. Mon.–Fri., 10 A.M.–6 P.M. Sat. June; 8:30 A.M.–5 P.M. Mon.–Fri., 10 A.M.–6 P.M. Sat. July–Aug.; 8:30 A.M.–4:30 P.M. Mon.–Fri., 10 A.M.–3 P.M. Sat. Sept.–May) runs a helpful visitor center stocked with information about the region. Their website lists scads of things to see and do.

GETTING THERE

Stratford is 150 kilometers (93 miles) southwest of Toronto, 45 kilometers (28 miles) southwest of Kitchener, and 60 kilometers (37 miles) northeast of London.

By Air

The closest airports to Stratford are in Waterloo (www.waterlooairport.ca) or London (www.londonairport.on.ca), but Toronto's **Pearson International Airport** (www.torontopearson.com) has far more flights from the greatest number of destinations. **Stratford Airporter Shuttle** (519/273-0057 or 888/549-8602, www.stratfordairporter.com, 2.5 hours, one-way $69/one person, $94/two people) provides transportation from Pearson to Stratford. They also run shuttles to the Waterloo and London airports.

By Train

You can catch the train to **VIA Rail's Stratford Station** (101 Shakespeare St., 888/842-7245, www.viarail.ca) from Toronto (2.25 hours, one-way adults $34–45, kids 2–11 $17–22) and London (1 hour, one-way adults $23, kids $12). From Toronto, it's possible to take the train, see a show, have an early dinner, and return that evening; you arrive in Stratford just before the matinee curtain.

By Bus

On some Saturdays in July, August, and September, the Stratford Festival (www.stratfordfestival.ca) runs the **TO Direct** (round-trip $48) and **KW Direct** (round-trip $30) buses for day-trippers. Buses bring theatergoers to Stratford in time for an afternoon matinee, leaving Toronto at 9:30 A.M. and Kitchener at 11 A.M. Buses depart the theater right after the show, returning to Kitchener at 5:45 P.M. and Toronto at 7 P.M. The main drawback to these festival buses is that you don't have any time to explore the town. The Toronto stop is on the city's north side, on Old York Mills Road at Yonge St. (subway: York Mills); the Kitchener stop is at the Kitchener Memorial Auditorium (400 East Ave.).

By Car

From Toronto, it's about a two-hour drive to Stratford. Take Highway 401 west to exit 278, Highway 8 west, toward Kitchener. Then follow Highway 7/8 west from Kitchener to Stratford. As you enter Stratford, Highway 7/8 becomes Ontario Street, the town's main east–west street.

GETTING AROUND

If you're staying in the downtown area, you can easily walk from your lodging to restaurants and shops. The Stratford Festival's theaters are scattered around the town center; two are right downtown, one is lakefront near downtown, and the largest, the Festival Theatre, is 1.5 kilometers (0.9 mile) east of downtown. To walk to the Festival Theatre, either follow the riverfront walking path or go east on Ontario Street, then north on Queen Street.

If you've come by car, stop into the offices of the **Stratford Tourism Alliance** (47 Downie St., 800/561-7926, www.welcometostratford.com, 8:30 A.M.–4:30 P.M. Mon.–Fri., 10 A.M.–6 P.M. Sat. June; 8:30 A.M.–5 P.M. Mon.–Fri., 10 A.M.–6 P.M. Sat. July–Aug.; 8:30 A.M.–4:30 P.M. Mon.–Fri., 10 A.M.–3 P.M. Sat. Sept.–May) and ask for a free one-day parking pass. Available to all visitors, it's good for free parking at several lots around the downtown area. Downtown street parking is metered, and while it's inexpensive, it's limited to two hours, so pull into a parking lot if you're going to see a show. There's free parking on the streets surrounding the Festival Theatre, but it fills quickly before curtain time; you can also park in the large Queen Street lot near the theater ($10). The Tom Patterson Theatre has its own lot with free parking. Street parking is free on Sunday.

City of Stratford Transit (519/271-0250, www.city.stratford.on.ca or www.welcometostratford.com, one-way adults $2.50, seniors and students $2.25) operates limited bus service around town Monday through Saturday. Buses run about every 30 minutes, but the last buses leave at 9:30 P.M. Monday through Friday and 7:30 P.M. on Saturdays, so they're not convenient for post-theater transportation. If you need a taxi, phone **City Cab** (519/272-2222) or **Radio Cab** (519/271-4242).

ST. MARYS

Known as "Stonetown" for the limestone dug from the area's quarries and the classical stone buildings that line the downtown streets, St. Marys is a small town with a big pool. It's home to **The Quarry** (Water St., 1–5 P.M. Sat.–Sun. June, 1–8 P.M. daily July–Aug., adults $4.50, seniors $4, kids $3), Canada's largest outdoor swimming pool, in a former stone quarry. Swimmers can use the changing rooms in the adjacent Lind Sportsplex and Curling Club. Also in town is a destination for baseball fans: the **Canadian Baseball Hall of Fame** (386 Church St. S., 519/284-1838, www.baseballhalloffame. ca, 10:30 A.M.–4 P.M. Sat., noon–4 P.M. Sun., May; 10:30 A.M.–4 P.M. daily, noon–4 P.M. Sun., June–early Oct., adults $7.50, seniors $6, kids 6–16 $3.75, family $15), crammed with memorabilia about baseball in Canada and Canadians who play baseball.

Accommodations and Food

You can stop off in St. Marys as part of a stay in Stratford or London. If you'd rather stay for a night or two, the town's best lodging is the **Westover Inn** (300 Thomas St., 519/284-2977 or 800/268-8243, www.westoverinn. com, $140–300 d). The nicest rooms are in the main building, a Victorian stone manor house built in 1867, with 11-foot ceilings, rich-hued linens, and period furnishings. The 12 rooms in the "terrace," a former church dormitory, are more modest and lack the manor's charms but

are fine if you just want to sleep. The four "cottage" rooms fall somewhere in between, more modern but without the manor's character. The manor also houses the white tablecloth dining room (lunch $10–15, dinner $23–36), serving dishes like grilled Ontario-raised ostrich, walnut- and blue cheese-crusted pork tenderloin with purple cabbage, or red pepper fettuccine tossed with seared shrimp and scallops. If you're dining with a special someone, book the alcove table in a secluded nook for two.

Stop into the **Darjeeling Tea Room** (83 Queen St. E., 226/661-0069, www.darjeelingtearoom.com, 10 A.M.–5 P.M. Mon.–Sat., $4–6) for a restorative cup of tea, a pastry, or a light lunch. They also serve a traditional afternoon tea with finger sandwiches, sweets, and, of course, tea.

Practicalities

St. Marys is 20 kilometers (12 miles) southwest of Stratford and 45 kilometers (28 miles) northeast of London. The town of St. Marys runs a **visitors information center** in the VIA Rail train station (5 James St. N., www. townofstmarys.com, 8:30 A.M.–5 P.M. Mon.–Fri., 9 A.M.–3 P.M. Sat. July–Aug.; 8:30 A.M.–4:30 P.M. Mon.–Fri., Sept.–June). Although **VIA Rail** (888/842-7245, www.viarail.ca) has train service to Toronto (2.75 hours, one-way adults $39–52, kids $19–26) and London (40 minutes, one-way adults $23, kids $12), you'll want a car unless the objective of your stay is to cocoon.

London

Canada's 10th-largest city makes a convenient stopover if you're traveling between Toronto and Lake Huron or if you're exploring southwestern Ontario. It's home to one of Canada's major universities—the University of Western Ontario—which gives the town a youthful feel, with lots of pubs and cool boutiques. London also has several worthwhile museums and an interesting pioneer village.

SIGHTS

Right in the city center, the six-hectare (15-acre) **Victoria Park** (bounded by Dufferin and Central Aves. and Clarence and Wellington Sts.) is a great place for a picnic. You'll often find festivals, concerts, and other special events here, as well. At the park's southwest corner is the grand **St. Peter's Cathedral** (196 Dufferin Ave., 519/432-3475, www.cathedral.rcec.london.on.ca), built in the 1880s to resemble a

LAKE ERIE TO LAKE HURON

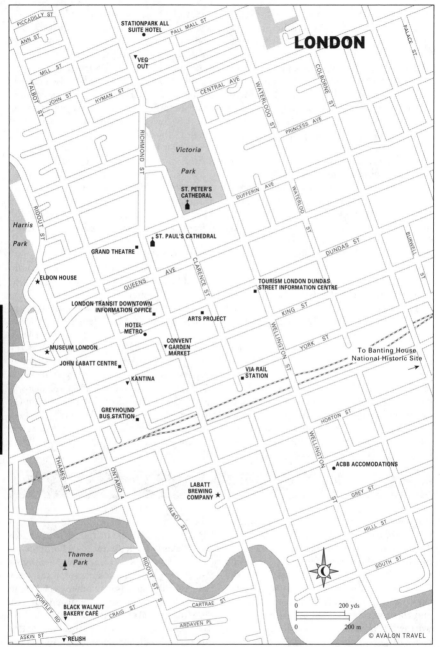

13th-century French Gothic cathedral. Visitors are welcome to take a peek inside the church or to attend mass.

Museum London (421 Ridout St. N., 519/661-0333, www.museumlondon.ca, noon–5 P.M. Tues.–Sun., noon–9 P.M. Thurs., admission by donation) exhibits a mix of historical art, contemporary art, and historical artifacts. Canadian architect Raymond Moriyama, who designed the Bata Shoe Museum and the Ontario Science Centre in Toronto, as well as the Canadian War Museum in Ottawa, also designed London's distinctive museum building.

Wander through London's oldest surviving residence, the 1834 **Eldon House** (481 Ridout St. N., 519/661-0333, www.eldonhouse.ca, noon–5 P.M. Tues.–Sun. June–Sept., noon–5 P.M. Wed.–Sun. Oct.–Dec., noon–5 P.M. Sat.–Sun. Jan.–Apr., noon–5 P.M. Wed.–Sun. May; adults $6, seniors and students $5, children age 13 and under $1, family $11, admission by donation Wed. and Sun.), and you can imagine yourself a guest of the well-to-do Harris family, who lived in this white clapboard home for four generations. Among its idiosyncratic furnishings are an umbrella stand made from an elephant's foot, gold-embossed faux leather wallpaper that the family brought back from Japan in 1897, and a melodeon (a miniature organ). In summer, you can take tea in the garden (2–4 P.M. Tues.–Sun. late June–Aug., tea $7, tea and house tour $10).

Founded in London in 1847, the Labatt Brewing Company still makes beer here. To learn more about the brewing process, take a two-hour **Labatt Brewery Tour** (150 Simcoe St., 519/850-8687 or 800/268-2337, www.labatt.com, Mon.–Fri., $10). You must book in advance by phone (8 A.M. and 4 P.M. Mon.–Fri.) or email (londontour@labatt.com).

London played an important role in medical history, when a local doctor, Frederick Banting (1891–1941), conceived the idea of extracting insulin from a pancreas as a treatment for diabetes. Thanks to Banting's research, insulin was first used successfully in a human trial in 1922, and Banting received the Nobel Prize in Medicine the following year. Dr. Banting's former home is now the **Banting House National Historic Site** (442 Adelaide St. N., 519/673-1752, www.diabetes.ca, noon–4 P.M. Tues.–Sat., adults $5, seniors and students 5 and older $4, family $12), which recounts the history of his life and his discovery.

Another aspect of London's history is on view at the **Fanshawe Pioneer Village** (Fanshawe Conservation Area, 1424 Clarke Rd., 519/457-1296, www.fanshawepioneervillage.ca, 10 A.M.–4:30 P.M. Tues.–Sun. mid-May–mid-Oct., adults and children 4 and older $7), which illustrates rural life in the region during the period 1820–1920. Costumed interpreters staff the restored buildings, demonstrating woodworking, printing, and cooking, or working in the general store or the school. If you're visiting with school-age kids, pick up a copy of the *Village Scavenger Hunt* to guide your explorations. The village is nine kilometers (5.6 miles) northeast of the city center, near the intersection of Clarke and Fanshawe Park Roads.

ENTERTAINMENT AND SHOPPING

The downtown **John Labatt Centre** (99 Dundas St., 519/432-8894 or 866/455-2849, www.johnlabattcentre.com) plays host to major concerts, theatrical productions, and sporting events. Also downtown, the **Grand Theatre** (471 Richmond St., 519/672-8800 or 800/265-1593, www.grandtheatre.com) has two stages for professional theater productions and also hosts concerts and other events.

For more experimental works, check what's on at the **Arts Project** (203 Dundas St., 519/642-2767, www.artsproject.ca), a gallery and performance space.

For a weekend in mid-July, world music performers from across Canada and farther afield converge on downtown London for **Sunfest** (Victoria Park, 519/672-1522, www.sunfest.on.ca, July), an outdoor festival of world music. All concerts are free (although donations are gladly accepted). Come on down to the fair, the **Western Fair** (519/438-7203 or 800/619-

4629, www.realseriousfun.ca, September), that is, London's old-time country fair, with rides, concerts, horse shows, animal exhibitions, and more. It's on County Road 2 (Florence Street) east of the city center.

Known as **Richmond Row** (www.richmondrowlondon.com), the downtown shopping district that runs along Richmond Street from the Grand Theatre north to Oxford Street is lined with boutiques and places to eat. Take some time to stroll and browse.

ACCOMMODATIONS

If you're looking for a basic chain motel, London has a slew of them south of downtown on Wellington Road. Otherwise, accommodations are clustered in the downtown area or near the University of Western Ontario campus north of the center.

Under $100

London's most centrally located budget lodging is the friendly **ACBB Accommodations** (190 Wellington St., 519/936-7823, www.guesthouselondon.ca, $25 dorm, $65 d), a small, privately run hostel. You can choose a bunk in the four- or six-bed mixed-gender dorms or opt for a private double; all the rooms share baths. The sleeping spaces are small, but with the comfortable lounges and shared kitchen, you won't spend much time there anyway. Rates include breakfast, parking, and Internet access.

A cross between a dormitory and a hotel, the **Guest House on the Mount** (Ignatia Hall, 1486 Richmond St., 519/641-8100, www.guesthouseonthemount.ca, $49–79 s, $59–89 d) is an excellent value, no-frills lodging that attracts guests of all ages. The spacious hotel-style rooms are simply furnished, with a bed, a TV, and not much else; you can choose no bath (and use the large washrooms down the hall), a "half bath" (with a toilet and sink), or a private bath. There's no food service, but you can prep your own in the shared kitchen. Other facilities include a lounge, a laundry, and free Wi-Fi. It's just north of the Western campus, but it's not easy to find; turn onto the grounds of the Windermere on the Mount retirement

home and follow the signs to Ignatia Hall. The guesthouse is on the second floor.

$100-150

One block from the Richmond Row shopping district, the **StationPark All Suite Hotel** (242 Pall Mall St., 519/642-4444 or 800/561-4574, www.stationparkinn.ca, $130–155 d) is popular with business travelers, who appreciate the suites with a bedroom and separate living area; they'd work for a family, too. The "superior" suites on floors 9–14 are a little brighter and have newer furnishings, but all rooms are equipped with mini-fridges, microwaves, and coffeemakers. Continental breakfast and Internet access are included; parking is $12/day.

Built in 1878 as a private home, the **Idlewyld Inn** (36 Grand Ave., 519/433-2891 or 877/435-3466, www.idlewyldinn.com, $130–200 d) is a rambling mansion with bay windows, stained glass, gingerbread trim, and a turret. The original owner, Charles Smith Hyman, served as London's mayor, a federal cabinet minister, and captain of Canada's national cricket team, and you can imagine this Victorian notable receiving guests in the formal parlor or in the traditional dining room. The 19 guest rooms feel a bit old-fashioned, furnished with antiques and period wallpapers, but they all have flat-screen TVs and Internet access (Wi-Fi is available only in the common areas). If you're celebrating a romantic occasion, ask for a suite with a whirlpool tub for two, or request champagne or chocolate-covered strawberries delivered to your room.

$150-200

In a lane facing the Covent Garden Market, the **Hotel Metro** (32 Covent Market Pl., 519/518-9000, www.hotelmetro.ca, $169–189 d) is London's first "boutique" hotel, set in a former shoe factory warehouse. The best of the 20 contemporary loft-style rooms, with iPod docks and coffeemakers, are on the fourth (top) floor, where they have exposed brick walls and oversized windows. There's no pool or workout room, but guests can request a pass to a nearby fitness club.

FOOD

You can find coffee, pastries, sandwiches, soups, salads, fresh produce, Thai food, sushi, falafel, and more at the **Covent Garden Market** (130 King St., 519/439-3921, www.coventmarket.com, 8 A.M.–6 P.M. Mon.–Sat., 8 A.M.–7:30 P.M. Fri., 11 A.M.–4 P.M. Sun.)—just the spot for a quick bite downtown. Outside on the market plaza is a seasonal **farmer's market** (8 A.M.–1 P.M., Thurs. and Sat., May–Nov.).

For scrumptious muffins, cookies, quiche, and other baked goods, head to the **Black Walnut Bakery Café** (134 Wortley Rd., 519/850-2253) in the Wortley Village neighborhood (www.wortleyvillage.com) south of downtown. The oatmeal date scones are deliciously crumbly, and if you're in a savory mood, try their flaky spinach pie; they also serve sandwiches and soups midday. In a brightly painted house along downtown's Richmond Row, vegan café **Veg Out** (646 Richmond St., 519/850-8688, www.vegoutrestaurant.com, 11:30 A.M.–9 P.M. Tues.–Wed., 11:30 A.M.–10 P.M. Thurs.–Sat., 11:30 A.M.–4 P.M. Sun., $7–14) serves meat-free sandwiches and salads, as well as smoothies and fresh juices.

In Wortley Village, locals flock to **Relish** (135 Wortley Rd., 519/667-0606, www.relishhamburger.com, noon–9 P.M. Sun.–Thurs., 11:30 A.M.–10 P.M. Fri.–Sat., $12–16) with good reason: the oversized "gourmet" burgers—which come in chicken, lamb, salmon, veggie, portobello mushroom, and bison varieties, in addition to the standard sirloin—are delicious. You can choose from more than three dozen funky burger toppings, like the "Hungry Frat Boy" (macaroni and cheese, double-smoked bacon, tomato, and pickles), the "P, B, & C" (peanut butter, bacon, and cream cheese), or the simpler "Stephen W. Andrus" (red onions, pickle, lettuce, and tomato), then add a signature housemade relish, from smoky avocado, to four pepper, to habanero peach. It's a super-casual joint, with brown-paper-topped tables and buckets full of condiments.

The chef at **Kantina** (349 Talbot St., 519/672-5862, www.kantina.ca, lunch 11:30 A.M.–2:30 P.M. Tues.–Fri., dinner 5:30–10 P.M. Tues.–Thurs., 5:30 P.M.–2 A.M. Fri.–Sat., noon–8 P.M. Sun., lunch $11–16, dinner $15–21) hails from Serbia, so the fare in this upscale contemporary bistro has influences from his home country. The Serbian salad includes peppers, tomatoes, cucumbers, onions, and feta cheese in a lemony dressing; *zhganci* (Balkan-style gnocchi) accompany the beef goulash; and even the hamburger comes with Serbian condiments.

INFORMATION AND SERVICES

Tourism London (www.londontourism.ca) runs two helpful visitor centers that provide information about the London area. The **Dundas Street Information Centre** (267 Dundas St., 8:30 A.M.–4:30 P.M. Mon.–Fri., 10 A.M.–5 P.M. Sat.–Sun.) is right downtown. If you're driving into town from Highway 401, take the Wellington Road exit, and you'll pass the **London Tourist Information Centre** (696 Wellington Road S., 8:30 A.M.–8 P.M. daily) on your way to the city center. The *London Visitors Guide* and their *Taste London* restaurant guide are both available online.

GETTING THERE
By Air

London International Airport (YXU, 1750 Crumlin Rd., 519/452-4015, www.londonairport.on.ca) is 10 kilometers (six miles) northeast of downtown. Air Canada (www.aircanada.com) flies to Toronto and Ottawa; WestJet (www.westjet.com) has direct flights to Winnipeg, Calgary, Orlando (FL), Las Vegas (NV), and Cancún, Mexico; and United (www.united.com) flies nonstop to Chicago (IL). A taxi between the airport and downtown London will cost $30–35.

If you need to rent a car, **Avis** (www.avis.com), **Budget** (www.budget.ca), **Enterprise** (www.enterpriserentacar.ca), and **National** (www.nationalcar.ca) all have offices at the London airport (1750 Crumlin Rd.).

London Transit (www.ltconline.ca) buses can take you between the airport and downtown (Mon.–Fri.), but you have to change

LAKE ERIE TO LAKE HURON

buses. Take bus #36 from the airport to Fanshawe College, where you can connect with bus #4 or #20 heading downtown. You'll find many more flight options into or out of **Toronto's Pearson Airport** (www.toronto-pearson.com). To travel between Pearson and London, you can take the **Robert Q Airbus** (105 Wharncliffe Rd. S., 519/673-6804 or 800/265-4948, www.robertq.com, 2.25 hours, one-way adults $54.52, seniors and students $51.67, kids under 12 $27.27).

By Train

London is easy to reach by train, since the Toronto–Windsor and Toronto–Sarnia trains all stop at London's **VIA Rail station** (205 York St., 888/842-7245, www.viarail.ca) downtown. Most of the trains between Toronto and London (one-way adults $50–68, kids 2–11 $25–34) make the trip in 2.25–2.5 hours, but check the schedule: a couple chug along for 3.5 hours. Windsor to London (one-way adults $47–63, kids 23–32) takes 1.75 hours.

By Bus

Greyhound operates numerous daily buses

from Toronto to the London **Greyhound Bus Station** (101 York St., 519/434-3250, www.greyhound.ca, 2–2.5 hours, one-way adults $30–44, children 2–11 $23–33) downtown.

By Car

London is 195 kilometers (120 miles) southwest of Toronto; it's a 2–2.5-hour drive. You can either take the QEW to Highway 403 to the 401 or just pick up the 401 directly. From the 401, take exit 187 and follow Wellington Road north toward downtown.

GETTING AROUND

Downtown London is compact enough to explore on foot, but to see more of the city's sights and neighborhoods, you'll need wheels. The city does have an extensive bus system, run by **London Transit** (519/451-1347, www.ltconline.ca, adults $2.75, kids 5–11 $1.35), although it may take some effort to figure out the route you want; call their customer service line or stop into the **Downtown Information Office** (150 Dundas St., near Richmond St.; 7:30 A.M.–7 P.M. Mon.–Fri., 8:30 A.M.–6 P.M. Sat.) if you need help.

Southwestern Ontario

In the 1800s, thousands of African-American slaves fled from the United States to freedom in Canada. Following what was known as the "Underground Railroad," a network of safe houses and churches that gave shelter to the refugees, the vast majority of those slaves crossed into Canada into what is now southwestern Ontario. Many remained in the region, with significant settlements in Windsor, Sandwich, Amherstburg, Chatham, Dresden, and Buxton, and many of their descendants live here today. A number of sights throughout southwestern Ontario enable you to explore this African-Canadian Heritage Route, tracing the history of the former slaves and their new life in Canada.

Windsor, now this region's largest city,

continues to be a magnet for newcomers, attracting immigrants from many nations. It's an industrial city, but it has several worthwhile museums, and its diverse population means that its restaurants offer up a multiethnic cornucopia.

Southwestern Ontario wears another hat, too. It's a small but growing wine-making region, where you can head out for a day or two of wine-tasting and exploring.

CHATHAM AND VICINITY

Many former slaves settled in the town of Chatham and the nearby communities of Dresden and Buxton, where several sites explore the history of these Afro-Canadian settlements.

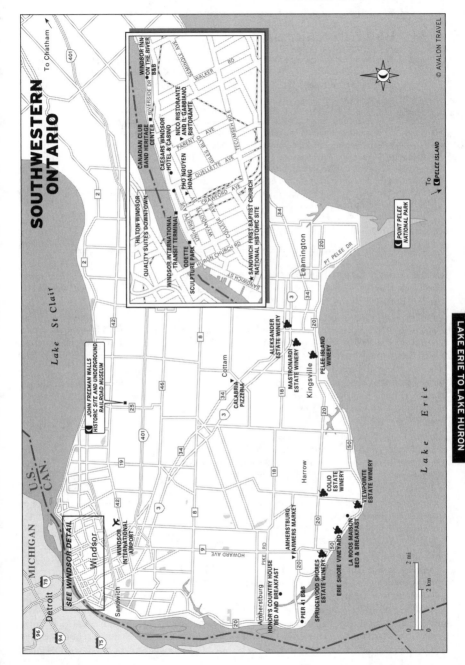

SOUTHWESTERN ONTARIO

LAKE ERIE TO LAKE HURON

© AVALON TRAVEL

Windsor Detail (inset):
- HILTON WINDSOR
- QUALITY SUITES DOWNTOWN
- WINDSOR INTERNATIONAL TRANSIT TERMINAL
- ODETTE SCULPTURE PARK
- CANADIAN CLUB BRAND HERITAGE CENTER
- WINDSOR INN ON THE RIVER B&B
- CAESARS WINDSOR HOTEL & CASINO
- NICO RISTORANTE AND IL GABBIANO RISTORANTE
- PHO NGUYEN HOANG
- SANDWICH FIRST BAPTIST CHURCH NATIONAL HISTORIC SITE

Streets: RIVERSIDE DR, WALKER RD, SEMINOLE AVE, UNIVERSITY AVE, WYANDOTTE AVE, COLLEGE AVE, CRAWFORD AVE, QUELLETTE AVE, GILES BLVD AVE, PARENT AVE, TECUMSEH RD E, HURON CHURCH RD, SANDWICH ST

Main map labels:
- To Chatham
- Lake St Clair
- MICHIGAN
- Detroit
- U.S. / CAN.
- Windsor
- WINDSOR INTERNATIONAL AIRPORT
- SEE WINDSOR DETAIL
- Sandwich
- JOHN FREEMAN WALLS HISTORIC SITE AND UNDERGROUND RAILROAD MUSEUM
- Cottam
- CALABRIA PIZZERIA
- ALEKSANDER ESTATE WINERY
- MASTRONARDI ESTATE WINERY
- Kingsville
- PELEE ISLAND WINERY
- Leamington
- PT PELEE DR
- POINT PELEE NATIONAL PARK
- To PELEE ISLAND
- Lake Erie
- Harrow
- COLIO ESTATE WINERY
- VIEWPOINTE ESTATE WINERY
- AMHERSTBURG FARMERS MARKET
- LA ROOS MAISON BED & BREAKFAST
- ERIE SHORE VINEYARD
- SPRUCEWOOD SHORES ESTATE WINERY
- PIER 41 B&B
- HONOR'S COUNTRY HOUSE BED AND BREAKFAST
- Amherstburg
- HOWARD AVE
- PIKE RD

Highways: 401, 2, 42, 8, 46, 25, 34, 3, 19, 18, 9, 20, 50, 75, 94, 96

Scale: 0 - 2 mi / 0 - 2 km

SLAVERY IN CANADA

Although by the mid-1800s, Canada was a safe haven for slaves escaping north from the United States along the Underground Railroad, Canada unfortunately had a history of slavery, as well. In 1629, the first slave was transported from Africa into the colony of New France. From that beginning, many of the early British and French settlers in Canada kept slaves throughout the 1600s and 1700s.

In 1793, Lieutenant Governor John Graves Simcoe prohibited the importation of slaves into the region then known as Upper Canada. By this decree, no new slaves could be brought into the province, but existing slaves were not freed. It wasn't until 40 year later, in 1833, that the British "Slavery Abolition Act" freed slaves across the British Empire, including Canada.

The migration of slaves from the United States into Canada began in earnest after the United States passed the 1850 Fugitive Slave Act, which required law enforcement officers to apprehend and return escaping slaves, even in the non-slave-holding northern states. The Underground Railroad developed to shelter fugitive slaves en route to Canada to prevent them from being returned to slavery in the South. Until the American Civil War in the 1860s, thousands of slaves fled north to freedom in Canada, many of them settling in Ontario.

Uncle Tom's Cabin Historic Site

The Uncle Tom's Cabin Historic Site (29251 Uncle Tom's Rd., Dresden, 519/683-2978, www.uncletomscabin.org, 10 A.M.–4 P.M. Tues.–Sat., noon–4 P.M. Sun., mid-May–Oct, also open 10 A.M. Mon. in July–Aug.; adults $6.25, seniors and students 13–17 $5.25, kids 6–12 $4.50, families $20) tells the story of the former slave and abolitionist Reverend Josiah Henson (1796–1883), who was born on a plantation in Maryland, then sold to a slave owner in Kentucky before following the Underground Railroad north to Canada. Settling in the Dresden area in 1841, he helped establish the Dawn Settlement, a community that became a refuge for former slaves. In 1852, American writer Harriet Beecher Stowe published her historic antislavery novel *Uncle Tom's Cabin,* which some historians say was based in part on Henson's memoirs.

Start your visit to the site by watching a video introducing Josiah Henson, the history of slavery in the United States and Canada, and the settlements that former slaves set up in southwestern Ontario. Then visit the gallery, where exhibits explore these topics in more detail. Outside the gallery, you can tour several restored buildings, including Henson House, the reverend's last residence, as well as a local church built in the 1880s. Inside the church, look for the booklet "Sounds of Freedom," which explains that many songs slaves sung contained coded messages. "The Gospel Train's a 'Comin'," for example, would alert other slaves that a group was planning an escape. You can also visit the small cemetery where Henson is buried.

The Uncle Tom's Cabin Historic Site is located just west of the town of Dresden, which is 30 kilometers (19 miles) north of Chatham. From Highway 401, the most direct route is to take exit 101, Kent Bridge Road/County Road 15, and continue north to Highway 21. Turn left (west) onto Highway 21 toward Dresden, then turn left onto Park Street and left again onto Uncle Tom's Road. If you're coming from Chatham, take Grand Avenue East, which becomes Longwoods Road. Then turn north on Kent Bridge Road/County Road 15 and follow the above directions.

Chatham-Kent Black Historical Society

In the 1850s, as more and more blacks established themselves in the Chatham area, the town became a center for Afro-Canadian intellectual life, and by 1861, Chatham had one of the largest black populations of any town in Upper

Canada. The Chatham-Kent Black Historical Society (177 King St. E., Chatham, 519/352-3565, www.ckblackhistoricalsociety.org, 9 A.M.–4 P.M. Mon.–Fri., $5) maintains a small museum about the region's Afro-Canadian heritage and about notable citizens from the black community from this period and beyond. The museum is located inside the W.I.S.H. Centre, a community center near downtown.

◖ Buxton National Historic Site and Museum

In 1849, an abolitionist organization called the Elgin Association purchased 3,650 hectares (9,000 acres) of land south of Chatham to establish a settlement for former slaves and free blacks. The new settlers would pay $2.50 per acre to buy a parcel of land, and within five years, approximately 150 families had settled here. The community opened a school, which not only successfully educated Afro-Canadian children, but also began attracting white students who lived nearby, becoming one of North America's first integrated schools. By the 1860s, more than 2,000 people lived in what became known as the Buxton Settlement; at the time, it was the largest black settlement in Canada.

The Buxton National Historic Site and Museum (21975 A. D. Shadd Rd., North Buxton, 519/352-4799, www.buxtonmuseum.com, 1–4:30 P.M. Wed.–Sun. May–June and Sept.; 10 A.M.–4:30 P.M. daily July–Aug.; 1–4:30 P.M. Mon.–Fri. Oct.–Apr.; adults $6, seniors and students $5, families $20) tells the fascinating story of this settlement and its black community. A 20-minute film introduces the settlement, and among the artifacts in the museum is a berth from a slave ship (its small size illustrating the horrifically cramped conditions on board) and original slave shackles, in both adult and child sizes.

Also on the site is an 1852 log cabin that was the oldest home in the settlement, a one-room schoolhouse used from 1861 until 1968, and the British Methodist Episcopal Church, built in 1866 and still in use today.

The museum is 15 kilometers (nine miles) southwest of Chatham. From Highway 401,

take exit 81, County Road 27/Bloomfield Road south, and turn right (west) onto 8 Line/County Road 14 and left (south) onto A. D. Shadd Road.

Accommodations and Food

Though options in Chatham are fairly limited, there is one surprisingly cool place to stay—the **Retro Suites Hotel** (2 King St. W., 519/351-5885 or 866/617-3876, www.retrosuites.com, $129–249 d). In a restored block of Victorian-era buildings, the 28 rooms are wildly different, from the "Chrome-e-Delic," a vibrantly colored '60s-style pad; to the "Easy Rider," with an antique motorcycle hanging from the ceiling; to the traditionally posh "King William." The hotel's dining room, the **Chilled Cork Restaurant and Lounge** (11 A.M.–10 P.M. Mon.–Sat., 8 A.M.–2 P.M. Sun., lunch $7–12, dinner $14–34), offers an appropriately eclectic menu that travels from pastas, steaks, and Ontario pickerel to kangaroo sirloin.

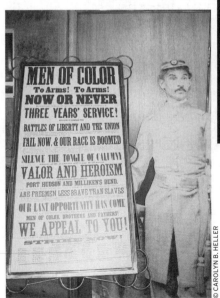

an army recruitment poster targeting African-Canadians at the Buxton National Historic Site and Museum

Otherwise, there are several basic roadside motels on Grand Avenue East. You'll find cafés and sandwich shops on and around King Street downtown.

Practicalities

Chatham is off Highway 401, 290 kilometers (180 miles) and 110 kilometers (68 miles) southwest of Toronto and London, respectively. Take exit 90, and go north on Highway 40/Communication Road toward Wallaceburg; then turn left onto Park Avenue East, which will take you toward the center of town. If you're coming from Windsor, take exit 81, Bloomfield Road, off the 401; follow Bloomfield Road north, then turn right (east) onto Park Avenue West. Chatham is 80 kilometers (50 miles) northeast of Windsor. **Chatham-Kent Tourism** (445 Grand Ave. W., Chatham, 519/351-7700 or 800/561-6125, www.visitck.ca) can provide information about traveling in the region.

KINGSVILLE AND LEAMINGTON

Along the Lake Erie shore, the towns of Kingsville and Leamington are popular with bird-watchers—Point Pelee National Park in Leamington is a highlight. The surrounding land is farm country. Leamington is known as the "Tomato Capital of Canada," both for the extensive tomato crop that grows nearby and for the large Heinz plant that dominates the town. You can also visit several nearby wineries. Kingsville and Leamington are the departure points for ferries to Pelee Island.

◖ Point Pelee National Park

The southernmost point on Canada's mainland is this waterfront national park (1118 Point Pelee Dr., Leamington, 519/322-2365 or 888/773-8888, www.pc.gc.ca or www. friendsofpointpelee.com, adults $7.80, seniors $6.80, kids 6–16 $3.80, families $19.60), a finger of land that juts into Lake Erie southeast of Leamington. At the park **Visitor Centre** (10 A.M.–6 P.M. daily late June–early Sept.; 10 A.M.–5 P.M. Apr., late May–late June, and early Sept.–Oct.; noon–5 P.M. Sat.–Sun.

Nov.–Mar.), you can walk through exhibits about the region's flora and fauna. Several short hiking trails start near the center, as well.

The park is an important stopover point for a vast number of migrating birds and butterflies. More than 370 bird species have been identified in the Point Pelee area, with the greatest variety of birds during the annual spring migration (typically the first three weeks of May). Songbirds are particularly prevalent in the spring. The Visitor Centre has extended hours (7 A.M.–5 P.M. daily) during the spring bird migration. Monarch butterflies also migrate through the Point Pelee region; visit from late August through early October for the best viewings or call the park's recorded information line (519/322-2371) to find out the butterfly status. Fall brings migrating hawks and other raptors.

Follow the **Marsh Boardwalk Trail,** a one-kilometer (0.6-mile) loop through the cattails to experience the marshy habitat that encompasses the park's eastern side. Near the Marsh Boardwalk, you can rent canoes ($12/hour; $25/4 hours) and bicycles (adults $10/hour, $15/4 hours; kids $5/hour, $8/4 hours) at the **Cattail Café** (519/322-1654, May–mid-Oct.), which also sells snacks.

The road between the Visitor Centre and the narrow spit of land at the park's southern end is closed to private vehicles during the busy spring through fall seasons. The park service runs the **Shuttle to the Tip** (Apr.–mid-Oct., call for hours), which takes visitors close to the park's endpoint. From the shuttle drop-off point, there's a one-kilometer (0.6-mile) loop trail to the tip and back. Swimming is prohibited near the tip, because the currents can be quite strong. To swim, head for one of the sandy beaches along the park's western shore.

The park is open year-round, although some services, including the Shuttle to the Tip, are seasonal. Park admission rates are reduced slightly from November through March.

Wineries

Canada's southernmost winery, the **Pelee Island Winery** (455 Seacliff Dr./County Rd.

20, Kingsville, 519/733-6551 or 800/597-3533, www.peleeisland.com, winery 9 A.M.–6 P.M. Mon.–Sat., 11 A.M.–5 P.M. Sun.; tours daily noon, 2 P.M., and 4 P.M., adults $5, seniors $4) grows its grapes on Pelee Island but makes most of its wines at this Kingsville location; only its ice wines are processed on the island, since the grapes need to be pressed while they are still frozen. The winery produces a wide range of wines, including pinot grigio, Riesling, cabernet merlot, cabernet franc, and ice wine. Tours include a video about the wine-making process, a walk through the winery, and a tasting.

Most of the other Kingsville-area wineries are small, family-owned properties, including **Mastronardi Estate Winery** (1193 Road 3 E., Kingsville, 519/733-9463 or 800/320-5040, www.mastronardiwines.com, 11 A.M.–5 P.M. daily; tours by appointment) and **Aleksander Estate Winery** (1542 County Rd. 34, Ruthven, 519/326-2024, www.aleksanderestate.com, 11 A.M.–6 P.M. Mon.–Fri., 11 A.M.–5 P.M. Sat.–Sun., tours by appointment).

Entertainment and Events

The **Festival of Birds** (www.friendsofpointpelee.com, May) at Point Pelee National Park (1118 Point Pelee Dr., Leamington, 519/322-2365 or 888/773-8888) celebrates the annual spring bird migration, with guided birding hikes, birding presentations, and other special events. A highlight of the three-day **Leamington Tomato Festival** (519/326-2878, www.leamingtontomatofestival.com, Aug.), which includes concerts, a parade, and, of course, tomato tastings, is the annual "tomato stomp." Don't wear white.

Accommodations and Food

At the **Hellemsfield Inn** (2 Mill St. W., at Division St. S., Kingsville, 519/733-5250, www.bbcanada.com/12468.html, $80 s, $95 d), owners Carol and Scott Sitler have created self-contained guest quarters in their 1872 Greek Revival–style home. Two crisp and comfortable guest rooms (one upstairs and one on the main level) share a common area. The bedrooms aren't large, so the space is well suited to sociable types or two

couples traveling together who'd enjoy hanging out in front of the wood-and-stone fireplace in the cheery living area. The owners serve a full breakfast on Saturday and Sunday, and a lighter continental spread during the week.

Built in the early 1900s, the stately brick **Inn 31** (31 Division St. S., Kingsville, 519/733-6900, www.jacksdining.com, $79–99 s, $109–129 d) houses a restaurant/pub with three guest rooms upstairs. Second-floor rooms have original dark woodwork and are furnished with antique-style pieces, mixed with modern accessories, puffy duvets on the queen-size beds, and flat-screen TVs. Rates include continental breakfast and Wi-Fi. Lively **Jack's Gastropub** (11:30 A.M.–9 P.M. daily, $10–22) serves sandwiches and burgers during the day, adding larger plates like barbecued ribs or pesto salmon in the evening. They stock a decent selection of Ontario beers, too.

You can practically roll out of bed and onto the Pelee Island ferry (at least when it's leaving from the Leamington docks) when you stay at the **Seacliffe Inn** (388 Erie St. S., Leamington, 519/324-9266, www.seacliffeinn.com, $119–159 d). The 23 nautical-themed motel-style rooms with sturdy wooden furnishings are comfortable enough, and you can grab a beer or a bite in the downstairs lounge.

Walk into **Tony's Tacos** (52 Erie St S., Leamington, 519/326-0110), and you'll think you've wandered out of Leamington and into a convivial cantina in small-town Mexico. The walls are bright orange, the merengue music blares, and the traditional tacos—heaped with meat—are only two bucks each. Ask for the housemade green hot sauce. On weekends, hunker down over a steaming bowl of *posole* (soup made with corn or hominy) or *menudo* (tripe stew).

Lit with strings of twinkling lights, the **Calabria Pizzeria** (123 Talbot Rd. W./Hwy. 34., Cottam, 519/839-5611, dinner Tues.–Sun., $12–25) is a casually romantic restaurant with a serious commitment to local food, masquerading as a pizza joint. Oh, they do make fine pizzas, topped with locally sourced ingredients, but they fry up an even more excellent fresh perch dinner. If tomatoes are in season, order the Bria salad, dripping with juices, along with olives, feta cheese, cucumbers, and red onions. The wine list is local, too. Worth a drive, the restaurant is in the town of Cottam, 12 kilometers (7.5 miles) north of Kingsville. From Highway 3, go north on Highway 27; at Talbot Road/Highway 34, turn left (west) for one block.

Information and Services

Ontario's most unusual tourism office may be the **Leamington Tourist Information Booth** (Talbot St. W. at Mill St. W., www.leamington. ca). Reflecting the town's tomato-growing and -processing heritage, it's shaped like a tomato! You can pick up local information and pose for tomato photos. **Tourism Windsor, Essex, and Pelee Island** (333 Riverside Dr. W., Suite 103, Windsor, 519/255-6530 or 800/265-3633, www. tourismwindsoressex.com) can also provide information about Kingsville and Leamington.

Getting There and Around

You'll want a car to explore the Kingsville-Leamington area. From Toronto (350 kilometers, or 215 miles) or London (170 kilometers, or 107 miles), take Highway 401 south to Highway 77 south to Leamington. Kingsville is 15 kilometers (nine miles) west of Leamington. County Road 20, which is Seacliff Drive in Leamington and Main Street in Kingsville, connects the two towns.

If coming from Windsor, follow Walker Road south to Highway 3 east. Exit at Division Road/County Road 29 for Kingsville (40 kilometers, or 25 miles) or at Erie Street for Leamington (50 kilometers, or 30 miles).

Ferries to Pelee Island (www.ontarioferries.com) leave from Leamington (Erie St. S., 519/326-2154, Mar.–July) and Kingsville (Lakeview Ave., at Park St., 519/733-4474, Aug.–Dec.). To travel between Kingsville/Leamington and northern Ohio, you can take the Pelee Island ferry to or from Sandusky.

◖ PELEE ISLAND

Canada's southernmost point is this laid-back little island in Lake Erie, where most visitors

the tourist information booth in Leamington, Canada's "Tomato Capital"

come simply to escape the mainland's hustle and bustle. In fact, the island's name, which locals pronounce "PEE-lee," comes from the French *pelée,* meaning "bare." Pelee is ringed with beaches—it's a peaceful spot for cycling and bird-watching, and there's even a winery—but otherwise, you won't find many "sights." As one island innkeeper said, "There's nothing to do here, but it takes at least three days to do it."

Pelee's summer population is about 1,500, but only 300 hardy souls live on the island year-round. Many accommodations and eateries are seasonal, opening in April or May and closing in October or November. Even during the "open" seasons, hours can be erratic; if few visitors are around, or if the owner has something else to do, places can close unexpectedly, so it's always a good idea to call ahead.

Travel on and off the island is also weather-dependent. While Pelee has some of the warmest weather in Canada, the winds can whip up along Lake Erie, causing the ferry to delay or even cancel service. While you can easily make a day trip to Pelee, don't go if you can't manage a delay of several hours or a potential overnight. Ferries to the island run from mid-March through mid-December. You can also fly to Pelee from Windsor; in winter, the only way to or from the island is by air.

Cycling is a popular option for getting around the island; from the west ferry dock, it's 10 kilometers (6.2 miles) north to the lighthouse (one-way), 1.2 kilometers (0.75 mile) south to the Pelee Island winery, and four kilometers (2.5 miles) south to Fish Point. You can bring your own bike on the ferry or rent one from **Comfortech Bike Rental** (West Shore Rd., 519/724-2828, www.comfortechbikerental.com) near the West Dock; they're behind the Westview Tavern.

Sights

Jam-packed with artifacts, photos, drawings, and fossils, the **Pelee Island Heritage Centre** (1073 West Shore Rd., 519/724-2291, www.peleeislandmuseum.ca, 10 A.M.–5 P.M. daily May–Oct., adults $3, seniors $2.50, students

watching the sea on a rocky Pelee Island beach

© CAROLYN B. HELLER

LAKE ERIE TO LAKE HURON

$2), a small museum opposite the ferry docks, is a good place to start your island explorations. Exhibits detail the island's geology, ecology, and human history, and you can also learn about shipwrecks that plagued the surrounding waters. Upstairs is the **Kite Museum** (www.thekitemuseum.com), an idiosyncratic collection of kites from around the world.

Pelee Island Winery (20 East West Rd., 519/733-6551 or 800/597-3533, www.pelee-island.com, 10 A.M.–4 P.M. Mon.–Thurs., 10 A.M.–7 P.M. Fri.–Sat. late May–late June and early Sept.–mid-Oct.; 10 A.M.–8 P.M. daily late June–early Sept.) grows 223 hectares (550 acres) of grapes on the island. At the Island Pavilion visitor center, find out more about the wine-making process and take a walk among the vines. Tours (noon and 2 P.M. daily late May–mid-Oct., additional tours 4 and 6 P.M. late June–early Sept., adults $5, seniors $4) run 90 minutes and include a wine tasting. Also on the grounds is the **Deli Hut,** a sandwich shop serving burgers, chili, and snacks. The winery is south of the ferry docks, at the intersection of West Shore Road.

On West Shore Road north of the dock, be on the lookout for **Stoneman,** a massive stone *inukshuk* sculpture, designed by local resident Peter Letkeman. The kids at the Pelee Island Public School gave Stoneman his name.

On the island's northeast tip, follow the short trail in the **Lighthouse Point Provincial Nature Reserve** (www.ontarioparks.com) that leads to the 1834 limestone lighthouse. There's a small pebbly beach, but no restrooms or other facilities.

At the **Stone Road Alvar Conservation Area** (www.erca.org, dawn–dusk daily year-round, free), you can see one of Pelee Island's distinctive natural features: alvars. Areas of limestone covered with a thin layer of topsoil, alvars allow unique vegetation to grow. You can wander along the rocky shore, and butterfly spotters have seen five rare species here, including the Giant Swallowtail, Tawny Emperor, Acadian hairstreak, Hackberry Butterfly, and Sachem Skipper. The conservation area is at the island's southeast corner; from the West Dock, take West Shore Road to East West Road, cross to the east side of the island, then turn south on Stone Road.

A popular bird-watching spot is the **Fish Point Provincial Nature Reserve** (519/825-4659, www.ontarioparks.com), a stopover point for migrating birds. There's also a beach, but no facilities. The reserve is at Pelee's southwestern tip. Follow West Shore Road south until it becomes McCormick Road, then continue south to Fish Point.

Other island beaches include **Sunset Beach** (West Shore Rd., north of the ferry docks) and **East Park Beach** (East Shore Rd., just north of East West Rd.).

Entertainment and Events

Birders and their friends flock to Pelee Island for the annual **Spring Song Weekend** (www.peleeislandmuseum.ca, May), which typically includes a bird-watching race, a pig roast, and an evening banquet with a presentation by a guest author.

A major event on the island is the annual **Pelee Island Pheasant Hunt** (www.pelee.org, Oct.–Nov.). The hunt started in the 1900s as a way to control the island's burgeoning pheasant population, but more recently, it's become a sporting event, with pheasants raised for the hunt on the Pelee Island Pheasant Farm. The hunt draws hundreds of visitors during the last two weeks of October and the first week of November; if hunting isn't your thing, visit during another time.

Accommodations and Camping

Pelee Island has a few small inns and B&Bs; on busy July and August weekends, you might want to arrange a place to stay before you hop on the ferry. Pelee isn't the place for deluxe lodgings, either. While most accommodations are comfortable, none are luxurious. One option is to rent a cottage, which is convenient if you want to prepare your own food; check the Pelee Island website (www.pelee.org) for links to rental cottages. The island does have restaurants, but not many.

The Anchor and Wheel Inn (11 West Shore

Rd., 519/724-2195, www.anchorwheelinn.com, Apr.–early Nov.) has a quirky variety of accommodations. Upstairs in the main building, six snug chambers ($65 s, $85 d) are furnished like grandmother's guest rooms; some retain their original tin ceilings. Guests share two baths, and rates include breakfast. Out back, there's a block of basic motel rooms with private baths ($125–175 d), as well as a camping area ($20 tent sites, $35 electrical sites). They also run a restaurant and bar (dinner Wed.–Sun. Apr.–early Nov.).

It's worth staying at **The Wandering Pheasant Inn** (1060 East West Rd., 519/724-2270, www.thewanderingpheasantinn.com) just for enthusiastic owner Sandra Laranja's wonderful breakfasts, which might include a frittata, homemade bread, a creative assortment of jams, and good conversation. The original Victorian inn building houses several simple guest rooms ($125 d) with shared baths. In an adjacent cottage-style block, the rooms ($175) are larger, furnished with Victoriana (and en suite baths). You can walk to the water in less than five minutes.

Near the lighthouse on the northeast corner of the island, the **Wavecrest Bed and Breakfast** (79 East Shore Rd., 519/724-1111, www.wavecrestpelee.com, May–early Nov., $160–170 d) faces a sandy beach. The "Fishing Suite" and the "Beachfront Suite" are both light and airy, with white antique furniture, while the smaller "Victorian Suite" lives up to its name with a sleigh bed and gold-framed portraits; all three rooms have private baths. Owners Thom Brown and Barry Wayman encourage guests to mingle over wine and cheese in the spacious living room and serve a full breakfast each morning.

The **East Park Campground** (1362 East Shore Rd., 519/724-2200, www.pelee.org, May–early Nov., $20) has 25 sites for tents and trailers, a short walk from East Beach. There are no electrical hookups, but there are washrooms with showers, as well as a small store.

Food

You can buy picnic supplies and groceries at the **Co-op Grocery Store** (West Pump Rd. and Centre Dyke Rd., 519/724-2910) on the island's north end. If there's something specific you want, though, bring it from the mainland. Tiny **Conorlee's Bakery and Delicatessen** (5 North Shore Rd., 519/724-2321, http://conorlee.bravehost.com, open year-round; call for seasonal hours; $4–7), in a little yellow cottage, serves pastries and coffee in the mornings, deli sandwiches and pizza later in the day. One Friday each month (May–Sept.), Conorlee's hosts their Wine and Dinner Series ($38/person), a five-course meal with wine pairings served in the garden at the Pelee Island Winery.

Crammed with buoys, shells, sailing flags, and other nautical geegaws, the funky dining room at **The Anchor and Wheel** (dinner Wed.–Sun. Apr.–early Nov., $15–35) looks like it washed ashore from a Jimmy Buffet song. You can start with a tropical drink (out in the Tiki Bar if the weather cooperates), but the real action is on the dinner plates, laden with bountiful portions of fish, prime rib, or pasta. The local perch is excellent.

Your basic island bar, the **Scudder Beach Bar and Grill** (North Shore Rd., 519/724-2902, www.scudderbeach.com, lunch and dinner daily May–Sept., $8–12) serves wings, wraps, fried fish, and other pub fare. Bands liven things up most summer weekends.

Information and Services

The **Municipality of Pelee Island** (519/724-2931 or 866/889-5203,www.pelee.org) is the best source of local island information. If you'd like a guide to organize your Pelee Island visit, contact **Explore Pelee: Pelee Island Tours** (519/325-8687 or 519/724-2285, www.explore-pelee.com). Owner Anne Marie Fortner can tell you anything you need to know about the island and offers several different bike tours ($25–40), as well as van-based tours ($50) that explore Pelee's geology, agriculture, or history.

Getting There

Pelee Island is located in Lake Erie, south

of Kingsville and Leamington and north of Sandusky, Ohio. Between late March and mid-December, the **Pelee Island Transportation Company** (519/724-2115 or 800/661-2220, www.ontarioferries.com) runs ferries to the island. Note that from the Ontario mainland, *the ferries leave from different points* depending on the season. March through July, the ferries depart from the **Leamington docks** (Erie St. S., 519/326-2154), while August to December, the boats leave from the **Kingsville docks** (Lakeview Ave., at Park St., 519/733-4474). The fare (one-way adults $7.50, seniors $6.25, kids 6–12 $3.25, bicycles $3.75, cars $16.50) is the same from either point, and the ride takes about 90 minutes. Because of weather conditions, the ferry will occasionally be rerouted to the alternate dock, so it's always smart to confirm your departure/arrival points.

In summer (late June–early Sept.), ferries run 3–4 times a daily in each direction, leaving the Ontario mainland at 10 A.M., 11 A.M., and 6 P.M. (additional departure at 2 P.M. Thurs.–Mon.). From Pelee Island, ferries depart at 9 A.M., 4 P.M., and 8 P.M. daily (additional departure at noon Thurs.–Mon.). Check the website for off-season hours (which vary significantly) and for any unexpected schedule changes.

Travelers from the United States can catch the ferry from the **Sandusky** docks (Jackson St., at Shoreline Dr., late Apr.–Sept., 1.75 hours, one-way adults $13.75, seniors $11.25, kids 6–12 $6.75, bicycles $6.50, cars $30). From late June through early September, ferries depart Sandusky daily at 3:30 P.M., with an additional departure at 8:30 P.M. on Fridays and Sundays. Boats leave Pelee for Sandusky daily at 1 P.M., with an added 6 P.M. departure on Fridays and Sundays. In spring (late Apr.–late June) and fall (Sept.), ferries between Pelee and Sandusky run weekends only.

If you're traveling between Sandusky and Pelee, remember your passports! You're crossing an international border and must clear customs and immigration.

If you're bringing a car on the ferry, whether from the Ontario mainland or from the United States, you must make a reservation in advance,

either by phone (519/326-2154 or 800/661-2220) or mail (Pelee Island Transportation, Pelee Island, ON N0R 1M0). You must provide your vehicle license number and a valid credit card.

From mid-December to late March, the only way on and off the island is by air. **Pelee Island Transportation Company** (519/724-2115 or 800/661-2220) flies regularly between Windsor and the **Pelee Island Airport** (Centre Dyke Rd., 519/724-2265). Griffing Flying Service (419/626-5161, www.griffingflying-service.com) flies to Pelee from Sandusky.

Getting Around

Pelee Island is about 13 kilometers (eight miles) from north to south and about six kilometers (3.8 miles) across. The island has no public transportation, but there are cabs, or you can bring a car from the mainland on the ferry.

AMHERSTBURG AND VICINITY

One of the oldest settlements in southwestern Ontario, Amherstburg, on the Detroit River south of Windsor, was occupied by American forces during the War of 1812. The British burned the town's original Fort Amherstburg, when U.S. troops forced them to retreat in 1813. After the war, the British regained control of the town and built Fort Malden, which is now a national historic site.

Amherstburg is also a gateway to the wine region known as the Lake Erie North Shore, with wineries around Amherstburg and in the adjacent community of Harrow.

Sights

In the first half of the 19th century, the British built fortifications in a strategic (and picturesque) setting on the Detroit River to protect the Amherstburg area from American attacks. What remains of Fort Malden, now the **Fort Malden National Historic Site** (100 Laird Ave., 519/736-5416, www.pc.gc.ca, 10 A.M.–6 P.M. daily late May–early Sept.; 1–5 P.M. Mon.–Fri., 10 A.M.–5 P.M. Sat.–Sun., early Sept.–Oct.; adults $3.90, seniors $3.40, kids 6–16 $1.90, families $9.80), dates to the 1830s. You can tour the soldiers' barracks, cookhouse, and other fort buildings; staff demonstrate musket drills, open-hearth cooking, and other elements of 19th-century military life.

Like other southwestern Ontario communities, Amherstburg was a destination for former slaves who escaped to Canada via the Underground Railroad. The exhibits at the **North American Black Historical Museum** (277 King St., 519/736-5433 or 800/713-6336 www.blackhistoricalmuseum.org, noon–5 P.M. Tues.–Fri., 1–5 P.M. Sat.–Sun., adults $5.50, seniors and kids $4.50, families $20) illustrate this history, as well as other elements of the black experience in North America. You can walk through a log cabin that belonged to a former slave family in the 1880s and explore one of the oldest surviving African Methodist Episcopal churches in Canada.

Wineries

Gord and Hannah Mitchell planted their first grapes in 1991 and now grow nine varieties, including chardonnay, pinot noir, merlot, and cabernet sauvignon. You can drop in for tastings at their family-run, Tuscan-style **Sprucewood Shores Estate Winery** (7258 County Rd. 50 W., Harrow, 519/738-9253 or 866/938-9253, www.sprucewoodshores.com, 11 A.M.–5 P.M. daily), but call ahead to arrange a tour (Mon.–Fri., wine $6/person, wine tour with cheese tasting $10/person). From May through October, you can purchase a picnic basket ($25) to enjoy on the patio or on the winery's lakefront beach.

A unique wine to sample at the friendly **Erie Shore Vineyard** (410 County Rd. 50 W., Harrow, 519/738-9858, www.erieshore. ca, 1–6 P.M. Mon.–Fri., 10 A.M.–6 P.M. Sat., noon–5 P.M. Sun.) is "Fire and Ice," a blend of slightly spicy red and sweet ice wine. They also make a variety of whites and reds, as well as ice wine.

The **Viewpointe Estate Winery** (151 County Rd. 50 E., Harrow, 519/738-0690 or 866/372-8439, www.viewpointewinery.com, 11 A.M.–6 P.M. daily) released its first vintage

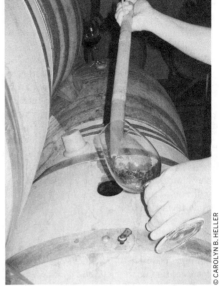

© CAROLYN B. HELLER

wine-tasting at the Colio Estate Winery

LAKE ERIE TO LAKE HURON

in 2007. It produces especially nice whites, including a simple Riesling and an unusual (but very good) Auxerrois. The winery also offers tours, as well as cooking classes.

Since opening in 1980, **Colio Estate Winery** (1 Colio Dr., just off Walker, Harrow, 519/738-2241 or 800/265-1322, www.colio-winery.com, winery 9 A.M.–5 P.M. Mon.–Fri., 10 A.M.–5 P.M. Sat., 11 A.M.–5 P.M. Sun.) has made a number of different wines, from the easy-drinking "Girls' Night Out" line to more premium varieties. Tours (1, 2, and 3 P.M. daily) visit the production facilities, crushing room, barrel room, and retail shop.

Entertainment and Shopping

Concerts, dinners, food demos, and, of course, wine tastings are all part of the annual four-day **Shores of Erie International Wine Festival** (268 Dalhousie St., Amherstburg, 519/730-1001, www.soewinefestival.com, Sept.), held on the grounds of the Fort Malden National Historic Site (100 Laird Ave.). Buy your tickets in advance; events do sell out.

Since the 1800s, **The Harrow Fair** (McAfee St., off County Rd. 20, Harrow, 519/738-3262, www.harrowfair.com, Sept.) has been showcasing the region's produce and livestock, and showing visitors a good old-fashioned time. Besides plenty of things to eat, activities include a horse show, a goat show, sheep shearing, a parade, concerts, and a pie-eating contest.

You can browse the shops and galleries along Dalhousie Street in Amherstburg. Founded by a group of local artists, the **Mud Puppy Gallery** (264 Dalhousie St., 519/736-7737, noon–8 P.M. Wed.–Sun.; call for winter hours) shows work by artists in the community. The gallery also sponsors periodic open-mic nights and other arts events.

Accommodations

The town of Amherstburg and the rural wine country nearby have a handful of B&Bs. For more accommodation options, consider staying in Kingsville or Windsor, which are within a short drive of the Amherstburg area.

The Lake Erie wine country's most upscale accommodation is **La Roos Maison Bed & Breakfast** (309 Martin Ln., Harrow, 519/890-1657, www.laroosmaison.com, $99–179 d), with five guest rooms in a sprawling modern home directly on the lakeshore. The ceilings in the common living room soar two stories high, and three rooms have balconies facing the water, including the huge "Lakefront 3" with vibrant rust-hued walls, black-and-white furnishings, and a gas fireplace. While only the spacious "Lakefront 1" unit has a private bath, the two luxuriously outfitted shared bathrooms are nearly as large as a New York studio apartment. Rates include Internet access and a full breakfast.

Located right on the Detroit River, the **Pier 41 Bed & Breakfast** (41 Mickle Dr., Amherstburg, 519/737-9187, www.pier41bb. com, $100 d) faces west for prime sunset vistas. Darlene and Jim McGuire's updated country-style home includes the Beachcomber Suite (which overlooks the water and has the best views), and the other room is done in a cottage–north woods style. Either way, you can

enjoy the water views at breakfast or out on the deck.

Robert Honor and his wife Debbie have been running **Honor's Country House Bed and Breakfast** (4441 Concession 4 S., Amherstburg, 519/736-7737 or 877/253-8594, www.honorscountryhouse.com, $80–90 s, $90–100 d) in their 1920 farmhouse for more than 25 years. The family has owned this farmland just east of Amherstburg since the late 1800s. The common areas, including a comfy living room with a TV/DVD player and a dining room with guest fridge and microwave, are done in Craftsman-style dark woods. Upstairs, the two simply furnished guest rooms both have private baths. After a hearty breakfast, you might not want to do more than sit on the front porch and watch the world go by.

Food

The **Amherstburg Farmers Market** (7860 County Rd. 20, Amherstburg, 519/730-1253, www.amherstburgfarmersmarket.com, 8:30 A.M.–1:30 P.M. Sat. June–Oct.) takes place at the Malden Community and Cultural Center, near the intersection of Howard Avenue.

With its curved wooden bar and stone walls, **Caldwell's Grant** (269 Dalhousie St., Amherstburg, 519/736-2100, www.caldwell-sgrant.com, 11:30 A.M.–9 P.M. Tues.–Sun., 11:30 A.M.–10 P.M. Fri.–Sat., lunch $8–10, dinner $15–28) feels like an old tavern, and the atmosphere is just as relaxing. You can order casual pub fare (gumbo, burgers, shepherd's pie), big salads, or more substantial dishes, like grilled pork chops, roast chicken, or local trout. The wine list includes lots of local labels.

One of the nicest settings for a summer meal is the patio overlooking the vineyards at the **(Viewpointe Estate Winery Restaurant** (151 County Rd. 50 E., Harrow, 519/738-0690 or 866/372-8439, www.viewpointewinery. com, noon–8 P.M. Thurs.–Fri., noon–5 P.M. Sat.–Sun., June–Sept., $9–16). In addition to salads, a tapas plate, and excellent pizzas, they serve "perch in a basket"—a local fish special—on Thursdays and Fridays.

Information and Services

The Town of Amherstburg's **Tourism Office** (268 Dalhousie St., 519/730-1309, www.amherstburg.ca) provides information about things to see and do in the area. You can also get information from **Tourism Windsor, Essex, and Pelee Island** (333 Riverside Dr. W., Suite 103, Windsor, 519/255-6530 or 800/265-3633, www.tourismwindsoressex.com), the regional tourism association. The **Southwestern Ontario Vintner's Association** website (SWOVA, www.swova.ca) has a listing of wineries in the region.

Robert Honor, co-owner of Honor's Country House Bed and Breakfast and a former Parks Canada staff member, leads the **Old Amherstburg Walking Tours** (519/736-7737 or 877/253-8594, $7–12/person), 45–90-minute walks that focus on different aspects of the town's history, including its architecture, churches, and general development.

Getting There and Around

Downtown Amherstburg is 35 kilometers (22 miles) west of Kingsville and 25 kilometers (15 miles) south of Windsor; County Road 20 connects these three communities. Most of the wineries are located on or near County Road 50, along the Lake Erie shore. While Amherstburg's town center is small and walkable, you'll need a car to visit the wineries and tour outside of town.

WINDSOR

If you're interested in history or in sampling ethnic foods, make a stop in Windsor. This ethnically diverse, industrial city sits on the Canadian side of the Detroit River, facing the Detroit skyline across the border in the United States. The region was one of Ontario's earliest settlements (it was the oldest French colony west of Montreal). In later years, its history entwined with America's, first over the issue of slavery and then during the Prohibition era.

More recently, the city has become a magnet for immigrants from around the world, with nearly a quarter of its 215,000 people born outside of Canada. Wyandotte Street, which runs east–west across downtown, offers a snapshot of Windsor's ethnic communities. Its east end, near Walker Street, is gentrifying near the Walkerville neighborhood of stately brick homes. Between Walkerville and the city center, Wyandotte is Middle Eastern, lined with Lebanese restaurants, bakeries, and markets. West of Ouillette Avenue downtown, Wyandotte turns toward Asia, with many Vietnamese, and some Chinese, eateries and shops. Windsor also has a "Little Italy" district; it's along Erie Street, just south of the city center.

Canadian Club Brand Heritage Center

On January 17, 1920, the U.S. Congress ratified the 18th Amendment to the U.S. Constitution, which banned the manufacture, sale, and transport of alcoholic beverages, ushering in the era that became known as Prohibition. Many Canadian provinces enforced a similar alcohol ban. In Ontario, the Liquor Control Act prohibited public drinking, but it didn't outlaw either the manufacture or export of liquor. Distilleries in the Windsor region capitalized on this loophole; more than 75 percent of the alcohol consumed in the United States during the 1920s and early 1930s traveled across the narrow Detroit River. Learn more about Prohibition and about Windsor's role as a "rum running" town at the Canadian Club Brand Heritage Center (2072 Riverside Dr. E., 519/973-9503, www.canadianclubwhisky.com, tours noon, 2 P.M., and 4 P.M. Wed.–Sat., noon and 2 P.M. Sun., May–Dec., adults $5, seniors $4), home of Canadian Club whiskey. Tours of the gorgeous 1894 building, with its dark oak woodwork and ornate marble fireplaces, typically last one hour and 20 minutes and include a whiskey tasting. In the basement, gangster Al Capone, who was heavily involved in the illicit liquor trade, allegedly fired a warning shot during a contentious meeting; you can still see the bullet hole in the wall.

Art Galleries

Showcasing Canadian art, particularly works by artists from southwestern Ontario, the **Art Gallery of Windsor** (401 Riverside Dr. W.,

519/977-0013, www.artgalleryofwindsor.com, 11 A.M.–5 P.M. Wed.–Sun., 11 A.M.–9 P.M. Thurs.–Fri., $5; free admission Wed.) has a cool contemporary building overlooking the river. On Sunday, the museum offers free drop-in art workshops for families (12:30–2 P.M.), as well as free gallery tours.

More artwork lines the Windsor waterfront in the **Odette Sculpture Park** (along Detroit River, between Huron Church Rd. and Church St., 519/253-1812, www.citywindsor.ca, free.), with over 30 outdoor sculptures. Windsor's Community Museum (519/253-1812, www.citywindsor.ca) offers one-hour **Art Cart Tours** (4–7:30 P.M. Wed.–Fri. July–Aug., 11 A.M.–4 P.M. Sat.–Sun. July–mid-Oct.) that cruise through the sculpture park in an electric golf cart.

Sandwich

Southwest of downtown, the neighborhood known as Sandwich is the oldest permanent European settlement in Ontario, inhabited by French pioneers in the 1700s; the City of Windsor publishes a *Sandwich Walking Tour*

booklet on its website (www.citywindsor.ca), which describes many of the community's historic structures. Sandwich was also important in the region's African-Canadian history, as a destination for former slaves who came to Canada along the Underground Railroad. The **Sandwich First Baptist Church National Historic Site** (3652 Peter St., 519/252-4917) is Canada's oldest active black church, beginning as a log structure built in the 1820s. The current church building, which is still used for services, opened in 1851. Historians have found evidence of a series of tunnels leading into the church cellar that were likely used by fugitive slaves.

◖ John Freeman Walls Historic Site and Underground Railroad Museum

Ring! Ring! When you arrive at the John Freeman Walls Historic Site and Underground Railroad Museum (859 Puce Rd., Lakeshore, 519/727-6555, www.undergroundrailroadmuseum.com, mid-May–early Sept., call for hours), ring the "Freedom Bell" to call the "conductor," who will

fugitive "slaves" hide in a wagon at the John Freeman Walls Historic Site

© CAROLYN B. HELLER

LAKE ERIE TO LAKE HURON

guide you around this open-air museum, built and operated by the descendents of John Freeman Walls and his wife Jane King Walls, fugitive slaves who traveled here from North Carolina on the Underground Railroad. As you walk into the nearby woods, following the path of former slaves, you hear the hound dogs attempting to track you down (fortunately, it's just a recording). You also tour the Walls' 1846 log cabin, where they raised nine children and which became a safe house for former slaves; watch a video about the family's history; and visit the family cemetery.

The museum is out in the countryside, 35 kilometers (22 miles) east of Windsor. Take Highway 401 to exit 28, Highway 25/Puce Road, and go north to the site. The site's hours can be irregular, so call before visiting.

Accommodations

Windsor has a cluster of high-rise chain hotels along, or near, the riverfront, as well as a few B&Bs around town. Built in the 1880s east of the city center, the white clapboard home that now houses the **Windsor Inn on the River Bed and Breakfast** (3857 Riverside Dr. E., 519/945-2110, www.windsorinnontheriver.com, $99–179 d) was once a private manor. Three of the five well-kept rooms look across the lawn to the river (a favorite, the Alexander Park Suite, has an antique queen bed, a fireplace, and an en suite bath), and a full breakfast is served in the formal dining room or out on the veranda.

The **Quality Suites Downtown** (250 Dougall Ave., 519/977-9707, www.choicehotels.ca, $110–140 d) may not have a riverside location, but it's a decent value for its central walk-to-everything setting. The suites all have a living room (with sleep sofa) and a separate bedroom, so there's ample room for a family. All rooms have mini-fridges, and some have kitchenettes. Local calls and Wi-Fi are both free; parking costs $3–10 per night.

The best rooms at the **Hilton Windsor** (277 Riverside Dr. W., 519/973-5555, www.hilton.com, $134–199 d), a 22-story tower on the waterfront, are the updated units with panoramic views over the river. Otherwise, expect standard Hilton amenities, including an indoor pool and fitness center, business services, and parking ($11/self-parking, $21 valet).

The city's top lodging is the glitzy **Caesars Windsor Hotel and Casino** (377 Riverside Dr. E., 519/258-7878 or 800/991-7777, www.caesarswindsor.com, $109–329 d), with 758 rooms in two riverfront towers (to stay in the Forum Tower, you must be at least 19 years old; all ages are welcome in the Augustus Tower). In addition to the gaming rooms, the hotel has a spa, an indoor pool, a fitness facility, and several restaurants.

Food

The Windsor area has a large Lebanese population and several excellent Middle Eastern restaurants. Its murals depict an idealized Mediterranean paradise, but the brightly lit **El-Mayor** (936 Wyandotte St. E., 519/258-7645, www.elmayorrestaurant.com, 10 A.M.–1 A.M. Mon.–Thurs., 10 A.M.–3 A.M. Fri., 10 A.M.–4 A.M. Sat., $5–25) is refreshingly down-to-earth. Like the many families who dine here, you'll want to bring a group, the better to share the overflowing platters of falafel, fattoush salad (lettuce, tomatoes, cucumber, herbs, and addictively crunchy pita bits), or kabobs. If you're by yourself, sample a shawarma sandwich with vinegary pickles, washed down with a glass of tart lemonade. Another excellent Lebanese eatery is the more upscale **Mazaar Lebanese Cuisine** (372 Ouellette Ave., 519/967-9696, www.mazaar.ca, 11 A.M.–9 P.M. Mon., 11 A.M.–10 P.M. Tues.–Thurs., 11 A.M.–11 P.M. Fri., noon–11 P.M. Sat., noon–9 P.M. Sun., $8–23), which also has bellydancing shows on Wednesday evenings.

If you're craving a bowl of hot beef noodle soup, or other inexpensive Vietnamese classics, the friendly but barebones **Pho Nguyen Hoang** (510 Wyandotte St. W., 519/977-0852, 9 A.M.–9 P.M. Thurs.–Tues., $4–12) can oblige. At the cozy **Taloola Café** (396 Devonshire Rd., 519/254-6652, www.taloolacafe.com, 7:30 A.M.–10 P.M. Tues.–Fri., 8:30 A.M.–11 P.M. Sat., 10 A.M.–4 P.M. Sun., $5–8), dine amid exposed brick walls and wood floors, from a menu of vegetarian-friendly salads, sandwiches, and rice bowls, as well as pastries, coffees, and teas.

Try the "Blue Green Salad" of kale, blue cheese, cranberries, walnuts, and fennel. Local musicians often perform on Friday and Saturday nights.

Erie Street, just south of the city center, is Windsor's "Little Italy." Locally popular choices in this district include **Nico Ristorante** (851 Erie St. E., at Elsmere, 519/255-7548, www.nicoristorante.com, 11:30 A.M.–2 P.M. and 5 P.M.–close Tues.–Fri., 5 P.M.–close Sat., 4 P.M.–close Sun., lunch $10–19, dinner $17–25) and **Il Gabbiano Ristorante** (875 Erie St. E., 519/256-9757, www.ilgabbiano.com, 11:30 A.M.–10 P.M. Mon.–Fri., 5–10 P.M. Sat., 4–9 P.M. Sun., lunch $10–22, dinner $15–37).

Information and Services

Tourism Windsor, Essex, and Pelee Island (333 Riverside Dr. W., Suite 103, 519/255-6530 or 800/265-3633, www.tourismwindsoressex. com, 8:30 A.M.–4:30 P.M. Mon.–Fri.) can supply lots of information about Windsor and the surrounding region. Their website is an excellent resource for travel planning, with listings for hotels, attractions, and upcoming events.

On the **Windsor Eats Wine Trail Rides** (www.winetrailride.ca, June–Oct., $50/person, $100 for tour plus bike rental), you can bicycle to several wineries in the Lake Erie North Shore wine district south of Windsor. You'll taste some wine and have lunch at a winery, park, or local farm.

Getting There

BY AIR

Windsor International Airport (YQG, County Rd. 42, 519/969-2430, www.yqg.ca) is located 12 kilometers (7.5 miles) southeast of downtown. Porter Airlines (www.flyporter.com) flies to Toronto's City Centre Airport, Air Canada (www.aircanada.com) goes to Toronto/Pearson, and WestJet (www.westjet.com) flies nonstop to Calgary. **Transit Windsor**'s (www.citywindsor. ca) #8 Walkerville bus runs between the airport and Riverside Drive downtown; however, service is infrequent. A taxi from the airport to most downtown points should be less than $10.

Across the U.S. border, **Detroit Metro Airport** (DTW, 734/247-7678, www.

metroairport.com) has many more options for flights to U.S. cities and overseas; flights might be cheaper than those into Windsor or Toronto. The airport is west of Detroit, about 40 kilometers (25 miles) from Windsor. **Robert Q Airbus** (519/673-6804 or 800/265-4948, www. robertq.com, 1.25 hours, one-way adults $42, seniors and students $39, kids under 12 $21) provides transportation between the Detroit airport and Windsor. Their Windsor pickup and drop-off location is at the Windsor Holiday Inn Select (1855 Huron Church Rd.). **Courtesy Transportation** (519/977-9700, www.courtesytransportation.com) and **Classic Shuttle** (519/796-4634, www.classicshuttle.ca) also provide transportation between DTW and downtown Windsor.

BY TRAIN

From the **VIA Rail Windsor Station** (298 Walker Rd., at Riverside Dr., 888/842-7245, www.viarail.ca), trains run to London (1.75 hours, one-way adult $47–63, kids $23–32) and Toronto (4.25 hours, one-way adult $62–118, kids $40–59). U.S. carrier **Amtrak** (800/872-7245, www.amtrak.com) has rail service from Chicago to Detroit, where you can cross the border into Windsor. Unfortunately, the convenient Windsor Tunnel Bus doesn't stop at the Detroit train station (11 W. Baltimore Ave.). The simplest option is to take a cab from the Amtrak station to one of the tunnel bus stops downtown. Alternatively, you could catch a Detroit Department of Transportation bus (DDOT, 313/933-1300 or 888/336-8287, www.ci.detroit. mi.us, adults US$1.50, seniors US$0.50, students US$0.75) from the train station to a Tunnel Bus stop; the ride takes about 20 minutes.

BY BUS

Windsor's bus station is the **Windsor International Transit Terminal** (300 Chatham St. W., 519/254-7575, www.city-windsor.ca) downtown. **Greyhound Bus** (www.greyhound.ca) runs several buses a day between Toronto and Windsor (5–5.5 hours, adults one-way $55–88, seniors $46–81, kids 2–11 $46–67). The same buses stop in London

(2–2.5 hours, adults one-way $32–48, seniors $19–43, kids 2–11 $27–37).

Between downtown Detroit and downtown Windsor, you can catch Transit Windsor's **Tunnel Bus** (www.citywindsor.ca, 519/944-4111, 5:30 A.M.–12:30 P.M. Mon.–Sat., 8 A.M.–midnight Sun., one-way $3.75). In Windsor, the bus arrives at and departs from the Windsor International Transit Terminal; you can also get off at the Caesars Windsor Hotel and Casino (377 Riverside Dr. E., 519/258-7878 or 800/991-7777, www.caesarswindsor.com). From Detroit, you can catch the bus at the Rosa Parks Transit Center (E. Park Place at State St.) or at the Detroit Tunnel Platform (Randolph St. at Renaissance Dr. N.), near the Mariner's Church opposite the Renaissance Center. Assuming no traffic or border delays, the trip takes only 15 minutes.

BY CAR

Windsor has two international border crossings (www.crossingmadeeasy.com): the **Detroit-Windsor Tunnel** (www.dwtunnel.com) and the **Ambassador Bridge** (www.ambassadorbridge.com). Both are open 24 hours a day. Tolls in the tunnel vary slightly depending on which direction you're traveling: from Detroit to Windsor (CDN$4.75/US$4) or from Windsor to Detroit (CDN$4.50/US$4). Bridge tolls (CDN$4.75/US$4) are the same in either direction.

Although border wait times vary, traffic tends to move relatively quickly at these busy crossings. Check the current border lineups online at **U.S. Customs and Border Protection** (http://apps.cbp.gov/bwt) and the **Canadian Border Services Agency** (www.cbsa-asfc.gc.ca). Always allow extra time if you're catching a plane, or if you have a time-critical appointment, on the opposite side. Remember that passports are required for travel between the United States and Canada.

To Windsor from Toronto, 365 kilometers (225 miles) to the northeast, it's a direct drive down Highway 401. Allow 4–4.5 hours. From London, it's 185 kilometers (115 miles).

Getting Around

Ouellette Avenue is the main north–south street in the downtown area and the dividing line between "east" and "west" addresses. Riverside Drive (along the river) and Wyandotte Street cross the city from east to west. If you're planning to stay downtown, **Transit Windsor** (www.citywindsor.ca, one-way adults $2.45, seniors and students $1.70) runs buses throughout the downtown area.

You'll want to have a car for exploring southwestern Ontario's wineries or the African-Canadian heritage sites. Car rental companies with Windsor offices include **Avis** (www.avis.com), **Budget** (www.budget.ca), **Discount** (www.discountcar.com), **Enterprise** (www.enterpriserentacar.ca), and **National** (www.nationalcar.ca).

LAKE ERIE TO LAKE HURON

Along Lake Huron

Lake Huron is famous for its sunsets. As the sun illuminates the darkening sky with streaks of gold, people come down to the beach just to watch, pausing as if to say good night to the day. And even though you know the sun will rise and set again tomorrow, there's something about watching it hover over the lake that makes you want to stop and watch it one more time.

During the day, the lake and its beaches are equally compelling, since Huron is lined with lovely stretches of sand. In the lakeside beach towns, you'll find lighthouses and small museums, galleries and theaters, but it's the beach—and the sunset—that will draw you again and again to the second-largest of the Great Lakes.

From Toronto, there's no direct highway to Lake Huron, so you'll need to slow down as you meander through the rural towns along the way. But that's okay—the leisurely drive will give you time to tune in to the laid-back vibe of the lakeshore. Once you reach Lake Huron, Highway 21, known as the Bluewater Highway, connects the lakeside towns from the Sarnia area north to Southampton.

GRAND BEND

Grand Bend has a long, sandy beach on Lake Huron and the honky-tonk feel of a summer tourist town. You've got ice cream stands and T-shirt shops, cheek-by-jowl rental cottages, and packs of young folks cruising the beach (and the bars) looking for a good time. There are plenty of families, too, who return to the beach year after year.

Visit outside of frenetic July and August, though, and Grand Bend becomes a quiet town with a pretty beach—a pleasant spot for a spring or fall weekend by the shore. Just outside of town is a provincial park with a spectacular dune-backed expanse of sand.

◖ The Pinery Provincial Park

One of the most beautiful beaches on the Lake Huron shore is just south of Grand Bend. At the Pinery Provincial Park (Highway 21, 519/243-2220, www.ontarioparks.com or www.pinerypark.on.ca, open year-round, $13–15/vehicle), the 10-kilometer (six-mile) powdery sand beach, backed by the undulating dunes topped with waving grasses, feels like it goes on forever. While the beach is wildly popular in summer, the day-use area is divided into nine different sections, so you can explore till you find a spot to lay your towel.

The park **Visitor Centre** (519/243-8574, 10 A.M.–5 P.M. daily July–Aug., call for off-season hours) is near the campgrounds on the west side of the park and runs various nature programs in summer. Near the visitor center, you can rent bicycles ($5–8/hour, $15–30/day), including mountain bikes and kids' bikes, and canoes and kayaks to paddle along the Old Ausable River Channel, which meanders through the park.

Ten short hiking trails, ranging from one to three kilometers (0.6–1.9 miles), wend

sand dunes at The Pinery Provincial Park on Lake Huron

© CAROLYN B. HELLER

through the park. With the exception of the challenging **Nipissing Trail,** which climbs up to a lookout atop the park's largest dune ridge, and the longer wilderness trail, most of the trails are easy enough to explore with kids. Pick up trail guide booklets and get information about trail conditions at the visitor center. The 14-kilometer (8.7-mile) **Savannah Multi-use Trail** loops through the park, more or less paralleling the road, making it a more pleasant (and safer) option for pedestrians and cyclists.

In winter, you can cross-country ski or snowshoe along 38 kilometers (24 miles) of trails. You can rent skis and snowshoes at the Visitor Centre (10 A.M.–4 P.M. Sat.–Sun., adults $2, children 6–17 $1).

The park entrance is eight kilometers (five miles) south of Grand Bend on Highway 21. Once you arrive, park your car and explore Pinery on foot or by bike. The park road is a 12-kilometer (7.5-mile) one-way loop, so if you want to revisit a spot you just passed, it's a long way around again.

Entertainment and Events

Several plays run in repertory every summer at the **Huron Country Playhouse** (B Line, off Highway 81, 519/238-6000 or 855/372-9866, www.draytonentertainment.com, mid-May–early Sept.). The theater, which began its productions in a tent more than 40 years ago, is located east of Grand Bend's town center. If you thought that old-time drive-in movies were long gone, think again. Grand Bend still has the **Starlite Drive-in Theatre** (36,752 Crediton Rd., 519/238-8344, www.starlitedriveintheatre.com/GrandBend.html) that screens films nightly in July and August and on weekends in the spring and fall.

Accommodations and Food

Motels, places to eat, and shops line Ontario Street (Highway 21) and Main Street. The **Bluewater Motel** (121 Ontario St. S./Hwy. 21, 519/238-2014, from $89 d) is a well-maintained, family-run—and family-friendly—property with an outdoor pool. The 22 rooms

are standard motel-style units, but they've got the basics: decent beds, fridges, TVs, and free Wi-Fi. Out back are three cottages that sleep 2–6. It's a one-kilometer (0.6-mile) walk along Lake Road to the town's South Beach and about the same distance along Highway 21 to the town center. Further south, the **Whispering Pines Motel** (10456 Lakeshore Rd./Hwy. 21, 519/238-2383, $89–148 d) has similar rooms and facilities.

The **Grand Bend Farmers' Market** (1 Main St., 8 A.M.–1 P.M. Wed. late May–early Oct.) sets up in the parking lot of the Colonial Hotel, at the intersection of Highway 21. The aroma of fresh baked goods may lure you into **Grandpa Jimmy's Scottish Bakery** (36 Ontario St. N., 519/238-5055 or 877/225-5907, www.grandpajimmys.com, 9 A.M.–5 P.M. daily). Don't resist; the scones are light, with just the right amount of sweetness (try a berry one, in season). For a beach picnic, pick up traditional sausage rolls, meat pies, breads, or pastries. Like any good grandfather's house, this one has toys for the kids (and magazines for the grown-ups).

Old-fashioned family dining has kept the tables full since the 1950s at friendly **Aunt Gussie's Country Dining** (135 Ontario St. S., 519/238-6786, www.auntgussies.ca, 7 A.M.–10 P.M. daily in summer; call for off-season hours; breakfast $4–9, lunch $7–11, dinner $10–17). Stop in for breakfast before heading to the beach; later in the day, you can fuel up on classics like burgers, open-faced turkey sandwiches with mashed potatoes and gravy, pot pies, and smoked pork chops. Aunt Gussie's is south of the town center, next to the Bluewater Motel.

CAMPING

The Pinery Provincial Park (Highway 21, 519/243-2220, www.ontarioparks.com or www.pinerypark.on.ca, $36.75–40.50 tent sites, $42.25–46 electrical sites) has the second-largest campground in the Ontario Provincial Park system (only Algonquin is larger), with 1,000 campsites in three camping areas; 404 of the sites have electrical hookups. Both the Dunes and Burley Campgrounds

(May–Sept.) have sites near the beach; the Riverside Campground (year-round) is inland near the river. All areas have flush toilets and showers.

The Riverside Campground also has 12 yurts ($91.50/night), with electricity and electric heat. The yurts have two sets of bunk beds, with one double and one single bunk, so you can sleep up to six people. You need to bring sleeping bags, as well as cooking gear and food. You can't cook inside the yurts, but outside you can use a gas barbecue.

Even though the camping area is large, it's extremely popular, so book your site in advance if you're visiting in summer or on any holiday weekend. Reservations are recommended for yurts anytime. To book campsites or yurts, contact the **Ontario Parks Reservation Service** (888/668-7275, www.ontarioparks.com, reservation fees $8.50 online, $9.50 by phone).

Practicalities

For tourist information, contact the **Grand Bend and Area Chamber of Commerce and Tourism** (81 Crescent St., 519/238-2001 or 888/338-2001, www.grandbendtourism.com, 10 A.M.–7 P.M. daily late May–early Sept., noon–4 P.M. Tues.–Sat. early Sept.–late May).

Grand Bend is 220 kilometers (137 miles) west of Toronto, about a 3.5-hour drive. Follow Highway 401 west to Kitchener, then take Highway 8 west to Stratford. From there, one option is to continue west on Highway 8 to Mitchell, then follow Highway 23 south to Highway 83, which meets Highway 21 just north of Grand Bend. Alternatively, pick up Highway 7 south from Stratford, then take Highway 20 toward Fullarton, where you'll connect with Highway 83.

BAYFIELD

If Grand Bend is a teenager in a bikini scarfing down hot wings or soft ice cream, Bayfield is her proper hat-wearing great aunt—more about heritage buildings, luxurious inns, and art galleries than catching rays in the sand.

In the mid-1800s, Bayfield became a well-to-do port town, shipping grain from area farms. Although the coming of the railroad (which didn't extend to Bayfield) ended the town's shipping industry, many stately lodgings and homes date to this prosperous era.

Sights and Recreation

Bayfield's town square, **Clan Gregor Square,** is now a park surrounded by historic structures, while shops, galleries, lodgings, and places to eat line Main Street, the sedate commercial district just off the square. A short walk from Main Street is **Pioneer Park,** overlooking Lake Huron, with steps that descend to the lovely town beach.

To find out more about the town's history, stop into the **Bayfield Historical Society** (20 Main St., www.bayfieldhistorical.ca), which runs a small museum and archives (1–5 P.M. Wed. and Sat. mid-Apr.–mid-Dec.) with photos, letters, and other documents about the town's history. The society also leads historical walking tours (July–Aug., call for schedule; $5) around the town.

For more active pursuits, visit **Outside Projects** (6 Main St., 519/565-4034, www.outsideprojects.ca, 10 A.M.–7 P.M. daily July–Aug., 10 A.M.–4 P.M. Fri.–Mon. Sept.–June), an outdoor gear store that rents bikes (half-/full-day $22/40), and, in winter, snowshoes. They also organize guided hikes, bike excursions, and snowshoe tours.

Entertainment and Events

The annual **Bayfield Writers' Festival** (June) brings authors to town for a weekend of readings and other events. Get information and tickets from the **Village Bookshop** (20A Catherine St., 519/565-5600, www.thevillagebookshop.com), which also hosts readings and literary events throughout the year.

Accommodations and Food

The Albion Hotel (1 Main St., 519/565-2641, www.thealbionhotel.com, $115–145 s, $125–155 d) has been taking guests since 1856, and it exudes a old-timey feel. Of the four guest rooms upstairs, the largest has a four-poster bed and a

© CAROLYN B. HELLER

The village of Bayfield is full of historic inns and restaurants.

fireplace; all are furnished in a simple country cottage style. Rates include continental breakfast. On the main floor, the pub is a popular local hangout; the dining room (11:30 A.M.–midnight Mon.–Sat., 11:30 A.M.–11 P.M. Sun., $10–30) serves burgers, ribs, fish 'n' chips, and steaks.

Ontario's longest continually operating inn, **The Little Inn of Bayfield** (26 Main St. N., 519/565-2611 or 800/565-1832, www.littleinn. com, $169–252 s, $202–285 d) was a stagecoach stop back in the 1830s. The original building now houses 18 traditionally appointed guest rooms, starting with the least expensive "original" rooms, which are quite tiny. For more space, opt for a larger "carriage house" room, still in the main inn, or a more luxurious junior suite, which has either a whirlpool tub or gas fireplace. In the separate "guest cottage" building across the street, the 10 rooms are more spacious and contemporary; the upstairs units have private decks. The main inn also houses an upscale **restaurant** (breakfast 8–10 A.M., lunch noon–2 P.M., dinner 5:30–8:30 P.M., lunch $15–20, dinner $24–33),

which is highly regarded for its creative, locally sourced cuisine. Main dishes might range from wild char caught in Lake Huron and served with cauliflower quinoa and yuzu mayonnaise to a Black Angus steak paired with purple potato confit and heirloom carrots. Basic lodging rates include a full breakfast; packages including dinner are also available.

If your style is more contemporary, consider the seven deluxe guest rooms at the **Red Pump Inn and Restaurant** (21 Main St., 519/565-2576 or 888/66-2576, www.theredpumpinn. com, Apr.–Dec., $250–425). With an eclectic mix of modern and traditional furnishings, the large units all have a king-size bed, a fireplace, roomy bathrooms, and a private balcony. The restaurant (lunch and dinner Wed.–Mon. Apr.–Dec., lunch $15–21, dinner $23–38), in an adjacent building, draws inspiration from cuisines around the world, with a menu that could feature shrimp pad Thai, chipotle turkey cutlet topped with charred corn salsa, or a local fish simply prepared with white wine, lemon, capers, and tomato concasse.

The relaxed **Black Dog Village Pub and Bistro** (5 Main St. N., 519/565-2326, www. blackdogpubbistro.ca, 11:30 A.M.–close daily in summer; call for off-season hours; lunch $13–16, dinner $13–27) serves burgers and sandwiches midday, adding pastas, curries, and steaks in the evening. They've got 20 beers on tap and a large whiskey selection, too, which help make it a cozy evening retreat.

Practicalities
Bayfield is 215 kilometers (134 miles) west of Toronto. Take Highway 401 west toward Kitchener, then continue west on Highway 8. At the town of Seaforth, pick up Highway 3 west, which meets Highway 21 (the Bluewater Highway) just south of Bayfield. From London (85 kilometers, or 53 miles, to the southwest, follow Highway 4 north to Brucefield, then take Highway 3 west to Highway 21.

Once you're in Bayfield, you don't need your car if you're staying in the village. It's a short walk between the inns, restaurants, and shops along Main Street and the town beach. You can get information about the town online from **Bayfield and Area Chamber of Commerce** (www.villageofbayfield.com).

KINCARDINE AND VICINITY
Settled by Scottish settlers in the mid-1800s, this Lake Huron town grew up from the lumber, fishing, and salt-producing industries. In 1968, a new technology changed the town's fortunes: a nuclear power plant—Canada's first commercial nuclear reactor—was built on the lakeshore north of town.

Sights and Recreation
In addition to its pretty, sandy town beach, which runs for over a kilometer (0.6 mile) along the lake, Kincardine's sights are linked to its marine past and its nuclear future. An active lighthouse since 1859, the lightstation that now constitutes the **Point Clark Lighthouse National Historic Site** (530 Lighthouse Rd., Huron-Kinloss, Point-Clark, 519/395-2494, www.pc.gc.ca or www.huronkinloss.com, 10 A.M.–5 P.M. daily late June–early Sept.; call

for fees) is one of six "imperial towers" that guided ships along Lake Huron and Georgian Bay. It's a 34-meter (110-foot) limestone tower, with a 12-sided lantern on top. The lighthouse keeper's house, which dates to the same era, is now a small museum. The lighthouse is 18 kilometers (11 miles) south of Kincardine and 35 kilometers (22 miles) north of Goderich. (As this book went to press, the lighthouse was under restoration; contact the Township of Huron-Kinloss at 519/395-3735 to confirm current hours before visiting.)

On the harbor in the center of Kincardine, the town's octagonal lighthouse was built in 1881. Still an operating light, it's now the **Kincardine Lighthouse and Museum** (Harbour St., off Queen Street, 519/396-3150 or 800/268-3838, www.sunsets.com, 11 A.M.–5 P.M. daily July–early Sept.).

One of the Lake Huron shore's most unusual attractions illustrates the role that nuclear power plays in the region. At the **Bruce Power Visitor Centre** (3394 Bruce Rd. 20, Tiverton, 519/361-7777 or 866/748-478, www.bruce-power.com, 9 A.M.–4 P.M. Mon.–Fri., free), you can learn more about the nuclear industry as well as the workings of the local nuclear power plants. Because it's run by the power company, the exhibits have a decidedly pro-nuclear bent, but it's still an educational stop. Outside are the spinning turbines of Ontario's first commercial wind farm (www.huron-wind.com), which provide a different type of power; the visitor centre has an exhibit about wind power, as well. The Bruce Power Visitor Centre is 20 kilometers (12.5 miles) north of Kincardine. From Kincardine, go north on Highway 21 to Highway 15/Main Street west toward Inverhuron; then take Highway 23 north to Concession 4 west.

Kincardine celebrates its Scottish heritage during the annual **Kincardine Scottish Festival and Highland Games** (www.kincardinescottishfestival.ca, July), with kilt-wearing pipe bands, Highland dancing, and "heavy events," a traditional athletic competition that includes stone and hammer throws and the caber toss.

Accommodations and Food

You can't get much closer to the lake than at the aptly named **Lakefront B&B** (328 Goderich St., 519/396-4345, www.lakefrontbb.com, $155–170 d). The largest unit is a cozy cabin with a sunroom facing Lake Huron and a separate bedroom. Two additional rooms are available on the lower level of the main house. Co-owner Katrena Johnston, who also plays bass in a local band, cooks a hearty breakfast that she serves in the "Crow's Nest," a nook overlooking the water. On Highway 21, there are a couple of newer chain motels. A few basic old-fashioned motels are scattered around town.

You'll find several restaurants along Queen Street in the town center, including the peanuts-on-the-floor-casual **Hawg's Breath Saloon and Deli** (894 Queen St., 519/396-6565), which serves beer, sandwiches, beer, burgers, and beer.

Practicalities

Kincardine is about 225 kilometers (140 miles) northwest of Toronto. By car, you can either head toward Guelph, where you can take Highway 7 north/west to Highway 9, which goes into Kincardine, or pick up Highway 10 north to Orangeville, where you turn west. It's difficult to explore the Kincardine area if you don't have a vehicle. The **Kincardine Visitor Information Centre** (1802 Hwy. 21, north of Hwy. 9, 519/396-2731 or 866/546-2736, www.sunsets.com/kincardine) can provide more information about the area and can assist with local cottage rentals.

SOUTHAMPTON AND VICINITY

As in many Lake Huron towns, summer life in Southampton revolves around the beach, and the town has a pretty, sandy one just a short walk from the laid-back downtown district. But Southampton also has a first-rate museum and it's the jumping-off point for an island lighthouse tour. Nearby, you can learn about the region's First Nations culture.

Sights and Recreation

You may not think about touring a museum on a sunny day in a beach town, but even if it's not raining, it's worth visiting the excellent **Bruce County Museum and Cultural Centre** (33 Victoria St. N., 519/797-2080 or 866/318-8889, www.brucemuseum.ca, 10 A.M.–5 P.M. Mon.–Sat., 1–5 P.M. Sun., adults $8, seniors and students $6, kids 4–12 $4). The modern, interactive exhibits focus on the region's heritage and culture, with displays about shipwrecks and marine history and local life. Sit around a farm kitchen table and listen to recordings recounting what it was like to live in Bruce County in the early 1900s, or learn about how ships in peril are rescued.

The **Chantry Island Lighthouse** was built in 1859 on an island off the coast of Southampton. Because the island is now a Federal Migratory Bird Sanctuary, home to nesting colonies of great blue heron, double-crested cormorant, and great egret, among others, access to the island is restricted. The best way to visit is on a two-hour trip with **Chantry Island Tours** (89 Saugeen St., 519/797-5862 or 866/797-5862, www.chantryisland.com, late May–early Sept., $30/person), which includes the boat ride to the island and a guided hike to the lighthouse. Tours depart from their base at Southampton Harbour; reservations are recommended.

The Southampton area is home to the Saugeen First Nation, an Ojibway people, who run the open-air **Saugeen Amphitheatre** (519/797-2781 or 800/680-0744, www.saugeenfirstnation.ca) and host workshops and cultural programs for visitors in July and August. A popular time to visit is during the annual **Saugeen Pow Wow** (July), with dancing, music, and traditional food. The amphitheater is 3.5 kilometers (two miles) north of Southampton on Highway 21.

Accommodations and Food

Restaurants, shops, and a few places to stay are clustered along High Street, Southampton's "downtown," on either side of Albert Street (Highway 21). The yellow brick Victorian

Southampton Inn & Spa (118 High St., 519/797-5915 or 888/214-3816, www.the-southamptoninn.com, $129–149 d) has a great location, one block from the beach and a block into town. Comfortable but far from fancy, the seven country-style rooms all have mini-fridges and private baths; three are suites that include separate sitting areas. If you need a massage, facial, or pedicure, simply walk downstairs to the spa. Room rates include Wi-Fi and a light breakfast; in the off-season (Nov.–Apr.), dinners are available on request.

Opposite the Southampton Inn, the **Chantry Breezes Bed & Breakfast** (107 High St., 519/797-1818 or 866/242-6879, www.chantrybreezes.on.ca, rooms $150–190 d, cottages $180–220) is similar in style, if a bit more upscale. Accommodations include five Victorian-style guest rooms, a two-room suite, and two small guest cottages out back. Guests gather in the large window-lined parlor, the formal dining room, or out on the porch.

Even when it's not the middle of summer, you can savor the soups and sandwiches at the **Mid Summers Café** (171 High St., 519/797-1122). You can also pop in for coffee, ice cream, or free Wi-Fi. Old favorite **Duffy's Restaurant and Bar** (151 High St., 519/797-5972, www.duffyssouthampton.com, 11:30 A.M.–9 P.M.

Tues.–Sat., 11:30–8 P.M. Sun. in summer; call for off-season hours) is known for its fish 'n' chips, but the pan-fried Lake Huron whitefish is a popular choice, too.

Practicalities

Saugeen Shores Tourism (201 High St., 519/797-2215 or 888/757-2215, www.saugeenshores.ca) is the regional tourism association for the Southampton area. The Southampton branch of the **Bruce County Public Library** (215 High St., 519/797-3586, www.library.brucecounty.on.ca) has free Wi-Fi.

Southampton is 225 kilometers (140 miles) northwest of Toronto. The most direct route is via Highway 10 to Owen Sound, where you can pick up Highway 21 south into Southhampton. Southampton can also be a jumping-off point for exploring the southern Bruce Peninsula. The town is just 20 kilometers (12 miles) south of Sauble Beach, via Highway 13. If you're traveling along the Lake Huron coast, it's 45 kilometers (28 miles) on Highway 21 between Kincardine and Southampton.

Once you get to town, you can leave the car parked. Southampton's town center is quite compact, and it's a short stroll from the shops to the beach or the museum.

OTTAWA

Canada's national capital brims with pomp and grandeur. Parliament, the Supreme Court, the homes of Canada's prime minister and governor general—along with numerous grand museums—are here. In summer, you can even take in the daily Changing of the Guard, the iconic fur hats and red uniforms echoing that other famous ceremony at London's Buckingham Palace. History is very present in present-day Ottawa.

Yet Ottawa isn't all about revolutions and representatives. It's an active, outdoorsy city, where residents are frequently out on foot, on skates, or on the water. The Rideau Canal, the oldest continuously operating canal in North America, transforms in winter into the world's longest skating rink. Just across the river from downtown is Gatineau Park, a sprawling nature reserve crisscrossed with trails for hiking, snowshoeing, and cross-country skiing.

Ottawa also knows how to party. The city hosts the nation's biggest Canada Day celebration every July 1, and throughout the year, there's one festival after another. Even in frigid February, Ottawa's long-running winter fest—known as Winterlude—draws thousands visitors from near and far.

Straddling the border with Quebec, this metropolitan area of more than a million people is one of Canada's most bilingual cities. It may not be as francophone as Quebec City or Montreal, but you'll hear plenty of French, not just in government buildings but all around.

If you think that Ottawa's bureaucratic culture means that its food is equally bland, think again—Ottawa is an unexpectedly

HIGHLIGHTS

LOOK FOR 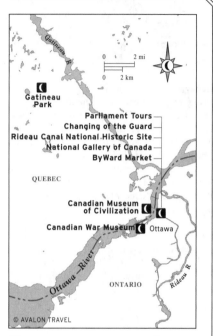 TO FIND RECOMMENDED SIGHTS, ACTIVITIES, DINING, AND LODGING.

Parliament Tours: Any visit to Ottawa should begin on Parliament Hill, in the ornate complex of copper-roofed buildings that house Canada's national legislature. Dozens of special events, including a nightly summer sound-and-light show and the nation's biggest Canada Day celebration, also take place in front of Parliament (page 201).

Changing of the Guard: Complete with red-coated, fur hat-wearing guards, this daily summer procession on Parliament Hill echoes its namesake ceremony at Buckingham Palace (page 204).

Canadian War Museum: The exhibitions in this striking contemporary museum west of Parliament Hill manage to put a human face on the grim periods of war throughout Canada's history (page 206).

Rideau Canal National Historic Site: Not only is the Rideau, which stretches from Ottawa south to Kingston, the oldest continuously operating canal in North America, in winter, the Canal's Ottawa section transforms into the world's longest skating rink (page 207).

National Gallery of Canada: Designed by Canadian architect Moshe Safdie, the country's national art gallery has particularly fine collections of Canadian and Inuit works. Wander out back for great city views, too (page 208).

ByWard Market: Named for both a food market and its surrounding neighborhood, this Ottawa district is foodie central, whether you're looking for a picnic lunch, a five-star meal, or a classic "beavertail" snack (page 210).

Canadian Museum of Civilization: You can learn almost anything you want to know about Canadian history and culture in this massive — and fascinating — museum, in a distinctive curved building on the Gatineau side of the Ottawa River (page 235).

Gatineau Park: This 361-square-kilometer (89-acre) green space in the Quebec hills just a short drive from Ottawa is the city's backyard — for hiking, cycling, swimming, cross-country skiing, snowshoeing, or just relaxing (page 237).

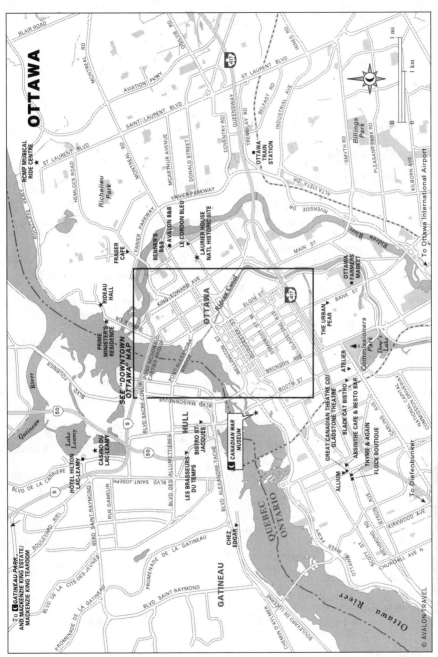

OTTAWA

OTTAWA

© AVALON TRAVEL

foodie destination. The city has a branch of Le Cordon Bleu culinary school, where you can take a workshop or have a classical French meal. To explore Ottawa in small bites, take one of several different food tours, or join one of the city's culinary events companies for an unusual (and fun) gourmet meal. The capital also has a growing number of innovative restaurants, where you can taste the latest creations when you've had your fill of history, culture, and the outdoors.

PLANNING YOUR TIME

Ottawa is a year-round destination. As long as you're prepared for serious cold (bring heavy coats, long underwear, warm hats, boots, and mittens), a winter visit means fewer crowds at Parliament, the museums, and other attractions (though some reduce their hours in the winter months). In spring, the capital shakes off its winter chill as a rainbow of colorful flowers bloom, particularly during the annual Tulip Festival. And if you want the best weather, schedule your visit during the crisp, clear days of autumn.

Still, it's summer when Ottawa really comes alive. Sure, the days can be hot and sticky, but the streets and museums fill with visitors, and every morning, crowds gather for the Changing of the Guard on Parliament Hill. Vendors set up their stalls around the ByWard Market, and one festival after another livens up the summer calendar.

If you have two or three days, you can take in many of Ottawa's highlights: tour the **Parliament** buildings; visit the **National Gallery** and the **Canadian Museum of Civilization;** stroll, cycle, or (in winter) skate along the **Rideau Canal;** and wrap up with a wander through the **ByWard Market** to snack on a "beavertail" (the city's iconic fried-dough treat) or have dinner at one of the many contemporary restaurants.

With at least four or five days, you can explore the capital in greater depth. If you're interested in government, politics, or the official life, tour Rideau Hall (the governor general's residence) and the Supreme Court. You'll have more time to explore the art galleries in and around the ByWard Market or venture further from downtown to shop and eat in the up-and-coming Wellington West neighborhood. If you're visiting with kids, don't miss the Museum of Nature or an afternoon outdoors in **Gatineau Park.** Or head west of the city to the **Diefenbunker,** a quirky—and somber—museum that takes you back to Canada's Cold War era.

Sights

Ottawa's main attractions are clustered in the city center on either side of the Rideau Canal. Parliament Hill and the main downtown district are west of the Canal; the ByWard Market, the National Gallery of Canada, and the Royal Canadian Mint are east of the Canal. Gatineau, across the Ottawa River from downtown, is where you'll find the Museum of Civilization and Gatineau Park. With so many major museums, Ottawa can induce a sort of museum fatigue, so be sure to balance sightseeing with more relaxing pursuits. A walk along the Rideau Canal or through the ByWard Market can help revive flagging energy.

Some of Ottawa's most interesting neighborhoods aren't known for their "sights," but they're still worth exploring. Head for Chinatown and Little Italy, both southwest of downtown, to browse the markets or look for a meal. The funky Glebe neighborhood, which runs along Bank Street south of downtown, and Wellington West, on the city's west side, are both fun districts to ramble through for shopping and eating.

PARLIAMENT HILL

Any visit to Ottawa should begin on Parliament Hill (Wellington St., at Metcalfe St.), the

A CRASH COURSE IN CANADIAN GOVERNMENT

Your visit to Ottawa will mean more if you know something about the workings of the Canadian government.

The federal government has three branches: executive, legislative, and judicial. Canada's **prime minister** is the country's chief executive, and **Parliament,** the national legislature, makes Canada's federal laws.

Parliament is made up of two bodies: the House of Commons, whose 308 members are elected, and the Senate, in which – unlike the U.S. Senate – the 105 legislators are appointed. Each House of Commons member, known as an MP or Member of Parliament, represents a geographically based "riding" or district. They're elected to five-year terms.

Senators can come from anywhere in the country. They can remain on the job until they reach age 75.

When a bill is introduced in Parliament, majorities in both the House of Commons and the Senate must approve it. The governor general, who is the British monarch's representative in Canada, then gives final approval – known as "royal assent" – to a bill before it becomes law.

Want to know more? The Parliament website (www.parl.gc.ca) is an excellent resource for information about the Canadian legislative system. And if you visit Parliament Hill in Ottawa, plan to tour the House of Commons and Senate Chambers and, if you can, arrange to watch a legislative session in action.

legislative headquarters of Canada's national government. Even if you're not interested in the work of the federal policy wonks, the strikingly ornate complex of copper-roofed Parliament buildings on Wellington Street above the Ottawa River is worth visiting for its architectural glamour alone.

Parliament Tours

The **Centre Block Guided Tour** (www.parl. gc.ca, year-round, free) takes you through the main Parliament building, which opened in 1920 after a fire destroyed most of the original structure. Tours typically begin in the foyer of the House of Commons, include an overview of Canada's parliamentary process, and (if Parliament isn't in session) visit the green **House of Commons chamber** (the color is modeled on that of the British House of Commons) and the red **Senate chamber.** Also on the tour is the gorgeous **Library of Parliament,** a circular Gothic Revival structure at the back of the Centre Block, which dates to 1876. It's one of the only parts of the original Parliament buildings that survived the devastating fire in 1916 (an employee closed the library's thick iron doors, saving it from the flames). Bedecked with elaborate wood carvings and ironwork, the library houses over one million books.

Another option is the **East Block Guided Tour** (www.parl.gc.ca, 10 A.M.–5:15 P.M., July–early Sept., free), which explores the 1860s building east of the Centre Block, which now houses legislative offices. The tour visits three rooms that have been restored to their 19th-century functions, including the office of the governor general, the office of Canada's first prime minister, and the Privy Council chamber.

To take either of these Parliament building tours, you must reserve a ticket in person on the day you wish to tour. Tickets are available beginning at 9 A.M., and they're issued for particular times during the day. The first tours of the day are generally less crowded, so arrive early if you can. On a busy summer day, you might show up in the morning and find that the first available tour is late in the afternoon, so be prepared to adjust your schedule.

Tours last between 20 and 60 minutes, depending on what's going on in the buildings on the day of your visit; tours don't enter the Senate or House of Commons chambers when Parliament is in session. Expect airport-style security screening before you enter the building.

Between mid-May and early September,

OTTAWA

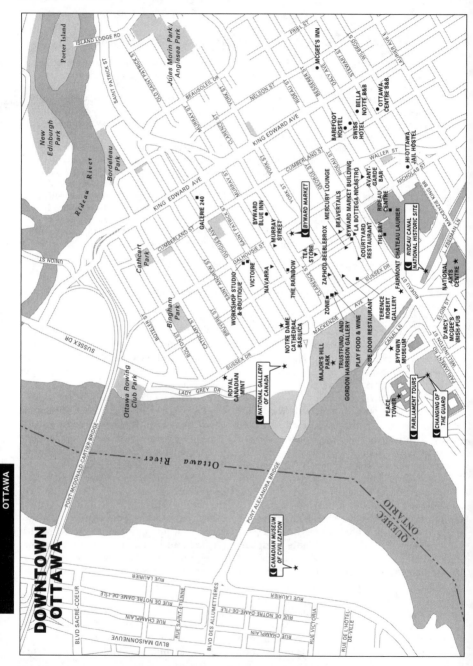

DOWNTOWN OTTAWA

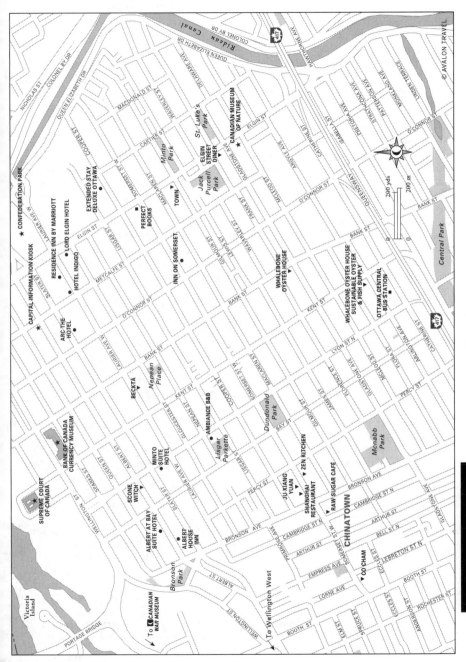

OTTAWA

from 9 A.M. to 5 P.M., make your tour reservations in the white **Info-Tent** on the Parliament lawn. In the evenings (5 P.M. to 7:30 P.M.), and outside the summer months (early September through mid-May, 9 A.M.–5 P.M.), arrange your Centre Block tour in the **Visitor Welcome Centre** just inside the Centre Block.

The Peace Tower and Memorial Chamber

In the middle of Parliament's Centre Block is the landmark Peace Tower, bedecked with gargoyles and ornate stonework, its clock face visible from blocks away. Completed in 1927, the tower is dedicated to the Canadian soldiers who died in World War I. Bells in the tower chime every quarter hour, and the tower also houses a carillon, with 53 bells ranging in size from 4.5 kilograms (10 pounds) to more than 10,000 kilos (over 22,000 pounds). From the Parliament lawn, you can listen to **free carillon concerts** (11 A.M.–noon July–Aug., noon–12:15 P.M. Sept.–June).

Take an elevator to the Peace Tower's **observation deck** (generally 9 A.M.–7:30 P.M. mid-May–early Sept., 9 A.M.–3:30 P.M. early Sept.–mid-May, free) for expansive views of the surrounding area, as well as an up-close look at the carillon's bells. You can go up in the Peace Tower at the end of the Centre Block tours, or ascend the tower without taking a tour first. Tickets aren't required, but expect lines, particularly in summer. Go up first thing in the morning to avoid the crowds.

Also in the tower is the Memorial Chamber, a chapel-like space lined with stained-glass windows, memorializing Canadian veterans. The chamber houses seven **Books of Remembrance** containing the names of Canadian men and women who died serving in the armed forces. Daily at 11 A.M., during the **Turning of the Page ceremony,** a page is turned in the Books of Remembrance, so that each name is visible at least once a year. Family members of the dead can make reservations to attend the ceremony (email memorial-souvenir@parl.gc.ca); the public can view the ceremony from the chamber's entryway.

Parliament Visitor Galleries

When Parliament is in session, visitors are welcome to watch the action from the Visitor Galleries in either the Senate or the House of Commons. The schedule varies, so check the Parliament website (www.parl.gc.ca) for hours. Seating in the galleries is first-come, first-served; go to the Info-Tent or Visitor Welcome Centre if you want to attend.

If you're Canadian, you can email or write to your Member of Parliament in advance of your visit to request a seat in the galleries. You'll then get a seat ahead of visitors who just turn up that day. Look up your MP's contact information on the Parliament website.

A popular time to visit the galleries is during the 45-minute **Question Period,** when the opposition is allowed to question the majority. When Parliament is in session, Question Period in the House of Commons is usually held 2:15 P.M. Monday to Thursday and at 11:15 A.M. Friday. The Senate Question Period takes place Tuesday through Thursday, but times vary.

You must remain quiet in the galleries—no talking is allowed—so don't bring the kids until they're old enough to sit without chatting.

C Changing of the Guard

If you're visiting Ottawa between late June and August, don't miss the Changing of the Guard ceremony (www.parl.gc.ca, 10 A.M. daily, free) on the lawn in front of the Parliament buildings. Dressed in ceremonial red coats and tall fur hats recalling their British counterparts at London's Buckingham Palace, the guards march in formation, accompanied by a military band. Most of the young guards are college or university students who are also Canadian Forces reservists (cool summer job, eh?).

The ceremony takes place rain or shine. Be on the lawn by 9:45 A.M.—earlier if you want a front-row "seat." Before and after the ceremony, the guards march along Wellington and Elgin Streets, where it's often easier to get close-up photos. Consider watching the full ceremony one day and taking more photos on the street the next.

Parliament Grounds

Visitors are welcome to explore the Parliament grounds, which are dotted with statues and monuments, including the **Centennial Flame** on the walkway leading to the Centre Block. It was first lit on January 1, 1967, honoring Canada's 100th birthday. Each of the twelve segments represents one of the provinces and territories (as of 1967). Do you know which current territory is missing? (That would be Nunavut, which became Canada's third territory in 1999.)

One monument to look for, east of the Centre Block, is *Women Are Persons!*, honoring five female reformers. In 1916, Emily Murphy was appointed a magistrate in the city of Edmonton, the first female magistrate in the British Empire. However, many people protested her appointment, arguing that under the British North America Act of 1867—Canada's founding document—only a qualified "person" could hold public office, and a woman was not legally a person. Murphy, along with Henrietta Muir Edwards, Louise McKinney, Nellie McClung, and Irene Parlby, eventually took the "Persons Case" to Canada's Supreme Court—and lost. They persisted, appealing to the Privy Council in Britain, which finally ruled in 1929 that, yes, women were persons, too.

Also on the grounds, west of the Centre Block, is the **Cat Sanctuary** (no kidding), which has been caring for abandoned felines, as well as needy birds, raccoons, and other critters, since the 1970s.

To guide your explorations, pick up *Discover the Hill: Outdoor Self-guiding Booklet* at the Info-Tent or in the Visitor Welcome Centre. It's also available in the **Capital Information Kiosk** (World Exchange Plaza, 111 Albert St., 613/239-5000 or 800/465-1867, www.canadas-capital.gc.ca, 10 A.M.–5 P.M. daily).

Parliament Sound and Light Show

Return to Parliament Hill in the evening for *Mosaika* (613/239-5000 or 800/465-1867, www.mosaika-sl.ca, early July–early Sept., free), a nightly 30-minute sound and light show that illuminates Canada's history and culture, with Parliament as its backdrop. The show begins at 10 P.M. in July, 9:30 P.M. in August, and 9 P.M. in September, weather permitting. Arrive at least an hour early, and bring a chair and/or blanket if you can.

DOWNTOWN

Extending west and south of Parliament Hill is Ottawa's downtown. Besides the many office and government buildings, several museums and attractions are downtown, as well as numerous hotels. The southern section of downtown, below Lisgar Street, is known as Centretown.

Supreme Court of Canada

With its headquarters a short walk west of Parliament Hill, the Supreme Court of Canada (301 Wellington St., 613/995-4330 or 888/551-1185, www.scc-csc.gc.ca, 9 A.M.–5 P.M. daily May–Aug., 9 A.M.–5 P.M. Mon.–Fri. Sept.–Apr., free) is the country's highest court. Every year, the court hears 80–100 cases that it considers to have "national importance," on appeal from the federal and provincial courts.

Nine judges sit on Canada's Supreme Court. By law, three justices must come from Quebec, and by convention, the remainder of the court includes three justices from Ontario, two from western Canada, and one from the Atlantic provinces.

Designed by Montreal architect Ernest Cormier (who later worked with the team designing the United Nations Headquarters in New York), the current court building was completed in 1941. From May through August, free 30-minute **tours** of the building are offered, with English-language tours starting on the hour, and French tours on the half-hour. Reservations aren't required. Between September and April, tours run Monday through Friday only, and you must book in advance by completing the online reservation request form on the court's website (www.scc-csc.gc.ca). Tours include an overview of Canada's judicial system, interesting historical tidbits about the court and the justices, and

OTTAWA

a walk through several rooms, including the court chambers.

The Supreme Court hears cases during three sessions each year, in winter (generally mid-Jan.–Mar.), spring (Apr.–June), and fall (mid-Oct.–Dec.). No sessions are held in July, August, or September. If you want to see the Supreme Court in action, you can; **court hearings** are open to the public on a first-come, first-served basis. Sessions normally begin at 9:30 A.M. Monday through Friday, and a second daily session is sometimes held starting at 2 P.M. Check the court website (www.scc-csc.gc.ca) for a schedule.

⬛ Canadian War Museum

A museum of military history could easily be dreary or downright depressing. Yet this engaging contemporary museum (1 Vimy Pl., 819/776-8600 or 800/555-5621, www.warmuseum.ca, 9 A.M.–6 P.M. Mon.–Fri., 9 A.M.–8 P.M. Thurs., 9:30 A.M.–6 P.M. Sat.–Sun. May–mid-Oct.; 9 A.M.–5 P.M. Mon.–Fri., 9 A.M.–8 P.M. Thurs., 9:30 A.M.–5 P.M. Sat.–Sun. mid-Oct.–Apr.; adults $12, seniors and students $10, children 3–12 $8, family $30; free admission 4–8 P.M. Thurs.; parking $3.50/hour or $10/day), located on LeBreton Flats, west of Parliament Hill, is neither. The exhibitions put a human face on periods of war, illustrating not just the conflicts, but also the societal issues of the times.

The four main galleries that make up the museum's permanent collection are organized chronologically. The first covers warfare on Canadian soil from the earliest days through 1885, including aboriginal conflicts, European conquests, and the War of 1812. The second (1885–1931) illustrates Canada's involvement in the South African War and World War I, while the third (1931–1945) addresses World War II. The fourth gallery begins in 1945 and continues to the present day. And because a war museum couldn't exist without tanks and airplanes, the LeBreton Gallery houses a large collection of military vehicles and artillery.

The building itself, which opened in 2005, has some interesting design features. Its plant-covered "green roof" is one of the largest in North America. Notice the windows on the north peak, where Morse Code spells out "Lest We Forget." The lead architect, Vancouver-born Raymond Moriyama, also designed Toronto's Bata Shoe Museum.

You can buy a combination ticket (adults $18, seniors and students $15, children $12, family $45) good for both the War Museum and the Canadian Museum of Civilization. Note, though, that the Civilization Museum is across the Ottawa River in Gatineau.

The War Museum is two kilometers (1.2 miles) west of the Parliament buildings. Bus #8, toward Gatineau, travels west on Albert Street and stops in front of the museum.

Canadian Museum of Nature

As you walk into this castle-like Tudor Gothic structure, built in the early 1900s as Canada's first national museum building, notice the **mosaic of a bull moose** on the floor of the entrance hall. Its prominent private parts apparently created a stir among proper Ottawans in the museum's early days.

Anatomically correct moose mosaics aside, Ottawa's natural history museum (240 McLeod St., 613/566-4700 or 800/263-4433, www.nature.ca, 9 A.M.–6 P.M. daily, 9 A.M.–8 P.M. Thurs.–Fri., May–early Sept; 9 A.M.–5 P.M. Tues.–Sun., 9 A.M.–8 P.M. Thurs. early Sept.–Apr.; adults $12, seniors and students 13–17 $10, children 3–12 $8; free admission 5–8 P.M. Thurs.), which focuses primarily on Canadian species, is great fun for the kids. Besides the ever-popular dinosaur skeletons, highlights include the "animalium," which houses a creepy collection of live tarantulas, hissing cockroaches, giant snails, and scorpions; a 19.8-meter (66-foot) blue whale skeleton (one of only two on view in Canada); and the Mammal Gallery, where classic 1950s dioramas of polar bears, moose, bison, and other Canadian beasts are paired with state-of-the-art computer-based activities. The Discovery Zone has more hands-on things to do.

The glass box that tops the entranceway is known as the **Queen's Lantern,** with great views over downtown from the top floor. Opened in 2010, it replaced the museum's original tower, which had to be dismantled back in 1916 when it began sinking into the ground.

THE RIDEAU CANAL

The Rideau Canal is not only a Canadian National Historic Site and a UNESCO World Heritage Site. In many ways, this rambling waterway and adjacent green space where both residents and visitors can stroll, boat, or skate is also the heart of Ottawa. Bordering the canal, just east of Parliament Hill, are two sights worth seeing if you're interested in Ottawa's heritage: the Bytown Museum and the Fairmont Château Laurier hotel.

◖ Rideau Canal National Historic Site

Running 202 kilometers (126 miles) from Kingston to Ottawa, the Rideau Canal (www.pc.gc.ca) is North America's oldest continuously operating canal. After the War of 1812 between the United States and Britain, Canadians were concerned that the St. Lawrence River—a vital shipping channel between Montreal and the Great Lakes—would be vulnerable to another U.S. attack, since the Americans controlled the river's southern banks. In 1827, led by Lieutenant Colonel John By, work began on the canal that would eventually connect the Ottawa region to Lake Ontario through a series of lakes, rivers, and canals linked by 24 lock stations that allow boats to navigate its changing water levels.

More than 1,000 people died constructing the canal, including By himself, who was one of many workers who contracted malaria working along the swampy canal route. After six years of construction, the canal opened in 1832.

The Ottawa section of the canal runs from the Ottawa River southward, separating downtown from the ByWard Market. Between mid-May and mid-October, you can watch boats transit through the **Ottawa Locks;** the lock station closest to downtown is just north of Wellington Street, between Parliament Hill and the Fairmont Château Laurier.

boats traveling through the Rideau Canal's Ottawa Locks

OTTAWA

Bytown Museum

To learn more about the history of Ottawa and the construction of the Rideau Canal, visit this small but well-designed museum (1 Canal Ln., 613/234-4570, www.bytownmuseum.com, 10 A.M.–5 P.M. daily, 10 A.M.–9 P.M. Thurs., mid-May–mid-Oct.; 11 A.M.–4 P.M. Tues.–Sun. mid-Oct. to mid-May; adults $6, seniors and students $4, children 5–12 $3, family $15; free admission 5–9 P.M. Thurs.) located in Ottawa's oldest stone building, next to the Ottawa Locks. It's built on the site where the construction of the Rideau Canal began back in 1826.

Start your visit with a 20-minute video about the canal's history and check out the working model of the locks. Upstairs, exhibits trace Ottawa's development from its early days as rough-and-tumble Bytown (it was renamed Ottawa in 1855, for the "Odawa," an Anishinabe tribe native to the area) until it became Canada's capital (in 1857) and beyond. The admission price includes a self-guided audio tour.

If you're visiting with children, look for the "scratch and sniff" cards illustrating local history (guess what the one about horses smells like?). Kids can also dress up in period costumes and play Victorian-era games.

Fairmont Château Laurier

Looming above the Rideau Canal, this grand hotel (1 Rideau St., 613/241-1414 or 866/540-4410, www.fairmont.com/laurier), built in 1912, is almost as recognizable a part of the Ottawa skyline as the nearby Parliament buildings. Even if you don't stay here, stroll through the posh lobby with its original marble floor and dark woodwork, or splurge on traditional afternoon high tea in **Zoe's Lounge** (613/241-1414, 2–5 P.M. Mon.–Fri., noon–5 P.M. Sat.–Sun., reservations required, adults $30–39, children $20).

BYWARD MARKET AND VICINITY

Home to one of Canada's oldest and largest public markets, the "ByWard Market" encompasses both the main market building and the surrounding neighborhood, bounded roughly by Sussex Drive and Guigues, Cumberland, and Rideau Streets. Whether your taste runs to museums, galleries, boutiques, or all manner of food shops and restaurants, you can easily spend days sampling the wares in and around the ByWard Market. South of the market area, the residential neighborhood of Sandy Hill is home to the University of Ottawa (www.uottawa.ca), the capital's largest educational institution.

◖ National Gallery of Canada

It's hard to say which makes a more notable landmark at Canada's national art gallery (380 Sussex Dr., 613/990-1985 or 800/319-2787, www.gallery.ca, 10 A.M.–5 P.M. Fri.–Wed., 10 A.M.–8 P.M. Thurs., May–Sept.; Tues.–Wed. and Fri.–Sun. 10 A.M.–5 P.M., 10 A.M.–8 P.M. Thurs. Oct.–Apr., adults $9, seniors and students $7, youth 12–19 $4, kids under 12 free, family $18, free admission 5–8 P.M. Thurs.). Is it the airy granite, glass, and steel building itself, which opened in 1988, designed by Canadian architect Moshe Safdie? Or is it the gigantic spider that sits on the museum's front plaza? The spider, a bronze sculpture known as *Maman,* by French-American artist Louise Bourgeois (1911–2010), guards the museum entrance, standing over nine meters (30 feet) high.

Inside, it's hard to pick just a few highlights; the museum houses the country's largest visual-arts collection. A good place to start is in the **Canadian art galleries,** which are organized chronologically and include a significant number of works by Ontario's Group of Seven, early 20th-century landscape artists; look for paintings like the striking *Maligne Lake, Jasper Park* (1924) by Lawren Harris (1885–1970) or *The Jack Pine* (1917) by Tom Thomson (1877–1917). More contemporary works include paintings by First Nations artist Norval Morrisseau (1932–2007) and quirky pieces like *You Let My Toast Burn Again* by Quebecois artist Pierre Ayot (1943–1995). Make sure to wander into the side rooms off the main galleries, too, which contain smaller-scale works. Also

© CAROLYN B. HELLER

Canadian architect Moshe Safdie designed the National Gallery of Canada.

visit the serene **Rideau Chapel,** a 19th-century chapel from Ottawa's Convent of Our Lady of the Sacred Heart that was saved from demolition in 1972 and reconstructed in its entirety within the museum.

Another highlight is the **Inuit art collection,** which includes many contemporary pieces like *Nunali* (1988–1989), which Iqaluit artist Jackoposie Oopakak sculpted from stone, antler, and bone. There are also comprehensive **photography** and **European** art galleries. In addition to the permanent collections, the museum typically mounts a major exhibition every summer, as well as 12 to 14 smaller exhibits throughout the year.

One strategy for tackling such a large, and at times overwhelming, museum is to visit for a short time (perhaps on Thursday evening when admission is free) to get your bearings, and then return for a longer visit to delve into one or more areas in depth. Or take a one-hour **guided tour** (613/998-8888, $7); call for tour topics and for reservations, which are required. To guide your own explorations, rent an **audio guide** ($6).

The museum hosts concerts, films, and other special events throughout the year, as well. Check their website or phone for schedules and other details.

If all this culture makes you hungry, head for the museum cafeteria. The menu runs to typical sandwiches and salads, but the view across the Ottawa River—to Parliament Hill on one side and the Museum of Civilization on the other—is one of the best in town.

Notre Dame Cathedral Basilica

Opposite the National Gallery, the twin spires of Ottawa's oldest surviving church (385 Sussex Dr., 613/241-7496, www.notredameottawa. com, 11:30 A.M.–6 P.M. Mon., 10 A.M.–6 P.M. Tues.–Sat., 8 A.M.–8 P.M. Sun., free) glint in the afternoon sun. If you think that North America has few churches to rival Europe's cathedrals, stop into this grand Gothic structure, built between 1841 and 1885, with its arched columns, stained-glass windows, and elaborate pipe organ. Visitors are welcome to attend church services (call or check the website for schedules), explore the architecture, or simply take sanctuary for a few moments of quiet contemplation.

Royal Canadian Mint

As the queen ages, what happens to her portrait on the country's coins? If you're interested in this and other pecuniary trivia, visit the Royal Canadian Mint (320 Sussex Dr., 613/993-8990 or 800/276-7714, www.mint.ca, 9 A.M.–6 P.M. daily; weekdays/weekends adults $6/4, seniors $5/3.75, children 5–17 $3/2.25, family $15/11.75). Although Canada's regular circulation coins are no longer made at this Ottawa facility (production moved to Winnipeg in 1976), the mint still manufactures investment and collection coins, military medals, and Olympic medals.

The only way to see the mint is by taking a 30-minute tour, where guides explain the production process, and you can look down on the surprisingly low-tech machines. Medals from the 2010 Winter Olympics, held in Vancouver, are also on display. Tours run frequently throughout the day; call for seasonal

OTTAWA

schedules. Tours do fill up, so make a reservation, particularly in the summer. Try to visit Monday through Friday to see the mint in full operation. On weekends, admission prices are lower than on weekdays, but the production lines are shut down, so you don't see as much.

Oh, and about the queen? Over the years, the portrait of Queen Elizabeth II that appears on Canada's coins has aged along with Her Majesty. Notice, though, that in newer coins, the monarch isn't wearing her crown. She apparently requested the crown-free likeness, so she'd appear more like a regular person.

❰ ByWard Market

The centerpiece of the ByWard Market neighborhood is the main market building (55 ByWard Market Sq., 613/562-3325, www.byward-market.com, free), which dates back to the 1820s. Lieutenant Colonel John By, who led the construction of the Rideau Canal, also designed the ByWard Market and its surrounding streets. He specified that George and York Streets should both be extra wide to accommodate the horse-drawn carriages that brought goods to the market.

Nowadays, the market building houses shops selling snacks, light meals, and souvenirs; there's also a **tourist information office** and restrooms. The more interesting part of the market, though, is outside, when vendors set up stalls (generally late April or May through October) to sell produce, prepared foods, and other goodies. You'll find dozens of small shops around the market building, as well.

As you wander the market area, make sure to explore the courtyards just east of Sussex Drive, from George to St. Patrick Streets. They house restaurants, shops, and cafés that aren't easily visible from the main streets.

Laurier House National Historic Site

Two of Canada's prime ministers lived in this Sandy Hill mansion that's now a national historic site (335 Laurier Ave. E., 613/992-8142,

© CAROLYN B. HELLER

The ByWard Market district is full of food shops and trendy restaurants.

www.pc.gc.ca, 9 A.M.–5 P.M. Mon.–Fri. Apr.–late May, 9 A.M.–5 P.M. daily late May–mid-Oct., adults $3.90, seniors $3.40, children 6–16 $1.90, family $9.80).

Canada had no official prime minister's residence when Sir Wilfrid Laurier took office in 1896; a group of friends and supporters raised money to build this home, where Laurier lived from 1897 until his death in 1919. When Laurier's wife Zoe passed away in 1921, she bequeathed the house to William Lyon Mackenzie King, Laurier's successor as Liberal Party leader. MacKenzie King, who became prime minister that same year, moved into the house (after extensive renovations) in 1923 and lived there until he retired from politics in 1948.

Guides in period costume take visitors through the house, which is furnished with many of Laurier's and MacKenzie King's belongings. You can also take an **evening candlelit tour,** where domestic "staff" offer up gossip and other tidbits about the politicians' lives; call for schedule and prices. In summer, stop in for a light **afternoon tea on the veranda** (1–4 P.M., Thurs.–Sat., June–Aug., adults $9.80, seniors $8.40, children $4.90); prices include house admission, and reservations are required.

Laurier House is just over two kilometers (one mile) east of Parliament Hill. If you don't want to walk, catch OC Transpo bus #5, which stops in front of the house.

Rideau Hall

Owing to Canada's history as part of the British Empire, the British monarch is still Canada's official head of state. Since the queen presumably has better things to do than worry about day-to-day governance of Britain's former colonies, however, Canada's governor general represents the British Crown. In practice, it's the prime minister who runs the governmental show in Canada, and the governor general's role is largely a ceremonial one. It's fitting, then, that the governor general's residence, Rideau Hall (1 Sussex Dr., 613/991-4422 or 866/842-4422, www.gg.ca, free), is a suitably ceremonial mansion, set in parklike grounds northeast of the ByWard Market.

The free 45-minute **tours of the governor general's residence** (10 A.M.–4 P.M. Sat.–Sun., by reservation Mon.–Fri., May–late June; 10 A.M.–4 P.M. daily late June–early Sept.; noon–4 P.M. Sat.–Sun., by reservation Mon.–Fri. early Sept.–Oct.; by reservation only Nov.–Apr.) explore the history of the building—built in sections from 1838 through 1940—and visit some of the grand public spaces. Imagine attending a soiree in the majestic ballroom or in the candy-striped "Tent Room," where the pink fabric-draped ceiling resembles a circus tent!

Tours are offered year-round, and reservations are recommended. From November through April, tours are by reservation only; call to book. The grounds are open daily from 8 A.M. to one hour before sunset. You can take a guided tour of the grounds (10 A.M.–4 P.M. daily May–Sept., free, reservations required), or if you prefer to explore

the grounds on your own, pick up a self-guided tour brochure at either entrance gate. Another tour option, for art lovers, is an art tour (free), exploring the mansion's art collection. Tours are offered year-round, but reservations are required.

Also on the grounds is a **skating rink** (noon–5 P.M. Sat.–Sun. Jan.–mid-Mar.) that's open for public skating on winter weekends, weather permitting.

To reach Rideau Hall from downtown or the ByWard Market, catch OC Transpo bus #9, which runs along Queen, Rideau, and Dalhousie Streets, before turning onto Sussex Drive; on weekends, check the schedule (www.octranspo.com) before heading out, since service can be infrequent. En route to Rideau Hall, you might catch a glimpse of the prime minister's residence (24 Sussex Dr.), but it's not open to the public.

RCMP Musical Ride

Canada's red-coated, Stetson-wearing Mounties, officially known as the RCMP (Royal Canadian Mounted Police), are the country's national police force. But a small group of Mounties have an additional (volunteer) duty: performing with the RCMP Musical Ride (www.rcmp-grc.gc.ca/mr-ce). With a troop of 36 horses and riders, the Musical Ride is a cavalry drill team, executing intricate formations choreographed to music. Between May and October, the Musical Ride is frequently on tour in other parts of Canada, but they do perform periodically in Ottawa; check their website for the performance schedule.

Even when the Musical Ride is on the road, you can tour the **RCMP Musical Ride Centre** (RCMP Rockcliffe Stables, 1 Sandridge Rd., 613/741-4285, www.rcmp-grc.gc.ca/mr-ce, 9 A.M.–3:30 P.M. Mon.–Fri. May–Aug., 10 A.M.–2 P.M. Tues. and Thurs., Sept.–Apr., free) to meet the horses and learn more about the performing troupe.

From Parliament Hill or the Rideau Centre, OC Transpo bus #7 will drop you near the stables.

FEELING THE CHILL OF CANADA'S COLD WAR

"Attention! Warning! Take cover immediately!" As the radio announcer issues this urgent alert, the air raid siren begins to wail. Is there an incoming bomber heading straight for Ottawa? No, but at the **Diefenbunker, Canada's Cold War Museum** (3911 Carp Rd., Carp, 613/839-0007 or 800/409-1965, www.diefenbunker.ca, adults $14, seniors $13, students $10, children 6-18 $8, family $40), the drama and fears of the Cold War are very much alive.

Built in 1961 as a safe haven for government officials, this four-level underground bunker in the countryside outside of Ottawa was designed to survive a five megaton bomb – more than 200 times stronger than the bomb dropped on Nagasaki during World War II. The bunker could house 500 people for up to 30 days following a nuclear attack. Fortunately, the potential nuclear catastrophe never occurred, but the bunker remained staffed and ready for use until 1994. The underground shelter, with 9,290 square meters (100,000 square feet) of living space, is now an unusual museum that vividly illustrates the Cold War era.

You can explore the Diefenbunker on your own, or with the free **DiefenGuide** (an hour-long audio-video iPod guide). However, it's definitely worth taking a **guided tour** (60-90 minutes, included with admission). As you enter the bunker through a 92-meter (300-foot) blast tunnel, your guide will ask each group to imagine that it's 1962 and you're joining others who've already taken refuge after a nuclear attack. You will experience a simulated decontamination procedure and medical exam, before making your way through the warren of underground chambers.

The tour visits the war cabinet room where elected officials would have plotted their strategies, the prime minister's bedroom, the CBC emergency broadcasting studio, and even the Bank of Canada vault designed to store 800 tons of gold. There's a recreation room with table tennis and pool tables, since you'll want to get some exercise while confined underground for 30 days. Also in the Diefenbunker are models of public fallout shelters, a cafeteria, and black rotary-dial phones, huge IBM computers, and other artifacts of the era.

Tours are appropriate for children of elementary school age and older; younger children may find it unsettling. The temperature in the underground museum is a cool 17-19°C (63-66°F) year-round, so bring a sweater or light jacket. The Diefenbunker is open daily year-round, but the hours and tour schedule vary seasonally.

- July–August: 10 A.M.-6 P.M. Fri.-Tues., guided tours hourly 11 A.M.-4 P.M.; 10 A.M.-9 P.M. Wed.-Thurs., guided tours hourly 11 A.M.-7 P.M.

- September–June: 11 A.M.-4 P.M. daily; guided tours 11 A.M. and 2 P.M. Mon.-Fri., 11 A.M., 1 P.M., and 2 P.M. Sat.-Sun.

On the third Tuesday of every month, the museum hosts the **Cold War Cinema** (7 P.M., $8), screening a Cold War-themed movie inside the bunker. You can take a mini-tour (6 P.M., $15) of the facility before the film.

You will need a car to visit the Diefenbunker, a 30-40-minute drive west of downtown Ottawa. Take Highway 417 west to Carp Road then continue north on Carp Road for 12 kilometers (7.5 miles) through the village of Carp to the Diefenbunker entrance.

Entertainment and Events

Ottawa may not have as active a nightlife scene as larger cities like Toronto or Montreal, but as the nation's capital, its arts venues not only promote local artists, but also feature Canadian performers from across the country. And with dozens of festivals year-round, there's almost always something going on.

NIGHTLIFE

The ByWard Market area is entertainment central, full of bars, pubs, and music venues. Oddly named nightclub **Zaphod Beeblebrox** (27 York St., 613/562-1010, www.zaphodbeeblebrox.com) offers music nightly, a mix of DJs and up-and-coming bands. **The Rainbow** (76 Murray St., 613/241-5123) books local, national, and international blues acts, with some R&B and jazz thrown in. DJs at **Mercury Lounge** (56 ByWard Market Sq., 2nd Fl., 613/789-5324, www.mercurylounge.com) play electronic, house, jazz, funk, and anything with "soul."

Local socialists—and socialites—say "Da" to the eclectic mix of Soviet propaganda posters, local art, and vast menu of Russian-themed drinks (how about a Red Square, Proletarian Omelet, or Comsomol Lust?) at the appropriately named **Avant-Garde Bar** (135 ½ Besserer St., at Dalhousie, 613/321-8908, www.avantgardebar.ca). If you're hungry, share a "bourgeois fish plate" or a bowl of Siberian *pelemeni* (dumplings). It's located one block south of Rideau Street.

In Chinatown, the **Shanghai Restaurant** (651 Somerset St. W., 613/233-4001, www.shanghaiottawa.com, closed Mon.), a typical Chinese eatery by day, morphs into a quirky club on weekend nights when the owners' son, a drag queen who goes by the name of China Doll, hosts a Saturday karaoke night and other events. Also in Chinatown, the **Raw Sugar Café** (692 Somerset St. W., 613/216-2850, www.rawsugarcafe.com) runs eclectic events ranging from experimental music to readings to "Stars on Vinyl" DJ nights.

Check the *Ottawa Xpress* (www.ottawaxpress. ca) or *Ottawa Citizen* (www.ottawacitizen.com) for listings and reviews of the latest hotspots.

THE ARTS

The capital's major arts venue is the **National Arts Centre** (NAC, 53 Elgin St., 613/947-7000 or 866/850-2787, www.nac-cna.ca, box office 10 A.M.–9 P.M. Mon.–Sat., additional hours on Sun. performance time). It's home to English- and French-language theaters, the NAC Orchestra, and a dance series. The NAC also hosts numerous festivals and special events.

To avoid paying service changes, buy your tickets for NAC events in person at the box office. You can purchase tickets online or by phone from Ticketmaster (www.ticketmaster. ca, 888/991-2787), but you'll pay a service fee. See the NAC website for more details on buying tickets.

Full-time students ages 13 to 29 can purchase last-minute **Live Rush tickets** (www. liverush.ca) to NAC theater, music, and dance events for only $12. Live Rush tickets are on sale between 10 A.M. the day before the show until 6 P.M. on show day.

In July and August, you can take a **free guided tour** of the hexagonal NAC building, which opened in 1969. The 45-minute tours leave from the main lobby at 11 A.M. and 1:30 P.M. on Tuesday, Thursday, and Saturday.

For a meal or snack before or after the show, try the NAC restaurant, **Le Café** (613/594-5127, 11:30 A.M.–4:30 P.M. and 5–9 P.M. Mon.–Fri., 5–9 P.M. Sat.). The restaurant stays open till 11 P.M. on show nights, and it opens for dinner on Sunday when there are Sunday performances; there are limited hours early Sept.–late May. The vibrantly colored mural above the café is called *Homage to RFK,* by Canadian contemporary artist William Ronald (1926–1998).

Outside the NAC, look—or listen—for **Oscar's Corner** (Elgin and Albert Sts.), a larger-than-life-size statue of Canadian jazz great Oscar Peterson. Recordings of Peterson's music play at the site, making it seem as if the musician (1925–2007) is still tinkling away on his piano. Canadian sculptor Ruth Abernethy created the bronze work, which was unveiled in 2010. A popular photo op: sit on the bench beside Peterson's likeness.

Theater

Every year, the **National Arts Centre English Theatre** (www.nac-cna.ca/en/theatre) typically presents five plays in their main 800-seat theater and three plays in the 290-seat studio theater, ranging from classics to contemporary Canadian works. They also produce family plays and other special presentations.

Established in 1975, the professional **Great Canadian Theatre Company** (GCTC, 1233 Wellington St. W., 613/236-5196, www.gctc. ca, adults $35–45, seniors and students $35) performs several contemporary plays each year, focusing on works by Canadian playwrights or with Canadian content. The first Sunday of each production's run is a pay-what-you-can performance; be at the box office at noon to buy a ticket (by donation) for the 2 P.M. show. In addition to the mainstage productions, smaller local companies present works in the black box studio theater.

The GCTC's modern building in the Wellington West neighborhood, the **Irving Greenberg Theatre Centre,** is one of Canada's only "green" theaters. Note the windows: what look like artistic designs on the glass are actually heat-conducting porcelain tiles. Upstairs, the **Fritzi Gallery** displays works that represent the current plays.

Fancy a good yarn? Look for shows by the **Ottawa Storytellers** (613/322-8336, www. ottawastorytellers.ca). From January to June, the group presents monthly professional storytelling performances at the National Arts Centre's Fourth Stage (adults $17, seniors and students $13.50); check their website for performance dates and details. On the first Thursday of every month, they host a story-swap/open-mic night (Library and Archives of Canada, 395 Wellington St., Room 156, 7–9:30 P.M., free) with tales by professional and amateur storytellers.

Music

The **National Arts Centre Orchestra** (www. nac-cna.ca/en/naco), directed by noted conductor and violinist Pinchas Zukerman, performs in the NAC's 2,323-seat Southam Hall. Concerts are typically held September through June.

Big-name rock, pop, county, and other musicians perform at **Scotiabank Place** (1000 Palladium Dr., 613/599-0140, www. scotiabankplace.com). The arena is a 25- to 30-minute drive (25 kilometers, or 16 miles) west of downtown via Highway 417. OC Transpo Connexion Route #403 bus (www. octranspo.com) will take you from downtown to Scotiabank Place in about 45 minutes.

Dance

Canadian and international ballet and contemporary dance companies perform as part of the **NAC Dance** series (www.nac-cna.ca/en/dance) at the National Arts Centre. The roster has included the National Ballet of Canada, the Royal Winnipeg Ballet, the Alvin Ailey American Dance Theatre, the Joffrey Ballet, and many other well-known and lesser-known troupes.

FESTIVALS AND EVENTS

Ottawa seems to host one festival after another, particularly during the summer months. The biggest events are the Canada Day festivities, celebrating the nation's birthday on July 1, and the winter festival known as Winterlude; make your travel arrangements in advance if you'll be in town for either of these.

For a complete calendar or more information about the festivities listed here, contact **Ottawa Festivals** (47 William St., 613/233-1085, www.ottawafestivals.ca), or check the websites of **Ottawa Tourism** (www.ottawa-tourism.ca) or the **Capital Information Kiosk** (www.canadascapital.gc.ca).

Spring

More than one million tulips herald the

beginning of spring in the nation's capital during the annual **Canadian Tulip Festival** (613/567-5757 or 800/668-8547, www.tulipfestival.ca, May). The festival runs for about two weeks, with most events in Major's Hill Park (Mackenzie Ave., behind the Fairmont Château Laurier) or at Commissioners Park (Preston St. and Queen Elizabeth Dr.) near Dow's Lake, south of downtown. Besides the opportunity to tiptoe through the tulips, the festival includes free concerts and garden parties, kids' programs, and the annual black-tie Tulip Ball.

Billed as "Canada's largest independent literary celebration," the semiannual **Ottawa Writers Festival–Spring** (Saint Brigid's Centre for the Arts and Humanities, 314 St. Patrick St., 613/562-1243, www.writersfestival.org, April/May) offers author readings, lectures, book launches, poetry cabarets, and other literary events at several venues around the city. Some events are free; others require tickets.

Summer

Are you a theater buff? Sample some of Canada's best contemporary theater productions during the **Magnetic North Theatre Festival** (613/947-7000 ext. 719 or 866/850-2787 ext. 719, www.magneticnorthfestival.ca, June). The festival is held in Ottawa every other year, at venues around town; in the alternate years, the event travels to other Canadian cities.

The **Canada Dance Festival** (www.canadadance.ca, June) presents several days of contemporary dance performances, featuring dancers from across Canada.

Although Quebec observes all of Canada's national holidays, the province has its own *Fête Nationale* (www.tourismeoutaouais.com or www.fetenationale.qc.ca, June), also known as Saint-Jean-Baptiste Day, which Ottawa-Gatineau celebrates with a big outdoor concert featuring Quebecois musicians.

Held in conjunction with National Aboriginal Day, the **Summer Solstice Aboriginal Arts Festival** (613/722-0315, www.nadottawa.ca, June) showcases aboriginal artists, musicians, and dancers, with lots of kids' activities, too.

It's been called "Canada's Biggest Party"— the annual **Canada Day Celebrations** (613/239-5000 or 800/465-1867, www.canadaday.gc.ca, July 1), which include scads of free activities, from official ceremonies, to street performers, to concerts; past headliners have included the Barenaked Ladies and Canadian rapper k-os. A highlight is the nighttime fireworks show on Parliament Hill.

Summer also brings a number of music events to town, including the **Ottawa International Jazz Festival** (613/241-2633, www.ottawajazzfestival.com, June/July), **Cisco Ottawa BluesFest** (613/247-1188 or 866/258-3748, www.ottawabluesfest.ca, July), and **Ottawa International Chamber Music Festival** (613/234-6306, www.chamberfest.com, July/August).

At the **Rideau Canal Festival** (613/288-0970, www.rideaucanalfestival.ca, July/August), historical tours, performances, and exhibits celebrate the canal's heritage, but the event also recognizes the canal's contribution to Ottawa's outdoor life, with bike tours, walks, even outdoor yoga.

Ottawa's Greek community welcomes visitors to join in **GreekFest** (613/225-8016 ext. 234, www.ottawagreekfest.com, August), a 10-day party of music, dancing, and of course, food. Culminating in a huge Pride Parade and outdoor concert, the **Capital Pride Festival** (613/252-7174, www.capitalpride.ca, August) has been celebrating Ottawa's gay, lesbian, bisexual, and transgendered community since 1986.

Fall and Winter

Like the spring version of this book festival, the **Ottawa Writers Festival-Fall** (Saint Brigid's Centre for the Arts and Humanities, 314 St. Patrick St., 613/562-1243, www.writersfestival.org, October) hosts readings, book talks, lectures, and other events for the literarily inclined.

In the world's coldest national capital (a dubious honor that both Moscow and Ottawa claim), what can you do but embrace the long winter? And Ottawa does just that during **Winterlude** (613/239-5000 or 800/465-1867, www.canadascapital.gc.ca/winterlude, February), a midwinter festival of outdoor fun that takes place on several February weekends. You'll find an ice sculpture competition, skating on the Rideau Canal, North America's largest outdoor snow playground, and other outdoor events. Bring your mittens!

During **Black History Month** (www.black-historyottawa.org, February), lectures, concerts, and other special events celebrating the Afro-Canadian experience take place around town.

Shopping

Ottawa's small but growing cohort of local fashion designers sell their wares at boutiques around town. The city also has an active art scene, with plenty of contemporary galleries for browsing (and buying). Besides the venues listed here, visit the shops in the major museums for unique souvenirs, books, jewelry, and children's gifts.

SHOPPING DISTRICTS

Far livelier than it seems from its uninviting stone exterior, the **Rideau Centre** (50 Rideau St., 613/236-6565, www.rideaucentre.net, 9:30 A.M.–9 P.M. Mon.–Fri., 9:30 A.M.–6 P.M. Sat., 11 A.M.–5 P.M. Sun.) is a large mall housing popular North American chain stores, from yoga-wear shop Lululemon, to clothing retailers like the Gap, Sears, and Jacob, to fast-food outlets like Tim Hortons and Starbucks. It's on the east side of the Rideau Canal, near the Fairmont Château Laurier. Across the street from the Rideau Centre is a branch of **The Bay** (73 Rideau St., 613/241-7511, www.hbc.com) department store.

The streets around the **ByWard Market** are happy hunting grounds for shoppers looking for unique boutiques. West of the market building, **Sussex Drive** is lined with high-end clothing shops. East of the market, head to **Dalhousie Street** for more eclectic, and more affordable, fashion and housewares.

Outside the city center, the increasingly trendy **Wellington West** district is another spot to find interesting boutiques, food shops, and cafés. Start around the intersection of Wellington and Holland and continue west along Wellington Street. From downtown,

it's about a 10-minute drive or 15-minute bus ride; take OC Transpo bus #86 to the corner of Holland and Wellington Streets.

ART GALLERIES

A number of contemporary art galleries are clustered around the ByWard Market. For an in-depth look at the community's art scene, take a **ByWard Market Art Gallery Walking Tour** (11 A.M. Sat., June–Oct., $8), a three-hour stroll that visits 8–10 of the neighborhood's galleries. Gallery owners or staff typically introduce their art spaces and discuss their current exhibitions. The tour begins at the **Gordon Harrison Gallery** (495 Sussex Dr., 613/746-6853, www.gordonharrisongallery.com, 11 A.M.–6 P.M. Wed., Sat., and Sun., 11 A.M.–8 P.M. Thurs.–Fri.), and reservations are recommended. Even if you don't take the tour, stop into the host gallery, which showcases the work of landscape painter Gordon Harrison, as well as works by other contemporary Canadian landscape artists.

One of the loveliest art spaces in the city, an airy multilevel venue with high ceilings and lots of glass, the **Terence Robert Gallery** (531 Sussex Dr., 613/860-9888, www.terencerobertgallery.com, 11 A.M.–5:30 P.M. Mon., Wed., and Sat., 11 A.M.–6 P.M. Thurs.–Fri., noon–5 P.M.) displays work by established and emerging Canadian artists.

One of Ottawa's most unusual gallery spaces is **Galerie 240** (240 Guigues Ave., 613/680-0866, www.galerie240.com, noon–6 P.M. Wed.–Sun.), which artist-owner Brenda Gale Warner runs in her 1870 wood-frame home, east of the ByWard Market. Warner shows her own work and that of other contemporary artists based in Ottawa and farther afield.

Several galleries have set up shop in Wellington West. On the first Thursday of the month, you can visit them all during the **Wellington West 1st Thursdays Art Walk** (www.wellingtonwest.ca, 5–9 P.M. Thurs., free); get a gallery map on the website.

BOOKS AND MAGAZINES

Every neighborhood needs a laid-back gathering place like the **Collected Works Bookstore and Coffeebar** (1242 Wellington St. W., 613/722-1265, www.collected-works.com, 8 A.M.–9 P.M. Mon.–Sat., 8 A.M.–8 P.M. Sun.), part independent bookstore and part local coffee shop. Check their website for readings and other events.

Another friendly independent bookshop with a knowledgeable staff is **Perfect Books** (258A Elgin St., 613/231-6468, www.perfectbooks.ca, 10 A.M.–9 P.M. Mon.–Sat., noon–5 P.M. Sun.) downtown.

CLOTHING AND ACCESSORIES

Focusing on wearable clothing by Canadian female designers, with roughly half their stock made in Ottawa, the funky **Workshop Studio and Boutique** (242 ½ Dalhousie St.,

613/789-5534, www.workshopboutique.ca, 10 A.M.–6 P.M. Mon.–Wed., 10 A.M.–8 P.M. Thurs.–Fri., 10 A.M.–6 P.M. Sat., noon–5 P.M. Sun.), near the ByWard Market, also carries accessories, purses, jewelry, and gifts. If you want to learn how to create your own clothing or jewelry, look for their one-day how-to classes.

The same owners operate **Flock Boutique** (1275 Wellington St. W., 613/695-0834, www.flockboutique.ca, 10 A.M.–6 P.M. Mon.–Wed., 10 A.M.–8 P.M. Thurs., 10 A.M.–6 P.M. Fri.–Sat., noon–5 P.M. Sun.), carrying similarly eclectic Canadian-made clothing in the Wellington West neighborhood.

Another creative boutique for dresses, jewelry, and other goods for women, **Victoire** (246 Dalhousie St., 613/321-1590, www.victoireboutique.com, 10 A.M.–6 P.M. Mon.–Wed., 10 A.M.–8 P.M. Thurs.–Fri., 10 A.M.–6 P.M. Sat., noon–5 P.M. Sun.) describes its style as "Rock 'n' Roll tea party...loved by rebel girls with good manners everywhere."

You've gotta love the cheeky spirit of a boutique named **Trustfund** (493 Sussex Dr., 613/562-0999, www.trustfundboutique.com, 10 A.M.–6 P.M. Mon.–Wed., 10 A.M.–9 P.M. Thurs.–Fri., 10 A.M.–6 P.M. Sat., noon–6 P.M. Sun.). Do you need your own trust fund to afford the *au courant,* and not inexpensive, fashions for men and women? No, but it wouldn't hurt.

Sports and Recreation

PARKS

With the park-lined Rideau Canal running through town, Ottawa feels like it has lots of green space. Downtown, you can relax in **Major's Hill Park** (Mackenzie Ave.), behind the Fairmont Château Laurier, or in **Confederation Park** (Elgin St. and Laurier Ave.), which hosts Canada Day festivities, as well as Winterlude events. The bigger **Commissioners Park** (Preston St. and Queen Elizabeth Dr.) is near Dow's Lake, south of the city center. The region's largest green space is **Gatineau Park** (33 Scott Rd., Chelsea,

819/827-2020 or 800/465-1867, www.canadascapital.gc.ca), in the hills on the Quebec side of the Ottawa River.

SUMMER SPORTS

The Ottawa-Gatineau region has more than 220 kilometers (137 miles) of cycling paths as part of the **Capital Pathway** network (www.canadascapital.gc.ca). The paths that are most accessible from the central city include the **Rideau Canal Pathway,** a flat, paved trail that runs for eight kilometers (five miles) on either side of the canal; the **Ottawa River Pathway,** with 20 kilometers

OTTAWA

(12 miles) of paved trail along the river heading west from Parliament Hill and another 13 kilometers (eight miles) of stone-dirt path running east from Rideau Hall; and the 12-kilometer (7.5-mile), paved **Rideau River Pathway**, which begins near Rideau Hall and follows the Rideau River south. Get cycling maps online at www.canadascapital.gc.ca or from the **Capital Information Kiosk** (World Exchange Plaza, 111 Albert St., 613/239-5000 or 800/465-1867, 10 A.M.–5 P.M. daily).

On **Sunday Bikedays** (www.canadascapital.gc.ca, late May–early Sept.), the city closes a number of roads to cars, creating additional cycling, in-line skating, running, and walking routes. In Ottawa, sections of the Ottawa River Parkway, Colonel By Drive, and Rockcliffe Parkway become bikeways; in Gatineau Park, it's the Gatineau, Champlain, and Fortune Lake Parkways. Note that the Gatineau routes are quite hilly!

You can rent bicycles from **RentABike** (2 Rideau St., at Colonel By Dr., 613/241-4140, www.rentabike.ca, 9 A.M.–5 P.M. daily mid-Apr.–Oct., $9–15/hour, $38–60/day), located at the Plaza Bridge near the Rideau Canal.

Capital BIXI (www.capital.bixi.com), a public bike-sharing system, was launched in 2011 with 10 bike stations located in downtown Ottawa and across the river in Gatineau. The basic rental fee is $5 for 24 hours (or $12 for 72 hours), and if you limit your rides to 30 minutes per trip, that's all you pay. Since the service is designed for short hops (especially convenient for touring around central Ottawa), you'll pay additional fees for each extra half-hour if you keep a bike for more than 30 minutes per trip. Their website has a map showing bike pickup and drop-off locations.

WINTER SPORTS

Even Ottawa's frigid winters don't keep locals indoors, and if you visit during the colder months, you should get outside, too. Skating on the Rideau Canal is a don't-miss experience. For cross-country skiing and snowshoeing, head for the trails in **Gatineau Park** (33

Scott Rd., Chelsea, 819/827-2020 or 800/465-1867, www.canadascapital.gc.ca).

The world's longest ice skating rink, the **Rideau Canal Skateway** (613/239-5000 or 800/465-1867 information, 613/239-5234 ice conditions, www.canadascapital.gc.ca/skateway, generally Jan.–early Mar., free) stretches 7.8 kilometers (4.8 miles), beginning just south of Wellington and Rideau Streets and continuing beyond Dows Lake.

You can rent skates at several points en route. Closest to downtown, **Capital Skates** (613/316-4977, www.capitalskates.com, generally 10 A.M.–9 P.M. daily, $16 for first 2 hours, $8/additional hour) is on the east side of the canal, between the MacKenzie King and Laurier Bridges; farther south, they have a second location on the west side of the canal near the intersection of the Queen Elizabeth Driveway and Fifth Avenue (6–10 P.M. Fri., 10 A.M.–10 P.M. Sat.–Sun.). Skate rentals are also available at **Dows Lake Pavilion** (1001 Queen Elizabeth Dr., 613/232-1001 ext. 5, www.dowslake.com, 9:30 A.M.–10 P.M. Mon.–Fri., 9 A.M.–10 P.M. Sat., 9 A.M.–9 P.M. Sun., adults $13/hour, $18/two hours, $8/additional hour, children $9/hour, $12/two hours, $6/additional hour).

Locals recommend bringing a backpack to carry your shoes, as well as water and snacks. Check the ice conditions before heading out, too, since even a brief stretch of warmer temperatures can unexpectedly close the canal to skaters.

It may seem rather sedate after cruising along on the canal, but you can also skate at the **Rideau Hall ice rink** (1 Sussex Dr., 613/991-4422 or 866/842-4422, www.gg.ca, noon–5 P.M. Sat.–Sun. Jan.–mid-Mar., free), on the grounds of the governor general's residence.

SPECTATOR SPORTS

The Senators aren't just Parliamentarians—they're also the capital's National Hockey League team. The **Ottawa Senators** (www.ottawasenators.com) play at **Scotiabank Place** (1000 Palladium Dr., 613/599-0140, www.scotiabankplace.com), which is just off Highway 417, 25 kilometers (16 miles) west of downtown, about a 25- to 30-minute drive. The regular season runs October to April.

OC Transpo (www.octranspo.com) runs buses between downtown and Scotiabank Place when there are hockey games or other events at the arena. Catch the Connexion Route #403 bus on Rideau or Albert Streets; it's about a 45-minute ride.

Accommodations

As in any large city, Ottawa has a range of accommodations from hostels to bed and breakfasts to boutique hotels to major chain lodgings. Many hotels are located in the downtown area, within walking distance of Parliament Hill. The ByWard Market neighborhood has several hotels, as well as a number of B&Bs, and you'll find more B&Bs south and east of the market in residential Sandy Hill.

Perhaps because the federal government attracts businesspeople and bureaucrats for long-term stays, the capital has numerous suite hotels, many of which would be comfortable options for families, even if you're visiting for just a day or two. Not only do you have more space, you can save money on food, since all have kitchen facilities. In addition to the suite hotels listed below, try **Premiere Executive Suites** (www.premieresuites.com), which rents studio, one-, and two-bedroom apartments around town for short-term stays.

DOWNTOWN

Many of Ottawa's larger hotels, as well as several small inns and B&Bs, are located in the city center. Expect to pay at least $100 per night, though, at least during the summer.

Under $100

The ambience of the **Ambiance B&B** (330 Nepean St., 613/563-0421 or 888/366-8772, www.ambiancebandb.com, $89–109 s, $99–129 d, suite $160 d) is that of a private home. Built in 1904, this brick Victorian has a snug parlor with an overstuffed sofa and gas fireplace; a three-course breakfast is served around the common dining room table. Upstairs, two of the homey guest rooms share a bath; the

other two are en suite. Just like at home, guests can help themselves to complimentary (nonalcoholic) drinks, or use the fridge and microwave. Free Wi-Fi.

Once the Embassy of Madagascar, this 1895 Victorian on a residential Centretown street was converted to an inn in 2000. Comfortably furnished with antiques and period pieces, the red brick **Inn On Somerset** (282 Somerset St. W., 613/236-9309 or 800/658-3564, www.innonsomerset.com, $75–117 s, $100–132 d) has 11 guest rooms, ranging from a small single to a spacious queen-bedded room with separate sitting area. A full hot breakfast is served in the cheerful sunroom, its walls lined with leaded-glass windows. Guests can use the third-floor laundry. The main drawback? Only four rooms have private baths.

$100-150

Built in 1875 as a private residence, the red brick **Albert House Inn** (478 Albert St., 613/236-4479 or 800/267-1982, www.albertinn.com, $108–180 d) is now a 17-room Victorian-style guesthouse downtown. Sure, some of the rooms are a bit old-fashioned, but they're well kept, with en suite baths, flat-screen TVs, and free Wi-Fi. First- and second-floor units have high ceilings that make them feel quite spacious, and guests are welcome to relax in the bay-windowed parlor. Rates include a full cooked-to-order breakfast. No kids under 10.

There's nothing flashy about the apartment-style **Extended Stay Deluxe Ottawa** (141 Cooper St., 613/236-7500, www.extendedstayhotels.com, $115–140 d) on a Centretown side street, but they cover the

OTTAWA

basics: comfortable studio and one-bedroom suites, all with fully equipped kitchen facilities. There's no restaurant or pool, but they do have a fitness center and hot tub, and you're just a block from the shops and restaurants on Elgin Street. Internet access is available for a onetime $5 fee.

Though not quite as posh as the nearby Château Laurier, the independently owned ◖ **Lord Elgin Hotel** (100 Elgin St., 613/235-3333 or 800/267-4298, www.lordelgin.ca, $139–184 d), built in 1941, still offers a traditionally elegant feel. This Ottawa institution, in a stately 11-story stone building topped with a green copper roof, has an excellent location just a short walk from Parliament Hill. Of the 355 guest rooms with classic Biedermeier-style furnishings, some of the nicest are the corner units overlooking the National Arts Centre; book these rooms in summer for great views of the Changing of the Guard procession marching up Elgin Street. Proper ladies and gentlemen (as well as the hoi polloi) sip cocktails in the gracious lobby lounge; photos of tulips by noted photographer Malek Karsh (brother of even more notable portrait photographer Yousuf Karsh) line the hallway nearby. On the lower level are a lap pool, hot tub, and fitness room. Dignified ambience notwithstanding, the hotel welcomes families and frequently offers substantial discounts that make it an excellent value (just check the fees for Internet service and parking).

An ample breakfast buffet, an indoor lap pool and fitness facility, free Internet service, and a guest laundry are among the features that make the 162-room **Residence Inn by Marriott** (161 Laurier Ave. W., 613/231-2020 or 877/478-4838, www.marriottresidenceinn-nottawa.com, $139–189) popular with both road warriors and traveling families. The studios, with a king bed and queen sofa bed, are about the size of typical hotel rooms, but the one- and two-bedroom suites are quite large, especially the corner units; all have kitchens. On some weekday evenings, the hotel hosts happy hours and other social events where guests can mingle.

the landmark Fairmont Château Laurier near the ByWard Market

© CAROLYN B. HELLER

Built around an open atrium in a historic six-story building, the hip **Hotel Indigo** (123 Metcalfe St., 613/231-6555 or 877/846-3446, www.hotelindigo.com, $132–225 d) appeals to travelers looking for boutique hotel style without the sky-high price. For a chain hotel, it feels surprisingly individual: in the 106 guest rooms, a floor-to-ceiling mural covers one wall, and rather than the ubiquitous white duvets, the quilt covers are bright floral prints. You've got all the modern amenities, from flat-screen TVs, mini-fridges, and coffeemakers to complimentary Internet access. Indigo guests share the fitness room and indoor pool with the Residence Inn by Marriott next door. The lobby café is nothing special, but it will do for coffee or a light breakfast.

Billing itself as Ottawa's first boutique hotel, **◖ ARC The.Hotel** (140 Slater St., 613/238-2888 or 800/699-2516, www.arcthehotel.com, $129–259 d) is still one of the capital's most stylish lodgings. The 112 guest rooms, with cream-colored upholstery and dark wood furniture, have a Zen feel, with the Egyptian linens and Frette bathrobes adding a luxurious touch. The lounge is one of the city's coolest meet-for-drinks spots, while the dining room (lunch $16–23, dinner $33–37) caters to trendy road warriors with dishes like elk ribs in cumin-coffee BBQ sauce with duck-fat smashed potatoes or duck breast in a dried cherry, chorizo, and foie gras *mole*. If a workout in the 24-hour fitness center doesn't sufficiently relax you, the concierge can book an in-room massage.

$150-200

The spacious one- and two-bedroom suites at the **Albert at Bay Suite Hotel** (435 Albert St., 613/238-8858 or 800/267-6644, www.albertatbay.com, one-bedroom $149–179 d, two-bedroom $239–249 d) are a good deal for families or couples traveling together. Even the smallest of the 197 traditionally furnished units are over 74 square meters (800 square feet)—more than double the size of many hotel rooms—and all have full kitchens. There's no pool, but the fitness room overlooks the rooftop terrace. Local phone calls and Internet service are free.

Drawing a mix of business travelers and vacationers, the 31-story **Minto Suite Hotel** (185 Lyon St. N., 613/232-2200 or 800/267-3377, www.mintosuitehotel.com, $158–197 d, two-bedroom $205–216 d) has 417 well-appointed studio, one-, and two-bedroom units. Though a bit smaller on average than those at the Albert at Bay, they're more upmarket; all have kitchen facilities, and some have in-suite washer/dryers. Other amenities include iPod docking stations, windows that open, a saltwater pool, and a fitness center. Staff will even stock your suite with groceries for a small fee.

BYWARD MARKET AND VICINITY

The ByWard Market and the adjacent Sandy Hill neighborhood (south of Rideau Street) have lots of lodging choices, from hostels to B&Bs to small hotels to big chain properties. Sandy Hill is primarily residential, surrounding the University of Ottawa, between the Rideau Canal and the Rideau River.

Under $100

Even if you don't usually stay in hostels, have a look at the **HI-Ottawa Jail Hostel** (75 Nicholas St., 613/235-2595 or 866/299-1478, www.hihostels.ca, $32–36 dorm, $57 s, $81–86 d), where some of the beds are in cells of the 19th-century former Carleton County Gaol (jail). The cells, as you might expect, feel claustrophobic and noisy, with heavy grates on the doors and transom windows open to the hallways, but you don't have to break any laws to sleep behind bars. More standard dorms and shared-bath doubles lack the cellblock ambiance, but rumors of ghosts abound. Guests share the kitchen or hang out in Mugshots, the pub. Free Wi-Fi.

The **Barefoot Hostel** (455 Cumberland St., 613/237-0335, www.barefoothostel.com, $29–43 dorm) is Ottawa's best budget lodging. Inside this red brick building near the ByWard Market, the common area with bright blue walls has space for lounging, with a flat-screen TV and several computers for guest use. Sleeping areas are in four dorms, each with four bunks, and while there's no room to spare, they're bright and cherry, with wood floors and individual storage lockers. Guests share three modern baths. Would-be chefs, take note: the kitchen has a microwave, fridge, and toaster, but no stove. The hostel is under the same ownership as the Swiss Hotel next door.

$100-150

Unlike many fussy Victorian B&Bs, the four rooms at the **Avalon Bed and Breakfast** (539 Besserer St., 613/789-4334 or 866/557-5506, www.avalonbedandbreakfast.com, $95–125 d) mix a few traditional furnishings with cool, contemporary pieces. The sleek, airy Pewter room, done in silver and white, has a private balcony, and all the rooms in this brick half-duplex, on a residential street in the east end of Sandy Hill, have en suite baths, wood floors, flat-screen TVs, and large windows. The location is a bit out of the way, but rates include parking, as well as a full breakfast. The young owners have created a website (www.exploreottawa.com) with tips for things to see and do around town. The other half of the Sandy Hill townhouse that houses the Avalon B&B is a bed and breakfast, as well: **Benner's B&B** (541 Besserer St., 613/789-8320 or 877/891-5485, www.bennersbnb.com, $95–130 d). The three rooms, all with private baths, have modern appointments; the largest, the King Loft, has exposed brick walls, a king bed, and a sitting area in front of an electric fireplace.

Owner Janis King is an avid traveler, and she's happy to swap travel tales with her guests at the **Ottawa Centre Bed & Breakfast** (62 Stewart St., 613/237-9494, www.ottawacenterbnb.com, $105–135 d), in her 1901 brick home just a short hop from the University of Ottawa campus. Though the appointments, particularly in the public areas, seem formal—the living room has a curved entryway and ornate wood mantel, the dining room, where a full hot breakfast is served, is filled with antiques and silver pieces—King makes her guests feel at home. Upstairs, the three bedrooms, all with en suite baths, have tall windows, wood floors, wingback chairs, oriental

rugs, and other traditional furnishings. Rates include breakfast, parking, and Wi-Fi.

Perhaps some of the rooms in the modest, European-style **ByWard Blue Inn** (157 Clarence St., 613/241-2695 or 800/620-8810, www.bywardblueinn.com, $109–149 d) should have been named "ByWard View," since the sunny, top-floor front units—the inn's nicest—have tiny terraces with views toward Parliament Hill. The rest of the 46 rooms in this six-story building, conveniently located just east of the ByWard Market, are more basic (and viewless; the cheapest are quite small and dark), but all have fridges, microwaves, and free Internet access. Rates include a continental breakfast; you can opt for a full breakfast for an extra $5.

Plenty of homey touches grace the three-story **McGee's Inn** (185 Daly Ave., 613/237-6089 or 800/262-4337, www.mcgeesinn.com, $118–198 d), from the teddy bear collection that lines the stairs to the hand-carved cherry fireplace mantel in the parlor. Built in 1886, as the home of Privy Council member John McGee and his family, this family-run inn now has 14 guest rooms. They're all somewhat different—some small, others quite large—but all have private baths and antiques or period furnishings. Several have original wood fireplaces, some have whirlpool tubs for two, and a couple have private porches. Parking, Internet access, and a full breakfast are included in the rates. While the inn might not be as child-focused as a generic chain hotel, kids under 12 stay free.

One of Ottawa's top midrange lodgings is the 22-room **C Swiss Hotel** (89 Daly Ave., 613/237-0335 or 888/663-0000, www.swisshotel.ca, $128–168). From the exterior of the 1872 stone building, you'd never know that that inside, the petite but stylish rooms are a riot of color, the lime green, orange, or charcoal gray walls balanced with crisp white duvets. Every room has an iPad, free for guests to use during their stay, as well as a flat-screen TV and free Wi-Fi. Owner Sabina Sauter, who has run the inn since the mid-1980s, is a tornado of energy and enthusiasm, swirling around the property offering advice and tending to guests' needs. Breakfast ($15) includes homemade

Swiss muesli, as well as freshly baked breads, cheeses, fruits, eggs, and more.

Co-owner Oscar Duplancic often serenades guests on the grand piano during breakfast at the aptly named **Bella Notte B&B** (108 Daly Ave., 613/565-0497 or 866/562-9569, www.bellanottebb.com, $138–158 d); Oscar and his wife Lillian are both professional musicians. Besides the high-ceilinged dining room with a marble fireplace, one of the nicest spaces is the cozy sitting room upstairs, with exposed brick walls, tall windows, and shelves stuffed with books. The three guest rooms are simpler, with carpeted floors and ceiling fans; the largest is the third-floor unit with sloped ceilings, but one on the second floor has a private balcony. The brick rowhouse, built in 1868, was once home to Sir Alexander Campbell, one of Canada's founding fathers.

Over $200

Ottawa's landmark hotel, the castle-like **(Fairmont Château Laurier** (1 Rideau St., 613/241-1414 or 866/540-4410, www.fairmont.com/laurier, $219–319 d), not only has a perfect location between the Rideau Canal and the ByWard Market, it also prides itself on its service. Some of the traditionally elegant rooms are on the small side, but others are quite spacious, and the public spaces, from the cozy reading lounge off the lobby to the Renaissance-style ballroom with 5.5-meter (18-foot) ceilings, are ever so posh. The classic Art Deco pool still has its original brass heat lamps; go up to the balcony overlooking the water to contemplate the bathing beauties. Before booking a visit, it's worth joining the President's Club, Fairmont's frequent-stay program; there's no cost to sign up, and you get free Internet access. Canadian portrait photographer Yousuf Karsh (1908–2002) and his wife lived in the hotel for many years; Karsh's photos of George Bernard Shaw, Ernest Hemmingway, and other notables hang in his former residence, which is now the multi-room Karsh Suite.

Food

Ottawa's reputation as a bland, beige bureaucrats' burg is changing, and no more so than in its dining scene. Yes, you can still find stuffy, old-fashioned "Continental" restaurants, but imaginative contemporary fare, small plates, and an increasing ethnic influence are all making Ottawa a surprisingly inspired choice for foodies.

Prices for this creativity don't come cheap, unfortunately. If you want to try one of Ottawa's high-end eateries but the dinner prices are beyond your budget, book a table at lunch. You'll often find equally inventive fare with a lower tab. Check the menus first, though; some restaurants get by with salads and sandwiches midday even as they pull out all the culinary stops in the evening.

DOWNTOWN

While the downtown area is filled with non-descript breakfast and lunch spots catering to local office workers or famished tourists, you can find a more interesting meal if you walk a few blocks south or west of Parliament Hill.

Bakeries and Cafés

In a little wood cottage incongruously set downtown, the **Scone Witch** (388 Albert St., 613/232-2173, 7 A.M.–4:30 P.M. Mon.–Fri., 8 A.M.–4 P.M. Sat.–Sun., scones from $2) casts its spell on lovers of the humble biscuit. Lemon poppyseed? Currant ginger? Orange cranberry? It's hard to choose a favorite flavor, so you might have to sample more than one. At midday, try an eponymous "sconewitch"—a sandwich served on a freshly baked scone.

Whether you've got the midnight munchies, crave breakfast at 3 P.M. in the afternoon, or need to refuel with a plate of meatloaf, a burger, or a pile of gooey *poutine,* the **Elgin St. Diner** (374 Elgin St., 613/237-9700, www.

OTTAWA

© CAROLYN B. HELLER

La Bottega Nicastro is a great place to get a sandwich.

elginstreetdiner.com, open 24 hours, $6–14) is your place. It's not gourmet, but it's wholesome, and they're open 365 days a year. If your kids can't find something they like here, send them home.

Contemporary

A dark, skinny room lined with a stainless-steel bar, neighborhood bistro **(Town** (296 Elgin St., 613/695-8696, www.townlovesyou. ca, 5–10 P.M. Tues., 11:30 A.M.–2 P.M. and 5–10 P.M. Wed.–Thurs., 11:30 A.M.–2 P.M. and 5–11 P.M. Fri., 5–11 P.M. Sat., 5–10 P.M. Sun., lunch $11–25, dinner $20–25) feels both homey and hip. It's the kind of spot where you could dine solo, bring a date, or hang out with a few pals. Italian-influenced small plates constitute most of the seasonally changing menu, where you might find creations like a beet salad topped with blue cheese *en carrozza*, the tangy cheese fried into a crisp, tempura-coated ball of creaminess. Among the pastas, look for cavatelli topped with chicken meatballs in a velvety foie gras–enriched sauce.

Seafood

Love oysters? The **Whalebone Oyster House** (430 Bank St., 613/231-8569, www. thewhalesbone.com, 11:30 A.M.–2 P.M. 5–10 P.M. Mon.–Wed., 11:30 A.M.–2 P.M. and 5–11 P.M. Thurs.–Fri., 11 A.M.–2 P.M. and 5–11 P.M. Sat., 11 A.M.–2 P.M. and 5–10 P.M. Sun., lunch $8–14, dinner $10–35) has 'em, shucking several varieties every day from North America's East and West Coasts. Yet it's not just bivalves that has Ottawa "sea-foodies" swimming into this laid-back Centretown joint, with its sturdy wooden tables and exposed brick walls; the menu includes a variety of fresh fish in intriguing preparations, like tuna with sunchokes, capers, bitters, goat cheese, and pollen or mackerel with prosciutto, popcorn, mushrooms, and spinach.

If you just want fresh fish without any fancy trappings (like tables and chairs), the same owners run the nearby **Whalebone Oyster House Sustainable Oyster & Fish Supply** (504 A Kent St., 613/231-3474). It's primarily a fish market, but they also sell a "Brownbag Lunch" (11 A.M.–2 P.M. Tues.–Sat., $7–10) with tasty fish sandwiches to go.

BYWARD MARKET AND VICINITY

Despite its touristy vibe, the ByWard Market (55 ByWard Market Sq., 613/244-4410) is still a working food market, with vendors setting up produce and other market stalls around the main market building from late April or early May through October.

This part of town is also home to many of the city's contemporary (and often high-end) dining rooms. Murray Street, particularly the stretch between Parent Avenue and Dalhousie Street, is locally known as "Gastro Alley" for its numerous restaurants.

Bakeries and Cafés

Even U.S. president Barack Obama couldn't resist the siren call of Ottawa's signature pastry, which gets its name from the flat, oblong tail of Canada's official animal. And

OTTAWA FOR FOODIES

It wasn't so long ago that you'd never hear "foodie" and "Ottawa" in the same sentence, unless that sentence was "Foodies lament the Ottawa culinary scene." No more. Ottawa has a rapidly growing food culture that encourages the use of local ingredients and culinary innovation. To learn more about the culinary landscape in Ottawa's neighborhoods, book an entertaining food walk with **C'est Bon Cooking** (613/291-9155, www.cestboncooking.ca). Their most popular tour is the 2.5-hour Foods of the ByWard Market ($45) that includes food shops, cafés, and restaurants around the market area. They also offer similar tours of Wellington West and of Beechwood Avenue in the New Edinburgh neighborhood, as well as cooking classes.

Even if you're not planning to become the top toque at a gastronomic temple, you can still take a cooking class at **Le Cordon Bleu Ottawa** (453 Laurier Ave. E., 613/236-2433 or 888/289-6302, www.cordonbleu.edu), the only Canadian branch of the famed French culinary school. Half-day, full-day, and multi-day programs are offered for "food enthusiasts;" previous cooking experience is not required. Courses vary from French regional cuisine to knife skills to chocolate making to pastry.

Want to get the skinny on vegetarian cooking? Learn from the city's master: Caroline Ishii, executive chef at Ottawa's gourmet vegan dining room, **Zen Kitchen** (613/233-6404, www.zenkitchen.ca). Chef Caroline offers vegetarian and vegan cooking classes at locations around town.

Savvy Company (613/728-8926, www.savvycompany.ca) organizes some of Ottawa's most informative and entertaining evenings. Cheese tastings are led by their in-house "cheese sommelier" and there are also wine tastings, Oktoberfest beer events, and multi-course dinners where guests mingle with local food producers. Great fun!

As you're exploring Ottawa's food shops, look for the **Savour Ottawa** (613/236-9300 ext. 305, www.savourottawa.ca) logo. Savour Ottawa is an organization whose mandate is to promote local food and support Ottawa's development as a culinary destination. Member businesses must meet minimum standards for using local food. Their website is also a useful resources for learning about eating local in Ottawa.

---

neither should you. **BeaverTails** (69 George St., 613/241-1230, www.beavertailsinc.com) cooks up pieces of whole-wheat dough and serves them hot from the fryer. You can have them slathered with all sorts of ridiculously sweet toppings, like chocolate hazelnut spread or Oreo cookies, but the simplest choices are the best: cinnamon sugar, either with or without a squeeze of lemon. In addition to the main location just outside the ByWard Market building, there's a BeaverTails stand along the Rideau Canal—a popular spot to take a break while skating.

Breathe deeply when you enter the **Tea Store** (53 York St., 613/241-1291, www.teastore.ca, 9 A.M.–7 P.M. Sun.–Wed., 9 A.M.–8 P.M. Thurs.–Sat.), the better to take in the spicy, fruity, and earthy aromas of their more than 200 varieties of tea. This tea shop and café makes a flavorful chai latte, which you can pair with pastries like tea-scented scones. A great escape from the ByWard Market hubbub.

To pick up a sandwich on the run, or to gather picnic supplies, squeeze into **La Bottega Nicastro** (64 George St., 613/789-7575, www.labottega.ca, 9 A.M.–6 P.M. Mon.–Wed. and Sat., 9 A.M.–8 P.M. Thurs.–Fri., 11 A.M.–5 P.M. Sun.), a jam-packed (or make that pasta-, cheese-, and *salumi*-packed) Italian deli and food shop. At their sandwich bar, choose your meat, cheese, bread, and toppings for custom-made panini ($5). If you're picnicking, try bread from local baker Art-Is-In (the rosemary focaccia is excellent), paired with cheese from Ontario or Quebec.

Contemporary

Craving a whole pig's head? Nose-to-tail bistro **Murray Street** (110 Murray St., 613/562-7244, www.murraystreet.ca, 11:30 A.M.–2:30 P.M. and dinner 5:30–10 P.M. Mon.–Fri., 11 A.M.–2:30 P.M. and dinner 5:30–10 P.M. Sat.–Sun., lunch $14, dinner $18–25) will smoke and roast a whole pig's head for you and nine or 10 of your porcine-craving pals (48 hours' notice required). If you're not ready to go whole hog, you can still pig out on the "Head and Shoulders" (a pulled pork shoulder and fried head cheese sandwich) or the "Knees and Toes" (a smoked ham and cheese–stuffed cabbage roll in smoked "trotter" broth). If you just want to graze, belly up to the charcuterie bar (11:30 A.M.–midnight daily) for a glass of wine and some smoked duck breast, elk salami, or housemade duck liver mousse. It's a friendly joint, but vegans? Uh-uh.

You know a place called **Play Food and Wine** (1 York St., 613/667-9207, www.play-food.ca, noon–2 P.M. and 5:30–10 P.M. Mon., noon–2 P.M. and 5:30–11 P.M. Tues.–Thurs., noon–2 P.M. and 5:30–11:45 P.M. Fri., noon–11:45 P.M. Sat., noon–10 P.M. Sun.; small plates $8–19) can't be too formal. In this airy space with baby blue walls, the kitchen sends out a fun assortment of small plates designed to share, from charcuterie and cheeses, to grilled Caesar salad, Digby scallops, or local mushrooms on toast. Wines by the "taste," glass, or bottle include options from Ontario and farther afield. Owner Stephen Beckta opened Play as a more casual sibling to his high-end **Beckta** (226 Nepean St., 613/238-7063, www.beckta.com, 5:30–10 P.M. daily, $27–41) downtown.

"Make tacos, not war," proclaims the menu at the sleek, chic **Side Door Restaurant** (20 York St., 613/562-9331, www.sidedoorres-taurant.com, Mon.–Sat., small plates $4–17, larger plates to $28), a loungey space with white leather barstools and black banquettes inside a stone heritage building. Indeed, who'd fight the eclectic, artistically arranged small plates, when they include tacos made from Chinese barbecue pork, soy-ginger shrimp, or lamb with "funky chili"? The rest of the vaguely Asian-inspired fare—salt-and-pepper squid, braised pork belly atop a mango salad, bok choy with fried garlic—pairs well with cocktails ($10) like the sake-politan (sake, Cointreau, cranberry, and lime) or the ginger mojito. If you're watching your loonies, come in for the happy-hour specials (5–7 P.M. Mon.–Fri.). The entrance is literally the building's "side door," on Clarendon Court, off York Street.

The Courtyard Restaurant (21 George St., 613/241-1516, www.courtyardrestaurant. com, lunch 11:30 A.M.–2 P.M. Mon.–Sat., 11 A.M.–2 P.M. Sun., dinner 5:30–9:30 P.M. Mon.–Sat., 5–9 P.M. Sun., lunch $14–17, dinner $22–35), a formerly staid landmark on Ottawa's culinary landscape, hired a creative young chef, Michael Hay—he wasn't even born when the restaurant first opened in 1980—who's been shaking up this elegant limestone building with, and earning kudos for, his innovative dishes. You might find duck breast sauced with a chocolatey *mole* alongside a confit duck leg, roasted beets, apricots, and runner beans, or Moroccan-spiced lamb paired with quinoa, black garlic, eggplant, and broccolini. Some desserts are even more over-the-top: chocolate "rocks" with Guinness ice cream, peanuts, pretzels, and toffee? Cherry sorbet, lemon cream, goat cheese, pistachios, and tobacco? Whoa. The lovely outdoor courtyard remains as romantic as ever.

Classic French cooking is alive and well at **Le Cordon Bleu Bistro @ Signatures** (453 Laurier Ave. E., 613/236-2499 or 888/289-6302, www. signaturesrestaurant.com, 11:30 A.M.–1:30 P.M. and 5:30–9:30 P.M. Wed.–Fri., 5:30–9:30 P.M. Sat., lunch $26, dinner $25–29), the white-tablecloth restaurant at the famous culinary school's only Canadian facility, set in an 1874 Sandy Hill mansion. Yet Canadian ingredients have their place, too; the fish paired with Puy lentils and an onion tart might be Arctic char, the pepper-crusted *steak au poivre* could be made with Alberta beef, the osso buco prepared with local elk. The gracious staff tempers French formality with Canadian affability.

Ask Ottawa foodies where to find some of the city's most interesting yet approachable eating, and they may send you across the Rideau River to the **Fraser Café** (7 Springfield Rd., 613/749-1444, www.frasercafe.ca, 11:30 A.M.–2 P.M. and 5:30–10 P.M. Tues.–Fri., 10 A.M.–2 P.M. and 5:30–10 P.M. Sat., 10 A.M.–2 P.M. and 5:30–10 P.M. Sun., lunch $12–16, dinner $24–26), a storefront bistro in the New Edinburgh neighborhood run by brothers Simon and Ross Fraser. The small menu emphasizes local and seasonal ingredients, perhaps barbecued mackerel paired with horseradish potato salad, roast duck with barley-mushroom risotto, or scallops with kohlrabi and balsamic beets. However, many diners eschew the menu and ask for "Kitchen's Choice"—whatever surprises the chefs have in store that day. OC Transpo bus #1 will take you from Parliament Hill or the Rideau Centre to the restaurant in about 15 minutes.

Spanish

Ottawa-born, Mexico-raised chef-owner René Rodriguez did stints at many of the capital's well-regarded eateries (including ARC The.Hotel and the Black Cat Café) before opening **Navarra** (93 Murray St., 613/241-5500, www.navarrarestaurant.com, dinner 5:30–10 P.M. Mon.–Sat., brunch 10:30 A.M.–2:30 P.M. Sat.–Sun., dinner $24–34), where he's cooking up Spanish-Basque fare, with some Mexican flavors and his own eclectic inspirations thrown in. Any restaurant that features oversized octopus as the background for its website must be serious about its cephalopods, and indeed, you might find a confit of octopus and scallops served with a preserved pineapple and coconut pudding. Plates of Basque-style charcuterie, tamales with *huitlacoche* (a corn fungus), crispy pig cheeks, and tuna grilled *a la plancha* all make their way onto the original menu, too. Come on Tuesday nights for tapas (3 for $25) and live flamenco music.

CHINATOWN, LITTLE ITALY, AND THE GLEBE

Ottawa's Chinatown (www.ottawachinatown.ca) is not strictly Chinese, particularly when it comes to eating. The neighborhood is home to a large concentration of Vietnamese eateries alongside Chinese, Korean, Japanese, even Middle Eastern options, as well as Ottawa's most distinctive vegetarian dining room. Somerset Street West, between Bay and Rochester Streets, is Chinatown's Main Street; you'll find restaurants both east and west of the colorfully painted Chinatown Gateway arch. OC Transpo bus #2 runs from downtown along Somerset through Chinatown.

Little Italy, along Preston Street southwest of downtown, still has some traditional red-sauce restaurants, but it's the more modern, non-Italian dining rooms that make the area worth an eating stop. Buses #3 or 14 will get you to the vicinity of Little Italy.

In the Glebe, centered along Bank Street south of downtown, food options include a mix of hip-grunge cafés, natural foods eateries, and contemporary restaurants, as well as the city's main farmers market. Buses #1 and 7 travel along Bank Street from downtown.

Asian

The cheapest meal in town may be a *banh mi* (Vietnamese sandwich) from **Co Cham** (780 Somerset St. W., 613/567-6050, 10:30 A.M.–9 P.M. Tues.–Sat., 10:30 A.M.–7 P.M. Sun., $2.25–8), where the bus fare to get here will cost more than your lunch. At this bare-bones Chinatown storefront, you can choose from several combinations of meat, pickled carrots and daikon, and fresh herbs on a bun—all for less than $3 each. The menu includes other Vietnamese classics, too, from *pho* (noodle soup) to *bun* (rice noodles with meat, bean sprouts, and herbs). To drink, opt for tea or a fruit shake.

Unlike many Chinatown eateries that serve southern Chinese (Cantonese) fare, the no-frills **Ju Xiang Yuan** (641 Somerset St. W., 613/321-3669, 4–11 P.M. Mon.,

OTTAWA

11 A.M.–11 P.M. Tues.–Thurs. and Sun., 11 A.M.–midnight Fri.–Sat., $5–16) cooks up the hearty, often spicy dishes of China's northeast. Specialties include *jiaozi* (steamed dumplings) filled with lamb or with pork and cabbage, a variety of stewlike hot pots, and skewers of barbecued meats, from cumin-scented lamb to grilled squid to more exotic chicken hearts or duck tongues. An interesting appetizer is the "tofu with chef sauce," a plate of cold bean curd tossed with an addictive garlic seasoning. Don't be shy about asking for recommendations or scouting out what other tables are eating.

Contemporary

Nitro Noodle Soup. Angry Octopus. Subterranean Homesick Alien. The menu names alone are (almost) worth the price of admission at chef-owner Marc Lepine's **Atelier** (540 Rochester St., 613/321-3537, www.atelierrestaurant.ca, 5–10 P.M. Tues.–Sat., prix fixe $88/person), Ottawa's first restaurant to experiment with molecular gastronomy techniques. Don't book a table unless you're ready to spend both big bucks and a leisurely evening; dinner is an elaborate 12-course tasting menu that has flush foodies all a-flutter. The kitchen will make modifications for "allergies, strong dislikes, and vegetarians" but otherwise, you get whatever wildly inventive dishes are on the menu that evening. Ottawa beige and bland? Not in this *atelier.*

One of the city's long-standing highly regarded restaurants, the ❰ **Black Cat Bistro** (428 Preston St., 613/569-9998, www.black-catbistro.ca, 5–10 P.M. Mon.–Sat., $20–33), has changed locations several times during its multidecade history. Now settled into a smart space in Little Italy, the "Cat" has gone bistro, serving French-inspired contemporary fare. You might start with the foie gras terrine paired with sour cherry jam and cocoa nibs or the grilled octopus with smoked paprika mayo, before moving on to the pan-roasted halibut with fingerling potatoes, truffled chicken breast with black pepper spaetzle, or classic steak frites. Vegetarians: Let the kitchen know

you don't eat meat, and they'll accommodate you. Everyone: Save room for the signature lemon tart.

A narrow sliver of a space just off Bank Street, with lime green walls and light wood banquettes, ❰ **The Urban Pear** (151 Second Ave., 613/569-9305, www.theurbanpear. com, 5:30–9 P.M. Tues., 11:30 A.M.–2 P.M. and 5:30–9 P.M. Wed.–Fri., 5:30–9 P.M. Sat., 11 A.M.–2 P.M. and 5:30–9 P.M. Sun., $28–33) is an unpretentious neighborhood bistro, where you could turn up in anything from jeans to a little black dress. Despite its casual atmosphere and small, frequently changing menu, there's some serious cooking going on, showcasing lots of local ingredients. Starters usually include a couple of savory soups, perhaps chilled beet or wild nettles and celeriac, while mains might range from a vegetarian plate—such as a preserved lemon and goat cheese gallette, paired with beet and barley risotto, grilled mushrooms, fried kale, and roasted squash—to a cocoa-spiced duck breast served with date-ginger chutney and sweet potatoes layered with rich duck rillettes. When the sun shines, nab a seat on the terrace.

Vegetarian

Executive chef Caroline Ishii isn't a vegan or even a vegetarian herself, but that hasn't stopped her from concocting some of the most imaginative, and delectable, vegan dishes that the capital has ever seen. Settle into the intimate, informal space at ❰ **Zen Kitchen** (634 Somerset St. W., 613/233-6404, www.zenkitchen.ca, 5 P.M.–close Tues. 11:30 A.M.–2 P.M. and 5 P.M.–close Thurs.–Fri., 5 P.M.–close Sat., 10 A.M.–2 P.M. and 5 P.M.–close Sun., lunch $14, dinner $19–22), where work by local artists adorns the warm peach- and rust-hued walls, order a flight of local beers or a kimchee Caesar cocktail (the kimchee provides a vegan alternative to the typical Clamato juice), and let the vegan adventure begin.

The world-roving menu changes regularly, but you might start with an Asian slaw topped with flash-fried mushrooms, a *sunomono*-style salad mixing sea and root vegetables, or savory Mexican *sopes,* corn cakes topped with grilled vegetables and a tomatillo salsa. Even die-hard carnivores won't complain if you feed them the homemade ravioli filled with a creamy "cheese" (yes, it's tofu, and no, you won't know), while the meaty seitan cutlets are (almost) as crisp and tasty as chicken schnitzel. Make sure you sample the homemade pickles, and finish on a sweet note with the lemon pie with coconut whipped "cream" or the chocolate cake with a spicy chili-chocolate sauce. For a complete vegan extravaganza, opt for the multicourse tasting menu ($48/person).

Groceries and Markets

At the large **Ottawa Farmers Market** (Lansdowne Park, 1015 Bank St., Gate 5, 613/986-2770, www.ottawafarmersmarket. ca, 8 A.M.–3 P.M. Sun. early May–Oct.) in the Glebe, vendors sell many types of organic produce, as well as baked goods, crafts, and prepared foods.

WELLINGTON WEST

Even though it's just a short ride west of downtown, you won't see too many tourists in the Wellington West neighborhood. What you will find is lots of interesting eating. Several cafés make good refueling stops if you're browsing the nearby boutiques, and a growing number of contemporary dining rooms serve up inventive food to a mostly local clientele.

Bakeries and Cafés

Thyme and Again Take Home Food Shop (1255 Wellington St. W., 613/722-6277, www. thymeandagain.ca, 8 A.M.–8 P.M. Mon.–Fri., 9 A.M.–6 P.M. Sat., 10 A.M.–5 P.M. Sun.) is part café and part takeout shop, carrying sandwiches, prepared foods, and luscious pastries. Look for locally made Pascale's Ice Cream (www.pascalesicecream.com), which has a devoted clientele for its all-natural frozen treats in flavors like peanut butter salted caramel, raspberry cassis, or dark chocolate bacon. On the second floor, the small **Exposure Gallery** (613/722-0093 ext. 225) shows work by emerging local artists.

Contemporary

Yes, you can sample cocktails made with the namesake green spirit at the **Absinthe Café and Resto Bar** (1208 Wellington St. W., 613/761-1138, www.absinthecafe.ca, 11:30 A.M.–2 P.M. and 5:30–10 P.M. Mon.–Fri., 5:30–10 P.M. Sat.–Sun., lunch $11–15, dinner $22–29); try the "Absinthe Minded," with absinthe, gin, triple sec, and vermouth, or the simpler "Death in the Afternoon" (absinthe and sparkling wine). If you're going to flirt with the "green fairy," you'd better eat something, too, and fortunately, the classic French bistro fare takes some modern twists. There's a traditional *steak frites,* but you might also find a bacon-wrapped pork tenderloin stuffed with mushrooms, spinach, and cheddar or halibut and prawns paired with a fennel-celery puree. The candlelit dining room is decorous enough for a business meal yet relaxed enough for a night on the town.

A mixed grill of maple-glazed quail, duck breast, and rabbit leg confit. Pan-fried rainbow trout with smoked mushrooms and pickled corn coulis. Roasted vegetable terrine paired with crispy polenta, butternut squash, and walnut pesto. These are just a few of the original dishes that might grace the oak tables at **Allium** (87 Holland Ave., 613/792-1313, www.alliumrestaurant.com, lunch 11:30 A.M.–2 P.M. Tues.–Fri., dinner 5:30–9:30 P.M. Mon., 5:30–9 P.M. Tues.–Thurs., 5:30–10 P.M. Fri.–Sat., lunch $12–16, dinner $23–32), a smart-casual bistro decorated with modern art. If you don't want to commit to a full meal, come for the Monday tapas night to sample from a changing assortment of small plates ($4–14), from seared scallops with kielbasa and mustardy-mayo, to Caesar salad made hearty with a topping of slow-roasted pork belly, to a simple wedge of Quebec cheese (try the camembert-like *La Sauvagine*). The restaurant is one block north of Wellington Street.

OTTAWA

Practicalities

INFORMATION AND SERVICES
Tourist Information

For planning a trip to Ottawa, the best source for information is **Ottawa Tourism** (130 Albert St., Suite 1800, www.ottawatourism.ca, 613/237-5150 or 800/363-4465, 8:30 A.M.–4:30 P.M. Mon.–Fri.). Their comprehensive website lists scores of details about the city's sights, activities, events, accommodations, restaurants, and shops.

Once you arrive in Ottawa, pick up tourist information or get your questions answered at the **Capital Information Kiosk** (World Exchange Plaza, 111 Albert St., 613/239-5000 or 800/465-1867, www.canadascapital.gc.ca, 10 A.M.–5 P.M. daily).

Media and Communications

Ottawa's daily newspapers are the *Ottawa Citizen* (www.ottawacitizen.com) and *Ottawa Sun* (www.ottawasun.com). Check *Ottawa Xpress* (www.ottawaxpress.com), an arts-and-entertainment weekly, for extensive listings of things going on around town. *Ottawa Magazine* (www.ottawamagazine.com), published monthly in print and available online, also covers the arts, restaurants, and things to do.

GETTING THERE
By Air

Ottawa International Airport (YOW, 1000 Airport Parkway, 613/248-2000, www.ottawa-airport.ca) is located about 15 kilometers (nine miles) south of downtown. **Air Canada** (888/247-2262, www.aircanada.ca) has nonstop flights to Ottawa from most major Canadian cities, several U.S. destinations (including Boston, New York, Washington, Ft.

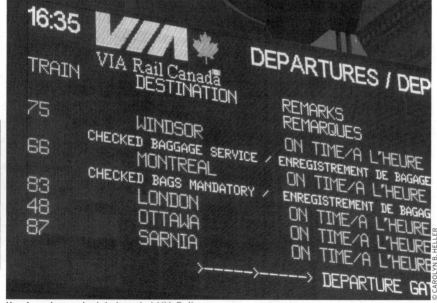

the departure schedule board at VIA Rail

© CAROLYN B. HELLER

OTTAWA

Lauderdale, and Orlando), as well as London (UK) and Frankfurt (Germany). **WestJet** (800/538-5696, www.westjet.com) flies to several Canadian and U.S. destinations, and **Porter Airways** (888/619-8622, www.flyporter.com) has flights to Toronto's City Centre Airport, Halifax (Nova Scotia), and Moncton (New Brunswick). Several U.S. carriers, including **American** (800/433-7300, www.aa.com), **Delta** (800/221-1212, www.delta.com), **United** (800/864-8331, www.united.ca), and **U.S. Airways** (800/428-4322, www.usairways.com), serve Ottawa, as well. Within Ontario, **Bearskin Airlines** (800/465-2327, www.bearskinairlines.com) flies to Ottawa from Kitchener/Waterloo and Sudbury.

The least expensive way to get from the airport to downtown is by public transit. Catch OC Transpo **bus #97** (613/741-4390, www.octranspo.com, adults $3.25 or two bus tickets, children 6–11 $1.60 or one bus ticket) outside the arrivals area; it will take you downtown in 30–35 minutes. The bus runs about every 20 minutes during the day and hourly late at night. Bus tickets ($1.30 each) are cheaper than the cash fare; at the airport, buy bus tickets at the Ground Transportation Desk in the arrivals area.

The **YOW Airporter** (613/260-2359, www.yowshuttle.com, one-way adults $16, children under 15 $9) is a convenient way to travel between the airport and hotels around the city. Shuttle buses leave the airport at 25 minutes and 55 minutes past the hour, from 6 A.M.–11 P.M. Buy a ticket at their booth in the ground-floor arrivals area; reservations aren't required, but you can book online or by phone if you want to make arrangements in advance. Tickets are cheaper if you have more than one person in your party; groups of two adults are $12/person one-way, and groups of three or more adults are $10 each. Round-trip tickets are $25 for one adult or $45 for two. To catch the shuttle from your hotel to the airport, check with your hotel or phone YOW Airporter for the pickup schedule.

A taxi from the airport to the downtown area will cost about $30–35.

By Train

If you're traveling to Ottawa from Toronto or Montreal, the train is a fast, efficient option. **VIA Rail** (200 Tremblay Rd., 888/842-7245, www.viarail.ca) has several trains a day to both Toronto (one-way adults $72–144, children 2–11 $36–72, 4.5 hours) and Montreal (one-way adults $32–64, children 2–11 $16–32, 2 hours). The Ottawa–Toronto trains all stop in Kingston (one-way adults $46–61, children 2–11 $23–31, 2 hours), and certain trains stop in Brockville, Belleville, and Cobourg, as well. Check www.viarail.ca for current schedules.

Ottawa's VIA Rail station is about five kilometers (three miles) southeast of the city center. By public transit, the trip between the train station and downtown takes about 15 minutes. Catch **bus #95** (613/741-4390, www.octranspo.com, adults $3.25 or two bus tickets, children 6–11 $1.60 or one bus ticket), which has frequent service (except during the middle of the night).

A taxi from the train station to downtown will cost about $10–15, depending on traffic conditions.

By Bus

Ottawa's **Central Bus Station** (265 Catherine St., 613/238-6668) is south of downtown on the edge of the Glebe neighborhood. **Greyhound** (www.greyhound.ca) runs most of the bus routes in and out of Ottawa, including service to Montreal (one-way adults $31–45, children 2–11 $24–34, 2.25–2.5 hours), Toronto (one-way adults $47–92, children 2–11 $47–70, 5–6 hours), Kingston (one-way adults $30–42, children 2–11 $23–32, 2.5–2.75 hours), North Bay (one-way adults $53–80, children 2–11 $47–60, 5 hours), and Sudbury (one-way adults $56–80, children 2–11 $47–60, 7 hours).

If you're traveling between Ottawa and either Montreal or Toronto, the train is more comfortable than the bus, but the buses run much more frequently. Consider the bus if the train schedule isn't convenient.

Greyhound also runs several buses daily between Ottawa and Montreal's Trudeau

FOLLOWING THE RIDEAU CANAL

A relaxing day or weekend trip from Ottawa is to follow the route of the Rideau Canal south toward Kingston. The canal runs 202 kilometers (126 miles), with 47 locks and several interesting small towns along the way.

Highway 15 is the main north-south route through the canal region. You can see many of the region's highlights in the triangle of three towns: Smiths Falls, Perth, and Westport.

The website for the **Rideau Heritage Route Tourism Association** (www.rideauheritageroute.ca) has lots of additional information about the Rideau region.

SMITHS FALLS

Stop in Smiths Falls (www.smithsfalls.ca) to learn more about the Canal's history. The **Rideau Canal Museum** (34 Beckwith St. South, 613/284-0505, www.rideau-info.com/museum, 10 A.M.-4:30 P.M. daily late May-mid-Oct., off-season by appointment; adults $4.50, seniors $4, kids 6-18 $3), the main interpretive center for the Rideau Canal National Historic Site, is housed in a 19th-century former mill, where exhibits detail the canal's construction (1826-1832) and its subsequent role in the region's development. You can also take a 50-minute guided tour of the Smiths Falls lockstation (adults $3, seniors and kids $2).

Smiths Falls' **Heritage House Museum** (11 Old Sly's Rd., 613/283-8560, www.smithsfalls.ca/heritagehouse, 10:30 A.M.-4 P.M. daily May-Dec., Mon.-Fri. Jan.-Apr.; adults $4.50, seniors $4, kids 6-18 $3) exhibits regional history in an 1860s Victorian home. If you have kids in tow, they'll only be interested in the house's curiosity: a two-story privy. And no, you don't want to sit on the lower level.

Smiths Falls is 75 kilometers (47 miles) southwest of Ottawa and 95 kilometers (59 miles) northeast of Kingston, along Highway 15.

PERTH

Many of the Scottish stonemasons who built the Rideau Canal settled in the 1800s in Perth, leaving a legacy of many elegant stone homes, including **Inge-Va** (66 Craig St., 613/498-3003, www.heritagetrust.on.ca, 10 A.M.-4 P.M. Wed.-Sun. mid-June-Aug., adults $3, kids 6-16 $1.50), an 1823 late-Georgian stone residence that is also the site of an archaeological mystery. When archaeologists excavated the site of a privy used by the Radenhurst family, who lived at Inge-Va in the mid-1800s, they were surprised to find thousands of pieces of dishes and glasses. Apparently, the family had thrown out all of their kitchenware! Historians speculate that

International Airport (one-way adults $31–45, children 2–11 $24–34, 2 hours).

To go downtown from the Central Bus Station by public transit, walk one block east, then one block north to the corner of Kent and Arlington Streets, and catch bus #4 (613/741-4390, www.octranspo.com, adults $3.25 or two bus tickets, children 6–11 $1.60 or one bus ticket).

By Car

Ottawa is located in eastern Ontario on Highway 417. It's closer to Montreal (2–2.5 hours by car) than it is to Toronto (about a five-hour drive). From Montreal to Ottawa (200 kilometers, or 125 miles), take Autoroute 40 west until it meets Highway 417 at the Ontario–Quebec provincial border.

From Toronto to Ottawa (450 kilometers, or 280 miles), the most straightforward route is to follow Highway 401 east, past Kingston and Brockville, then turn north on Highway 416, which joins Highway 417 just south of Ottawa. A more scenic route would be to pick up Highway 7 east of Toronto and follow it northeast until it meets Highway 417. You could also take the 401 east to Kingston, then meander north on Highway 15, through the small towns along the Rideau Canal.

From Kingston to Ottawa (200 kilometers, or 125 miles), it's about two hours by car.

From the east gate of Algonquin Park to

they may have desperately hoped to stop the spread of infectious diseases that claimed five of their 10 children.

Murphys Point Provincial Park (County Rd. 21, 613/267-5060, www.ontarioparks.com or www.friendsofmurphyspoint.ca, $14/vehicle) tells the story of a different heritage. The Silver Queen Mine was a mica mine that operated from 1903 to 1920 in what is now the park, with the minerals shipped out along the Rideau Canal. In summer, you can take a guided tour of the former mine and learn more about life as an early 20th-century miner. Murphys Point also has 20 kilometers (12.5 miles) of hiking trails and a 160-site campground ($36.75–$40.50 tent sites, $42.25–46 electrical sites. The park is 19 kilometers (12 miles) south of Perth, via County Roads 1 and 21.

A good place to stay in Perth is the **Code's Mill Inn and Spa** (82 Peter St., 613/326-0082 or 866/906-0082, www.codesmillinnandspa.ca, $139-159 d), which has 51 spare but comfortable guest rooms. Rates include Internet access and continental breakfast.

Perth and District Chamber of Commerce (34 Herriott St., 613/267-3200 or 888/319-3204, www.perthchamber.com) can give you more information about the region. Perth is off Highway 7, a scenic alternative connecting Toronto and Ottawa. It's also 20 kilometers (12 miles) west of Smiths Falls, via Highway 43.

WESTPORT

One of the prettiest towns in the Rideau region is Westport, perched on the shores of Upper Rideau Lake, 30 kilometers (18 miles) southwest of Perth, along Highway 10. Stroll around town, or head up the ridge overlooking both the town and the lake to the 325-hectare (800-acre) **Foley Mountain Conservation Area** (105 Perth Rd. N., 613/273-3255, www.rvca.ca, dawn-dusk daily, $6/vehicle). Several hiking trails wend through the woods; the lookout at Spy Rock has the best views.

A traditional, family-run country inn, **The Cove Inn** (2 Bedford-on-the-Water, 613/273-3636 or 888/268-3466, www.coveinn.com, $120-165 d) has nine simple, well-kept guest rooms in the 1872 main building (which was originally a private home) and six additional rooms in the Victorian-style 1876 Fredenburgh House across the street. The Cove's waterview dining room (lunch $7-14, dinner $11-30) serves pub-style dishes – burgers or hot turkey sandwiches – as well as more substantial dinner fare, with live music several nights a week.

Ottawa, it's about 240 kilometers (150 miles), but the roads aren't fast, so allow 3.5 hours. Take Highway 60 east to Highway 17 east, which will join Highway 417 as you continue east into Ottawa.

GETTING AROUND

The majority of Ottawa's attractions are clustered in and around the downtown area, so it's easy to get around on foot. You can even walk across the bridge to the Museum of Civilization in Gatineau (although to reach Gatineau Park and other Gatineau destinations, you'll need to have wheels of some sort). The city has a comprehensive bus system that's useful if you're traveling farther afield, or if you just need to give your feet a rest.

By Bus

Ottawa's public transit system, **OC Transpo** (613/741-4390, www.octranspo.com), includes an extensive network of buses that travel through the city center and out to the suburbs. Most buses operate between 6 A.M. and midnight Monday through Saturday and between 7 A.M. and 11 P.M. Sunday; service is frequent on weekdays, with buses running every few minutes at peak times, but less so on weekends. Bus #97 between the airport and downtown operates 24 hours. Many buses that run into or out of downtown use the Transitway, a dedicated lane for buses only.

OTTAWA

You can either pay cash (with exact change) when you enter the bus or pay with a bus ticket. It's less expensive to use bus tickets, but you must purchase tickets in advance, before you board the bus. Many convenience stores, drugstores, and groceries around Ottawa sell bus tickets, including Loblaws, Mac's Milk, Pharma Plus, Quickie, Shoppers Drug Mart, and Zellers. You can also buy tickets or get bus information at Rideau Center—the **OC Transpo Sales and Information Centre** (50 Rideau St., 8:30 A.M.–9 P.M. Mon.–Fri., 9:30 A.M.–6 P.M. Sat., 11 A.M.–5 P.M. Sun.) is on the third floor, near Sears—or inside Ottawa City Hall (110 Laurier Ave., 8:30 A.M.–4:30 P.M., Mon.–Fri.).

Cash fares are $3.25 for adults, $1.60 for children ages 6–11. Bus tickets cost $1.30, and most regular trips require two tickets for adults ($2.60) and one ticket ($1.30) for kids. Whether you pay cash or use a ticket, get a transfer from the driver when you board the bus. It's your proof of payment, and it's also valid for 90 minutes if you need to transfer to another route.

If you're going to use the buses several times in one day, buy a **DayPass** ($7.50), good for unlimited trips on the day that you purchase it. Buy the pass directly from the bus driver when you board. The DayPass is a great deal on weekends, when the whole family (two adults and up to four kids under 12) can travel all day on a single DayPass.

Use the Travel Planner on the OC Transpo website (www.octranspo.com) to figure out what bus to take and when the buses run. You can enter an address or select a landmark (including hotels) for your starting point and destination to plot your route.

Downtown, many of the east–west buses run on Albert Street going westbound and Slater Street going east; some lines instead stop on Wellington Street, near Parliament. Going north–south, buses run on Elgin and Bank Streets. On the east side of the Rideau Canal near the ByWard Market, Rideau Street, around Rideau Centre, is a main transit point for buses heading in many directions.

By Light Rail

Ottawa has a limited light rail system, the **O-Train** (613/741-4390, www.octranspo.com, $2.85). The single north–south line currently has only five stations that are not conveniently located for reaching most of Ottawa's visitor attractions. Plans to expand the light rail network, with service through the downtown area, have been in the works for some time. Get updates at www.ottawalightrail.ca.

By Taxi

You can usually find taxis near major attractions and hotels, and at the airport, train station, and bus depot. Taxi stands are also located at several points throughout downtown. Taxis are metered. Local companies include **Blue Line Taxi** (613/238-1111, www.bluelinetaxi.com) and **Capital Taxi** (613/744-3333, www.capitaltaxi.com).

By Car

Highway 417, also known as the Queensway, is the region's main east–west highway. A network of parkways winds along the rivers and the canal.

If you're driving in the city center, pay attention to the many one-way streets. Wellington Street runs east–west in front of Parliament, while Elgin and Bank Streets are main north–south streets downtown.

On the east side of the Rideau Canal, Sussex Drive heads north, skirting the ByWard Market neighborhood, and continuing toward Rideau Hall, the governor general's residence. Rideau Street is the main east–west road between the canal and the Rideau River.

Parking can be a challenge in downtown Ottawa. On-street parking is limited to a maximum of three hours between 7 A.M. and 7 P.M., so if you need to leave your car for a longer time, park it in a lot. Most lodgings charge extra—sometimes a lot extra—for parking; be sure to ask before you book.

The good news is that on Saturdays and Sundays, **parking is free** downtown at on-street parking meters and in city-owned parking lots. The free parking zone is bounded by

Wellington Street on the north, the Rideau Canal on the east, Catherine Street on the south, and Bronson Avenue on the west. City parking lots in this area include 212 Gloucester Street and 234–250 Slater Street, both between Bank and Kent Streets. Check the city website (www.ottawa.ca) for additional parking information.

Between November 15 to April 1, you cannot park overnight on city streets (between 1 A.M. and 7 A.M.) when Environment Canada forecasts a snow accumulation of seven centimeters or more. To find out if an overnight parking ban is in effect, call the city information line at 311.

Tours

A fun way to explore Ottawa is on an **Urban Quest** (613/853-2886, www.urbanquest.com, year-round, $20/team), where you solve a series of clues that lead you from place to place around town. You can do a quest with any number of people, but most are designed for two to four, just right for vacationing pals or families. Typically lasting around 1.5 hours, the quests end at a mystery restaurant where you can have lunch or dinner (not included in the quest fee).

Plunge into the Ottawa River on the **Lady Dive Amphibus Tour** (613/524-2221 office or 613/223-6211 ticket kiosk, www.ladydive.com, May–early Sept., adults $31, senior and students $28, children 6–12 $21, children under 6 $11, family $87), which combines a circuit of the city's main attractions with a river cruise in an amphibious vehicle. Buy your ticket at their kiosk at Sparks and Elgin Streets.

With **Ottawa Walking Tours** (613/799-1774, www.ottawawalkingtours.com, adults and children 11 and older $15, kids 10 and under free), you get a two-hour guided historical walk around the city's main attractions. Tours depart from the Terry Fox statue opposite Parliament Hill (90 Wellington St. at Metcalfe St.). Advance reservations are required; tour schedules are posted on their website.

Gatineau

Cross the Ottawa River from downtown, and you enter the district of Gatineau in the province of Quebec. You're still in metropolitan Ottawa, but at times it can feel as if you've wandered into another country. While much of Ottawa's population is bilingual, once you enter Gatineau, the first language is definitely French. Several bridges connect this Quebec region, known as the Outaouais (pronounced "Ooo-ta-WAY"), with the rest of the Ottawa metropolitan area.

Before a municipal amalgamation back in 2003, Gatineau's downtown area was previously the city of Hull, and some people still use the older name. If an address is located in "Hull," head for downtown Gatineau.

SIGHTS

Even if you don't explore farther afield in Quebec, it's worth crossing the bridge for one of the region's best museums: the Canadian Museum of Civilization. Ottawa's largest green space, Gatineau Park, is also on the Quebec side of the river.

◧ Canadian Museum of Civilization

The most-visited museum in Canada is this massive museum of human history and culture (100 Laurier St., 819/776-7000 or 800/555-5621, www.civilization.ca, 9 A.M.–6 P.M. Mon.–Wed. and Fri., 9 A.M.–8 P.M. Thurs., 9:30 A.M.–6 P.M. Sat.–Sun. May–mid-Oct.; 9 A.M.–5 P.M. Mon.–Wed. and Fri., 9 A.M.–8 P.M. Thurs., 9:30 A.M.–5 P.M. Sat.–Sun. mid-Oct.–Apr.; museum only/museum and IMAX theater adults $12/18, seniors and students $10/15, children 3–12 $8/12, family $30/35; free admission 4–8 P.M. Thurs.; parking $3.50/hour or $10/day), on the banks of the Ottawa River.

OTTAWA

© CAROLYN B. HELLER

The Canadian Museum of Civilzation is in Gatineau, across the river from downtown Ottawa.

The building itself, which opened in 1989, is one of Ottawa's most distinctive structures, notable for its curved, undulating walls. Alberta-born architect Douglas Cardinal, who is of Métis heritage (his other credits include the Smithsonian Institution's National Museum of the American Indian in Washington, D.C.), was responsible for the museum's design.

Inside, a good place to start your visit is in the first-floor **First Peoples** galleries. Besides containing one of the world's largest collections of totem poles, the exhibits traces the history of Canada's aboriginal communities. In the Great Hall, look for the sculpture *Spirit of Haida Gwaii,* by noted First Nations artist Bill Reid (1920–1998).

On the third floor, the **Canada Hall** covers Canadian civilization from A.D. 1000 until modern times (no small task!). In **Face to Face: The Canadian Personalities Hall,** on the fourth level, you can learn about 27 notable Canadians who played a unique role in the country's development.

Also included with the regular admission are two "museums within the museum": the **Canadian Children's Museum** and the **Canadian Postal Museum.** There's an IMAX theater, as well (which charges an additional ticket fee).

In addition to these extensive permanent collections, the museum organizes a changing roster of temporary exhibitions. Check their website, or phone for information.

The museum has created a free app that includes maps of the galleries, a calendar of events, and audio tours. Get download instructions and more details on the museum's website.

You can buy a combination ticket good for both the Museum of Civilization and the Canadian War Museum (on the Ottawa side of the river). Combo ticket prices are adults $18, seniors and students $15, children $12, and families $45.

The easiest way to walk to the museum from the Ottawa side of the river is to walk to St. Patrick Street at MacKenzie Avenue (near the National Gallery of Canada), then continue across the Alexandra Bridge.

By bus, take bus #8 from Albert Street

downtown to the Museum of Civilization stop. You can also catch the Société de transport de l'Outaouais (www.sto.ca) bus #77 (direction: Magnus) on Wellington Street at Metcalfe, and get off at Maisonneuve/Papineau, which is about a five-minute walk to the museum. From the ByWard Market area, take STO bus #31 (direction: Parc de la Montagne) from Rideau Street at Cumberland to Allumettières/Laurier, also about a five-minute walk from the museum.

Gatineau Park

When Ottawans want to escape from the city, they head for their backyard—this vast green space in the Gatineau Hills. Measuring 361 square kilometers (89 acres), Gatineau Park has plenty of room for hiking, cycling, picnicking, canoeing, or just relaxing.

Start your visit at the **Gatineau Park Visitor Centre** (33 Scott Rd., Chelsea, 819/827-2020 or 800/465-1867, www.canadascapital.gc.ca, 9 A.M.–5 P.M. daily), where you can pick up maps and get advice from the staff to plan your explorations. The park also has a seasonal **Welcome Area** (Gamelin Blvd. at Gatineau Pkwy., June–mid-Oct.) where you can stop for information.

Gatineau Park has 165 kilometers (103 miles) of **hiking** trails. Download a trail map from the www.canadascapital.gc.ca website, or pick up a free copy at the Gatineau Park Visitor Centre or in Ottawa at the Capital Information Kiosk (World Exchange Plaza, 111 Albert St., 613/239-5000 or 800/465-1867, www.canadascapital.gc.ca).

In summer, you can swim in several of the park's lakes, including Meech, Philippe, and La Pêche Lakes (parking $10/vehicle). At Philippe and La Pêche Lakes, you can rent canoes, rowboats, and kayaks ($17/1.5 hours, $22/two hours, $29/three hours).

Also in the park is the **MacKenzie King Estate** (819/827-2020, 11 A.M.–5 P.M. daily mid-May–early Sept.; 11 A.M.–5 P.M. Mon.–Fri. and 10 A.M.–5 P.M. Sat.–Sun. early Sept.–mid-Oct., parking $8/vehicle), the country home of William MacKenzie King, Canada's 10th prime minister. You can tour the house and gardens, or stop to refuel with a sandwich,

This way to Gatineau Park, Ottawa's largest green space.

salad, or afternoon tea at the **MacKenzie King Tearoom** (819/827-3405, 11 A.M.–5 P.M. daily mid-May–mid-Oct., $8–19).

Fall is one of the best times to visit Gatineau Park, when the leaves change color and the weather is mild. Come midweek if you can to avoid the crowds. In October, the park hosts its **Fall Rhapsody,** with a variety of special events.

The park grounds are open all year. In winter, you can hike, snowshoe, or cross-country ski; purchase a trail pass at the visitors center or at any of the park's any of the 15 departure points. The visitors center also has trail maps.

In February, thousands of skiers from around the world race in the annual **Gatineau Loppet** (819/778-5014 ext. 22, www.gatineauloppet.com), the largest cross-country ski event in Canada. Even if you're not up for marathon ski racing, you can join one of the Loppet's recreational events, including a "mini" two-kilometer (1.2-mile) course for kids and their parents, complete with stops for cookies and hot chocolate.

OTTAWA

To get to Gatineau Park, you really need a car. The park visitors center is about 20–30 minutes from downtown Ottawa.

Casino du Lac-Leamy

Gambling, as well as concerts and other shows, is another reason to cross the bridge from Ottawa to Gatineau's swanky casino (1 Blvd. du Casino, 819/772-2100 or 800/665-2274, www.casino-du-lac-leamy.com, 24 hours/day).

The **Société de Transport de l'Outaouais** (STO, 819/778-8327, www.sto.ca) bus #21 travels from downtown Ottawa to the casino. The casino supplies free bus tickets to guests at many downtown hotels; ask the concierge at your lodging.

ACCOMMODATIONS AND FOOD

If you can't drag yourself away from the black-jack tables till the wee hours, or if you just want a comfortable place to stay on the Gatineau side of the river, you can crash at the **Hôtel Hilton Lac-Leamy** (3 Blvd. du Casino, 819/790-6444 or 866/488-7888, www.hilton.com, $229–339 d), where original works by glass artist Dale Chihuly decorate the lobby. Besides the 349 comfortable Hilton-standard rooms, the hotel has indoor and outdoor pools, a fitness center, tennis courts, a large spa, six restaurants, and three bars. Parking is free in the outdoor lot; Internet access is available for $7.95/day.

Microbrewery **Les Brasseurs du Temps** (170 rue Montcalm, 819/205-4999 ext. 1, www.brasseursdutemps.com, 11:30 A.M.–mid-night Mon.–Tues., 11:30 A.M.–1 A.M. Thurs.–Fri., 11:30 A.M.–2 A.M. Sat., 3 P.M.–midnight Sun., lunch $8–20, dinner $12–27) brews a variety of different beers that you can taste in their restaurant and pub. The food menu features international pub fare, from burgers and sandwiches to lamb shanks, *moules frites,* and poutine. They even try to make beer drinking educational with an exhibit on the history of brewing in the Outaouais.

Chez Edgar (60 rue Bégin, 819/205-1110, www.chezedgar.ca, 10 A.M.–6:30 P.M. Wed.–Fri., 10 A.M.–5 P.M. Sat., 9:30 A.M.–5 P.M. Sun.)

is a popular purveyor of contemporary comfort food, in the form of pastries, soups, creative sandwiches, and salads. It's on a residential street in Gatineau's Hull section.

When in Quebec, eat as the Quebecois do, but that doesn't mean old-fashioned rib-sticking fare. One place that serves French-Quebecois bistro fare with plenty of modern twists is the chic **Bistro St. Jacques** (51 rue St. Jacques, 819/420-0189, www.bistrostjacques.ca, lunch 11:30 A.M.–2:30 Mon.–Fri., dinner 5–11 P.M. Mon.–Sat., lunch $13–17, dinner $18–30). You can have traditional steak frites, but you might also try quail stuffed with foie gras and figs, rare tuna served with Asian-style rice and sprouts, or poached chicken with sweet potato chips and ginger foam.

PRACTICALTIIES

Ottawa and Gatineau have separate bus systems. Some Ottawa (OC Transpo) buses go to Gatineau, but Gatineau's own bus system, **Société de Transport de l'Outaouais** (STO, 819/778-8327, www.sto.ca), operates within Gatineau and between Gatineau and downtown Ottawa; the STO website has route maps and a useful trip planner. The regular STO adult cash fare is $3.40. You can purchase an STO day pass, called *La Passe-temps,* for $6.50, good for unlimited travel for one day on either STO or OC Transpo buses. You can also buy a booklet of six STO bus tickets for $17.70.

Regular OC Transpo bus tickets are not accepted on the STO system. However, you *can* use an OC Transpo DayPass on STO buses.

Taxi companies serving the Gatineau area include **Crown Taxi** (819/777-1645) and **Regal Taxi** (819/777-5231).

For information about the Gatineau area, contact **Outaouais Tourism** (103 Laurier St., 819/778-2222 or 800/265-7822, www. tourismeoutaouais.com). Moon Handbooks' *Montreal and Quebec City* guide has more details about travel in the Outaouais region. For other foodcentric stops in Gatineau and vicinity, check out the **Outaouais Gourmet Way** (www.outaouaisgourmetway.com), an interactive map of regional food experiences.

EASTERN ONTARIO

As you travel along the shores of Lake Ontario, the St. Lawrence River, the network of interconnected lakes in the Kawartha region, or the Rideau Canal, you're never far from a beach or a boat. If it's an island getaway you seek, you have literally thousands to choose from. Eastern Ontario is home to the Thousand Islands, and another island destination, Prince Edward County, has a booming food and wine scene that draws gourmets and oenophiles from Toronto and beyond.

Kingston, the region's largest city, was the first capital of Upper Canada back in 1841, and many historic structures dating from the 1800s still dot the city. Whether at a 19th-century fort, the grand city hall, or any number of restored downtown buildings, history is very present in present-day Kingston.

Kingston serves as a good base here for day-trips to the Thousand Islands, to Prince Edward County, or into the backcountry at provincial parks just north of town.

Eastern Ontario offers far more opportunities for adventures, whether it's going back in time at a pioneer village, exploring an aboriginal community or ancient native rock carvings, following the route of the Rideau Canal, or simply vacationing in a lakeside cottage. Whether you're organizing a brief holiday, or traveling across the province, the eastern districts serve up plenty of fun—and tasty—detours along the way.

PLANNING YOUR TIME

Many Eastern Ontario destinations are close enough to Toronto or Ottawa for a weekend

© CAROLYN B. HELLER

HIGHLIGHTS

LOOK FOR TO FIND RECOMMENDED SIGHTS, ACTIVITIES, DINING, AND LODGING.

◖ Canadian Canoe Museum: This well-designed museum in Peterborough traces Canadian historical and cultural developments through the country's waterways and water-craft (page 242).

◖ Petroglyphs Provincial Park: One of the largest concentrations of petroglyphs in North America, Petroglyphs Provincial Park is a sacred First Nations site with more than 900 symbols carved into a massive marble slab (page 244).

◖ Prince Edward County Wineries: If you enjoy good wine and local food, this booming wine region is a great place for a getaway and is an easy drive east of Toronto (page 253).

◖ Sandbanks Provincial Park: Like the beach? This expansive and popular Prince Edward County park has some lovely ones and giant sand dunes, too (page 257).

◖ Fort Henry: There's always something happening at these 19th-century fortifications overlooking the city of Kingston. You can tour

the barracks, attend "Victorian school," watch the Sunset Ceremonies, and even spend the night at the fort (page 264).

◖ Thousand Islands Boat Tours: The best way to see the Thousand Islands is by water. Choose from a variety of cruises around the islands, departing from Gananoque or from the nearby town of Rockport (page 276).

◖ Fulford Place: George Taylor Fulford made his fortune selling "Pink Pills for Pale People," and he used the considerable proceeds to build this opulent 35-room mansion overlooking the St. Lawrence River in Brockville (page 280).

◖ Upper Canada Village: Travel back to the 1860s at one of Ontario's largest and best-preserved historic villages. You can chat with costumed interpreters as they go about their daily business as millers, bakers, or blacksmiths, and join in a variety of traditional activities, from milking the cows to riding in a horse-drawn barge (page 282).

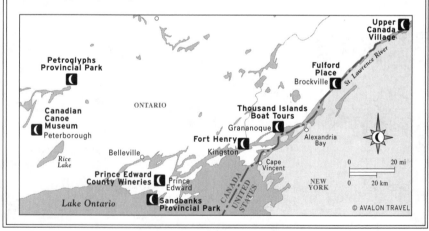

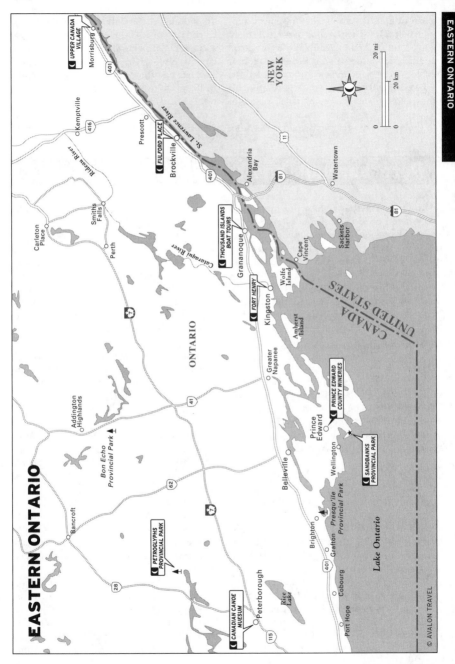

EASTERN ONTARIO

© AVALON TRAVEL

getaway, and they also make convenient stopping points if you're traveling between Toronto and Montreal. You can easily spend a weekend at a lakeside resort around **Peterborough** or exploring the museums in **Kingston. Prince Edward County,** with its wineries, comfortable inns, and contemporary restaurants, is ideal for a couple of days of exploration, too.

If you have a week, you could travel from Toronto along **Lake Ontario,** stopping off in the lakeside towns of Port Hope or Cobourg, spend a couple of days wine touring in Prince Edward County, explore Kingston for a day or two, and continue east through the **Thousand Islands.** In 10 days to two weeks, you could make a loop from either Toronto or Ottawa, adding stops at some of the beautiful provincial parks in the region and time by the lakes in the Kawarthas.

Peterborough and the Kawartha Lakes

The city of Peterborough, with a year-round population of 135,000, is the gateway to the Kawartha region. Just two hours northeast of Toronto (traffic permitting) you can get away to the Kawartha Lakes, a lovely district of lakes and waterways, provincial parks, and lakeside resorts. While the Kawartha Lakes region historically hasn't had the cachet of the Muskoka Lakes "Cottage Country," it's still worth visiting, especially to explore the region's aboriginal heritage.

SIGHTS

While several of Peterborough's attractions, including the Canoe Museum, the Locks, and the Art Gallery, are within the city, others are in the surrounding countryside and lake regions. In planning your itinerary, allow time to travel between these far-flung sites.

◖ Canadian Canoe Museum

If you think that a canoe museum would appeal only to boating enthusiasts, think again. The well-designed exhibits at the Canadian Canoe Museum (910 Monaghan Rd., 705/748-9153 or 866/342-2663, www.canoemuseum.ca, 10 A.M.–5 P.M. Mon.–Sat., noon–5 P.M. Sun., adults $9.25, seniors and students $7.25, families $22.12) aren't just about watercraft. They trace Canada's history and culture, exploring how the lakes and rivers that cross and connect the country—and the boats that provided vital transportation links along those waterways—have influenced the nation's development. Yes,

the exhibits illustrate how different peoples across Canada built and used canoes, from the West Coast First Nations' massive whaling canoes to the birchbark canoes of central and eastern Canada, but they also detail cultural developments, like how canoes became and continue to be an integral part of Ontario's recreational culture. Canoe making was also important in Peterborough's development, beginning in the 1880s; several canoe companies once operated in the region.

In the summer, you can often watch artisans at work in the galleries, carving paddles, building canoes, or doing other related crafts. The museum also offers periodic workshops where you can learn these skills yourself.

Trent-Severn Waterway National Historic Site

Since at least 9000 B.C., aboriginal people have traversed the network of interconnected lakes and waterways across Ontario. When the European fur traders arrived in the 17th century, they, too, used these water routes to explore and trade. In the 1800s, settlers lobbied for an inland canal in the hope to make water travel easier and to gain access to markets across what is now Ontario.

The first lock on this waterway was built in 1833 at the town of Bobcaygeon in the Kawarthas region; by the 1880s, additional locks made it possible to travel smoothly through several of the Kawartha Lakes. Steamboats began plying the lakes, opening

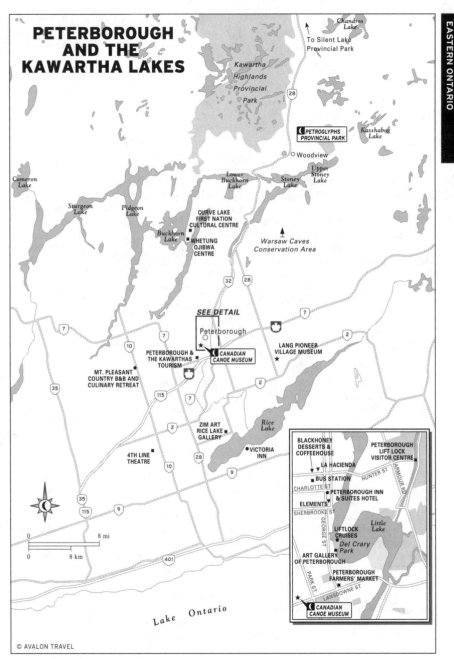

PETERBOROUGH AND THE KAWARTHA LAKES

Chandros Lake

To Silent Lake Provincial Park

Kawartha Highlands Provincial Park

(28)

Kasshabog Lake

PETROGLYPHS PROVINCIAL PARK

Woodview

Cameron Lake

Lower Buckhorn Lake

Stoney Lake

Upper Stoney Lake

Sturgeon Lake

Pidgeon Lake

CURVE LAKE FIRST NATION CULTURAL CENTRE

Warsaw Caves Conservation Area

Buckhorn Lake

WHETUNG OJIBWA CENTRE

(32) (28)

SEE DETAIL

(7)

(7)

Peterborough

(2)

(7)

(10)

PETERBOROUGH & THE KAWARTHAS TOURISM

CANADIAN CANOE MUSEUM

LANG PIONEER VILLAGE MUSEUM

MT. PLEASANT COUNTRY B&B AND CULINARY RETREAT

(35)

(115)

(7)

(2)

Rice Lake

ZIM ART RICE LAKE GALLERY

(2)

(28)

VICTORIA INN

4TH LINE THEATRE

(10)

(9)

(35)

(115)

9

(401)

0   8 mi
0   8 km

Lake   Ontario

© AVALON TRAVEL

Detail inset:

BLACKHONEY DESSERTS & COFFEEHOUSE

PETERBOROUGH LIFT LOCK VISITOR CENTRE

LA HACIENDA

HUNTER ST

ARMOUR RD

BUS STATION

CHARLOTTE ST

PETERBOROUGH INN & SUITES HOTEL

GEORGE ST

ELEMENTS

SHERBROOKE ST

LIFTLOCK CRUISES

Little Lake

Del Crary Park

ART GALLERY OF PETERBOROUGH

PETERBOROUGH FARMERS' MARKET

PARK ST

LANSDOWNE ST

CANADIAN CANOE MUSEUM

the area to tourism. New lakeside resorts and cottage colonies catered to the growing number of visitors. Though the invention of the automobile led to the decline of steamship travel in the 1900s, the Kawartha Lakes region continued to develop as a holiday destination.

Today, the Trent-Severn Waterway, with a system of more than 40 locks, connects Lake Ontario with Georgian Bay, running for 386 kilometers (241 miles) across central Ontario. Recreational boaters are the waterway's primary users.

Peterborough's **Lock 21,** which opened along the waterway in 1904, is the highest hydraulic lift lock in the world; rising 19.8 meters (65 feet), it's essentially an elevator for boats. You can learn more about the lock and the waterway system at the **Peterborough Lift Lock Visitor Centre** (Hunter St. E. at Ashburnham Dr., 705/750-4950, www.pc.gc.ca/trent, 9 A.M.–6 P.M. daily July–Aug., 10 A.M.–5 P.M. daily mid-May–June and Sept.–mid-Oct.).

To see the Trent-Severn Waterway from the water, take a two-hour sightseeing cruise with **Liftlock Cruises** (Little Lake Peterborough Marina, George St., 705/742-9912 or 888/535-4670, www.liftlockcruises.com, daily mid-May–mid-Oct., call for seasonal schedules; adults $19.50, seniors and students $17.50, kids 4–13 $10).

Art Gallery of Peterborough

There's usually something new to see at Peterborough's lakeside art museum (250 Crescent St., 705/743-9179, www.agp.on.ca, 9 A.M.–5 P.M. Mon.–Fri., 9 A.M.–8 P.M. Wed., 11 A.M.–5 P.M. Sat.–Sun. July–Aug.; 11 A.M.–5 P.M. Tues.–Sun. Sept.–June; free). The gallery hosts more than a dozen exhibitions every year, emphasizing Canadian contemporary art. It also organizes the weekend-long **Kawartha Studio Tour** every September, when local artists open their studios to visitors.

Lang Pioneer Village Museum

Many settlers came to the Peterborough area in the 1800s from England, Scotland, and Ireland. You can learn about the lives of these pioneers as you explore the Lang Pioneer Village Museum (104 Lang Rd., off Highway 34, Keene, 705/295-6694 or 866/289-5264, www.langpioneervillage.ca, 10 A.M.–3 P.M. Mon.–Fri. late May–mid-June; 10 A.M.–4 P.M. daily late June–early Sept., adults $8, seniors and students $7, kids 5–14 $4, families $20).

More than 25 buildings here date from the 1820s to the 1880s. When settlers first arrived, they would typically build a simple log cabin, like the 1820s Fife Cabin. As they became more established, they would construct larger homes, like the 1840s Fitzpatrick House or the comparatively more comfortable 1870s Milburn House. In addition to touring these restored homes, visit the general store, church, and schoolhouse, as well as the reconstructed shops of the village carpenter, tinsmith, printer, and blacksmith. Costumed guides help bring the village to life.

The pioneer village is 18 kilometers (11 miles) southeast of Peterborough. Take Highway 7 east for 10 kilometers (6.2 miles), then turn south on County Road 34 (Heritage Line). From there, it's six kilometers (3.7 miles) to Lang Road and the village entrance.

◖ Petroglyphs Provincial Park

Containing one of the largest concentration of petroglyphs (native rock carvings) in North America, this provincial park (2249 Northey's Bay Rd., Woodview, 705/877-2552, www.ontarioparks.com, 10 A.M.–5 P.M. daily late June–early Sept.; 10 A.M.–5 P.M. Wed.–Sun. mid-May–late June. and early Sept.–mid-Oct., $14/vehicle) is also an active sacred site for First Nations people.

No one knows for sure when the Algonquian people carved the more than 900 symbols onto the massive crystalline marble slab, now protected in a large glass building constructed around the rock. Experts date the carvings, which include human figures as well as snakes, turtles, and other animals, at somewhere between 600 and 1,100 years old. Park interpreters can help identify some of the carvings and share ideas about their traditional meanings.

Before you head for the petroglyphs, go first

to the **Learning Place Visitor Centre,** where all visitors must register. Watch a 20-minute film about the site and its history, then have a look at the exhibits about the region's aboriginal traditions.

On several evenings in July and August, park staff run a special 90-minute "light show," in which the glyphs are illuminated and become more visible than they are during the day. Even if you've seen the petroglyphs in daylight, it's worth returning for these special evening events.

Although the park is regularly open until 5 P.M., staff advise arriving no later than 3:30 P.M., so you have time to drive to the site, visit the Learning Place, and see the glyphs. The park service manages the site in partnership with the local Curve Lake First Nation. Due to the site's spiritual importance, no photos are allowed.

The park is 55 kilometers (34 miles) northeast of Peterborough. Take Water Street/ Highway 29 north, continue north on Highway 28, and turn right (east) onto Northey's Bay Road, which leads to the park entrance. There are no camping facilities or other accommodations within the park.

Curve Lake First Nations Reserve

If a visit to the petroglyphs piques your curiosity about the region's First Nations' heritage and cultural, your next stop should be the Curve Lake First Nations Reserve (www.curvelakefirstnation.ca). More than 750 Ojibway people live on this reserve, with several hundred more in the surrounding communities.

The small exhibit area at the **Curve Lake First Nation Cultural Centre** (1024 Mississauga St., 705/243-1646, www.curvelakeculturalcentre.ca, 8:30 A.M.–4:30 P.M. Mon.–Fri., weekends by appointment; adults $3, seniors and kids 5 and older $2) doesn't look like much, but curator Anne Taylor (the "cultural archivist" who manages the facility), or one of her staff, uses the displays of drums, baskets, and beadwork to introduce visitors to the culture and history of the Curve Lake

turtle crossing on the Curve Lake First Nations Reserve

© CAROLYN B. HELLER

people. The staff will discuss traditional teachings, explain how particular items are made and used, and answer your questions. The Cultural Centre is on the main floor of the reserve's government offices. (Look for the "Curve Lake Business Centre" sign, which is easier to see than the smaller sign for the museum.)

Up the road from the Cultural Centre, the **Whetung Ojibwa Centre** (875 Mississauga St., 705/657-3661, www.whetung.com, 9 A.M.–5 P.M. daily, free) is part souvenir shop, part art gallery, and part museum. It stocks everything from inexpensive doodads to high-quality works by local and regional aboriginal artists. Poke around the museum room on the lower level, which is crammed with buffalo bones, arrowheads and other artifacts, photographs, and traditional craftwork.

Another way to experience First Nations culture here is to attend the annual **Curve Lake Pow Wow** (www.curvelakefirstnation.ca, third weekend of Sept.), a festival of traditional music and dance that is open to the public.

The Curve Lake Reserve is located 35

kilometers (22 miles) northwest of Peterborough on a peninsula that's surrounded by lakes; the only direct road access is from the north. From Peterborough, take Water Street/Highway 29 north, then continue north on Buckhorn Road/Highway 23. At Curve Lake Road/Highway 22, turn left (west); the road (called Mississauga St.) will turn south onto the reserve.

Warsaw Caves Conservation Area

If you're claustrophobic, you might want to skip the Warsaw Caves (289 Caves Rd., Warsaw, 705/652-3161 or 877/816-7604, www.warsawcaves.com, caves daily mid-Apr.–Nov.; park and campground daily mid-May–mid-Oct.; $10/vehicle), a series of seven narrow caverns formed in the limestone bedrock. But if you—or your kids—enjoy underground exploring, you can climb, slither, and crawl through these caves that range in size from 40 meters (130 feet) to 91 meters (300 feet) long. While you don't need technical climbing skills, you do need to climb over and around the rocks and scoot through narrow passageways—it's like an underground jungle gym. Kids younger than eight or nine may find the caves difficult or frightening, but adventurous older ones should enjoy exploring them.

There's no light in the caves, so you'll need a flashlight—a headlamp is best to keep your hands free (purchase one at the gatehouse if you don't have your own). Wear sturdy shoes and clothes that can get dirty or wet, since you will get dirty, and don't enter the caves alone. Ask at the gatehouse for the park's *Spelunkers' Guide,* which gives tips for tackling each of the caves.

The conservation area also has several short hiking trails, including one that leads to the **Disappearing River,** a quirk of nature in which the Indian River disappears into the limestone, reemerging further downstream. Beyond this underground section, the Indian River is typically a placid place to canoe. Rentals are available ($8.50/hour, two-hour minimum, $34/day).

The caves are 25 kilometers (15 miles) northeast of Peterborough via County Road 4.

Kawartha Highlands Provincial Park

The vast wilderness expanse of Kawartha Highlands (613/332-3940, www.ontarioparks.com) encompasses 37,587 hectares (92,879 acres) and is Ontario's largest park south of Algonquin. With a series of interconnected lakes and waterways, this is an excellent spot for canoeing, and park staff have mapped out six recommended canoe routes, with stopovers at some of the 108 backcountry campsites within the park. (You can reach the campsites only by canoe, and a permit is required; there are no walk-in sites, and there is no car camping.)

The park doesn't rent canoes. For canoes and other gear, contact **Adventure Outfitters** (1828 County Rd. 18, Lakefield, 705/652-7986, www.adentureoutfitters.ca, $30/day, $50/weekend) or **Wild Rock Outfitters** (169 Charlotte St., Peterborough, 705/745-9133 or 888/945-3762, www.wildrock.net, $39–49/day, $25–35/additional days).

You can reach the park's east side via Highway 28 and west side from Highway 507. From Peterborough, the park's closest entrance is about 50 kilometers (30 miles) to the north.

Silent Lake Provincial Park

For an outdoor stopover en route to Algonquin Provincial Park's East Gate, visit Silent Lake Provincial Park (Highway 28, Cardiff, 613/339-2807, www.ontarioparks.com, $16.25/vehicle). The park has hiking trails, beaches, three mountain-bike routes, canoeing, and two campgrounds.

The day-use area has a sandy beach and a large, grassy picnic area. From here, you can reach the easy, 1.5-kilometer (0.9-mile) **Lakehead Loop** hiking trail, which is good for kids. Serious hikers may want to circle the lake on the 15-kilometer (9-mile) **Lakeshore Hiking Trail** (4–6 hours, strenuous). You can rent canoes and kayaks at the **Pincer Bay**

FROM ZIMBABWE TO ONTARIO

One of the Peterborough area's most unexpected attractions is out in the farmland south of the city. At the **Zim Art Rice Lake Gallery** (855 Second Line, Bailieboro, 705/939-6144, www.zimart.ca, hours by appointment), Fran Fearnley showcases high-quality stone carvings by artists from Zimbabwe.

After doing volunteer work in South Africa, Fearnley was introduced to the stonework, known as Shona sculpture, from nearby Zimbabwe. She now returns to Africa for three or four months every winter to scout out new artworks to exhibit and sell back in Ontario. She has established an artist-in-residence program that brings a stone sculptor to Pe-

terborough every summer to work and teach sculpting skills.

For two weeks every September, Fearnley sets up a sprawling outdoor exhibition, showing more than the sculptures outdoors among her trees and gardens. Outside of this September period, she shows work informally in her home. Just phone ahead to let her know you'd like to stop by.

The gallery is 23 kilometers (14 miles) south of downtown Peterborough, outside the town of Bailieboro. From Highway 115, take Bensfort Road south to County Road 2. Turn right and follow County Road 2 for about eight kilometers (five miles), then turn right onto Second Line.

canoe launch (8:30 A.M.–5 P.M. July–Aug.). In the spring and fall, rentals are available at the park gatehouse.

Silent Lake is 75 kilometers (47 miles) northeast of Peterborough, off Highway 28. For groceries and other services, head south of the park to the town of Apsley or north to Bancroft.

ENTERTAINMENT AND EVENTS

Since 1991, the **4th Line Theatre** (The Winslow Farm, 779 Zion Line, Millbrook; box office 4 Tupper St., Millbrook, 705/932-4445 or 800/814-0055; www.4thlinetheatre.on.ca, July–Aug.) has performed plays with Canadian historical themes in an outdoor space on a farm 30 kilometers (19 miles) southwest of Peterborough.

Peterborough's **Little Lake Musicfest** (Del Crary Park, www.littlelakemusicfest.ca, late June–Aug.) presents free outdoor concerts every Wednesday and Saturday night in summer. Concerts start at 8 P.M.

Canoe excursions, demonstrations, and races, a barbecue, and an open house at the Canadian Canoe Museum are all part of the festivities for **National Canoe Day** (www.nationalcanoeday.net, June).

ACCOMMODATIONS

Peterborough has some standard chain motels on Landsdowne Street, both east and west of the city center. Outside of town, inns and cottage resorts sit on the shores of many of the surrounding lakes, and there are B&Bs out in the countryside as well.

Hotels and B&Bs

Jackie DeKnock and her family purchased an old farmhouse west of Peterborough and have restored it into the (**Mt. Pleasant Country B&B and Culinary Retreat** (2398 Queen Mary St./County Rd. 10, Cavan, 705/799-2999, www.gourmetsafari.com, $100 s/d). The two cozy country-style rooms mix antiques with souvenirs from the family's travels; they share a large modern bath, with a rock-floor shower that feels great on your feet! The real showpiece of the house is the spacious, contemporary kitchen, where Jackie serves breakfast and also offers cooking classes. She'll customize a class to your interests, whether it's local food, a particular foreign cuisine (her Moroccan cooking classes are popular), or a cooking lesson for men. Jackie and her husband, Dan, are well traveled (she formerly worked for an airline) and enjoy swapping travel and food tales with their guests.

If you want to stay downtown, the **Peterborough Inn and Suites Hotel** (312 George St. N., 705/876-6665 or 866/446-4451, www.peterboroughinn.com, $120–150) has a convenient central location. The 32 rooms are fairly generic, but all have fridges and microwaves, and you get free Wi-Fi, parking, and continental breakfast.

Lake Resorts

The Irwin family opened the **Irwin Inn** (1390 Irwin Rd., Douro-Dummer, 705/877-2240 or 800/461-6490, www.irwininn.com) on the south shore of Stoney Lake back in 1947, and a stay here feels like going off to an old-fashioned summer camp. In July and August, the full roster of activities includes swimming, horseback riding, and canoeing to the weekly "Fish Fry" dinner; even in the off-season, staff will still help you organize adventures. The accommodations vary, from old-fashioned B&B rooms in the main inn, to the more upscale lakefront units in the Spa Suites Building, to the one- to four-bedroom country-style cottages scattered around the property. Except for the B&B rooms ($149 d), lodging rates (which start at about $150/person per day) include hearty breakfasts and dinners. Seasonal packages are available, including free stays for kids. The inn is about 40 kilometers (25 miles) northeast of Peterborough, via County Roads 4 and 6.

The **Viamede Resort** (595 Mt. Julian Viamede Rd., Woodview, 705/654-3344 or 800/461-1946, www.viamede.com, $155–365 d) mixes traditional lake resort activities with more modern amenities. There's a full range of watersports, including kayaks, canoes, and hydro bikes, a small beach, an outdoor pool, and a hot tub, tennis, and shuffleboard. The resort has three restaurants: a casual pub, the traditional main dining room, and the elegant 32-seat **Inn at Mount Julian** in an 1875 waterfront house. Accommodations, including 33 inn rooms and 19 cottages (some with kitchens), range from rustic to newer; the best overlook the lake. Rates include breakfast and most activities. As you stroll

around the property, peek into the beautifully restored 1877 wedding chapel, with its original wood paneling and pews. Viamede is on Stoney Lake's north shore, 40 kilometers (25 miles) northeast of Peterborough, off Highway 28, a short drive from Petroglyphs Provincial Park.

On the south shore of Rice Lake, the old-timey **Victoria Inn** (5316 Rice Lake Scenic Dr., Gore's Landing, 905/342-3261, www.thevictoriainn.ca, mid-Feb.–Dec., $80–125 s, $95–175 d) has nine simple, cozy guest rooms, including the octagonal turret room with great lake views. The 1902 building is a little creaky, but the lakefront grounds, with an outdoor pool, are lovely. Owner Donna Cane, who's lived in the area for more than 40 years, is a great resource for things to do; ask about the scavenger hunt she created to explore the Rice Lake region. Rates include a full breakfast; the country-style dining room, which features local lamb, trout, and produce when available, also serves lunch and dinner. The inn is 40 kilometers (25 miles) south of Peterborough and 20 kilometers (12.5 miles) north of Cobourg.

Camping

The **Warsaw Caves** (289 Caves Rd., Warsaw, 705/652-3161 or 877/816-7604, www.warsawcaves.com, daily mid-May–mid-Oct., $10/vehicle. $35/site) has a wooded 52-site campground. The individual sites don't have water or electrical hookups, but there's a comfort station with flush toilets and showers, and drinking water is available throughout the campground.

Kawartha Highlands Provincial Park (613/332-3940, www.ontarioparks.com, $9.50 reservation fee) has 108 backcountry campsites. You can reach the campsites only by canoe—there are no walk-in sites and there is no car camping—and a permit is required.

Silent Lake Provincial Park (Highway 28, Cardiff, 613/339-2807, www.ontarioparks.com, day use $16.25/vehicle, tent sites $36.75, electrical sites $42.25) has two campgrounds, with a total of 167 campsites and

10 yurts ($91.50). Most of the campsites are set amid the evergreens away from the lake. Campers who don't mind carrying their gear a short distance might choose one of the walk-in sites close to the lakeshore, at the corner of the Pincer Bay Campground; you're a longer walk from the showers, though. Each of the two campgrounds has a comfort station with showers, flush toilets, and laundry facilities.

FOOD

In downtown Peterborough, restaurants cluster on and around George Street, while funky Hunter Street, between George and Aylmer, has lots of cafés, pubs, and other eateries. The dining rooms at most lake resorts are open to the public.

The **Peterborough Farmers' Market** (Lansdowne St. W., at George St. S., 705/742-3276, www.peterboroughfarmersmarket. com, 7 A.M.–1 P.M. Sat.) operates outdoors in Morrow Park on the south end of downtown from May through October. It moves into the park's Morrow Building November through April.

"There's always room for dessert" is the motto of **Blackhoney Desserts and Coffeehouse** (221 Hunter St. W., 705/750-0014 or 877/350-0014, www.blackhoneydesserts.com, 8 A.M.–10 P.M. Mon.–Thurs., 8 A.M.–11 P.M. Fri., 10 A.M.–11 P.M. Sat., 10 A.M.–5 P.M. Sun., $5–10). At this cheery little café, you can have a sandwich or a salad, but don't leave without sampling the sweets.

Craving enchiladas, *pollo con mole* (chicken with a chocolatey mole sauce), or traditional Mexican tacos? **La Hacienda Restaurante Mexico** (190 Hunter St. W., 705/742-1559, www.lahaciendamexico.com, 11 A.M.–11 P.M. Mon.–Sat., $7–17) is your place. Ask for their selection of salsas to spice up your dish.

Elements Restaurant (140 King St., 705/876-1116, www.elementsrestaurant.ca, lunch $9–18, dinner $18–33) has all the "elements" of a first-rate meal. Plants line the garden-like dining room, where the sunny yellow walls, green tables, and purple chairs give the space a whimsical feel. The kitchen sources locally whenever possible, and everything tastes fresh, from the delicious pear, watercress, and blue cheese salad, to the hearty sandwiches (the pulled, barbecued wild boar is popular), to pasta with fresh fava beans and smoked bacon. In the evening, you can graze a selection of tapas ($8–14). When the weather is mild, nab a seat on the patio.

INFORMATION AND SERVICES

Peterborough and the Kawarthas Tourism runs a year-round **Visitor Information Centre** (1400 Crawford Dr., 705/742-2201 or 800/461-6424, www.thekawarthas.ca, 9 A.M.–5 P.M. Mon.–Fri., 10 A.M.–5 P.M. Sat.) just off Highway 115/7 south of the city center.

GETTING THERE AND AROUND

Peterborough is 140 kilometers (87 miles) northeast of Toronto. By car, the most direct route is to take Highway 401 east to Highway 115 north. **Greyhound** (www.greyhound.ca) runs frequent buses between Toronto and the **Peterborough Bus Station** (220 Simcoe St., 705/743-8045, 1.75–2 hours, adults $18.50–40, seniors $13–37, students $12.30, kids 2–11 $14–31).

You need a car to explore Peterborough and vicinity, since many attractions are outside the city proper, and even in town, sights aren't within easy walking distance. Car rental companies with Peterborough offices include **Discount Car and Truck Rentals** (705/749-6116, www.discountcar.com) and **Enterprise** (705/745-7275, www.enterpriserentacar.ca).

Outside of town, navigating around the Kawartha region requires patience and careful attention to your map (or GPS), since there are few direct roads and many lakes to circumnavigate. Allow more time to reach your destination than the mileage might indicate.

Lake Ontario

As you head east from Toronto along Highway 401, suburban sprawl and industrial developments begin to give way to farms, orchards, and beaches. A string of towns along Lake Ontario—including Port Hope, Cobourg, Grafton, and Brighton—make convenient stops en route to Prince Edward County, Kingston, or points farther east, or as getaway destinations for a quick holiday.

Northumberland Tourism (600 William St., Cobourg, 905/372-3329 ext. 6257 or 866/401-3278, www.northumberlandtourism.com) can provide information about the region, including details about festivals, special events, cycling routes, and other activities.

PORT HOPE

Port Hope's draw is its historic downtown district, where many of the well-preserved buildings date to the late 1800s. Wander along Walton Street, where you can browse in the boutiques, antique shops, and bookstores, or hang out in one of the cafés. You might check what's happening at the **Capitol Theatre** (20 Queen St., 905/885-1071, www.capitoltheatre.com), a restored 1930s theatre that hosts plays, concerts, and films. You can also pick up a brochure outlining self-guided walking or driving tours of the historic district at the **Municipality of Port Hope Tourism Office** (20 Queen St., 905/885-2004 or 888/767-8467, www.porthopetourism.ca).

Port Hope is 100 kilometers (60 miles) east of Toronto, just off Highway 401. It's just over an hour's ride on **VIA Rail** (888/842-7245, www.viarail.com, one-way adults $24–33, seniors $21–30, students $23, kids 2–11 $12–17) to Port Hope Station (Hayward St.).

Accommodations and Food

If you want to stay the night, try **The Waddell** (1 Walton St., 905/885-2449 or 800/361-1957,

along the Lake Ontario "Apple Route"

© CAROLYN B. HELLER

www.thewaddell.ca, $159–199), a traditionally furnished inn in an 1845 brick building that fits right in with downtown's historic ambience. Rates include breakfast in the trattoria downstairs.

The colorful dining room at **Zest Bar + Bistro** (64 John St., 905/885-7200, www.zestfoods.ca, 11:30 A.M.–4 P.M. Sun.–Tues., 11:30 A.M.–8 P.M. Wed.–Thurs., 11 A.M.–9 P.M. Fri.–Sat., $10–32) sets the scene for a modern menu that ranges from simple fare—Cobb salad, roast turkey sandwich, or meatloaf—to creative updates on pasta (with portobello mushrooms and slow-roasted tomatoes), chicken, or rack of lamb. They operate a takeout shop, too, if you need a quick bite for the road.

At **Black Beans Steakhouse and Lounge** (63 Walton St., 905/885-1888, www.blackbeans.ca, 4:30–9:30 P.M. Sun.–Thurs., 4:30–10:30 P.M. Fri.–Sat., $14–24), the menu takes its flavors from Cajun country and the Southwest. Tuck into a steak, tapas, or crab cakes with jalapeo aioli and guacamole or blackened catfish. The real draw at this popular watering hole, though, is bartender Wes Galloway's innovative, carefully constructed cocktails. He infuses his own syrups and makes his own bitters, as the basis for his fresh and flavorful creations. If you're not a drinker, or if you're the designated driver, ask him to concoct a nonalcoholic libation.

COBOURG

Like nearby Port Hope, the town of Cobourg has a historic downtown district, and it also has a pretty, sandy beach, just a short stroll from the town center. Before you get too sandy, though, wander along King Street and take a peek into the stately **Victoria Hall** (55 King St. W., 8 A.M.–5 P.M. Mon.–Fri., 1–4 P.M. Sat.), built in 1860. The courtroom on the first floor is a replica of London's Old Bailey. On the top floor is the **Art Gallery of Northumberland** (905/372-0333, www.artgalleryofnorthumberland.com, 10 A.M.–4 P.M. Tues.–Fri., 1–4 P.M. Sat., admission by donation), which shows contemporary works.

The **Town of Cobourg Business and Tourism Centre** (212 King St. W., 905/372-5481 or 888/262-6874, www.cobourgtourism.ca) can tell you more about what's happening around town.

Cobourg is off Highway 401, 120 kilometers (75 miles) east of Toronto. **VIA Rail** (888/842-7245, www.viarail.com) trains stop in Cobourg (563 Division St.) en route between Toronto (1.25–1.5 hours, one-way adults $30–40, seniors $25–36, students $28, kids 2–11 $15–20) and Kingston (1.25–1.5 hours, one-way adults $43–59, seniors $37–53, students $41, kids 2–11 $21–29).

Accommodations and Food

What do you get when you cross an upscale hotel with a jail? You get something like the weirdly fun **King George Inn and Spa** (77 Albert St., 905/373-4610, www.thekinggeorginn.com, $89–163 d), set inside the former Cobourg Jail (www.cobourgjail.com), which housed prisoners as recently as 1997. Even if you don't stay here, visit a small exhibit area in the basement in the cells that were used for solitary confinement. Many of the 23 guest rooms retain the cell bars, bunks, or original stainless-steel jail showers, although some are simply standard hotel rooms. Bring your own handcuffs.

Like pie? At **Betty's Pies and Tarts** (7380 County Rd. 2 btw. Port Hope and Cobourg, 905/377-7437) the tasty pastries come in both full-size and convenient single-serving sizes—the better to sample more varieties! The apple pies are good, but resisting the gooey pecan butter tarts is futile.

If you're in town on a Saturday, stop into the **Cobourg Farmers' Market** (Market Square, Second and Albert Sts., 7 A.M.–1 P.M. Sat. May–Oct., 8 A.M.–1 P.M. Sat. Nov.–Dec.), which has been supplying residents and visitors with locally grown produce, cheeses, meats, breads, and pastries since 1839.

GRAFTON

Grafton is 130 kilometers (80 miles) east of Toronto and 10 kilometers (6 miles) east of Cobourg. The main attraction in town—St.

Anne's Spa—is north of Highway 401; Grafton Village lies to the south.

Accommodations and Food

Set on nearly 200 hectares (500 acres) high in the hills, **☾ St. Anne's Spa** (1009 Massey Rd., Grafton, 905/349-2493 or 888/346-6772, www.spavillage.ca) feels like a secluded European health retreat, where you can escape for a day (or more) of pampering. The sprawling property is built around the elegant stone main inn, but you may not care about the resort's heritage once you've had a chakra-balancing massage, mud wrap, or lymphatic drainage treatment. You can take a yoga or meditation class, go for a swim (the outdoor pool has great views across the hills to Lake Ontario), rejuvenate in the eucalyptus steam room, or indulge in a wide range of other spa treatments.

Overnight guests can choose from a traditionally furnished room in the main inn, or from one of several cottages around the property. Some of the cottages are quite a distance from the main inn and spa building (the hotel does offer shuttle services), so they're best for a girlfriends' getaway or for couples who want to cocoon.

Spa services start at $65 for a half-hour massage, but you can choose from a variety of packages. Day spa packages include a "Stress Express Day" ($245/person), which includes round-trip transportation from Toronto (on VIA Rail), $100 worth of spa services, a yoga or other wellness class, lunch, afternoon tea, and use of the pools and other facilities. Overnight packages, including three meals as well as spa treatments, start at $525/person (single) or $425/person (double).

Most visitors to the spa stay put, so you don't need a car here. You can arrange for spa staff to pick you up at the VIA Rail station in Cobourg.

If you're just passing through the town of Grafton and want a bite to eat, the **Grafton Village Inn** (10830 County Rd. 2, 905/349-3024, www.graftonvillageinn.ca, hours vary, lunch $14–17) makes excellent (if somewhat pricey) sandwiches. Try the BLT (bacon,

lettuce, and tomato), made richer with the addition of melted Brie cheese.

BRIGHTON

This part of Ontario is apple-growing country, and Highway 2, which parallels Highway 401 closer to the lake, is dotted with apple orchards and farm stands. The online Apple Route guide (www.appleroute.com) directs visitors to fruit vendors and orchards. Brighton celebrates the rosy fruit every autumn with a weekend-long **Applefest** (www.applefest.reach.net, Sept.). You can pick your own apples at **Cricklewood Farm** (27 Grandview Rd., Brighton, 613/475-4293, www.cricklewood.ca). Another highlight, especially for the kids, is their **corn maze** (9:30 A.M.–4:30 P.M. daily, 9:30 A.M.–6 P.M. Sat., Aug.–early Nov.), where you have to find your way through the maze-like rows of corn. The farm is just off County Road 2, about three kilometers (1.9 miles) west of Brighton.

Presqu'ile Provincial Park

As its French name suggests, this provincial park (328 Presqu'ile Parkway, Brighton, 613/475-4324, www.ontarioparks.com or www.friendsofpresquile.on.ca, $14/vehicle) is "almost an island." Set on a peninsula jutting out into Lake Ontario, it's like two parks in one; the section closest to the mainland is lined with flat, wide beaches, while the section extending between Presqu'ile Bay and the lake has both marshes and woods.

The park sees an abundance of migrating birds in the spring and fall; May and September are particularly popular with birders. Many birders walk across the shallow water from Owen Point (follow the trail from the south end of the beach) to **Gull Island,** which has ample bird life. However, access to the island is restricted from mid-March to mid-September to avoid disturbing the birds' habitat.

Frogs, fish, and other creatures entertain kids at the **Nature Centre** (10 A.M.–4 P.M. daily July–early Sept.); in summer, park staff organize guided hikes, kids' programs, and evening campfires. A lighthouse stands guard at the far end of the park, and the nearby **Lighthouse Interpretive Centre** (10 A.M.–5 P.M. daily July–early Sept., 10 A.M.–4 P.M. Sat.–Sun. late May–June and early Sept.–mid-Oct.) has exhibits about the area's natural and nautical past.

On Wednesdays and Saturdays in July and August, you can hop on the free shuttle bus that runs to Presqu'ile from downtown Brighton (Chamber of Commerce office, 74 Main St.) on the hour between 10 A.M. and 3 P.M. Park admission is also free when you arrive on the shuttle.

Accommodations and Camping

Presqu'ile's campgrounds are popular with families. The park (328 Presqu'ile Parkway, Brighton, 613/475-4324, www.ontarioparks.com or www.friendsofpresquile.on.ca, $14/vehicle) has 394 campsites, including 234 tent sites ($36.75–40.50) and 160 electrical sites ($42.25–46). The most requested, particularly among RV campers, are the waterfront sites in the High Bluff campground, although they are not very shaded.

If you're not a camper, a comfortable place to stay in town is the **Brighton Inn Bed & Breakfast** (40 Young St., Brighton, 613/475-9706 or 888/895-5807, www.brightoninn.com, $85–95 s, $105–115 d), with four guest rooms in an 1890s Victorian. Lemon crepes are one of owners Don and Nikki Parks' breakfast specialties, and they'll keep your coffee cup filled while giving you tips about the area.

Practicalities

Brighton is 160 kilometers (100 miles) east of Toronto, via Highway 401. It's about a 45-minute drive to the Prince Edward County wineries. Learn more about the region at the **Brighton and District Chamber of Commerce** (74 Main St., Brighton, 613/475-2775 or 877/475-2775, www.brightonchamber.ca).

Prince Edward County

Once a predominantly agricultural area, Prince Edward County has been reborn as a wine-producing district. County farms have always raised tomatoes, apples, and other produce, too (more than 70 canneries once operated here), but the region has jumped on the local-food bandwagon, with numerous restaurants, both modest and fine, featuring the county's bounty. What does that mean for visitors? Wine tasting and good eating!

Prince Edward County is located along Lake Ontario between Toronto and Kingston, south of the mainland towns of Trenton, Belleville, and Napanee. Lodgings, restaurants, galleries, and shops are concentrated in the towns of Picton, Bloomfield, and Wellington. The largest group of wineries is in the Wellington/Hillier area on the county's west side, with others scattered around the region.

High season here is May through mid-October, and the county is especially busy in July and August. For fewer crowds, try to come midweek in summer or visit in June or September. In early spring and late fall, some businesses reduce their hours (many restaurants close Tues.–Wed. off-season), and from January till March the county seems to hibernate. Some lodgings remain open for winter getaways, but if you're hoping to visit particular wineries or eateries, confirm first that they're not on holiday themselves.

Lastly, don't mistake Prince Edward *County* for Prince Edward *Island,* the province in Atlantic Canada, even though, confusingly, Prince Edward County is also on an island. Even more confusingly, the county was once a peninsula connected to the mainland by a narrow strip of land, known as "the Carrying Place." In 1889, the Murray Canal was built at the Carrying Place, linking the Bay of Quinte with Lake Ontario but severing the county from the mainland.

◖ WINERIES

Wine making is a relatively new venture in Prince Edward County. The first winery

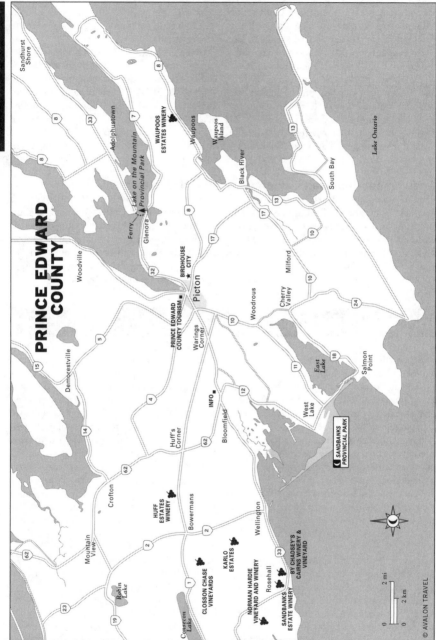

PRINCE EDWARD COUNTY

Sandhurst Shore

Adolphustown

Woodville

Demorestville

Mountain View

Crofton

Bowermans

Wellington

Rosehall

Casseron Lake

Robin Lake

HUFF ESTATES WINERY

KARLO ESTATES

CLOSSON CHASE VINEYARDS

NORMAN HARDIE VINEYARD AND WINERY

SANDBANKS ESTATE WINERY

BY CHADSEY'S CAIRNS WINERY & VINEYARD

Huff's Corner

Bloomfield

INFO

Warings Corner

Woodrous

West Lake

East Lake

Salmon Point

Cherry Valley

Milford

South Bay

Black River

Waupoos

Waupoos Island

WAUPOOS ESTATES WINERY

Lake on the Mountain Provincial Park

Glenora

Ferry

PRINCE EDWARD COUNTY TOURISM

Picton

BIRDHOUSE CITY

SANDBANKS PROVINCIAL PARK

Lake Ontario

2 mi

2 km

© AVALON TRAVEL

© CAROLYN B. HELLER

table for two overlooking the lake at The County Cider Company

opened in 2001, and most of the region's more than 30 producers are still quite small. That means that at many properties you might meet the winemaker, and tours, if offered, tend to be informal. The county is best known for its white wines, although a number of wineries now produce reds, as well.

The **Prince Edward County Winegrowers Association** (613/921-7100, www.thecounty-wines.com) has additional wine-touring tips on their website. They publish a helpful wine-touring map that you can pick up at tourist offices, hotels, and wineries around the county.

Most wineries are open daily from late May until mid-October. Many remain open with more limited hours year-round, while others close January to March. They typically charge a small fee for tastings, which they'll often waive if you purchase wine.

And lest you think the county is only about wine, there's a brewery, too: **Barley Days Brewery** (13730 Hwy. 33, Picton, 613/476-7468, www.barleydaysbrewery.com,

noon–5 P.M. Tues.–Sat., noon–4 P.M. Sun.) is just west of Picton, en route to Bloomfield.

Wellington

Ira Chadsey, who lived on this property just east of the present-day town of Wellington back in the 1800s, erected a series of stone cairns on the land. According to legend, Ira believed he'd be reincarnated as a white horse and the cairns would mark his way home. He needed that guidance, perhaps, because he shot and killed himself in his maple syrup shack.

So what does this legend have to do with wine? Nothing, really, except it gave its name to the **By Chadsey's Cairns Winery and Vineyard** (17432 Hwy. 33, www.bychadseys-scairns.com, 11 A.M.–6 P.M. daily June–Oct., 11 A.M.–6 P.M. Sat.–Sun. Mar.–May and Nov.–Dec.), a laid-back producer of rieslings, gamay noir, a dry rose, and the county's only chenin blanc. Their tasting room is in a brick apple storehouse, and they make their wine in the former carriage barn. There are no official tours, but you're welcome to explore the property, which includes an old cemetery. And if you ask, they'll tell you about the cairns and other legends.

Owner Norman Hardie is a well-known promoter of the county's wines, and you'll often find him on the grounds of his **Norman Hardie Vineyard and Winery** (1152 Greer Rd., 613/399-5297, www.normanhardie.com, 11 A.M.–5 P.M. daily Mar.–May, 10 A.M.–6 P.M. daily June–Nov., 11 A.M.–5 P.M. Sat. Dec.–Feb.). Hardie specializes in pinot noir and chardonnay, and also produces pinot gris, muscadet, and cabernet franc. The tasting bar, in a cool, industrial, hut-like structure, is open year-round. Tours are available, too, but staff suggest that you phone ahead. In summer, you can lunch on their Pizza Patio, where a wood-fired oven churns out freshly baked pizzas.

The winery harvests their grapes by hand, and you can, too: during the fall **Harvest Weekends** (usually the first two weekends of Oct.), visitors can join in the harvest. Make no mistake, this is hard work, but your reward, besides the experience of being out in the fields, is a celebratory pig roast when you're done (reservations required).

Known for their chardonnay and pinot noir, **Rose Hall Run** (1243 Greer Rd., 613/399-1183 or 888/399-1183, www.rosehallrun.com, 11 A.M.–6 P.M. daily Apr.–mid-Oct., 11 A.M.–5 P.M. Sat.–Sun. mid-Oct.–Dec.) is a casual place where you might meet owners Dan and Lynn Sullivan in the wine shop or around the tasting bar. There's no official tour schedule, but they'll arrange a "casual tour" if you phone ahead.

Want more wine stops? Other Wellington-area wineries include **Closson Chase Vineyards** (629 Closson Rd., Hillier, 613/399-1418 or 888/201-2300, www.clossonchase.com, 11 A.M.–5 P.M. Mon.–Thurs., 10 A.M.–6 P.M. Fri.–Sun. mid-Apr.–Nov.; 11 A.M.–5 P.M. Sat.–Sun. Dec.–mid-Apr.), **Karlo Estates** (561 Danforth Rd., 613/399-3000, www.karloestates.com, 11 A.M.–6 P.M. daily May–Oct.; 11 A.M.–5 P.M. Fri.–Mon., 11 A.M.–6 P.M. Sat.–Sun. Nov.–Dec. and Mar.–Apr.; 11 A.M.–6 P.M. Sat.–Sun. Jan.–Feb.), and **Sandbanks Estate**

Wintery (17598 Hwy. 33, 613/399-1839, www.sandbankswinery.com, 10 A.M.–6 P.M. daily May–Oct.; 10 A.M.–5 P.M. Sun.–Thurs., 10 A.M.–6 P.M. Fri.–Sat. Nov.–Dec.; 10:30 A.M.–5 P.M. Sat.–Sun. Feb.–Apr.).

Bloomfield

One of the county's more established wineries is **Huff Estates** (2274 County Rd. 1, 613/393-5802, www.huffestates.com, 10 A.M.–6 P.M. daily), which makes rieslings, chardonnays, pinot gris, and pinot noir. Unlike smaller properties, they do offer organized tours (10 A.M., 2 P.M., and 4 P.M. daily May–Sept., $5), where you can learn about the county's wine history, how to match local wines with food, and taste several varieties. Locally notable chef Michael Hoy runs the outdoor restaurant, **Hoy at Huff** (11 A.M.–5 P.M. Thurs.–Mon. spring–fall, weather permitting, $9–19), offering salads, sandwiches, and pasta with locally sourced ingredients.

Adjacent to the winery, the **Oeno Gallery** (2274 County Rd. 1, 613/393-2216, www.oenogallery.com, 10 A.M.–6 P.M. daily) features high-end contemporary art by international artists, including some with Ontario connections. Outside, you can wander among the more than 40 works on view in the Sculpture Garden (suggested donation $2).

Waupoos

The county's oldest winery, **Waupoos Estates Winery** (3016 County Rd. 8, 613/476-8338, www.waupooswinery.com, 10:30 A.M.–6 P.M. daily May–mid-Oct., 11 A.M.–5 P.M. Thurs.–Mon. mid-Oct.–Dec, 11 A.M.–5 P.M. Sat.–Sun. Mar.–Apr., call for winter hours) opened in 2001, east of Picton. It's a lovely spot, set on manicured grounds overlooking the water. While they produce a variety of wines, they're best known for their riesling (white) and baco (red). They also make the county's first ice wine.

Tastings and several tour options are available. The basic tour ($5) runs daily at 11 A.M., 1 P.M., and 3 P.M. in July and August, and on Saturdays and Sundays in May, June, September, and October.

The winery's **Gazebo Restaurant**

© CAROLYN B. HELLER

the Gazebo Restaurant at Waupoos Estates Winery

(11:30 A.M.–3 P.M. and 5–9 P.M. daily May–mid-Nov., call for off-season hours, lunch $12–18) serves sandwiches, salads, and a couple of larger plates midday, with contemporary, locally focused fare in the evenings. They're also open for light bites on summer afternoons (3–5 P.M.).

Just up the road from the Waupoos Winery, **The County Cider Company** (657 Bongards Crossroad, at County Rd. 8, 613/476-1022, www.countycider.com, 10 A.M.–6 P.M. daily May–Oct.; call for off-season hours) makes both "hard" (alcoholic) and nonalcoholic apple cider, as well as a unique "ice cider," a sweet dessert wine that's similar to grape-based ice wine. They fire up their pizza oven from late May to mid-October (11 A.M.–4 P.M. daily), serving pizzas, burgers, and salads outdoors while looking across a vineyard to the lake.

SIGHTS

At the **Macaulay Heritage Park** (35 Church St., at Union St., Picton, 613/476-3833, www.pe-county.on.ca/museums.html, 10 A.M.–4:30 P.M. Tues.–Sun., Wed. 10 A.M.–7 P.M., July–Aug.;

1–4:30 P.M. Tues.–Sun., Wed. 1–7 P.M., mid-May–June and Sept.; adults $4.50, seniors and students $3.50, kids 5–12 $2.50, families $11.50), the 1820s **Church of St. Mary Magdalene** is now a museum of county history. Follow the timeline exhibit to learn about the area's settlement and development. Many of the county's earliest settlers were Loyalists, British supporters who came from the United States in the late 1700s, following the American Revolutionary War. In the room adjacent to the altar is one of the county's curiosities: a tombstone belonging to a Mr. Pierce, whose stone says he died on the nonexistent February 31, 1860. (Historians have never been able to unravel the source of this error.)

Next door to the church is the 1830 **Macaulay House,** where costumed guides will tell you about Reverend William Macaulay (1794–1874) and other settlers who lived in the county in the middle of the 19th century.

◖ Sandbanks Provincial Park

Blessed with some of the best beaches on

© CAROLYN B. HELLER

the dunes at Sandbanks Provincial Park

Lake Ontario, this lakefront provincial park (County Rd. 12, 613/393-3319, www.ontarioparks.com, late Apr.–mid-Oct., $16.25/vehicle), one of the most visited destinations in the Ontario Park system, is also known for its giant sand dunes.

The largest of the park's beaches is the long, sandy **Sandbanks Beach,** which extends along Lake Ontario for nearly 11 kilometers (7 miles). Access to the beach is only from the south end, but you can walk along the beach literally for miles. You can also hike to the dunes along the 2.5-kilometer (1.5-mile) **Dunes Trail.**

The three-kilometer (1.8-mile) **Outlet Beach,** on a sliver of land between Lake Ontario and East Lake, is another long stretch of sand. **Dunes Beach,** which is where you'll find the famous sand dunes, is on West Lake, where the water can be a little warmer than in less protected Lake Ontario. The Outlet River is a good spot for canoeing. You can rent canoes at the Wood Yard, adjacent to the river.

The park's **Visitor Centre** (10 A.M.–4:30 P.M. daily mid-June–early Sept.) has

exhibits about the animals and plants that live in the Sandbanks area and often has snakes, fish, or other creatures on hand. In summer, the park offers **guided dunes walks,** evening campfire programs, and other activities. Because the park gets so crowded in summer, particularly on weekends, it can feel noisy and congested. Try to visit in late spring or early fall if you can, particularly if you're camping.

Sandbanks is 18 kilometers (11 miles) west of Picton; take County Road 10 to County Road 11. From Bloomfield, it's 13 kilometers (eight miles) southwest on County Road 12. Coming from Bloomfield, you can bypass the park's main gate and pay your admission fee at the parking area, which may save you some time on busy days.

Birdhouse City

The county's birds nest in style at the quirky Birdhouse City (Macaulay Mountain Conservation Area, 224 County Rd. 8, Picton, 613/968-3434, www.quinteconservation.ca, dawn–dusk daily, free), a large field populated with nearly 100 birdhouses designed as replicas of historic structures and other buildings from near and far. There's a log cabin, a church, and a B&B, even a McDonald's and the Leaning Tower of Pisa! The birdhouses are just east of Picton; take Union Street east, which becomes County Road 8.

Lake on the Mountain Provincial Park

If you don't know the story behind Lake on the Mountain (County Rd. 7, 613/393-3319, www.ontarioparks.com, dawn–dusk daily, free), you might think it's just a pretty little body of water. But what makes the lake a curiosity is that it has a constant flow of fresh water, with no obvious source.

Early settlers to the region assumed it must be a bottomless lake, and even modern scientists, who believe that underground springs now feed the lake, haven't been able to unravel how it formed, since the lake is 60 meters (195 feet) higher than nearby Lake Ontario.

The lake is east of Picton; follow Highway 33 to County Road 7. The parking lot overlooks Picton Bay; Lake on the Mountain is across the road.

ENTERTAINMENT AND EVENTS

Built in the 1920s, the **Regent Theatre** (224 Main St., Picton, 613/476-8416, www.theregenttheatre.org) shows movies and hosts concerts and other special events. **Taste the County** (www.tastecelebration.ca, Sept.) celebrates the county's local food and wine, with a variety of tastings and special events. If you want to sample some of the county's more expensive dining rooms, while still watching your budget, visit during **Countylicious** (www.countylicious.ca, Mar.–Apr. and Nov.), when local restaurants offer good-value prix-fixe menus.

SHOPPING

Shops, galleries, and cafés line the Main Streets of Picton, Bloomfield, and Wellington. Farther afield, you'll find farm stands, cheese makers, and orchards. And of course, all the wineries have shops where you can buy wine and wine-related souvenirs.

Art Galleries

Numerous artists work in the county, and you can follow the **Arts Trail** (www.artstrail.ca), a self-guided tour of galleries and studios. Wellington, Bloomfield, and Picton each have clusters of galleries, while others are in the countryside around the county. Access the Arts Trail guide online or pick up a brochure at county tourist offices, hotels, and galleries.

Arts on Main (223 Main St., Picton, 613/476-5665, www.artsonmaingallery.ca, call for seasonal hours), an artist cooperative, shows works by its members, who all live and work in the county.

The Red Barns (167 White Chapel Rd., Picton, 613/476-6808, www.theredbarns.com, 10 A.M.–5 P.M. Tues.–Sun. May–mid-Oct.) bills itself as "an artisan's playground," and whether you want to make art, see it made, or browse locally created works, there's something here for you on this former farm. There's a small shop and gallery, and you can watch several artists-in-residence at work or choose from a variety of classes and workshops in stained glass, glass blowing, pottery, painting, wood carving, and blacksmithing. Most workshops are designed for adults, but some are suitable for teens. The property is about two kilometers (1.2 miles) north of downtown Picton, off Highway 49.

F A D (3 Corey St., Bloomfield, 613/393-5235, www.shopfad.com, 10 A.M.–5 P.M. Wed.–Mon. July–Oct., 11 A.M.–4 P.M. Sat.–Sun. Apr.–June and Nov.–Dec.) sells high-quality contemporary crafts and fine art by Ontario artisans.

Bookshops

Books and Company (289 Main St., Picton, 613/476-3037, www.pictonbookstore.com, 9 A.M.–6 P.M. Mon.–Thurs., 9 A.M.–8 P.M. Fri.–Sat., 10 A.M.–5 P.M. Sun.) is a large independent bookstore that often hosts readings and other literary events. It's connected to **Miss Lily's Cafe** (613/476-9289, $4–7), a light and airy spot to have a coffee, pastry, or light lunch—or curl up with a book.

Gourmet Treats

Fifth Town Artisan Cheese Company (4309 County Rd. 8, Waupoos, 613/476-5755, www. fifthtown.ca, 10 A.M.–6 P.M. daily July–early Sept.; 10 A.M.–5 P.M. daily early Sept.–Dec.; call for off-season hours) makes its goat-, sheep-, and cow's-milk cheeses by hand (you can watch through the window into their production room), with milk sourced from within 100 miles (160 kilometers). The dairy itself is a "green" building, made from more than 80 percent recycled materials. Sample the cheeses in their tasting room, or in summer, come for a one-hour wine and cheese pairing session—with tastes, of course ($12). If you're really keen, sign up for the Cheese Maker for a Day program ($275), which includes a tour of the facilities, cheese-making lessons, breakfast and lunch, a wine and cheese tasting, and your own cheese to take home and age.

Established in 1901, the **Black River Cheese Company** (913 County Rd. 13, Milford, 613/476-2575 or 888/252-5787, www.blackrivercheese.com, 9 A.M.–7 P.M. daily July–early Sept., 9 A.M.–5 P.M. early Sept.–June) specializes in cheddar cheese, aged 1–8 years (the eight-year variety is deliciously flavorful). In their cheese shop, 11 kilometers (eight miles) south of Picton, you can sample at least a couple of varieties (and they're all available for purchase). Aficionados know that fresh curds are made on Tuesdays, Thursdays, and Saturdays.

ACCOMMODATIONS
Wellington

You may feel like a guest at a private cottage when you stay at the **Devonshire Inn on the Lake** (24 Wharf St., Wellington, 613/399-1851 or 800/544-9937, www.devonshire-inn.com, $150–235 d), particularly when you're lounging in the library stocked with books and games. The building, which dates to 1850, still has its original staircase, pocket doors, and fireplace.

the menu at Fifth Town Artisan Cheese Company

Four of the traditionally furnished guest rooms are on the main floor, two on the second floor, and the top floor is a two-bedroom suite with skylights and a water view you can enjoy from the bathroom. Guests take their breakfast in the waterfront dining room, which is also open to the public for dinner. There's a small beach, too, although it's a rocky one. The inn stays open year-round; the restaurant is closed in January and February.

Bloomfield

Owners Diane and Bruce Milan used to be organic farmers in Minnesota before decamping to the county's milder Canadian climate. Now they operate the cozy **Hillsdale House** (332 Main St., Bloomfield, 613/393-2952, www.bbcanada.com/625.html, $125 d), a two-room B&B in their 1890s home. Diane serves a three-course hot breakfast each morning, and Bruce is also a blacksmith; stop into his Island Forge Studio out back to see what he's working on.

On the grounds of the Huff Estates winery,

Inn at Huff Estates (2274 County Rd. 1, Bloomfield, 613/393-1414 or 866/484-4667, www.huffestates.com, $199–269 d) is a modern building (it opened in 2006), but the 21 guest rooms are done in a woodsy, cottage style. All have private patios; some overlook the interior courtyard, while others look out onto the vineyards. Rates include a breakfast buffet.

Picton

You don't have to be an artist to stay at the **The Red Barns** (167 White Chapel Rd., Picton, 613/476-6808, www.theredbarns.com, May–Oct., $90–125 d), just north of downtown Picton, but owners and artists Heather Watson and Peter Josic have decorated the three guest rooms in their farmhouse with original stained glass inspired by artists like Frank Lloyd Wright and Charles Rennie MacIntosh. Families might prefer the one-bedroom coach house ($200/night), with midcentury modern furnishings, kitchen, living room with sleep sofa, and more stained glass. Rates for the farmhouse rooms, but not the coach house, include breakfast.

The former owner of the county's oldest inn moved it from the other side of the island and spent more than 40 years painstakingly putting it back together. The current owners of the **Hayes Inn** (2319 County Rd. 8, Picton, 613/476-6904 or 877/928-8667, www.hayes-inn.com, $165–180 d), on the road to Waupoos, finished the job, reopening this bright and airy four-room lodging with cream-colored furnishings, white duvets, flat-screen TVs, and new bathrooms. You get a full breakfast that might include crepes with local cheeses and fruit or eggs with freshly made salsa—nothing like its early rough-hewn tavern days.

Don't go for a fussy Victorian look? The **Loyalist Lofts** (56 Mary St., Picton, 613/471-1169, www.loyalistlofts.ca, $175 d), in a restored 1877 brick home, take a more streamlined path, renting two spacious apartments furnished in a relaxed mix of modern and historic features. The first-floor Wellington Suite has a large front bedroom, a smaller second bedroom, and a comfy living area. Both this unit and the upstairs Picton suite have full

kitchens and renovated bathrooms. Breakfast isn't provided, but you can cook for yourself and you're just one block from Picton's Main Street. There's free Wi-Fi, too.

Food is an important part of a stay at the **Merrill Inn** (343 Main East, Picton, 613/476-7451 or 866/567-5969, www.merrillinn.com, Feb.–Dec., $155–299 d), a 13-room lodging in an 1878 brick Victorian. Not only does the inn have a fine restaurant (5:30–9 P.M. Tues.–Sat.), but you get a copious breakfast buffet, as well as afternoon tea (or lemonade, or hot cider, depending on the season), with freshly baked cookies. In the quieter months (Feb.–Apr.), the inn hosts wine and cheese hours where guests can mingle with local winemakers. The guest rooms, spread out over three floors, are all different, but all are furnished with antiques and period pieces; some have fireplaces, and the Fireplace Suite even has a working wood-burning one.

The property that now houses the **Waring House Inn** (395 Sandy Hook Rd., Picton, 613/476-7492 or 800/621-4956, www.waringhouse.com, $149–229 d) was once a farm. The main inn and restaurant are in the 1860s stone farmhouse; the guest rooms upstairs are cozy but tiny. Rooms are more spacious in two newer lodges, furnished with classic pieces from the local Gibbard Furniture company. For a romantic getaway, cuddle in the stone "Vineyard View" cottage ($299 d) overlooking the gardens. Also on the property is the **Folkworks Studio Gallery** (613/471-0346, www.danielis.ca), where you can often chat with artist Robert Danielis as he works. The Waring House runs a cooking school, as well.

Under the same ownership as the Waring House, the **◖ Claramount Inn & Spa** (97 Bridge St., Picton, 613/476-2709 or 800/679-7756, www.claramountinn.com, $195–225 d) is its posh cousin, a sunny yellow Colonial Revival mansion, built in 1906. The seven spacious suites in the main inn are all different, but expect antiques, large soaker tubs, and some fireplaces; three suites in the neighboring carriage house have a more rustic country style. The spa on the lower level is one of the few places in

Canada to offer Hawaiian-style lomi lomi massage, among its other services, and you can swim in the heated saltwater pool year-round (it has a retractable roof). **Clara's Restaurant** (breakfast $8–14, dinner $24–32), where the chef emphasizes local ingredients in his contemporary dishes, overlooks the harbor.

Camping

Sandbanks Provincial Park (County Rd. 12, 613/393-3319, www.ontarioparks.com, late Apr.–mid-Oct., $16.25/vehicle, $37–41 tent sites, $43–46 electrical sites) has 549 campsites in five campgrounds, including 140 sites with electrical service. The prime sites are at Camper's Beach, right on the lake. You'll need to reserve far ahead to nab one of these sites; the park accepts reservations five months in advance, and eager campers book the Camper's Beach sites on the day they become available. Some of the sites in the Outlet River Campground are also on the water (the river). From Richardson's Campground, it's a short walk to Sandbanks Beach and a slightly longer walk to the Dunes Beach. All the campground comfort stations, except Richardson's, have showers and flush toilets, although as this book went to press, the park was planning a new comfort station for Richardson's, as well.

The park also has two cottages that are available for rent. The **Maple Rest Heritage House** ($312/night) is a four-bedroom, four-bathroom brick Victorian home that sleeps eight. The smaller lakeside **Jacques Cottage** ($140/night) can sleep up to six; the small master bedroom upstairs has a double bed, an adjacent open loft space has two twins, and there's a sleep sofa in the living room. Both cottages have kitchens, and linens are provided. Book either cottage—well in advance—through the Ontario Parks reservation service (519/826-5290 or 888/668-7275, www.ontarioparks.com).

FOOD

As you travel around the county, you'll see farm stands on many of the local roads, including a couple that are especially worth seeking out. Many county regulars make a beeline for

Schroedter's Farm Market (1492 Hwy. 62, at Hwy. 1, Bloomfield, 613/393-2823) for one reason: freshly made donuts.

Near the Black River Cheese Company, **Vicki's Veggies** (81 Morrison Point Rd., off County Rd. 13, Milford, 613/476-7241, www.vickisveggies.com) is a self-service roadside stand selling organically grown vegetables. Vicki's supplies many local restaurants and sells her wares as far away as Toronto. Tomatoes are a highlight in season; look for their annual **heirloom tomato festival** in September.

Wellington

With a mix of sleek black candlelit tables and wide board pine floors (plus a friendly knowledgeable staff), **(East and Main Bistro** (270 Main St., Wellington, 613/399-5420, www.eastandmain.ca, lunch noon–2:30 P.M., dinner 5:30–9 P.M. Thurs.–Mon. Feb.–Dec., lunch $10–14, dinner $19–29) feels both stylish and totally relaxed. The menu walks that hip-homey line, too; the duck confit might come with a potato, apple, and pea hash, the smoked pork tenderloin might be served with Stilton polenta and bourbon sauce, and the stuffed pepper might be filled with local veggies, grains, and Fifth Town cheese. The wines are local, of course.

Bloomfield

An old-fashioned "from scratch" pastry shop, **Just Sweets Retro Bakery** (5 Corey St., Bloomfield, 613/393-5365, www.justsweetsretrobakery.com, call for seasonal hours) bakes cupcakes, butter tarts, individual lemon Bundt cakes, and delicious date squares, among other goodies. Cash only (as they say, "How retro is that?").

Picton

Even simple eateries like the funky **Chesterfields Homegrown Café** (126 Main St., Picton, 613/476-2233, www.chesterfieldscafe.ca, 7 A.M.–3 P.M. daily, $6.50) support the county's locally grown philosophy. Case in point: the delicious, 100 percent local breakfast sandwich called the "Berkzerker," made with locally raised Berkshire pork sausage, cheese from the county's Black River Cheese company, local eggs, and homemade mayo on a bun baked at **The Pastry House** (125 Main St., Picton, 613/476-6560, www.pastryhouse. com), the bakery across the street.

Looking like an old-time sweet shop, with white wainscoting, a tin ceiling, and turquoise walls, the **Regent Café** (222 Main St., Picton, 613/476-9833, www.theregentcafe.com, 8 A.M.–6 P.M. Mon., 8 A.M.–8 P.M. Tues.–Sat., 10 A.M.–5 P.M. Sun. in summer; call for off-season hours, $4–9), adjacent to the theater of the same name, is a cheerful spot for breakfast, coffee, or a pre-theater bite. The menu includes breakfast burritos, oatmeal, sandwiches, pizzas, and pastries, and yes, the coffee they brag about is good. Free Wi-Fi.

Even hot dogs are hip at **Buddha Dog** (172 Main St., Picton, 613/476-3814, http:// buddhafoodha.com, open daily in summer; 11 A.M.–5 P.M. Fri.–Sat. and Mon., 11 A.M.–4 P.M. Sun. fall–spring), where you can top your all-beef dog ($2.50) with local cheese and homemade ketchup, wasabi-lime mayo, jalapeño tequila jelly, or other eclectic sauces.

Even if you're not staying at the **◖ Merrill Inn** (343 Main E., Picton, 613/476-7451 or 866/567-5969, www.merrillinn.com, Feb.–Dec., 5:30–9 P.M. Tues.–Sat., $25–36), call in advance for a reservation for their cozy garden-level dining room; they serve some of the most interesting food in the county. Start with their fresh and hearty signature salad—baby spinach and other greens topped with local cheddar, apples, and spicy-sweet pecans—or perhaps calamari braised in a lemon-parsley brown butter or a salad of smoked trout and beans. Entrées might include local perch topped with lemon aioli, cornish hen paired with garlicky mashed potatoes, or locally raised lamb; the kitchen takes great care with the accompanying vegetables, too. For the sweet finale, you might sample the summery peach and frangiapane tart or the cheesecake-like *mousse au fromage blanc* made from Fifth Town cheese and topped with local berries.

Bustling, casual, and modern, the **Blumen Garden Bistro** (647 Hwy. 49, Picton, www. blumengardenbistro.com, 613/476-6841, lunch 11:30 A.M.–2 P.M. Thurs.–Sun., dinner 5–9 P.M. Wed.–Mon., lunch $11–15, dinner $21–29) takes influences from chef-owner Andreas Feller's Swiss-German background and sprinkles them into interesting contemporary dishes. The duck breast, sauced with a red wine–cherry reduction, might come with spaetzle, or the gnocchi might be topped with braised rabbit and oyster mushrooms. If anything with a chocolate brownie—more like a rich and delicious flourless cake—is on the menu, save room.

INFORMATION AND SERVICES

Prince Edward County Chamber of Tourism and Commerce (116 Main St., Picton, 613/476-2421 or 800/640-4717, www.visitpec. ca) can provide event listings, maps, wine-touring guides, and lots of other helpful information for planning a county visit.

The county tourism association also operates several seasonal information kiosks, including **Bloomfield Information Kiosk** (Bloomfield Town Hall, 289 Main St., lower level, 613/393-2796), **Wellington Information Kiosk** (Lakeshore Farms, 467 Main St. W.), and **Hillier Information Kiosk** (The County Way Restaurant, Hwy. 33, at County Rd. 1).

Cooking Classes

With its emphasis on local food, perhaps it's not surprising that the county has several cooking programs to help you learn to use local ingredients. All post upcoming class schedules on their websites.

From the Farm Cooking School (www. fromthefarm.ca, May–Oct.) offers small classes, from bread baking to French country cooking, that include lunch.

The **Waring House Cookery School** (613/476-7492 or 800/621-4956, www.waringhouse.com), at the Waring House Inn, offers a variety of cooking classes, which typically run three hours (including a meal), in their large commercial kitchen. Topics might include breakfast dishes, fall vegetables, or bistro desserts.

Chef Michael Hoy (613/476-3811, www.chefmichaelhoy.com), who runs the restaurant at Huff Estates Winery, also offers three-hour cooking classes.

GETTING THERE AND AROUND

Prince Edward County is 215 kilometers (135 miles) east of Toronto. Take Highway 401 east to either Exit 522 (Wooler Road South) or Exit 525 (Highway 33, Trenton). You need a car to get to around the county.

From Kingston, you can either take the 401 west to Exit 566 (Marysville) and continue south on Highway 49, or follow the slower but shore-hugging Loyalist Parkway (Highway 33) to Adolphustown and then take the 10-minute

Glenora-Adolphustown Ferry (www.prince-edward-county.com, 6 A.M.–1:15 A.M., free). The ferry leaves from the Adolphustown side at 15 minutes before and 15 minutes after the hour; it departs Glenora on the hour and the half-hour.

The main road across the county is Highway 33, the Loyalist Parkway, which becomes "Main Street" in Wellington, Bloomfield, and Picton. If you're coming from the west and heading to Picton, it's faster to cut across on Highway 1 east from Consecon, which rejoins Highway 33 just west of Picton.

If you don't want to wine-taste and drive, contact **Prince Edward County Wine Tours** (613/393-8988 or 866/900-3703, www.pecwinetours.com), which offers half-day (from $69/person) and full-day (from $125/person) winery tours, including transportation.

Kingston

On June 15, 1841, Kingston became the first capital of the fledgling nation of Canada. If you're interested in history, it's worth exploring this city of 150,000, located midway between Toronto and Montreal. There's a 19th-century fort, a majestic city hall, the oldest continuously running public market in Ontario, and the well-regarded Queen's University, founded the same year that Kingston took on its capital-city duties.

Kingston is sometimes nicknamed "The Limestone City" for its many well-preserved stone structures (some of which are now inns or B&Bs) that date to the 1800s. Located on Lake Ontario at the southern end of the Rideau Canal, Kingston's waterfront is an important part of its heritage, too, and it makes the present-day city even more pleasant, whether you're strolling along the eight-kilometer (five-mile) waterfront trail or looking out across the water from your hotel window.

Yet even with all this history, there's nothing stuffy about this entertaining little city. It's compact and easy to walk around, with a number of eclectic, contemporary restaurants,

casual cafés, and leafy parks. Perhaps its blend of history and fun makes it—as its hometown band would have it—"Tragically Hip."

SIGHTS
◀ Fort Henry

Standing majestically on a point overlooking the city of Kingston and the St. Lawrence River, Fort Henry (1 Fort Henry Dr., at County Rd. 2, 613/542-7388, www.forthenry.com, 10 A.M.–5 P.M. daily late May–early Sept., adults $14.25, seniors $13, kids 5–18 $9.95, kids 2–4 $3, parking $4.50) was built in the 1830s to protect the town, the nearby Royal dockyards, and the mouth of the adjacent Rideau Canal. Kingston was a major stop on the supply routes between Montreal, Ottawa, and points farther west, making it a strategic location for the British. British troops were stationed at the fort until 1870.

Today, you can tour the restored fort to learn more about the history of Kingston—and Canada—in the 1800s and visit the soldiers' barracks, the officers' quarters, and the

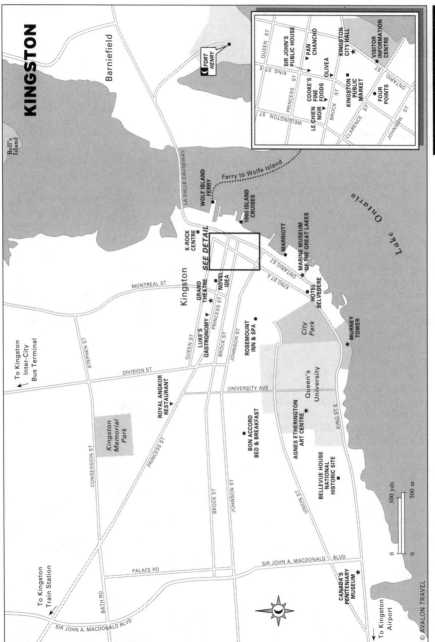

KINGSTON

Barniefield

Bell's
Island

FORT
HENRY

Inset detail:

QUEEN ST
SIR JOHN'S PUBLIC HOUSE
PAN CHANCHO
KING ST E
OLIVEA
KINGSTON CITY HALL
VISITOR INFORMATION CENTRE
PRINCESS ST
COOKE'S FINE FOODS
KINGSTON PUBLIC MARKET
BROCK ST
LE CHIEN NOIR
WELLINGTON ST
CLARENCE ST
ONTARIO ST
FOUR POINTS
JOHNSON ST

Ferry to Wolfe Island

LA SALLE CAUSEWAY

WOLF ISLAND FERRY

1000 ISLAND CRUISES

SEE DETAIL

K-ROCK CENTRE

MARRIOTT

MARINE MUSEUM OF THE GREAT LAKES

Lake Ontario

Kingston

MONTREAL ST

GRAND THEATRE

NOVEL IDEA

ONTARIO ST

KING ST E

HOTEL BELVEDERE

LUKE'S GASTRONOMY

Queen ST

Princess ST

Brock ST

Johnson ST

ROSEMOUNT INN & SPA

City Park

MURNEY TOWER

STEPHEN ST

To Kingston Inter-City Bus Terminal

DIVISION ST

ROYAL ANGKOR RESTAURANT

UNIVERSITY AVE

Queen's University

KING ST E

CONSESSION ST

PRINCESS ST

Kingston Memorial Park

BON ACCORD BED & BREAKFAST

AGNES ETHERINGTON ART CENTRE

BELLEVUE HOUSE NATIONAL HISTORIC SITE

BROCK ST

JOHNSON ST

UNION ST

BATH RD

To Kingston Train Station

PALACE RD

SIR JOHN A. MACDONALD BLVD

CANADA'S PENITENIARY MUSEUM

SIR JOHN A. MACDONALD BLVD

To Kingston Airport

0   500 yds
0   500 m

© AVALON TRAVEL

fort's schoolroom, kitchen, and other facilities. Costumed interpreters portray soldiers, as well as schoolteachers, soldiers' wives, and other civilian residents of the fort. Explore the fort on your own or take a 50-minute guided tour, which departs several times daily (10:30 A.M.–4 P.M.). (As this book went to press, a Discovery Centre was under construction. When complete, it will introduce visitors to the history of the fort and its time period.)

When planning your visit, check the daily schedule (available online or at the fort) for other activities that take place throughout the day. You might train as a British soldier, become a student (circa 1867) at "Victorian school," or participate in the trial of a misbehaving private. If you're visiting in July or August, try to attend the **Sunset Ceremonies** (7:30 P.M. Wed.), when "soldiers" perform precision military maneuvers, accompanied by period military music and gun salutes, culminating in fireworks over the harbor.

In the fall, Fort Henry transforms into **Fort Fright** (6–10 P.M. Wed.–Sat. late Sept.–Oct., $13/person including parking), an elaborate haunted house with shaking coffins, ghouls that jump out at you, and other creepy effects, plus Halloween-themed performances. The fort reopens during the first half of December for the **Victorian Holiday Festival,** which includes a craft show, Christmas caroling, and other activities illustrating the history of Christmas at the fort.

An on-site snack bar will keep your little soldiers from starving while touring the fort, or you can sit down to a traditional British lunch in the **Bonnycastle Lunch and Tea Room** (613/530-2550, www.foodandheritage. com, daily late May–early Sept.). In the evenings, dine by candlelight in the **Fort Henry Officers' Mess** (613/530-2550, www.foodandheritage.com, 5–9 P.M. daily July–Aug.) on traditional (and not-so-traditional) foods.

Fort Henry is 2.5 kilometers (1.5 miles) east of downtown. If you don't have a car, you can catch Kingston Transit Bus #12 (Princess Street, near King), which will drop you off at the top of the fort road.

Kingston City Hall

Built in the 1840s when Kingston was the first capital of Canada, Kingston City Hall (216 Ontario St., 613/546-0000, www.cityofkingston.ca) is both a working government building and a National Historic Site. One of the building's highlights is Memorial Hall, with its arched ceiling, 12 stained-glass windows, and massive portrait of Sir John A. Macdonald, the Kingston resident who became Canada's first prime minister.

In July and August, you can take a free guided tour (11 A.M.–3 P.M. Sat.–Sun.) of the building. Free tours are also offered on weekdays between mid-May and the end of September (10 A.M.–4 P.M. Mon.–Fri.), but you must make a reservation at least two weeks in advance (613/546-4291, ext. 1520). Tours are not offered October through mid-May, but you can still explore the building on your own; pick up a tour brochure at the City Hall reception desk.

© CAROLYN B. HELLER

Kingston City Hall was built in the 1840s.

Murney Tower

In the 1840s, the British built four small fortifications along the Kingston waterfront, which are known as the Martello Towers. The British copied these stocky round towers from a similar French structure constructed on Mortella Point on the island of Corsica (the "Martello" name is apparently an Anglicized corruption of "Mortella"). Kingston's Martello Towers are among only 13 similar fully intact structures in the world.

One of these fortifications, the 1846 Murney Tower (King St. W., at Barrie St., www.kingstonhistoricalsociety.ca, 10 A.M.–5 P.M. daily mid-May–early Sept., adults $5, seniors and students $4, families $12) is open to the public. Cannons still point out from the narrow windows at the top of the tower, and inside, a small historical museum describes the lives of the 19th-century soldiers and their families who lived in the tower.

Canada's Penitentiary Museum

Directly across the street from the maximum-security Kingston Penitentiary is a quirky, fascinating, and sobering museum about the region's prison past. Housed in the former Kingston Pen's warden's residence is Canada's Penitentiary Museum (555 King St. W., at Sir John A. Macdonald Blvd., 613/530-3122, www.penitentiarymuseum.ca, 9 A.M.–4 P.M. Mon.–Fri., 10 A.M.–4 P.M. Sat.–Sun., May–Oct., admission by donation). The museum includes a "punishment room," which displays various disciplinary measures used over the years—from the strapping board that inmates were strapped to, to be paddled (used as recently as 1969), to "The Box," a creepy casket-like container used for solitary confinement in the 1840s. You can peek into actual jail cells, and in the "contraband room" you'll see all manner of handmade weapons and devices used for attempted escapes. Not your everyday tourist attraction, but definitely worth seeing.

Bellevue House National Historic Site

The former home of Sir John A. Macdonald, Canada's first prime minister, the Bellevue House National Historic Site (35 Centre St., 613/545-8666, www.pc.gc.ca/lhn-nhs/on/bellevue/index.aspx, 10 A.M.–5 P.M. daily Apr.–Oct., adults $3.90, seniors $3.40, kids 6–16 $1.90) is a sprawling 20-room white stucco mansion that Macdonald, his wife, Isabella, and their infant son rented in 1848. Macdonald hoped that the peaceful atmosphere of this country house (located about 1.5 kilometers, or one mile, from central Kingston) would improve Isabella's poor health.

Unfortunately, the Macdonalds' son died shortly after they moved into the house. Isabella continued to ail (she may have suffered from tuberculosis), and Macdonald found himself in financial trouble. The family left Bellevue House after only one year, relocating to a smaller and less costly home in town. A few of the Macdonalds' possessions remain at Bellevue House, although most of the furnishings are other pieces from the 1840s. Costumed guides are on hand to tell you about Macdonald, his family, and the home. On Thursdays, Fridays, and Sundays in July and August, you can take afternoon tea in the garden, served by staff in period costume.

Agnes Etherington Art Centre

On the Queen's University campus, this contemporary art museum (University Ave. at Bader Ln., 613/533-2190, www.aeac.ca, 10 A.M.–4:30 P.M. Tues.–Fri., 1–5 P.M. Sat.–Sun., adults $5, seniors $3, students and children free) mounts exhibits of works by artists from Canada and around the world. On the third Thursday of every month, you can take a free 45-minute guided tour of the current exhibitions. During the school year (Sept.–Apr.), the museum stays open until 9 P.M. every Thursday.

ENTERTAINMENT AND EVENTS

First opened in 1879, the **Grand Theatre** (218 Princess St., 613/530-2050, www.kingston-grand.ca) now hosts numerous theater, dance,

BON ECHO PROVINCIAL PARK

Combining a striking outdoor setting with interesting aboriginal history, Bon Echo Provincial Park (16151 Hwy. 41, RR 1, Cloyne, 613/336-2228, www.ontarioparks.com or www.bonechofriends.ca, early May-mid-Oct., $14/vehicle) is worth the trip, whether for a day or more. The park is 100 kilometers (60 miles) northwest of Kingston and 130 kilometers (80 miles) northeast of Peterborough, located roughly between Toronto and Ottawa.

ABORIGINAL PICTOGRAPHS

The park's centerpiece is **Mazinaw Rock,** jutting 100 meters (325 feet) out of Mazinaw Lake and now preserved as a National Historic Site. On the front surface of the predominantly granite rock are 260 aboriginal pictographs.

Unlike the aboriginal markings at Petroglyphs Provincial Park, which were carved into the rock, the Bon Echo pictographs were drawn or painted onto the rock face. But as at Petroglyphs, the exact date of the drawings, which include turtles, canoes, and underwater creatures, is unknown. Estimates put them at somewhere between 300 and 900 years old.

You can see the Bon Echo pictographs only from the water. In the summer, the **Wanderer Ferry** (round-trip adults $6.50, kids under age 12 $4) runs 45-minute tours across the lake to the pictographs. The ferry departs from the docks near the park visitors center. The lines for the boat, which seats only 26, can be long; it's typically less crowded first thing in the morning.

Another way to reach the pictographs is by canoe or kayak. You can't disembark at this section of the rock, but you can paddle near the drawings. Rent canoes and kayaks at the lagoon.

ON TOP OF THE ROCK

If you're atop Mazinaw Rock, you can't see the pictographs; the rock is too steep to hike (or climb) down. But you can hike the 1.5-kilometer (0.9-mile) **Cliff Top Trail** to a lookout on the rock's summit; in the fall, you'll have a great vista across the reds, golds, and greens of the surrounding forests. The trail is steep, but there are stairs in the steepest sections.

Like the pictographs, the Cliff Top Trail is accessible only from the water. The **Mugwump Ferry** (round-trip adults $3.25, kids under 12

musical, and other productions every year by local, national, and international performers. For rock concerts, sports events, ice shows, and other big productions, head to the **K-Rock Centre** (1 Barrack St., 613/650-5000, www.k-rockcentre.com).

Every year on June 15, Kingston celebrates **First Capital Day** (www.cityofkingston.ca), commemorating the city's role as Canada's first capital. During Fort Henry's annual **1812 Overture Weekend** (www.forthenry.com, mid-July), the Kingston Symphony performs Tchaikovsky's 1812 Overture, accented with 1860s cannons firing and closing with a finale of fireworks. Clowns, contortionists, crooners, and all manner of street performers take over downtown during the **Kingston Buskers Rendezvous** (www.kingstonbuskers.com, July).

SHOPPING

Princess Street is the main downtown shopping street, with a mix of local and chain clothing shops, cafés, and other boutiques, including the independent bookstore **Novel Idea** (156 Princess St., 613/546-9799, www.novelideabooks.ca), which carries a good selection of both fiction and nonfiction. Most of the shops are between Ontario and Sydenham Streets.

One block south of Princess, Brock Street has a few interesting shops, as well, including **Cooke's Fine Foods** (61 Brock St., 613/548-7721, www.cookesfinefoods.com, 9:30 A.M.–5:30 P.M. Mon.–Sat.), which opened in 1865. It still has the original counters and tin ceiling, and its shelves are packed with coffees, jams, cheeses, chocolates, and other specialty foods.

$2.25) will shuttle you from the lagoon to the start of the trail. You can also canoe across from the lagoon to the trailhead.

BEACHES AND HIKING TRAILS
So what else is there to do at Bon Echo? You can swim in Mazinaw Lake from either **Main Beach** or **North Beach**. North Beach is sandy and good for kids, although the water tends to be a little colder. Take a short hike to **The Narrows,** a point just across a narrow section of water from the rock. You can't see the pictographs from here, but at sunset, the setting sun reflects its colors on Mazinaw Rock.

The park has several other hiking trails, ranging from the easy one-kilometer (0.6-mile) **Bon Echo Creek** route, to the rugged, 17-kilometer (10.5-mile) **Abes Loop.**

PRACTICALITIES
Bon Echo has 532 **campsites** spread out over several areas, including 333 tent sites ($36.75-40.50), 169 electrical sites ($42.25-46), and 30 backcountry sites (adults $10, kids 6-17 $4.75). There are also six yurts ($91.50). Sawmill Bay is designed primarily for tent camping; there are five walk-in sites directly on Upper Mazinaw Lake, and other sites within a short walk of North Beach. Some sites in the Fairview Campground are near (but not on) the lake. Across Highway 41 from Mazinaw Lake, the Hardwood Hill Campground is a wooded area high up on a hill and feels much more secluded than the lakeside campgrounds. The drawback, naturally, is that you're farther from the lake. Also on this side of the park is a series of canoe-in back-country campsites on Joeperry and Pearson Lakes.

If you don't want to camp, rent the **Cabin on the Hill** ($113), an 1870s log cabin that's been updated with electricity, indoor plumbing, and a kitchen. It's a short walk from North Beach and has great views of the rock. The cabin has one bedroom, plus two sleeper sofas in the living room.

The park has no food concessions, although on summer weekends, there's usually a lunchtime **barbecue** (noon-2 P.M. Sat.-Sun.). There's a small market in the village of Cloyne, about a 10-minute drive south of the park, and a larger grocery in Northbrook, farther south on Highway 41.

ACCOMMODATIONS
If you like staying in inns or B&Bs in stately historic buildings, you'll enjoy staying in Kingston. You may find a creaky floor here or a bit of chipped paint there, but the atmosphere is more distinctive than in a cookie-cutter chain. That said, if these quirks bother you, you can opt for one of the more modern chain hotels downtown.

Downtown Kingston also has several business-friendly chain hotels, which would be convenient for families, too. The **Radisson Hotel Kingston Waterfront** (1 Johnson St., 613/549-8100 or 800/967-9033, www.radisson.com, $200 d) and the newer **Marriott Residence Inn Kingston Water's Edge** (7 Earl St., 613/544-4888, www.marriottresidenceinnkingston.com, $230 d) are on the waterfront; the **Four Points by Sheraton** (285 King St. E., 613/544-4434, www.fourpointskingston.com, $190 d) is centrally located, as well.

Under $100
Want to know what it was really like to be a soldier in 1800s Kingston? You won't be issued a musket or army rations, but you can spend the night at **Fort Henry** (County Rd. 2, 613/542-7388, www.forthenry.com, $50 s, $100 d, $40/person for families or groups). The fort has two small brick-walled guest rooms, one with a double bed, another with two twins, and two larger dormitory-style rooms with rows of single beds, available to families or groups. The billets are basic—you have a quilt-topped bed and not much else—but you won't have to use 19th-century privies. The fort has modern washroom facilities, including hot showers, although you have to walk across the open courtyard to reach

them from the guest rooms, so come prepared for the weather. Flashlights are provided.

$100-150

The **Bon Accord Bed & Breakfast** (275 Albert St. at Earl St., 613/540-2378 www.bbcanada.com/bonaccordbb, $139 d) is an unusual-for-Kingston contemporary house near the Queen's University campus. Owners Suzanne and Brian are artists who've decorated their home and three first-floor guest apartments with their paintings and sculptures. The rooms have kitchenettes, though a full breakfast is provided, as well. The house's best feature is the secluded top-floor lounge and spacious roof deck; it's like a grown-up tree house overlooking the neighboring rooftops. The B&B rooms are typically available April through August; during the Queen's academic year, the units are often rented for long-term stays.

Conveniently located between downtown and the Queen's campus, the **Hotel Belvedere** (141 King St. E., 613/548-1565 or 800/559-0584, www.hotelbelvedere.com, $119–259 d) was built in 1880 as a private home. Now an inn, it's traditionally appointed without feeling frilly or formal. Many of the 20 antiques-filled rooms, in sizes that vary from snug to spacious, have little nooks and crannies; a set of stairs might lead into a closet, or a kitchenette might hide behind the door. Rates include Wi-Fi, parking, and a light continental breakfast (English muffin, juice, tea or coffee) delivered to you in your room or in the ample, high-ceilinged guest parlor.

Over $150

Guests are encouraged to mingle at the **Rosemount Inn & Spa** (46 Sydenham St., 613/531-8844, www.rosemountinn.com, $175–299 d), whether it's over afternoon tea and cookies in the lounge, on the spacious front porch, or at breakfast, where a set menu is served around the community table. The nine rooms in the main inn, a statuesque ivy-covered stone villa built in 1850, are all different, but throughout the building you'll find

leaded-glass windows, oriental rugs, wingback chairs, and four-poster beds. Two suites in the adjacent coach house are more modern; one two-level unit has a living area on the main floor and a bedroom and bath above.

FOOD

For a small city, Kingston has a large selection of good places to eat, from basic ethnic joints to upscale contemporary dining rooms. Most are clustered in the downtown area, around Princess, King, and Ontario Streets.

Bakeries and Cafés

Need a foccacia, muffin, or scone? **Pan Chancho Bakery and Café** (44 Princess St., 613/544-7790, www.panchancho.com, $3–16) is your place. The bakery (7 A.M.–6 P.M. Mon.–Sat., 7 A.M.–5 P.M. Sun.) sells tasty baked goods and prepared foods to go, or you can sit down to a meal in the café (7 A.M.–4 P.M. daily): pastries or egg dishes in the morning, salads, cheese plates, or creative, world-rambling entrées later in the day.

Asian

Southeast Asian eateries, serving Cambodian and Thai food in particular, are popular in Kingston. An excellent choice, if you don't mind venturing out of the downtown core, is the barebones but welcoming **Royal Angkor Restaurant** (523 Princess St., 613/544-9268, www.royalangkor.ca, daily 11:30 A.M.–3 P.M. and 5–10 P.M., $7–10), where a few photos above the Formica tables constitute the "decor." No matter—the food is fresh and flavorful. Try the "Samlaw Khmer," a hot-and-sour mix of chicken, shrimp, long beans, onions, and chunks of tomatoes flavored with tamarind and basil. The "Golden Chicken" (with peanuts and lemongrass) and the "Kako Khmer" (chicken with green papaya, jackfruit, and eggplant) are also popular choices.

Contemporary

Chef Luke Hayes-Alexander was just 15 years old when he became executive chef at **⟨ Luke's Gastronomy** (264 Princess St., 613/531-7745, www.lukesgastronomy.com, 6–9 P.M. Sun.–Thurs., 6–10 P.M. Fri.–Sat., $26–36), the narrow downtown bistro, owned by his parents, that bears his name. Though he's still barely out of adolescence, he continues to serve some of the most eclectic, and innovative, fare in town. His ever-changing menu might include "The Taste of Money" (beef cheeks, with foie gras, champagne, rose, and hippocras, a spiced wine), "Blues Junkie Goat, or How Coffee Was Discovered" (goat cooked with yogurt, coffee, chilies, pomegranate, dates, and almonds), or "Flight to First-Century Rome," sausages served with wild blueberries, must bread, an herb cheese called moretum, and makshufa (a traditional Mediterranean nut candy). Like living with a teenager, there's never a dull moment at Luke's.

The exposed brick walls, tin ceiling, and rust-hued banquettes say "traditional bistro," and you'll find plenty of traditional bistro fare at 【 **Le Chien Noir** (69 Brock St., 613/549-5635, www.lechiennoir.com, 11:30 A.M.–11 P.M. daily, lunch $12–27, dinner $17–39), from omelets to burgers to steak frites. But chef Derek Macgregor likes to push the bistro envelope, too, topping his poutine with duck confit and a triple-cream Brie, adding crispy pig ears to his frisée salad, or tarting up a dessert with a bit of bacon. You'll be equally at home here in jeans or a little black dress.

Italian

Decked out with stone walls, wooden tables, and a searingly hot pizza oven, **Woodenheads Gourmet Pizza** (192 Ontario St., 613/549-1812, www.woodenheads.ca, lunch and dinner daily, $9–21) is wildly popular for its eponymous pies, as well as salads and fusion variations on classic Mediterranean fare (calamari Mumbai-style, anyone?). The pizzas range from traditional tomato-and-cheese to the creative Citta (topped with Brie, prosciutto, caramelized onions, and basil) to quirky combos like the Nonna Mela, with blackened chicken, cheddar cheese, roasted garlic, and apple butter.

At the friendly, bustling trattoria **Olivea** (39 Brock St., 613/547-5483, www.olivea.ca, 11:30 A.M.–4:30 P.M. Mon.–Wed., 11:30 A.M.–9 P.M. Sun.–Thurs., 11:30 A.M.–10 P.M. Fri.–Sat., $9–25), with a wall of windows facing Market Square, you can order appetizers, salads, and pastas in both full and half portions, the better to sample more tasty dishes from the Italian-Mediterranean menu, share with your friends, or sate you as a solo diner. The salad with buttery tuna confit, white beans, and arugula pairs well with one of the pastas, perhaps penne with a spicy tomato-based arrabbiata sauce. If you're feeling creative, design your own pasta dish, selecting your noodle and sauce, and adding a vegetable if you like.

Pubs

In the 1850s, John A. Macdonald had his office in the King Street building that now houses **Sir John's Public House** (343 King St. E., 613/530-2550, www.foodandheritage.com, call for hours, lunch $8–10, dinner $11–14). The restaurant is part Scottish pub and part homage to Canada's first prime minister; notice the original bust of Sir John on the dining room wall. The menu gives basic pub fare a Scottish twist: you can get bangers and mash (pork sausages served with "tatties," or mashed potatoes, and "neaps," mashed turnips), fish 'n chips, or chicken pie with dark ale gravy. You can even sample the Scottish classic—haggis—though here it's fried into more palatable fritters and served with a tangy piccalilli sauce. The drink menu includes many Scotch whiskeys, of course.

Groceries and Markets

Located behind City Hall, the **Kingston Public Market** (Springer Market Sq., King St. E., between Brock and Clarence Sts., www.kingstonpublicmarket.ca) is the oldest market in Ontario, in operation since 1801. Selling local produce and prepared foods that change with the seasons, the market is open Tuesdays, Thursdays, and Saturdays, April to November; official hours are 6 A.M.–6 P.M., but you won't find much action before 8 A.M., and many vendors are packing up by 4 P.M.

INFORMATION AND SERVICES

Located in the former train station, the **Tourism Kingston Visitor Information**

Centre (209 Ontario St., 613/548-4415 or 888/855-4555, www.tourism.kingstoncanada. com) is in Confederation Park opposite City Hall. From mid-May to mid-October, the information center is open 9:30 A.M.–5 P.M. daily, with extended hours between July and early September until 8 P.M. Sunday through Wednesday and 9 P.M. Thursday through Saturday. From mid-October through April, hours are 10 A.M.–4 P.M. daily.

The information center has two computers with **free Internet access.** While the building nominally has free Wi-Fi, as well, it's difficult to get a signal inside; surprisingly, you might have better luck picking up the signal in the park just outside.

GETTING THERE
By Air
From the small **Kingston/Norman Rogers Airport** (YGK, www.kingstonairport.ca), eight kilometers (five miles) west of the city center, Air Canada (www.aircanada.com) flies to Toronto several times a day. The closest major international airports are in Ottawa (www. ottawa-airport.ca) and in Syracuse, New York (www.syrairport.org), although you have more flight options, and more direct transportation, through Toronto's Pearson airport (www.torontopearson.com). To travel between Ottawa airport and Kingston, you'll either need to rent a car or go from the airport to the train or bus station and then continue to Kingston on VIA Rail or by the Greyhound bus service.

Coach Canada (800/461-7661, www.coachcanada.com) runs several daily buses between Toronto Pearson Airport and Kingston (3.5–4 hours, one-way adults $59, seniors and students $53, kids 2–11 $30). You can get on or off either at the main bus terminal (1175 John Counter Blvd., 613/547-4916) or on the Queen's University campus (Goodes Hall, Union St.).

By Train
If you're coming to Kingston from another major Canadian city, the train is a convenient option, since VIA Rail's Toronto–Ottawa and Toronto–Montreal trains both stop at the

Kingston Train Station (1800 John Counter Blvd., 888/842-7245, www.viarail.ca). The station is 6.5 kilometers (four miles) northwest of downtown. It's a short cab ride, or you can take Kingston Transit Bus #18.

By Bus
From the **Kingston Inter-City Bus Terminal** (1175 John Counter Blvd., 613/547-4916), **Greyhound** (800/661-8747, www.greyhound. ca) operates several daily buses to Ottawa (2.75 hours; one-way adults $34–45, seniors $29–42, students $23, kids 2–11 $26–35). **Megabus** (705/748-6411 or 800/461-7661, www.megabus.com) runs buses throughout the day between Kingston and Toronto (2.75–3 hours, one-way $25–38) and from Kingston to Montreal (3–3.25 hours, one-way $25–38).

From the bus terminal to downtown (five kilometers, or three miles), either take a cab or catch Kingston Transit Bus #2 or 18.

By Car
Kingston is 265 kilometers (165 miles) east of Toronto, via Highway 401. If you're coming from the west, the easiest way to reach downtown Kingston is to take Exit 615 and follow Sir John A. Macdonald Boulevard south for about six kilometers (3.7 miles). Turn left onto King Street, which will pass the Queen's University campus and continue toward downtown.

From Ottawa, which is 195 kilometers (123 miles) northeast of Kingston, the fastest route is to follow Highway 416 south to Highway 401 west. Exit the 401 at Highway 15 (Exit 623) and continue south to Highway 2. Turn right (west) onto Highway 2. You'll pass Fort Henry and then cross the bridge into downtown Kingston.

GETTING AROUND
You can explore Kingston without a car, since the city's downtown core is compact and easy to walk around. You can also walk from the Queen's University campus to downtown (about 1.5 kilometers, or 0.9 mile). If you do have a car, you might want to leave it at your hotel when you're exploring downtown, since

parking can be somewhat limited in the downtown core.

The city has a public bus system, **Kingston Transit** (www.cityofkingston.ca, adults $2.50, seniors and kids 6–18 $2.25), which can take you to most visitor destinations. Use the "Trip Planner" feature on their website to plot your route.

Walking Tours

Kingston writer Arthur Milnes, in partnership with the city of Kingston, created a one-hour, self-guided walking tour, **In Sir John A.'s Footsteps,** highlighting sights important to the city during the time that Sir John A. Macdonald, Canada's first Prime Minister, lived and worked here. You can download MP3 audio files of the narration accompanying the tour from the City of Kingston website (www.cityofkingston.ca), and you can even choose your narrators: one tour features former Canadian prime minister Jean Chrétien and former speaker of the House of Commons Peter Milliken, while another version is narrated by hockey players Don Cherry and Jim Dorey. Or pick up an audio player preloaded with the tour from the Kingston Visitor Information Centre (209 Ontario St.).

If you prefer a human guide, Milne also leads tours himself. Tours (adults $6, seniors and kids $4, families $14) depart from the Visitor Centre at 11:30 A.M. and 1 P.M. in July and August.

The visitor center can also give you pamphlets for several other self-guided historic walking tours around town.

Boat Tours

If you want to see Kingston's sights from the water, take one of the **1000 Islands Cruises** (1 Brock St., 613/549-5544 or 800/848-0011, www.1000islandscruises.ca, early May–mid-Oct., call or check website for schedules) that depart from the pier at the foot of Brock Street, near Confederation Park. The 90-minute "Discovery Cruises" (adults $24.50, kids $12.25) will introduce you to local history while cruising along the waterfront from Fort

Henry to the Kingston Penitentiary. The three-hour "Heart of the Islands" trip combines a Kingston waterfront tour with a cruise around the westernmost 1000 Islands.

Food Tours

Young entrepreneur and recent Queen's grad Julia Segal launched **Kingston By Fork** (613/888-2327, www.kingstonbyfork.com, June–mid-Sept., call or check website for tour schedule). This food-tour company introduces visitors to the flavors of Segal's adopted hometown. She leads two different food walks, "A Taste of the World" (adults $20, seniors and students $15, kids $10), a two-hour sampling tour with stops at local shops for chocolate, cheese, Italian food, Indian snacks, and more, and a three-hour "Homegrown Eats Tour" (adults $35, seniors and students $30, kids $20), a guided local food walk through the Kingston Public Market and some downtown food venues, followed by lunch at a local restaurant. Reservations are recommended.

VICINITY OF KINGSTON
Wolfe Island

Wolfe Island (www.wolfeisland.com) is an easy day trip from Kingston. The island measures 32 kilometers (20 miles) long, and up to 11 kilometers (seven miles) wide, and is the largest of the Thousand Islands. You can see the island's wind turbines as you look across Kingston harbor.

Most day-trippers head to the beach at **Big Sandy Bay** (www.bigsandybay.ca, 9 A.M.–7 P.M. daily July–Sept., Sat.–Sun. mid-May–June, adults $8, children 6–17 $3) on the southwest corner of the island. It's a 1.3-kilometer (0.8-mile) walk from the parking area to the beach. Bicycles aren't allowed on the walking trail, so cyclists must lock their bikes at the trail gatehouse. The beach is open year-round, but staffed only during the summer; in the off-season, leave a donation in the box on the trail gate.

Bicycling is a popular way to tour the island. You can rent a bike from **Cycle Wolfe Island** (37 Leander St., Marysville, 613/329-5805, http://cyclewolfeisland.blogspot.com/, $15–25), located three blocks from the ferry dock. Cycle Wolfe Island accepts advance reservations by phone or email (cyclewolfeisland@gmail.com). The Wolfe Island website (www.wolfeisland. com) includes a map of island cycling routes.

The Wolfe Island Business and Tourism Association runs a seasonal **Tourist Information Centre** (Main St., Marysville, 613/385-1875, www.wolfeisland.com, May–Oct.) that can help you get oriented. The 20-minute **Wolfe Island Ferry** (www.wolfeisland.com, free) transports passengers, bicycles, and cars between Kingston (Ontario St., at Barrack St.) and the island year-round. There's also a seasonal car ferry from the United States, leaving from Cape Vincent, New York (www.hornesferry.com, May–Oct.); passports are required.

Frontenac Provincial Park

You don't have to venture far from Kingston to get out into the wilderness. The 5,200 hectares (12,849 acres) of Frontenac Provincial Park (1090 Salmon Lake Rd., Sydenham, 613/376-3489, www.ontarioparks.com or www.frontenacpark. ca, $14/vehicle) begin less than an hour's drive north of the city. Situated on the southernmost projection of the Canadian Shield, Frontenac has a northern Ontario landscape that doesn't require a long trek to the north. It's a popular spot for **day-hiking,** with more than 160 kilometers (100 miles) of trails ranging in length from 1.5 to 21 kilometers (0.9–13 miles).

The 22 lakes in the park make for good canoeing, too. Although rentals aren't available in the park, you can rent a canoe from nearby outfitters such as **Frontenac Outfitters** (6674 Bedford Rd., Sydenham, 613/376-6220 or 800/250-3174, www.frontenac-outfitters.com, 9 A.M.–5 P.M. Mon.–Fri., 8:30 A.M.–5 P.M. Sat.–Sun., Apr.–Oct., $37–45/day), south of the park entrance.

If you want to work on your outdoor skills, park staff offer a series of **wilderness skills workshops** year-round, including kayaking, snowshoeing, fishing, wilderness navigation, winter camping, and more. For some workshops, there's no fee beyond the park admission, while others may have an added charge.

Frontenac has no car camping sites, but there are 48 back-country **campsites** (adults $11.75, kids 6–17 $5) throughout the park, accessible either on foot or by canoe. Reservations are recommended on weekends from May to October; contact the Ontario Parks Reservations Service (888/668-7275, www.ontarioparks.com, booking fee online/phone $8.50/9.50).

The park entrance is north of the village of Sydenham, 40 kilometers (25 miles) north of Kingston. From Kingston, take Sydenham Road/Frontenac County Road 9 north for about 20 kilometers (12.5 miles). Turn left onto County Road 5 into Sydenham and watch for the park sign on your right, directing you to County Road 19. From here, it's a winding 13-kilometer (eight-mile) drive to Salmon Lake Road, which enters the park.

The Thousand Islands and the St. Lawrence

The region known as the Thousand Islands extends roughly 80 kilometers (50 miles) from Kingston to Brockville, straddling both sides of the St. Lawrence River, which divides Canada and the United States. The "Thousand Islands" is more of an estimate; officially, this area has 1,864 islands. On some islands, you'll see a single home or cottage, while others support year-round communities. To be counted among the Thousand Islands, an island must

be above water year-round and have at least two living trees. Two-thirds of the islands are in Canadian waters, although the overall area of the Thousand Islands is split equally between Canada and the United States.

The Thousand Islands are part of the Frontenac Arch Biosphere Reserve (www.explorethearch.ca), a United Nations designation designed to protect and promote "globally significant ecological features." The Biosphere

Reserve is a 270,000-hectare (667,000-acre) region, rather than a single "sight," bounded roughly by the towns of Gananoque, Brockville, and Westport, and the area surrounding Frontenac Provincial Park. The Frontenac Arch's significant feature is a ridge of ancient granite that's part of the Canadian Shield, more commonly associated with the rugged landscape of the Canadian north than with southern Ontario's flatter topography.

Long part of traditional Iroquois and Mohawk territory, the region along the St. Lawrence River's northern banks has linked its fortunes to U.S.–Canadian relations. During and after the American Revolution in the late 1700s,

"loyalists" (American colonists who remained loyal to the British crown) fled across the border into Canada. Many of these loyalists settled along the St. Lawrence in towns like Brockville, Prescott, and Morrisburg, which still have historic sites reflecting the loyalist legacy.

GANANOQUE AND VICINITY

The town of Gananoque—pronounced "Gan-uh-NOCK-way"—is the gateway to the region known as the Thousand Islands. You can learn more about the history of the area at the small **Arthur Child Heritage Museum** (125 Water St., Gananoque, 613/382-2535 or 877/217-7391, www.1000islandsheritagemuseum.

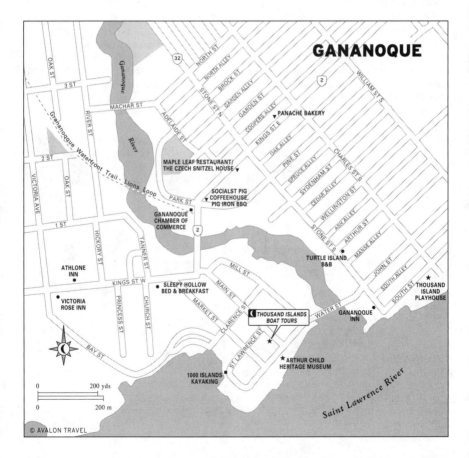

com, 10 A.M.–8 P.M. daily late June–Aug., 10 A.M.–4 P.M. daily late Apr.–late June and Sept.–Oct., admission by donation) near the waterfront, where the exhibits trace the region's development from its original First Nations settlers to the War of 1812 to the "Golden Age" of the Thousand Islands in the late 1800s, when the region became a popular tourist destination for wealthy Americans.

For views across the Thousand Islands, ride the elevator to the top of the **1000 Islands Skydeck** (Hill Island, www.1000islandsskydeck.com, 9 A.M.–8 P.M. summer, 9 A.M.–6 P.M. spring and fall; adults $9.75, kids 6–12 $5.75), which has three observation levels. The Skydeck, on Hill Island, is located between the Canadian and U.S. spans of the 1000 Islands International Bridge, 20 kilometers (12.5 miles) east of Gananoque and 40 kilometers (25 miles) west of Brockville. It's in Canadian territory, so you don't need your passport if you're coming from the Ontario side. From Highway 401, take Exit 661 (Bridge to USA/Hill Island). If you're coming from the

U.S. side, follow I-81 to the bridge and clear Canadian customs (remember your passport!), and you'll see the Skydeck on your right.

◖ Thousand Islands Boat Tours

The best way to appreciate the Thousand Islands is from the water. The **Gananoque Boat Line** (280 Main St., Gananoque, 613/382-2144 or 888/717-4837, www.ganboatline.com, May–mid-Oct.) operates one-, 2.5-hour, and five-hour cruises around the islands, leaving from the Gananoque waterfront. Gananoque Boat Lines' one-hour trips (10:30 A.M., noon, 1:30 P.M., 3 P.M., 4:30 P.M., and 7 P.M. late June–early Sept., call for spring and fall schedule; adults $20, seniors $17, kids 6–12 $11) are primarily nature tours, cruising around some of the islands closest to shore, with commentary about their flora and fauna.

The 2.5-hour tours (9:30 A.M., 11 A.M., 12:30 P.M., 2 P.M., 3:30 P.M., and 5 P.M. late June–early Sept.; call for spring and fall schedule; adults $30, seniors $25, kids 6–12 $11) include recorded commentary about the

The best way to see the Thousand Islands is on a boat tour.

© CAROLYN B. HELLER

history and development of the islands, giving you a more detailed picture of who has lived on various islands, past and present. These tours cruise past, but don't stop at, Boldt Castle.

BOLDT CASTLE

A highlight is a visit to Boldt Castle (Heart Island, New York, www.boldtcastle.com, 10 A.M.–7:30 P.M. daily late June–early Sept., 10 A.M.–6:30 P.M. early May–late June and early Sept.–early Oct., 10 A.M.–5:30 P.M. early/mid-Oct., adults $7, kids 6–12 $4.50). George C. Boldt, owner of New York City's Waldorf Astoria Hotel, began constructing the grandiose 120-room stone castle in 1900 in honor of his wife, Louise. For several years, a crew of more than 300 worked on building the castle. Unfortunately, Louise died suddenly in 1904, and George ordered that all work be halted. He never returned to the property. The castle was abandoned until 1977, when the Thousand Islands Bridge Authority acquired and began restoring the property, which is now available for tours.

The **Gananoque Boat Line**'s Boldt Castle tours (5 hours, adults $36, seniors $32, kids 6–12 $11) depart the Gananoque docks daily at 10 A.M. and 3 P.M. late June–early September, and on Saturdays and Sundays only from late May to late June and early September through early October. The cruise includes a two-hour stopover at Boldt Castle. Admission to Boldt Castle is not included in the boat tour prices.

If you want to tour Boldt Castle but you're short on time, trips run by the **Rockport Boat Line** (23 Front St., Rockport, 613/659-3402 or 800/563-8687, www.rockportcruises.com, daily late June–early Sept., San.–Sun only late May–late June and early Sept.–mid-Oct.; adults $32, seniors $28, kids 5–12 $12) take 3.5 hours, including two hours to explore the castle. They depart from the town of Rockport, which is closer to the castle, 19 kilometers (12 miles) east of Gananoque. Departures from Rockport are generally at 10:30 A.M., 12:30 P.M., and 2:30 P.M., but call to confirm any seasonal variations. Rockport Boat

Line offers a variety of shorter island cruises, as well.

Note that Heart Island, where Boldt Castle is located, is in the United States. Coming from Canada, you're crossing an international border and *you must have a valid passport.*

Sports and Recreation

A fun way to explore the Thousand Islands is by kayak, and **1000 Islands Kayaking** (110 Kate St., Gananoque, 613/329-6265, www.1000ikc.com, May–Oct., half-day/full-day single $35/55, tandem $55/70) rents kayaks to head out on your own or take a guided trip (half-day, adults $85, kids $45; full-day, adults $135, kids $65). They'll tailor an excursion to your interests and abilities, whether you want to learn about the history or natural life of the islands or get a good workout. They accept walk-ins, but if you have specific interests or requests, give them a call in advance.

Entertainment and Events

From May through October, the well-regarded **Thousand Islands Playhouse** (185 South St., 613/382-7020 or 866/382-7020, www.1000islandsplayhouse.com), a professional company established in 1982, presents 7–10 plays in repertory in two riverfront theaters. The deck of the Springer Theatre, overlooking the river, must be one of the prettiest theater lobbies anywhere.

Accommodations

Gananoque has several inns and B&Bs in historic buildings around the center of town. If you're looking for chain motels, they're jumbled together on King Street East.

In many First Nations legends, North America was called "Turtle Island." Ted and Chris, owners of the **Turtle Island B&B** (415 Stone St. S., 613/382-7261 or 855/382-7261, www.turtleislandbb.com, $109 d), chose this name for their relaxed lodging, where they display their collection of aboriginal arts and crafts. The three guest rooms in this 1922 brick Victorian are simple but cozy, with quilt-topped beds and First Nations prints on the walls. Ted's

© CAROLYN B. HELLER

The Victoria Rose Inn is one of Gananoque's many historic lodgings.

other venture is a brewery, so one of his breakfast specialties is waffles made with beer!

It's easy to spot the **Sleepy Hollow Bed & Breakfast** (95 King St. W., 613/382-4377 or 866/426-7422, www.sleepyhollowbb.ca, $100–170 d), a Victorian "painted lady" decked out in yellow, purple, and green. This rambling 1905 home still has its original tin ceiling and oak wainscoting on the first floor. Upstairs, the seven guest rooms are homey and a bit old-fashioned, with period furnishings. There's a pool table for guests, and you can make yourself at home in the octagonal dining room, where owners Don and Marion Matthews serve a full hot breakfast.

Jason and Miranda McMillan (he's the chef, she's the innkeeper) are the enthusiastic young owners of the **Athlone Inn** (250 King St. W., 613/382-3822 or 888/382-7122, www.athloneinn.ca, $120–200 d), a nine-room lodging and restaurant in a stately 1877 brick villa. Furnished with antiques, three of the rooms in the main inn have original marble fireplaces, and the fourth is a two-bedroom suite

that could accommodate two couples or a family (with well-behaved kids). Five additional rooms in the "Cottage Suites" (a 1940s brick addition) are simpler, and more, well, cottagey. The restaurant (dinner from 5 P.M. Tues.–Sun. mid-May–mid-Oct., Thurs.–Sun. mid-Oct.–mid-May, $21–32) serves updated French fare; the menu might include filet mignon with grilled asparagus, pork tenderloin served on a Gruyère polenta cake, or pickerel paired with quinoa and a salad of baby sprouts.

Imagine having this grand brick mansion, surrounded by gardens, as your summer home. Built in 1872, the **Victoria Rose Inn** (279 King St. W., 613/382-3368 or 888/246-2893, www.victoriaroseinn.com, May–Oct., $159–265 d) was originally the summer residence of Gananoque's first mayor. The main level has high ceilings, arched windows, and its original oak floor, as well as three guest rooms; the remaining nine stylish guest units (some with fireplaces) are on the second and third floors, furnished with antiques and creamy beige linens. If you've always wanted to bathe in a turret, book the Tower Suite, with a whirlpool tub in the top-floor tower. Rates include a full breakfast and Wi-Fi.

Gananoque's only waterfront hotel is the **Gananoque Inn** (550 Stone St. S., 613/382-2165 or 888/565-3101, www.gananoqueinn.com, $209–400) with 53 rooms in several different buildings. If you want a water view, choose one of the traditional rooms in the 1896 main inn (some have verandas overlooking the water) or the more basic units in a motel-like block out back that are even closer to the river. The newer annex units are large and more upscale, some with whirlpool tubs and fireplaces, although only those on the upper floor have peek-a-boo water views. The small spa offers the expected range of massages, facials, and other treatments, and the inn has two restaurants: the more formal, riverview **Watermark** (daily July–Oct., Sat.–Sun. only Nov.–June, dinner $23–38) and the mellow **Muskie Jake's Tap and Grill** ($9–20).

Food

If you don't want to dine at one of the inns, wander along King Street East to find more casual eateries. You're also close enough to Kingston that you could head there for more dining choices.

Stop into **Panaché Bakery** (164 King St. E., Gananoque, 613/382-1412, www.panachebakery.ca, 9 A.M.–5:30 P.M. Mon.–Sat.) for breakfast, a light lunch, or a snack. They bake fresh muffins (try the cranberry walnut), scones, mini quiche, and breads, and they make up a few sandwiches, too.

Get a cup of coffee or a glass of wine and check your email (there's free Wi-Fi) at the quirky **Socialist Pig Coffeehouse** (21 King St. E., Gananoque, 613/583-2199, www.axleworks.info; 7 A.M.–10 P.M. Mon.–Thurs., 7 A.M.–11 P.M. Fri., 8 A.M.–11 P.M. Sat., 8 A.M.–11 P.M. Sun. in summer; call for off-season hours), where several of the tables are made from old suitcases.

The same owners run the adjacent **Pig Iron Barbecue** (613/463-8800, call for seasonal hours, $8–16), a super-casual, order-at-the-counter joint, dishing out hearty portions of smoked ribs, brisket, chicken, and pulled pork that you eat at the picnic tables out on the deck (there are a few tables inside, too). Grab a lemonade, a sweet tea, or a beer to wash it down.

Part Canadian diner and part Eastern European schnitzel parlor, the homey **Maple Leaf Restaurant/The Czech Snitzel House** (65 King St. E., Gananoque, 613/382-7666, www.mapleleafrestaurant.ca, 4–9 P.M. Mon., 10:30 A.M.–9 P.M. Tues.–Fri., 10 A.M.–9 P.M. Sat.–Sun. May–mid-Oct.; 10:30 A.M.–9 P.M. Wed.–Fri., 10 A.M.–9 P.M. Sat.–Sun. mid-Oct.–late Dec., $7–20) serves homemade borscht, spaetzle, and delicious schnitzel (in either chicken or pork varieties), alongside burgers, omelets, and deli sandwiches.

Information and Services

The **Gananoque Chamber of Commerce and Visitors Services Centre** (10 King St. E., 613/382-3250 or 800/561-1595, www.1000islandsgananoque.com, 8 A.M.–8:30 P.M. daily in summer; 10 A.M.–4 P.M. Tues.–Fri., 10 A.M.–2 P.M. Sat. in winter) can provide information about the town and surrounding area.

The **1000 Islands International Tourism Council** (800/847-5263, www.visit1000islands.com) is another source of information about the islands on both the Canadian and U.S. sides of the border.

Getting There and Around

Gananoque is 30 kilometers (19 miles) east of Kingston, 290 kilometers (180 miles) northeast of Toronto and 160 kilometers (100 miles) south of Ottawa. If you're traveling east on Highway 401, take Exit 645 or 647; heading west, take Exit 645 or 648.

The prettiest route between Gananqoue and Brockville is the 52-kilometer (32-mile) Thousand Islands Parkway, which hugs the shore parallel to Highway 401. Note that the parkway is not the same road as Highway 2, which also parallels the 401.

While you don't need a car within Gananoque—it's a short walk between downtown, the waterfront, and many of the accommodations—there's no convenient bus or train service into town.

ST. LAWRENCE ISLANDS NATIONAL PARK

The first Canadian national park east of the Rockies, established in 1904, the St. Lawrence Islands National Park (613/923-5261 or 888/773-8888, www.pc.gc.ca, late May–mid-Oct.) includes more than 20 islands in the St. Lawrence River. There's no boat transportation to the islands, unfortunately (unless you have your own), but on the mainland, you can stop into the **Mallorytown Landing Visitor Centre** (1121 Thousand Islands Pkwy., Mallorytown, 613/923-5261, 10 A.M.–4 P.M. Sat.–Sun. late May–early June, 10 A.M.–4 P.M. Wed.–Mon. early June–early Sept.), between Gananoque and Brockville, to learn more about the natural and cultural history of the region. A short (1.7-kilometer, or 1.1-mile) walking trail starts at the Visitor Centre.

For additional hiking options, head to the park's Jones Creek area, east of the Visitor Centre, off the Thousand Islands Parkway. West of the Visitor Centre (closer to Gananoque), you can hike at the **Landon Bay Centre** (302 Thousand Islands Parkway, 613/382-2719, www.landonbay.org).

BROCKVILLE AND VICINITY

As you wander through the town of Brockville, on the St. Lawrence River at the east end of the Thousand Islands, you'll notice a number of grand Victorian homes, though none is grander than the mansion that local resident George Fulford built at the turn of the 20th century.

◖ Fulford Place

Entrepreneur and politician George Taylor Fulford (1852–1905) made his fortune hawking "Pink Pills for Pale People." He had bought the rights to these pills, a simple iron supplement, for $53.01, and successfully marketed his wonder drug as he traveled the world in the late 1800s.

Fulford used the considerable proceeds to build Fulford Place (287 King St. E., 613/498-3003, www.heritagetrust.on.ca, adults $5, seniors, students, and kids 7 and older $4), an opulent 35-room Edwardian mansion overlooking the St. Lawrence River, where he lived with his wife Mary White Fulford (1856–1949) and their three children. The house was completed in 1901, but sadly, Fulford was able to enjoy the fruits of his labors for only a few years. In 1905, he became the first Canadian to die in an automobile accident.

The 1,900-square-meter (20,000-square foot) home is made of marble and filled with all sorts of sumptuous details—from Honduran mahogany ceilings, to silk wallpaper, to original stained-glass windows. Many of the furnishings on view belonged to the Fulford family. Frederick Law Olmsted, who designed New York's Central Park, landscaped the Fulford Place gardens.

Tours of Fulford Place run 11 A.M.–4 P.M. daily from late June through early September, and Tuesday through Sunday from late May through late June; the last tour departs at 3:10 P.M. The rest of the year, tours are available at 1 P.M. Tuesdays, Wednesdays, and Thursdays, and 11 A.M.–4 P.M. Saturdays and Sundays.

Fulford Place is just east of downtown Brockville on King Street, which becomes Highway 2 on either end of town.

Homewood Museum

One of the oldest houses in Ontario, a Georgian-style stone home built in 1799–1800, is now the Homewood Museum (Hwy. 2, Maitland, 613/498-3003, www.heritagetrust.on.ca, 10 A.M.–4 P.M. Wed.–Sun. mid-June–early Sept., adults $3, kids under 16 $1.50). Seven generations of the Jones family lived here, and unlike many historic homes, all the furnishings belonged to the family, from the four-poster bed, to the china and silver, to the early 19th-century surgical tools; the original owner, Solomon Jones (1756–1822), was a Loyalist and the area's first physician. Guides take you on 30–45-minute tours of the house.

The Homewood Museum is located just east

of the town of Maitland, between Brockville and Prescott. From Highway 401, take the Maitland exit and go south to Highway 2. Turn east onto Highway 2, and continue about two kilometers (1.25 miles) to the house. If you're also planning to visit Fulford Place, you can buy a $6 combination ticket that includes admission to both properties.

Many members of the Jones family are buried in the **Blue Church Cemetery,** where numerous graves date to the late 1700s and early 1800s. The cemetery is also the final resting place of Barbara Heck, a founder of the Methodist Church. You'll find the graveyard three kilometers (1.8 miles) east of Homewood, on Highway 2.

Sports and Recreation

Hundreds of ships were sunk in the St. Lawrence River over the past several centuries, and many of these wrecks are now accessible to scuba divers. **Dive Brockville** (12 Water St. E., 613/345-2800, www.divebrockville.com) can organize dives and supply you with gear.

Accommodations and Food

It's okay to sleep in church—at least if you're staying at the **Green Door Bed and Breakfast** (61 Buell St., 613/341-9325, www.greendoorbb. com, $105–125 d), a 1928 former Pentecostal tabernacle that owners and welcoming hosts Lynne and Peter Meleg converted into a funky B&B. The common spaces are striking, with 4.5-meter (15-foot) ceilings and original arched windows. The former altar is now a library, where they occasionally host small concerts, and guests gather in the airy dining space for full breakfasts that might include ricotta pancakes or poached eggs served on a bed of spinach. The three guest rooms on the main floor aren't large, but they're full of character. The Boathouse room has a ship-shape platform bunk and a second twin bed, while the Victorian-style Mrs. Brown's Chamber has a brass bed and clawfoot tub. Two lower-level rooms feel quiet and more modern (although less distinctive). The Pastor's Suite, in an adjacent 1890s house (connected to the main

building), is set up as a separate apartment, with a kitchen, living room with sofa bed, and bedroom, where the headboard is made from a former church pew.

Pick up a coffee and pastry at the long-standing **Tait's Bakery** (31 King St. W., 613/342-3567, www.taitsbakery.ca, 6:30 A.M.–5:30 P.M. Mon.–Wed., 6:30 A.M.–6 P.M. Thurs.–Fri., 7 A.M.–5 P.M. Sat. summer; call for winter hours). For a light lunch, try **Boboli** (32 King St. W., Brockville, 613/498-2957), which makes homemade soup and deli sandwiches on freshly baked bread.

At the **Georgian Dragon Tavern** (72 King St., 613/865-8224; 11 A.M.–11 P.M. Mon.–Thurs., 11 A.M.–2 A.M. Fri., 9 A.M.–2 A.M. Sat., 9 A.M.–11 P.M. Sun., $10–15), a traditional English pub, you can hang out over a beer, a burger, or a hearty Guinness pie. On weekends, they serve good-value breakfast specials.

Information and Services

For more information about the Brockville area, contact the **Brockville and District Chamber of Commerce Tourism Office** (10 Market St. W., 613/342-4357 or 888/251-7676, www. brockvilletourism.com, 8 A.M.–8 P.M. Mon.–Fri., 8 A.M.–4 P.M. Sat.–Sun. mid-June–early Sept; 9 A.M.–5 P.M. Mon.–Fri., 9 A.M.–3 P.M. Sat. early Sept.–mid-Oct.; 8:30 A.M.–4:30 P.M. Mon.–Fri. mid-Oct.–late May; 8 A.M.–5 P.M. daily late May–mid-June).

The **Brockville Public Library** (23 Buell St., 613/342-3936, www.brockvillelibrary.ca) has free Wi-Fi and Internet access.

Getting There and Around

Brockville is 55 kilometers (35 miles) northeast of Gananoque and 110 kilometers (68 miles) south of Ottawa, via Highway 401 or Highway 2.

VIA Rail trains (888/842-7245, www.viarail. ca) run to Brockville Station (141 Perth St.) from Toronto (3.25–3.75 hours; one-way adults $88–104, seniors $88–94, students $73, kids 2–11 $44–52), Kingston (0.75 hour; one-way adults $21–29, seniors $18–26, students $20, kids 2–11 $11–15), and Ottawa (1.25 hours, one-way adults

$27–37, seniors $23–33, students $26, kids 2–11 $14–19). The train station is about a kilometer (0.6 mile) northwest of downtown.

Megabus (705/748-6411 or 800/461-7661, www.megabus.com) stops in Brockville from Kingston (one hour, one-way $17–23), Montreal (2.5 hours, one-way $47), and Toronto (4 hours, $30–45). The bus drops you in the parking lot of the Food Basics store (3049 Jefferson Dr.), north of Highway 401, about two kilometers (1.2 miles) from downtown. Since the Megabus depot is on the north side of Highway 401, and downtown is on the south, take a cab rather than trying to walk.

It's easiest to explore the region if you have a car, but Brockville's downtown area is compact and walkable. Fulford Place is 1.5 kilometers (0.9 mile) east of downtown.

PRESCOTT

Settled by the British in 1787, the town of Prescott became a military post to defend Canada's border. Fort Wellington, now the **Fort Wellington National Historic Site** (370 Vankoughnet St., at King St., 613/925-2896, www.pc.gc.ca, 10 A.M.–5 P.M. daily late May–Sept., adults $3.90, seniors $3.40, kids 6–16 $1.90, families $9.80), was built during the War of 1812 to protect shipping routes along the St. Lawrence River from U.S. attack. Nowadays, guides in period costumes demonstrate 19th-century games, crafts, open-hearth cooking, and rifle and cannon handling. In summer, you can take a free guided tour of the fort (1:30 P.M. Sat.–Sun. July–Aug.), or an evening candlelight tour (8 P.M. Thurs. mid-July–mid-Aug., $4.90/person, reservations recommended). The fort is especially busy during **Prescott Loyalist Days** (613/925-3559, www.prescottloyalistdays. ca, August), a weekend-long event that includes military reenactments (including a mock battle for the kids), a parade, and fireworks.

MORRISBURG
◀ Upper Canada Village

Walk back into the 1860s when you enter the gates of Upper Canada Village (13740 County Rd. 2, 613/543-4328 or 800/437-2233, www.

uppercanadavillage.com, 9:30 A.M.–5 P.M. daily late May–early Sept., 9:30 A.M.–5 P.M. Wed.–Sun. early Sept.–mid-Oct.; adults $20.95, seniors $19.95, students 13–18 $13.95, kids 5–12 $11.95, kids 2–4 $3.95), one of Ontario's largest and best-preserved historic villages.

Not only do costumed interpreters staff all the village buildings, going about their business as 19th-century millers, shopkeepers, tavern-keepers, and bakers, they'll enthusiastically tell you about "their" life and work on the cusp of the Industrial Revolution, as Upper Canada was transforming from farm country to a more mechanized society. In the woolen mill, staff operate original carding and spinning machines, powered by a water turbine that replaced the "old" technology of the spinning wheel. In the grist mill, staff grind grains that the village bakers use to bake bread, and in the saw mill, they're splitting logs with their newfangled machines. There's a cheese factory and a school, a dressmaker and a village doctor, a tinsmith, a print shop, a blacksmith, a tavern, even a farm, complete with live animals.

Start by visiting the absorbing multimedia Discovery Centre, which puts the village into its historical context, with lots of video, audio, and high-tech displays. The story begins with the original First Nations inhabitants (you can listen to audio clips in the Mohawk language) and continues with the "loyalists" who settled here after the Revolutionary War in the United States. More exhibits explain the region's ongoing development from the Industrial Revolution into the 20th century.

Kids have plenty of special activities, too. They can dress in traditional garb, learn to milk a cow, and ride along the village canal on a horse-drawn barge.

The village is 110 kilometers (68 miles) northeast of Gananoque and 155 kilometers (96 miles) southwest of Montreal. From Highway 401, take exit 758 (Upper Canada Road), go south, then turn left on County Road 2. From there, it's two kilometers (1.25 miles) east to the village. You can also easily visit Upper Canada Village on a day trip from Ottawa, 80 kilometers (50 miles) to the

© CAROLYN B. HELLER

Explore life in the 1860s at Upper Canada Village.

northwest. Head south on Bank Street, which becomes Highway 31 and continues south all the way to the town of Morrisburg. Turn left (east) on County Road 2; the village is 11 kilometers (6.8 miles) to the east.

Upper Canada Bird Sanctuary

Every fall, thousands of geese pass through the Upper Canada Bird Sanctuary (County Rd. 2, Ingleside, 613/545-3704 or 800/437-2233, www.uppercanadabirdsanctuary.com, trails open year-round) as they migrate south for the winter. At this 9,000-hectare (22,000-acre) preserve of woods, marsh, pastures, and waterways, you might also see great blue heron, wild turkeys, hawks, ducks, and a wild variety of common and less common birds. Even if you're not a birder, the sanctuary is a pleasant for a walk or hike, with eight kilometers (five miles) of self-guided nature trails; in winter, the trails are open for cross-country skiing. The Visitor Centre (mid-May–late Oct.) has nature exhibits about the area.

The sanctuary is 14 kilometers (nine miles) east

of Morrisburg, off County Rd. 2, near Ingleside. From Highway 401, take Exit 758 or 770.

Entertainment and Events

While you're in town, take in a show at the **Upper Canada Playhouse** (12320 County Rd. 2, 613/543-3713 or 877/550-3650, www.uppercanadaplayhouse.com, Apr.–Dec.), a professional theater company that presents several comedies and other light plays every year. The theater is a former toothbrush factory.

Accommodations and Food

Sleep like a pioneer (but in more comfortable lodgings) at **Upper Canada Village** (613/543-4328 or 800/437-2233, www.uppercanadavillage.com). Montgomery House ($150/night), a 19th-century log cabin, looks rustic from the outside, but inside, between the log walls and wide pine floors, are comfy accommodations for a couple, a family, or a group of friends. The main floor has a living room with couches and a flat-screen TV, a double Murphy bed (that will fold into the wall when you're not using it), a fully equipped kitchen, and two bathrooms. Upstairs, in a dormitory-style space under the eaves, are six single beds. Linens are provided, but (since you're supposed to be a pioneer, after all), there's no Internet service. The larger "The Guest House" ($275/night) is a restored farmhouse with a main-floor living area, a country kitchen, a TV/DVD, and even a computer with Internet access and a washer/dryer. Upstairs, you can sleep eight in the three bedrooms.

Along County Road 2 near Upper Canada Village are a couple of basic motels, including the **Riverside Motel** (13339 County Rd. 2, 613/543-2162 or 877/885-5078, www.stayriverside.ca, $85–99).

About 10 kilometers (six miles) west of Upper Canada Village in the town of Morrisburg, you won't be roughing it at all if you stay at the lavishly decorated ◖ **Russell Manor B&B** (36 First St., 613/543-3871 or 866/401-7472, www.russellmanorbb.com, $115–140 s, $125–150 d). Owners Michael Burton (the interior decorator) and Ron Currie (the chef) have created an elegant, romantic retreat in their 1870s manor house that feels like a getaway with your cool urban friends. The three guest accommodations upstairs are all two-room suites with separate sitting areas, Victorian furnishings, voluminous draperies, and fine linens. On the main floor, in addition to the posh parlor with its cream-hued rugs and overstuffed sofas, is the **Manor Bistro** (dinner Thurs.–Sat., $19–27), where a menu of starters, three entrées, and a dessert or two are served in one of the extravagantly appointed rooms or secluded private nooks. The bistro is open to guests and nonguests; reservations are suggested.

Part curio store, part art gallery, and part old-time coffee shop, the **Basket Case Cafe** (27 Main St., 613/543-0002, 9 A.M.–6 P.M. Tues.–Sat., 9 A.M.–8 P.M. Fri., 10 A.M.–5 P.M. Sun., $5–7), in a strip mall on County Road 2, is as crammed with stuff as your grandmother's attic. But no matter, they'll cook up a tasty hot breakfast, bowl of soup, hearty sandwich, or slice of pie. If you can't decide between breakfast and lunch, try the breakfast sandwich, laden with eggs, bacon, cheese, and tomato.

CAMPING

The **St. Lawrence Parks Commission** (613/543-4328 or 800/437-2233, www.parks.on.ca), which operates Upper Canada Village and the Bird Sanctuary, also manages several campgrounds in the Morrisburg area. As a camper you'll receive discounts of 40 percent at Upper Canada Village and at Fort Henry in Kingston if you purchase your tickets at the same time as you make your camping reservations. Contact the Parks Commission or use their online reservation service to reserve a campsite (reservation fee $11.43).

The 301-site **Riverside-Cedar Campground** (13180 County Rd. 2, 613/543-3287, late May–mid-Oct., tent sites $29.25–31.25, electrical sites $34.50–38.25, cabins $85–95), along the St. Lawrence River, is closest to Upper Canada Village. Three cabins are available for rent. If you don't have your own tent or RV, you might consider the instant camping service ($36.95–39.95)—a pre-assembled tent that sleeps up to six on a raised wooden platform. You still need to bring sleeping bags or bed linens for both the cabins and the instant camping service, but it's much easier than pitching your own tent.

The 69-site **Upper Canada Migratory Bird Sanctuary Campground** (late May–mid-Oct., tent sites $31.25–33.25, electrical sites $36.25–39.75) is on the bird sanctuary grounds. Campsites have both water and electricity. The campground has showers, and there is a swimming beach along the river.

Getting There and Around

From Ottawa, County Road 31 runs 80 kilometers (50 miles) south to Morrisburg. Following the speedier Highway 416 to Highway 401 is longer (120 kilometers, or 75 miles), but it will take you about the same amount of time. Morrisburg is 140 kilometers (87 miles) northeast of Kingston, along Highway 401. **VIA Rail** (www.viarail.ca) trains from Toronto or Ottawa stop in Brockville (west of Morrisburg) and in Cornwall (east of Morrisburg), but you really need a car to get around the area.

GEORGIAN BAY AND COTTAGE COUNTRY

If you're looking for a getaway to the outdoors, whether to be soothed and healed or exhilarated by the adventure, head to Georgian Bay and Ontario's "Cottage Country."

The eastern finger of Lake Huron, Georgian Bay is 320 kilometers (200 miles) long and 80 kilometers (50 miles) wide, and it's surrounded by some of Ontario's most spectacular scenery. The Georgian Bay region has three national parks, several large provincial parks, dramatic rock formations, Caribbean-blue water, and a network of red-and-white lighthouses standing guard along the shore. There are ski slopes and canoe routes, as well as the world's longest freshwater beach, and offshore, the bay waters are dotted with more than 30,000 islands and some of the finest scuba diving in the north. The region is a hugely popular destination for hikers, too, since it contains the northern portions of the Bruce Trail, Canada's longest hiking route.

You won't want to miss the stunning Bruce Peninsula, with its unusual rock formations, offshore islands, and network of hiking trails. The Georgian Bay Islands National Park is the gateway to the 30,000 islands region, and splurging on a floatplane tour is a new level of thrill. Winter sports enthusiasts should head to the Blue Mountains, Ontario's top ski and snowboarding region. If you prefer history and culture with your outdoor adventures, the towns of Midland, Penetanguishene, and Parry Sound will oblige.

To escape the city's frenzy, many Torontonians head north to Cottage Country. Cottage Country begins just 100 kilometers (60 miles)

HIGHLIGHTS

LOOK FOR ◖ TO FIND RECOMMENDED SIGHTS, ACTIVITIES, DINING, AND LODGING.

◖ **Bruce Peninsula National Park:** This national park is among Ontario's most beautiful settings. Its intricate rock formations, turquoise waters, and more than 40 species of orchids draw hikers, kayakers, and other nature lovers (page 293).

◖ **The Bruce Trail:** This iconic Canadian hiking route stretches 845 kilometers (525 miles) from the Niagara region to the end of the Bruce Peninsula (page 294).

◖ **Fathom Five National Marine Park:** One of only three national marine conservation areas in Canada, this marine park is best known for its distinctive "flowerpot" rock formations. It also has some of the finest scuba diving in North America (page 297).

◖ **Sainte-Marie Among the Hurons:** This historic village "reimagines" the first European settlement in Ontario, where French Jesuits lived and worked with the native Wendat (Huron) people in the 1600s (page 316).

◖ **The Georgian Bay Islands National Park:** Of the thousands of islands that dot Georgian Bay, 63 are protected in this island national park. Visit for a day of hiking and swimming, or try an "all-inclusive" camping experience (page 321).

◖ **Flight-Seeing:** The most thrilling way to take in Georgian Bay's 30,000 Islands is on a floatplane tour. Soar above the bay by day or take a romantic sunset flight – complete with champagne (page 325).

◖ **Killbear Provincial Park:** This waterfront area near Parry Sound offers granite cliffs, sandy beaches, and a lovely destination for hiking, canoeing, swimming, and camping (page 327).

◖ **Canoeing in Algonquin Provincial Park:** Ontario's largest provincial park is one of the province's best destinations for canoeing, whether you're paddling on the numerous lakes and rivers or taking a multiday trip across the backcountry (page 347).

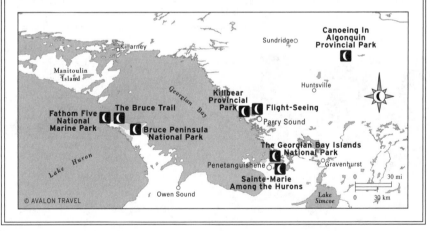

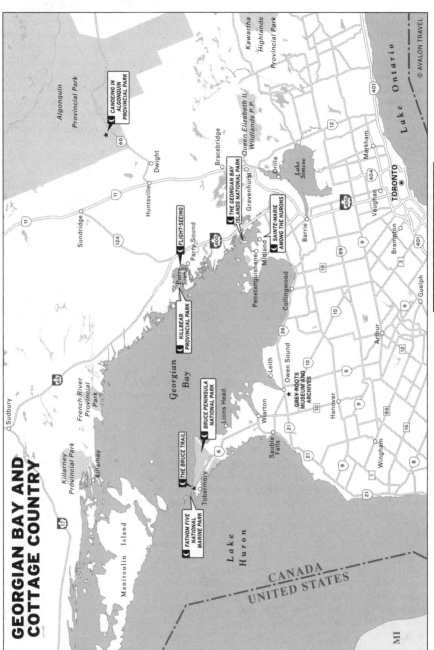

GEORGIAN BAY AND COTTAGE COUNTRY

GEORGIAN BAY

© AVALON TRAVEL

CANOEING IN ALGONQUIN PROVINCIAL PARK

FLIGHT-SEEING

THE GEORGIAN BAY ISLANDS NATIONAL PARK

SAINTE-MARIE AMONG THE HURONS

KILLBEAR PROVINCIAL PARK

BRUCE PENINSULA NATIONAL PARK

THE BRUCE TRAIL

FATHOM FIVE NATIONAL MARINE PARK

GREY ROOTS MUSEUM AND ARCHIVES

Algonquin Provincial Park

Kawartha Highlands Provincial Park

Queen Elizabeth II Wildlands P.P.

Lake Ontario

Dwight

Huntsville

Sundridge

Bracebridge

Gravenhurst

Orillia

Lake Simcoe

Markham

TORONTO

Vaughan

Brampton

Parry Sound

Penetanguishene

Midland

Barrie

Guelph

Collingwood

Owen Sound

Leith

Georgian Bay

Wiarton

Lions Head

Hanover

Arthur

Wingham

French River Provincial Park

Sudbury

Killarney Provincial Park

Killarney

Tobermory

Sauble Falls

Lake Huron

Manitoulin Island

CANADA
UNITED STATES

MI

GEORGIAN BAY AND COTTAGE COUNTRY

north of Toronto and includes Gravenhurst, Bracebridge, and Huntsville. Dotted with inland lakes, ski hills, and waterfront towns along Lake Muskoka and numerous smaller lakes, this region offers numerous opportunities for outdoor adventure and relaxation. Don't-miss attractions include Algonquin Provincial Park, one of Ontario's largest protected green spaces. Algonquin is one of the province's highlights; visit for a day or a week and take a short hike, paddle across an inland lake, or set out on a multiday wilderness adventure.

PLANNING YOUR TIME

This region is packed with outdoors highlights, but many attractions and services around Georgian Bay and Cottage Country don't begin operation till mid- or late May and close in mid-October after the Canadian Thanksgiving weekend. One exception is the Blue Mountains, which draws winter visitors for skiing and snowboarding.

For a long weekend, do a quick tour of the **Bruce Peninsula,** ski or snowboard at **Blue Mountain,** pair a visit to **Midland**'s historic sights with a day trip to the **Georgian Bay Islands National Park,** or base yourself in **Parry Sound** and explore the nearby provincial parks. A weekend trip could also take you to **Algonquin** for a relaxing getaway to the Muskokas.

You can easily spend a week exploring the Bruce Peninsula, particularly if you want to hike sections of the Bruce Trail or scuba-dive in the **Fathom Five National Marine Park.** Between May and October, a ferry runs between the Bruce Peninsula and **Manitoulin Island,** for further exploration.

The Bruce Peninsula

From limestone cliffs to crystal blue waters to forested hiking trails and even a wide variety of orchids, the Bruce Peninsula's striking natural scenery is the main reason to visit this finger of land that juts out between Lake Huron and Georgian Bay. The must-see attractions are its two national parks—The Bruce Peninsula National Park and Fathom Five National Marine Park—located at the peninsula's north end, around the town of Tobermory. Yet beyond these natural attractions, it's the friendly, low-key atmosphere that draws vacationers. Though the region attracts plenty of visitors, it hasn't lost its small-town warmth, with people greeting each other on the street and on the trail.

For pre-trip research, check out the detailed **County of Bruce Tourism website** (www.explorethebruce.com), which lists vast amounts of information about the Bruce Peninsula and surrounding communities. Also pick up the extremely useful **Grey-Bruce Official Visitor Map** (www.explorethebruce.com) at information centers around the region; it shows both major and minor roads across the peninsula.

TOBERMORY

To explore the Bruce Peninsula National Park and the Fathom Five National Marine Park, it's most convenient to base yourself in Tobermory, a pretty waterfront town at the northern tip of the Bruce Peninsula. Highway 6, the peninsula's main north–south road, ends in Tobermory.

National Park Visitor Centre

Start your visit at the National Park Visitor Centre (120 Chi Sin Tib Dek Rd., 519/596-2233, www.pc.gc.ca, adults $5.80, seniors $4.90, children $2.90), which has information about both Bruce Peninsula National Park and Fathom Five National Marine Park. You can watch a short film about the area's highlights and explore exhibits about the local ecology. In summer, a variety of interpretive programs, including guided hikes and children's activities, are offered; schedules are posted online at the

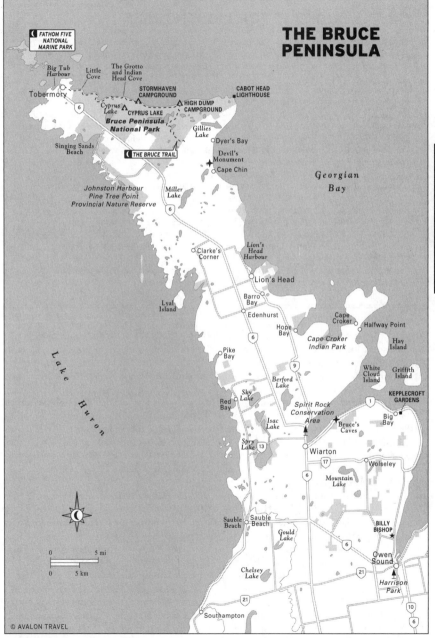

THE BRUCE PENINSULA

FATHOM FIVE NATIONAL MARINE PARK

Big Tub Harbour

Little Cove

The Grotto and Indian Head Cove

STORMHAVEN CAMPGROUND

CABOT HEAD LIGHTHOUSE

Tobermory

Cyrus Lake

CYPRUS LAKE

HIGH DUMP CAMPGROUND

Bruce Peninsula National Park

Gillies Lake

Singing Sands Beach

THE BRUCE TRAIL

Dyer's Bay

Devil's Monument

Cape Chin

Georgian Bay

Johnston Harbour Pine Tree Point Provincial Nature Reserve

Miller Lake

Clarke's Corner

Lion's Head Harbour

Lion's Head

Lyal Island

Barro Bay

Edenhurst

Cape Croker

Halfway Point

Lake Huron

Hope Bay

Cape Croker Indian Park

Hay Island

Pike Bay

White Cloud Island

Griffith Island

Berford Lake

Sky Lake

KEPPLECROFT GARDENS

Red Bay

Isac Lake

Spirit Rock Conservation Area

Big Bay

Spry Lake

Bruce's Caves

Wiarton

Wolseley

Mountain Lake

Sauble Beach

Sauble Beach

BILLY BISHOP

Gould Lake

Owen Sound

Chelsey Lake

Harrison Park

Southampton

0   5 mi

0   5 km

© AVALON TRAVEL

GEORGIAN BAY

ON THE LOOKOUT FOR LIGHTHOUSES

What is it about lighthouses that draw people like a beacon? If you're a lighthouse lover, the Lake Huron and Georgian Bay coasts are prime territory for lighthouse touring. Many of the region's lighthouses were built in the mid- to late 1800s or early 1900s during the heyday of Great Lakes shipping.

On Lake Huron, visit the **Chantry Island Light** (www.chantryisland.com) near Southampton and the **Kincardine Lighthouse** (www.sunsets.com), a lighthouse-turned-museum just a short walk from Kincardine's downtown. The Bruce Peninsula has several lighthouses, including the **Big Tub Lighthouse** in Tobermory, the **Cabot Head Lighthouse and Museum** (www.cabothead.ca), the **Lion's Head Lighthouse** on Lion's Head Beach, and the **Cape Croker Lighthouse** at the tip of Cape Crocker, a First Nations reserve. On Flowerpot Island in the Fathom Five National Marine Park, you can visit the **Flow-**erpot Island Lightstation. One of the most picturesque light stations is the **Killarney East Lighthouse,** on the bay near Killarney Provincial Park.

Today the lonely job of lighthouse keeper has generally gone the way of the dodo bird, as most lighthouse operations are now computerized. For a glimpse of old-fashioned lighthouse-keeping life, book a stay at **Cabot Head Lighthouse** (www.cabothead.ca), where you can spend a week as part of the assistant lightkeeper's program (late May–mid-Oct.). It's a working holiday where you help greet visitors to the lighthouse, assist in the gift shop, and pitch in with some housekeeping duties. For reservations, contact the **Friends of Cabot Head** (mailing address: P.O. Box 233, Lion's Head, ON, N0H 1W0; email cabothead@hotmail.com). The lighthouse stays are quite popular, so make your plans well in advance.

center and on the Friends of the Bruce District Parks Association (www.castlebluff.com). If you plan to camp on Flowerpot Island in the Fathom Five Marine Park, or to scuba-dive in any of the park territory, you must register at the Visitor Centre before heading out.

The Visitor Centre is the northernmost point on the Bruce Trail. Check out the "sculpture" made from hikers' worn boots in the lobby and the **Bruce Trail Cairn** out front marking the end of the Bruce Trail. If you've hiked the entire trail, this is the spot to take your photo. Two hiking trails start at the center. It's an easy 800-meter (half-mile) walk to the **Little Dunks Bay Lookout.** The 3.5-kilometer (two-mile) **Burnt Point Loop Trail** meanders through the forest to Georgian Bay, where you can look out over the Fathom Five islands. Near the Visitor Centre is a 20-meter (65-foot) **Lookout Tower.** Climb the 112 steps for views out across the peninsula and the nearby islands.

Visitor Centre hours vary seasonally. From mid-July through early September, the center is open daily 8 A.M.–8 P.M. (and until 9 P.M. on Fri.). From early September through mid-October, hours are 10 A.M.–6 P.M. Sunday through Friday and 8 A.M.–6 P.M. Saturday. For the rest of the year, the center is open 10 A.M.–4 P.M. Tuesday through Saturday. The Visitor Centre is located under a 10-minute walk from Tobermory's Little Tub Harbour along a flat, partly paved section of the Bruce Trail. By car, look for the park sign on Highway 6, just south of town.

Little Tub Harbour

Most of Tobermory's shops and services are clustered around Little Tub Harbour. Boats to the Fathom Five islands leave from Little Tub, as do a variety of sightseeing cruises (mid-May–mid-Oct.) around Tobermory and the Fathom Five islands.

The two-hour Great Blue Heron glass bottom boat tour, run by **Blue Heron Tours** (Little Tub Harbour, 519/596-2999, www.blue-heronco.com, adults $35.31, seniors $33.37, children 4–12 $25.76), sails around Russel Island, Cove Island, the Otter Islands, and Flowerpot Island. You can do this two-hour tour as a sunset cruise for the same price.

G+S Watersports (8 Bay St. South, 519/596-2200, www.gswatersports.net) also offers sightseeing cruises. They run a two-hour Flowerpot Island Cruise ($25), a two-hour Cove Island Lighthouse Tour (also $25), and a 45-minute Sweepstakes Tour($15) to see the shipwrecks in Big Tub Harbour.

Big Tub Harbour

Tobermory has a second port area, known as Big Tub Harbour. The first lighthouse at Big Tub was constructed in 1885 to guide ships safely into port. The present-day **Big Tub Lighthouse,** a hexagonal tower that was automated in 1952, still performs that role at the harbor's mouth. The lighthouse isn't open to the public, but you can walk around the exterior and along the rocky shore. You can also swim or snorkel here.

The remains of two 19th-century ships lie in the shallow water of Big Tub Harbour. The *Sweepstakes,* a two-masted schooner, ran aground near Cove Island Lighthouse in 1885; the boat was towed to Big Tub Harbour, where it sank. The steamer *City of Grand Rapids* caught fire in 1907 while docked in Little Tub Harbour. The boat was towed out of the harbor to prevent the fire from spreading to other nearby ships; the burning ship then drifted into Big Tub Harbour and sank there.

You can see the shipwrecks on one of the boat tours out of Tobermory or on several of the Flowerpot Island boats. Scuba diving is allowed around the wrecks, but only at designated times, since boat traffic in the area can be heavy. Check with the National Park Visitor Centre (519/596-2233, www.pc.gc.ca) for details.

Entertainment and Shopping

Looking for a unique way to spend an evening? Storytellers Leslie Robbins-Conway and Paul Conway open their home to visitors as hosts of **Voyageur Storytelling: Country Supper**

Storytelling Concerts (56 Brinkman's Rd., Miller Lake, 519/795-7477, www.voyageurstorytelling.ca, Tues.–Sat., mid-June–early Sept., adults $46, seniors and students $42, children $36), pairing a multicourse home-cooked meal with a storytelling performance.

At the annual **Orchid Festival** (www.orchidfest.ca, late May), you can join guided orchid-viewing walks, take flower drawing or photography workshops, or learn more about the peninsula's orchid population. Check the website for a schedule, or stop into festival headquarters at the Bruce Peninsula National Park Visitor Centre (120 Chi Sin Tib Dek Rd., Tobermory, 519/596-2233).

Most of the shops around Little Tub Harbour sell T-shirts and other ordinary souvenirs. One exception is **Circle Arts** (14 Bay St., 519/596-2541, www.circlearts.com) and its sister location, **Circle Arts Too** (10 Bay St., 519/596-2543). These fine-art galleries showcase prints, paintings, sculpture, photographs, jewelry, textiles, one-of-a-kind furniture, and other works crafted by Canadian artists, many of whom have ties to the Bruce Peninsula. You might find everything from a $15 ceramic candleholder to a $20,000 painting. Both galleries are open mid-May to mid-October.

Accommodations

A number of motels and B&Bs are clustered around, or within walking distance of, Little Tub Harbour. Other accommodations dot Highway 6 south of town; if you don't want to take your car everywhere, try to stay near the harbor. In July and August, and on holiday weekends, even basic motel rooms go for over $100 per night; it's a good idea to book in advance, or at least arrive early in the day. The **Tobermory Chamber of Commerce** (www.tobermory.org) has a list of local accommodations on its website.

Inside this nondescript vinyl-sided house about a 15-minute walk from Little Tub Harbour is the surprisingly stylish **Molinari's B&B** (68 Water Dr., 877/596-1228, www.themolinaris.com, $115–125 d). The three contemporary guest rooms are done in richly hued textiles and outfitted with microwaves, fridges, coffeemakers, and small flat-screen TVs. Guests take their breakfast in the sleek industrial kitchen; there's no other common space, though, so it's not a sit-around-and-chat kind of lodging. Owners Maria and Bob, who relocated from Montreal after falling in love with the Bruce Peninsula during scuba-diving visits here, also run **Molinari's Espresso Bar and Italian Restaurant** (53 Bay St., 519/596-1228) in town. The B&B is open year-round; the restaurant is open May through October.

The friendly **Blue Bay Motel** (32 Bay St., 519/596-2392, www.bluebay-motel.com, May–mid-Oct., $130–160 d), right above Little Tub Harbour, has 16 basic but comfortable rooms with fridges and coffeemakers; the best are the renovated ones with more modern linens and wood floors, or the second-floor units with water views (the first-floor rooms face the parking lot). There's also a large three-bedroom suite with a full kitchen.

The **Maple Golf Inn** (22 Maple Golf Crescent, 519/596-8166, www.maplegolfinn.ca, $100–125 d, $145–175 suite), in a suburban home about a 10-minute drive south of Tobermory, is popular with hikers, since there's an access point to the Bruce Trail nearby. On the main floor are two comfortable rooms decorated in a modern country style, with quilts, wood floors, and private baths. Hosts Jill and Lawrence Stewart serve a full English breakfast, and guests can lounge in the living room, which looks onto the Cornerstone Golf Club. Downstairs, with a private entrance, is a family-friendly basement suite, which includes a living room with a sofa bed, a separate bedroom with king bed, and a kitchenette. The B&B is open year-round, but the downstairs suite, which has no central heating, is available only in milder weather.

Looking for a true get-away-from-it-all place? At **◖ E'Terra** (www.eterra.ca, $395–560 d), a sumptuous wood and stone manor house hidden in the woods, the phone number is unlisted, the property has no sign, and the owners won't divulge the address until

you make a reservation. The inn's philosophy is "eco-epicurean," pairing over-the-top luxury with environmental sensitivity. Four of the six guest rooms are two-story suites, and all have French linens, silk duvets, and heated flagstone floors. Guests can unwind in the spacious living room or in the cozy third-floor library and take a sauna or a dip in the saltwater pool. As you climb higher in the house, the vistas of Georgian Bay become more expansive, although the most striking views may be from the multilevel Douglas fir deck behind the building, tiered into the rocks above the water. You could drive to Tobermory in just a few minutes, but why would you want to leave?

Food

Most of Tobermory's dining options are in or near Little Tub Harbour, with a few other eateries along Highway 6.

Just south of town, in a little house off Highway 6, the **Little Tub Bakery** (4 Warner Bay Rd., 519/596-8399, www.littletubbakery.org, 9 A.M.–6 P.M. Mon.–Fri. in summer; call for off-season hours) is justifiably famous for their gooey butter tarts. The cinnamon rolls and freshly baked pies are also popular, or you can pick up a sandwich or homemade pizza for a picnic.

A Mermaid's Secret Café (7433 Hwy. 6, 519/596-8455, www.amermaidssecret.com, seasonal hours vary, $6–10), an eclectic eatery decorated in a cheerful chaos of Caribbean colors, serves some of the most interesting food in town. Besides organic fair-trade coffees and teas, the morning fare includes pastries, bagels, waffles, and fruit smoothies, while midday, there's a range of grilled sandwiches, from avocado, Brie, and red onion to grilled chicken with roasted red pepper and mango. Vegetarians have several options, including the Sumzie salad—a mountain of greens, veggies, dried fruit, and nuts. In July and August, they're open for dinner and often feature live music. Service can be leisurely, so don't dash in if you're rushing to catch the ferry.

Several places in Tobermory serve fish 'n' chips, but you can't miss the bright blue and yellow facade of **The Fish and Chip Place** (24 Bay St. S., 519/596-8380, www.thefishand-chipplace.com, open late May–mid-Oct. with seasonal hours, $7–12). The small menu includes the eponymous whitefish and French fries; their fish taco won't put any Baja joints out of business, but this far north of the border, it will do. On a sunny afternoon, particularly if you've been hiking, a beer on their deck is a perfect reward.

Information and Services

The **Tobermory Chamber of Commerce Information Centre** (Hwy. 6, just south of Little Tub Harbour, 519/596-2452, www.to-bermory.org) can provide maps and information about attractions, lodging, and services. You can also park your car here for the day at no charge. **County of Bruce Tourism** (www.explorethebruce.com) has extensive information about Tobermory and the rest of the Bruce Peninsula.

The **Foodland Market** (9 Bay St., 519/596-2380, 7 A.M.–9 P.M. daily) at Little Tub Harbour stocks basic supplies for picnics or camping and also has a laundromat.

Getting There and Around

Tobermory is approximately 300 kilometers (186 miles) northwest of Toronto. It's about a four-hour drive, weather and traffic permitting. Parking around Little Tub Harbour is restricted to two hours. If you're planning a longer stay in town, or heading out on a boat tour, leave your car in one of the free long-term parking lots. There's one at the Tobermory Chamber of Commerce Information Centre on Highway 6, two smaller lots on Head Street (between the Information Centre and Little Tub Harbour), and another on Legion Street, west of Highway 6.

Without a car, you can easily walk around Tobermory or to the National Park Visitor Centre, catch a boat to Flowerpot Island, and take other short hikes in the area. Some hotel or B&B owners will drop you at the trailhead for a day hike, so inquire when making lodging reservations. **Thorncrest Outfitters** (7441

Hwy. 6, 519/596-8908, www.thorncrestoutfit-ters.com) runs a shuttle service for hikers or paddlers (they'll also transport your canoe or kayak) between Tobermory and Cyprus Lake, Dyer's Bay, or Lion's Head.

While there's no direct bus service to Tobermory, you can connect through Owen Sound. **First Student Canada bus service** (2180 20th St. E., Owen Sound, 519/376-5712, one-way adults $28, children 12 and under $14) runs one bus a day in each direction between Owen Sound and Tobermory on Fridays, Saturdays, Sundays, and holiday Mondays from July through early September. The schedule is timed to connect with the Manitoulin Island ferry. **Greyhound Bus Lines** (800/661-8747, www.greyhound.ca) can get you to Owen Sound from Toronto and from points farther afield.

The **M.S. Chi-Cheemaun Ferry** (519/376-6601 information, 800/265-3163 reservations, www.ontarioferries.com), nicknamed "The Big Canoe," runs mid-May to mid-October between Tobermory and South Baymouth on Manitoulin Island. The crossing takes about two hours, and the ship accommodates 638 passengers and 143 cars. The ferry cuts out several hours of driving time, compared to the road route between Southern Ontario and Manitoulin. Reservations are recommended, particularly if you're taking a car. The Tobermory ferry terminal is at 8 Eliza Street (519/596-2510).

◖ BRUCE PENINSULA NATIONAL PARK

Intricate rock formations. Caribbean-blue water. Centuries-old trees. Inland lakes. More than three dozen types of orchids. The Bruce Peninsula National Park (www.pc.gc.ca, open year-round, $11.70/vehicle), which encompasses 156 square kilometers (60 square miles) spread out over several parcels of land, protects these natural features that are unique in Ontario. The park is at the northern tip of the Bruce Peninsula near the town of Tobermory.

The Grotto and Indian Head Cove

The park's most visited sights are the Grotto, a

waterside cave, and the adjacent Indian Head Cove. And with good reason. Through centuries of erosion, the waters of Georgian Bay have sculpted the area's soft limestone cliffs, leaving dramatic overhangs, carved rocks, and underwater caves, such as the Grotto. At Indian Head Cove, the rocks are sculpted into pillars, narrower at the bottom and wider at the top, resembling smaller versions of the "flowerpots" in the Fathom Five National Marine Park. Particularly on bright sunny days, the contrast between the brilliant blue-green bay, the polished white rocks along the shoreline, and the layered rock cliffs is striking.

You can climb down to sea level to explore the cave-like Grotto, but even if scrambling down steep rocks isn't your thing, you can still view the Grotto from above. At Indian Head Cove, the rock formations are on the pebbly beach, so no climbing is required. You can swim in Georgian Bay here, although the water is cold year-round.

It's a moderate hike to the Grotto from the day-use parking area near the **Cyprus Lake Park Office** (Cyprus Lake Rd., off Highway 6, 519/596-2263), where several trails lead to Georgian Bay. Once at the shore, head north along the rocky shore to Indian Head Cove and then to the Grotto. Allow about 30–45 minutes to walk each way from the parking area. You must stop at the park office to pay a day-use parking fee ($11.70 per car) before you set out. There are restrooms at the Cyprus Lake office and near the Grotto, but no other services, so bring whatever food and water you need.

Cyprus Lake

From the Cyprus Lake day-use parking area (Cyprus Lake Rd., off Highway 6), you can walk down to the lake itself in just a few minutes. There's a sandy beach with somewhat warmer water than in chilly Georgian Bay, as well as picnic tables.

The **Cyprus Lake Trail** follows the lakeshore. A mostly flat, 5.2-kilometer (3.2-mile) loop trail, it's a popular spot for bird-watching. Paddlers looking for a calm body of

water to canoe or kayak can head out into Cyprus Lake. In winter, you can snowshoe along Cyprus Lake and on to the Grotto. Park at the Cyprus Lake main gate, then follow the Cyprus Lake Trail to the Georgian Bay Trail.

There are no boat rentals at the lake, but in Tobermory, **Thorncrest Outfitters** (7441 Hwy. 6, 519/596-8908, www.thorncrestoutfitters.com) rents canoes and kayaks and can transport them to the lake. They also offer a number of full- and half-day guided paddling trips at various locations on the northern Bruce Peninsula and rent snowshoes ($15/day) in winter.

◖ The Bruce Trail

Serious hikers often plan their holidays to hike the Bruce Trail (www.brucetrail.org), doing sections of this 845-kilometer (525-mile) route in two-day, three-day, or week-long increments. They return to the trail until they've completed the entire route from the Niagara region to Tobermory. Yet you don't have to be an indomitable whole-trail hiker to enjoy the Bruce Trail. You can easily take day hikes along the trail, in and around the Bruce Peninsula National Park.

From the Grotto, the Bruce Trail extends along Georgian Bay in both directions. If you continue to the west, you can hike all the way to Tobermory (18 kilometers, or 11 miles). Between the Grotto and Little Cove (12.6 kilometers, or 7.8 miles), the trail is quite difficult, with very rocky terrain, but you're rewarded with sweeping views of Georgian Bay. From Little Cove to Tobermory (5.4 kilometers, or 3.4 miles), the trail flattens out and wends through the cedar forest.

Heading east from the Grotto along the bay, the Bruce Trail hugs the shore to Stormhaven (2.4 kilometers, or 1.5 miles), where there's a primitive camping area and restroom. The trail then gets more difficult for the next 9.5 kilometers (6 miles) to the High Dump camping area.

Because many sections of the Bruce Trail are quite rugged, get details about your route

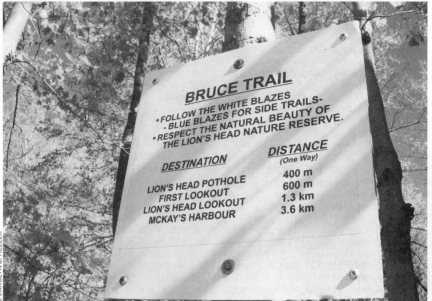

BRUCE TRAIL

- FOLLOW THE WHITE BLAZES
  - BLUE BLAZES FOR SIDE TRAILS-
- RESPECT THE NATURAL BEAUTY OF
  THE LION'S HEAD NATURE RESERVE.

DESTINATION	DISTANCE (One Way)
LION'S HEAD POTHOLE	400 m
FIRST LOOKOUT	600 m
LION'S HEAD LOOKOUT	1.3 km
MCKAY'S HARBOUR	3.6 km

© CAROLYN B. HELLER

GEORGIAN BAY

The Bruce Trail runs from the Niagara region to the Bruce Peninsula.

before you set out. The staff at the Cyprus Lake Park Office or the National Park Visitor Centre can help match a hike to your ability level.

Singing Sands Beach

On the west side of the peninsula, Singing Sands Beach (Dorcas Bay Rd.) looks like it's part of a completely different natural environment than the rocky eastern shores—and it is. The flat, sandy beach spreads out around Dorcas Bay with vistas out across Lake Huron; it's a popular swimming spot. A short boardwalk trail loops around an adjacent marsh, and the three-kilometer (1.9-mile) **Forest Beach Loop Trail** is another easy walk that's good for bird-watching.

Camping

Within Bruce Peninsula National Park, the **Cyprus Lake Campground** (Cyprus Lake Rd., $23.40 mid-Apr.–mid-Oct., $15.70 mid-Oct.–Apr.) has 242 drive-in campsites

in three camping areas. All three areas border Cyprus Lake and have restroom facilities with flush toilets and cold-water taps, but no showers. No electrical or sewer hookups are available. There are showers at Little Tub Harbour in Tobermory, about 15 kilometers (9 miles) north of Cyprus Lake. The campground is open year-round. Between May and mid-October, you can reserve campsites through the Parks Canada Campground Reservation Service (877/737-3783, www.pccamping.ca). Reservations are recommended, particularly during July and August. Reservations aren't taken between mid-October and April, when sites are first-come, first-served.

Also in the park are two primitive backcountry campgrounds ($9.80/person): **Stormhaven** and **High Dump**. Stormhaven is 2.4 kilometers (1.5 miles) east of the Grotto along Georgian Bay. High Dump is 9.5 kilometers (6 miles) east of Stormhaven, or eight kilometers (five miles) from the parking area at Crane Lake

THE BRUCE TRAIL

One of Canada's iconic outdoor experiences is a hike along Ontario's Bruce Trail, an 845-kilometer (525-mile) hiking route that extends from the Niagara region to the tip of the Bruce Peninsula. How long does it take to complete the whole trail? If you hiked eight hours a day, covering about 30 kilometers (19 miles), it would take you roughly a month to hike "end to end." However, unless you're an experienced hiker, this pace will likely be much too fast. And while some hikers do the entire trail straight through, far more "end to end" hikers complete the trail in a series of shorter excursions over several months or years.

Some sections of the trail are flat and easy, while others are quite rugged – get information about your route before you set out. A good source of trail information is the **Bruce Trail Conservatory** (905/529-6821 or 800/665-4453, www.brucetrail.org), a charitable organization committed to protecting and promoting the trail. They have a free online overview map, and you can download detailed maps of individual trail sections ($3/map). If you're serious about hiking the entire trail, consider purchasing the **Bruce Trail Reference** ($36.95), available on the conservatory website or through Canadian bookseller Chapters/Indigo (www.chapters.indigo.ca). Many Canadian libraries stock the guide, too. It's updated regularly – and there are changes and additions to the trail – so check for the most recent edition.

If you'd like to find hiking companions or join in group hikes, check out one of the nine Bruce Trail clubs, which help maintain the trail and arrange group activities in different regions. The **Peninsula Bruce Trail Club** (www.pbtc.ca) organizes hikes throughout the year on the Bruce Peninsula and also publishes guides to peninsula day hikes. You can get a list of all the trail clubs from the Bruce Trail Conservatory website (www.brucetrail.org).

The Bruce Trail Conservatory website includes a list of campgrounds that are accessible to the trail, as well as B&Bs and inns that welcome trail hikers. Many innkeepers whose lodgings are close to the trail will pick up or drop off hikers at nearby trailheads.

Another option for hikers who don't want to camp or lug gear is the **Home-to-Home B&B Network** (888/301-3224, www.hometohome-network.ca). Stay at any lodgings in this network of B&Bs, located between Wiarton and Tobermory, and hike to your next destination. The B&B owners will move your luggage to your next lodging, where dinner will be waiting. In the morning, you'll have a hot breakfast before beginning the day's hike. If you want a picnic lunch to eat on the go, that can be arranged, too. A Home-to-Home coordinator will help plan your hiking route and arrange accommodations. Reservations are required at least two weeks in advance.

(from Highway 6, take Dyers Bay Road east to Crane Lake Road). To reach either area, you need to backpack in along the Bruce Trail. You must register at the Cyprus Lake Park Office (Cyprus Lake Rd., off Highway 6) before heading out. Between May and October, you can register by phone (519/596-2263) or in person at the office; the rest of the year, register at the self-service kiosk outside the office.

Stormhaven and High Dump each have nine sites with tent platforms and a composting toilet. No water is available, so bring your own or purify the water from the bay.

If you don't want to camp, the closest accommodations to the national park are in Tobermory.

Information and Services

For general information about the Bruce Peninsula National Park, phone or visit the **National Park Visitor Centre** (120 Chi Sin Tib Dek Rd., Tobermory, 519/596-2233, www.pc.gc.ca). Between May and October, you can also contact the **Cyprus Lake Park Office** (Cyprus Lake Rd., off Highway 6, 519/596-2263).

FATHOM FIVE NATIONAL MARINE PARK

One of only three national marine conservation areas in Canada, Fathom Five National Marine Park (519/596-2233, www.pc.gc.ca) includes 22 islands in Georgian Bay off the northern end of the Bruce Peninsula. Access to the park is by boat from the town of Tobermory. Formed over 400 million years ago, these rocky islands are composed primarily of dolomite, a type of limestone. The main attractions for visitors are the distinctive rock formations are known as "flowerpots." Narrow at the bottom and wider at the top, these rock stacks resemble massive stone pots. While the waves have slowly worn away the softer limestone on the pillars' lower end, the harder dolomite tops have survived, creating the unusual shape.

More than 20 shipwrecks lie within the Fathom Five park's territory, making it a popular destination for scuba divers. In fact, the park gets its name from William Shakespeare's play *The Tempest*, in which the following lines describe the father of Ferdinand, who is feared dead in a shipwreck:

> *Full fathom five thy father lies;*
> *Of his bones are coral made;*
> *Those are pearls that were his eyes:*
> *Nothing of him that doth fade*
> *But doth suffer a sea-change*
> *Into something rich and strange.*
> *Sea-nymphs hourly ring his knell*
> *Hark! now I hear them, ding-dong, bell.*

A "fathom" is a unit of measure roughly equal to 1.8 meters, or six feet, so "fathom five" is nine meters, or about 30 feet. A long way down!

Scuba Diving

While you might not think of such a northern location as a prime scuba destination, Fathom Five has some of the world's best freshwater diving. Not only is the water generally clear, but the combination of underwater cliffs, caves, and other geological formations, along with the more than 20 shipwrecks in the area, give divers plenty to explore.

All divers must register in person at the National Park Visitor Centre in Tobermory (120 Chi Sin Tib Dek Rd., 519/596-2233, www.pc.gc.ca, adults $5.80, seniors $4.90, children $2.90). The park charges divers a per-person daily fee of $4.90 in addition to the park admission fee and the cost of boat transport. If you're planning to dive at least four days, buy an annual divers' pass for $19.60. Several companies in Tobermory run single-day and multiday dive trips to the Fathom Five islands and surrounding areas. They also offer scuba lessons and gear rentals. Contact **Divers Den** (3 Bay St., 519/596-2363, www.diversden.ca), **G+S Watersports** (8 Bay St. South, 519/596-2200, www.gswatersports.net), or **Tobermory Aquasports** (7037 Hwy. 6, 519/596-8474, www.tobermoryaquasports.com).

Flowerpot Island

Unless you have your own boat, only one of the park's 22 islands is accessible to visitors: Flowerpot Island, named for the two towering

one of the "flowerpots" in the Fathom Five National Marine Park

© CAROLYN B. HELLER

GEORGIAN BAY

rock pillars known as the "flowerpots." These rock stacks sit waterside on the island's eastern shore.

Tour boats from Tobermory dock at Beachy Cove on the east side of Flowerpot Island. The island isn't large (about 2 square kilometers, or 0.77 square mile), so it's only about a 15-minute walk from Beachy Cove to the first **small flowerpot** (which is 7 meters, or 23 feet, high), and a few minutes farther to the **large flowerpot,** which stands 12 meters (40 feet) tall. From the flowerpots, you can follow the **Loop Trail,** passing a small cave. (The path up to the cave is easy to miss; it's on the left just beyond the flowerpots.) You can't go inside the cave, but you can peer into the entrance.

Beyond the cave, the Loop Trail continues to the **Flowerpot Island Lightstation** on the island's northeast tip. The first lighthouse on the island went into service in 1897; in the 1960s, the original light was replaced with a steel lighthouse tower that's still flashing its beacon today. You can walk out to the tower and to an adjacent observation deck with a view across Georgian Bay. Near the lightstation is the lightkeeper's house, which contains a small museum (July–Aug.).

To return to Beachy Cove from the lighthouse, either backtrack along the trail past the flowerpots or continue on the Loop Trail up and over the bluffs in the middle of the island. This latter section of the Loop Trail is much more rugged; park staff advise allowing at least an extra hour to return via this route.

If you can tolerate cold water, you can swim or snorkel off Flowerpot Island. The beaches are rocky, so you might want to wear protective footwear. The best spots to swim are near Beachy Cove (either near the picnic shelter or the campground) or around the flowerpots. In either location, be alert for boat traffic.

CAMPING

Camping is your only option if you want to spend the night on Flowerpot Island. The park accepts camping reservations (519/596-2233, ext. 221) each year beginning in early May. The **Flowerpot Island Campground** ($9.80/

person) has six basic tent sites, all a stone's throw from the shore and a 5–10-minute walk from the Beachy Cove boat dock. There's a composting toilet nearby but no showers or running water. You need to bring your own water or purify the bay water for drinking.

No supplies are available on the island, so bring food and anything else you might need. Parks Canada cautions that campers should bring enough food, water, and warm clothing to last extra days, since the boat service back to the mainland can be canceled if the weather turns bad.

INFORMATION AND SERVICES

Park staff are frequently on duty at Flowerpot Island's Beachy Cove during the summer months. Otherwise, staff may or may not be available on the island, so if you have questions, check at the visitor center (120 Chi Sin Tib Dek Rd., 519/596-2233, www.pc.gc.ca, adults $5.80, seniors $4.90, children $2.90) before you leave Tobermory.

A small volunteer-run snack bar near the lighthouse is open during the summer, but hours are erratic; be sure to bring water and snacks with you. There are restrooms at Beachy Cove between the ferry dock and the campground, as well as near the lighthouse. It's almost worth hiking to the lightstation just to use the "Loo with a View," with its vistas across the bay.

GETTING THERE

The park service does not run its own boats; instead, it works with a private company, **Blue Heron Tours** (Little Tub Harbour, 519/596-2999, www.blueheronco.com, mid-May–mid-Oct.) that offers several types of boat trips to Flowerpot Island. The sailing schedules vary seasonally, so check their website or phone for details. Also confirm when the last boats leave Flowerpot Island to return to the mainland, and get back to the dock at Beachy Cove in plenty of time. You don't want an unexpected overnight stay!

If you just want to get to Flowerpot Island, take Blue Heron's 15-minute direct shuttle boat (adults $33.19, seniors $31.42, children

4–12 $24.34 round-trip) between Little Tub Harbour and Beachy Cove. Boats drop off and pick up passengers several times a day.

For a few dollars more, you can add a brief ride through Big Tub Harbour to look at the remains of two shipwrecks on the 25-minute island shuttle and shipwrecks tour (adults $37.62, seniors $35.85, children 4–12 $28.77 round-trip). You don't see much—the wrecks look like shadows under the water—but it's as close as you can get to the sunken ships without scuba diving.

On the one-hour *Blue Heron V* glass bottom boat tour (with Flowerpot Island: adults $37.62, seniors $35.85, kids 4–12 $28.77; boat tour only: adults $28.77, seniors $26.99, kids 4–12 $19.92) you can visit the Big Tub shipwrecks and cruise around Flowerpot Island with an option to disembark on the island.

You must pay the national park admission fee (adults $5.80, seniors $4.90, children $2.90) in addition to the price for the boat trips. Park admission includes access to the National Park Visitor Centre in Tobermory, as well as admission to Flowerpot Island.

DYER'S BAY

Unlike many of the Bruce Peninsula's lighthouses, which you can see only from the exterior, at the **Cabot Head Lighthouse** (www.cabothead.ca, 10 A.M.–7 P.M. daily late May–mid-Oct., suggested donation $3), you can venture inside. The lower levels of the red-and-white wooden structure are a museum with exhibits about local marine history. You can climb up to the observation tower for a lightkeeper's-eye-view out across the bay. The original Cabot Head Lighthouse began operation in 1896. It remained in use until 1968, when it was torn down and replaced with the current light, which is an automated beacon.

The lighthouse is about 40 kilometers (25 miles) southeast of Tobermory, about a 45–50-minute drive. From Highway 6, go east on Dyer's Bay Road. Once you pass through the village of Dyer's Bay, the road becomes a winding gravel track that twists along the shoreline to the lighthouse.

LION'S HEAD

Lion's Head is a friendly little village on Georgian Bay in the approximate north–south midpoint of the Bruce Peninsula. With its central location, it's a convenient base for exploring the peninsula, particularly if you want to visit sights beyond the Tobermory area. And if you want to stay put, you can stroll or swim at the beach, browse in the village shops, or have a beer in the local pub. Set on the bay at the mouth of Lion's Head harbor, **Lion's Head Lighthouse** is a re-creation of the original lightstation built here in 1903. Students at the local high school constructed the current lighthouse in 1983, using plans for the original structure. The lighthouse is particularly photogenic, perched on the shore with the bay and the cliffs of the Niagara Escarpment behind.

On the south side of town, **Lion's Head Provincial Park** (519/389-9056, www.ontarioparks.com, free) is known for its "potholes," deep, cylindrical holes carved by erosion into the limestone rocks. It's about a 15–20-minute walk along a flat section of the Bruce Trail to two of the large potholes. The trail continues toward Georgian Bay, where it becomes much more difficult as it hugs the cliffs. The reward for the climb up and along the tops of the rocks is a spectacular view of the cliffs and the bay. This section of the trail isn't recommended for small children, as the trail veers quite close to the cliffs. Access to the potholes trail is from Moore Street. Don't be deterred by the "No Exit" sign on Moore Street; it just means that the road dead-ends. The trail starts opposite 128 Moore Street. The park has no restrooms or other services.

The **Central Bruce Peninsula Chamber Of Commerce** (519/793-3178, www.centralbrucepeninsula.ca, daily July–Aug., Sat.–Sun. mid-May–June and Sept.–mid-Oct.) runs a seasonal tourist information center on Highway 6 in Ferndale, at the intersection of Highway 9 (the Lion's Head turnoff). The rest of the year, staff answer questions by phone. Lion's Head is about 250 kilometers (160 miles) north of Toronto, and there's no public transportation to or around the area.

Accommodations and Food

Big rooms, a beachside location, and a warm welcome are the reasons to stay at the **Lion's Head Beach Motel and Cottages** (1 McNeil St., 519/793-3155, www.lionsheadbeachmotelandcottages.ca, $95–105 s, $109–119 d). Although the motel rooms won't win any design prizes, they're well maintained and larger than average, and they include kitchenettes. They're spacious enough to accommodate a family, but the newer two- and three-bedroom cottages would be even more comfortable if you've brought Grandma or the kids.

If you're not a regular at **The Lion's Head Inn & Restaurant** (8 Helen St., 519/793-4601, www.lionsheadinn.ca, lunch and dinner daily May–Oct., Wed.–Sat. Nov.–Apr., $10–20), you may feel like one after you've dined in this convivial restaurant and pub. The food is a notch above your basic pub fare, starting with burgers and pasta and moving on to grilled whitefish, steak, even chicken Cordon Bleu. The best value is the Friday all-you-can-eat fish 'n' chips special ($15); you need a hearty appetite to tackle more than three pieces of fish, but the last I heard, the fish-eating record was 11! Built as a boardinghouse in 1879, the inn also has three simple guest rooms upstairs ($65 d with shared bath, $80 d with private bath).

It's worth visiting the small **Lion's Head Farmers' Market** (9 A.M.–noon Sat. late May–mid-Oct.) just for its open-air setting right on Lion's Head Beach. Vendors sell produce, muffins, and other baked goods, as well as crafts.

Perfect for a country getaway, hiker's respite, or a plentiful farm-style supper, the **☾ Cape Chin Connection Country Inn** (418 Cape Chin North Rd., 519/795-7525, www.capechin.ca, $70s, $90 d with shared bath, $105 s or d with private bath, open year-round) is set on a 40-hectare (100-acre) homestead about 25 kilometers (16 miles) north of Lion's Head Village. Although additions have been made over the years, the original 1853 log farmhouse remains and now contains one of the dining rooms. On the main floor, there's one guest room with private bath; upstairs, the five smallish bedrooms, with floral wallpaper and

country quilts, share two bathrooms. Room rates include a full breakfast, and packages including breakfast, a packed lunch, and a five-course dinner are also available. Nonguests are welcome in the restaurant for the five-course prix-fixe dinners (6–9 P.M. daily, $27–33) by reservation; the beer-braised pork ribs are a favorite among the hearty homestyle dishes. Owners Ann and Don Bard, who've run the inn since 1988, can tell you pretty much anything you need to know about the region; they were founding members of the Home-to-Home B&B network, which provides lodging and meals to Bruce Trail hikers (the Bruce Trail crosses the inn's property).

Craving butter tarts, hearty potato-filled "pasties," or homemade multigrain bread? Then pull off Highway 6 at the **Harvest Moon Organic Bakery** (3927 Hwy. 6, 519/592-5742, www.harvestmoonbakery.ca, 9 A.M.–4:30 P.M. Wed.–Sun. July–Aug., Thurs.–Sun. May–June and Sept.–Oct.). Besides sampling the treats that come out of this riotously colorful little house, you can stroll around the quirky sculpture garden (free). The bakery is about 10 minutes north of Ferndale, on the west side of Highway 6.

WIARTON AND VICINITY

The town of Wiarton sits on Colpoys Bay, an inlet off of Georgian Bay, with the cliffs of the Niagara Escarpment towering above the water. Highway 6, the peninsula's main north–south route, runs straight through town, where it's called Berford Street. While it's not a big city (the year-round population is under 2,500), Wiarton does have all the basic services you need, including a 24-hour grocery store. Many of Wiarton's limestone or brick buildings downtown date to the mid-1800s; the village was incorporated in 1880, and the railway reached the area the following year. The former railway station is now the town's information center. Two fingers of land jutting into Georgian Bay on either side of Wiarton are worth exploring. To the north, Cape Crocker is a First Nations reserve; to the east, you can head toward the village of Big Bay, visiting caves, gardens, and an ice cream shop en route.

Wiarton's most famous resident may be **Wiarton Willie**, a weather-forecasting groundhog. Similar to the American "Punxsutawney Phil," Wiarton Willie comes out of his burrow annually on Groundhog Day (Feb. 2). If he sees his shadow, Canada's winter will last for another six weeks; if he doesn't, spring is supposedly on the way. Between May and September, and again in early February, you can view "Willie" in his pen outside the Wiarton branch of the Bruce County Public Library (578 Brown St., at William St.). Local sculptor Dave Robinson crafted a 4.5-ton limestone statue of the town's notable groundhog. *"Willie Emerging"* sits near the beach in **Bluewater Park** (William St.). Also in the park is Wiarton's former train station, an ornate wooden building built in 1904 and moved to its present site in 1971.

East of Wiarton, in the hamlet of Big Bay, you can stroll among the irises, lilacs, poppies, and lavender in the peaceful, privately owned **Kepplecroft Gardens** (504156 Grey Rd. 1, Big Bay, 519/534-1090, www.keppelcroft.com, 10 A.M.–5 P.M. Wed.–Sun. May–mid-Oct., suggested donated $3). Walking paths wend through the property, which includes a Zen garden, a woodland garden, and rock sculptures. The Kepplecroft Gardens are part of a regional network of private gardens, known as the **Rural Gardens of Grey and Bruce Counties** (www.ruralgardens.ca), that are open to visitors. The website lists gardens hours and locations; you can also pick up a "Rural Gardens" map at any of the information centers on the Bruce Peninsula.

Wiarton celebrates its weather-forecasting groundhog during the annual **Wiarton Willie Festival** (519/534-5492, www.wiartonwillie. com), a winter carnival that includes a parade, fireworks, concerts, pancake breakfasts, sleigh rides, and, of course, Willie's prediction for the end of winter. The festival takes place for several days around Groundhog Day (February 2). Get an event schedule on the festival website or from the local tourism offices.

Stop into the **Wiarton Information Centre** (Bluewater Park, 519/534-3111 or 519/534-2592, www.wiartonchamber.ca, May–early

Sept.), run by the local Chamber of Commerce in the former train station. You can also get visitor information from the **Town of South Bruce Peninsula** (315 George St., 519/534-1400 or 877/534-1400, www.southbrucepeninsula.com, 8:30 A.M.–4:30 P.M. Mon.–Fri.), or call the main office for the **County of Bruce Tourism** (578 Brown St., 519/534-5344 or 800/268-3838, www.explorethebruce.com), located in Wiarton. Wiarton is about 220 kilometers (137 miles) northwest of Toronto. There's no public transportation in the area, and it's difficult to explore without a car.

Cape Croker

Part of the Saugeen Ojibway First Nations Territory, the 6,000-hectare (14,825-acre) Cape Croker Peninsula juts out into Georgian Bay north of Wiarton. The peninsula's Ojibway name, *Neyaashiinigmiing*, means "a point of land nearly surrounded by water," and the name is apt—except for a sliver of land connecting the peninsula to the mainland, it's ringed by the waters of the bay. Cape Croker is a pretty spot for a drive or hike, particularly on the north side of the peninsula with views across the water to the limestone bluffs of the Niagara Escarpment. You can drive out to the **Cape Croker Lighthouse,** built in 1902 on the tip of the cape, but the interior isn't open to the public, and the setting behind a chain-link fence isn't that picturesque.

The waters off Cape Croker are popular with kayakers. **Suntrail Source For Adventure** (60 Queen St. E. aka Hwy. 6, Hepworth, 519/935-2478 or 877/882-2958, www.suntrail.net) offers full-day kayak excursions ($99 per person) on Sydney Bay, departing from the Cape Croker Indian Park. They rent kayaks and offer a delivery service, as well. Near the mainland end of the peninsula, the **Cape Croker Indian Park** (519/534-0571, www.capecrokerpark. com, $10/vehicle) has a lovely beach and hiking trails, as well as a campground.

To experience the music, dance, and other traditions of the local First Nations community, visit the Bruce Peninsula during the **Cape Croker Powwow** (www.nawash.ca, late Aug.,

$7), held at Cape Croker Indian Park (519/534-0571, www.capecrokerpark.com, $10/vehicle). Visitors are welcome as long as they are respectful of local customs. Ask permission before taking photos or videos, and leave the beer at home—the powwow is an alcohol-free event.

Accommodations and Food

In the late 1990s, Evan LeBlanc and Dave Peebles bought a basic roadside motel overlooking Colpoys Bay just east of Wiarton, and they've been steadily upgrading the property that is now the three-story **Waterview on the Bay** (501205 Island View Dr., 519/534-0921 or 877/534-0921, www.waterview.ca, Apr.–Dec., $95–155 d). The rooms range from simple motel style with two double beds and a fridge to more deluxe; the nicest are the "luxury suites," with whirlpool tubs, sleigh beds, and expansive bay views. There's a swimming pool out back, and it's a short stroll down to the sandy beach, where complimentary kayaks and paddleboats are available. In summer, an all-you-can-eat breakfast buffet is served daily ($10). The Waterview is family-friendly, pet-friendly, and just overall friendly.

While many people dream of abandoning the city for a simpler rural life, Bonnie Howe and Phil Howard actually made the move when they purchased a farm east of Wiarton and opened the **Longlane Bed & Breakfast** (483078 Colpoy's Range Rd., 519/534-3901, www.longlane.ca, $80 s, $100 d). They raise cattle and chickens (guests can help gather eggs) and grow an expanding array of organic vegetables. Upstairs in the 1902 farmhouse, the three guest rooms are decorated with quilts and country curtains; on the walls are black-and-white photos of the family who originally established the farm. Guests share two bathrooms, as well as a sitting area with a TV, and in the morning, they tuck into hearty farm breakfasts around the communal kitchen table. The owners will shuttle hikers to the Bruce Trail nearby.

Wiarton's best restaurant, the **Green Door Café** (563 Berford St., 510/534-3278, www.thegreendoorcafe.com, contact for seasonal hours) looks like a small-town coffee shop, where local retirees stop in for coffee and grilled cheese sandwiches. At this unassuming eatery, though, the straightforward sandwiches ($5–10) and hearty main dishes ($11–14) are well prepared from fresh ingredients. Try the delicious, garlicky Caesar salad or the meaty cabbage rolls.

The tiny **Big Bay General Store** (Big Bay Sideroad at Grey Rd. 1, 519/534-4523, daily late May–early Sept., Sat.–Sun. only spring and fall), east of Wiarton, doesn't stock many groceries, but if you're looking for delicious homemade ice cream, this is the place. They make more than 80 different flavors, with 10 to 12 available at a time. Call to confirm their hours before making a special trip.

CAMPING

Owned and operated by the Chippewas of Nawash First Nation, the **Cape Croker Indian Park** (519/534-0571, www.capecrokerpark.com, early May–mid-Oct., $25–31 per site) has an enviable waterfront location on Sydney Bay. The 210-hectare (520-acre) property has 315 campsites, with showers, flush toilets, laundry facilities, a swimming beach, and canoe rentals. Prime waterfront sites look across to the cliffs of the Niagara Escarpment, while other sites are tucked into the woods. A small camping cabin with two bunks ($65) is also available. Reservations aren't required, but you may want to book ahead for the popular waterfront sites, for the cabin, or for holiday weekend stays; definitely reserve in advance for the August powwow.

SAUBLE BEACH

On the shore of Lake Huron at the south end of the Bruce Peninsula, Sauble Beach is a full-fledged beach-holiday town. This sun-and-fun community has burger stands and soft-serve ice cream shops, T-shirt sellers and bikini boutiques, and, oh, yes, a sandy lakeshore beach that seems to go on and on.

The world's second-longest freshwater beach, Sauble Beach (Lakeshore Dr.) is a flat paradise of sand that extends for 11 kilometers (nearly seven miles); only Wasaga Beach, east of Collingwood, is longer. The early French explorers who traversed this area named it "La Rivière au Sable" ("River to the Sand") for the nearby Sauble River, but by the end of the 19th-century, the town was known as Sauble Beach for its major geographical asset. Since the water is fairly shallow, Sauble Beach is a good choice for families with younger kids. The atmosphere in July and August can be rather honky-tonk, but the farther you go from the heart of town, the easier it is to find a peaceful spot to lay your towel. And despite the summer crowds, the beach is undeniably beautiful, and sunsets over the lake can be spectacular. Outside summer high season, you'll sometimes have the fine golden sand almost to yourself. Beach parking ($3/hour or $15/day in season) is available in lots right on the sand and along Lakeshore Road. Prepare for epic summer traffic jams. The **Sauble Beach Sandfest** (Lakeshore Blvd., 519/422-2457) takes place the first weekend in August and turns the beach into a giant outdoor sand sculpture gallery, drawing both professional and amateur sand sculptors.

Sauble Beach has a large assortment of standard beach motels and cottages. The **Sauble Beach Information Centre** (672 Main St., 519/422-1262, www.saublebeach.com, call for hours) has information about cottage rentals and lists of area accommodations. If you prefer a more peaceful atmosphere, you could stay in Wiarton (about 20 kilometers, or 12.5 miles, from Sauble Beach) and come to the beach during the day. Restaurants in town tend to serve burgers, pizza, and other eat-and-run fare. Eateries are clustered along Main Street and on Second Avenue North (one block east of the beach).

Sauble Beach is about 220 kilometers (137 miles) northwest of Toronto via Highways 6/10. After you pass through Owen Sound, continue on Highway 6 to Bruce Road 8, which heads west into Sauble Beach.

Sauble Falls Provincial Park

About one kilometer (0.6 mile) north of Sauble Beach, this small provincial park (Sauble Falls Parkway/County Rd. 13, 519/422-1952, www.

ontarioparks.com, late Apr.–Oct., $10–13/vehicle) couldn't feel more different than the frenzied tourist crush of the nearby town. Although it does get busy in summer, it still feels more like an escape into the woods.

The petite waterfalls along the Sauble River that give the park its name descend in tiers, almost like an aquatic wedding cake, over a staircase of dolomite limestone. You can watch the falls from a small viewing platform or along either side of the river; it's a lovely spot for a picnic. In spring and fall, you may see salmon and rainbow trout attempting to swim upstream over each ledge of the falls. You can also go canoeing or kayaking on a stretch of the Sauble River that winds through the park. Canoe and kayak rentals (daily mid-June–early Sept., weekends only early Sept–mid-Oct., call for fall hours) are available off Sauble Falls Parkway just north of the river.

Sauble Falls Provincial Park has 152 campsites ($36.75 tent sites, $42.25 electrical sites). In both the East Campground and the larger, radio-free West Campground, the nicest sites front the Sauble River. Both areas have flush toilets and showers; the West Campground has laundry facilities. You can reserve a campsite up to five months in advance though the Ontario Parks Reservations Service (888/668-7275, www.ontarioparks.com, reservation fees $8.50 for online, $9.50 by phone).

OWEN SOUND

It's hard to imagine that this small community of about 22,000 was once known as "Chicago of the North." From 1885 through 1912, when the Canadian Pacific Railway (CPR) made Owen Sound the terminus of its steamship line, the town's port was the busiest in the upper Great Lakes. Many of the town's Victorian homes and buildings date to this era. Alas, in 1912, the Canadian Pacific Railway moved its shipping operations farther east to Port McNicoll, Ontario, which had better rail connections, thus ending Owen Sound's glory years.

If you're more of a city person than the outdoors type, you could use Owen Sound as a base for exploring the peninsula's sights. From

Owen Sound, it's about a 45-minute drive to Wiarton and 75–90 minutes to Tobermory.

For a small city, Owen Sound has a large number of museums and historic attractions. To stroll through the town's history, pick up the *Historic Downtown Walking Tour* brochure at the **Owen Sound Tourist Information Centre** (1155 First Ave. W., 519/371-9833, www.owensoundtourism.com). Many of the community's grand historic homes, built in the late 1800s, are along First Avenue West, while many Victorian-era commercial buildings still stand along Second Avenue East. To learn about Owen Sound's Afro-Canadian heritage, follow two self-guided tours of sites that were important to the African-Canadian community. Pick up brochures about these tours—*The Freedom Trail*, a 10-kilometer (six-mile) walking or cycling tour, and the *Owen Sound Underground Railroad Driving Tour*—at the Owen Sound Tourist Information Centre (1155 First Ave. W., 519/371-9833, www.owensoundtourism.com) or get details online from the City of Owen Sound's Black History website (www.osblackhistory.com).

Grey Roots Museum and Archives

If you think that a museum about a region's roots is a musty trove of papers and old tools, think again. This contemporary museum (102599 Grey Rd. 18, 519/376-3690 or 877/473-9766, www.greyroots.com, 10 A.M.–5 P.M. daily late May–mid-Oct., 10 A.M.–5 P.M. Tues.–Sat. mid-Oct.–late May) showcases the history and culture of Owen Sound and the surrounding region with cool multimedia features that include films, radio stories, and computer-based displays.

Start in the Grey County gallery, where the permanent "Grey Roots" exhibit introduces you to the people who settled the region—from the local First Nations to early pioneers to notable citizens such as Agnes Macphail, a Grey County native who became Canada's first female member of Parliament. Other galleries host temporary and traveling exhibitions; recent exhibits have focused on First Nations storytelling, Victorian-era death and mourning

customs, and the history of Grey County's African-Canadian population.

If you have kids in tow, explore the **Moreston Heritage Village** (10 A.M.–5 P.M. daily June–early Sept.), a pioneer village on the site that's staffed by costumed volunteers. Watch the blacksmith at work, visit the 1850s log cabin, or check out the schoolhouse.

Museum admission rates vary seasonally. From late May to early September, adults are $8, seniors $6, children 5–13 $4, and families $20. The rest of the year, adults are $6, seniors $5, children $3.50, and families $18.

The museum is located on the south edge of Owen Sound, about seven kilometers (4.4 miles) south of downtown.

Tom Thomson Art Gallery

Artist Tom Thomson (1877–1917) grew up outside Owen Sound in the town of Leith. A member of Ontario's Group of Seven—notable landscape artists of the early 20th century—Thomson is best known for the paintings he created in Algonquin Park between 1912 and 1917, until his death (reportedly by drowning) in Algonquin's Canoe Lake. The small, modern Tom Thomson Art Gallery (840 First Ave. W., 519/376-1932, www.tomthomson.org, 10 A.M.–5 P.M. Mon.–Sat., noon–5 P.M. Sun. late May–mid-Oct.; call for off-season hours; adults $5, seniors and students $3, kids under 12 free) mounts changing exhibits of work by Thomson and other Ontario artists. On Wednesdays and on the third Sunday of every month, admission is by donation. In July and August, the gallery also hosts both a film series and a series of Wednesday-afternoon concerts.

Billy Bishop Home and Museum

Owen Sound native William Avery Bishop (1894–1956), a fighter pilot with the British Royal Flying Corps, became one of the most decorated Canadians serving in World War I. Bishop's childhood home, in a restored Victorian mansion, is now the Billy Bishop Home and Museum (948 3rd Ave. W., 519/371-0031, www.billybishop.org, 10 A.M.–5 P.M. Mon.–Sat., noon–5 P.M. Sun. late May–early

Sept.; call for off-season hours; adults $5, seniors and students $4, children 3–12 $2) that includes artifacts from Bishop's life and from World Wars I and II, with an emphasis on aviation history. A musical about Bishop's life, *Billy Bishop Goes to War,* premiered in 1978 and is one of Canada's most widely produced plays.

Owen Sound Marine and Rail Museum

Located in Owen Sound's former Canadian National Railway station (the station's waiting room now houses the Owen Sound Tourist Information Centre), the Owen Sound Marine and Rail Museum (1155 First Ave. W., 519/371-3333, www.marinerail.com, 10 A.M.–5 P.M. Mon.–Sat., noon–5 P.M. Sun. late May–early Sept.; call for off-season hours; adults $5, seniors and students $4, children 3–12 $2) commemorates the region's glory days as a ship and rail hub in the late 1800s. There are ship models, trains, and an exhibit about working on the railroad; outside the museum, you can climb on board a restored caboose.

Harrison Park and the Black History Cairn

Owen Sound was one of the northernmost stops on the Underground Railroad, the network of safe houses that protected slaves fleeing from the United States in the 1800s.

The Black History Cairn (www.osblackhistory.com), located in Harrison Park (Second Ave. E.), memorializes the slaves' journey to the north. This outdoor sculpture includes eight tiles inlaid in the ground, incorporating quilt patterns that represented coded messages to escaping slaves—according to legend, the patterns were originally sewn into quilts. One pattern symbolizes the North Star, which guided slaves to freedom; a log cabin symbol indicates a safe house along the Underground Railroad; another is a sailboat, signifying a water crossing. Around the tiles is a stone structure representing the ruins of a church, with windows looking out toward the Sydenham River. According to Bonita Johnson de Matteis, the artist who designed the cairn, newly freed slaves might have looked out similar church windows in Owen Sound as they gave thanks for their freedom. Johnson de Matteis herself is a descendent of a slave who escaped from the United States and settled in Owen Sound.

Harrison Park is located off 2nd Avenue East, south of downtown. Once you arrive in Harrison Park, to find the Black History Cairn, walk north from the parking area near the Harrison Park Inn; the cairn is just past the playground. The park is a lovely spot for a picnic, and it's crisscrossed with trails for hiking, running, and cycling; it also has three playgrounds, as well as canoe rentals.

Entertainment and Shopping

Owen Sound is an arts hub for the surrounding region, with theater, concerts, films, and special events year-round. The historic downtown **Roxy Theatre** (251 9th St. E., 519/371-2833 or 888/446-7699, www.roxytheatre.ca), built in 1912, hosts live theater and musical performances throughout the year.

The first weekend in August, Owen Sound's annual **Emancipation Celebration Festival** (Harrison Park, 2nd Ave. E., www.emancipation.ca) recalls the struggles of the former slaves who traveled the Underground Railroad to freedom in Canada. It began in 1862 and is now the longest continuously running emancipation festival in North America. Events include a speaker's forum, music, and a picnic.

From photography to metalwork to jewelry, the **Owen Sound Artists' Co-op** (279 10th St. E., 519/371-0479, www.osartistscoop.com, 9:30 A.M.–5:30 P.M. Mon.–Sat. and noon–4 P.M. Sun. July–Aug.) displays and sells the work of its roughly 40 member artists, all from the local area.

Accommodations and Food

Owen Sound has plenty of lodging options, ranging from standard chain motels to Victorian-style bed and breakfasts. Several of the chains are on the east side of town along Highway 6/10; the Owen Sound Tourist Information Centre (www.owensoundtourism.com) has online listings.

The most romantic place to stay in town is the ◖ **Highland Manor** (867 4th Ave. "A" W., 519/372-2699 or 877/372-2699, www.highland-manor.ca, $120 s, $140–160 d, children under 12 not permitted), a grand brick mansion on a shady residential street. On the first floor, the high ceilings, polished wood floors, and marble fireplaces create an elegant feel; guests can browse books about the area in the library, take their elaborate breakfasts in the formal dining room, and sip drinks in the music room (with a 1902 grand piano) or outside on the veranda. Upstairs, the guest rooms are equally refined, with working fireplaces, antique furnishings, and diaphanous drapes. Owners Linda Bradford and Paul Neville are passionate about local history, and they're a wealth of information about things to see and do nearby.

Although it's out of the town center on a charmless stretch of road and most of its 100 rooms are standard chain accommodations, the **Best Western Inn on the Bay** (1800 2nd Ave. E., 519/371-9200 or 800/780-7234, www.bestwesternontario.com, $140–240 d) does have rooms that overlook Georgian Bay. There's no pool, but the hot tub faces the waterfront.

If you'd like to wander and check out food options, head downtown to 2nd Avenue East, between 10th and Seventh Streets. The **Owen Sound Farmers' Market** (114 8th St. E., 519/371-3433, www.owensoundfarmersmarket.ca, 7 A.M.–2:30 P.M. Sat.) sells baked goods, snacks, and crafts in addition to seasonal produce. Located downtown opposite City Hall, the market is open Saturdays year-round.

As its name suggests, the **Ginger Press Bookshop and Café** (848 2nd Ave. E., 519/376-4233, www.gingerpress.com) is part bookstore and part casual café. You can browse or linger over a coffee during regular bookshop hours (9:30 A.M.–6 P.M. Mon.–Fri., 9 A.M.–4 P.M. Sat.). The kitchen is open for soup, sandwiches, and other light meals (9:30 A.M.–2 P.M. Mon.–Fri., 9 A.M.–noon Sat.). Fresh-pressed apple ginger juice is their specialty. Free Wi-Fi.

At the eclectic **Rocky Raccoon Café** (941 2nd Ave. E., 519/374-0500, www.rockyraccooncafe.

com, noon–10 P.M. daily, $15–25), local ingredients join Asian and global influences to create world-beat dishes that ramble from Thai-style venison to elk curry to whitefish with dill-mango tartar sauce. Weekday buffet lunches ($15) typically feature curries from chef-owner Robin Pradhan's native Nepal.

Practicalities

The **Owen Sound Tourist Information Centre** (1155 First Ave. W., 519/371-9833 or 888/675-5555, www.owensoundtourism.com), just north of downtown, shares a building with the Marine and Rail Museum. You can pick up lots of information about attractions and lodgings around town. The regional tourism association, **Grey County Tourism** (102599 Grey Rd. 18, 519/376-3265 or 877/733-4739, www.visitgrey.ca), has a helpful information desk in the lobby of the Grey Roots Museum.

Owen Sound is 190 kilometers (120 miles) northwest of Toronto, about a 2.5-hour drive via Highways 6 and 10. **Greyhound Bus Lines** (City Transit Centre, 1020 3rd Ave. E., 519/376-5375 or 800/661-8747, www.greyhound.ca) runs two direct buses daily in each direction between Toronto and Owen Sound (about four hours, $33–43 per person).

The **Grey Bruce Airbus** (800/361-0393, www.greybruceairbus.com, one-way/round-trip adults $70/125) operates four trips daily in each direction between Toronto's Pearson Airport and the Owen Sound Days Inn (950 6th St. E.).

The majority of Owen Sound's roadways are numbered streets and avenues (streets run east–west, avenues run north–south). The Sydenham River divides the east and west sides, so a "West" address, such as the Tom Thomson Gallery on 1st Avenue West, is west of the river, while an "East" address is the east of the river.

Owen Sound's attractions are clustered in two main areas—around downtown and south of the center. The main downtown shopping street is 2nd Avenue East, south of 10th Street and east of the river. From downtown, you can continue south on 2nd Avenue East to reach Harrison Park and the Grey Roots Museum.

Owen Sound has a walkable downtown core and you can get around town on **Owen Sound Transit** buses (Downtown Transit Terminal, 1020 3rd Ave. E., 519/376-3299, www.owensound.ca, adults $2, students $1.50, kids under 5 free). Buses operate 6:30 A.M.–6 P.M. Monday through Friday and 9 A.M.–5:30 P.M. Saturday. (Note that there's no evening or Sunday service.) One useful route is the Crosstown loop, which circles between downtown and Harrison Park.

To explore the surrounding towns or further up the Bruce Peninsula, it's much easier to have your own wheels. Car rental companies with offices in Owen Sound include: **Enterprise Rent-A-Car** (669 10th St. W., 519/371-9777 or 800/736-8222, www.enterpriserentacar.ca), **Thrifty Car Rental** (2055 16th Ave. E., 519/371-3381 or 800/371-3381, www.thrifty.com), and **Discount Car Rentals** (677 6th St. E., 519/372-0532, www.discountcar.com).

Collingwood and the Blue Mountains

The Blue Mountain Resort, just outside the town of Collingwood, is Ontario's top ski destination. If you're expecting the Alps or the Rockies, you may chuckle when you see the size of the "mountains" here, but these rolling hills should have plenty of terrain to keep most skiers or snowboarders occupied for at least several days. Besides the winter snow-sports season, the busiest times are midsummer (for mountain biking, hiking, golfing, and other outdoor activities) and fall weekends, when the trees are blazing with color.

Collingwood (population 17,000) serves skiers and other outdoor adventurers with grocery stores, movie theaters, and restaurants; it's also a good base for exploring the region. If your goal is skiing, snowboarding, or other outdoor pursuits, it's most convenient to stay in the Village at Blue Mountain, the resort area at the base of the mountain. If you want more options for dining, shopping, or touring, or if you like lodging with more personality, stay in or near Collingwood.

BLUE MOUNTAIN RESORT
Owned by resort giant Intrawest, Blue Mountain (108 Jozo Weider Blvd., 705/445-0231 or 877/445-0231, www.bluemountain.ca) may remind you of other North American ski towns (at least those with a big corporate parent). The village is car-free, and casually up-scale restaurants, bars, and outdoor clothing shops line the pedestrian streets. You can easily

walk from village lodgings to the lifts, or if you stay in one of the condo developments around the village, a free shuttle will pick you up.

Blue Mountain Activity Central (705/445-5522, www.activitycentral.ca) acts as an activity "concierge" for guests. They keep a schedule of regular events, including free guided hikes or snowshoe tours, sleigh rides, scavenger hunts, toboggan tours, and more, as well as activities for kids and teens. They can also book activities for you, both on and off the mountain.

Blue Mountain's newest attraction is the **Ridge Runner Mountain Coaster** (10 A.M.–8 P.M. late June–early Sept., call for off-season hours; adults and kids 12 and older $15/ride, $24/two rides; kids 3–12 $5/ride), which twists and turns from the top of the Glades area through the trees and down to the village. One or two people can ride together in each car, and the riders control the car's speed. At least one of the riders must be at least 12 years old and 137 centimeters (54 inches) tall.

Still looking for more things to do? Hiking, tennis, golf, miniature golf, indoor rock climbing, and riding the **Blue Mountain Gondola** (late May–mid-Oct., $4–7) are among the many other mountain activities.

Special events take place at Blue Mountain nearly every weekend from July through early October and on select weekends during the rest of the year. Highlights include the **May Long Weekend Music and Fireworks** (late May),

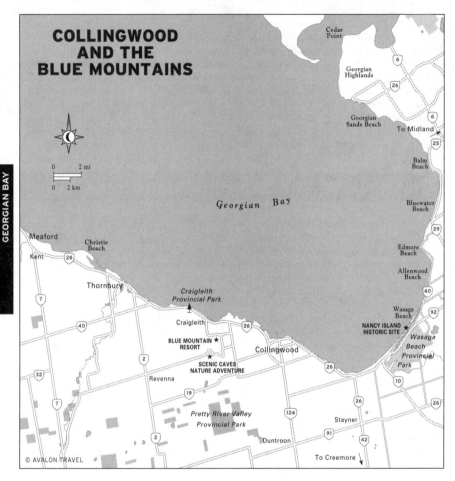

COLLINGWOOD AND THE BLUE MOUNTAINS

Cedar Point

6

Georgian Highlands

26

Georgian Sands Beach

To Midland

6

25

Balm Beach

Georgian Bay

Bluewater Beach

29

Meaford

Christie Beach

Edmore Beach

Kent

26

Allenwood Beach

Thornbury

60

7

Craigleith Provincial Park

Wasaga Beach

92

40

Craigleith

26

NANCY ISLAND HISTORIC SITE

2

BLUE MOUNTAIN ★ RESORT

Collingwood

Wasaga Beach Provincial Park

32

★ SCENIC CAVES NATURE ADVENTURE

26

Revenna

19

10

Pretty River Valley Provincial Park

124

26

26

7

Stayner

2

Duntroon

91

42

To Creemore

© AVALON TRAVEL

Salsa at Blue Mountain (late June), **Village Beach Party** (early Aug.), **Apple Harvest Festival** (early October), and **Oktoberfest at Blue** (late Oct.).

Skiing and Snowboarding

Blue Mountain Resort (108 Jozo Weider Blvd., 705/445-0231 or 877/445-0231, www. bluemountain.ca) began life as a winter sports mecca and now has 15 lifts serving 36 trails. At 720 vertical feet, it's not a tall mountain, nor does it get buried in snow like the western

resorts, but an extensive snow-making operation supplements the average annual snowfall of 280 centimeters (110 inches). The winter season typically starts in December and runs through March. Come midweek to avoid the crowds.

Lift tickets (adults $59, seniors and children 6–17 $40) are good for either day skiing (9 A.M.–4:30 P.M.) or afternoon/night skiing (12:30–10 P.M.). If you just want to ski in the evening (4:30–10 P.M.), when 25 of the 36 trails are open, tickets are $40. Ski and

WILD WINTER ADVENTURES

Ontario may not have the towering mountains of western Canada, but that doesn't mean you can't take to the slopes. Not only do the Georgian Bay and Cottage Country regions north of Toronto have several spots for downhill skiing and snowboarding, but there are also plenty of opportunities for cross-country skiing, snow-shoeing, dogsledding, and other winter adventures. The Ottawa Valley region, a short drive from the nation's capital, is the other major Ontario destination for winter sports.

The **Blue Mountain Resort** (705/445-0231 or 877/445-0231, www.bluemountain.ca) is the largest downhill ski resort in Ontario and also offers mountain biking and other outdoor sports when the snow season ends. Even closer to Toronto, the **Horseshoe Resort** (1101 Horseshoe Valley Rd., Barrie, 705/835-2790 or 800/461-5627, www.horseshoeresort.com), just north of Barrie off Highway 400, has downhill skiing and snowboarding, golf, even a treetop trekking course.

If you're looking for more places to ski or snowboard, check the **Ontario Snow Resorts Association** (www.skiontario.ca) or make tracks to one of the following mountain resorts:

- **Calabogie Peaks Resort** (30 Barrett Chute Rd., Calabogie, 613/752-2720 or 800/669-4861, www.calabogie.com)

- **Dagmar Ski Resort** (1220 Lakeridge Rd., Ashburn, 905/649-2002, www.skidagmar.com)

- **Hidden Valley Highlands Ski Area** (1655 Hidden Valley Rd., Huntsville, 705/789-1773 or 800/398-9555, www.skihiddenvalley.on.ca)

- **Hockley Valley Ski Resort** (R.R. 1, Orangeville, 519/942-0754, www.hockley.com)

- **Lakeridge** (790 Chalk Lake Rd., Uxbridge, 905/649-2058, www.ski-lakeridge.com)

- **Mount Pakenham** (McWatty Rd., Pakenham, 613/624-5290, www.mountpakenham.com)

- **Mount St. Louis Moonstone** (R.R. 4, Coldwater, 705/835-2112, www.mslm.on.ca)

- **Searchmont Ski Resort** (103 Searchmont Resort Rd., Searchmont, 705/781-2340, www.searchmont.com)

GEORGIAN BAY

snowboard rentals, lessons, and kids camps are all available.

For snowboarders, a **terrain park** (10 A.M.–9 P.M. daily) has its own chairlift. To access the park, you must purchase a $10 park pass, in addition to your lift ticket.

Mountain Biking

From late May through mid-October, mountain bikers take over the trails at Blue Mountain (705/445-0231 or 877/445-0231, www.bluemountain.ca). The lifts are open to bikers 10 A.M.–8 P.M. daily late June to early September and 10 A.M.–5 P.M. Friday, Saturday, and Sunday in spring and fall. Daily trail passes are $6 (no lift access), $12 (one lift access), or $30 (unlimited lift access). You can rent bikes and safety gear.

If you don't want to hit the trails on your own, a variety of guided mountain-biking options are available, for youth, teens, adults, and families, both novice and experienced riders.

Swimming and Water Sports

If you or your kids love water, check out the **Plunge Aquatic Centre** (200 Mountain Dr., 705/444-8705, www.plungebluemountain.ca, adults $11–13, seniors and children 3–13 $7–10) adjacent to the Westin Trillium House. This year-round water-activity center has indoor and outdoor swimming pools, several water slides, rope swings, hot tubs, and a water playground for toddlers. Schedules vary seasonally, but in general, Plunge is open daily in summer and winter, weekends only in spring and fall. Admission tickets are good for a three-hour period, and prices vary by time of day.

In summer, Blue Mountain Resort maintains a **private beach** (Blue Mountain Activity Central, 705/443-5522 or 800/955-6561) on Georgian Bay, that's open only to resort guests. A complimentary shuttle will take you from the village to the beach; it's about a 10-minute ride.

Accommodations

Blue Mountain Village has several hotel and condominium properties, and just outside the village are additional condo and townhouse complexes. Except for the Westin Trillium House, which you have to contact directly, you can book lodgings through **Blue Mountain Central Reservations** (877/445-0231, www.bluemountain.ca). When booking, ask whether the lodging is ski-in/ski-out or within walking distance of the lifts. Winter room rates typically start at about $150 per night for a double room, and a variety of lodging and lift ticket packages are available.

The **Blue Mountain Inn** was the village's original lodging, and while it's starting to show its age, it offers moderately priced accommodations. You can walk to the Century Express chair lift. For more style, the boutique **Mosaïc** has 163 contemporary suites, ranging from studios to three-bedroom units. The smaller units have kitchenettes, and the larger suites, some of which are multilevel townhouses, have full kitchens. There's a fitness center, as well as a year-round outdoor pool and hot tub. It's not as close to the lifts as the **Weider Lodge** or the **Grand Georgian**—both slightly older condo hotels—but the rooms are more stylish and you can walk to the gondola in a few minutes.

The village's most posh accommodation, located a short walk from the gondola, is the **Westin Trillium House** (220 Mountain Dr., 705/443-8080 or 800/937-8461, www.westinbluemountain.com, $195–550 d), designed like a grand Georgian Bay lodge. The 222 rooms, including standard guest rooms and one-, two-, and three-bedroom suites, have modern furnishings in ski-lodge beiges and browns, as well as TV/DVDs and kitchenettes. There's a 24-hour gym, a year-round outdoor pool, a sauna, and hot tubs, and if you're too tired to walk downstairs to the restaurant or lounge, you can order from room service.

Food

Food in the village tends toward either fuel-up-fast-and-get-back-on-the-slopes fare or simple but hearty pub-style eats. Start your day with coffee and pastry at the **Royal Majesty Espresso Bar Bakery** (190 Jozo Weider Blvd., 705/812-3476, www.royalmajestyatblue.com, generally open 7 A.M.–9 P.M. daily), or stop in later for a bowl of soup or a sandwich. Free Wi-Fi.

A popular après-ski spot, with live music most nights, is **Windy O'Neill's** (170 Jozo Weider Blvd., 705/446-9989, www.windyoneills.com, 11 A.M.–2 A.M. daily, $10–15), an Irish pub that says it's owned by "genuine Irish people." They usually have at least 20 beers on tap, along with basic pub grub, from burgers to fish 'n' chips to traditional Irish stew.

The local outpost of a Toronto-based restaurant group, **Oliver and Bonacini Café Grill** (Westin Trillium House, 220 Mountain Dr., 705/444-8680, www.oliverbonacini.com, 7 A.M.–10 P.M. daily, $13–30) is one of the best places to eat in the village. It's not cheap, but the contemporary dishes are both crowd-pleasing and creative. Try the Japanese-influenced chicken Caesar salad with edamame, shiitake mushrooms, and wasabi peas or the rock shrimp linguine with basil-almond pesto.

Practicalities

The Blue Mountain Resort is 170 kilometers (105 miles) northwest of Toronto and 11 kilometers (7 miles) west of Collingwood, off Highway 26. Depending on traffic and weather conditions, it's about a two-hour drive from metropolitan Toronto. For resort information or reservations, contact **Blue Mountain Resorts Limited** (108 Jozo Weider Blvd., Blue Mountains, ON, 705/445-0231 or 877/445-0231, www.bluemountain.ca) or the **Blue Mountain Village Association** (705/445-0231, www.villageatblue.com).

If you're staying in the Village at Blue Mountain, you don't really need a car. The village is car-free (and ringed with parking lots where you can leave yours). A free **resort shuttle** (www.bluemountain.ca) loops through the village daily every 15–20 minutes between 8 A.M. and 10:30 P.M. Outside of these hours, you can call for a pickup by dialing extension 8280 on any resort phone.

COLLINGWOOD

While many people come to Collingwood to ski or snowboard at nearby Blue Mountain, it's also a pleasant spot for a weekend getaway, even if you're not mountain-bound. The Collingwood area draws gourmets to its many first-rate restaurants. The **Georgian Trail** (705/445-7722, www.brucegreytrails.com) is a flat, 32-kilometer (20-mile) rail trail for hiking and cycling that runs west from Collingwood to the nearby towns of Thornbury and Meaford, passing several beaches en route. In winter, it's a cross-country ski and snowshoeing trail.

To soothe those post-adventure sore muscles, sink into the outdoor baths at the **Scandinave Spa at Blue Mountain** (152 Grey Road 21, Blue Mountains, 705/443-8484 or 877/988-8484, www.scandinave.com, 10 A.M.–9 P.M., $45), which offers a Scandinavian-style "bath experience." First, warm up with heat in one of the Finnish saunas, steam baths, or outdoor hot tubs. Then immerse yourself in a chilling plunge pool. After recovering in one of the relaxation areas, repeat the process until you feel totally tranquil; the average stay is 2–4 hours. The experience is even more magical when snow falls on the hot pools. Bathing suits are required, and you must be at least 19 years old. Prices are $10 less on Wednesdays.

For several days in July, Collingwood is overrun with Elvis Presley lookalikes. The annual **Collingwood Elvis Festival** (866/444-1162, www.collingwoodelvisfestival.com) features a parade, as well as more than 100 tribute concerts. Not only is it the region's biggest event, but it ranks among the world's largest Elvis festivals. If you didn't pack your blue suede shoes, the **Collingwood Music Festival** (519/599-

5461, www. collingwoodmusicfestival.com) presents a series of classical and world music concerts in July and August. Performances are held at the New Life Brethren in Christ Church (28 Tracey Lane, at Hurontario St.).

Scenic Caves Nature Adventures

Located high in the hills outside Collingwood, Scenic Caves Nature Adventures (260/280 Scenic Caves Rd., 705/446-0256, www. sceniccaves.com, 9 A.M.–5 P.M. Mon.–Fri., 9 A.M.–6 P.M. Sat.–Sun. May–Oct.) is a sprawling outdoor playground. Walking trails wend through the woods, and you can explore a network of underground caves (try to squeeze yourself through "Fat Man's Misery," a narrow rock channel). A highlight, at least if you're not afraid of heights, is a stroll across the 126-meter (413-foot) suspension bridge, Ontario's longest suspension footbridge, with panoramic views across Georgian Bay. Basic admission rates (adults $20.80, seniors $18.36, and children 3–17 $16.82) include access to the caves, suspension bridge, and walking trails.

If you're more adventurous, consider the three-hour guided eco-tour (adults $95, seniors and children 10–17 $85.), which includes a short hike to the suspension bridge, followed by a treetop canopy tour through the trees on a network of narrow wooden bridges. You'll also tour the caves and whiz through the air on not one, but two, zip lines, including a 305-meter (1,000-foot) plunge from the top of the Niagara Escarpment.

In winter, the eco-tours aren't offered, but the park is open for cross-country skiing and snowshoeing (9 A.M.–5 P.M. daily Dec.–Mar., full-day weekend/weekday pass: adults $18.50/14.50, seniors and children 6–17 $14.50/$12.50). You can even snowshoe across the suspension bridge. Ski and snowshoe rentals are available, and on weekends, you can purchase a half-day admission (adults $16.50, seniors/children $12.50).

Allow a minimum of two hours to explore the site, but you can easily spend most of the day. Wear running or hiking shoes. There's a

GEORGIAN BAY

small snack bar, but for more variety, pack your own picnic lunch.

Accommodations

A number of Collingwood's restored Victorian homes are now inns or B&Bs, and in the hills around town, you'll find more small accommodations. Contact the **Collingwood Area Bed and Breakfast Association** (www.bbcanada. com/associations/cabba) for additional lodging options. Motels are clustered along Highway 26, west of town. Most area lodgings are open year-round.

The **Beild House Country Inn** (64 Third St., 705/444-1522 or 888/322-3453, www. beildhouse.com, $140 d) isn't in the country—it's just a block from Collingwood's main downtown street—but it has the faded charm of a country estate. The parlor, with its dark woodwork, chintz sofas, and portraits of Victorian gentlemen, and the dining room, where elaborate multicourse dinners are served by candlelight, recall its glory days as a private residence (it was built in 1909). Drawing couples who come to cocoon, the 11 guest rooms are romantic in a cozy, if slightly fussy, Victorian style. Rates start at $140 for a double room including a full breakfast and afternoon tea; on weekends, guests must also include dinner ($60 per person). If you're not staying at the inn, you can have dinner here with advance reservations.

As the name might suggest, the four guest rooms at the romantic **Bacchus House** (142 Hume St., 705/446-4700, www.bacchushouse.ca, call for rates) are decorated with a wine theme. All the bedrooms in this 1880 yellow-brick Victorian have hardwood floors, TV/DVD players, and iPod docking stations, but each has slightly different features: the purple Pinot Noir Suite has an ornate four-poster bed, the Merlot Suite (done in brown and burgundy) has a gas fireplace, and the Cabernet Sauvignon Suite has a clawfoot tub. There are several common spaces for guests, including the living room with a fireplace and overstuffed sofas, a den with a TV, a deck with a hot tub, and the dining room, where a full

breakfast is served. Only the location on a busy street mars the elegance of this upscale lodging; if you're sensitive to traffic noise, choose the golden-hued Chardonnay Suite at the rear of the house.

Set on a 15-acre property with gardens, walking trails, a swimming pool, and a gaggle of ducks and hens, the **Willow Trace B&B** (7833 Poplar Side Rd., 705/445-9003, www. collingwoodbedandbreakfast.com, $125–150 d) feels like a rural getaway, yet it's only a five-minute drive from downtown. The rooms are bright and modern, with two upstairs and one on the lower level facing the gardens (the downstairs room is family-friendly). Co-owner and chef Philip Tarlo runs the B&B with his wife Leanne Calvert and allows guests to choose from a menu of breakfast options that he'll prepare to order—perhaps cinnamon French toast, a customized omelet, or a full English breakfast.

Food

Collingwood's restaurants range from the foodie to the ardently epicurean. Most are located on or near Hurontario Street in the town center. Even hot dogs go gourmet at **Buddha Dog** (48 Pine St., 705/444-2005, www.buddhafoodha.com), which upgrades the lowly tube steak with locally raised beef and homemade buns.

Hidden in a lane downtown, **Tesoro** (18 School House Ln., 705/444-9230, lunch and dinner Mon.–Sat., dinner only Sun., $14–27), with its sturdy pine tables and vibrant red chairs, is the sort of welcoming, casual Italian eatery everyone would like to have in their neighborhood. There's a long list of creative pizzas (try the Tre Funghi with black olives and three types of mushrooms), as well as updated versions of Italian classics, like penne *arrabiatta* (pasta with spicy sausage and hot peppers), chicken *parmigiano,* or lasagna.

One of Ontario's most distinctive dining destinations is ◖ **Eigensinn Farm** (449357 Concession Rd. 10, Singhampton, 519/922-3128), which draws well-heeled gourmets from far and wide. Chef-owner Michael Stadtlander left Toronto for a quieter country life here; he accommodates no more than a dozen diners per night, creating extravagant eight-course tasting menus ($275). And that's not including wine (the restaurant has no liquor license, so guests must bring their own). The restaurant's schedule can be as wildly personal as the dining experience, so make reservations well in advance. To get here from Collingwood, take County Road 124 south for about 13 kilometers (eight miles).

The owners of Eigensinn Farm also run the nearby **Haisai Restaurant & Bakery** (794079 County Rd. 124, Singhampton, 705/445-2748, www.haisairestaurantbakery.com). The bakery (8:30 A.M.–6 P.M. Wed.–Sat., 9 A.M.–6 P.M. Sun.) sells freshly baked breads, buns, and pastries, along with a selection of prepared foods. The restaurant (Fri.–Sat. evenings) serves elaborate multicourse tasting menus by reservation only. No credit cards.

Practicalities

The **Georgian Triangle Tourist Association** (30 Mountain Rd., 705/445-7722 or 888/227-8667, www.visitsouthgeorgianbay.ca) runs a tourist information center that provides information about the Collingwood/Blue Mountain region. **Greyhound Bus Lines** (800/661-8747, www.greyhound.ca) operates two buses a day in each direction between Toronto and Collingwood; the same buses also go on to Blue Mountain. The trip takes about 3 hours. In town, the buses depart from Collingwood's **Transportation Centre** (22 Second St., 705/445-7095). On the mountain, buses stop at the **Blue Mountain Inn** (www.bluemountain.ca).

Simcoe County Airport Service (137 Brock St., Barrie, 705/728-1148 or 800/461-7529, www.simcoecountyairportservice.ca) runs regular vans from Toronto's Pearson airport to Collingwood and the Blue Mountain Resort. Prices vary depending on the number of people in your party. From Pearson to Collingwood, the one-way price is $88 for one person, $119 for two; to Blue Mountain, it's $99 for one, $130 for two. **Colltrans** (705/446-

1196, www.collingwood.ca, 7 A.M.–6 P.M. Mon.–Sat., 9 A.M.–5 P.M. Sun., $1) is the town's public-transportation service, with three routes around the community (but not out to Blue Mountain). The main bus "terminal" (Second St. at Pine St.) is an outdoor bus shelter.

VICINITY OF COLLINGWOOD

Several small towns around Collingwood, including Thornbury and Meaford to the west and Creemore to the south, are worth exploring for their galleries, shops, and restaurants. Wasaga Beach, the world's longest freshwater beach, is also an easy day trip from Collingwood.

Creemore

This village of about 1,300 people makes a great day trip if you're looking for that elusive "small-town charm." The main downtown street—Mill Street—is lined with art galleries, cafés, and shops, ready-made for wandering and browsing. Creemore's main "tourist attraction" is the **Creemore Springs Brewery** (139 Mill St., 705/466-2240 or 800/267-2240, www. creemoresprings.com, 10 A.M.–6 P.M. Mon.–Sat., 11 A.M.–5 P.M. Sun.), which was started in 1987 by three beer-loving guys who retired to the area and decided they needed a hobby. The brewery now produces several varieties of beer, including their signature Creemore Springs Premium Lager. You can take a free 30-minute tour of their production facility, which wraps up with a beer tasting. Tours are offered several times a day year-round. The brewery shop sells beer and brew-related souvenirs.

The **Mad and Noisy Gallery** (154 Mill St., 705/466-5555, www.madandnoisy.com, 11 A.M.–5 P.M. Mon.–Fri., 10 A.M.–5 P.M. Sat., noon–4 P.M. Sun.) is neither—it's named for the two rivers that meet near Creemore. It showcases high-quality work of painters, sculptors, photographers, and other artists, most of whom hail from the Southern Georgian Bay area. The **Maplestone Gallery** (142 Mill St., 705/520-0067, http://maplestonegallery.com, 11 A.M.–5 P.M. Thurs.–Fri., 10 A.M.–5 P.M. Sat., 11 A.M.–4 P.M. Sun.) is unique in Canada

The Creemore Jail is North America's smallest prison.

for displaying only contemporary mosaic art. Many of the works are surprisingly ornate and, not surprisingly, beautiful. Want to learn to create mosaics yourself? The gallery runs periodic workshops for beginners.

Mill Street has several café's, bakeries, and restaurants, as well as the **100 Mile Store** (176 Mill St., 705/466-3514, www.100milestore. ca), a local grocery that lives up to its name by sourcing its products—from produce to grains to meats—within 100 miles of town. Stop in for locally made snacks, cheeses, or ice cream. A good choice for a sit-down meal is **Chez Michel** (150 Mill St., 705/466-3331, www.chezmichel.ca, lunch and dinner Wed.– Sun., $26–60), decorated in sunny yellows and bright Provençal blues. The kitchen uses local Ontario ingredients to create classic French dishes from *escargots* (snails) to *steak au poivre*.

When you're done shopping and snacking, venture east of Mill Street to find the **Creemore Jail** (Library St., between Elizabeth and Caroline Sts.). This diminutive stone structure, built in 1892, claims to be the smallest jail in North America.

Creemore is about 30 kilometers (19 miles) southeast of Collingwood. If you're not in a hurry, you can meander here through the countryside along a series of back roads. Otherwise, the fastest route is to take Highway 26 east from Collingwood to Highway 42 south; then go west on Highway 9 into Creemore and turn left onto Mill Street.

Wasaga Beach

The Wasaga area played a role in the War of 1812, through a trading ship called the *Nancy,* built in 1789. In 1814, American troops attacked the Nancy on the Nottawasaga River. The ship sank, and eventually the silt and sand flowing through the river collected around the ship's hull, forming an island. Today, at the **Nancy Island Historic Site** (late May–early Sept., 705/429-2728, www.wasagabeachpark. com), you can see the *Nancy*'s hull, watch a video about her story, and join in as park staff reenact elements of the *Nancy*'s history.

Along Georgian Bay east of Collingwood, **Wasaga Beach Provincial Park** (11 22nd St. N., Wasaga Beach, 705/429-2516, www.ontarioparks.com, 8:15 A.M.–10 P.M. daily Apr.–mid-Oct., $13–18/vehicle) is the world's longest freshwater beach. This stretch of sand extends for 14 kilometers (nearly nine miles) and is divided into eight different sections, each with a different personality. Beaches 1–4 are closer into town and have more restaurants, shops, and other services; they're also more crowded and honky-tonk. As you move farther from the town center—to Beaches 5 and 6 to the south and New Wasaga and Allenwood Beaches to the north—the sand becomes less populated and more peaceful. Because the beach is flat and the bay is shallow, Wasaga is a popular destination for families. (Note that a new Wasaga Beach Welcome Centre is slated to open in 2012).

Although most people come for the beach, Wasaga also has 50 kilometers (31 miles) of hiking trails. The park service leads guided hikes on Wednesdays in July and August. In winter, there are 30 kilometers (19 miles) of trails for cross-country skiing. Access the trail network from the **Wasaga Nordic Centre** (705/429-0943, 9 A.M.–5 P.M. daily mid-Dec.–mid-Mar., adults $9.50, children 6–17 $4.75).

For information about Wasaga Beach, contact the provincial park office (705/429-2516, www.ontarioparks.com), or check the informative **Friends of Wasaga Beach** (www.wasagabeachpark.com) website. The **Town of Wasaga Beach** (705/429-3844, www.wasagabeach.com) and the **Wasaga Beach Chamber of Commerce** (705/429-2247 or 866/292-7242, www.wasagainfo.com) are good sources of information about accommodations and services in the Wasaga area. Wasaga Beach has the usual assortment of modest beach motels, as well as privately run campgrounds (the provincial park has no camping facilities). Cottage rentals are also popular; contact the Chamber of Commerce (705/429-2247 or 866/292-7242, www.wasagainfo.com) for details.

Located about 20 kilometers (12.5 miles) east of Collingwood, Wasaga Beach is an easy day trip from the Collingwood area; take Highway 26 to Highway 92.

Midland and Parry Sound

This peninsula on Georgian Bay's southwestern side houses the towns of Midland and Penetanguishene. It once played an important role in Ontario's early history. Long populated by First Nations people, in the 1600s a site near present-day Midland became the region's first European settlement, when a group of French Jesuits established a village there. The area retains a strong French and First Nations heritage. Several interesting historic sites, particularly the well-designed Sainte-Marie among the Hurons, illuminate the region's past.

Like the other areas around Georgian Bay, the Midland region has its share of beautiful outdoor destinations, particularly Wye Marsh in Midland and the large Awenda Provincial Park in Penetanguishene. It's also a gateway to the 30,000 Islands that dot Georgian Bay, some of which are protected in the Georgian Bay Islands National Park.

You can visit the Georgian Bay Islands National Park in a day trip from either Midland or Penetanguishene; it's less than an hour's drive to Honey Harbour, where the boat to the park islands departs.

North along Georgian Bay is Parry Sound, a pleasant community that's both a base for outdoor activities and a cultural destination. Less than an hour's drive away, the ruggedly beautiful Killbear Provincial Park draws travelers to its waterfront campgrounds.

MIDLAND

The largest community along this part of Georgian Bay, Midland is still a fairly small town (population 17,000), and it retains its low-

GEORGIAN BAY

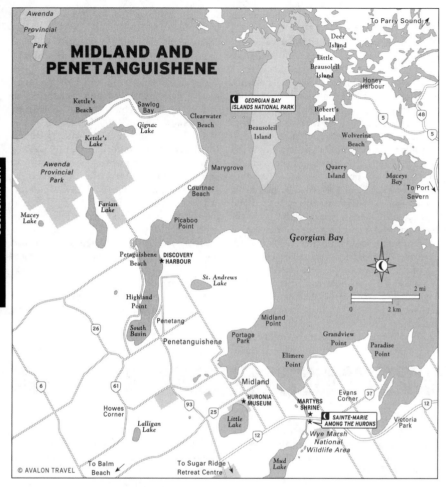

key feel along King Street, the main downtown street. The town has begun to sprawl out from the center, with malls and other developments on its edges, and its sights are spread out around the area. But it's a convenient base for exploring the region's mix of historic and outdoor attractions.

As you walk around downtown Midland, be on the lookout for the 34 **murals** (www.downtownmidland.ca) painted on walls around town. One mural, painted on silos along Midland Harbor, depicts a Jesuit priest and a Huron native at Sainte-Marie; it is reportedly

the largest outdoor historic mural in North America. Pick up a mural map at the **Southern Georgian Bay Chamber of Commerce** (208 King St., 705/526-7884) or contact the **Downtown Midland Business Improvement Association** (212 King St., 705/527-7246, www.downtownmidland.ca), which offers free guided mural tours by appointment.

Sainte-Marie Among the Hurons

In 1639, a group of French Jesuit missionaries

began constructing a community near present-day Midland, establishing the first European settlement in Ontario. Their goal was to bring Christianity to the native Wendat people, whom they called the "Huron." The Jesuits worked with the Huron for 10 years, until hostilities worsened between the Huron and the nearby Iroquois people. After the Iroquois killed two of the priests, the Jesuits abandoned the settlement and burned it to the ground to protect it from desecration. Centuries later, in 1930, Pope Pius XI canonized the murdered priests, Father Jean de Brébeuf and Father Gabriel Lalemant.

What you see today at this fascinating historic village (Hwy. 12 E., 705/526-7838, www.saintemarieamongthehurons.on.ca, 10 A.M.–5 P.M. daily mid-May–mid-Oct., 10 A.M.–5 P.M. Mon.–Fri. late Apr.–mid-May and late Oct., adults $11.25, seniors $9.25, students $9.75, children 6–12 $8.50) is a "re-imagination" of the 17th-century settlement. Because the Jesuits left no records, historians can only theorize what the community actually looked like. It wasn't until the 1940s and '50s that archeologists began excavating the area, providing clues to the village's history and structure.

Sainte-Marie was reconstructed replicating French construction styles of the period. Surrounded by a high wooden fence, the settlement has 25 buildings in three main areas. The **North Court** was the mission's primary living and working quarters, including a cookhouse, chapel, carpentry shop, a chicken run, and stables. The **South Court** was where supplies arrived (following an 800-mile canoe journey from Quebec). The South Court includes a reconstructed waterway with working locks that may have allowed canoes to enter the mission from the river. The third section of the settlement was the **Native Area,** where a church, a longhouse, a hospital, and other structures illustrate the mix of French and Huron building styles and cultures.

You can easily spend several hours exploring the settlement. Start your visit with the 15-minute movie that introduces the site's history. In summer, costumed guides staff the village buildings, demonstrating elements of village life, from cooking to blacksmithing to Wendat storytelling. In spring or fall, when fewer staff are on duty, rent the audio guide ($3) to help understand the site. Following your walk through the village, you can explore museum exhibits that provide more background and history about the settlement.

Sainte-Marie Among the Hurons (www.saintemarieamongthehurons.on.ca) organizes a number of special events throughout the year. Highlights include the annual **Aboriginal Festival** (June), which honors the Hurons' heritage with traditional dancing, music, games, and crafts, and the **First Light Festival** (late Nov.), which lights up the Sainte-Marie site with more than 3,000 candles.

The site is five kilometers (three miles) east on Highway 12 from the intersection of Highway 93.

Wye Marsh Wildlife Centre

A lovely spot to enjoy the outdoors is this nature center and marshlands (16160 Hwy. 12 E., 705/526-7809, www.wyemarsh.com, 9 A.M.–5 P.M. daily, adults $11, seniors and students $8.50, children 6–12 $8) on the east side of Midland, next to Sainte-Marie Among the Hurons. The visitor center has exhibits about local ecology, and kids enjoy the live animal presentations, but the real action is outdoors, where one can follow a network of walking trails around the marsh. Rent an audio guide for details about the plants and wildlife, or simply follow the interpretive signs and climb up the observation tower for views over the marsh.

The marsh is a nesting habitat for trumpeter swans, and one highlight of a visit here is the chance to observe these majestic birds. You can canoe or kayak on the channels that wend through the marsh, and guided canoe excursions are offered.

In winter, there are 22 kilometers (14 miles) of groomed trails for cross-country skiing and 10 kilometers (six miles) of snowshoeing trails. Ski ($15) and snowshoe rentals ($5–10) are available. You can also take a snowshoe eco-tour, a three-hour guided walk to learn about the local waterfowl, plants, and wetlands. A wide variety of other nature programs are offered throughout the year.

Martyrs' Shrine

Located across the highway from Sainte-Marie Among the Hurons, this 1926 church (16163 Hwy. 12 W., 705/526-3788, www.martyrs-shrine.com, 8:30 A.M.–9 P.M. daily mid-May–mid-Oct., adults and children 10 and older $4), with its two soaring spires, honors the memory of the Jesuits who worked at Sainte-Marie but were killed in a 1649 Iroquois raid. Mass is celebrated several times a day, and you can stroll around the gardens and walkways. The site draws religious pilgrims from all over the world. An onsite café serves basic breakfasts and lunches.

Huronia Museum

Exploring the Huronia Museum (549 Little Lake Park, 705/526-2844, www.huroniamuseum.com, 9 A.M.–5 P.M. daily May–Oct., Mon.–Fri. Nov.–Apr., adults $8.60, seniors $7.55, children 5–17 $5.40), an old-fashioned regional history museum, feels like a treasure hunt. You might find everything from washtubs to wheelchairs, sewing machines to the "Slenderizer" (an old-time exercise machine). Most of the hodgepodge of artifacts dates from the 1800s and 1900s. Also on the site is the Huron Ouendat Village, a modest re-creation of a 16th-century First Nations settlement.

Sports and Recreation

The Midland/Penetanguishene peninsula is surrounded by water, but many of the beaches are private. One exception is the small, sandy **Balm Beach** (www.visitbalmbeach.com) on Georgian Bay. From Midland, take Highway 25/Balm Beach Road directly west to the water. The west-facing beach is a pretty spot to watch the sunset. The **Miss Midland 30,000 Islands Boat Cruises** (705/549-3388, www.midlandtours.com, mid-May–mid-Oct., adults $27, seniors $25, students $20, children 5–14 $14) are two-hour tours around the Georgian Bay Islands

National Park and some of the other 30,000 islands. Cruises depart from the Midland Town Dock at the foot of King Street.

Accommodations

Midland has the usual selection of chain motels, clustered along King Street near Highway 12 or on Yonge Street off Highway 93. Try the **Best Western Highland Inn** (924 King St., 705/526-9307 or 800/461-4265, www.bestwesternmidland.com) or the **Midland Comfort Inn** (980 King St., 705/526-2090 or 888/274-3020, www.comfortinnmidland.com). For bed-and-breakfast options, check the website for the **Southern Georgian Bay B&B Association** (www.southerngeorgianbaybb.com).

Want to get away from it all? Set amid tall grasses and marshlands on a secluded country road and about a 15-minute drive south of downtown Midland, the (● **Sugar Ridge Retreat Centre** (5720 Forgets Rd., Wyebridge, 705/528-1793 or 866/609-1793, www.sugar-ridge.ca, $120/night with breakfast) may be one of the quietest places you'll ever stay. While many guests come for yoga retreats and other workshops, artists, writers, and anyone looking for a peaceful escape is also welcome. Ten sturdy cabins dot the fields around the main lodge building, a contemporary Zen-style retreat center with an airy yoga studio, guest lounge, and large dining room. The cabins, which sleep up to four, are simply furnished with warm duvets, electric heat, and ceiling fans. They have no plumbing, phones, or Internet service; however, the area does have cell phone coverage, and restrooms, showers, and Wi-Fi are available in the lodge, where vegetarian meals are also served. Rates vary depending on the number of guests and meals, and whether you're part of a group retreat. Guests are welcome to join in yoga and meditation classes (drop-in fee $15). Owners Liz and Kurt Frost, both psychotherapists and yoga instructors, also accommodate B&B guests in their home down the road (5790 Forgets Rd., $95–115 d).

Food

For places to eat in Midland, wander along

King Street downtown. At **Ciboulette et Cie** (248 King St., 705/245-0410, www.ciboulet-teetcie.ca, 8:30–9 A.M. until 6–7 P.M. daily; call for specific hours), a cheerful café and takeout shop (the name is French for "Chive and Company"), the day starts with freshly baked scones and other pastries. Then creative sandwiches and delicious ready-to-eat salads, perhaps Brussels sprout slaw or roasted sweet potatoes with cranberries, make a quick lunch or early supper.

With its walls of books, maps, and photos of faraway lands, **The Explorers Cafe** (345 King St., 705/527-9199, www.theexplorerscafe.com, noon–10 P.M. Tues.–Sat., lunch $10–12, dinner $17–25) resembles a Victorian-era adventurer's residence. The menu wanders the world, too; there's always an Indian-style curry and a New Zealand meat pie, and you might find an Argentinean steak, Spanish grilled sardines, or a Singapore noodle bowl. Despite the international emphasis, there's usually a "100 mile meal," as well, with most of its ingredients sourced locally. Although the restaurant is right downtown, you may need a compass to find it, since it's set back from the main road; look for their signboard on King Street.

Craving Texas-style barbecued pork ribs? Jerk chicken? BBQ brisket? Then head for the little yellow bungalow, about 10 minutes south of Midland, that houses **MAD Michael's Restaurant and Bakery** (8215 Hwy. 93, Wyebridge, 705/527-1666, www.madmichaels.com, noon–8 P.M. Thurs.–Sun. May–mid-Oct., lunch $13–16, dinner $15–20). This isn't any ordinary BBQ shack; chef "Mad Michael" White smokes ribs in his outdoor kitchen, bakes bread, and even makes his own ketchup (in his spare time, he crafts rustic wood furniture). Save room for a slice of homemade pie.

Practicalities

The helpful staff at the **Southern Georgian Bay Chamber of Commerce and Tourism Information Centre** (208 King St., 705/526-7884 or 800/263-7745, www.southerngeorgianbay.on.ca) in downtown Midland can provide lots of information about the region.

The Midland/Penetanguishene area is about 160 kilometers (100 miles) from Toronto. From Highway 93, take Highway 12 east, then turn left onto King Street for downtown Midland or continue east on Highway 12 to Sainte-Marie Among the Hurons, the Martyrs' Shrine, and Wye Marsh. The attractions in Midland and Penetanguishene are spread out over a fairly wide area. It's difficult to explore the region without a car.

PENETANGUISHENE

Smaller than nearby Midland, the town of Penetanguishene (population 9,300) has a strong French heritage; roughly 16 percent of the residents speak French as their first language. Penetanguishene's main attractions are the restored naval base at Discovery Harbour and the sprawling Awenda Provincial Park, which has the region's best beaches. Penetanguishene Harbor is also the departure point for the area's most interesting 30,000 Islands cruise.

Discovery Harbour

Following the War of 1812, the British built a naval base at Penetanguishene to protect the Upper Great Lakes region from possible future American attacks. Today, you can visit the restored base now known as Discovery Harbour (93 Jury Dr., 705/549-8064, www.discoveryharbour.on.ca, 10 A.M.–5 P.M. daily July–early Sept.; 10 A.M.–5 P.M. Mon.–Fri. late May–June, adults $6, seniors and students $5.25, children 6–12 $4.25) to learn more about naval and military life here in the 1800s. While only one original building remains (the 1845 Officers' Quarters), the reconstructed site reflects life on the base during the period from 1817 to 1822. Guides in period costumes conduct tours of the 19 historic buildings and demonstrate various aspects of sailors' life, from cooking to ropework to games. You can also tour replicas of two majestic 18th-century British sailing vessels, the H.M.S. *Bee,* a supply schooner, and the H.M.S. *Tecumseth,* a warship.

Awenda Provincial Park

Fronting Georgian Bay 11 kilometers (seven

miles) northwest of Penetanguishene, this 2,915-hectare (7,200-acre) provincial park (Awenda Park Rd., off Concession Rd. 16 E./ Lafontaine Rd. E., 705/549-2231, www.ontarioparks.com, $13/vehicle) is a beautiful destination for hiking and swimming. One of the largest parks in central Ontario, Awenda is in a transition zone between north and south, making it home to a diverse array of plants and trees, as well as roughly 200 bird species and many reptiles and amphibians. In summer, park staff offer a variety of nature programs, theatrical productions, and other special events; call the park office or check online (Friends of Awenda, www.awendapark.ca) for schedules.

Awenda is open year-round, and you can cross-country ski here in winter.

30,000 Island Cruises

What makes the island cruises special on the **M.S. Georgian Queen** (705/549-7795 or 800/363-7447, www.georgianbaycruises.com, May–mid-Oct., adults $20–27, seniors $18–24, children 5–14 $9–11) is the onboard commentary that the companionable captain provides. As you cruise out of Penetanguishene Harbor and out among the 30,000 Islands, Captain Steve will not only point out the "sights," but he'll tell you who lives on what island (many are private), which properties are for sale (and at what price), and how locals manage to build homes, transport goods, and spend summers on these isolated chunks of rock. The cruises depart from the Town Docks at the foot of Main Street and range from 1–3 hours. Take one of the longer cruises if you can, since the shortest excursions stay in the harbor area rather than travel out to the islands.

Sports and Recreation

Awenda Provincial Park (Awenda Park Rd., off Concession Rd. 16 E./Lafontaine Rd. E., 705/549-2231, www.ontarioparks.com, $13/ vehicle) has approximately 30 kilometers (19 miles) of multiuse trails throughout the park. The most popular is the easy **Beach Trail,** which connects the park's four beaches. Off the Beach Trail, you can follow the easy, one-

kilometer (0.6-mile) **Beaver Pond Trail,** most of which is along a boardwalk, to an area that had extensive beaver activity.

Longer park trails include: the **Robitaille Homestead Trail,** a three-kilometer (1.9-mile) round-trip trail past ancient sand dunes, that begins in the day parking lot near Bear Campground; the five-kilometer (three-mile) **Wendat Trail,** which starts near Kettle's Lake; and the 13-kilometer (eight-mile) **Bluff Trail,** which circles the campgrounds and connects the camping areas to the beach.

Some of the nicest swimming spots in the Midland/Penetanguishene area are within the provincial park, which has four beaches along Georgian Bay. **First Beach,** closest to the parking area, is a sheltered, family-friendly sand beach that also has rocks for the kids to climb on. You can continue along the beach trail to **Second Beach; Third Beach,** which has particularly soft sand; and eventually to the more secluded **Fourth Beach.** It's about two kilometers (1.25 miles) from First to Fourth Beach.

You can also swim at **Kettle's Lake,** an inland lake with an easy boardwalk trail to the water. The lake is also a calm spot for canoeing, particularly for beginning paddlers; in summer, canoe rentals are available. Around the lake, you might see otters, beaver, loon, or great blue heron.

Entertainment and Events

Located at Discovery Harbour, the **King's Wharf Theatre** (97 Jury Dr., 705/549-5555 or 888/449-4463, www.draytonentertainment. com) is a professional summer theater that produces several plays every year between June and early September. Discovery Harbour celebrates the region's Métis traditions through music, art, and games at the annual **Métis Day Bo'jou Neejee event** (early Aug., www.discoveryharbour.on.ca). The Métis are an aboriginal group of mixed First Nations and European heritage; more than 10 percent of Penetanguishene's current population is of Métis descent.

Accommodations and Food

Catering primarily to boaters and their guests,

the **Hindson Marina Floatel-Motel** (79 Champlain Rd., 705/549-2991, www.hindsonmarine.on.ca, $109–132 d) is a floating lodging, right on the docks on the west side of Penetanguishene Harbor. The three rooms and one two-room suite are ordinary motel units, but you can't get much closer to the water than this. Entrance is through the marina gates.

Surrounded by lush gardens and tall pines, the **Copeland Woods B&B** (47 Copeland Creek Dr., 705/549-1330, www.copelandwoodsbb.com, May–Oct., $115–135 d) feels like an escape into nature. Because the owners built the home as a combination residence and B&B, the accommodations are well designed for guests. Of the three stylish-country guest rooms, one is on the main level, and the other two are on the lower level facing the garden and woods. There's a kitchenette with a fridge and microwave for guests' use, and a full breakfast is served either on the deck or around the Arts and Crafts–style dining table. The B&B is in a quiet residential subdivision on Penetanguishene's west side.

Do you fantasize about having your own cottage right on Georgian Bay? Awenda Provincial Park's **Stone Cottage** (Awenda Park Rd., off Concession Rd. 16 E./Lafontaine Rd. E., 705/549-2231, www.ontarioparks.com, May–Oct.) can be yours, at least for a week or two. Down an unmarked lane deep in the park, the lodging looks like the classic Canadian hideaway, made of solid fieldstone, with a spacious terrace directly above the water. Inside, the huge open living room has a stone fireplace and a wall of windows facing the bay. There are two bedrooms, one with a double bed and two bunks and a second with twin beds. So what's not to love? Like the classic cottages of the 1940s, when the Stone Cottage was built, it has no running water; large jugs of drinking water are provided, and there's an outhouse but no shower. You also need to bring sleeping bags or linens, as well as food and cooking gear. The cottage rents by the week ($1,040/week) from late June through early September; you can book stays of two days or more ($150/night) in the spring or fall. Make reservations (Ontario Parks Reservation Service, 888/668-7275, www.ontarioparks.com, $8.50

for online bookings, $9.50 for telephone bookings) well in advance.

Just up the hill from Penetanguishene harbor, the **Froth Café** (102 Main St., 705/549-7199, www.frothcafe.com, 8 A.M.–5 P.M. Tues.–Sun.) is a convenient spot for breakfast, lunch, or a sightseeing coffee break. The menu is simple: scones, bagels, French toast, and omelets in the morning (all under $5); salads and sandwiches ($6–10), including a warm chicken panini, at midday. Jazz on the stereo and local art on the walls make it feel cool and arty. Free Wi-Fi.

CAMPING

The six campgrounds at **Awenda Provincial Park** (Awenda Park Rd., off Concession Rd. 16 E./Lafontaine Rd. E., 705/549-2231, www.ontarioparks.com, mid-May–mid-Oct., $36.75 tent sites, $42.25 electrical sites) are set amid maple and oak forests, so the 333 shaded sites feel comparatively private. All the camping areas have flush toilets and showers, and three have laundry facilities. Although the park has lovely beaches, none of the campgrounds is on the water. The Snake, Wolf, and Deer areas are closest to the bay, but it's still a long walk. Bring bicycles if you can. To book a campsite, contact the Ontario Parks Reservation Service (888/668-7275, www.ontarioparks.com, $8.50 for online bookings, $9.50 for telephone bookings).

Practicalities

The **Penetanguishene Tourist Information Centre** (1 Main St., 705/549-2232, www.penetanguishene.ca, 10 A.M.–6 P.M. Wed.–Sun. mid-to-late May, 10 A.M.–6 P.M. daily June and Sept., 10 A.M.–8 P.M. daily July–Aug.) is at the town docks.

The Midland/Penetanguishene area is about 160 kilometers (100 miles) from Toronto. Highway 93 connects Midland to Penetanguishene, where it becomes Main Street. You really need a car to explore the region.

◖ THE GEORGIAN BAY ISLANDS NATIONAL PARK

Georgian Bay is dotted with at least 30,000 islands. Some are not much more than a big

GEORGIAN BAY

GEORGIAN BAY

THAT'S A LOT OF ISLANDS

Many people outside of Ontario know about the Thousand Islands, the chain of islands along the St. Lawrence River in the eastern part of the province. After all, there's even a salad dressing with the Thousand Islands name. Yet the Georgian Bay region has far more than just a thousand isles. Depending on who's counting, Georgian Bay is dotted with at least 30,000 islands. It's one of the world's largest freshwater archipelagoes.

Some of these islands are hardly more than specks of bare rock, while others are quite substantial. Manitoulin Island, which measures 2,765 square kilometers (1,067 square miles) on the bay's northern side, is the largest freshwater island in the world.

What created these many different islands? During the ice age, more than 10,000 years ago, glaciers covered what is now Canada. According to one theory, the movement of these glaciers compressed and reshaped the land, fashioning the distinctive landscape of islands and coves that today surrounds Georgian Bay.

UNESCO has recognized the unique geography of the Georgian Bay region and its islands, designating 347,000 hectares (857,455 acres) of the shoreline between the Severn and French Rivers as the **Georgian Bay Biosphere Reserve** (705/774-0978 or 866/495-4227, www.gbbr.ca). One of 15 such reserves in Canada, it's home to more than 100 species of at-risk animals and plants, including the eastern wolf, the lake sturgeon, and the Massasauga rattlesnake. The biosphere's mission is to assist in the conservation of these species and to support both education and sustainable development in the region, working with the provincial and national parks, local municipalities, and private businesses and landowners along the bay.

The 30,000 Islands are a mix of public and private lands. Some, like the 63 islands of the **Georgian Bay Islands National Park** (705/526-9804, www.pc.gc.ca) or **Fathom Five National Marine Park** (519/596-2233, www.pc.gc.ca), are government-protected natural areas. Many others are privately owned, with a cottage or two offering their owners a waterfront getaway. Visitors to this island region can cruise around the bays and harbors, explore the island parks, and even soar above the islands by floatplane.

So come back again and again. To tour even a tiny fraction of these 30,000 islands will take you years – no, decades – of exploring.

---

rock jutting out of the water, while others are substantial enough to house entire communities. A visit to Georgian Bay Islands National Park (www.pc.gc.ca, open year-round), established in 1929 and encompassing 63 islands across Georgian Bay, is perhaps the easiest way to sample the island experience.

With numerous hiking trails, beaches, and campgrounds, as well as a visitor center, Beausoleil Island, the largest of the park's islands, is the most accessible area. Parks Canada runs a seasonal boat service from Honey Harbour to Beausoleil to take day-trippers to the island (in fact, the boat is named *DayTripper*). To reach islands other than Beausoleil Island, you need to have your own boat, make arrangements with a local outfitter, or hire a water taxi.

Most of the boats traversing the islands are powerboats. While experienced kayakers and canoeists can explore the park islands on their own, the park service advises extreme caution, due to the frequently heavy boat traffic and to the many rocks just under the surface that can surprise the unwary. The park service has partnered with **White Squall Paddling Centre** (19 James St., Parry Sound, 705/746-4936, www.whitesquall.com) to offer guided kayak day trips to some of the park's northern islands.

Honey Harbour is the jumping-off point to visit the park. It's about 168 kilometers (104 miles) northwest of Toronto and 35 kilometers (22 miles) northwest of Midland, the nearest major town.

Georgian Bay Islands National Park is technically open year-round, but park services, including boat transportation between Honey Harbour and Beausoleil Island, operate only between mid-May and mid-October.

Beausoleil Island

The main destination for visitors exploring the Georgian Bay Islands National Park (www. pc.gc.ca, open year-round) is this 11-square-kilometer (4.2 square mile) island, 15 minutes by boat from the Parks Canada marina in Honey Harbour. A unique feature of Beausoleil Island is that it encompasses two different natural environments. The northern part of the island is typical of the Canadian Shield, which extends into Northern Ontario, with its rocky shoreline and its windblown juniper and pine forests. On Beausoleil's southern half, you'll see more hardwood trees, especially maples, beech, oak, and birch, and land that's grassy or marshy, rather than rocky. The best sandy beaches are on the southern end, but you can swim almost anywhere that looks inviting.

Bring your own food and water, along with anything else you need for the day (hiking shoes, swim suit, towel, and insect repellent). While park rangers are on duty on Beausoleil Island during the summer months, there are no snack bars or other services.

Beausoleil Island has about a dozen marked hiking trails, ranging from a 0.3-kilometer (0.2-mile) passage across the island's narrowest point, to an 8.2-kilometer (5-mile) path that traverses between the island's north and south. Most are for hikers only, but bicycles are allowed on two of the routes. Pick up a copy of the park *Visitor Guide,* available free at any of the park offices or at the Beausoleil information kiosk. It includes a trail map with trail distances and approximate hiking times.

Parks Canada runs the *DayTripper* boat service (705/526-8907, adults $15.70, seniors $13.45, children 6–16 $11.70) to transport visitors from Honey Harbour to Beausoleil Island. The *DayTripper* makes the 15-minute trip several times a day (except Wednesdays) in July and August and on Saturdays in the spring and fall. The *DayTripper* rates include park admission. Reservations are recommended.

Two privately owned water taxis also shuttle visitors from Honey Harbour to the park's islands: **Georgian Bay Water Services** (705/627-3062, www.gbws.ca) and **Honey Harbour Boat Club** (705/756-2411). If you take a water taxi to Beausoleil, park admission is $5.80 for adults, $4.90 for seniors, and $2.90 for children 6–16.

Accommodations and Food

Within the national park, the only accommodation option is camping. If you don't want to camp, you'll need to stay on the mainland. The village of Honey Harbour, where the park service boat dock is located, has a handful of places to stay and eat. Most are seasonal, opening in late May or June and closing in September or October. Port Severn is a blink-and-you'll-miss-it town off Highway 400 (exit 153), just south of the Honey Harbour turnoff, but the town does have the nicest lodging in the vicinity of the national park.

If you want to stay somewhere a bit more lively, with more food and entertainment options, sleep in the Midland area and spend the day in the national park; it's about an hour's drive.

In Honey Harbour, the old-school **Delawana Inn Spa and Conference Resort** (42 Delawana Rd., 705/756-2424 or 800/627-3387, www.delawana.com, late May–mid-Oct.) has been operating its summer camp–like property since the 1890s, and it's the closest lodging to the national park. Sprawling over 10 hectares (25 acres), the family-friendly resort includes blocks of 120 motel-style rooms set amid broad lawns and evergreen trees. Some of the old-fashioned rooms could do with an upgrade, but with a pool, a beach, a nine-hole golf course, mini-golf, canoes, kayaks, and tennis courts, you won't lack for things to do. Boats shuttle guests to nearby Royal Island for hikes and nature programs, and in July and August, there are organized camp activities for kids and teens. Prices vary depending on the season, type of room, and the number of meals included; kids stay free during certain times. Nonguests can purchase a day pass to the resort for $30 per person. At the casual **Lake**

GEORGIAN BAY

Country Grill (Nautilus Marina, 2755 Honey Harbour Rd., 705/756-0303, www.lakecountrygrill.com, May–mid-Oct., $9–20), which overlooks the water, pasta is a specialty, but you can also get pizza, burgers, and other pub fare. Or just have a beer while you watch the sunset.

In Port Severn, the **Rawley Resort and Spa** (2900 Kellys Rd., Port Severn, 705/538-2272 or 800/263-7538, www.rawleyresort.com) feels like a waterfront estate, particularly as you sit in the dining room, looking across the manicured lawns to the water. The restaurant feels quite formal, serving classic dishes such as veal scaloppini, grilled steak, or roasted Alaskan halibut, with live jazz several nights a week. Accommodations are spread over several buildings and range from upscale guest rooms, to large one- or two-bedroom suites, to two-story loft units overlooking the water. There's an outdoor pool, as well as a small beach.

CAMPING
Beausoleil Island has eight campgrounds. The largest is **Cedar Spring Campground** (705/526-8907, $25.50/site, reservation fee $9.80 per campsite), near the boat dock on the southeast side of the island, with 36 tent sites and four camping cabins, as well as flush toilets and showers.

The remaining primitive campgrounds ($15.70/site) are first-come, first-served with either pit or composting toilets. Payment is by self-registration permits available at each campground's docking area. Campers must bring their own water.

- **Honeymoon Bay** (13 sites), at the island's northernmost end
- **Chimney Bay** and **Oaks** (13 sites total)
- **Sandpiper** (eight sites)
- **Tonch North** (four sites)
- **Tonch East** (seven sites)
- **Tonch South** (seven sites)
- **Thumb Point** (eight sites)

Campers staying in the primitive areas can use the showers at Cedar Spring for a small fee. The park service also provides a drop-off and pickup service for campers staying in the primitive areas. Otherwise, if you arrive on the park service's *DayTripper* boat, which docks at Cedar Spring, you'll need to hike to your campsite. The walks to Christian Beach, Beausoleil Point, and Thumb Point campgrounds are under an hour; the others are much farther, so be prepared to carry your gear.

On several weekends in September and early October, the park service offers an **"All-Inclusive" Camping Experience** (705/526-8907, $299 for two adults, $179 for one adult, and $49 each child age 16 and under), handy for anyone who's new to camping or who doesn't want the hassle of assembling all the gear. Park staff will transport you to The Oaks, a seven-site camping area on a sheltered bay near the north end of Beausoleil Island. Staff provide comfortable, preassembled tents, with cots for the adults and sleeping pads for the kids, as well as drinking water, cooking equipment, camp chairs and table, a lantern, a canoe, and kayaks. They'll also cook your dinner on Friday night, but you'll need to bring your own sleeping bags and your food for the rest of the weekend. The all-inclusive weekend isn't a luxury experience—you'll still use an outhouse, and there are no shower facilities nearby—but a park staff person will be on-site to help throughout your stay.

Reservations are required, and because there are only seven campsites, it's a good idea to book early. Bookings are accepted beginning in April for the following autumn.

Information and Services
The administrative office of **Georgian Bay Islands National Park** (705/526-9804, email info.gbi@pc.gc.ca, 8 A.M.–4 P.M. Mon.–Fri.) is located in Midland. You can contact them for information by phone or email year-round.

The **Parks Canada Welcome Centre** (Port Severn, 705/538-2586, mid-May–mid-Oct) is just off Highway 400 (exit 153) between Midland and Honey Harbour. It's not in the national park, but they can give you information about park activities. The Welcome Centre is located at Lock 45 on the 386-kilometer

(240-mile) **Trent-Severn Waterway** that connects Lake Ontario with Georgian Bay; the lock station has a small exhibit area about the waterway and the lock system, and you can watch boats transiting the lock.

From mid-June until early September, the park service runs an **information kiosk** (8:30 A.M.–4 P.M. Sun.–Thurs., 8:30 A.M.–7:30 P.M. Fri.–Sat.) on Beausoleil Island, near the Cedar Spring Campground.

PARRY SOUND

Fronting Georgian Bay, Parry Sound is a jumping-off point for exploring the 30,000 Islands, which dot the waters just offshore. It's a popular destination for kayaking, whether you're just getting started or you're an experienced paddler. For a relatively small community (the year-round population is about 6,000), Parry Sound has a surprisingly robust cultural life, drawing music lovers in particular to the beautifully designed performing-arts center.

Parry Sound's most famous native son may be hockey player Bobby Orr, whose legacy lives on in the **Bobby Orr Hall of Fame** (Charles W. Stockey Centre for the Performing Arts, 2 Bay St., 705/746-4466 or 877/746-4466, www.bobbyorrhalloffame.com, 9 A.M.–5 P.M. Tues.–Sun. late June–early Sept., Wed.–Sat. early Sept.–late June; adults $9, seniors/children $6). The first-floor exhibits document Orr's legendary National Hockey League career, beginning in 1962, when the Boston Bruins recruited him for their junior team at age 14. If you have kids in tow, they'll likely head right to the second floor to play a variety of hockey skills games.

30,000 Islands Cruises

Off the Parry Sound coast, Georgian Bay is dotted with thousands of islands, and one of the best ways to explore this coastal region is on a cruise. The 550-passenger *Island Queen* (9 Bay St., 705/746-2311 or 800/506-2628, www.islandqueencruise.com), which bills itself as Canada's largest sightseeing boat, runs a three-hour cruise (1 P.M. daily, June–mid-Oct., adults $33, children 5–12 $16.50) that

passes by Killbear Provincial Park and circles a number of the islands. In July and August, there's also a two-hour morning cruise (10 A.M. daily, adults $25, children 5–12 $12.50) that sticks closer to shore and the inner islands, where you can catch glimpses of cottages and vacation homes.

After years of service as Niagara Falls' *Maid of the Mist,* the **M.V. Chippewa III** (Spirit of the Sound Schooner Company Ltd., Seguin River Parkette, off Bay St., 705/746-6064 or 888/283-5870, www.spiritofthesound.ca, July–Aug.) now tours the waters off Parry Sound. They offer a variety of island cruises, including a two-hour afternoon cruise (adults $24, children under 17 $12), a sunset cocktail cruise (adults $30, children under 17 $15), and a dinner cruise (adults $60, children under 15 $4 per year). They also run trips to **Henry's Fish Restaurant** on Frying Pan Island (adults $36, children under 17 $18), combining a cruise with a stop for a fish 'n' chips lunch.

◖ Flight-Seeing

Touring the 30,000 Islands by boat is a lovely way to spend an afternoon, but seeing the islands by air is an entirely different thrill. Run by husband and wife pilots Keith and Nicole Saulnier, **Georgian Bay Airways** (11A Bay St., 705/774-9884 or 800/786-1704, www.georgianbayairways.com, May–Oct.) flies Cessna floatplanes that take off from Parry Sound Harbor and soar over the nearby islands.

Seeing the islands from above gives you a much clearer picture of both their number and their diversity. The chain of islands extends far across the horizon; some are barely more than a boulder in the bay, while others support entire towns. Keith and Nicole both know the region well, and can tell you all about the various islands as you circle.

The basic tour runs 25–35 minutes (adults $95–119), or you can opt for a variety of special flights, from a sunset champagne flight ($295 per couple) to a fish 'n' chips meal at Henry's Fish Restaurant (705/746-9040, mid-May–Sept., adults $159) on Frying Pan Island. They've hosted in-flight marriage proposals, and even a wedding, so if you have something special in mind, let them know.

Canoeing and Kayaking

The Parry Sound area is an excellent starting point for canoe or kayak tours, and one well-established local outfitter has two locations to help you get out on the water. The **White Squall Paddling Centre** (53 Carling Bay Rd., Nobel, 705/342-5324, www.whitesquall.com, 9 A.M.–5:30 P.M. daily Apr.–mid-Oct.), on Cole Lake, rents canoes and kayaks, offers lessons, and organizes a variety of day-trips, as well as multiday kayak tours. It's located off Highway 559 en route to Killbear Provincial Park.

In downtown Parry Sound, the **White Squall Outdoor Gear Store** (19 James St., 705/746-4936, www.whitesquall.com, 9:30 A.M.–5:30 P.M. Mon.–Sat., 11 A.M.–4 P.M. Sun.) is primarily a gear shop, but you can get information about their rentals and trips here, too. In July and August (Tues. 6:30–8 P.M.), they offer free kayaking and canoeing at Waubuno Beach (Prospect St.).

Entertainment and Shopping

The hub of cultural life in Parry Sound—indeed, in this entire region of Ontario—is the **Charles W. Stockey Centre for the Performing Arts** (2 Bay St., 705/746-4466 or 877/746-4466, www.stockeycentre.com). This striking contemporary building right on the bay, built of local timber and stone, hosts concerts, lectures, and other events year-round.

Parry Sound's major cultural event, held at the Stockey Centre, is the annual **Festival of the Sound** (42 James St., 705/746-2410 or 866/364-0061, www.festivalofthesound.ca). Since 1979, this classical-music festival has been drawing Canadian and international musicians—and music lovers—for three weeks of concerts in July and August.

Accommodations

Parry Sound has several B&Bs and small inns located between downtown and the harbor. If you're a porch lover, **Mariner's Rest Bed and Breakfast** (14 Belvedere Ave., 705/746-9011, www.bbcanada.com/8153.html, $80 s, $95 d), in a 1910 Arts and Crafts–style home, has two: a big front porch with wicker chairs for lounging and a screened-in porch for summer breakfasts. The two upstairs bedrooms are furnished with solid dark wood pieces and floral wallpaper. The house is on a residential street between downtown and the harbor.

Want more porch options? The nicest spots to relax at the homey **40 Bay Street Bed & Breakfast** (40 Bay St., 705/746-9247 or 866/371-2638, www.40baystreet.com, $125–140 d) are the two sunporches overlooking the harbor. The Bay Room, the smallest of the three cozy guest quarters (all with private baths), has expansive harbor views, too. The Retreat Room's special feature is the oversized bathroom, and the Garden Room lives up to its name with a private deck facing the flower-filled yard. Children under 11 are not permitted.

Built in 1882 (with a 1950s addition), the rambling 11-room **Bayside Inn** (10 Gibson St., 705/746-7720 or 866/833-8864, www.psbaysideinn.com, $128–143 d) is conveniently located near downtown. The rather ramshackle exterior belies the well-turned-out rooms, done in a modern country style, that all have air-conditioning, flat-screen TVs, wireless Internet, and refrigerators. Unlike many small inns, the family-owned Bayside welcomes families; ask for a room with two sleeping areas separated by a divider. Free coffee and tea are available every morning, and guests can have breakfast for a small additional charge (continental $4, full breakfast $8).

Though rustic on the outside, the six units (in three cabins) at the **Log Cabin Inn** (9 Lil Beaver Blvd. at Oastler Park Dr., 705/746-7122, www.logcabininn.net, $150 d) are country-contemporary inside, with a king or two queen beds, fireplaces, and modern baths. Rooms overlook the river, and while not plush by city standards, they'd make a comfortable spot for a getaway. Rates include continental breakfast, and packages including breakfast and dinner in the upscale restaurant are available. The property is three kilometers (1.9 miles) south of town.

Food

The downtown area, around the intersection of Seguin and James Streets, has several basic places to eat. Along the harbor, Bay Street has a couple of seasonal eateries, open only in the summer.

The stacks of newspapers (plus books for the kids) encourage lingering at **Hanson's Mad Hatter Café** (35 Seguin St., 705/746-8992, www.hansonsmadhatter.com, 7 A.M.–4 P.M. Mon.–Fri., 8:30 A.M.–4 P.M. Sat.), where you can stop in for coffee and muffins, settle in for lunch, or pick up a sandwich to go. Roast beef, chicken, and bacon all figure prominently among the sandwiches, but several options, like the avocado-veggie wrap, are vegetarian-friendly.

Families and couples, tourists and locals, even the occasional visiting hockey team all turn up at **Wellington's Pub and Grill** (105 James St., 705/746-1333, $9–19), a friendly pub-restaurant downtown decorated with black-and-white photos from Parry Sound's past. From salads to steaks to schnitzel, the food is decent enough (you can't go wrong with the bacon-topped chicken sandwich), and the bar stocks plenty of local brews; you also get free Wi-Fi.

For more gourmet dining, head south of town to the **Log Cabin Inn** (9 Lil Beaver Blvd. at Oastler Park Dr., 705/746-7122, www.log-cabininn.net, lunch $8–15, dinner $20–40), where you can sample grilled elk chops, pan-seared rainbow trout, or roast chicken in, yes, a log cabin. Don't expect pioneer hardship, though; the solid log structure with a soaring ceiling overlooks the river, with a fireplace, twinkling candles, and a lengthy wine list setting the mood.

Practicalities

Georgian Bay Country Tourism (1A Church St., 705/746-4455 or 888/746-4455, www.gb-country.com) can provide information about the Parry Sound region. If you're heading toward Parry Sound from the south, stop into their

Georgian Bay Country Visitor Centre (1 Horseshoe Lake Rd., 705/378-5105 or 888/229-7257) at Exit 214 off Highway 400/69.

The **Rainbow Country Travel Association** (2726 Whippoorwill Ave., Sudbury, 705/522-0104 or 800/465-6655, www.rainbowcountry.com) is another source of information about Parry Sound.

Parry Sound is 222 kilometers (138 miles) northwest of Toronto along Highway 400/69. It's 163 kilometers (105 miles) south of Sudbury via Highway 69. **Ontario Northland** (800/461-8558, www.ontarionorthland.ca) runs buses to Parry Sound from Toronto and Sudbury. There are two buses daily in each direction between Toronto and Parry Sound (3.5 hours, adults $53) and between Parry Sound and Sudbury (2 hours, adults $37). Buses stop at Richard's Coffee (119 Bowes St., 705/746-9611), about 1.8 kilometers (1.1 miles) east of downtown.

Three times a week, the VIA Rail *Canadian* between Vancouver and Toronto stops at **Parry Sound Train Station** (70 Church St., 888/842-7245, www.viarail.ca), about one kilometer (0.6 mile) north of downtown, but the schedule is much less convenient than the bus.

Parry Sound's attractions are clustered along the harbor, which is a short walk from downtown. The town has no public transit, so if you don't have a car, choose a lodging near the harbor or downtown and take a cab from the station to your accommodations. You can then walk to attractions and restaurants. For taxi service, try **Parry Sound Taxi** (705/746-1221).

◖ KILLBEAR PROVINCIAL PARK

With pink granite cliffs, windblown pines, and several long sandy beaches along Georgian Bay, Killbear Provincial Park (35 Killbear Park Rd., Nobel, 705/342-5492, www.ontarioparks.com, $13/vehicle) is a spectacular location for outdoor activities, from hiking to canoeing to swimming. Lesser known than Ontario's "destination" provincial parks like Algonquin or Killarney, Killbear is less than an hour's drive from Parry Sound, which makes it an easy day trip. If you'd like to stay longer, Killbear's campgrounds are the third largest in the Ontario provincial park system (only Algonquin and The Pinery have more campsites).

The park **Visitor Centre** (705/342-5492, 10 A.M.–5 P.M. daily mid-May–mid-Oct.) has a variety of exhibits about the geology, natural history, and cultural history of the Killbear area. Particularly popular with the kids (well, with most of them) are the snake exhibits; in summer, naturalists give "snake talks" where you can learn about and touch local reptiles. In July and August, you can join in a daily interpretive program; there are guided hikes, slide shows, kids' activities, and more. And be sure to walk around to the back of the Visitor Centre for great views of Georgian Bay.

Killbear is home to the endangered Massasuaga rattlesnake. While it's not likely you'll see one, if you do come upon a rattlesnake near the campgrounds or along the road, notify a park staff person, who will relocate the snake to a less-traveled area. Don't try to pick up or move the snake yourself.

The park is officially open mid-May through mid-October, but in the off-season, you can walk in for winter hiking, cross-country skiing, or snowshoeing.

Sports and Recreation

Several easy hiking trails wend through the park, making Killbear good for novice hikers. Heading along the shoreline out to the far end of the park, the **Lighthouse Point Trail** is an easy one-kilometer (0.6-mile) route that passes a 1904 lighthouse. The 3.5-kilometer (2.2-mile) **Lookout Point Trail** goes through the forest to a lookout above Georgian Bay. For the bayside views of the park's pink granite rocks, follow the **Twin Points Trail,** a 1.5-kilometer (0.9-mile) path loop from the day-use parking area. A six-kilometer (3.7-mile) walking and cycling trail runs from the park entrance past several of the campgrounds to Lighthouse Point.

Killbear's three kilometers (1.9 miles) of sandy beaches include a popular swimming beach at the day-use area. You can swim near most of the campgrounds, as well. **Harold**

Point, with both a sand beach and rocky cliffs, is a pretty spot to watch the sunset.

Surrounded by water on three sides, Killbear is a popular destination for canoeing and kayaking. The most sheltered waters are near the park's day-use area. Canoe and kayak rentals are not available inside the park, but you can rent boats from nearby outfitters (mid-May–mid-Oct.). **Killbear Park Mall** (Hwy. 559, Nobel, 705/342-5747, www.killbearparkmall.com), a general store and gear-rental shop just outside the park entrance, rents canoes ($23/day), single kayaks ($29/day), and double kayaks ($45/day). Located four kilometers (2.5 miles) east of the park, **The Detour Store** (401 Hwy. 559, Nobel, 705/342-1611, www.thedetourstore.ca) rents canoes ($20–22/day) and kayaks ($20–35/day single, $40/day double), too. **White Squall Paddling Centre** (53 Carling Bay Rd., Nobel, 705/342-5324, www.whitesquall.com), located off Highway 559 en route to Killbear, also rents a variety of different types of canoes ($28–38/day) and kayaks ($22–45/day single, $30–65/day double). White Squall has a shuttle service to deliver boats to various locations in and around the park.

Camping

Killbear Provincial Park (35 Killbear Park Rd., Nobel, 705/342-5492, www.ontarioparks.com, $34.25 tent sites, $37.75 premium sites, $39.25 sites with electrical service) has seven different campgrounds, with a total of 880 campsites, most within a five-minute walk of the shore. All the campgrounds, except for the more remote, 55-site Granite Saddle area, have restrooms, showers, and laundry facilities. About a quarter of the sites have electrical hookups.

Among the prime sites are the waterfront campsites fronting the beach at **Kilcoursie Bay.** Other campgrounds with waterfront sites include **Beaver Dams, Harold Point,** and **Lighthouse Point.**

Killbear's campgrounds are exceedingly popular, and they book up early, so make reservations (Ontario Parks Reservation Service, 888/668-7275, www.ontarioparks.com, reservation fees $8.50 online, $9.50 by phone) well in advance. You can make reservations up to five months before your stay.

Practicalities

Contact the **Killbear Provincial Park office** (35 Killbear Park Rd., Nobel, 705/342-5492, www.ontarioparks.com) or check online (Friends of Killbear, www.friendsofkillbear. com) for more information. Several small stores along Highway 559 stock food and other provisions. For a better selection, do your shopping in Parry Sound.

By road, Killbear Provincial Park is 35 kilometers (22 miles) northwest of Parry Sound, about a 45-minute drive. From Parry Sound, take Highway 69 north to Nobel, where you pick up Highway 559 west to the park. There's no public transportation to or around the park, so you'll need to come by car.

Muskoka Cottage Country

With more lakes than you can count, the Muskoka region is one of Ontario's vacation lands. For many Ontarians, Muskoka is "Cottage Country," a place to escape from the city's frenzy, where your obligations are nothing more than to sit on the porch of your summer cottage and relax. Even people who don't have cottages of their own (or friends with cottages who invite them for weekends) head to Cottage Country, to stay in B&Bs, hotels, or the many cottage resorts that still dot the lakes.

The Muskoka region, north of Toronto, encompasses the towns of Gravenhurst, Bracebridge, and Huntsville, among others, extending northwest to Georgian Bay and northeast to Algonquin Provincial Park. Tourism to Muskoka began in earnest in the 1800s when steamboats transported visitors across the lakes. These days, nearly all the steamboats are gone (except for a couple used for sightseeing cruises), but the tourists continue to come. And if you're looking for a place to get outdoors, whether to hike, canoe, or just sit on the porch, you should, too.

BARRIE

Barrie isn't really part of the Muskoka region, but you'll likely pass through the city on your way north. Even though it's 105 kilometers (65 miles) north of Toronto, it feels like an extension of the metropolitan area (and people do commute daily from Barrie to Toronto), rather than the start of a cottage holiday. Still, it's a handy spot to break up your drive, whether to have a bite to eat or to stay for a day or two. And if you're continuing north from Barrie, stop in the town of Orillia to tour the former home of noted Canadian humorist Stephen Leacock.

Barrie spreads out along the shore of Lake Simcoe, so even in the heart of the city, you can stroll along the lake. Dunlop Street is the main downtown thoroughfare; most sights and shops are on or around Dunlop.

Barrie has a small but worthwhile art museum, the **Maclaren Art Centre** (37 Mulcaster St., 705/721-9696, www.maclarenart.com, 10 A.M.–5 P.M. Mon.–Fri., 10 A.M.–4 P.M. Sat., noon–4 P.M. Sun., adults $5), which exhibits work by established Canadian and emerging regional artists. Half of the building was Barrie's original public library, built in 1917; the other half is an airy contemporary addition built in 2001. In the main lobby, look for the door that designer and goldsmith Donald A. Stuart reworked into a multimedia art installation, bejeweled with drawing pencils, rulers, rocks, and luminous slabs of wood. If you're looking for a gift for an arty friend, browse the jewelry and works by local artists in the gallery shop.

You can cruise the lake on the **Serendipity Princess** (Bayfield St., at Simcoe St., 705/728-9888, www.midlandtours.com, June–Sept., adults $25, seniors $23, students $20, kids $5–14, families $67), a paddle-wheel boat that offers daily summer sightseeing excursions. Boats depart from the Barrie Town Dock.

If you're heading north and need outdoor gear, Barrie has an outpost of the massive **Mountain Equipment Co-op** (61 Bryne Dr., 705/792-4675, www.mec.ca, 10 A.M.–7 P.M. Mon.–Wed., 10 A.M.–9 P.M. Thurs.–Fri., 9 A.M.–6 P.M. Sat., 11 A.M.–5 P.M. Sun.), a Canadian chain that stocks clothing, camping equipment, cycling gear, and other supplies for outdoor adventures. You must be a member to make a purchase, but anyone can join simply by paying the $5 lifetime membership fee. The Barrie store is just off Highway 400 (exit 94, Essa Rd.).

Accommodations

Several chain motels cluster along Hart Drive (take the Dunlop Street exit off Highway 400), in an area that has nothing much to recommend it except views of the highway. Closer to downtown, you'll find more appealing B&Bs and small inns.

Owners Pam and Bob Richmond have set up a separate wing for guests on the second floor of their 1911 brick Georgian-style home east of downtown. The **Richmond Manor B&B** (16 Blake St., 705/726-7103, www.bbcanada. com/1145.html, $75–100 d) has two large, traditionally furnished guest rooms with peek-a-boo views of Kempenfelt Bay. A shared bath is located between the rooms, and across the hall is a guest lounge with a TV/DVD player. Breakfast is a formal affair, served on fine china in the stately dining room.

Catering to business travelers and people relocating to the Barrie area, the **Harbour View Inn** (1 Berczy St., 705/735-6832, www. harbourviewinn.ca, $129–349) has eight rooms and suites—some with lake views— in a brick Victorian just east of downtown. While the accommodations aren't large, they all have kitchenettes, with a microwave, a mini-fridge, a coffeemaker, a toaster, and dishes; some have sleep sofas to accommodate an extra guest. Free Wi-Fi.

Food

One of Ontario's largest and longest running farmers' markets, the year-round **Barrie** **Farmers' Market** (Collier St. at Mulcaster St., www.barriefarmermarket.com, 8 A.M.–noon Sat.) has been operating since 1846. You can buy seasonal produce, prepared foods, baked goods (mmm, butter tarts), and crafts. From May to October, the market is outside on the plaza in front of City Hall; from November to April, it moves inside the City Hall building.

Some of Barrie's most interesting food isn't in the downtown area—it's in the strip malls and industrial parks off Highway 400. A good example is **Cravings Fine Food** (131 Commerce Park Dr., 705/734-2272, www. cravingsfinefood.ca, 9 A.M.–6 P.M. Mon.–Tues., 9 A.M.–7 P.M. Wed.–Fri., 9 A.M.–5 P.M. Sun.), a café and gourmet shop that sells beautifully crafted (and scrumptious) pastries, sandwiches, salads, and other prepared foods, perfect for a quick meal on the road or to take north to the cottage.

If you love butter tarts (and who doesn't?), find your way to the strip mall that houses **The Sweet Oven** (75 Barrie View Dr., #103A, 705/733-9494, www.thesweetoven.com, 10 A.M.–6 P.M. Mon.–Sat.), which makes these tasty tarts ($2, or $10 for six) in numerous varieties. Flavors like peanut butter, mint, or chai are novelties, but the classics—plain, pecan, or raisin—are the best.

Barbecue tastes best when you have to hunt for it in an out-of-the-way locale, doesn't it? At least it does at the **Big Chris BBQ Smokehouse** (110 Anne St., #8, 705/721-7427, www.big-chrisbbq.ca, 11 A.M.–11 P.M. daily, $8–20) in an industrial park between Highway 400 and downtown. The Texas-sized portions of ribs, pulled pork, and burgers come with cole slaw, baked beans, and a heap of French fries. If the flavors are more mild-mannered Canadian than Texas badass, just add some hot sauce and dig in. The interior is about as charming as a fast-food franchise, but service is nearly as speedy.

Information and Services

You can pick up all sorts of information about Barrie and the surrounding region at the helpful **Tourism Barrie Visitor Information**

Centre (205 Lakeshore Dr., 705/739-9444 or 800/668-9100, www.tourismbarrie.com, 9 A.M.–5 P.M. Mon.–Fri., 10 A.M.–4 P.M. Sat.), located on the south side of Lake Simcoe. In July and August, they're also open Sunday (10 A.M.–4 P.M.). Tourism Barrie also staffs a seasonal **Downtown Information Kiosk** (Bayfield St. at Simcoe St., 9 A.M.–7 P.M. daily May–mid-Oct.).

The provincially run **Ontario Travel Information Centre** (21 Mapleview Dr. E., 705/725-7280 or 800/567-1140, www.ontariotravel.net, 8 A.M.–8 P.M. daily June–Aug., 8:30 A.M.–4:30 P.M. daily Sept.–May), just off Highway 400, can help with travel questions about Barrie and points north.

Getting There and Around

Both **Ontario Northland** (800/461-8558, www.ontarionorthland.ca, adults $22 one-way) and **Greyhound Bus Lines** (800/661-8747, www.greyhound.ca, adults $19–28 one-way) stop at the Barrie Bus Terminal (24 Maple Ave., 705/739-1500) downtown. Between Barrie and Toronto, there are frequent buses throughout the day in both directions; it's about a 90-minute trip. Ontario Northland buses continue north from Barrie to Gravenhurst, Bracebridge, Huntsville, and North Bay; another travels toward Parry Sound and Sudbury.

Simcoe County Airport Service (137 Brock St., 705/728-1148 or 800/461-7529, www.simcoecountyairportservice.ca, one-way $62/person, $87/two, $111/three, $134/four) runs door-to-door van service from Toronto's Pearson airport to Barrie. Book online or by phone.

Barrie Transit (705/739-4209, www.barrie.ca, $2.75/ride), the city's bus service, can take you around town if you don't have a car. Get a transfer when you board, since it's good for 60 minutes (even if you're heading back in the same direction), and parents, take note: up to three elementary school kids ride free with a paying adult.

If you're heading farther north from Barrie, you can rent a car here, which may be less expensive than picking up a rental in Toronto. Many car rental companies have Barrie offices, including **Avis** (425 Dunlop St. W., 705/726-6527 or 800/879-2847, www.avis.com), **Budget** (520 Bryne Dr., #10, 705/737-0333 or 800/268-8900, www.budget.ca), **Discount Car Rentals** (15 George St., 705/722-8900, www.discountcar.com), and **Enterprise Rent-A-Car** (304 Dunlop St. W., Unit 4, 705/728-1212 or 800/736-8222, www.enterpriserentacar.ca).

ORILLIA

Though his "day job" was as a political science professor at Montreal's McGill University, Stephen Leacock (1869–1944) became famous as a writer and humorist. He published 35 humor books over his career, including *Sunshine Sketches of a Little Town* (1912) and *Arcadian Adventures of the Idle Rich* (1914).

In 1928, Leacock built a summer house near Old Brewery Bay in the town of Orillia. The home became his permanent residence following his retirement from McGill in 1936 until his death 12 years later. It is now the **Stephen Leacock Museum** (50 Museum Dr., Orillia, 705/329-1908, www.leacockmuseum.com, 9 A.M.–5 P.M. daily June–Sept., 9 A.M.–5 P.M. Mon.–Fri. Oct.–May, adults $5, seniors $4, students $3, kids $2). Some parts of the house are (nearly) as Leacock left them, including the sunroom with his work table, his study, and his living room facing the lake. On the main floor are signed original portraits of Leacock that noted photographer Yousuf Karsh took at the home in 1941.

Orillia is 40 kilometers (25 miles) northeast of Barrie. Go north on Highway 11 to Highway 12, then turn left on Atherley Road and follow the signs to the museum.

GRAVENHURST

You know you've arrived in Cottage Country when you pass by the **world's largest Muskoka chair** (1170 Muskoka Rd. S.), located outside the Gravenhurst Home Hardware store at the south end of town. What's a "Muskoka chair," you may ask? It's the laid-back wooden porch chair that most Americans call an Adirondack chair. This symbol of relaxation gives you a clue of what Gravenhurst is all about.

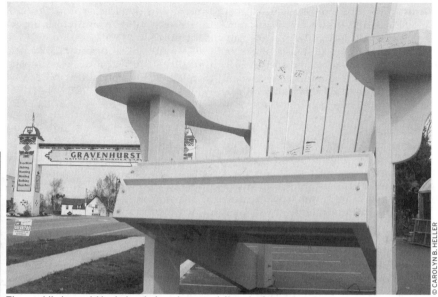

© CAROLYN B. HELLER

The world's largest Muskoka chair welcomes visitors to Gravenhurst.

Gravenhurst's main attractions are at Muskoka Wharf (www.muskokawharf.ca), the lakefront development where you can tour a boat museum or cruise the lake in a traditional steamship. The town is also the birthplace of Norman Bethune, a Canadian doctor who became wildly famous in China, where he's still considered a hero long after his death.

Gravenhurst Opera House (295 Muskoka Rd. S., 705/687-5550 or 888/495-8888, www. gravenhurstoperahouse.com), built in 1901, now hosts concerts, plays, and films. **Music on the Barge** (Gull Lake Rotary Park, Brock St., at Bethune Dr., 7:30 P.M. Sun. mid-June–mid-Aug.) has brought toe-tapping summer concerts, from big band to Dixieland to folk, to the waterfront since 1959.

Muskoka Wharf

The Muskoka Lakes Navigation Company opened in 1866 and during its heyday operated the largest fleet of inland lake steamships in North America. The ships carried both passengers and freight across the Muskoka Lakes, providing service where the railroads didn't reach and roads either didn't go or were difficult to navigate. At one time, there were more than 100 lakeside hotels in the Muskokas whose guests all arrived by steamship.

One of these ships, the **R.M.S. *Segwun*,** was built in 1887 and used as an official "Royal Mail Ship." Today, it's North America's oldest operating steamship. **Muskoka Steamships** (185 Cherokee Ln., 705/687-6667 or 866/687-6667, www.segwun.com, mid-June–mid-Oct.) offers a variety of sightseeing cruises on the *Segwun,* departing from their Muskoka Wharf docks. The schedules vary with the seasons, but you can choose from 1–4-hour trips (adults $17.95–48.95, kids $10.95–34.95).

Back on land, explore the region's steamship traditions at the **Muskoka Boat and Heritage Centre** (275 Steamship Bay Rd., 705/687-2115, www.realmuskoka.com, 10 A.M.–6 P.M. Tues.–Fri., 10 A.M.–4 P.M. Sat.–Mon. summer; 10 A.M.–4 P.M. Tues.–Sat. winter; adults $7.50, seniors $5.50, kids $3.50, families $18.50), a creatively designed museum, filled with multimedia exhibits. One section of the museum is a re-created lakeside hotel, where the owner welcomes you (in a video) when you enter the lobby and you can pretend that you're holidaying in the 19th century. Another exhibit is a re-created steamship that you can go aboard. You can also visit the Grace and Speed Boathouse, North America's only in-water exhibit of working antique boats, with up to 20 spiffy craft on view.

Bethune Memorial House National Historic Site

Born in Gravenhurst, Henry Norman Bethune (1890–1939) became a legendary physician, known largely for a brief tour of service on the other side of the world. Bethune was a surgeon, working in Montreal during the Depression of the 1930s. Not only did he develop new surgical techniques and devices (one of these inventions, the Bethune rib shears, is still used today), he was also something of a radical, becoming an early advocate for socialized medicine in Canada. He joined the Communist Party in 1936.

In 1938, after China and Japan went to war, Bethune decided to travel to China to tend to the injured. Arriving at the front, he was appalled to discover that the Chinese had few trained medical personnel. He implemented a medical education program and established mobile medical facilities, including an operating theater that two mules could carry. The legend of the foreign doctor's commitment to the Chinese began to spread across China. After spending less than two years in the country, however, Bethune accidentally cut his finger while performing an operation. He developed a particularly aggressive form of blood poisoning, which killed him within the month. Chinese leader Mao Tse-tung wrote an essay, "In Memory of Norman Bethune," which became required reading for Chinese students and helped solidify Bethune's memory.

The Bethune Memorial House National Historic Site (297 John St. N., 705/687-4261, www.pc.gc.ca, 10 A.M.–4 P.M. daily June–Oct., adults $3.90, seniors $3.40, kids 6–16 $1.90,

families $9.80) consists of two buildings: one is a museum that recounts Bethune's history; the other is the 1880 home next door where Bethune was born. Bethune lived in the house only a short time, so most of the contents are from the period rather than the family.

Try to visit on a weekday if you can, when the house's diminutive rooms are less crowded and staff have more time to tell you about Bethune's legacy.

Tree Museum

One of Cottage Country's most offbeat attractions is this outdoor art gallery outside of Gravenhurst. No, the Tree Museum (1634 Doe Lake Rd., 705/684-8185, www.thetreemuseum.ca, dawn–dusk daily, free) isn't a museum of trees—it's a gallery set outside in the woods. As you wander along the hiking trails through the 80-hectare (200-acre) woodland, spy imaginative sculptures and other eclectic works set among the trees. Be prepared for a lot of walking along the sometimes muddy paths. It's one kilometer (0.6 mile) from the parking area to the first sculpture, and another 1.2 kilometers (0.75 mile) to the center of the site; return the way you came. The museum has no restrooms or other facilities, so bring some water and a snack.

To get to the Tree Museum, follow Highway 11 north past Gravenhurst, then exit at Doe Lake Road (Muskoka Road 6). Go east about eight kilometers (five miles) farther till you see museum signs on your right.

Accommodations

The **Residence Inn by Marriott** (285 Steamship Bay Rd, Muskoka Wharf, 705/687-6600 or 866/580-6238, www.marriott.com, $165–399 d) is located at Muskoka Wharf, overlooking Lake Muskoka. The 106 modern suites all have kitchen facilities and include studios with sleeper sofas and larger units with one or two bedrooms. Rates include a buffet breakfast, parking, and Internet access.

In the woods on Lake Muskoka north of town, the expansive (and expensive) **Taboo Resort** (1209 Muskoka Beach Rd., 705/687-2233 or 800/461-0236, www.tabooresort.com, mid-Feb.–Oct., $299–639 d) feels like two resorts in one. Some of the 101 guest rooms have a traditional Muskoka feel, with overstuffed chairs and wooden cottage-style furniture, while others are sleek and modern, all satiny woods and chrome; the best rooms of both types are right above the lake. Thirty condos, ranging from two to four bedrooms, are scattered around the property; they're individually decorated, giving them each a distinct personality, although most don't have lake views. You won't be bored here, with a private beach, three outdoor pools, an indoor pool, and one pool just for the kids, plus golf, a spa, two restaurants, and a poolside bar. Expect to pay a resort fee that covers various activities, including the use of canoes and kayaks.

Food

Though it looks a bit twee, with its floral café curtains and blue-and-white china, the **Blue Willow Tea Shop** (900 Bay St., Muskoka Wharf, 705/687-2597, www.bluewillowteashop.ca, 11 A.M.–3 P.M. Tues.–Thurs., 11 A.M.–8 P.M. Fri.–Sat., $7–14) overlooks the lake and makes a good rest stop while visiting Muskoka Wharf. They serve soups, salads, and sandwiches at lunch, along with a large selection of black, green, and fruit teas. Midafternoon, you can take a tea break with a scone, a tart, or a slice of cake, or settle in for a traditional high tea.

Hip, urban **North Restaurant and Lounge** (530 Muskoka Road N., 705/687-8618, www.northinmuskoka.com, Apr.–Dec., call for seasonal hours, lunch $9–16, dinner $20–40) would be right at home in the big city, with its contemporary decor and dishes. Lunch runs from sandwiches—like glazed ham, Brie, and arugula served with lemon-apple slaw on raisin bread—to traditional eggs Benedict to a hearty plate of spaghetti with homemade meatballs. In the evening, choices might include roast Cornish hen with root veggies or beer-braised bison short ribs. If you want a bite to go, come around back to the **Back Door Fish with Chips** ($7–15), their to-go fish shack.

Information and Services

Muskoka Tourism (800/267-9700, www.muskokatourism.ca) provides information about the entire Muskoka Lakes region, including the Gravenhurst area. They operate a travel information center on Highway 11 south of Gravenhurst in the town of Kilworthy. The **Gravenhurst Chamber of Commerce** (685-2 Muskoka Rd. N., 705/687-4432, www.gravenhurstchamber.com, 8:30 A.M.–4:30 P.M. Mon.–Fri.) publishes an annual visitors' guide, with details on attractions, accommodations, restaurants, and events. It's available online or from their office.

Getting There and Around

Gravenhurst is 180 kilometers (112 miles) north of Toronto and 75 kilometers (47 miles) north of Barrie. From Toronto, pick up Highway 400 north to Barrie, then continue north on Highway 11 into Gravenhurst.

Ontario Northland trains and buses both stop at **Gravenhurst Station** (150 Second St. S., 705/687-2301 or 800/461-8558, www.ontarionorthland.ca, 2–2.5 hours, one-way adults $36.45, seniors and students $31, kids 2–11 $18.20) en route from Toronto's Union Station.

Shuttle Ontario (317 Carmichael Dr., North Bay, 705/474-7942 or 800/461-4219, www.shuttleontario.com, 2 hours, one-way adults $83) makes two scheduled trips a day in each direction between Toronto's Pearson Airport and Gravenhurst.

Exploring Gravenhurst is easiest if you have a car, although you can walk between Muskoka Wharf and the town center. **Discount Car Rentals** (1011 Airport Rd., 705/645-4878, www.discountcar.com) is located between Gravenhurst and Bracebridge. **Enterprise Rent-A-Car** (800/736-8222, www.enterpriserentacar.ca) has an office in Bracebridge.

BRACEBRIDGE

Like many Muskoka towns, Bracebridge's tourism industry goes back to the late 1800s, when visitors from Toronto came to the region by train and boat. Most of the old-time resorts are gone, but the town's main street, Manitoba Street, has an old-timey feel that makes for a pleasant stroll. Bracebridge is a good base for exploring the region—it's an easy drive to Gravenhurst or Huntsville and to other towns dotting the surrounding lakes—and with comfortable B&Bs and excellent restaurants, it's also a spot where you can just unwind.

Since the "lakes" are an important part of the Muskoka Lakes experience, get yourself out on the water. One option is to head out with **Lady Muskoka Cruises** (300 Ecclestone Dr., 705/646-2628 or 800/263-5239, www.ladymuskoka.com, late May–mid-Oct.), which operates sightseeing boats on Lake Muskoka. Cruises run at noon daily in July and August; in May and June and in September and October, there are noontime cruises on Saturdays, Sundays, and (except in May) on Wednesdays.

Bracebridge's own microbrewery, **Muskoka Brewery** (13 Taylor Rd., 705/646-1266, www.muskokabrewery.com), welcomes visitors to their shop, where they'll share their enthusiasm for beer brewing and maybe give you a taste or two.

A Bracebridge summer tradition is the free **Bandshell Concert Series** (Memorial Park, Manitoba St., www.bracebridge.ca) on Thursday evenings from June through early September.

Accommodations

Sandy Yudin has run **Century House B&B** (155 Dill St., 705/645-9903, www.bbmuskoka.com/centuryhouse, $60–70 s, $80–90 d), the 1855 brick farmhouse she shares with her husband Norman Yan, for nearly two decades, and she knows how to make guests feel at home. Sandy is warm and chatty, offering restaurant suggestions and ideas of things to do. The simple, traditional B&B rooms are furnished with quilts, wicker chairs, and antiques and have all the essentials—comfortable beds, reading lamps, bathrobes—but no extraneous frills. Located on the second floor, the three guest rooms share two baths. Sandy's a great cook, too, serving multicourse breakfasts with fresh fruit, eggs, smoked trout, and toast with homemade jams (mmm, tangy peach marmalade).

The B&B is in a residential neighborhood about a 15-minute walk from the shops and restaurants on Manitoba Street.

Although it's just a short walk from the town center, the **Bay House Bed and Breakfast** (2 Dominion St., 705/645-7508, www.bbmuskoka.com/bayhouse, $128–168) feels like a cottage in the woods. The three guest rooms are on the lower level, done in cheery pastel colors. The largest, the Bay Suite, has an electric fireplace and four-poster bed, while the Garden Room opens onto the patio. Jan and Peter Rickard are experienced innkeepers who are full of tips for things to do, although after their hearty breakfasts (which might include lemon ricotta pancakes or eggs hollandaise), you may be tempted just to soak in the outdoor hot tub.

Food

You can have a sandwich at **Marty's "World Famous" Café** (5 Manitoba St., 705/645-4794, www.martysworldfamous.com), but the shop's self-proclaimed fame is for the gooey, caramel butter tarts. Though some might bridle at the in-your-face self-promotion (and the excessively runny tart filling), no one disputes their advice not to eat these runny pastries in your car, or, as they warn, "You'll end up wearing them!"

A friendly joint for hanging out and having a an interesting microbrew, **The Griffin Gastropub** (9 Chancery Ln., 705/646-0438, www.thegriffinpub.ca, noon–midnight Tues.–Wed., noon–2 A.M. Thurs.–Sat., $8–13) also serves inventive pub grub, from addictive risotto balls to bison burgers to sticky toffee pudding. They usually have live folk, rock, blues, or jazz starting around 9 P.M. Thursday through Saturday. The pub is at the top of a narrow alleyway, off Manitoba Street.

Don't be put off by the strip mall setting behind the Tim Hortons. There's some serious sushi savvy in this chic Japanese restaurant. At **Wabora Fusion Japanese Restaurant** (295 Wellington St., #17, 705/646-9500, www.waborasushi.com, 11 A.M.–11 P.M. daily, $5–15), the cavernous room has a bar at one end, with

GEORGIAN BAY

What's Marty famous for? Butter tarts!

artfully arranged bottles, and a well-lit sushi bar where the chefs ply their trade. The specialties on the huge menu are the wildly imaginative *maki* rolls, like the Bracebridge (salmon, crab, asparagus, and gobo wrapped in cucumber with lemon-ponzu-caramel sauce) or the Spicy Cottage (shrimp tempura, crab, spicy tuna, greens, cucumber, mango, and avocado in a rice paper roll with creamy wasabi sauce), but the straight-up *nigiri* is first-rate, too. If it's your birthday, they'll ring a gong and serenade you.

Colorful original artwork seems to pop out from the white walls at **⟨ One Fifty Five** (155 Manitoba St., 705/645-1935, lunch 11:30 A.M.–2:30 P.M. Tues–Sat., dinner 5–9:30 P.M. Tues–Sun., lunch $11–16, dinner $18–36), Bracebridge's white-tablecloth restaurant. The menu is colorful, too, with choices like chicken stuffed with Oka cheese from Quebec or panko-crusted pickerel. For dessert, it's hard to choose between the warm chocolate tart or the "zesty" lemon tart topped with fresh berries.

Information and Services

Tourism Bracebridge (1 Manitoba St., 705/645-8121 or 866/645-8121, www.tourism-bracebridge.com) provides information about the area, including an annual visitors' guide listing special events.

Getting There and Around

Bracebridge is 195 kilometers (121 miles) north of Toronto and 18 kilometers (11 miles) north of Gravenhurst. From Toronto, pick up Highway 400 north to Barrie, then continue north on Highway 11 to Bracebridge.

Ontario Northland (800/461-8558, www.ontarionorthland.ca, 2.5 hours, one-way adults $39.30, seniors and students, $33.40, kids 2–11 $19.65) runs the daily *Northlander* train from Toronto's Union Station to the **Bracebridge train station** (88 Hiram St.), right downtown. Ontario Northland buses stop at the Riverside Inn (300 Ecclestone Dr., 705/646-2239 or 800/461-8558, www.ontarionorthland.ca), south of downtown. From Toronto, bus fares are the same as the train fares. Both buses and trains continue to Huntsville, North Bay, Temagami, and points farther north.

Shuttle Ontario (317 Carmichael Dr., North Bay, 705/474-7942 or 800/461-4219, www.shuttleontario.com, 2.25 hours, one-way adults $85) makes two scheduled trips a day in each direction between Toronto's Pearson airport and Bracebridge.

Bracebridge is fairly small and compact, so you could arrive by train or bus and amuse yourself in town without a car. If you want to use Bracebridge as a base to explore the Muskoka region, though, you need to have your own vehicle. Car rental companies with Bracebridge offices include **Enterprise Rent-A-Car** (1 Armstrong St., 705/645-5952 or 800/736-8222, www.enterpriserentacar.ca) and **Discount Car Rentals** (15 Keith Rd., 705/645-4878, www.discountcar.com).

Huntsville and Vicinity

Located just west of Algonquin Provincial Park, the attractive town of Huntsville is a favorite destination in its own right, with lots of outdoor activities, good places to eat, and a cute downtown. But it's also close enough to Algonquin that you can easily stay in town and make day trips into the park.

SIGHTS

Start your Huntsville visit walking around downtown, looking for the colorful wall murals that decorate the town buildings. The murals constitute the **Group of Seven Outdoor Gallery** (www.groupofsevenoutdoorgallery.ca); they're replicas of works by the artists from the "Group of Seven" who worked in Ontario in the early 1900s. To do a complete mural tour, pick up a brochure from the **Huntsville/Lake of Bays Chamber of Commerce** (8 West St. N., 705/789-4771, www.huntsvilleadventures.com).

Muskoka Heritage Place

If you're interested in the history and development of the Muskoka region, there's lots to see and do at Muskoka Heritage Place (88 Brunel Rd., 705/789-7576, www.muskokaheritageplace.org, 10 A.M.–4 P.M. daily late May–mid-Oct.; last admission at 3 P.M.; adults $15.50, seniors $14, and kids 3–12 $10.50). Your first stop should be in the **museum** (open year-round; off-season: 10 A.M.–4 P.M. Mon.–Fri. mid-Oct.–late May), which traces the region's roots from the early First Nations people, through the first European contact, the fur trading and lumber eras, and the evolution of the Muskokas as a tourist destination.

More fun for the kids is the **pioneer village** (open seasonally), where wandering around the 20 restored buildings takes you back to the period between 1880 and 1910. Costumed interpreters demonstrate blacksmithing, woodworking, and other trades. You can also explore a trapper's cabin, a one-room schoolhouse, and a First Nations encampment.

You can also catch a ride on the **Portage**

Flyer steam train (100 Forbes Hill Dr., departs at noon, 1 P.M., 2 P.M., and 3 P.M., Tues.–Sat. July–Aug.; check website for off-season schedule; adults $5.25, seniors $4.75, and kids 3–12 $3.25), which ran from 1904 to 1959 in nearby Dwight, along the world's smallest commercial railroad. It operated on a 1.8-kilometer-long (1.125-mile) narrow-gauge track, as a "portage," ferrying supplies and tourists across a sliver of land between Peninsula Lake and Portage Bay.

The trip on the steam train today runs about 30 minutes and includes a stop at the **Rail Museum,** a re-creation of a 1920s train station, where you can learn more about the role of railroads and steamboats in the Muskokas' development. If you're a train enthusiast, note that the steam engine pulls the train only in July and August; in spring and fall, a diesel locomotive does the work, to help preserve the steam engine's life.

Muskoka Heritage Place is just a few minutes' drive from downtown Huntsville. From Main Street, just west of the bridge, go south on Brunel Road. The train depot is a short distance from the main entrance to Muskoka Heritage Place; watch for the signs.

Arrowhead Provincial Park

Through far smaller and less well known than nearby Algonquin, this provincial park (451 Arrowhead Park Rd., 705/789-5105, www.ontarioparks.com, $14/vehicle) is a worthwhile destination for day hiking, with several easy-to-moderate trails ranging from 1–7 kilometers (0.6–4.3 miles). In winter, these paths become cross-country ski trails (per day adults $9.50, kids 6–17 $4.75). Ski rentals are available, and you can also rent canoes, kayaks, and bicycles in the park. In July and August, go to the Beach Information Building at the day-use beach for rentals, and to the main park office in the spring and the fall.

The park is located 10 kilometers (six miles) north of Huntsville. If you're coming from Huntsville, take Highway 3 north; you can also reach the park via Highway 11.

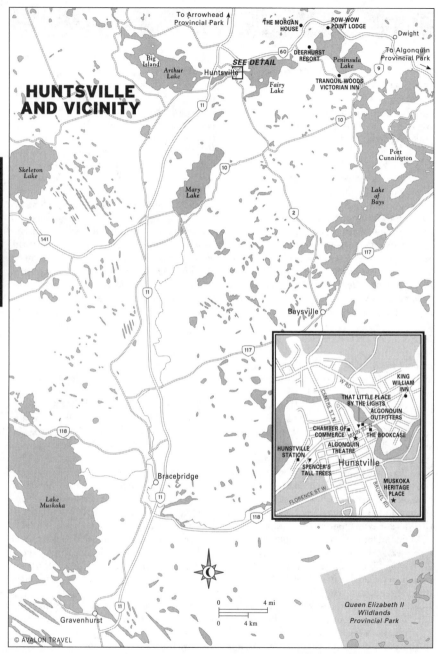

GEORGIAN BAY

HUNTSVILLE AND VICINITY

To Arrowhead
Provincial Park
THE MORGAN
HOUSE
POW-WOW
POINT LODGE
Dwight
60
DEERHURST
RESORT
To Algonquin
Provincial Park
Peninsula
Lake
9
Big
Island
Arthur
Lake
SEE DETAIL
Huntsville
Fairy
Lake
TRANQUIL WOODS
VICTORIAN INN
11
10
Port
Cunnington
Skeleton
Lake
10
Mary
Lake
Lake
of
Bays
2
141
117
11
Baysville
117
118
Bracebridge
11
Lake
Muskoka
118
0   4 mi
0   4 km
11
Gravenhurst
© AVALON TRAVEL
Queen Elizabeth II
Wildlands
Provincial Park

Detail:
W RD
KING
WILLIAM
INN
THAT LITTLE PLACE
BY THE LIGHTS
ALGONQUIN
OUTFITTERS
CHAMBER OF
COMMERCE
THE BOOKCASE
HUNSTVILLE
STATION
ALGONQUIN
THEATRE
Hunstville
SPENCER'S
TALL TREES
MUSKOKA
HERITAGE
PLACE
FLORENCE ST W
BRUNEL RD

Limberlost Forest and Wildlife Reserve

An excellent, less-visited hiking destination is the privately owned Limberlost Forest and Wildlife Reserve (South Limberlost Rd., 705/635-1584, www.limberlostlodges.com, dawn–dusk daily, free), where more than 70 kilometers (44 miles) of trails circle many of the property's 20 lakes as they crisscross the forested 4,045-hectare (10,000-acre) reserve. Check the website for the extremely detailed *Master Trail Guide,* which tells you about each of the trails and their notable features; it also includes trail maps. The trail guide is also available in the reserve office.

To find the reserve from Huntsville, follow Highway 60 east for about 10 kilometers (six miles), then turn left (north) onto Limberlost Road (Muskoka Road 8). Continue another nine kilometers (5.6 miles), and turn right onto South Limberlost Road and follow it for three kilometers (1.8 miles) to the reserve entrance. The gates of the reserve look rather imposing, but don't worry; pull up to the gates and they'll slide open.

ENTERTAINMENT AND SHOPPING

The **Algonquin Theatre** (37 Main St. E., 705/789-4975 or 888/696-4255, www.algonquintheatre.ca) stages concerts, plays, and lectures, featuring performers from near and far. All summer long, the **Huntsville Festival of the Arts** (705/789-4975, www.huntsvillefestival.on.ca) brings concerts, art workshops, and other events to venues around town. Many events are outdoors and free. For ticketed events, you can buy tickets online, by phone, or in person at the Algonquin Theatre.

What's a cottage holiday without time curled up with a good book? If you need something to read, stop into independent bookstore **The Bookcase** (93 Main St. E., 705/789-9111, www.thebookcase.ca, 10 A.M.–5 P.M. Mon.–Sat., noon–4 P.M. in spring; 9 A.M.–9 P.M. Mon.–Sat., 10 A.M.–5 P.M. Sun. in summer). Other shops along Huntsville's Main Street sell outdoor gear (useful if you need clothing or

supplies for your excursions into Algonquin), artwork, and souvenirs. **Algonquin Outfitters Huntsville** (86 Main St. E., 705/787-0262 or 800/469-4948, www.algonquinoutfitters.com, 9:30 A.M.–6 P.M. Mon.–Wed., 9:30 A.M.–8 P.M. Thurs.–Fri., 9 A.M.–5:30 P.M. Sat., 11 A.M.–4 P.M. Sun. July–early Sept.; 10 A.M.–6 P.M. Mon.–Fri., 9 A.M.–5 P.M. Sat., 11 A.M.–4 P.M. Sun. early Sept.–June) has a large selection of outdoor clothing and gear. They also rent canoes, kayaks, and bikes.

ACCOMMODATIONS

The Huntsville area has a wide range of places to stay, from basic in-town motels, to B&Bs hidden in the woods, summer camp–style cottage colonies, and upscale resorts. A number of these accommodations are off Highway 60, just east of Huntsville. Closer to Algonquin's West Gate, in the tiny town of Dwight (which seems to exist primarily to provide lodging and other services to travelers heading into Algonquin), there's a cluster of accommodations around Oxtongue Lake.

Huntsville

The **King William Inn** (23 King William St., 705/789-9661 or 888/995-9169, www.kingwilliaminn.com, $129–165 d) is the nicest of the in-town motels. Although it sits on a charmless stretch of road opposite a fast-food joint and a car dealership, the King William has upgraded its rooms with crisp white linens and new furnishings. The standard rooms, with either two doubles or one double and one queen, are slightly smaller but otherwise similar to the queen rooms, which have one queen bed and a sleep sofa. The largest rooms are the kings with a whirlpool tub. Free Wi-Fi.

East of Huntsville

A stay at **The Morgan House** (83 Morgans Rd., 705/380-2566 or 866/311-1727, www.morganhousewoolworks.ca, $70 d, $100 d), a bed-and-breakfast in a comfortable, stone country home, is like a holiday with good friends on their (mostly) organic farm. Co-owner Pam Carnochan is a wool artist who also teaches at the Algonquin Art Centre, and she welcomes guests on the screened-in porch or in the parlor with its overstuffed furniture. Upstairs, the two simple guest rooms, with traditional quilts on the beds, share one large bathroom. Breakfast includes homemade baked goods and eggs from the farm's hens. Families are welcome.

A suburban home set amid lovely gardens, and, yes, tranquil woods, the **Tranquil Woods Victorian Inn** (50 North Portage Rd., 705/788-7235, www.tranquilwoods.ca, $120–135 d) is Victorian in style, but it's in a newly built house with high ceilings and an airy feel. Personable owners Judy and Dan enjoy helping guests organize their day and offer touring tips while serving up a hearty breakfast. The largest of the three guest rooms is on the main floor, with a private patio. Upstairs, the Red Oak room has a sleigh bed and Victorian furnishings, while the red-walled Scarlett Maple room is more country cottage.

Over breakfast at the 🌙 **Pow-Wow Point Lodge** (207 Grassmere Resort Rd., 705/789-4951 or 800/461-4263, www.powwowpoint-lodge.com), staff ring a bell and announce the activities for the day, from sandcastle contests to swimming races to movie nights—just like at summer camp. And even if you don't go for organized fun, there's plenty to do, with a lakeside beach for swimming, canoeing, and kayaking, tennis courts, shuffleboard, a kids' play area, and an indoor pool for rainy days. Accommodations include basic, knotty pine–walled lodge rooms and cottages and more updated units, but all feel homey. Owners Doug and Dee Howell have been running the lodge since 1989, and many of their guests, including lots of multigenerational families, return year after year. Daily rates, which range $268–417 per person for a two-night stay, include three ample meals; kids' and teens' rates are discounted, and the daily rate is cheaper the longer you stay.

You won't be bored at the classy **Deerhurst Resort** (1235 Deerhurst Dr., 705/789-6411 or 800/461-4393, www.deerhurstresort.com, $239–719 d), where activities run the gamut from golf, tennis, squash, and Ping-Pong, to swimming, canoeing, kayaking, and more. The lakeside "Splash Zone" is summer fun central, with water trampolines, a climbing wall (anchored in the lake), beach volleyball, sunset

summer fun at the Deerhurst Resort

© CAROLYN B. HELLER

boat tours, and all kinds of watersports. The resort's sports desk organizes regular activities, too, including trail rides, kids' crafts, and both hiking and canoeing excursions to Algonquin Park. Accommodations at this sprawling property range from basic hotel rooms to condos with one, two, or three bedrooms (all the condos have full kitchens). You can spend a lot of time just navigating the grounds, so if you (and the kids) are going to spend most of your time at the lake, you might choose a room in the Bayshore building (it's right at the beach) or in one of the lakefront condos. If you'd rather be closer to the indoor pool, tennis courts, gym, spa, and restaurants, stay in the main inn or in one of the "sports villas." **Eclipse** is the resort's main dining room, serving contemporary fare overlooking the lake, but several more casual eateries are scattered around the property.

Dwight and Oxtongue Lake

If you don't want to camp, the cheapest beds in the Algonquin vicinity are at the laid-back **Wolf Den Bunkhouse and Cabins** (4568 Hwy. 60, Oxtongue Lake, 705/635-9336 or 866/271-9336, www.wolfdenbunkhouse.com, year-round, $25 dorm, $42 s, $66–84 d, $80–135 cabins), a hostel located between Dwight and the park's West Gate. It's not as picturesque as lakeside lodgings, but it's a friendly spot, where you can often meet other travelers to explore Algonquin Park. The main lodge has a shared kitchen and large lounge, as well as several guest rooms (each accommodating one or two people) on the lower level. Two log bunkhouses each have an eight-bed dorm on the upper floor and rooms sleeping four to five on the main level. Two more private cabins with kitchenettes sleep four to six. In addition to a shared washroom in the main lodge, there's a wash house with showers, toilets, and sinks in the center of the property, but none of the units has a private bath. There's no meal service, so bring your own provisions.

A small cluster of lodgings sits along Oxtongue Lake, just off Highway 60, about a 10-minute drive from Algonquin's West Gate. It's a pretty setting, although the proximity of Highway 60 and its traffic noise can be bothersome.

Under the same ownership as the Bartlett Lodge in Algonquin Park, **The Pines Cottage Resort** (1032 Oxtongue Lake Rd., Dwight, 705/635-2379, www.algonquinparkaccommodations.com, late May–mid-Oct., $125–225) has several family-friendly one- and two-bedroom cottages (with fully equipped kitchens) in the woods just above Oxtongue Lake, where there's a sandy beach. Rates include the use of canoes and kayaks.

More modern, but a little closer to Highway 60, the **Blue Spruce Resort** (4308 Hwy. 60, Dwight, 705/635-2330, www.bluespruce.ca, $132–303) has both hotel-style suites and standalone cottages, ranging from one to three bedrooms, all with kitchens. There are tennis courts and a swimming beach, with a water trampoline. The Blue Spruce, which has Wi-Fi as well as a coin-operated laundry for guests, is open year-round.

Camping

Arrowhead Provincial Park (451 Arrowhead Park Rd., 705/789-5105, www.ontarioparks.com, $14/vehicle) has three campgrounds (mid-May–mid-Oct., $32.52 tent sites, $37.39 electric sites), with a total of 378 campsites, 185 with electrical service. The campgrounds have comfort stations with flush toilets and showers.

FOOD
Huntsville

Two of the best spots for picnic supplies or a meal to go are located on Highway 60, just east of town, and both have similar names. The **Farmer's Daughter** (118 Hwy. 60, 705/789.5700, www.fresheverything.ca, 8 a.m.–6 p.m. Mon.–Wed., 8 a.m.–7 p.m. Thurs.–Fri., 9 a.m.–6 p.m. Sat., 9 a.m.–5 p.m. Sun.) is a combination farm stand, prepared food counter, bakery, and gourmet market. They sell fresh produce, sandwiches made to order, and fancy fixings like smoked fish pâté or homemade jams. Their baked goods, including the addictive trail mix bars, are excellent. If your accommodations have a kitchen, you can pick up dishes like macaroni and cheese or chicken pot pie to heat up back at the cottage.

Across the road, the **Butcher's Daughters** (133 Hwy. 60, 705/789-2848, www.butchersdaughters.ca, 9 A.M.–6 P.M. Mon.–Sat., 10 A.M.–4 P.M. Sun. July–Aug.; 9 A.M.–6 P.M. Mon.–Sat. June and Sept., 9 A.M.–6 P.M. Tues.–Sat. Oct.–May, $4.50–8) makes good deli sandwiches, including the popular peameal bacon, as well as interesting soups and salads. There's a small seating area, or you can take your food to go. They also make heat-and-eat main dishes like lasagna, shepherd's pie, or beef bourguignon, useful if you have kitchen facilities.

For many Ontarians, a trip to Cottage Country isn't complete without a stop at the old-style, family-friendly **West Side Fish and Chips** (126 Main St. W., 705/789-7200, 8 A.M.–8 P.M. daily, $4–15) for a hearty plate of halibut and chips and a gooey slice of coconut cream pie. They're always busy, but you can amuse yourself with trivia game cards while you wait.

You know **That Little Place by the Lights** (76 Main St. E., 705/789-2536, www.thatlittleplacebythelights.ca, 9 A.M.–9 P.M. Mon.–Sat., 11 A.M.–4 P.M. Sun., lunch $5–10, dinner $11–14)? It's a cozy Italian trattoria masquerading as a touristy ice cream parlor and coffee shop. The sauces for the pastas and pizzas are homemade (try the spicy, salty linguini puttanesca, with olives, capers, anchovies, and hot peppers), and the salads are simple but fresh. It's family friendly, too, especially if you promise the kids some gelato for dessert.

One of Huntsville's highly regarded upscale restaurants is **Spencer's Tall Trees** (87 Main St. W., 705/789-9769, www.spencerstalltrees.com, 5 P.M.–close Mon., 11:30 A.M.–2 P.M. and 5 P.M.–close Tues.–Fri., 5 P.M.–close Sat., call for seasonal hours, lunch $10–21, dinner $18–49) set in a heritage house amid the trees. They serve updated versions of classics like filet mignon with béarnaise sauce, veal Oscar (topped with crab), or pickerel in a maple-thyme-butter sauce. Lunch options range from lighter salads and sandwiches to pastas. To finish with something sweet, try the chocolate pâté or a seasonal fruit crumble.

Dwight and Oxtongue Lake

The perpetual lines attest to the popularity of **Henrietta's Pine Bakery** (2868 Hwy. 60, Dwight, 705/635-2214, 9 A.M.–5 P.M. daily May–mid-Oct.), where the specialties include sticky buns and a highly-recommended scone-like cranberry pastry called the Muskoka cloud. They do sell breads and other savories, but it's the sweets that make it worth the stop. Come early in the day, since they close early if they sell out of goodies.

INFORMATION AND SERVICES

The **Huntsville/Lake of Bays Chamber of Commerce** (8 West St. N., 705/789-4771, www.huntsvilleadventures.com), just off Main Street, can provide more information about events and things to do in the Huntsville/Algonquin region.

Algonquin Outfitters Oxtongue Lake (1035 Algonquin Outfitters Rd., Dwight, 705/635-2243 or 800/469-4948, www.algonquinoutfitters.com, 8 A.M.–6 P.M. Mon.–Thurs., 8 A.M.–7 P.M. Fri.–Sun. July–early Sept.; 9 A.M.–5 P.M. Mon.–Thurs., 8 A.M.–6 P.M. Fri.–Sat., 9 A.M.–6 P.M. Sun. May–June and early Sept.–mid-Oct.; 9 A.M.–5 P.M. daily mid-Oct.–Apr.) stocks outdoor clothing and gear; rents canoes, kayaks, and bikes; and offers guided canoe and kayak trips in and around Algonquin Park.

GETTING THERE
By Car

Huntsville is 215 kilometers (133 miles) north of Toronto and 35 kilometers (22 miles) north of Bracebridge. From Toronto, pick up Highway 400 north to Barrie, then continue north on Highway 11 to Huntsville.

By Train

Ontario Northland (800/461-8558, www.ontarionorthland.ca, 3 hours, one-way adults $48.15, seniors and students, $40.90, kids 2–11 $24.10) runs the convenient *Northlander* train from Toronto's Union Station to **Huntsville Station** (26 Station Rd.), just off Main Street west of downtown. From Huntsville, trains continue to North Bay, Temagami, Cochrane, and other points north. The *Northlander* operates Sunday through Friday.

By Bus

Ontario Northland (705/789-6431 or 800/461-8558, www.ontarionorthland.ca, 3.75–4 hours, one-way adults $48.15, seniors and students, $40.90, kids 2–11 $24.10) operates buses to Huntsville from the Toronto Central Bus Station on Bay Street. The bus is a little slower than the train (the fares are the same), but departures are more frequent. The **Huntsville Bus Depot** (77 Centre St. N.) is one kilometer (0.6 mile) north of Main Street. Buses continue from Huntsville to North Bay, Temagami, Cochrane, and other northern destinations.

If you're coming to Huntsville directly from Toronto's Pearson airport, you can take the **Shuttle Ontario** (317 Carmichael Dr., North Bay, 705/474-7942 or 800/461-4219, www.shuttleontario.com, 2.75 hours, one-way adults $91) shared van service, which runs two scheduled trips a day in each direction. It's convenient, since it takes you right from the airport, but it's much more expensive than the Ontario Northland trains or buses.

GETTING AROUND

While it's easy to get to Huntsville without a car, and the downtown area is quite compact, exploring the region around the town, including Algonquin Park, is difficult without your own wheels. If you don't have your own car, take the bus or train into Huntsville and then rent a car for a couple of days to explore Algonquin. **Enterprise Rent-A-Car** (174 Main St. W., 705/789-1834 or 800/736-8222, www.enterpriserentacar.ca) has an office on the west end of Main Street. **Discount Car Rentals** (10 Howland Dr., 705/788-3737, www.discountcar.com) is north of town.

Algonquin Provincial Park

If you visit only one of Ontario's many outdoor destination, the province's first provincial park is an excellent choice. Measuring 763,000 hectares (1,885,000 acres), Algonquin Provincial Park (www.ontarioparks.com or www.algonquinpark.on.ca) is not just big—it's massive, stretching across a wide swath of Northeastern Ontario. Covered with hardwood and coniferous forests, the region was a major logging area in the 1800s, and many visitors are surprised to learn that limited logging is still allowed in some sections of the park. When the park was created in 1893, it wasn't to bring a halt to logging, but rather to protect the region's wildlife.

The park's earliest tourists arrived by train, disembarking at a rail depot near Cache Lake in the southwest quadrant of the park; a nearby hotel housed passengers from Toronto and points south. In the 1930s, Highway 60 was built across Algonquin's southern sections. Sadly, as more and more tourists came by road, the rail service was discontinued. The prevailing wisdom at the time was that eliminating train service would keep the park more "natural."

Highway 60 is still the main access route for most park visitors entering the West Gate from Huntsville (or Toronto) or the East Gate from Ottawa. If your time is limited, pick a few stops—perhaps a paddle at Canoe Lake, hiking one or two of the shorter trails—and spend an hour at the exhibits in the park Visitor Centre.

Despite the park's popularity, you can still find plenty of quiet trails and canoe routes to explore even if you stay near Highway 60. But Algonquin also has a vast backcountry, offering ample opportunities to get out into the wilderness. Most of Algonquin's backcountry is reachable only by canoe.

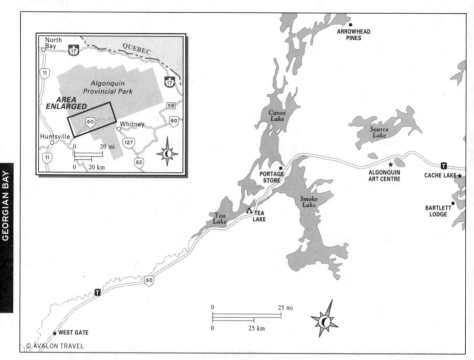

Algonquin Park is open year-round, although many park services and sights operate only from April or May until mid-October.

SIGHTS

The park's main sights are listed from west to east along Highway 60, the direction you'll reach them if coming from Toronto or from elsewhere in the Muskoka region. Distances are from the park's West Gate, so a sight at "KM 20" is 20 kilometers east of the West Gate. If coming from Ottawa, Peterborough, and the Kawarthas, or from elsewhere in Eastern Ontario, enter the park from the East Gate (at KM 56) and follow these locations in reverse.

West Gate (Hwy. 60, KM 0)

At Algonquin's western entrance, you can purchase your park permit ($16.25/vehicle), which all visitors must have. (If you're simply driving across the park on Highway 60 without

stopping, you do not need a park permit. If you stop anywhere in the park, even to use the bathroom, you need to have a permit, or you risk being fined.) Display the permit on your dashboard, so that it's visible from outside. If the park warden can't see the permit, you'll get a ticket. Permits are available at the East and West Gates and at the Algonquin Park Visitor Centre.

If you're going to spend several days in the park, or if you're visiting multiple parks, consider purchasing an **Ontario Parks seasonal pass,** which allows unlimited day visits to any Ontario provincial parks. You can buy a summer-only pass (valid Apr.–Nov., $107.50), a winter-only pass (Dec.–Mar., $70), or a full-year pass valid from April until the following March ($150.50)

The on-site staff can help you get oriented and provide information about things to see and do, which is particularly helpful if your time is limited.

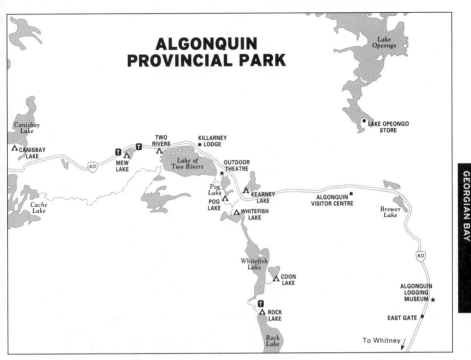

ALGONQUIN PROVINCIAL PARK

Canoe Lake (Hwy. 60, KM 14.1)

The history of Canoe Lake is inextricably linked to the mysterious disappearance of the painter Tom Thomson (1877–1917), a member of the Group of Seven artists who lived and worked in Ontario in the early 1900s. Thomson spent several years visiting and painting in Algonquin Park, beginning in 1912, mostly on and around Canoe Lake. Thomson was last seen on July 8, 1917, in the vicinity of Canoe Lake—and then he vanished. His overturned canoe was found behind the lake's Wapomeo Island, and several days later, his body was pulled from the lake. The exact circumstances of his death remain a puzzle that has never been solved. In his memory, the **Tom Thomson memorial cairn** was erected in 1930 on one of Thomson's favorite Canoe Lake campsites. The cairn is accessible only by canoe.

The **Portage Store** (Hwy. 60, KM 14.1, 705/633-5622, www.portagestore.com, late Apr.–mid-Oct.) on Canoe Lake rents canoes and can give you tips on where to go, including how to get to the Thomson cairn. They also offer half- and full-day guided paddles.

Algonquin Art Centre (Hwy. 60, KM 20)

This art center (705/633-5555, www.algonquinartcentre.com, 10 A.M.–5 P.M. daily June–mid-Oct.) has a small gallery (admission by donation) that shows changing exhibits of works by artists who have an Algonquin connection. The center also offers drop-in art activities (10:30 A.M.–4:30 P.M. daily July–Aug.), for both children and adults, which are great for a rainy day or when the kids need a break from hiking and swimming. You might paint a wooden canoe paddle or miniature canoe, make a mobile, or create a clay sculpture. Activities take place in a screened outdoor gazebo. Prices vary by activity, but most range $10–25. On Tuesdays, Wednesdays, and Thursdays in summer, the

GEORGIAN BAY

HOWLING WITH THE WOLVES

One of the many animals who live in the Algonquin Provincial Park wilderness is the wolf. And one of the most popular (and eeriest) activities at Algonquin Park is the Wolf Howl.

These events typically attract more than 1,500 visitors, who assemble at the park's Outdoor Theatre (Hwy. 60, KM 35.4) for a presentation about wolves and their habitat. Then everyone gets in their cars and drives caravan-style to a designated spot where park naturalists have heard a wolf pack on the previous night. Once everyone is in place, the naturalists begin a sequence of howls – hoping that the wolves will respond with howls of their own. Sometimes they do, and sometimes they don't, but if you're lucky enough to hear the wolf pack howling, it's a unique experience.

The Wolf Howls are typically held during the month of August (or occasionally the first week of September), the only time of year when wolves are likely to remain in one place for days at a time. The howls are held once a week, on Thursday evenings, beginning at 8 P.M., and last about three hours.

Check event bulletin boards throughout the park, or phone the Visitor Centre (613/637-2828) to confirm if the week's Wolf Howl will be held. Howls are canceled if no wolves are in an area (along Hwy. 60) or if the weather is inclement, so you generally won't know till the day of the event whether it will take place. Updates on the Wolf Howls are also posted on the Friends of Algonquin Park website (www.algonquinpark.on.ca), where you can sign up to receive an email update on the week's Wolf Howl.

---

art center runs art classes, as well, for children and adults. Suitable for beginning and more advanced students, the classes typically last 90 minutes. Pre-registration is required; call or visit the center in advance to sign up.

Cache Lake (Hwy. 60, KM 23.5)

Cache Lake was once the center of activity in Algonquin Park. From the 1890s, when the park was first established, until the 1950s, this lake area had a rail depot—Algonquin Park Station—as well as a large hotel. All that remains today, aside from the lovely lake itself, is a short historical walking trail, where several signs with historical photos along a wooded path tell you about the area's interesting past.

Another reason to stop at Cache Lake is to eat or stay at **Bartlett Lodge** (Cache Lake, 705/633-5543, 705/633-5746, or 866/614-5355, www.bartlettlodge.com, mid-May–late Oct.). Boat service to the lodge runs across the lake from the Cache Lake Landing.

Lake of Two Rivers (Hwy. 60, KM 31)

Lake of Two Rivers is a busy place. In addition to the large **Two Rivers Campground** (519/826-5290 or 888/668-7275, www.ontarioparks.com, reservation fee $9.50 phone, $8.50 online, $35.25–40.50 tent sites, $46 RV sites), there's a snack bar, grocery store, and mountain bike rentals. East of the campground, **Killarney Lodge** (Lake of Two Rivers, Hwy. 60, KM 33.2, 705/633-5551 or 866/473-5551, www.killarney-lodge.com) is set on the Lake of Two Rivers. Just east of the lodge is a public swimming beach.

Algonquin Visitor Centre (Hwy. 60, KM 43)

Even if you've entered the park from the west and gotten oriented at the West Gate, it's worth stopping into the Algonquin Visitor Centre (9 A.M.–5 P.M. daily late Apr.–late June and mid-late Oct.; 9 A.M.–9 P.M. daily late June–early Sept.; 9 A.M.–6 P.M. daily early Sept.–mid-Oct.; 10 A.M.–4 P.M. Sat.–Sun. Nov.–late Apr., with daily hours during holiday weeks) to learn more about the park. Start by watching a 12-minute film about the park's history and natural features, and then visit the exhibit area, which covers these topics in more detail. In summer, many of the park's interpretive programs are based at the Visitor Centre. A shop sells detailed park maps and guides, as well as books about wildlife, camping, and the outdoors. There's a basic cafeteria, and free Wi-Fi, too. The best feature of the Visitor Centre, though, is outside the building. The deck out back overlooks a wide swath of park territory and helps you appreciate Algonquin's vast expanse.

Algonquin Logging Museum (Hwy. 60, KM 54.5)

Logging was an important part of Algonquin's heritage, and you can learn more about that history and about the delicate balance between industry and preservation at the Algonquin Logging Museum (9 A.M.–5 P.M. daily late June–mid-Oct., free). Inside the exhibit building, you can watch a short video about Algonquin's logging history, but the most interesting parts of this museum are outdoors. Follow a walking trail through a re-created logging camp, continuing along the trail, where you can see how loggers cut and squared the trees, hauled them across the lakes, and drove them through water "chutes" to transport them down the river to the cities. You can climb aboard an "alligator," a steam-powered tugboat used to haul logs. The trail also takes you past a working log dam and chute, a restored blacksmith shop, a locomotive, and a classic 1950s truck. There are enough things to touch and climb on that kids may enjoy it, even if they don't appreciate the historical angle.

East Gate (Hwy. 60, KM 55.8)

Like the West Gate, Algonquin's eastern entrance has an information office that sells the required park permits ($16.25/vehicle), provides park maps, and offers suggestions about things to see and do. There's no need to stop here if you're coming from the west and leaving the park, although if you're driving east toward Ottawa, you might stop and use the restrooms before hitting the road.

SPORTS AND RECREATION
Bicycling

Algonquin Park has two cycling trails that are easy to reach from Highway 60. The 10-kilometer (6.2-mile) **Old Railway Bike Trail** follows the route of a former rail line. Connecting the Mew Lake and Rock Lake Campgrounds, the trail also passes the campgrounds at Lake of Two Rivers, Kearney Lake, Pog Lake, Whitefish Lake, and Coon Lake. The trail is relatively flat and good for families.

The **Minnesing Mountain Bike Trail** (Hwy. 60, KM 23, mid-June–mid-Oct.) is more challenging; the park rates it as "moderate" on the scale of technical difficulty. It includes four hilly loops of 4.7, 10.1, 17.1, and 23.4 kilometers (2.9, 6.3, 10.6, and 14.5 miles). The trail is often quite muddy in June and July.

You can rent bikes at the **Two Rivers Store** (Hwy. 60, KM 31.4, 705/633-5622) and the **Opeongo Store** (Lake Opeongo, 6.2 kilometers, or 3.9 miles, north of KM 46.3, 613/637-2075 or 888/280-8886, www.algonquinoutfitters.com).

C Canoeing

Algonquin Park (www.ontarioparks.com or www.algonquinpark.on.ca) is one of Ontario's most popular destinations for canoeing. Not only can you paddle on the park's numerous lakes and rivers, but Algonquin also has more than 2,000 kilometers (1,240 miles) of canoe routes across the backcountry, ideal for overnight or multiday canoe trips. A useful planning resource is the *Canoe Routes of Algonquin Provincial Park Map* (www.algongquinpark. on.ca, $4.95), which you can order online or purchase at any of the park stores or information centers. It details all the lakes, access points, portages, and campsites across Algonquin.

Within the park, you can rent canoes at the **Portage Store** (Canoe Lake, Hwy. 60, KM 14.1) and the Opeongo Store (6.2 km or 3.9 miles north of KM 46.3), run by **Algonquin Outfitters** (613/637-2075 or 888/280-8886, www.algonquinoutfitters.com). Both outfitters offer shuttle services to take you and your canoe to various launch points. Many outfitters outside the park will rent canoes with car-top carriers, so you can transport them to launch points in Algonquin.

If you're new to canoeing, or if you'd prefer to go out with a guide, both the Portage Store and Algonquin Outfitters offer guided canoe day trips. The Portage Store runs a full-day trip (9:30 A.M.–4:30 P.M., adults $57.95, kids under 14 $29) on Canoe Lake, which includes an orientation about the park, basic canoe instruction, and a daylong paddle with a stop for a picnic lunch. Trips run daily from late June through early September, and every day except Tuesday and Thursday from mid-May to late June and from early September to mid-October. In July and August, they also offer a half-day trip (1–5 P.M., adults $32.95, kids under 14 $17. Reservations are recommended for both trips.

Algonquin Outfitters' guided day trips include departures from the Opeongo Store and from their location just outside the park's West Gate on Oxtongue Lake. From the Opeongo Store, options include a half-day Costello Creek trip (Mon.–Fri. mid-May–Oct., $69.98/person for two, $46.98/person for three, $34.98/person for four) and a full-day Hailstorm Creek nature-reserve trip (Mon.–Fri. mid-May–Oct., $152.48/person for two, $121.65/person for three, $111.23/person for four). They also offer a full-day guided canoe trip (Mon.–Fri. mid-May–Oct., $139.98/person for two, $93.98/person for three, $69.98/person for four) departing from their Oxtongue Lake store at 9 A.M. Rates for kids are discounted by 25 percent.

Hiking

All along the Highway 60 corridor are trails for day hikes, ranging from an easy boardwalk path to strenuous all-day excursions. More experienced hikers can tromp along more than 140 kilometers (87 miles) of backpacking trails through the park's interior.

Following are the most accessible park trails, their locations along Highway 60, their length, and difficulty:

- Whiskey Rapids (KM 7.2, 2.1 km, moderate)
- Hardwood Lookout (KM 13.8, 0.8 km, moderate)
- Mizzy Lake (KM 15.4, 11 km, moderate)
- Peck Lake (KM 19.2, 1.9 km, moderate)
- Track and Tower (KM 25, 7.7 km, moderate)
- Hemlock Bluff (KM 27.2, 3.5 km, moderate)
- Bat Lake (KM 30, 5.6 km, moderate)
- Two Rivers (KM 31, 2.1 km, moderate)
- Centennial Ridges (KM 37.6, 10 km, strenuous)
- Lookout (KM 39.7, 1.9 km, moderate)
- Big Pines (KM 40.3, 2.9 km, moderate)
- Booth's Rock (KM 40.5, 5.1 km, moderate)
- Spruce Bog Boardwalk (KM 42.5, 1.5 km, easy)
- Beaver Pond (KM 45.2, 2 km, moderate)

Trail guides, with more details about each of these hikes, are available at the trailheads (from spring through fall) and online (www.algonquinpark.on.ca).

Winter Sports

If you want to try dogsledding, these outfitters can get you out on the Algonquin trails. **Voyageur Quest** (416/486-3605 or 800/794-9660, www.voyageurquest.com) offers an introductory day of dogsledding (Dec.–Mar., $185/person) that includes orientation, harnessing the dogs, and a four-hour mush. They also offer weekend-long and multiday dogsledding trips.

Snow Forest Adventures (705/783-0461, www.snowforestadventures.ca) runs half-day (10 A.M.–12:30 P.M. or 1–3:30 P.M., late Dec.–Mar., $125/person) and full-day (10 A.M.–3 P.M. late Dec.–Mar., $190/person) dogsledding trips that depart from the Sunday Lake dogsledding trails (Hwy. 60, KM 40). No experience is necessary, and kids under 12 can ride on a sled with a paying adult for a small fee ($25/half-day trip, $50/full-day trip).

© CAROLYN B. HELLER

Algonquin Provincial Park is a popular destination for hikers.

Algonquin Park has three areas that offer trails for cross-country skiing. At the West Gate, the groomed **Fen Lake Ski Trail** has four loops, ranging 1.25–13 kilometers (0.75–8 miles). One kilometer (0.6 mile) west of the East Gate, the groomed **Leaf Lake Trail** has routes measuring 5–51 kilometers (3–32 miles). For more challenging wilderness skiing, head to the **Minnesing Trail** (Hwy. 60, KM 23), where four ungroomed loops range 4.7–23.4 kilometers (2.9–14.5 miles).

For snowshoeing, you can explore nearly anywhere in the park, including any of the hiking trails along the Highway 60 corridor. Snowshoes are not allowed on the cross-country trails.

You must have a park permit ($16.25/vehicle) for any winter activities. Also remember that daylight is much more limited in the winter, so make sure you have ample time to get off the trails before dark. Ensure, too, that you have warm clothes, particularly hats, gloves, boots, and multiple layers appropriate for your outdoor activity.

Outfitters

A number of outfitters, both within and outside Algonquin Park, can help you organize canoeing, camping, and hiking trips; rent you the gear you need; or take you on a guided journey. Some even organize dogsledding excursions.

Algonquin Outfitters (800/469-4948, www.algonquinoutfitters.com) has locations throughout the Muskoka region, including the Opeongo Store on Lake Opeongo within the park, Oxtongue Lake outside the West Gate, and Huntsville. They offer a variety of services and trips, including half-day, full-day, and multiday canoe and kayak trips, either guided or self-guided, departing from several different locations.

Located on Canoe Lake, the **Portage Store** (Hwy. 60, KM 14.1, 705/633-5622, www.portagestore.com, late Apr.–mid-Oct.) organizes canoe trips and offers half-, full-, and multiday guided paddles.

Outside the East Gate, **Opeongo Outfitters** (Hwy. 60, Whitney, 613/637-5470 or 800/790-1864, www.opeongooutfitters.com, mid-Apr.–mid-Oct.) can rent the gear you need for a multiday canoe trip, including a canoe, tent, a pack, a sleeping bag, food, cooking utensils, and other supplies. You can also rent a kayak or canoe for the day.

Voyageur Quest (416/486-3605 or 800/794-9660, www.voyageurquest.com) organizes several different Algonquin excursions, from three- to five-day canoe trips (including trips designed for families), to winter dogsledding trips.

Snow Forest Adventures (705/783-0461, www.snowforestadventures.ca) offers half-day and full-day dogsledding trips, from late December through March, weather permitting.

ACCOMMODATIONS AND FOOD

If you want to stay within the park, you can choose from three upscale lodges (which also operate restaurants), rustic former ranger cabins, or camping. The lodges, cabins, and most of the campgrounds are open from spring to fall. In winter, you can camp at Mew Lake, off Highway 60, or out in the backcountry. The park cafeterias and snack bars also operate seasonally.

Park Lodges

From hiking to swimming to canoeing, there's plenty to do at **Arowhon Pines** (Arowhon Rd., 705/633-5661 or 866/633-5661, www.arowhonpines.ca, late May–mid-Oct., $198–440/person). When you're ready to bed down for the night, you can choose from 50 rooms, in either shared or private cabins. The private cabins are just that: your own cottage, with a queen bed, lounge area, and private deck. The shared cabins come in two flavors. In the two-bedroom cabins, you have a private room and bath, but share the lounge space with guests in the other room. The shared cabins are more like mini-lodges, where your room and bath are private, but all the guests use the common living area. Lodging rates, which include breakfast, lunch, and dinner, as well as use of all the recreational facilities, go up depending on the level of privacy. To reach Arowhon Pines, follow Highway 60 to KM16, then turn north onto Arowhon Rd., which winds through the woods to the lodge.

Getting to **Bartlett Lodge** (Cache Lake, 705/633-5543, 705/633-5746, or 866/614-5355, www.bartlettlodge.com, mid-May–late Oct.) is half the fun. Set on the opposite side of Cache Lake from Highway 60, the lodge is accessible only by boat. They run a motorboat shuttle to bring guests back and forth, making a stay here feel like a true getaway into the woods. Most of the accommodations are in cottages, ranging from studios to three bedrooms. The studio units ($155–185/person), in a historic log cabin, are named for Group of Seven artists A. Y. Jackson and Lawren Harris and feature the artists' work. Some of the cabins ($167–238/person) were built back in the early 1900s, while others were constructed more recently; they're all lakeside or a short walk away. Rates in the studios and cabins include a buffet breakfast and a multicourse dinner. The lodge also offers a "glamping" (glamorous camping) option: accommodations in two furnished **platform tents** ($80–100/person), which are more like staying in an outdoor room than camping in a tent. A washroom with showers is in an adjacent building. Tent rates include a buffet breakfast. To get to Bartlett Lodge, turn off Highway 60 at KM 23.5, Cache Lake. Park your car and use the lodge phone at Cache Lake Landing to contact the lodge. They'll send their water taxi to pick you up.

Killarney Lodge (Lake of Two Rivers, Hwy. 60, KM 33.2, 705/633-5551 or 866/473-5551, www.killarneylodge.com, mid-May–mid-Oct., $169–339/person) is the easiest to reach of the park lodges. Just off Highway 60, it's a convenient base for exploring the rest of the park. The 25 log cottages are set in the woods, with neat-as-a-pin knotty-pine or rough-hewn log interiors. The "one-bedroom" cabins are one room, with a king or queen bed; the "two-bedroom" cabins have two rooms, one with a king bed, a second with twin beds. Most (but not all) of the cottages are right on the lake, and each comes with your own canoe.

Ranger Cabins

Algonquin has 14 ranger cabins (mid-Apr.–mid-Oct., $58–134) that essentially offer indoor camping. They're rustic log structures without running water or electricity that were built in the early 1900s; rangers patrolling the park would travel from cabin to cabin where they'd overnight. You can reach five of the cabins by car, including cabins at Rain Lake, Bissett Creek Road, Kiosk, and two cabins at Brent. The remainder are in the backcountry. The cabins are basic, equipped with a table and chairs, a wood stove, and an outdoor toilet; most have bunks but not necessarily mattresses, so bring a sleeping pad as well as a sleeping bag. You also need to bring any dishes, pots, or cooking utensils that you want.

The Friends of Algonquin Park (www.algonquinpark.on.ca) has detailed descriptions of each cabin and their facilities.

Camping

Algonquin is a popular destination for campers, with the largest number of campsites of any Ontario provincial park. Reserve your campsite (519/826-5290 or 888/668-7275, www.ontarioparks.com, reservation fee $9.50 phone, $8.50 online, $35.25–40.50 tent sites, $46 RV sites) in advance, particularly for summer and fall weekends. Eight of the front-country campgrounds are accessible by car near Highway 60. Most are seasonal, opening in late April or mid-May and closing in mid-October. Only the Mew Lake campground is open year-round.

The front-country campgrounds (and their distance from the West Gate) are:

- Tea Lake (KM 11.4, 42 sites) has pit toilets and no other facilities.
- Canisbay Lake (KM 23.1, 242 sites) has secluded campsites, swimming beaches, showers, and flush toilets.
- Mew Lake (KM 30.6, 131 sites) also has seven **yurts** ($91.50/night), available year-round. The yurts, which sleep six, are furnished with two sets of bunk beds (a double below and a single above), a table and chairs, a propane barbecue, cooking utensils, and dishes. They

have electric lights and heat. You still need to bring sleeping bags or other bedding, as well as food and other personal items.

- Two Rivers (KM 31.8, 241 sites) is the most centrally located, and frequently the most crowded. It has a beach, a laundry, flush toilets, and showers.
- Pog Lake (KM 36.9, 286 sites) has secluded campsites, and comfort stations with showers, laundry, and flush toilets.
- Kearney Lake (KM 36.5, 103 sites) has two beaches, showers, and flush toilets.
- Coon Lake (six kilometers south of KM 40.3, 48 sites) has a beach and pit toilets.
- Rock Lake (eight kilometers south of KM 40.3, 121 sites) has two beaches, showers, flush toilets, and laundry.

Algonquin has three more drive-in campgrounds (late Apr.–mid-Oct.) farther north. **Achray** (45 sites), **Brent** (30 sites), and **Kiosk** (22 sites) campgrounds are all accessible from Highway 17 but far more secluded than the Highway 60 camping areas. Achray and Kiosk have flush toilets, and Achray also has a yurt, but none of these three campgrounds has showers.

Algonquin Park also has numerous **backcountry campgrounds** (adults $11.75, kids 6–17 $5) that you can't reach by car; most are accessible only by canoe. The Friends of Algonquin Park (www.algonquinpark.on.ca) has detailed information to help plan a trip into the backcountry. Several outfitters also organize backcountry trips.

Outside the Park

A short drive outside the park's East Gate, the **Couples Resort** (Galeairy Lake Rd., Whitney, 866/202-1179, www.couplesresort.ca, $152–798 d) has an entirely different ambience than the cottage-style park lodges. The decor, in the 36 suites and 12 cabins, all within 15 meters (50 feet) of the waterfront, is unabashedly romantic, even over-the-top, designed for couples who want to cocoon. Many rooms, which range from large to huge, have four-poster beds, ornate wallpapers and window treatments, hot tubs or whirlpool baths (or both), as well as wood-burning fireplaces and iPod docks with CD players and radios. If you ever come out of your room, you can have a dip in the outdoor heated saltwater pool (late May–mid-Oct.), play pool or table tennis, take a sauna, or work out in the fitness room. There's an on-site spa, too.

Prices include breakfast, served either in the dining room or in your suite, and a five-course dinner. Plan to dress for dinner; jeans, shorts, and sandals are forbidden, and men must wear a dress shirt with a collar. If you must get online, Internet access is available ($20/stay). Check the resort website for midweek or last-minute specials.

Couples Resort is in the town of Whitney. From Highway 60, go south on Galeairy Lake Road.

Food

If you're not a lodge guest, you can still come for a meal in the dining room at **Arowhon Pines** (Arowhon Rd., 705/633-5661 or 866/633-5661, www.arowhonpines.ca, late May–mid-Oct.). Meals are a fixed price: breakfast (8–10 A.M., $25/person), weekday lunch (12:30–2 P.M., $32/person), weekend lunch buffet (12:30–2 P.M., $45/person), and an abundant multicourse dinner (6:30 P.M. only, $70/person). The dining room doesn't have a license to serve alcohol, but you can bring your own.

The **Bartlett Lodge** dining room (Cache Lake, 705/633-5543, 705/633-5746, or 866/614-5355, www.bartlettlodge.com, mid-May–late Oct.) is open to nonguests for breakfast ($15/person) and in the evening, when an elaborate five-course, prix-fixe dinner ($59/person) is served; kids have a three-course dinner option ($25/person). The dining room isn't licensed to serve alcohol, but you can bring your own.

The main lodge building at **Killarney Lodge** (Lake of Two Rivers, Hwy. 60, KM 33.2, 705/633-5551 or 866/473-5551, www.killarney-lodge.com, mid-May–mid-Oct.) dates to 1935 and now houses the dining room. The dining room is open to the public, serving hearty, fixed-price, three-course menus at lunch (noon–2 P.M. daily, $25) and dinner (5:45 P.M.–7:30 P.M., $50). If you're not a lodge guest, reservations

are recommended for dinner. Also, the dining room keeps slightly shorter hours in May and June, so phone to confirm.

In addition to the lodges' dining rooms, you can get casual meals at the **Portage Store** (Canoe Lake, Hwy. 60, KM 14.1, 705/633-5622, www.portagestore.com), which serves breakfast, lunch, and dinner from late April through mid-October, and at the **Sunday Creek Café** (Hwy. 60, KM 63, 613/637-1133), the basic cafeteria in the Algonquin Visitor Centre. A seasonal snack bar sells sandwiches and ice cream at the **Two Rivers Store** (Hwy. 60, KM 31.4).

INFORMATION AND SERVICES

For general information about Algonquin Park, phone the **Algonquin Park Information Office** (705/633-5572, 9 A.M.–4 P.M. daily Apr.–Oct., 9 A.M.–4 P.M. Fri–Sun. Nov.–Mar., www.algonquinpark.on.ca). You can also get visitor information at the park's West Gate, East Gate, and Visitor Centre. Online, the best source of information is the **Friends of Algonquin Park** (www.algonquinpark.on.ca). **Ontario Parks** (www.ontarioparks.com) will give you an overview of the park facilities but doesn't provide as much detail.

Mobile phones do work in Algonquin Park, if you're within about three kilometers (1.9 miles) on either side of Highway 60. There are dead spots, though, and outside of this zone, don't count on picking up a phone signal.

Within the park, three stores sell camping supplies (including mosquito repellent, rain ponchos, and basic first aid) and a small selection of groceries. The **Portage Store** (KM 14.1) is on the west end of Highway 60 at Canoe Lake, the **Two Rivers Store** (KM 31.4) at the Lake of Two Rivers Campground is at roughly the midway point on Highway 60, and the **Opeongo Store** is to the east, a short drive north of KM 46.3.

GETTING THERE
By Car

Algonquin's West Gate is 45 kilometers (28 miles) east of Huntsville, via Highway 60. The

East Gate is five kilometers (three miles) west of the town of Whitney. From Toronto (270 kilometers, or 168 miles), the most direct, if most heavily trafficked, route is to take Highway 400 north to Highway 11 north, which will take you to Huntsville, where you can pick up Highway 60 to the West Gate.

An alternate route from Toronto takes you to the East Gate. Go east on Highway 401, then pick up Highway 115 into Peterborough; from there, take Highway 28 north to Bancroft, Highway 62 north to Maynooth, then Highway 127 north to Highway 60, which will bring you to the park's East Gate. While this route sounds more complicated, it's clearly marked; it's about 310 kilometers (193 miles) from the Toronto metropolitan area.

From Ottawa, pick up Highway 417/17 west to Highway 60, which will take you into the park. It's 240 kilometers (150 miles) from Ottawa to the East Gate.

You can buy gas at the Portage Store (KM 14.1, early May–mid-Oct.). Otherwise, the nearest gas stations are in Oxtongue Lake and Dwight west of the park and in Whitney to the east.

By Bus

Launched in 2010, the **Parkbus** (800/928-7101, www.parkbus.ca) provides direct bus service from Toronto to Algonquin. It's a non-profit initiative designed to get people out of the city—and out of their cars. The bus runs on select weekends throughout the summer season. The bus departs from several points in Toronto, including 30 College St. (between Yonge and Church Streets, one block from the College subway station) and Dufferin Street, at Bloor Street West, which is at Dufferin station.

You can get off the bus at several points, including the Wolf Den Hostel near Oxtongue Lake, the West Gate, the Portage Store at Canoe Lake, Lake of Two Rivers Campground, Pog Lake, and the Algonquin Outfitters store on Lake Opeongo. These locations either have accommodations (you can camp at Lake of Two Rivers or Pog Lake, or bunk at the Wolf Den), or they're departure points for outfitters who organize guided trips. The Parkbus works with several outfitters, so you can buy an all-inclusive trip, if you prefer.

If you're coming from Huntsville, there's another bus option that can take you to the park. **Hammond Transportation** (705/645-5431, www.hammondtransportation.com, one-way $36) runs a bus from Huntsville to Algonquin, on Mondays, Wednesdays, and Fridays from late June through August. The bus leaves the Huntsville depot at 1:15 P.M. and makes three stops: at Algonquin Outfitters on Oxtongue Lake (1:50 P.M.), at the Portage Store on Canoe Lake (2:00 P.M.), and at Lake of Two Rivers General Store, near the campground (2:15 P.M.). The return bus leaves Lake of Two Rivers at 2:30 P.M., the Portage Store at 2:45 P.M., and Algonquin Outfitters at 3 P.M., returning to Huntsville at 3:30 P.M. Since the bus operates only three times a week, you need to stay at least two days to catch the bus back to Huntsville. Still, it's a useful option if you're camping or going on a guided trip with one of these outfitters.

GETTING AROUND

There is no public transportation within Algonquin. If you arrive on the **Parkbus** (800/928-7101, www.parkbus.ca), you can camp at Lake of Two Rivers or Pog Lake, which are both centrally located and have hiking, cycling, and canoeing options nearby, so it's feasible to do without a car. You can also arrive by bus and do a canoeing or hiking trip that you've booked through an outfitter; the bus will drop you at one of several outfitters' locations.

Otherwise, unless you're comfortable bicycling or hiking long distances, you need a car to explore the park. The most convenient place to rent a car in the vicinity of the park is in Huntsville.

GEORGIAN BAY

THE NORTH

Biggest, deepest, longest—Northern Ontario is a place of geographical superlatives. It has the largest body of freshwater in the world (Lake Superior), the deepest Great Lake (again Lake Superior), the world's largest and second-largest freshwater islands (Manitoulin and St. Joseph), and vast—really vast—tracks of wilderness stretching north from Lake Huron to Hudson Bay and west to the Manitoba border. Adventurous travelers could explore for years before covering this immense region.

If it's eco-adventure you crave, Northern Ontario is your place. Temagami, dotted with lakes and forests, is a prime destination for canoe trips, and Killarney is a stunning canoeing destination as well. From Sault Ste. Marie, you can take a one-day rail journey into the wilderness of Agawa Canyon. The shores of Lake Superior are lined with spectacular beaches and rocky cliffs crisscrossed with hiking trails.

While the North is a natural choice for outdoor adventures, it's ripe for cultural explorations, too. Aboriginal people have lived in Northern Ontario for thousands of years, and many aboriginal communities are welcoming visitors who want to learn about their culture and traditions. Manitoulin Island's Great Spirit Circle Trail is a leader in aboriginal tourism, and if you venture farther north, to the remote communities of Moosonee and Moose Factory Island on the shores of James Bay, you can explore the culture of the Cree First Nation, one of Canada's largest aboriginal groups.

Northern Ontario also has a large Francophone population, so don't be surprised to see bilingual signs or hear *"Bonjour"* and *"Merci."* The city of

© CAROLYN B. HELLER

HIGHLIGHTS

LOOK FOR 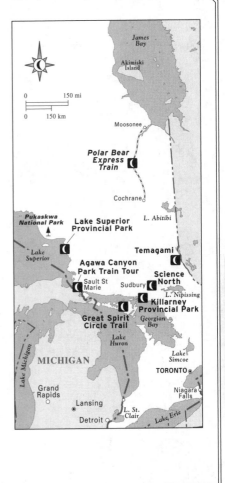 TO FIND RECOMMENDED SIGHTS, ACTIVITIES, DINING, AND LODGING.

❰ Temagami: This lakeland region is one of the most accessible places in the north for canoe-tripping, whether you're a novice or experienced paddler (page 359).

❰ *Polar Bear Express Train:* Go where no roads go, on this rail trip north to James Bay, where you can explore the Cree First Nations communities of Moosonee and Moose Factory Island (page 363).

❰ Science North: Sudbury's cool, contemporary science museum is filled with "please touch" exhibits that are particularly eco-friendly (page 368).

❰ Killarney Provincial Park: Escape to the wilderness of this vast and dramatic provincial park, with its rugged white dolomite ridges, pink granite cliffs, pine forests, and crystal clear lakes (page 371).

❰ Great Spirit Circle Trail: Explore aboriginal culture on Manitoulin Island, the largest freshwater island in the world. Take a guided "Mother Earth" nature hike or a workshop on traditional dance, drumming, and food, and stay on a First Nations reserve (page 377).

❰ Agawa Canyon Park Train Tour: A car-free day-trip into the northern wilderness, this rail journey is particularly spectacular during the fall foliage season (page 383).

❰ Lake Superior Provincial Park: One of Ontario's most beautiful outdoor destinations, this provincial park extends along the eastern shore of the world's largest body of freshwater. You'll find sandy beaches, rocky coves, rugged hiking trails, even ancient rock paintings (page 386).

THE NORTH

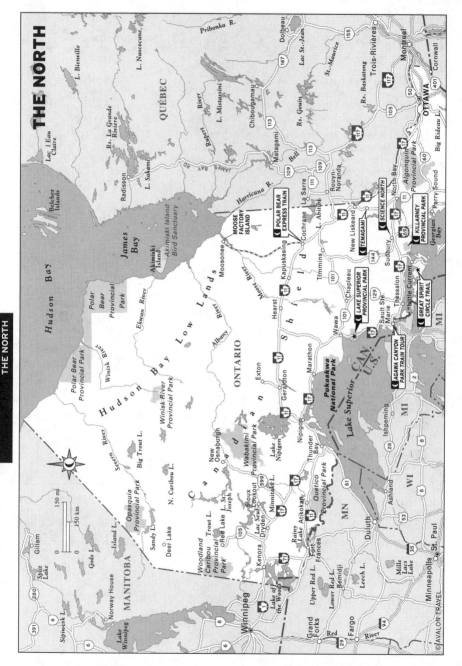

THE NORTH

© AVALON TRAVEL

Sudbury is particularly bilingual; it's Canada's third-largest French-speaking community outside Quebec. In some northern towns, you'll find French-Canadian influences in the food, too, with *tortière* (meat pie) and *poutine* (French fries topped with cheese curds and gravy) almost as common as burgers and fries.

Looking for outdoor adventure? Cultural adventure? Just plain adventure? Then head north.

PLANNING YOUR TIME

Distances between northern destinations are far, so pick just one place to visit if your time is short. For a long weekend from Toronto, take a canoe trip in **Temagami** or hop on the ferry to **Manitoulin Island.** With several days to spare,

explore the shores of Lake Superior, canoe in **Killaryn Provincial Park,** take the *Polar Bear Express Train* north to Cochrane, and travel onward to the Cree communities of **Moosonee** and **Moose Factory Island.**

July and August are the busiest months for travel in the North. While winter temperatures dip well below freezing, summers can be hot and humid, with daytime highs above 30°C (86°F). Early autumn (Sept.–mid-Oct.) is popular, when temperatures are milder. From mid-October through April, many lodgings and restaurants shut down except for those catering to cross-country skiers, snowshoers, snowmobilers, dogsledders, or other outdoor adventurers.

North Bay to James Bay

Traveling north from Algonquin Provincial Park or northeast from the Ottawa Valley, the towns get farther apart and the forests get denser. Mining and logging have historically formed the backbone of local economies here, but tourism, particularly outdoor adventure and ecotourism, is a growing business. From the city of North Bay, it's a short trip to the lakeland town of Temagami, which has excellent canoe-trip options. Farther north, you can tour a former gold mine, with retired miners as your guide, or board the train for a unique journey to First Nations communities along James Bay.

NORTH BAY
Sights

On May 28, 1934, quintuplets were born to Oliva and Elzire Dionne, a French-Canadian couple living in Corbeil, outside North Bay. These five identical girls—the now-famous Dionne Quintuplets—became an immediate media sensation. By an act of Parliament, they were removed from their parents, who already had five other children under age seven, and designated the property of the Ontario government, which built an "observation playground" where the quints lived—in view of more than

three million visitors—until 1943. Although they were returned to their family, the transition to "normal" life was difficult, and their treatment eventually drew public indignation.

The house where the quints were born, which was moved to its current location adjacent to North Bay's Regional Tourist Information Centre east of downtown, is now the **Dionne Quints Museum** (1375 Seymour St., 705/472-8480 or 888/249-8998, www.northbaychamber.com, 9 a.m.–7 p.m. daily July–Aug., 9 a.m.–5 p.m. Mon.–Fri. and 10 a.m.–4 p.m. Sat.–Sun. Sept.–June; adults $3.50, seniors and students 13–18 $3, children 5–12 $2), filled with memorabilia about their lives. It's worth taking the free guided tour, available on request, to learn more about the quintuplets and their complicated history.

The **Heritage Railway and Carousel** (Memorial Dr., 4 p.m.–dusk Fri., 10 a.m.–dusk Sat.–Sun. mid-May–late June; 10 a.m.–dusk daily late June–early Sept.; 10 a.m.–dusk Sat.–Sun. early Sept.–mid-Oct., $2/ticket) is an old-time miniature train and merry-go-round that will appeal to kids.

The **Discovery North Bay Museum** (100 Ferguson St., 705/476.2323, www.

THE NORTH

NIPPING INTO NIPISSING

The big woods of Algonquin give way to farm country as you drive north on Highway 11, then turn west toward the small village of Nipissing (pronounced "NI-pi-sing"). Nipissing is attracting modern-day pioneers who are simultaneously getting back to the land and welcoming visitors into their lives. It's a funky, little-touristed destination for a weekend getaway.

Pop in for a quick look through the quirky **Nipissing Museum** (Hwys. 654 at 534, 705/724-2938, 11 A.M.-5 P.M. mid-June-early Sept., admission by donation), and you may find you're there for an hour or more. The museum is a labor of love for the local resident nicknamed "Museum Joe," who has assembled several buildings packed with artifacts reflecting life in Nipissing since the early 1900s. There's the dress of a local woman who met with British royalty, the cash register from the general store, a wide variety of household items, and scads of photos – and Joe can give you the details about every one.

The family-run **Board's Honey Farm** (6866 Hwy. 534, 705/729-2939 or 888/363-2827, www.boardshoneyfarm.com, 10 A.M.-5 P.M. May-Oct.), between Nipissing and Restoule, houses more than 300 colonies of bees and sells a variety of homemade honeys and honey products. On Thursdays in July and August, you can take a guided tour of the beekeeping operations (1:30 P.M.); otherwise, explore the gardens, walking trails, and hives on your own.

Continue west of Highway 534 to quiet **Restoule Provincial Park** (705/729-2010, www.ontarioparks.com), where you can swim in the lake and perhaps spot deer, moose, or other wildlife nearby.

WHERE TO STAY

Staying at the **Piebird Bed & Breakfast** (113 Chapman's Landing Rd, 705/724-1144, www.piebird.ca, $125-150 d) is like escaping to a laid-back farm run by your cool, socially conscious friends. Upstairs in the 100-year-old farmhouse are three country bedrooms, two with queen beds and one with a single. They share a bathroom with an old clawfoot tub; there's also a solar shower outside. Owners Sherry and Yan, who grow their own vegetables and use local produce whenever possible, share their love of organic farming and vegetarian food with their guests. They serve vegetarian breakfasts, and they'll prepare lunches and dinners by reservation. Even if you're not staying here, you can book a meal if your group includes at least four (or if you're able to join an existing group). They also organize workshops about vegetarian food, herbs, canning, and other topics related to organic and local food, and they host periodic concerts on the property, including the annual **Picnic Marathon and Garden Concert,** a day of music and outdoor eating; check their website for schedules and other details.

The homey **Settlers Guesthouse Bed & Breakfast** (5260 Hwy. 534, 705/729-1633, www.settlersguesthouse.com, $75 s, $90-100 d), set on 100 acres of farmland, has three country-style guest rooms in a 1917 farmhouse. The kitchen was once the entire original house (it was subsequently expanded); the owners raised 10 children in that one room! You have more space now, particularly in the comfortable living room, and outdoors, you can hike or bird-watch along nearby trails. On Saturdays (10 A.M.-2 P.M.), owner Marcy Rohn, who moved here from Toronto in 2005, sells her homemade baked goods from the house, so it's worth a snack stop even if you're not staying the night.

GETTING THERE

Nipissing is 340 kilometers (210 miles) north of Toronto and 110 kilometers (68 miles) beyond Huntsville. Turn off Highway 11 at Highway 534 and continue west for about 13 kilometers (eight miles). For Nipissing Village, go north on Highway 654; Highway 534 continues west toward Restoule.

discoverynorthbay.com, 9:30 A.M.–4:30 P.M., Mon.–Wed. 9:30 A.M.–8:30 P.M. Thurs.–Sat., noon–4 P.M. Sun. July–Aug., $6) has model trains and other transportation exhibits housed in the former train station.

Lake Nipissing is a short walk from downtown. You can explore the lake on a sightseeing cruise aboard the *Chief Commanda II* (200 Memorial Dr., 705/494-8167 or 866/660-6686, www.georgianbaycruise.com, mid-May–early Oct.).

Accommodations and Food

Chain motels line Lakeshore Drive south of the city center. Downtown, try the 42-room **Inn on the Bay** (340 Main St. W., 705/495-6461 or 877/937-8483, www.innonthebay.ca, $85–140 d), which isn't actually on the bay, but it's a short walk from the lake.

Main Street has several eateries, including the vegetarian-friendly **Cedar Tree Lebanese Restaurant** (183 Main St. E., 705/472-2405, www.cedartreelebaneserestaurant.com, 11 A.M.–8 P.M. Mon.–Thu., 11 A.M.–9 P.M. Fri.–Sat., $5–12), which serves tasty falafel, tabbouleh, shawarma, and other Middle Eastern classics. Just off Main, **Veg Out Organic Beverage Bar** (207 Ferguson St., 705/495-0020, 8 A.M.–2 P.M. Tues.–Fri., 9 A.M.–2 P.M. Sat.) blends up fresh juices and smoothies, as well as sandwiches and snacks.

Information and Services

North Bay's **Regional Tourist Information Centre** (1375 Seymour St., at Hwy. 11, 705/472-8480 or 888/249-8998, 8:30 A.M.–8:30 P.M. daily July–Aug., 9 A.M.–5 P.M. Mon.–Fri. and 10 A.M.–4 P.M. Sat.–Sun. Sept.–June.) can assist with information about the area.

Getting There and Around

At the junction of Highways 11 and 17, North Bay is roughly equidistant to Toronto and Ottawa (355 kilometers, or 220 miles, from each), and 130 kilometers (80 miles) east of Sudbury. **Ontario Northland** (www.ontarionorthland.ca) has train and bus service to Toronto, while **Greyhound** (www.greyhound.ca) runs buses to Sudbury and Ottawa. The **train and bus station** (100 Station Rd., 705/495-4200) is east of downtown, near Highway 17.

You really need a car to explore North Bay. Local rental agencies include **Avis** (705/476-9730, www.avis.com), **Enterprise** (705/840-7777, www.enterprise.com), and **National** (705/474-3030, www.nationalcar.com).

TEMAGAMI

If you love to canoe or hike, Temagami, a wilderness region dotted with lakes large and small, makes a great getaway. Outdoor adventurers flock here in summer, increasing the population from 1,000 to over 10,000. If it's winter in the outdoors you crave, Temagami can oblige, with snowshoeing, cross-country skiing, and dogsledding.

Unlike many outdoor destinations, Temagami is relatively easy to reach without a car, since it's on a direct train line from Toronto, and local outfitters help organize active trips. Allow at least a long weekend for your visit; if you're a paddler, you'll find scores of opportunities for multiday canoe trips.

The town's name (pronounced Te-MAWG-a-mee) is an Ojibway word, roughly translated as "Deep Water by the Shore," a fitting moniker for this lakeland country.

Sights

For an expansive aerial view of the surrounding lakes and forests, climb the **Temagami Fire Tower** ($3). At 396 meters (1,300 feet) above sea level, it's the highest point on Yonge Street/Highway 11, which runs more or less all the way to Toronto (and at one time was named the longest street in the world).

Shops and restaurants are clustered along Highway 11 near the train station—which also houses a tiny **rail museum** (10 A.M.–5 P.M. daily, $1) and gift shop—and on Lakeshore Drive, bordering Lake Temagami.

Two kilometers (1.2 miles) south of town, **Finlayson Point Park** (Finlayson Park Rd., off Hwy. 11, 705/569-3205, www.ontarioparks.com, late May–late Sept., $13/vehicle) has two small sandy beaches for swimming on Lake Temagami. You can also rent canoes. A

THE NORTH

museum has exhibits about the park's natural environment.

A vast protected wilderness surrounds Temagami, with a network of backcountry parks. The largest is **Lady Evelyn Smoothwater Provincial Park** (www.ontarioparks.com) to the northwest. Exploring this rugged region isn't for outdoor novices; as the park service warns, "Visitors should be backcountry veterans and well-experienced in white-water canoeing and other wilderness skills." Contact local outfitters for information about backcountry trips.

Sports and Recreation

Smoothwater Wilderness Lodge (705/569-3539 or 888/569-4539, www.smoothwater.com) can organize canoe, kayak, or hiking adventures. Another well-established local outfitter is the **Temagami Outfitting Company** (6 Lakeshore Dr., 705/569-2595 mid-May–mid-Sept.; 484/467-1068 mid-Sept.–mid-May, www.icanoe.ca). They run an outdoor gear store and organize canoe, kayak, and hiking trips.

To get into the wilderness surrounding Temagami, **Lakeland Airways** (705/569-3455, www.lakelandairways.ca) can take you around by floatplane. They'll even strap your canoe to the plane and drop you off on a remote lake. Another way to explore is by houseboat, which you can pilot along the interconnected lakes that wind through the region. Contact **Leisure Island Houseboat Rentals** (705/569-3261, www.leisureislandhouseboats.com) or **Three Buoys Houseboat Rentals** (705/569-3455, www.threebuoyshouseboats.ca) for rentals.

For winter excursions, contact **Wolf Within Adventures** (705/840-9002, www.wolfwithin.ca), which runs dogsledding expeditions with a team of Alaskan huskies.

Accommodations and Food

Temagami's best place to stay is the **C Smoothwater Wilderness Lodge** (Smoothwater Rd., off Hwy. 11, 705/569-3539 or 888/569-4539, www.smoothwater.com, $30 dorm, $140 d, lodging and meal packages available). The rustic guest building with several petite doubles and a bunkhouse is comfortable enough, but it's the knowledgeable staff, excellent food, and friendly vibe that make Smoothwater so special. The hearty meals feature local ingredients, and breakfast and dinner are served family-style, so guests can trade tales about their day's adventures. And the staff can organize whatever adventures you have in mind, from paddling on the property's lake to multiday canoeing and camping excursions. In winter, you can snowshoe or cross-country ski on 50 kilometers (31 miles) of trails. When they're not out adventuring, guests lounge lakeside or in the high-ceilinged "Gathering Hall," outfitted with comfy sofas, books, and games. Smoothwater is 14 kilometers (8.7 miles) north of Temagami; staff can pick you up at the train station (for an additional fee).

If you just need a place to sleep, try the **Wildflower Motel** (7 Wildflower Ave., 705/569-2618, www.wildflowermotel.com, $97 d), with four neat, basic rooms above a pub. It's across Highway 11 from the station, opposite the grocery store.

Although the sign at this roadside stand says **B&D Burgers** (6731 Hwy. 11, $2.50–12), everyone calls it "The Chip Shop," because that's what you should order: chips (French fries), specifically the French-Canadian specialty known as *poutine*. Oh, you can get a hamburger, hot dog, or fried fish if you must, but it's the mounds of fries topped with gooey cheese and brown gravy that keep the picnic tables packed. When they ask if you want "shredded or curds" on your poutine, they're inquiring about the cheese; to be authentic, you want curds.

You can't miss the bright yellow sign for the **Busy Bee Restaurant** (6710 Hwy. 11, 705/569-2705) opposite the station. This friendly diner buzzes all day, though the fare runs to basics like sandwiches and pizza.

CAMPING

Finlayson Point Park (Finlayson Park Rd., off Hwy. 11, 705/569-3205, www.ontarioparks.com, late May–late Sept., $31.30–36.75 tent sites, $36.75–42.25 electrical sites) has 117 campsites, many right on Lake Temagami.

The campground has showers, flush toilets, and laundry facilities.

Campers are welcome to pitch a tent on the lawn at **Smoothwater Wilderness Lodge** (705/569-3539 or 888/569-4539, www.smoothwater.com, $10/night); you can use the washrooms and showers in the nearby bunkhouse.

Practicalities

The cheerful staff at the **Temagami Chamber of Commerce Information Centre** (Lakeshore Dr., off Hwy. 11, 800/661-7609, www.temagamiinformation.com) can give you information about the area.

Ontario Northland (www.ontarionorthland.ca) has both train and bus service to **Temagami station** (Hwy. 11, 705/569-3310). From Toronto, 455 kilometers (285 miles) to the south, take the train if you can; train and bus fares are the same (one-way adults $92.35, seniors and students $78.50, children $46.20), but the seven-hour trip on the *Northlander* train is faster and more comfortable than the eight-hour bus.

Ontario Northland trains and buses also connect Temagami to North Bay, 100 kilometers (60 miles) south.

TIMMINS

Many Northern Ontario communities make their living from mining, and Timmins, a workaday town of 45,000 with a large French-speaking population, is no exception. But Timmins is one of the few places where visitors can experience life underground—if only for a day—on an in-depth tour of a former mine. Timmins is also home to a glitzy museum celebrating the life of local girl turned country music sensation, Shania Twain.

Timmins Underground Gold Mine Tour

Suit up in coveralls, a hardhat, rubber boots, and a tool belt before descending into the former Hollinger Gold Mine for the Timmins Underground Gold Mine Tour (1 Shania Twain Dr., 705/360-2619, www.timminsgoldminetour.com, tours daily 9:30 A.M., 11:30 A.M., 1:30 P.M., and 3 P.M. July–Aug., 10:30 A.M.

THE NORTH

© CAROLYN B. HELLER

Suit up before descending into the Timmins Underground Gold Mine.

and 1:30 P.M. Wed.–Sun. mid-May–June and Sept.–Oct.; adults $19, seniors and children $17). Retired miners lead the tours, so you get a real flavor of mine life. As you walk down the damp, muddy walkways, guides explain the workings of the gold mine (which operated from 1909 until the 1980s), demonstrate different mining techniques, and answer your questions about what it's like to spend your days beneath the earth.

The temperature in the mine is 3°C (37°F) year-round, so wear a sweater or jacket, and don't forget warm socks. Tours are suitable for older children (kid-sized coveralls and boots are available); younger ones may be frightened by the dark or by the loud noises when the guides demonstrate jackhammers and other clamorous machinery.

Adjacent to the Gold Mine Tour is the **Shania Twain Centre** (1 Shania Twain Dr., 705/360-2619, www.shaniatwaincentre.com, 10 A.M.–5 P.M. daily, adults $9, seniors and children $7), which chronicles the singer's life with photos, costumes, videos, and recordings. You can even sing along with Shania, karaoke-style.

If you plan to visit the Shania Twain Centre and take the Gold Mine Tour, buy a discounted combination ticket (adults $23, seniors and children $20).

Accommodations and Food

Timmins has the usual chain motels along Highway 101, both east and west of downtown.

A cross between an upscale motel and a full-fledged "resort," **Cedar Meadows Resort & Spa** (1000 Norman St., 705/268-5800 or 877/207-6123, www.cedarmeadows.com, $100–195 d), set amid farmland and forests, is a less generic alternative to the chains. The large, family-friendly rooms have refrigerators, microwaves, and free Wi-Fi; some have fireplaces, whirlpool tubs, and kitchenettes. The surprisingly elegant **Voyageur Dining Room** (7 A.M.–10 P.M. Mon., 6:30 A.M.–10 P.M. Tue.–Fri., 8 A.M.–10 P.M. Sat.–Sun.) is popular for its lavish Sunday brunch. You can explore walking trails around the property, or take a guided "wilderness tour" (3 P.M. daily year-round and

daily 7 P.M. in summer, adults $12, seniors $10, students 13–17 $8, children $6). At the spa, indulge in a **Scandinavian nature bath** (10 A.M.–10 P.M. daily, $35), alternating between a hot soak, sauna, or steam bath and an invigorating cold dip. The spa, baths, and wilderness tours are open to the public.

Built in 1921 to house the manager of the local McIntyre mine, this stately log home is now the **McIntyre Lodge B&B** (150 Highway 655, 705/268-5242, www.bbcanada.com/mcintyrebb, $124 s, $134 d). As mine executives and their visitors once did, you can lounge by the massive stone fireplace in the grand parlor and have breakfast on the window-lined porch. Upstairs, the five guest rooms—all different—are furnished with period details like quilts and clawfoot tubs. Also on the wooded property are a swimming pool and sauna, as well as a more rustic two-bedroom guest cottage ($200–250 d).

Every town needs an all-day breakfast joint like **Restaurant Nadeau** (293 Wilson Ave., 705/268-2664, 5 A.M.–3 P.M. Mon.–Fri., 6 A.M.–3 P.M. Sat., 7 A.M.–3 P.M. Sun.). They've got the usual eggs and sausages, but a Francophone influence turns up in dishes like savory Quebec-style beans, peameal bacon, and freshly made crepes, and in the French you'll hear spoken all around. Get the home fries grilled, with onions. And if you're a pie-for-breakfast person, have a slice of the traditional sugar variety.

For a complete old-time French-Canadian dining experience, **La Chaumière** (32 Mountjoy St. N., at Algonquin Blvd., 705/266-8016, 6:30 A.M.–8 P.M. Mon.–Sat., 8 A.M.–8 P.M. Sun., $5–15), next to the Centre Culturel La Ronde (French cultural center), is your place. Settle into the stocky wooden chairs and (if you're a hungry carnivore) order the massive "special plate" of *tortière*, beans, pork hock stew, and mashed potatoes—it's essentially meat pie and meat stew with meatballs! Otherwise, tuck into hearty all-day breakfast, burgers, spaghetti, or fish.

Information and Services

For regional information, stop into the

Timmins Chamber of Commerce Tourism Information Centre (76 McIntyre Rd., at Hwy. 101, 705/360-1900, www.timminschamber.on.ca, 9 A.M.–6 P.M. Mon.–Fri., 10 A.M.–5 P.M. Sat.) on the town's east side, or contact **Tourism Timmins** (220 Algonquin Blvd. E., 705/360-2619 or 800/387-8466, www.tourismtimmins.com).

Getting There and Around

Timmins is 710 kilometers (440 miles) north of Toronto, 300 kilometers (186 miles) north of Sudbury, and 110 kilometers (68 miles) southwest of Cochrane.

Air Creebec (705/264-9521 or 800/567-6567, www.aircreebec.ca) connects **Timmins Victor M. Power Airport** (705/360-2636) with Moosonee and with remote points farther north. **Air Canada** (www.aircanada.com) flies to Toronto, but fares for the 90-minute hop rival prices for cross-country trips.

Ontario Northland (www.ontarionorthland.ca) runs buses to **Timmins Station** (54 Spruce St. S., at 3rd Ave., 705/264-1377) from Toronto (one-way adults $134.45, seniors and students $114.30, children $67.20; 11–13 hours), Sudbury (one-way adults $56.40, seniors and students $47.95, children $28.20; 4 hours), and Cochrane (one-way adults $17.85, seniors and students $15.20, children $8.90; 1–2 hours).

Unless you're just going from the bus station to the Gold Mine and back (two kilometers, or 1.2 miles, each way), Timmins is difficult to explore without a car. Car rental agencies in Timmins include **Avis** (www.avis.ca), **Budget** (www.budget.ca), **Discount** (www.discountcar.com), **Enterprise** (www.enterpriserentacar.ca), and **National** (www.nationalcar.ca).

◖ POLAR BEAR EXPRESS TRAIN

You won't see polar bears en route (it's still too far south), nor is the Ontario Northland train particularly "express," yet this 299-kilometer (186-mile) rail journey (800/265-2356, www.ontarionorthland.ca, one-way adults $52.45, seniors and students $44.60, children $26.20, Sun.–Fri. July–Aug., Mon.–Fri. Sept.–June; 5

hours) gives you a fascinating glimpse of life in the north. From Cochrane, the train chugs through stands of birch and poplar toward swampier lowlands dotted with skinny, green-tufted black spruce, before pulling into the predominantly Cree community of Moosonee, where you can also visit nearby Moose Factory Island, another Cree settlement.

It's not a luxury train, but there's a dome car with broader views of the surrounding terrain, a dining car, an entertainment car (where local bands often perform), and a family car, offering activities and movies to help kids pass the time. You can rent a worthwhile audio tour ($15) that provides background about the region, points out highlights of Moosonee and Moose Factory Island, and introduces you to Cree culture.

Many people take the *Polar Bear Express* from Cochrane, make a quick tour of Moosonee and Moose Factory Island, and return the same night. If you have time, though, stay at least one night in the north to better experience the Cree culture.

The best months for the journey are July and August, when day-trippers have almost four hours to walk around Moosonee and Moose Factory before the southbound train departs. The rest of the year, the train's tourist amenities are discontinued, and the southbound train leaves three hours after the northbound train arrives, making a day trip less feasible, particularly since the train can be delayed.

Practicalities

Ontario Northland's *Polar Bear Express Train* (705/336-2210 or 800/265-2356, www.ontarionorthland.ca, one-way adults $52.45, seniors and students $44.60, children $26.20, Sun.–Fri. July–Aug., Mon.–Fri. Sept.–June) departs Cochrane at 9 A.M. and reaches Moosonee Station (705/336-2210) about 5 hours later. The return train leaves Moosonee at 6 P.M. in July and August and at 5 P.M. the rest of the year.

Advance reservations are recommended; pay for your tickets at least three days in advance and receive a 10 percent discount. Family discounts may be available for at least one adult and one child traveling together.

If you're short on time, you can fly at least

one way to Moosonee. **Air Creebec** (705/264-9521 or 800/567-6657, www.aircreebec.ca) flies between the **Moosonee Airport** (705/336-2731) and Timmins (one hour), where you can make connections farther south. Reflecting the destination's remoteness, though, fares tend to be quite high.

Cochrane

The main reason to come to Cochrane is to leave again. This windswept town with a remote, almost Wild West feel, is the starting point for the *Polar Bear Express Train* that runs north toward James Bay, at the edge of the arctic. While Cochrane itself isn't far enough north to support arctic wildlife, the town capitalizes on its polar bear connection as the home of the small **Polar Bear Habitat and Heritage Village** (1 Drury Park Rd., 705/272-2327 or 800/354-9948, www.polarbearhabitat.ca, 9 A.M.–5 P.M. daily May–Oct., call for off-season hours; adults $20, seniors and students $18, children 2–14 $12), a polar bear sanctuary. It's worth a visit if you're passing through,

particularly with children. You can even swim with the bears for an extra fee ($5). Also on the grounds is a modest one-street "heritage village" that re-creates a pioneer settlement and a snowmobile museum. (In 2011, the center had closed temporarily, so check the status before making a special trip.)

If you still have time to kill, visit the **Tim Horton Museum** (7 Tim Horton Dr., off Fourth St. E., 705/272-5084, call for hours, $2), inside the Tim Horton Event Centre, 2.5 kilometers (1.6 miles) east of the station. Born in Cochrane in 1930, Horton played 22 seasons in the National Hockey League, but he's equally well known as the founder of the ubiquitous Canadian donut shop chain that bears his name.

For tourist information, look for the giant polar bear. Chimo, an 11-meter (35-foot) bear statue (its name is an Inuit word meaning "Welcome"), greets visitors outside the **Town of Cochrane Information Centre** (3 Third Ave./Hwy. 11, 705/272-4926, www.town.cochrane.on.ca).

Cochrane's polar bear welcomes visitors to this northern town.

© CAROLYN B. HELLER

ACCOMMODATIONS AND FOOD

Cochrane's accommodations are clustered near the train station, with additional chain motels on Highway 11 south of town. Behind a grim stone facade opposite the station is Cochrane's most upscale lodging, the **Best Western Swan Castle Inn** (189 Railway St., 705/272-5200 or 800/265-3668, www.bestwesternontario.com, $120–140 d), which has 39 middle-of-the-road rooms and a helpful staff. Rates include continental breakfast.

You can roll out of bed and onto your train from the **Station Inn** (200 Railway St., 705/272-3500 or 800/265-2356, www.ontarionorthland.ca, $100 d), with 23 smallish rooms above the depot. The **coffee shop** ($5–16) serves three meals daily, from eggs and sandwiches to pastas and pork chops. The low-rise **Commando Motel** (80 Seventh Ave. S., 705/272-2700, www.commandomotel.com, $60 s, $70 d) is another option, one block from the station.

To rustle up some grub, your best bet is the **J.R. Bar-B-Q Ranch** (63 3rd Ave., 705/272-4999), where the family-friendly room, decorated with saddles and trophy fish, feels like the love child of a cowboy and a north-woods fisherman. The hearty barbecued ribs ($18/half rack, $24/full rack) are worth hooting over, and the menu includes ample portions of BBQ chicken, burgers, steaks, and pizza.

GETTING THERE AND AROUND

Cochrane is off Highway 11, 725 kilometers (450 miles) north of Toronto and 375 kilometers (235 miles) beyond North Bay. *Polar Bear Express* passengers who've arrived in Cochrane by car can leave their vehicles in the station parking lot during their journey north.

Despite Cochrane's seemingly remote location, you don't need a car to get here. The **Cochrane train station** (200 Railway St., 705/272-4228), which is also the bus depot, is the terminus for the *Northlander,* Ontario Northland's train from Toronto, via Huntsville, North Bay, and Temagami. The Toronto train (www.ontarionorthland.ca, one-way adults $142.25, seniors and students $120.90, children $71.10; 10 hours) arrives in the early evening, so if you're continuing to Moosonee, you'll need to stay the night.

If you're making stops en route to Cochrane, Ontario Northland buses may be more convenient than the train. A northbound bus arrives in Cochrane midday, giving you ample time to tour the town before the *Polar Bear Express* departs the next morning.

Cochrane has no public transit, but you can easily walk around the small town.

Moosonee

If you look at a map of northeastern Ontario,

THE NORTH

WHERE'S THE FACTORY ON MOOSE FACTORY?

The James Bay region in Northern Ontario has been traditional Cree territory for thousands of years. More recently (in the 17th century, that is), the Hudson Bay Company established Ontario's first English-speaking settlement on Moose Factory Island, just south of James Bay. Traders came to the island in 1673, which makes Moose Factory Ontario's oldest fur-trading community.

It was this fur-trading heritage that gave the island its unusual name. The "Moose" referred to the Moose River, where the island is located, but there wasn't (and still isn't) a factory on the island, at least in the modern sense of the word.

In the 17th century, the chief agent in a fur-trading post was called a "factor." And the place where a factor worked was called, logically enough, a "factory."

Today, little of this fur-trading era remains on Moose Factory Island. On Front Street, near the Quickstop Convenience Store, is the **Hudson's Bay Staff House** that was once part of the Hudson's Bay Post. A more permanent legacy, perhaps, is the island **cemetery** (Pehdabun Rd.) where some of these early settlers were laid to rest.

© CAROLYN B. HELLER

The *Polar Bear Express Train* heads north to Moosonee.

you'll notice one important thing is missing: roads. The only way to reach the remote area around James Bay, which has a predominantly First Nations population, is by rail or air.

The *Polar Bear Express Train* travels to Moosonee, a town of about 3,500 near James Bay. The Moosonee area has two main settlements: the dusty frontier town of Moosonee itself on the mainland, and the island of Moose Factory in the Moose River just offshore. Local websites with information about the region include the Moose Cree First Nation (www.moosecree.com) and the town of Moosonee (www.moosonee.ca).

Moosonee's main street is First Avenue, which runs from the train station to the river, where you can catch a water taxi to Moose Factory Island. Stop first at the **Railway Car Museum** (First St., hours vary, free), opposite the station, to check out the exhibits about the area's culture and history. Down the street is **Northern College** (First St., 705/336-

2913, www.northernc.on.ca, 8 A.M.–4 P.M. Mon.–Fri., free), where displays of native crafts, including leather and beadwork, line the hallways.

MOOSE FACTORY ISLAND

Home to 2,700 people, Moose Factory is 4.8 kilometers (three miles) long and 3.2 kilometers (two miles) wide; the Moose Cree First Nation Reserve occupies much of the island.

The island's main attraction is the **Cree Culture Interpretive Centre** (Pehdabun Rd., 705/658-4619 ext. 265, www.moosecree.com, 9 A.M.–4:30 P.M. Sun.–Fri. July–Aug., off-season by appointment, adults $10, children under 12 $5), which has well-designed exhibits about Cree culture, language, traditional medicine, and food. Outside the building, you can peek into several tepees. Located on the island's east side, the center is about a 25-to-30-minute walk from the Cree Village Ecolodge or from the town docks. The waterfront views along Pehdabun Road are lovely.

You can explore the surrounding waterways with **Kway Journey Tours** (July–Aug., $35–75), which runs boat trips from Moose Factory to nearby Fossil Island and up to James Bay (15 kilometers, or nine miles, to the north). Each tour is offered twice a day, weather and tides permitting. Book through the Cree Village Ecolodge.

The whole island seems to gather at the **Moose Cree Complex** (Mookijuneibeg Dr.), part shopping mall and part community center. There's a grocery store, pharmacy, coffee shop, bank, and post office, and residents often sell homemade baked goods or crafts. The building also houses the Moose Cree Tourism Office (705/658-4619 ext. 265).

ACCOMMODATIONS AND FOOD

Opposite the docks in Moosonee, the friendly **Polar Bear Lodge** (705/336-2345, $115 d) has 27 barebones rooms—half have one double bed, the remainder have two—and a **restaurant** (year-round) that serves three meals a day. In July and August, they run a free shuttle to and from the train station. On First Street are the **Northern Store** (a large grocery), a bank, and the post office. Note the Cree script on signs around town.

It's much nicer to stay on Moose Factory Island, where the Moose Cree First Nation run the **(Cree Village Ecolodge** (Hospital Dr., 705/658-6400 or 888/273-3929, www.creevillage.com) on the banks of the Moose River. The 20 rustically comfortable rooms have organic cotton bedding, birch blinds, and Wi-Fi, and the staff help arrange tours around the island. The lodge's showpiece is the dining room—the best place to eat in the area—with a soaring ceiling and a multistory wall of windows facing the water. The kitchen uses traditional First Nations ingredients in its bison chili, baked pickerel, venison, and other dishes ($17–33).

In a teepee opposite the Ecolodge, you'll often find Cree women cooking *bannock*—a traditional biscuit-like bread—over an open fire. Hours are irregular, so if you see the fire going, stop for a snack.

THE NORTH

© CAROLYN B. HELLER

The Moose Cree First Nation run the Cree Village Ecolodge.

For a casual meal, join the locals at **Gunner's Grill** (Moose Cree Complex, Mookijuneibeg Dr., 8 A.M.–7 P.M. Mon.–Sat., 9 A.M.–7 P.M. Sun.), a coffee shop that serves bacon and eggs, sandwiches, and other diner-style chow.

The **Northern Store** (Moose Cree Complex, Mookijuneibeg Dr., 705/658-4552, 10 A.M.–6 P.M. Mon.–Wed. and Sat., 10 A.M.–8 P.M. Thurs.–Fri.) is a well-stocked grocery, although prices—as in many northern towns—are significantly higher than they are down south. You can also pick up provisions at **G. G.'s Corner** (Center Rd., 705/685-4591, 11 A.M.–9 P.M. daily) or **Quickstop Convenience** (Front St., 705/658-4086, noon–7 P.M. daily).

GETTING AROUND
From Moosonee's train station, it's about a 15–20-minute walk to the docks; a taxi will cost about $5. In summer, **water taxis** ($10/person) cross the river between Moosonee and Moose Factory Island in 10–15 minutes.

Boats typically wait at the docks on both the Moosonee and Moose Factory sides. The Cree Village Ecolodge has its own dock, on the opposite side of the island from the main public dock, so be sure to tell the boatman if you're heading to the lodge. Ontario Northland operates a **ferry** (705/336-2210 or 800/265-2356, www.ontarionorthland.ca, $10) that shuttles passengers between Moosonee and Moose Factory Island.

In midwinter, the river freezes solid enough to support an **ice road** between Moose Factory and the mainland; taxis and other vehicles can drive across. During the fall "freeze-up" and spring "break-up" periods, when the river is too icy for boats to cross but not solid enough for cars, the only way on and off Moose Factory Island is by helicopter.

Taxis typically meet trains arriving in Moosonee. For a cab on Moose Factory Island, call **Creeway** (705/658-5256) or **Northway** (705/658-4131).

Sudbury

Sudbury reveals its charms slowly. This industrial city of 157,000 is ringed with the belching smokestacks and rocky pits of its many active mines. Yet if you find yourself here, en route to Manitoulin Island, Killarney Provincial Park, or wilderness spots farther north, it's worth exploring. The city's science museum is a don't-miss sight if you have children in tow, and the compact downtown is reviving, with interesting restaurants and a few galleries.

SIGHTS
Worth a stop, **Artists on Elgin** (168 Elgin St., 705/674-0415, www.artistsonelgin.ca, 10 A.M.–5 P.M. Mon.–Sat.) features local artists' work.

◖ Science North
Kids (and their parents) could easily spend a day or more at Sudbury's cool, contemporary science museum (100 Ramsey Lake Rd.,

705/523-4629 or 800/461-4898, www.sciencenorth.ca, 9 A.M.–6 P.M. daily late June–early Sept.; call for off-season hours; adults $20, seniors and youth 13–17 $18, children 3–12 $16). Built into a massive rock on the edge of Ramsey Lake (you enter the exhibit halls through a tunnel blasted from the bedrock), this hands-on museum is packed with "please touch" exhibits. In the Nature Exchange, kids can bring in something they've found—a plant, a rock, a bug—learn something about it, and exchange it for something in the museum's collection. Other exhibits focus on the environment, animals, or the human body.

Science North is open daily year-round, except December 24–26 and the first two weeks in January. Admission packages including Science North and the on-site IMAX theatre or planetarium are available, as are combination tickets to Science North and Dynamic Earth (adults $35, seniors and youth $31, children $27).

Dynamic Earth

In a region where mining, primarily for nickel and copper, is such a big part of the local economy, it's no surprise that a major attraction is this high-tech mining museum (122 Big Nickel Rd., 705/523-4629 or 800/461-4898, www.dynamicearth.ca, 9 A.M.–6 P.M. daily late June–early Sept., call for off-season hours; adults $20, seniors and youth 13–17 $18, children 3–12 $16). A highlight is the Underground Tour through a simulated mine, where you walk through 100 years of mining technology, from the dark, narrow tunnels of the early 1900s to the more high-tech mines of today. It's a rather promotional pitch for the mining industry but still makes for an interesting tour. Another fun exhibit is the Mining Command Centre, where you use computers to drill or smash rocks and track mine activities (you can even spy on the Underground Tour groups).

Although Dynamic Earth operates in conjunction with Science North and you can buy a combination ticket to both, the two attractions are about five kilometers (three miles) apart.

ENTERTAINMENT AND EVENTS

Sudbury hosts a variety of arts festivals, including **Northern Lights Festival Boreal** (www.nlfbsudbury.com, July), a long-running music fest on Ramsey Lake; the **Cinéfest Sudbury International Film Festival** (www.cinefest.com, Sept.), and the **Sudbury Jazz Festival** (www.jazzsudbury.ca, Sept.). A unique food-and-music party is the **Canadian Garlic Festival** (www.ukrseniors.org, Aug.), sponsored by the Ukrainian Seniors' Centre; bring your own breath mints.

ACCOMMODATIONS

The "artisan" at the **Artisan Upstairs Guesthouse** (318 Jeanne D'Arc Ave., 705/674-4387, www.personainternet.com/artisanupstairs, $95 s, $125 d), on a residential street east of downtown, is co-owner Pete Lautenschlager, who carved much of the furniture and woodwork in these two second-

floor guest rooms. Popular with couples and business travelers, the bedrooms have sponge-painted walls and private baths. Guest can use the fully equipped kitchenette and relax on the deck overlooking the nearby woods. Rates include a full breakfast.

The **Southbay Guesthouse Sudbury** (1802 Southbay Rd., 705/671-9611 or 877/656-8324, www.southbayguesthouse.com) has an enviable waterfront location in a private home on Ramsey Lake. The larger Luna de Miel suite ($149 d) has a king bed, two-person whirlpool tub, and a fireplace, while the queen-bedded Sunrise suite ($109 d) opens onto a lakeside deck. Rates include breakfast. The same family runs Manitoulin Island's Southbay Guesthouse.

Among the nicest of Sudbury's many chain motels along Regent Street south of downtown is the 121-room **Hampton Inn-Sudbury** (2280 Regent St., 705/523-5200, www.sudburyontario.hamptoninn.com, $125–150 d), which makes both business travelers and vacationing families feel at home. The beds are topped with crisp white duvets, and kids will appreciate the indoor pool.

FOOD

Head downtown to the Durham Street area for a selection of restaurants and cafés. A seasonal farmers' market operates at **Market Square** (85 Elm St., 705/670-9121, www.mysudbury.ca/marketsquare; 8 A.M.–3:30 P.M. Sat., 10 A.M.–3:30 P.M. Sun., June–Oct.).

Regulars line up for the inexpensive daily specials—such as homemade ravioli or hearty pasta and sausage soup—at sunny ◖ **Bertolo's Homemade Foods** (149 Durham St., 705/670-0599, $5.50–7), a tiny Italian-influenced café, where chef-owner Natalie Bertolo McAloney prepares fresh salads, sandwiches, and pastas like your grandmother used to make. Her dark chocolate chip cookies are pretty irresistible, too.

A chill downtown spot for vegetarians (and their non-veg companions) is the **Laughing Buddha** (194 Elgin St., 705/673-2112, www.laughingbuddhasudbury.com, 11 A.M.–2 A.M.

daily), a café/bar that hums till the wee hours. Whether you want herbal tea or booze, a "tree-hugger salad" (a hearty bowl of romaine, tomatoes, mushrooms, raisins, and cashews) or a "Swiss and sow" (aka a ham and cheese sandwich), the laid-back staff will oblige.

At **Leinala's** (272 Caswell Dr., 705/522-1977), a traditional Finnish bakery, it's difficult to choose among the delicious sweet breads and fresh-cooked doughnuts, including their specialty, jelly pigs (glazed and filled with jam). It's in a strip mall off Regent Street, south of downtown.

INFORMATION AND SERVICES

Sudbury Tourism (200 Brady St., 705/673-4161 or 866/451-8252, www.sudburytourism.ca) has details about the city on its website. You can also get information about Sudbury and the surrounding region from the **Rainbow Country Travel Association** (2726 Whippoorwill Ave., 705/522-0104 or 800/465-6655, www.rainbowcountry.com).

GETTING THERE

Sudbury is well served with air, train, and bus connections, but all its transportation terminals are inconveniently located outside the city center.

By Air

The **Greater Sudbury Airport** is 25 kilometers (15 miles) northeast of downtown. **Air Canada** (www.aircanada.com) flies to Toronto's Pearson Airport, but you can sometimes find better deals on **Porter Airlines** (www.flyporter.com) to Toronto City Centre Airport. **Bearskin Airlines** (705/693-9199 or 800/465-2327, www.bearskinairlines.com) serves Ottawa, Sault Ste. Marie, and Thunder Bay.

From the airport, take the **Sudbury Airport Shuttle** (705/566-0375 or 866/230-3332, www.sudburyairportshuttle.ca, $35–40 for one, $5 for each additional person), a door-to-door shared van. A taxi from the airport to in-town hotels will cost $40–60.

By Train

VIA Rail's transcontinental Toronto–Vancouver train stops three days a week at **Sudbury Junction** (2750 Lasalle Blvd., 705/524-1591), 10 kilometers (six miles) northeast of the city center. The Sudbury–Toronto leg (one-way adults $70) takes seven hours. Note that the only trains using the **Sudbury downtown station** (233 Elgin St.) travel to the remote town of White River, between Sault Ste. Marie and Thunder Bay.

By Bus

From Sudbury's **Intercity Bus Terminal**

NAUGHTY KIDS GET LIVER AND ONIONS

If you despair of finding anything to eat along Highway 69 between Parry Sound and Sudbury, detour to the fun and funky **Little Britt Inn** (1165 Riverside Dr., Britt, 705/383-0028 or 888/383-4555, www.zeuter.com/~lilbritt, noon-8 P.M. daily year-round, $11-20). Besides burgers, steaks, and roast chicken, the kitchen turns out local classics like a Georgian Bay "shore lunch" (fish, fried potatoes, baked beans, coleslaw, and crusty bread) – or you might find specials like hearty elk stew.

The hospitable owner encourages guests to introduce themselves to neighboring diners and swap travel tales. Families are welcome, although the tongue-in-cheek menu cautions that noisy kids will be served liver and onions, while polite youngsters get free ice cream!

If you can't bear getting back into the car after a leisurely meal, head upstairs to where four spacious guest rooms ($105-125 d) await, all with separate sitting and sleeping areas. Front rooms look out over the river.

To find the Little Britt Inn, take Highway 69 to the Britt exit, then drive west for about five minutes. The Inn is on the right in the village of Britt.

(854 Notre Dame Ave., 705/524-9900), three kilometers (1.9 miles) north of downtown, **Ontario Northland** (www.ontarionorthland. ca) runs buses to Toronto (one-way adults $73.15, seniors and students $62.20, children $36.60; six hours), Timmins (one-way adults $56.40, seniors and students $47.95, children $28.20; four hours), and Cochrane (one-way adults $74.25, seniors and students $63.10, children $37.10, six hours). **Greyhound** (www.greyhound.ca) connects Sudbury with Sault Ste. Marie (one-way adults $52–63, four hours) and Toronto (one-way adults $63–81, five hours).

A taxi from the bus station to downtown will cost about $15.

By Car
Sudbury is at the intersection of Highway 69 south to Toronto and Highway 17, which goes west to Sault Ste. Marie and east to North Bay and Ottawa. The city is 390 kilometers (242 miles) north of Toronto, a five- to six-hour drive. Sudbury is 90 minutes north of Killarney Provincial Park and about the same distance to Manitoulin Island's swing bridge.

GETTING AROUND
Although the city center is compact and walkable, Sudbury's attractions are all outside downtown. You can get around by bus (if you're patient) or taxi, but having your own wheels is more convenient.

Greater Sudbury Transit (www.city.greatersudbury.on.ca) runs the city's bus network. Local cab companies include **Lockerby Taxi** (705/522-2222) and **Aaron Taxi** (705/523-3333). **Avis** (www.avis.ca), **Enterprise** (www.enterpriserentacar.ca), and **National** (www.nationalcar.ca) rent cars at the airport; **Enterprise** has other city locations, as does **Budget** (www.budget.ca).

Killarney

Located on Georgian Bay south of Sudbury, Killarney ranks among Ontario's most beautiful natural destinations. This wilderness park juts out into the bay with white dolomite ridges and pink granite cliffs providing a striking backdrop for hiking, canoeing, and kayaking.

◖ KILLARNEY PROVINCIAL PARK
One of Ontario's premier outdoor destinations, Killarney Provincial Park (Hwy. 637, Killarney, 705/287-2900, www.ontarioparks.com, $14/vehicle) is known for its striking scenery, particularly the white quartzite and pink granite cliffs that dominate the hilly ridges throughout the park. Dense pine forests surround more than 40 crystal blue lakes, and the park is home to approximately 100 bird species. Killarney's rolling hills are what remains of the La Cloche Mountains. Worn down over millions of year, the La Cloche range once had peaks taller than the present-day Rockies. Today, white rocks peek out through the woods near the peaks, and the granite cliffs that surround many of the lakes and the shores of Georgian Bay glow with a pinkish cast, particularly in the early-morning and late-afternoon sun.

At 493 square kilometers (190 square miles), Killarney is tiny compared to the mammoth Algonquin Provincial Park. Yet it feels more remote, with secluded wilderness territory just a short hike or paddle away. This wilderness naturally takes some effort to reach. The park is located off Highway 69 between Parry Sound and Sudbury. Within the park, services are limited and camping is the only accommodation option. Otherwise, the area's lodgings, restaurants, and services are located in the village of Killarney, just west of the park.

For most Killarney visitors, the first stop is **George Lake** (off Highway 637), where the main park office and campground are located. You can swim or canoe here, and it's the starting point for two of the park's hiking trails.

At the **Killarney Park Observatory** (George Lake), evening astronomy programs are held about once a week in summer. During the summer, the park also hosts various events, from nature presentations to concerts, at the George Lake Amphitheatre. Get schedules from the park office or the Friends of Killarney Park (www.friendsofkillarneypark.ca).

Killarney Provincial Park is open year-round, but many businesses in the village close from mid-October to May. And at any time of year, be prepared for sudden storms and rapid weather changes. Even if it's sunny when you head out in the morning, a storm can blow in by afternoon.

Beaches

Killarney's most accessible swimming beaches are two sandy stretches along George Lake. The main beach at **George Lake** is in the day-use area; it's a launching point for canoes and kayaks, so just watch for paddling traffic. **Second Beach** is in the George Lake Campground. You can also swim in the park's numerous interior lakes and rivers.

Canoeing and Kayaking

With more than 40 lakes throughout the park, Killarney is a popular destination for multiday canoe trippers. **George Lake** is the park's most popular spot for canoeing. You can easily paddle around here for an hour or two, appreciating the striking scenery, with pink granite cliffs surrounding sections of the lake. **Bell Lake,** on the park's east side, is another good canoeing spot. From the Bell Lake Road turnoff from Highway 637—21 kilometers (13 miles) east of George Lake or 38 kilometers (24 miles) west of Highway 69—it's about nine kilometers (5.5 miles) farther to the lake. For kayakers who want to venture beyond George and Bell Lakes, other good kayaking destinations include **Chikanishing Creek** (Chikanishing Road, off Highway 637) and areas along Georgian Bay.

Two companies rent canoes and kayaks at both George and Bell Lakes: **Killarney Outfitters** (Hwy. 637, 705/287-2828 or 800/461-1117, www.killarneyoutfitters.com) and **Killarny Kanoes** (Bell Lake, 705/287-2197 or 888/461-4446). Killarny Outfitters organizes guided canoe and kayak excursions, as well as canoe/hike combinations (half- and full-day trips starting at $35 per person). They also provide a shuttle service for canoeists whose excursions start at one point and end at another. Their trip planning service ($45) includes planning a route according to your specifications (length, difficulty, things you'd like to see and do), arranging for permits, and preparing a detailed trip plan; they also provide gear packages ($80 per person per day) for multiday canoe or kayak trips, including canoe/kayak rental, camping gear, and cooking equipment. Killarney Outfitters offers several sailing cruises ($45–95 per person) on Georgian Bay, from a leisurely afternoon sail to a full-day sailing/hiking combination, as well as motorboat tours of the Georgian Bay coast and islands ($45–105 per person).

Based in Parry Sound, the **White Squall Paddling Centre** (705/746-4936 or 705/342-5324, www.whitesquall.com) is another outfitter who organizes multiday kayak trips in the Killarney area.

Hiking

Killarney Provincial Park isn't really a beginner's hiking destination, but the park rates several of the trails "moderate," suitable for people who can manage some steep sections and rocky terrain. Hiking times are estimates only; it's a good idea to talk with park staff before you head out.

Opposite the George Lake park office, you can pick up the **Granite Ridge Trail,** which winds through the forest and climbs up to two lookout points, one overlooking Georgian Bay and the other onto the rocky cliffs of La Cloche Range. This two-kilometer (one-mile) loop trail is one of the park's easiest; most people should be able to complete it in an hour or so.

The longer **Cranberry Bog Trail** (four kilometers, or 2.5 miles) starts in the George Lake Campground; the trailhead is near site

#101. As the name suggests, it passes through bogs and marshes, and then goes along A. Y. Jackson Lake, which is named for one of the Group of Seven artists. Allow about two hours round-trip.

A short hike that gives you beautiful views of Georgian Bay's rocky shores is the **Chikanishing Trail.** Allow one hour for this three-kilometer (1.9-mile) loop that involves some scrambles across massive granite boulders (best save this hike for a dry day, as the rocks are quite slippery when wet). The trailhead is at the end of Chikanishing Road, off Highway 637 about two kilometers (1 miles) west of George Lake.

Serious hikers may want to climb up through the boulders of **The Crack** for some of the best views across the La Cloche Mountains. This six-kilometer (3.7-mile) route is quite difficult, and the trail is not a loop, so you must return the same way you came in. Pick up the trail off Highway 637, seven kilometers (4.3 miles) east of the George Lake park office. Save this hike for a clear day to appreciate the views. The trail to The Crack is part of the 100-kilometer (62-mile) **La Cloche Silhouette Trail,** a difficult backpacking route that will take many hikers at least seven days. For experienced backcountry hikers only!

On the east side of the park, the **Lake of the Woods Trail** is a 3.5-kilometer (2.2-mile) loop around Lake of the Woods; part of the route crosses a beaver dam. The trail starts from Bell Lake Road, which is off Highway 637, 21 kilometers (13 miles) east of George Lake or 38 kilometers (24 miles) west of Highway 69.

Skiing and Snowshoeing

The park has 30 kilometers (19 miles) of trails for cross-country skiing and snowshoeing. The trails all start at the George Lake Park Office, which also offers snowshoe rentals. You can usually expect plenty of snow from December through March.

Camping

Killarney's car-camping area is the **George Lake Campground** ($40.50 July–mid-Oct.;

$29.75 mid-Oct.–June), which has 126 campsites, with flush toilets, showers (July–mid-Oct. only), and laundry facilities, but no electricity. The most secluded spots are near Second Beach, along Blue Heron Circle, although those sites are also the farthest from the showers.

To reserve a campsite, contact **Ontario Parks Reservations** (888/668-7275, www.ontarioparks.com, reservation fees $8.50 online, $9.50 by phone). You can make a reservation up to five months in advance; early reservations are recommended, particularly for summer weekends. Campsites can be reserved from May to October; the rest of the year, sites are first-come, first-served.

If you don't want to bring your own tent, book one of Killarney's six **yurts** ($91.50/night), located in the George Lake Campground. Modeled on the traditional octagonal tents used on the Mongolian grasslands, the Killarney yurts are aluminum-framed structures that sleep up to six people. Each yurt has two bunk beds, with a double lower bunk and single upper bunk, as well as a table and chairs, lights, and electric heat. Adjacent to the yurt is a deck with a picnic table, a propane-fueled barbecue, and a bear-proof box for storing your food. You can't park directly in front of the yurts; you must walk a few minutes from the yurt-access parking area (spring–fall); each yurt has a cart for hauling your gear. In winter, the yurt parking is closed, so you must ski or snowshoe 500 meters (about 550 yards) from the front gate. Toilets and water taps are located near the parking area. The yurts are open year-round, and reservations are required.

For a true wilderness experience, head for one of Killarney's year-round **backcountry campsites** (705/287-2900, www.ontarioparks.com, adults $11, children 6–17 $4.75). You can hike in to 33 of these sites; another 140 backcountry campsites are accessible only by canoe.

Killarney Kanoes (Bell Lake, 705/287-2197 or 888/461-4446, www.killarneykanoes.com) rents tents, sleeping bags, and other camping gear.

The Village of Killarney

About 500 people live in the village of Killarney, which is on the harbor approximately 10 kilometers (six miles) west of the provincial park. Until 1962, when Highway 637 was built between Killarney and Highway 69, the only way to get to the village was by water (or in winter, across the ice to Manitoulin Island). Killarney was originally known by its Ojibway name, *Shebahonaning,* and many of the present-day residents have aboriginal roots.

Most of the town's lodgings and services are located on or near Channel Street, named for the Killarney Channel, which the street follows. The nicest time to stroll along the waterfront is in the early evening, as the sun begins to set.

The land you see directly across the channel is George Island. Formerly a logging area, the island is now primarily wilderness. You can hike around the island on the 7.5-kilometer (4.7-mile) **George Island Trail,** which is rated moderate-to-difficult; make sure you have sturdy hiking boots and enough food and water for the day. Both the Killarney Mountain Lodge (705/287-2242, www.killarney.com) and the Sportsman's Inn (705/287-9990, www.sportsmansinn.ca) arrange boat transportation to and from George Island.

Originally built in 1868 and rebuilt in 1909, the **Killarney East Lighthouse** (Ontario St.) is at the mouth of the channel on the east side of the village. You can hike or swim nearby, and it's especially pretty just before sunset.

ACCOMMODATIONS AND FOOD

None of the places to stay in the village of Killarney are particularly posh, but most are comfortable enough. Several of the inns have restaurants or pubs, and unless you bring your own provisions to picnic, or eat at the wildly popular Herbert Fisheries, most people eat at one of the lodgings. Many accommodations and other services close between mid-October and early May.

Opposite the harbor, **The Pines Inn** (36 Channel St., 705/287-1068, www.bbcanada.com/4791.html, $90–95 s or d, year-round) is a comfortable, old-time lodge with a popular pub and restaurant. Upstairs, the six simple guest rooms with quilt-covered beds share two bathrooms; washbasins in the rooms help minimize bathroom waits. Owners Paul and Adele Malcew offer guests a warm welcome, with Paul serving up cold beer behind the bar and Adele cooking bacon-and-eggs breakfasts, burgers, grilled fish, and other homestyle fare. Even if you're not staying here, stop in for a drink and a chat; the pub is a local hangout.

At the **Sportsman's Inn** (37 Channel St., 705/287-9990 or 877/333-7510, www.sportsmansinn.ca, mid-May–mid-Oct.) on the harbor, there are several different room types, from plain rooms in a separate motel building ($109 d) to more upscale units overlooking the waterfront ($159 d) to large two-bedroom suites ($320 d). The main dining room serves straightforward traditional fare, from grilled chicken to whitefish to steak ($20–29), while the pub sticks with nachos, burgers, and other basics.

The nicest place to stay in the Killarney area is the (**Killarney Mountain Lodge** (3 Commissioner St., 705/287-2242 or 800/461-1117, www.killarney.com, mid-May–mid-Oct.) on the waterfront, a five-minute walk from the village. A holiday here feels like a trip back to summer camp, from the 46 simple pine-paneled rooms, suites, and cabins to the long list of daily activities, from hiking to canoeing to sailing. Owners Maury and Annabelle East, who've run the lodge since 1962, also operate the Killarney Outfitters store, gear rental, and guide service, so they offer a wide variety of activities and packages to lodge guests. There's a pool, a sauna, a game room, and Ping-Pong tables, as well as two large dining areas serving three meals a day and the circular **Carousel Bar,** lined with windows overlooking the water. You can watch TV or get Wi-Fi in the main lodge, but the rooms have no phones, TVs, or Internet access (hey, you're on vacation, right?). Rates start at $75 single/$150 double for a room with breakfast; accommodations plus breakfast and dinner run $115–195/person, and lodging plus three meals a day costs $135–215/person. Ask about packages combining room, meals, and activities.

Lines are legendary at **Herbert Fisheries** (21 Channel St., 705/287-2214, lunch and dinner daily June–Aug., Fri.–Sun. only May and Sept.–early Oct.), which dishes out first-rate fish 'n' chips (from $13) from a red-and-white trailer on the waterfront.

Information and Services

For general information about the Killarney region and surrounding areas, contact the **Rainbow Country Travel Association** (2726 Whippoorwill Ave., Sudbury, 705/522-0104 or 800/465-6655, www.rainbowcountry. com). A good first stop when you arrive in the Killarney area is the **Killarney Provincial Park** main office (Hwy. 637, 705/287-2900), located at the George Lake park entrance. You can pick up a copy of the free park information guide and ask questions of the park staff. The **Friends of Killarney Park** store (George Lake Campground, 705/287-2800, www.friendsofkillarneypark.ca, year-round) sells park guides, maps, books, and other souvenirs; they have a second location at Bell Lake. You can also order canoeing and hiking guides online—a boon for trip planning.

The online **Friends of Killarney Park** (www.friendsofkillarneypark.ca) is a useful supplement to the main Killarney Park website (www.ontarioparks.com). The park information guide is online at the Friends of Killarney site, as is information about park events, hiking trails, and other activities. The Friends also run an online forum, where you can post questions about hiking and canoe trips and read trips reports from others who have explored the park.

The **Killarney Outfitters store** (Hwy. 637, 705/287-2828 or 800/461-1117, www. killarneyoutfitters.com, hours vary) is located

between the village and the main park entrance at George Lake. They sell outdoor clothing and camping supplies; rent canoes and kayaks ($29–37), as well as other gear; and can arrange a variety of outdoor excursions.

You can pick up snacks and basic groceries year-round at **Pitfield's General Store** (7 Channel St., 705/287-2872), but prices are much higher than in Parry Sound or Sudbury. They also have a laundromat.

Getting There and Around

Killarney is 425 kilometers (265 miles) northwest of Toronto, about a 5–6-hour drive. Sudbury is the closest city, about a 90-minute drive to the north; Parry Sound is about two hours' drive to the south. The only road access to Killarney Provincial Park is from the east, via Highway 637, which is off Highway 69 between Parry Sound and Sudbury. From the Highway 69/637 interchange, it's 67 kilometers (42 miles) to the village of Killarney, about an hour by car.

It's not easy to get to Killarney without a car. The **Ontario Northland** buses (www. ontarionorthland.ca) between Parry Sound and Sudbury will stop at Highway 637, but you're still an hour's drive from town or the park. **Killarney Outfitters** (705/287-2828 or 800/461-1117, www.killarneyoutfitters. com) can provide a shuttle ($130 each way) from the bus stop into town, although it's pricey unless you can split the cost between travelers.

While the village of Killarney is only about 20 nautical miles from the eastern tip of Manitoulin Island, there's no public boat service between Manitoulin and Killarney. By car, it's a three-hour drive from Killarney to Little Current, a distance of about 220 kilometers (137 miles). From Killarney, return to Highway 69 and travel north toward Sudbury; then take Highway 17 west to Espanola, where you pick up Highway 6 south, which will cross the bridge to Manitoulin.

Manitoulin Island

Bordered by Lake Huron to the west and Georgian Bay to the east, Manitoulin isn't Canada's largest island (that honor belongs to Baffin Island). Yet Manitoulin is still tops for its size: it's the largest freshwater island in the world.

Don't expect to make a quick loop around Manitoulin in a couple of hours. Measuring 2,765 square kilometers (1,067 square miles), with good but meandering roads, Manitoulin is a place for leisurely exploration.

One of the most significant things to explore is the island's aboriginal culture. Manitoulin and the surrounding mainland region are home to eight First Nations, collectively known as the Anishinabe people. An innovative aboriginal tourism association, the **Great Spirit Circle Trail,** offers a variety of cultural programs to introduce visitors to local First Nations traditions. The First Nations

communities hold traditional **powwows** that welcome visitors, too.

Because the island is so large, consider your interests in deciding where to stay. If you're interested in aboriginal culture, base yourself on the island's eastern half, where you'll be close to more First Nations attractions. For the best beaches, head south; the nicest sandy spot is Providence Bay, on the south shore. And if you're looking for a remote getaway, go west, where villages like Gore Bay and Meldrum Bay have comfortable inns.

Scientists believe that millions of years ago, Manitoulin was connected by land to the Bruce Peninsula. Today, the only land access is from the north, via Highway 6, where a "swing bridge"—similar to a drawbridge, except that it swings sideways instead of lifting—links the island to the mainland.

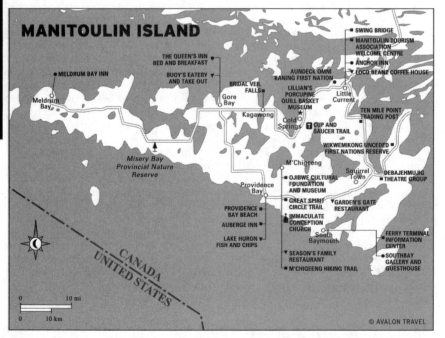

If you're coming from Toronto and southern Ontario, the most direct route to Manitoulin is by boat. From mid-May to mid-October, a ferry runs between Tobermory, on the Bruce Peninsula, and South Baymouth, on the southeast corner of Manitoulin Island. The island's high season mirrors the ferry schedule, so when the ferry docks for the winter, many Manitoulin lodgings close and restaurants shut down or reduce their hours.

SIGHTS

Just across the swing bridge onto the island is the town of Little Current. The small "downtown" runs along Water Street, with a handful of shops for browsing. You can also stroll along the harbor, which fronts Lake Huron's North Channel, watching the sailboats (and the occasional cruise ship).

(Great Spirit Circle Trail

Based in M'Chigeeng, this aboriginal tourism association (705/377-4404 or 877/710-3211, www.circletrail.com) offers a number of activities to introduce visitors to First Nations traditions. The M'Chigeeng First Nation (the "M" is silent) is 34 kilometers (21 miles) southwest of Little Current and 78 kilometers (48 miles) northwest of South Baymouth.

The headquarters for the Great Spirit Circle Trail, the **Ojibwe Cultural Foundation and Museum** (15 Hwy. 551, 705/377- 4902, www. ojibweculture.ca, 9 A.M.–6 P.M. Mon.–Fri., 10 A.M.–4 P.M. Sat., noon–4 P.M. Sun. mid-June–Sept.; 9 A.M.–4:30 P.M. Mon.–Fri. Oct.– mid-June; adults $7.50, seniors and students $5) is also an intriguing gallery and cultural center. Exhibits focus on First Nations history and contemporary aboriginal arts, explained in a worthwhile, one-hour guided tour (generally

---

PLANNING TO POWWOW

One of the most interesting ways to experience aboriginal culture is to attend a traditional powwow, a festival that encompasses dance, music, and food. And one of Ontario's best places to find powwows is on Manitoulin Island.

WHERE TO POWWOW

Manitoulin's largest and longest-running powwow is the **Wikwemikong Cultural Festival and Powwow** (www.wikwemikongheritage. org), held annually in late July on the Wikwemikong Reserve on the island's east side.

Most of Manitoulin's other First Nations communities hold annual traditional powwows, as well, including the **Aundeck Omni Kaning** (June), **Sheguiandah** (July), and **M'Chigeeng** (early September).

Get a powwow schedule and details about any of these events from the Great Spirit Circle Trail office (705/377-4404 or 877/710-3211, www.circletrail.com).

POWWOW ETIQUETTE

Traditional powwows are generally open to the public. Some are free (although donations are accepted), while others charge admission for a day or for the duration of the event. A master of ceremonies leads the powwow and explains the various dances and ceremonies. You can purchase food and traditional crafts on-site.

During certain ceremonial songs or dances, photography and video recording are prohibited; the master of ceremonies will usually explain when these ceremonies are taking place. At other times, you may take photos or videos, but it's polite to ask for permission first, particularly when you're photographing a dancer in traditional regalia. Because many believe that the regalia (which should never be called "costumes") have their own spirit, and frequently are handmade or passed down from an ancestor, you should never touch the regalia, either. Powwows are also alcohol-free events.

To learn more about powwow customs and etiquette, request a copy of the Great Spirit Circle Trail's *Powwow Visitor Guide* (705/377-4404 or 877/710-3211, www.circletrail.com). *Miigwetch* (Thank you)!

11 A.M. and 3 P.M. Mon.–Fri.). In summer, the museum offers great workshops on traditional First Nations dance, drumming, and crafts, from pottery to quillwork to shield making; call for schedule and details.

Opposite the Ojibwe Cultural Foundation, the **Immaculate Conception Church** (Hwy. 551, 705/377-4985, donations accepted) mixes First Nations and Catholic religious traditions. The round structure with a conical roof recalls a traditional tepee; on the bright blue front door, a yellow sun with four rays in the shape of a cross is a native symbol of Christ. Inside, look for other native paintings and carvings.

Part shop and part gallery, **Lillian's Porcupine Quill Basket Museum** (5950 Hwy. 540, 705/377-4987, 10 A.M.–6 P.M. Mon.–Fri., 10 A.M.–5 P.M. Sat.–Sun., free) displays a local First Nations craft: baskets and boxes intricately woven from colorful porcupine quills. Make sure you see the exhibits done by master craftspeople in the back room. The front room sells more typical native souvenirs.

Sheguiandah and Wikwemikong

South of Little Current along Highway 6, stop at the **Viewpoint at Ten Mile Point,** where vistas stretch east across Sheguiandah Bay. Adjacent to the viewpoint, the **Ten Mile Point Trading Post and Gallery** (12164 Hwy. 6, Sheguiandah, 705/368-2377) looks like a standard souvenir shop, but amid the T-shirts and trinkets are high-quality works, from jewelry to leather to prints, by First Nations artists. They also carry a large selection of books about Manitoulin and First Nations culture, including books for kids.

On the peninsula jutting out from Manitoulin's eastern shore is the **Wikwemikong Unceded First Nations Reserve**—"unceded" because the group never agreed to any treaty that would give title of its land to the government. It's Canada's only officially recognized unceded Indian reserve. The Wikwemikong offer a variety of tours and cultural experiences, including a bannock-making workshop, walking tours, and canoe excursions. Contact the **Wikwemikong Tourism Information Center** (888/801-9422, www.wikwemikong.ca) for details.

If you visit during July or August, don't miss a production by the **Debajehmujig Theatre Group** (office: 8 Debajehmujig Ln., 705/859-2317, www.debaj.ca). They perform works with aboriginal themes in the ruins of Wikwemikong's Holy Cross Mission.

SPORTS AND RECREATION
Hiking

One of Manitoulin's most popular hikes is the **Cup and Saucer Trail** (Hwy. 540 at Bidwell Rd., dawn–dusk daily, mid-May–mid-Oct.), which climbs the Niagara Escarpment to spectacular lookouts from the 70-meter (230-foot) cliffs. This 12-kilometer (7.5-mile) route is divided into several shorter trails, including the adventure trail (2 kilometers/1.2 miles), which takes hikers up and down ladders and along narrow ledges to a viewpoint overlooking the North Channel. The trailhead is 18 kilometers (11 miles) west of Little Current, just north of M'Chigeeng.

Off Highway 551, south of the Ojibwe Cultural Foundation, is the **M'Chigeeng Hiking Trail,** which climbs the bluff above the M'Chigeeng powwow grounds to look out across the North Channel. A fascinating way to explore the trail is on a two-hour **Mother Earth Nature Hike,** led by an aboriginal guide, who will help you identify local plants and understand how they're used in aboriginal medicine and cooking; contact the Great Spirit Circle Trail (705/377-4404 or 877/710-3211, www.circletrail.com) to book.

Legend has it that, back in the 1880s, a farmer was cutting down grass in southwest Manitoulin, when two men approached and asked the place's name. "Misery," the hot, tired farmer called, and the name stuck. Today, it's the antithesis of misery for hikers who stroll the trails in the **Misery Bay Provincial Nature Reserve** (400 Misery Bay Park Rd., 705/966-2315, www.miserybay.org, 10 A.M.–5 P.M. daily July–Aug., Sat.–Sun. mid-May–June and Sept.–mid-Oct.). The Misery Bay turnoff is 35 kilometers (22 miles) west of Gore Bay along Highway 540.

Water Sports

Although Manitoulin is ringed with beaches, the best sandy spots are on the south shore, west of South Baymouth. And the best of the best? **Providence Bay Beach,** a long strip of soft sand along Lake Huron, backed by swaying grasses and a boardwalk trail. The beach has a snack shack with restrooms and, wonder of wonders, an espresso bar.

Heading west from M'Chigeeng on Highway 540, you reach Kagawong, a cute village just down the path from **Bridal Veil Falls,** where (at least if it's a hot enough day), you can swim under the waterfall. You can kayak or canoe nearby; **Manitoulin Wind and Wave** (55 Main St./Hwy. 540, 705/282-1999 or 800/385-9673, www.paddlemanitoulin.ca) rents boats and gear. In eastern Manitoulin, off Highway 6 between Sheguiandah and Manitowaning, is the largest of the island's 108 freshwater lakes, Lake Manitou.

ACCOMMODATIONS AND FOOD

Manitoulin lodgings include cottages, B&Bs, small inns, and summer camp–style resorts. No chains or megaresorts have set up shop (yet). It's a good idea to book ahead, especially in July and August. Manitoulin isn't a "fine dining" destination—it's much easier to find burgers and fish 'n' chips than a gourmet meal—but most towns have someplace to get a bite.

Little Current

Both sailors and landlubbers wash into the **Anchor Inn** (1 Water St., 705/368-2023, www.anchorgrill.com, 7 A.M.–11 P.M. July–Aug., call for off-season hours, $5–15 lunch, $8–25 dinner) for a beer or for chow that ranges from burgers and sandwiches to more substantial steaks and fish plates. The whitefish sandwich is excellent. Upstairs, the inn has several simple rooms and apartments ($50–60 s, $70–90 d), although light sleepers should note that rooms

You can stay in a teepee on Manitoulin Island.

© CAROLYN B. HELLER

THE NORTH

over the bar can be noisy, particularly on weekends when bands are playing.

Have coffee and check your email at **Loco Beanz** (7 Water St., 705/368-2261, 7 A.M.–6 P.M. Mon.–Fri., 7:30 A.M.–6 P.M. Sat., 8 A.M.–4 P.M. Sun. summer; call for off-season hours), a cheery café with free Wi-Fi.

Aundeck Omni Kaning

On this First Nations reserve off Highway 540, five kilometers (three miles) west of Little Current, **Endaa-aang "Our Place"** (705/368-0548, www.aokfn.com, May–Oct.) rents four well-kept cabins in parklike grounds near the North Channel waterfront. The wood-paneled cabins sleep six, with a double bedroom, a twin-bedded room, and a living room with a sofa bed; they have full kitchens, as well as decks with barbecues.

Also on the property are **tepee rentals.** The tepees sleep eight but are unfurnished. Bring sleeping bags and other camping gear; restrooms are nearby.

Guests can use the reserve's beach along the

North Channel, but it's otherwise not open to the public. For reservations, contact "Our Place" directly, or book through the Great Spirit Circle Trail (705/377-4404 or 877/710-3211, www.circletrail.com).

M'Chigeeng

A convenient place to eat before or after you visit the Ojibwe Cultural Foundation, **Season's Family Restaurant** (Hwy. 551, 705/377-4344, 7 a.m.–7:30 p.m. Mon.–Sat.) serves bacon and eggs, sandwiches, and other family-style dishes.

South Baymouth and Tehkummah

The closest accommodations to the ferry terminal, the **Southbay Gallery and Guesthouse Manitoulin** (14–15 Given Rd, South Baymouth, 877/656-8324, www.south-bayguesthouse.com, May–Sept., $90–140 d) has several guestrooms (two with private baths) with stocky wooden furniture, in two different buildings. The property also includes a self-contained guest cottage, hot tub, and art gallery/shop. The same family runs the Southbay Guesthouse in Sudbury.

One of the island's best restaurants is unobtrusively set in the countryside 26 kilometers (16 miles) north of South Baymouth. In a homey white house at the end of a garden path, ◖ **Garden's Gate Restaurant** (Hwy. 542, Tehkummah, 705/859-2088 or 888/959-2088, www.manitoulin-island.com/gardens-gate, lunch Tues.–Sun. and dinner nightly July–Aug., call for off-season hours, $13–15 lunch, $16–23 dinner), with its floral tablecloths and cozy screened porch, looks more grandmotherly than gourmet, but the food—updated country fare made with fresh, local ingredients—is first-rate. Save room for the homemade pie.

Providence Bay

A five-minute walk from Providence Bay Beach, the **Auberge Inn** (71 McNevin St., 705/377-4392 or 877/977-4392, www.aubergeinn.ca, $39 dorm, $90 d), the island's only hostel, is a super-friendly place. There's one dorm room

that sleeps six (in three bunk beds) and a private room with a double bed; guests share a large bathroom upstairs and a smaller washroom off the kitchen. Owners Alain Harvey and Nathalie Gara-Boivin offer great tips on things to do, and you can rent bicycles, kayaks, or canoes for your island explorations. Rates include self-serve continental breakfast. Wi-Fi is available (guests free, nonguests $5/hour). Open year-round.

What's a day at the beach without fish 'n' chips? **Lake Huron Fish and Chips** (20 McNevin St., 705/377-4500, late May–Sept., cash only) is just inland from Providence Bay.

Gore Bay

One of Manitoulin's most elegant accommodations is **The Queen's Inn Bed and Breakfast** (19 Water St., 705/282-0665, www.thequeensinn.ca, May–Dec., $125–190 d), overlooking the harbor in Gore Bay. Built in the late 1800s, this Victorian manor has a formal antiques-filled parlor and a saloon-turned-breakfast-room where a hot morning meal is served. On the second and third floors are eight Victorian-style guest rooms (five with private bath). Sit on either of the two verandas to enjoy the harbor views.

Buoys Eatery and Take Out (1 Purvis Dr., off Water St., 705/282-2869, www.buoystake-out.com, lunch and dinner daily June–Sept., Wed.–Sun. Oct.–May, $9–15) looks like your ordinary fish shack (albeit one with a lovely deck), but their two specialties make it worth the stop: fish 'n' "wedges" (broiled or fried local whitefish paired with thick slices of roasted potato) and pizzas with out-of-the-ordinary toppings; the "Greek Obsession" sports tzatziki sauce, gyro meat, feta cheese, and olives, while the "Morning Pizza" is made with bacon and eggs.

Meldrum Bay

To get way, way away from it all, book a stay at the **Meldrum Bay Inn** (25959 Hwy. 540, 705/283-3190 or 877/577-1645, www.meldrumbayinn.com, $130–160 d) on Manitoulin's far west end. The seven simple rooms with quilt-topped beds share two baths; rates include continental breakfast. The homestyle dining room specializes in local whitefish and barbecued ribs. The inn is open year-round, the restaurant from May through October. Meldrum Bay is 167 circuitous kilometers (104 miles) from South Baymouth and 134 kilometers (83 miles) from Little Current; allow at least two hours from the island's east side.

INFORMATION AND SERVICES

Just over the swing bridge, stop into the **Manitoulin Tourism Association Welcome Centre** (Hwy. 6, Little Current, 705/368-3021, www.manitoulintourism.com), where obliging staff provide maps and brochures, book ferry reservations, and offer advice about things to do and places to stay. Their website is an excellent resource for planning your island visit; it has a good map with descriptions of Manitoulin's various communities. If you arrive on the ferry, pick up maps and brochures at the **ferry terminal information center** (41 Water St., South Baymouth, 705/859-3161).

For information about aboriginal tourism on Manitoulin, contact the **Great Spirit Circle Trail** (15 Hwy. 551, M'Chigeeng, 705/377-4404 or 877/710-3211, www.circletrail.com). The **Wikwemikong Tourism Information Center** (888/801-9422, www.wikwemikong.ca) can tell you about activities on the Wikwemikong Reserve.

GETTING THERE
By Ferry

From Toronto or other Southern Ontario destinations, the quickest way to Manitoulin is by ferry from the Bruce Peninsula. The **M.S. Chi-Cheemaun Ferry** (800/265-3163, www.ontarioferries.com, mid-May–mid-Oct., one-way adults $16.25, seniors $14.10, children 5–11 $8.10, cars $27.75–35.40)—its Ojibway name means "The Big Canoe"—makes the two-hour run between Tobermory and South Baymouth several times daily. Discounts are available for families and for same-day returns.

Make a reservation if you're taking a car; a $15 reservation fee applies to many sailings.

When the ferry is running, it's possible—though not easy—to get from Toronto to Manitoulin without a car. Take the Greyhound bus to Owen Sound, where you catch another bus operated by First Student Canada to the ferry terminal in Tobermory. Then take the ferry to South Baymouth.

By Car

By road, it's a long slog (about 510 kilometers, or 320 miles) from Toronto to Manitoulin. After taking Highway 400/69 north to Sudbury, it's still 90 minutes further on Highway 17 west and Highway 6 south to Manitoulin's **swing bridge.** In summer, every hour on the hour (dawn–dusk), the bridge swings sideways to allow boats to pass underneath, halting road traffic for 15 minutes. The bridge is only one lane, so even when it's open, traffic alternates in each direction. Don't be in a rush to make the crossing.

GETTING AROUND

Highway 6 runs along the island's east side between Little Current and South Baymouth, passing Sheguiandah and Wikwemikong en route. From Little Current, Highway 540 goes west to M'Chigeeng, Kagawong, Gore Bay, and Meldrum Bay.

From South Baymouth to M'Chigeeng, take Highway 6 north to Highway 542 west, then, at Mindemoya, pick up Highway 551 north to M'Chigeeng. To Providence Bay, turn south onto Highway 551. For Gore Bay, continue west on Highway 542.

Manitoulin has no public transportation. If you're an avid cyclist able to ride fairly long distances, **bicycling** is a reasonable way to tour the island. From South Baymouth, it's 30 kilometers (19 miles) to Providence Bay and 62 kilometers (39 miles) to Little Current. For cycling tips, check with the **Manitoulin Tourism Association** (705/368-3021, www.manitoulintourism.com) or with the owners of the **Auberge Inn** (71 McNevin, Providence Bay, 705/377-4392 or 877/977-4392, www.aubergeinn.ca).

Sault Ste. Marie and Vicinity

With an Ojibway community here for centuries, and a French Jesuit mission established in 1668, Sault Ste. Marie, on the St. Mary's River opposite the U.S. city of the same name, is one of North America's oldest settlements. Its riverside location helped it become an important fur-trading post in the 1700s and eventually an industrial city of 75,000 people. While "the Sault" (pronounced "Soo") has several interesting museums, the best attractions take you out of town, including a train tour to Agawa Canyon, a drive north along the shores of Lake Superior, or a day trip east to St. Joseph Island.

SIGHTS

Most of the Sault's attractions are downtown between Queen Street East and the river.

Stroll the riverfront boardwalk and take a break in **Roberta Bondar Park,** which honors Canada's first woman astronaut, a Sault native who flew aboard the space shuttle *Discovery* in 1992. The park pavilion hosts frequent summer concerts.

At the city's west end is the **Sault Ste. Marie Canal National Historic Site** (1 Canal Dr., 705/941-6262, www.pc.gc.ca, 8:30 A.M.–4:30 P.M. daily late June–early Sept., Mon.–Fri. early Sept.–late June; tours 11 A.M. and 2 P.M. July–Aug., by appointment Sept.–June, $3). Opened in 1895, the Sault canal was the last link in a system of Canadian waterways connecting Lake Superior to the Atlantic Ocean. At the time, it was the world's longest lock and the first in Canada to operate on electric power. Although the original lock was replaced in the

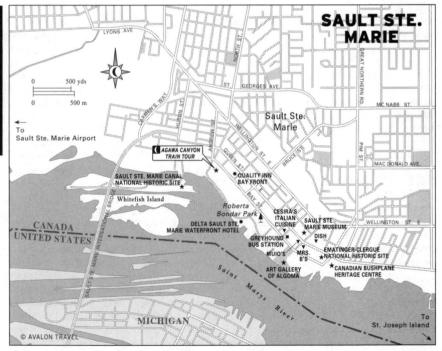

the Clergue Blockhouse at the Ermatinger-Clergue National Historic Site

1990s, recreational boaters now pass through a smaller lock within the historic one. At the visitor center, you can explore exhibits about the lock and the region's shipping history.

Two unusual historic buildings constitute the **Ermatinger-Clergue National Historic Site** (831 Queen St. E., 705/759-5443, www.city.sault-ste-marie.on.ca). The stately, Georgian-style Old Stone House, built in 1814, was home to wealthy fur trader Charles Oakes Ermatinger, his Ojibway wife Mananowe (Charlotte), and their 13 children. Next door is the Clergue Blockhouse, a replica of a frontier fort cantilevered above a former gunpowder magazine. Francis Hector Clergue, an industrialist and (ultimately failed) entrepreneur, had this odd structure built in 1895 as his home and office. Costumed interpreters guide you through both buildings and explain about 19th-century local life.

The waterfront **Art Gallery of Algoma** (10 East St., 705/949-9067, www.artgalleryofalgoma.ca, 11 A.M.–6 P.M. Wed.–Sun., admission by donation) has three galleries with contemporary art exhibits that rotate every eight to 10 weeks. The main gallery showcases established local artists, the "project room" features emerging artists, and the education gallery shows student work, from preschool to university. The gallery shop sells jewelry, cards, and other work, many by Northern Ontario artists.

Climb aboard several of the 25 historic airplanes at the **Canadian Bushplane Heritage Centre** (50 Pim St., 705/945-6242 or 877/287-4752, www.bushplane.com, 9 A.M.–6 P.M. daily mid-May–mid-Oct., 10 A.M.–4 P.M. daily mid-Oct.–mid-May; adults $10.50, seniors $9.50, students $5, children $2). Located in a cavernous former air service hangar, exhibits include forest-fire fighting, becoming a pilot, and aircraft radio. You can also take a video flight tour of Agawa Canyon.

◖ Agawa Canyon Park Train Tour

It's all about the scenery on the Agawa Canyon Train (Algoma Central Railway, 129 Bay St., 705/946-7300 or 800/242-9287, www.

© CAROLYN B. HELLER

climbing to the lookout over Agawa Canyon

agawacanyontourtrain.com, Tue.–Thurs. mid-June, daily late June–mid-Oct., adults $79–99, seniors $70–99, youth 5–18 $35–64, children 2–5 $30–39), a one-day trip into the wilderness. Agawa Canyon is tiny compared to the United States' Grand Canyon or Mexico's Copper Canyon, but with a river winding amid the trees and below the rock walls, it's an attractive—and car-free—destination.

After the train pulls out of Sault station at 8 A.M., the city's mills and factories give way to forests, hills, and lakes. With the surrounding foliage, the most popular times for the trip are the last two weeks of September and the first week of October, when fall colors are typically at their peak.

For much of the four-hour, 184-kilometer (114-mile) ride north, the best views are from the right (east) side of the train, but as you near the canyon, be sure to look left; near Mile 100, you can see all the way to Lake Superior. You can also take in the "engineer's view" en route; cameras mounted on the engine project onto flat-screen monitors inside the coaches.

Visitors on the Agawa Canyon tour disembark at the canyon, where they then have about 90 minutes to explore before the return train leaves. The prettiest hike climbs 320 steps up the **Lookout Trail** (30–40 minutes round-trip), the best vantage point for photos over the canyon.

The flatter **Bridal Veil Falls Trail** (30 minutes round-trip) goes to the 68.5-meter (225-foot) waterfall of the same name. You can picnic at the falls, but if you climb the Lookout Trail, too, you won't have time to sit and eat (have lunch on the train before you reach the canyon or when the dining car reopens heading south). As you walk back from the falls, take the path across the train tracks (carefully) to follow the **Black Beaver Falls Trail** to a second, smaller waterfall.

The train gets you back to the city around 6–6:30 P.M.

From January to March, the canyon trip runs Saturdays only as the **Snow Train.** Although the views from the train are more expansive when the surrounding trees are bare, you can't disembark at the canyon—there's too much snow!

ACCOMMODATIONS

Among the chain hotels downtown, the **Quality Inn Bay Front** (180 Bay St., 705/945-9264, www.qualityinn.com, $150–180 d, $200–220 suite) is most convenient to the Agawa Canyon train, while the most upscale is the 195-room riverfront **Delta Sault Ste. Marie Waterfront Hotel** (208 St. Mary's River Dr., 705/949-0611 or 888/713-8482, www. deltahotels.com, $150–190 d).

If you have a car, an excellent-value lodging that draws both families and business travelers is **Algoma's Water Tower Inn** (360 Great Northern Rd., 705/949-8111 or 888/461-7077, www.watertowerinn.com, $125–155 d). Although the surroundings are typically suburban, once you're inside, it feels like a mini-resort, particularly in the "Aqua Spa," with its indoor pool and indoor/outdoor hot tubs. The best of the guest rooms are the contemporary "top of the inn" units.

Other chain hotels line Great Northern

Road, including the newer **Fairfield Inn** (633 Great Northern Rd, 705/253-7378, www.marriott.com, $140–170).

FOOD

Dining options are plentiful around Queen Street East downtown and amid Great Northern Road's strip malls. The city has a large Italian population, which makes Italian eating a good choice; finding the best pizza seems to be a competitive sport.

Dish (740 Queen St. E., 705/946-3474, 8 A.M.–10 P.M. Mon.–Fri., 10 A.M.–4 P.M. Sat., $4–6), a loungey espresso bar–café, may be downtown's coolest place to hang out. Besides coffee drinks and fruit smoothies, they serve soups, salads, and creative sandwiches, like pesto chicken or roasted red pepper hummus. Free Wi-Fi.

Popular with everyone from young folks on dates to old folks on pensions, **Muio's** (685 Queen St. E., 705/254-7105, www.muios.com, 7 A.M.–close daily, $5–10 lunch, $10–20 dinner) is so retro, it's hip. The must-have dish is "broasted" chicken (the Soo's version of southern fried), which comes as "chicken on a bun" or as a heaping platter with potatoes and salad or coleslaw; either way, it's a hefty—and delicious—meal. The ravioli is another favorite, and other options include pizza, burgers, and steaks. Breakfast, too.

With its dark wainscoting and white tablecloths, **Cesira's Italian Cuisine** (133 Spring St., 705/949-0600, www.cesiras.com, lunch 11 A.M.–2:30 P.M. Mon.–Fri., dinner 5–10 P.M. Mon.–Sat., $7–14 lunch, $13–27 dinner), in an old house downtown, has a faded elegance that belies the great value of its traditional Italian fare, particularly the inexpensive specials ($6.99 lunch, $12.99 dinner). The handmade pastas are excellent.

Among pizza partisans, popular picks include **Mrs. B's** (76 East St., 705/942-9999, 11 A.M.–11 P.M. Mon.–Thu., 11 A.M.–midnight Fri.–Sat., 1–7 P.M. Sun.) in a bright red building downtown, and **Fratelli's** (522 Great Northern Rd., 705/256-1313, www.giovanisrestaurant.ca, 11 A.M.–11 P.M. Mon.–Sat.,

11 A.M.–10 P.M. Sun.), which also makes tasty *panzarotti,* Ontario's version of a calzone.

PRACTICALITIES

The helpful crew at **Tourism Sault Ste. Marie** (99 Foster Dr., 705/759-5442 or 800/461-6020, www.saulttourism.com), and their equally informative website, can clue you into things to do in the Soo.

Across the river from its Michigan namesake, Sault Ste. Marie is closer to the United States than to many Ontario points. Michigan's I-75 crosses the **International Bridge** into the Canadian Sault's downtown. Locals will tell you that, years ago, residents on both sides of the border would regularly go back and forth for shopping, dining, or last call at the bars. More recently, heightened border security has increased the separation between the Canadian and U.S. cities; border wait times vary but can run to an hour or more. Remember that passports are required for travel between the United States and Canada.

From **Sault Ste. Marie Airport** (www.saultairport.com), 20 kilometers (12 miles) west of downtown, Air Canada (www.aircanada.com) and Porter Airlines (www.flyporter.com) fly to Toronto. Bearskin Airlines (www.bearskinairlines.com) has flights to Thunder Bay.

The **Greyhound Bus Station** (73 Brock St., 705/949-4711 or 800/661-8747, www.greyhound.ca), off Queen Street East downtown, has buses to Sudbury ($44–66, 4.5 hours), Toronto ($87–149, 11 hours), and Thunder Bay ($87–149, 10 hours), among other destinations.

Within Ontario, it's an easy 3.5-hour drive between Sault Ste. Marie and Sudbury, 300 kilometers (186 miles) to the east. The Sault is roughly equidistant (700 kilometers, or 435 miles) between Toronto and Thunder Bay.

The city's attractions are clustered in the walkable downtown, so if you stay downtown, you don't need a car. However, to explore Lake Superior Provincial Park or other day-trip sights, you'll need your own wheels. Local car rental companies include **Budget** (705/942-1144, www.budget.com), **Discount** (705/253-

1075, www.discountcar.com), **Enterprise** (705/254-3227, www.enterprise.com), and **National** (705/949-5121, www.nationalssm. com).

ST. JOSEPH ISLAND

The second-largest freshwater island in the world (after Manitoulin), rural St. Joseph is dotted with farms, beaches, and two tiny villages. It's a leisurely day-trip from the Sault.

The island's main "attraction" is the **Fort St. Joseph National Historic Site** (Fort Rd., 705/246-2664, www.pc.gc.ca, 9:30 A.M.–5 P.M. daily June–early Oct., adults $3.90, seniors $3.40, children $1.90). The British built the fort in the 1790s; the Americans burned it to the ground during the War of 1812. What remains are the excavated ruins of the fort buildings, from the powder magazine to the kitchen to a surprisingly intact chimney. The Visitor Centre exhibits explain about life in this remote outpost and the alliances between the British and First Nations; guided tours are available ($4). The fort is on St. Joseph's southwestern tip, 37 kilometers (23 miles) from the bridge onto the island.

North of the fort, stop to stroll around lovely **Adcocks' Woodland Gardens** (4757 5th Side Rd., www.adcockswoodlandgardens.com, generally 11 A.M.–4 P.M. mid-May–late Sept., admission by donation), part cultivated grounds and part wild woods.

You can get a bite to eat in the villages of Richards Landing and Hilton Beach. Have a burger or a sandwich on homemade bread at the homey **Dry Dock Restaurant** (Marks St., Hilton Beach, 705/246-0850, 8 A.M.–8 P.M. daily), decorated with lighthouse paraphernalia.

The St. Joseph turnoff from Highway 17 is 45 kilometers (28 miles) east of Sault Ste. Marie.

BATCHAWANA BAY

Batchawana Bay Provincial Park (Hwy 17, 705/882-2209, www.ontarioparks.com, mid-May–mid-Oct., $10/vehicle), on Lake Superior 70 kilometers (44 miles) north of the Sault, has a long, sandy beach that's a pleasant place to swim or lounge by the lake.

Even lovelier is the smooth stretch of sand backed by dunes and trees at **Pancake Bay Provincial Park** (Hwy 17, 705/882-2209, www.ontarioparks.com, early May–mid-Oct., $13/vehicle), 10 kilometers (6.2 miles) farther north. Hikers may want to follow the **Edmund Fitzgerald Lookout Trail** (Lookout Trail Rd.) to a viewing platform above the section of the lake where the S.S. *Edmund Fitzgerald* sank in 1975; allow 2–3 hours to hike the seven-kilometer (4.4-mile) trail. The trailhead is across the highway from the rest of the park, two kilometers (1.2 miles) to the north.

A popular place for **camping** ($36.75–40.50 tent sites, $42.25–46 electrical sites), Pancake Bay has 328 campsites along the water; try to book a lakefront site or one up in the Hilltop Campground, as others are quite close to the highway. The campground has showers, flush toilets, and laundry facilities, as well as five **yurts** ($91.50) that each sleep six. Reserve campsites and yurts through the **Ontario Parks Reservations Service** (888/668-7275, www.ontarioparks.com).

For a bite to eat in Batchawana Bay, try the hearty fare at **Voyageurs' Lodge and Cookhouse** (Hwy. 17, 705/882-2504, www. voyageurslodge.com). They're especially busy Friday evenings for their weekly fish fry.

◖ LAKE SUPERIOR PROVINCIAL PARK

One of Ontario's most beautiful outdoor destinations, this provincial park (Hwy. 17, 705/856-2284, www.ontarioparks.com, early May–late Oct., $13/vehicle) stretches 115 kilometers (72 miles) along Lake Superior's eastern shore. As you sit on a sandy beach or scramble up the rocky cliffs, you could be forgiven for thinking you were actually at the ocean, as surf crashes onto the rocks and the steely blue-gray water disappears into the horizon, with no land in sight.

For park information, contact the main park office, located in the northern half of the park

Surf's up at Lake Superior Provincial Park.

near Red Rock Lake; or the Agawa Bay Visitor Centre (705/882-2026, mid-May–mid-Oct.).

Sights

At the south end of the park, stop first at the modern **Agawa Bay Visitor Centre** (705/882-2026, 9 A.M.–8 P.M. daily mid-June–early Sept., 9 A.M.–5 P.M. daily mid-May–mid-June and early Sept.–mid-Oct.), where you can learn more about Lake Superior, which is not just the largest, deepest, and coldest of the Great Lakes—it's the largest body of freshwater in the world. Other exhibits illustrate the lake's legendary storms, including the one that sank the freighter S.S. *Edmund Fitzgerald* in 1975, immortalized in Ontario-born singer Gordon Lightfoot's ballad "Wreck of the Edmund Fitzgerald." The knowledgeable staff here can help you plan your time in the park. Internet access is available ($2/20 minutes), too.

A few kilometers north of Agawa Bay, a short (0.5-kilometer, or 0.3-mile) but steep and rocky trail leads to the **Agawa Rock Pictographs,** red ochre graphics that Ojibway people painted on a lakefront rock face several hundred years ago. Park staff are usually on hand in July and August to tell you more about the aboriginal people and their history. The rocky shore here is especially beautiful. Because you have to scramble out onto slippery rocks to see the pictographs, you can visit only when the lake is calm; otherwise, the surf can crash dangerously onto the rocks.

Continuing north is **Katherine Cove,** with a sheltered beach of fine white sand that is a pretty picnic spot. If the surrounding trees were palms instead of evergreens, you could imagine that you were in the Caribbean.

The terrain changes again at **Old Woman Bay,** approaching the park's northern boundary. Evergreen hills rise and fall around the bay, and waves pound the broad sandy beach.

Recreation

Hikers will find a wide variety of terrain, ranging from easy paths like the two-kilometer (1.2-mile) **Crescent Lake Trail** or the longer (six kilometer, or 3.7 mile) but still fairly flat

Pinguisibi/Sand River Trail to the rugged 65-kilometer (40-mile) **Coastal Trail** that extends from Agawa Bay north beyond Gargantua Harbour; allow five to seven days to hike the entire coastal route, but you can do sections as dayhikes. Pick up hiking information and maps at the park office or the Agawa Bay Visitor Centre.

You can swim in Lake Superior, at least if you're hardy; not only is the surf often strong, but even in August, the average surface temperature is a chilly 14.5°C (58°F). Head for one of the more sheltered bays to find warmer water. The park also has several interior lakes, which are warmer, calmer places to swim or boat. You can rent **canoes** (mid-June–early Sept., $10/hour, $30/day) at Agawa Bay, Rabbit Blanket Lake, and Crescent Lake, and from the Red Rock Park Office near Mijinemungshing Lake.

Camping

The park has 248 campsites in three different areas. To camp beside Lake Superior, book a site at the **Agawa Bay Campground** (early May–mid.–Oct., $36.75–40.50 tent sites, $42.25 electrical sites), where the premium sites are right on the beach. The park's largest and most popular campground, Agawa has showers, flush toilets, and laundry facilities, as well as an outdoor amphitheatre where a variety of nature programs are offered in summer.

In the park's northern half, away from Lake Superior but on a smaller interior lake, you can camp at the **Rabbit Blanket Lake Campground** (early May–late Oct., $36.75 tent sites, $42.25 electrical sites). This area has flush toilets, showers, and laundry facilities, as well.

To reserve campsites at Agawa Bay and Rabbit Blanket Lake, contact the **Ontario Parks Reservations Service** (888/668-7275, www.ontarioparks.com).

Near the park's southern boundary, the small, rustic **Crescent Lake Campground** (mid-June–mid-Sept., $31.50 tent sites), with a swimming beach on this interior lake, has vault toilets, but the nearest running water is at Agawa Bay. Reservations aren't accepted at Crescent Lake.

If you don't want to camp, the closest accommodations are north of the park in Wawa.

Getting There

Highway 17 from Sault Ste. Marie to Wawa bisects Lake Superior Provincial Park; you can tour the park on a day-trip from either town. From the Sault, it's 140 kilometers (87 miles)—less than two hours by car—to the Agawa Bay Visitor Centre, and another 64 kilometers (40 miles) from Agawa Bay to Old Woman Bay.

WAWA

Wawa is an Ojibway word meaning "wild goose," so it's fitting that the chief landmark in this community is the 8.5-meter (28-foot) tall **Wawa Goose,** created by sculptor Dick Vandercliff. The goose sits perched outside the **Wawa Visitor Information Centre** (Hwy. 17 at Hwy. 101, www.wawa.cc, 8 A.M.–8 P.M. July–Aug., 9 A.M.–5 P.M. mid-May–June and Sept.–mid-Oct.), south of town. After taking your obligatory goose photo, head inside to pick up information about the Lake Superior region or to check your email (Internet $2/20 minutes). The town also has an attractive beach on **Wawa Lake.**

Outfitter **Naturally Superior Adventures** (www.naturallysuperior.com) is based in the Rock Island Lodge. Rent kayaks, take kayaking lessons, or sign up for day hikes, canoe or kayak excursions, or a variety of adventure trips.

The best place to stay in the Wawa area is the small **⬛ Rock Island Lodge** (800/203-9092, www.rockislandlodge.ca, mid-May–early Nov., $98–109 d). The four rooms don't have phones or TVs, but they do have private baths and awesome views of Lake Superior. Out on the deck, the lake is so close, you're practically in the water. Wi-Fi is available, but cell service is spotty. Rates include breakfast, and staff will prepare lunch and dinner on request, or you can use the lodge kitchen to cook your own meals.

Between Wawa and Lake Superior Park, the **Best Northern Motel** (Hwy. 17, 705/856-7302 or 800/434-8240, www.best-northern.ca, $65–75 s, $75–89 d, $135 cottages) is an updated motel with 11 guest rooms, all with microwaves, refrigerators,

© CAROLYN B. HELLER

The *Wawa Goose* sits atop the local tourist information center.

coffeemakers, and flat-screen TVs, as well as three two-bedroom cottages. You're right off the highway, though, so beware of road noise. The main lodge has a sauna, a rec room and pool table, and a restaurant that serves Polish specialties along with the more common burgers, fish, and steaks. You'll find more motels and places to eat in town, particularly along Mission Road and Broadway Avenue, Wawa's main streets.

Wawa is 230 kilometers (145 miles) north of Sault Ste. Marie.

BACKGROUND

The Land

Covering 1.1 million square kilometers (425,000 square miles), Ontario is nearly as large as the countries of France, Italy, and Germany combined. It's not Canada's largest province (Quebec has that honor), but it's twice as big as Texas, the second-largest U.S. state, and just slightly smaller than Alaska. Ontario's northernmost regions share the same latitude as southern Alaska, while Point Pelee, the southernmost point on the Ontario mainland, is the same latitude as the northern California wine country. No wonder, then, that southern Ontario is a major wine-producing region.

Ontario sits between Manitoba to the west and Quebec to the east, but if you think it's landlocked in the middle of the country, think again. The province borders four of the five Great Lakes—Ontario, Erie, Huron, and Superior—along more than 3,000 kilometers (2,300 miles) of shoreline. Ontario even has over 1,000 kilometers (680 miles) of saltwater shores on its northern boundary with Hudson Bay.

Beyond these major bodies of water, Ontario has nearly a quarter-million lakes (holding one-third of the world's freshwater!), as well as numerous rivers and streams. Of course, the province's most impressive "water feature" may be Niagara Falls, which thunder down the Niagara River, while separating Canada from the United States.

© CAROLYN B. HELLER

GEOGRAPHY

With its granite rock formations and pine forests, the Canadian Shield covers two-thirds of Ontario, extending from the Manitoba border across the province nearly to Ottawa and to the Thousand Islands farther south. In the far north, in the Hudson Bay lowlands along Hudson and James Bays from Moosonee to Fort Severn, the rocks and pines give way to swamps and meadows.

In the south, in the ecological zone known as the mixedwood plain, more lowlands (along the Great Lakes) are flat farm country, while the woodlands include a mix of deciduous trees and evergreens. Bisecting a 725-kilometer (450-mile) section of southern Ontario, extending roughly between the Niagara and Bruce Peninsulas, is the Niagara Escarpment, a forested ridge of sedimentary rock that juts above the region's otherwise flatter terrain. The highest point on the escarpment is 510 meters (1,625 feet) above sea level.

CLIMATE

Although Toronto is northwest of Buffalo, Torontonians are quick to point out that the "lake effect" that dumps piles of snow on their New York State neighbors has a different result in their city. Toronto's position on Lake Ontario's northern shore moderates the winter weather, and the city averages 115 centimeters (45 inches) of snow per year, less than Buffalo can get on a single day. Winter is still cold—January's average temperatures range from -10°C (14°F) to -2°C (28°F)—but at least you might not always be battling major blizzards if you visit midwinter.

Toronto's spring is fairly short, beginning in late April or May, and summers can turn hot and humid. In July, the average temperatures range from a low of 15°C (59°F) to a high of 27°C (81°F). Fall is a lovely time of year, and the best season to travel across much of the province, particularly in late September and early October when the trees put on their annual autumn color show.

South of Toronto, on the Niagara Peninsula, the Niagara wineries claim that the region's climate is similar to that of France's Burgundy region and Loire Valley, with Lake Ontario again moderating the more extreme winter weather found in nearby New York

ONTARIO'S AVERAGE TEMPERATURES

The following chart shows the average annual temperatures in several of Ontario's cities. Keep in mind that these are averages and that temperatures can fluctuate on a given day. On a typical July day in Toronto, for example, the temperature might vary from 18°C (64°F) at night to 26°C (79°F) during the day.

City	January	April	July	October
Toronto	-4°C, 25°F	7.5°C, 45.5°F	22°C, 71.5°F	10.5°C, 51°F
Niagara Falls	-4.5°C, 24°F	7.5°C, 45.5°F	22°C, 71.5°F	10.5°C, 51°F
Ottawa	-10.5°C, 13°F	6°C, 43°F	21°C, 70°F	8°C, 46°C
Windsor	-4.5°C, 24°F	8°C, 46°C	23°C, 74°F	11°C, 52°F
Sudbury	-13.5°C, 7.5°F	3°C, 38°F	19°C, 66°F	6°C, 43°C
Thunder Bay	-15°C, 5°F	3°C, 38°F	18°C, 65°F	5°C, 41°C

Source: Environment Canada

State. Temperatures are slightly more moderate than in Toronto, too, slightly hotter in summer, not quite as frigid in winter. Niagara's warm summers and temperate autumns are the busiest times here, when tourism is in full swing.

As you travel north of Toronto, into the Muskoka Cottage Country and along Georgian Bay, the slightly cooler summers have made these regions popular with Torontonians escaping the city's heat and humidity. It's still hot midsummer, but at least you can cool off with a swim in the lake. In winter, a snowbelt starts north of Toronto around the city of Barrie. It can be snowing in Barrie (and on the ski hills between Barrie and Collingwood) when it's raining or dry in Toronto.

Ottawa residents will maintain, with a certain perverse pride, that their city is the coldest capital in the world. Moscow may also claim that honor, but there's no disputing that winter in Ottawa—320 kilometers (200 miles) north of Syracuse, New York—can be frigid. While Ottawa may not get the heavy snows that towns like Syracuse do, it's definitely in the snowbelt, averaging 235 centimeters (nearly eight feet) of snow per year. Still, the city celebrates its winter weather with the popular Winterlude Festival in February and with lots of outdoor activities. Spring comes late to Ottawa (it might begin to warm in April, but it's not consistently springlike till May), and summers, as in Toronto, are hot and sticky. Fall, as it is throughout Ontario, is one of Ottawa's best seasons.

Across northern Ontario, winter temperatures, as you'd expect, dip well below freezing and snowfall is heavy. Summers, though, can be surprisingly hot and humid, with daytime highs above 30°C (86°F). Even along Hudson and James Bays, expect warm temperatures if you're traveling in July and August.

FLORA

Although you might not know it from a downtown Toronto street corner, forests dominate Ontario's landscape, covering more than 60 percent of the province's land. The types of trees you'll find vary from the southern to northern regions.

In the south, along Lake Erie and Lake Ontario and extending to Lake Huron's southeastern shore, deciduous forest is dominant. Trees common to this region include maple, oak, and walnut. You'll find the white trillium, Ontario's official provincial flower, blooming in deciduous forests in late April and early May.

Moving north, the forests become a mix of deciduous and coniferous trees, the former including red maples, sugar maples (accounting for most of the province's maple syrup production), yellow birch, and red oak, and the latter including eastern white pine (which is Ontario's official provincial tree), eastern hemlock, red pine, and white cedar. This forest region, known as the "Great Lakes–St. Lawrence Forest" extends across the central part of the province, along the St. Lawrence River, on the Lake Huron shores, and in the area west of Lake Superior.

If you think of orchids as tropical plants, you may be surprised to learn that more than 40 species of orchids grow on the Bruce Peninsula, which juts into Lake Huron. The best time to see the orchids in bloom is mid-May through early June.

Boreal forest covers most of northwestern Ontario, extending for 49 million hectares (roughly 121 million acres). The predominant species here are jack pine and black spruce, as well as white birch, poplar, and balsam fir.

In the far north's Hudson Bay Lowlands, constituting the remaining 25 percent of Ontario's land and bordering the subarctic tundra, trees include black spruce, white spruce, white birch, balsam fir, and balsam poplar. This area is also one of the world's largest expanses of wetlands.

Ontario's provincial government owns more than 90 percent of the province's forests. About a third is classified as "production forest," meaning that it's available for logging.

Although some provincial parks and reserves, like Algonquin Provincial Park, are protected from further development, logging has historically been part of their economy, and limited logging is still allowed.

Even in its urban areas, Ontario is beginning to realize that its trees are an important asset. In Toronto, the city is working toward a goal of doubling its tree canopy from 17 percent to 34 percent by the year 2050. The city hosts annual tree-planting days and plants free trees on residential streets.

FAUNA

Southern Ontario is home to the white-tailed deer, as well as other small animals, including raccoons, skunks, beavers, red foxes, and gray squirrels. In autumn, thousands of monarch butterflies pass through the province's southwest, crossing Lake Erie as they migrate south to Mexico. Point Pelee National Park is one of the best spots to witness the monarch migration. The Point Pelee region is also prime bird-watching territory. More than 370 species of birds have

been recorded in the vicinity, and in the spring, thousands of birders come to witness the migration of songbirds returning to the north.

In the Canadian Shield region that covers much of central Ontario, the animals get bigger. While you'll still see foxes, squirrels, and beavers, this region is also home to both the eastern timber wolf and the gray wolf, white-tailed deer, caribou, Canadian lynx, and black bear. One of the most popular events in Ontario's Algonquin Provincial Park is the summer **Wolf Howl,** when park naturalists imitate wolf calls and wild wolves may howl in response. Many of the fish, including pike, lake trout, and walleye, that you see on Ontario tables come from this region.

In the far north, caribou, moose, and black bears become more prevalent, and in the extreme northern reaches, including the vast protected territory of Polar Bear Provincial Park (accessible only by air), there's a small population of polar bears. Seals, walruses, and beluga whales can sometimes be spotted off the northern coasts.

© CAROLYN B. HELLER

Birdwatchers flock to Southwestern Ontario, a major migration area.

History

ABORIGINAL PEOPLES AND THE FIRST EUROPEANS

Archaeologists have found evidence of human settlement in Ontario dating back more than 7,000 years. In the north, early aboriginal people hunted and fished, while farther south, they were the region's first farmers. The province's name, Ontario, comes from an Iroquoian word that's loosely translated as "sparkling water."

The first Europeans to explore Ontario arrived in the early 1600s. French explorer Étienne Brulé sailed along the St. Lawrence River into Lake Ontario in 1610, while his countryman Samuel de Champlain followed in 1615, after overseeing the construction of a fort at what is now Quebec City. British explorer Henry Hudson claimed the northern Ontario region that now bears his name—Hudson Bay—for Britain in 1611.

A group of French Jesuit missionaries began constructing a community near present-day Midland in 1639, establishing the first European settlement in Ontario. Their mission was to bring Christianity to the native Wendat people, whom they called the "Huron." You can visit a re-created version of this settlement, where the Jesuits worked with the Huron for 10 years. It's now known as Sainte-Marie Among the Hurons.

In 1670, the Hudson's Bay Company was established, when the British monarch granted the company the exclusive trading rights to the land around Hudson Bay. Over the next 100 years, the fur trade flourished across northern Ontario and the rest of Canada's far north. Aboriginal hunters sold furs to the Hudson's Bay Company in exchange for knives, kettles, and what became the company's signature wool blankets.

FRANCE VS. BRITAIN

Both France and Britain staked claims to territory in present-day North America during the 1600s and 1700s, and battles broke out as the two countries fought over these territorial claims.

During the Seven Years' War (1756–1763),

while many conflicts took place in what is now Quebec and Eastern Canada, others were waged on Ontario soil, along Lake Ontario and in the Niagara region. In 1759, the British defeated the French in Quebec City, during the Battle of the Plains of Abraham, which turned the tide of the war. The Canadian territories became part of the British Empire.

Over the subsequent decades, the British found that their vast colony was difficult to govern. In 1791, the British Parliament passed the "Constitutional Act," which divided the territory in two. The region encompassing present-day Ontario became "Upper Canada," and what is now Quebec became "Lower Canada."

Upper Canada's first capital was the town of Newark, which is now called Niagara-on-the-Lake. In 1793, the capital was moved farther north, away from the volatile American border, to the settlement of York, which eventually grew to become the city of Toronto.

THE UNITED EMPIRE LOYALISTS

In the late 1700s, a wave of immigration to Upper Canada came from south of the border. The 13 British colonies south of Canada declared their independence from Britain, launching the American Revolutionary War, which resulted in the creation of the United States. After the war, many "Loyalists"—Americans who remained loyal to the British Crown—found that they were no longer welcome in the new United States.

The Loyalists came north to the still-British colony of Upper Canada, where many received land grants from the British government. Many of the early settlers to eastern Ontario, along the Thousand Islands, in Kingston, in Prince Edward County, and in what is now the Rideau Canal region, were Loyalists, who kept British traditions alive and well in their new colony.

THE WAR OF 1812

Tensions between Britain and France flared up again in the early 1800s. The British navy eventually set up a blockade, preventing French ships from reaching the Americas and stopping American ships heading for Europe. In North America, where Britain and the United States still had an uneasy relationship in the aftermath of the American Revolution, the shipping blockade became one more significant source of conflict. In 1812, the United States attacked the closest outpost of the British Empire: Canada.

Many battles during the War of 1812, which lasted until 1815, were fought on Ontario soil, in the regions bordering the United States: the Niagara Peninsula, Toronto, the Windsor-Detroit area, and along the St. Lawrence in Eastern Ontario. The Americans burned the legislative buildings in Toronto; the British in turn attacked Washington, D.C., and set the White House aflame.

The British and American governments eventually negotiated a settlement, and the war officially ended with the Treaty of Ghent, signed on December 24, 1814, and ratified February 16, 1815.

BUILDING CANALS AND WATERWAYS

After the War of 1812, Canadians were concerned that the St. Lawrence River—a vital shipping channel between Montreal and the Great Lakes—could be vulnerable to another U.S. attack, since the Americans controlled the river's southern banks. In 1826, British lieutenant colonel John By arrived on the site of what is now Ottawa and made plans both for a new town—christened "Bytown"—and for a canal that would run south to Lake Ontario through a series of connected lakes, rivers, and waterways. The canal, which opened in 1832, became the Rideau Canal.

During the same time period, entrepreneur William Hamilton Merritt proposed the idea of a canal across the Niagara Peninsula, to provide a passage for ships traveling between Lake Ontario and Lake Erie. The Niagara River connected the two lakes, but a significant natural feature prevented the river from becoming a shipping route: the unnavigable Niagara Falls. Construction began on the Welland Canal, which

included a series of locks to help ships "climb the mountain"—the Niagara Escarpment—between the two lakes. The canal opened in 1829.

Settlers in Ontario were also looking to improve shipping routes across the central sections of the province. In 1833, the first lock was built on what would eventually become the Trent-Severn Waterway, connecting Lake Ontario with Georgian Bay.

FIRST STEPS TO A UNITED CANADA

Upper and Lower Canada, which had been split apart in 1791, were joined together again in 1840 as the Province of Canada. Toronto had been the capital of predominantly British Upper Canada, while Quebec City was the capital of francophone Lower Canada. However, when the two provinces were united, neither would accept the other's capital as the seat of government. As a compromise, the city of Kingston became the first capital of the Province of Canada. But the political wrangling continued, and two years later, the capital was moved to Montreal. In the meantime, the frontier outpost of Bytown that Lieutenant Colonel John By settled in the 1830s had become the city of Ottawa. By 1857, when the legislature still hadn't been able to agree on a permanent home for the Canadian capital, they referred the problem to the British monarch, Queen Victoria. The queen and her advisors unexpectedly chose the comparatively remote outpost of Ottawa.

Situated between English Upper Canada and French Lower Canada, Ottawa had a relatively central location. But another important factor was that other potential capitals—Toronto, Kingston, and Montreal—were extremely close to Canada's boundary with the United States. Ottawa, in contrast, was situated at a safer distance from the American border. Since 1857, Ottawa has been the nation's capital.

THE UNDERGROUND RAILROAD

In the mid-1800s, thousands of African-American slaves fled from the United States to freedom in Canada. Following what was known as the "Underground Railroad," a network of safe houses and churches that gave shelter to the refugees, the vast majority of those slaves crossed into Canada into what is now southwestern Ontario. Many remained in the region, with significant settlements in Windsor, Sandwich, Amherstburg, Chatham, Dresden, and Buxton, and many of their descendants live here today.

CONFEDERATION

The Province of Canada was split once again in the 1860s, creating the new provinces of Quebec and Ontario. But this time, these provinces joined with Nova Scotia and New Brunswick to establish a new country: the Dominion of Canada. The British Parliament passed the British North America Act in 1867, which officially created this fledgling country, joining these four original provinces at "Confederation" on July 1, 1867. Kingston lawyer and politician John A. MacDonald became the first prime minister of the new nation of Canada. Today, Canadians celebrate Confederation on July 1, Canada Day.

ONTARIO'S DEVELOPING INDUSTRIES

In the late 1800s and early 1900s, Ontario began the transition from a primarily agricultural province to a more industrial one.

In 1903, a huge silver vein was discovered in northern Ontario, near the town of Cobalt, launching the mining industry in this region. In southwestern Ontario, the industry was automobiles; the year after Henry Ford founded the Ford Motor Company, the company set up a manufacturing plant across the river from Detroit, in the Ontario city of Windsor.

During this same era, tourism became important to the Ontario economy as the railroads and steamships ferried visitors to lakeside resorts in the Muskoka region, the Kawarthas, the Thousand Islands, and Niagara Falls. The falls also became a source of hydroelectric power, beginning in 1906.

The province's industrial development continued throughout the 20th century, during and after the two World Wars, and into the 1950s and '60s. The Toronto subway—Canada's first—opened in 1954, and the Macdonald-Cartier Freeway (Highway 401), which crosses the province from Windsor to the Quebec border, opened in 1968. And more recently, an Ontario company developed a now-ubiquitous communication device when Waterloo-based Research in Motion introduced the BlackBerry. At the turn of the 20th century, nearly 60 percent of Ontarians lived on farms or in rural communities. By 1981, more than 80 percent lived in the cities, a pattern that continues to the present day.

Government and Economy

GOVERNMENT

Canada has a three-tiered governmental structure, with federal, provincial (or territorial), and municipal governments. The federal government, headquartered in Ottawa, is responsible for foreign policy, national defense, immigration, and other national issues. The provincial governments handle health care, education, policing, and the highways, among other things. Local issues, such as zoning, city police and firefighting, snow removal, garbage, and recycling, are the municipal governments' purview.

Retaining its roots as a British Commonwealth country, Canada is a constitutional monarchy. The country's head of state is officially the monarch of the United Kingdom. That means that the Queen of England is also the Queen of Canada. Although Canada has preserved many of its British influences and traditions, including the summer Changing of the Guard ceremony in Ottawa, the monarch's role in Canada has become largely symbolic, and it's Canada's **prime minister** who is the country's chief executive.

the House of Commons chambers, Parliament Hill, Ottawa

The queen's official representative in Canada is the **governor general.** This, too, is largely a ceremonial role. The governor general is something of a governmental ambassador, officiating at ceremonies, bestowing awards, and opening and closing Parliament sessions. With the prime minister's advice, the queen appoints the governor general for a five-year term.

Parliament is the national legislature, which has two bodies: the elected 308-member House of Commons and the appointed 105-member Senate.

The governmental structure at the provincial level parallels that of the federal government. The head honcho of each provincial government is the premier, a position analogous to a U.S. state governor. Each province and territory has its own legislature. Toronto is Ontario's provincial capital; the Legislative Assembly building is in Toronto's Queen's Park.

ECONOMY

In Ontario's early days, the region's economy was based on its natural resources, including timber, fur, and minerals. Logging, trapping, and mining are still important components of northern Ontario's economy. In cities like Sudbury and Timmins, mines dominate the skyline, and across the north, you'll share the highways with massive logging trucks.

Southern Ontario was formerly agricultural, and while you'll see plenty of farms, orchards, and vineyards, the province's southern sector is now heavily industrial. Manufacturing, particularly in the automotive, pharmaceutical, and aerospace sectors, has been a foundation of Ontario's economy for many years. The province produces more than half of all manufactured goods that are exported from Canada.

As in many other countries, the service industries have become larger and larger components of Ontario's economy. Toronto is Canada's financial capital; not only is Canada's major equities market, the Toronto Stock Exchange, based here, but so are the headquarters of scores of banks and financial services companies.

High technology has become a major Ontario business, too. Greater Toronto, the Kitchener-

Waterloo region, and Ottawa are major centers for software and hardware development, telecommunications, and biotechnology. Toronto is a hub for Canada's communications industries, as well, including TV and film production, broadcasting, publishing, performing arts, design, and advertising.

With more than 30 colleges and universities, education is a significant component of Ontario's economy. Canada's largest university—the University of Toronto—is based in Ontario. Other major Ontario universities include York University, Ryerson University, and the Ontario College of Art and Design, all based in Toronto; McMaster University in Hamilton; the University of Waterloo and Wilfred Laurier University in Waterloo; the University of Western Ontario in London; the University of Windsor; Carlton University, and the University of Ottawa in the nation's capital; and Queen's University in Kingston.

ENVIRONMENTAL ISSUES

Like many heavily industrialized regions, Ontario has its environmental challenges. Along the lakeshores, particularly sections of Lake Erie, Lake Ontario, and Lake Huron, you'll still see power plants and other reminders of the province's industrial heritage—some still active, some long abandoned. In northern towns like Sudbury and Timmins, where mining remains an important part of the local economy, barren rocky pits mar parts of the landscape, and smoke can darkens the skies. Similarly, the logging industry has cut wild swaths across Ontario's north; even in protected areas like Algonquin Provincial Park, limited logging is still allowed.

Another industrial legacy, unfortunately, is water pollution. The Great Lakes can be plagued with poor water quality, although significant efforts have been made in recent years to clean up the lakes and make them again fit for recreation. Many beaches now have a "Blue Flag" program in place, where a blue flag identifies areas that are clean and safe for swimming.

As Ontario's cities continue to grow, urban sprawl, increasing traffic, and worsening air quality are challenges to address. These issues are most acute in Toronto, the province's largest metropolitan area, and in the "Golden Horseshoe," the suburban ring around metropolitan Toronto. But Ontario is continuing to promote alternatives to car travel, with increasing options for train, bus, and ferry travel across the province.

People and Culture

Ontario is Canada's most populous province, home to more than 13 million people, or nearly 40 percent of all Canadians. Most of Ontario's population lives in the cities, with over five million concentrated in the region known as the "Golden Horseshoe" with Toronto at its center. The "Golden Horseshoe" extends around the western end of Lake Ontario from the Niagara Peninsula to Toronto's eastern suburbs.

DEMOGRAPHY

Canada's government actively encourages immigration as a way to counterbalance the country's declining birthrate and provide workers for the nation's growing economy. Due to these immigration policies, which began in earnest in the 1970s, Canada's largest cities have become among the most multicultural on the planet. Half of all immigrants to Canada settle in Ontario.

Toronto, in particular, is a city of immigrants. Roughly half of the metropolitan area's residents were born outside Canada, and approximately 100,000 new immigrants move to the city every year. While the majority of Toronto's early settlers were of British origin, immigrants now come from all over the globe. In recent years, Toronto's Chinese community has increased by more than 15 percent, the Indian community by 25 percent, and the Filipino community by over 30 percent.

After English and French, Chinese is the most widely spoken language in Ontario. Ontario also has significant Italian- and German-speaking populations.

RELIGION

Christianity is the major religion in Canada. More than 40 percent of Canadians are Catholic, and about a quarter are Protestant; in Ontario, Protestants are the predominant religious group, with Catholics a close second. Recent census figures indicate that more than 15 percent of Canadians claim no religious affiliation at all.

Although only about 1 percent of Canada's population, or roughly 350,000 people, is Jewish, Canada has the fourth-largest Jewish population in the world, after Israel, the United States, and France. More than half of Canada's Jews live in Toronto.

Canada's largest non-Christian religious group is Muslim, representing about 2 percent of the population nationwide. In Ontario, Canada's Muslim communities are concentrated in the large urban areas of Toronto and Ottawa.

FRENCH LANGUAGE AND CULTURE

Ever since European explorers first landed on Canada's shores, the country was settled by both English- and French-speaking colonists. While many people assume that Quebec is Canada's only French-speaking region, Ontario, in particular, had a large francophone population during colonial times. Even as late as the mid-1800s, more than half of Ontario's population were native French speakers.

Today, English is the first language throughout most of the province of Ontario, and there's no need to brush up on your *bonjour* and *merci* to travel here. However, since the province shares a long border with francophone Quebec, French is widely spoken throughout the region, and Ontario's francophone community is the largest in Canada outside of Quebec. Roughly a half million Ontario residents, or just under 5 percent of the population, speak French as

More than 40 percent of Canadians are Catholic.

their first language. More than 60 percent of Ontario's francophones live in the province's eastern and northeastern regions, not surprising since those areas border Quebec.

Ottawa has a particularly large francophone and bilingual community. In fact, as the capital of bilingual Canada, Ottawa is itself a bilingual city, closer in linguistic mindset—and physical proximity—to Montreal than to Toronto. The Ottawa metropolitan area spans two provinces, Ontario and Quebec. The city of Ottawa is on the Ontario side of the Ottawa River, but on the opposite riverbank is the community of Gatineau in French-speaking Quebec. Residents easily go back and forth across the bridges between the two provinces, many living on one side and working on the other. Reflecting this linguistic diversity, nearly half the population of the Ottawa region is fully bilingual. The government operates in both languages, as do many businesses.

Across the province, Ontario's francophone community continues to grow through immigration, as French-speaking immigrants from

Africa, the Caribbean, and Europe have settled here. Today, about 10 percent of Ontario's francophones are members of a visible racial minority.

ABORIGINAL CULTURE

Canada has three "officially recognized" aboriginal groups: the First Nations, the Inuit, and the Métis. "First Nations" is the politically correct term for aboriginal people who are neither Inuit or Métis. The Inuit people live primarily in Canada's far north, while the Métis—descendants of French settlers and their First Nations spouses—have historically settled in the prairies and the west.

Canada's aboriginal peoples—totaling just over one million individuals—make up about 4 percent of the nation's population. Roughly a quarter of Canada's aboriginal people, most of whom fall under the "First Nations" designation, live in Ontario.

Canada's aboriginal people are divided primarily into two groups, based on their linguistic heritage. The Cree, Oji-Cree, Algonquin, Ojibway, Odawa, Potawatomi, and Delaware, whose historical territory has spread across central and northern Ontario, speak languages that derive from Algonquian, while the Six Nations people, who are concentrated in the southern part of the province and include the Mohawk, Oneida, Onondaga, Cayuga, Seneca, and Tuscarora, are Iroquoian-speaking.

Some of Ontario's aboriginal peoples—including the Anishinabe on Manitoulin Island, the Cree along James Bay, the Ojibway near Peterborough in eastern Ontario, and the Six Nations near Brantford and Hamilton—are beginning to open their communities to tourism, offering opportunities for visitors to learn about their cultures while bringing in new revenue.

The Arts

As you travel around Ontario, you can't help but see works by the "Group of Seven," Canadian landscape painters who worked primarily in the 1920s and whose works have become associated with Ontario. The original members, Franklin Carmichael, Lawren Harris, A. Y. Jackson, Frank Johnston, Arthur Lismer, J. E. H. MacDonald, and Frederick Varley, were all based in Ontario. Although artist Tom Thomson died (under mysterious circumstances in Algonquin Provincial Park) before the group was officially formed, he worked with most of its members and is normally considered part of the group. The National Gallery of Canada in Ottawa has an extensive collection of Group of Seven works, as does Toronto's Art Gallery of Ontario. In Owen Sound, there's a small museum, the Tom Thomson Art Gallery, devoted to Thomson's work.

LITERATURE

Many of Canada's notable contemporary authors live and work in Ontario or have made the province their home.

The artist Tom Thomson was a member of the Group of Seven.

© CAROLYN B. HELLER

Margaret Atwood, born in Ottawa in 1939, is one of Canada's best-known novelists. She writes on themes ranging from feminism (*The Edible Woman,* 1969) to science fiction (*The Handmaid's Tale,* 1985) to life in Toronto (*The Robber Bride,* 1993) to ancient Greece (*The Penelopiad,* 2005).

Another of Canada's most notable writers, Carol Shields, was born in the United States but moved to Canada at age 22. She lived in Ottawa, Winnipeg and Victoria, authoring 10 novels, three collections of short fiction, three volumes of poetry, and four published plays. She won the Pulitzer Prize for *The Stone Diaries* (1993). Her other books include *A Fairly Conventional Woman* (1982), *Larry's Party* (1997), and *Unless* (2002).

Short-story writer and novelist Alice Munro, who was born and continues to live in Ontario, writes frequently about growing up female in the province's rural communities in the 1940s and 1950s. Among her works are *Lives of Girls and Women* (1971), *Who Do You Think You Are: Stories* (1978), and *The View from Castle Rock* (2006). Her stories also appear periodically in *The New Yorker* and *The Atlantic.*

Timothy Findley was born in Toronto and began his professional career as an actor, performing with the Stratford Festival in 1953. He later became the first playwright-in-residence at Ottawa's National Arts Centre and author of more than a dozen novels, including *The Wars* (1977).

Sri Lankan–born novelist Michael Ondaatje has lived and worked in Ontario for many years, teaching at the University of Western Ontario, York University, and the University of Toronto. His best-known works, including *The English Patient* (1992) and the more recent *Anil's Ghost* (2000), don't draw on Ontario life, but one of his earlier novels, *In the Skin of a Lion* (1987) is set in 1930s Toronto.

With so many Ontarians hailing from abroad, it's no surprise that many of the province's modern writers deal with immigrant themes. Rohinton Mistry, born in India and now living in Toronto, writes about the Indian and Indo-Canadian communities in novels such as *A Fine Balance* (1995) and *Family Matters* (2002).

Toronto novelist M. G. Vassanji also tackles immigrant themes, particularly about Indians and Africans. His books include *No New Land* (1991), *The In-Between Life of Vikram Lall* (2003), and *The Assassin's Song* (2007).

Another Toronto writer, Dionne Brand, born in Trinidad in 1953, considers immigrant issues in her works, as well, including the 2005 novel *What We All Long For,* as does Barbados-born novelist and memoirist Austin Clarke in books such as *The Meeting Point* (1967), *Storm of Fortune* (1971), and *The Bigger Light* (1975).

Born in Ontario in 1959, Nino Ricci drew on his experiences as an Italian-Canadian in his first novel, *Lives of the Saints* (1990). His subsequent books include *In a Glass House* (1993), *Where She Has Gone* (1997), *Testament* (2003), and *The Origin of Species* (2008).

One of Ontario's earliest "immigrant" writers was Susanne Moodie, who came with her husband from England in 1832 and settled in Upper Canada, in what is now Ontario. She described their experiences in her autobiographical works, *Roughing It in the Bush; or, Life in Canada* (1852) and the sequel, *Life in the Clearings Versus the Bush* (1853).

Humorist Stephen Leacock offered up a different take on small-town Ontario life in *Sunshine Sketches of a Little Town* (1912), which was among his 35 books of humor. His former home in Orillia, north of Barrie in central Ontario, is now a museum.

Ontario-born playwright and novelist Robertson Davies set many of his novels, such as *Fifth Business* (1970) and *What's Bred in the Bone* (1985), in his home province. More recently, novelist Jane Urquhart, who was born in the small northern Ontario town of Little Long Lac and now lives in the southern part of the province, also considers regional themes, in works such as *The Stone Carvers* (2001).

MUSIC

Ontario has contributed many performers to the music and dance worlds. Rock-and-roll legend

Neil Young hails from Toronto, as does classical pianist and composer Glenn Gould (1932–1982), where a concert hall in the Canadian Broadcasting Company building bears his name. Singer/songwriter Gordon Lightfoot, born in Orillia, is perhaps best known for "The Wreck of the Edmund Fitzgerald," his ballad about a Lake Superior shipwreck. Stratford's hometown heartthrob is teen pop sensation Justin Bieber. The town has even created a "Bieberific" map to Justin's Stratford, highlighting the schools he attended, the skate park where he hung out, and his favorite ice cream shop. Country singer Shania Twain was born in Windsor and raised in Timmins, where you can visit a museum built in her honor. The bands Barenaked Ladies and Tragically Hip both have Ontario roots, as do singer/songwriters Alanis Morissette (1974–), who was born in Ottawa, and Avril Lavigne, born in Belleville.

THEATER AND FILM

Toronto is a major center for English-language theater, with more than 90 theater venues around the metropolitan region. A number of the city's professional repertory companies focus on Canadian plays. Toronto is also home to a theater landmark. The Elgin and Winter Garden Theatres are Canada's only "double-decker" theater—one auditorium is stacked atop the other—and one of fewer than a dozen ever built worldwide.

In Ottawa, the National Arts Centre (NAC) is the theater hub. The NAC has resident English- and French-language companies and often hosts national and international theater troupes and special events.

North America's two largest theater festivals take place in Ontario: the Stratford Shakespeare Festival and the Shaw Festival in Niagara-on-the-Lake. The Stratford productions, which run annually from late April through October, include works by the Bard and by many other classical and more contemporary playwrights. Similarly, the Shaw Festival was launched in 1962 to produce works by Irish playwright George Bernard Shaw but now mounts plays by Shaw, his contemporaries, and more modern-day authors during its annual April-to-October season.

Toronto is often called "Hollywood North" for the number of movies made here. Among the films shot on location in Toronto are *Chicago, Hairspray, The Time Traveler's Wife, Mean Girls, Harold and Kumar Go to White Castle,* and *Cinderella Man.* To see what's currently filming in the city (so you can be on the lookout for the stars), check the lists that the Toronto Film and Television Office publishes on their website (www.toronto.ca/tfto).

Every September, Ontario hosts one of the industry's major film fests: the Toronto International Film Festival. Headquartered in the distinctive glass TIFF Bell Lightbox theater building, the festival screens more than 300 movies from around the world and draws celebrities from across the globe, too.

Ontario has also contributed many actors to Hollywood. Among the many film-industry notables who were born in Ontario are Dan Aykroyd (Ottawa), John Candy (Toronto), Jim Carrey (Newmarket), Ryan Gosling (London), Rachel McAdams (London), Sandra Oh (Ottawa), Catherine O'Hara (Toronto), Christopher Plummer (Toronto), and Martin Short (Hamilton). Even early film star Mary Pickford, who became known as "America's Sweetheart," was actually born in Toronto.

ESSENTIALS

Getting There

BY AIR

If you're flying to Ontario from abroad, Toronto will likely be your gateway city. The province's largest metropolitan area is also its transportation hub. Ottawa, Canada's national capital, has an international airport, as well, with flights from across Canada, several U.S. cities, and some European destinations.

Ontario Airports

Toronto's **Pearson International Airport** (YYZ, 416/247-7678 or 866/207-1690, www.torontopearson.com) is Ontario's major airport, with flights from across Canada, the United States, and many European and Asian countries. Canadian carriers **Air Canada** (888/247-2262, www.aircanada.ca) and **WestJet** (800/538-5696, www.westjet.com), along with a number of U.S., European, and Asian airlines, fly into Pearson.

Toronto has a second, smaller airport, the **Toronto City Centre Airport** (YTZ, www.torontoport.com), that's located on the Toronto Islands a short ferry ride from downtown. You can fly here from the New York area, Boston, and Chicago, and from several Canadian cities. **Porter Airways** (888/619-8622, www.flyporter.com) is the main carrier serving the City Centre Airport, although Air Canada also flies here from Montreal.

© CAROLYN B. HELLER

Ottawa International Airport (YOW, 613/248-2000, www.ottawa-airport.ca) has flights from most major Canadian cities, several U.S. destinations (including Boston, New York, Washington, Ft. Lauderdale, and Orlando), and London (UK) and Frankfurt (Germany). **Air Canada** and **WestJet,** along with a number of U.S. airlines, fly to Ottawa.

Most of Ontario's other large cities, including two that are within 90 minutes' drive of Toronto, have airports with flights from other parts of Canada. You can fly nonstop to **Hamilton International Airport** (YHM, 905/679-1999, www.flyhi.ca), southwest of Toronto, from Calgary, Edmonton, Winnipeg, Halifax, and Moncton. In the Kitchener-Waterloo area, the **Region of Waterloo International Airport** (YFK, 519/648-2256 or 866/648-2256, www.waterlooairport.ca) has nonstop flights from Calgary, Ottawa, and Montreal.

Other regional Ontario airports include:

- London International Airport (YXU, 519/452-4015, www.londonairport.on.ca)
- Windsor International Airport (YQG, 519/969-2430, www.yqg.ca)
- Greater Sudbury Airport (YSB, 705/693-2514, www.flysudbury.ca)
- Sault Ste. Marie Airport (YAM, 705/779-3031, www.saultairport.com)
- Thunder Bay International Airport (YQT, 807/473-2600, www.tbairport.on.ca)

U.S. Airports

If you're flying to Ontario from the United States, it's worth checking airfares into nearby airports that are just across the U.S. border. Airline taxes are lower in the United States than in Canada, and airfares may be cheaper, too.

For Toronto and the Niagara region, check the **Buffalo-Niagara International Airport** (BUF, 716/630-6000 or 877/359-2642, www.buffaloairport.com). For Windsor and points in southwestern Ontario, look at flying into **Detroit Metro Airport** (DTW, 734/247-7678, www.metroairport.com).

BY TRAIN
VIA Rail

Canada's national rail carrier, VIA Rail (888/842-7245, www.viarail.ca), can take you to Ontario from across the country.

VIA's flagship route, **The Canadian,** crosses Canada from Vancouver to Toronto, via Jasper, Edmonton, Saskatoon, and Winnipeg. If you do the trip nonstop, it takes 3.5 days. There are departures three times a week in each direction.

From Atlantic Canada, **The Ocean** travels overnight from Halifax to Montreal, where you can make connections for Ottawa, Toronto, or other Ontario destinations. The train runs six days a week.

From Montreal to Toronto, VIA Rail runs several trains a day in each direction; depending on the train and how many stops it makes en route, the trip takes between five and six hours. Between Montreal and Ottawa, a quick two-hour ride, there are also several trains a day.

You can purchase train tickets online, by phone, or in person at most stations. VIA Rail fares are cheaper when you buy your tickets in advance. You'll get the lowest fare if you're willing to buy a nonrefundable ticket at least four days before you plan to travel. Fares are typically lowest from mid-October through May.

Fares also depend on the class of service. On shorter routes, such as Montreal–Toronto, you can choose between economy and business class. The main benefit of business class is that your ticket includes a multicourse meal with cocktails and wine onboard the train; you also get to wait in the more comfortable Panorama lounge, with complimentary drinks and newspapers, in the station. On long-haul routes, like *The Canadian,* your options range from a basic economy seat to several types of sleeping berths and cabins; all the sleeper tickets include meals for the duration of your trip, as well as access to a shower room and an observation car.

VIA Rail periodically runs last-minute specials, offering significantly discounted rates for travel within the upcoming weeks. If you're flexible in your plans, you might be able to snag a great deal. They post the specials on their website. It's worth checking their website,

Toronto's Union Station is the hub of VIA Rail's train network.

© CAROLYN B. HELLER

signing up for their newsletter, or following them on Twitter if you're planning a lot of train travel, because you can often learn about other sales and discount offers, as well.

VIA Rail sells several different rail passes that are good for multiple trips during a specified period. The Ontario–Quebec **Canrailpass** (adults $347–479, seniors, students, and kids 2 and older $312–431) is valid for seven one-way trips within a 10-day period along the Windsor–Toronto–Quebec City route. VIA also sells systemwide Canrailpasses, good for seven one-way trips within a 21-day period, anywhere in Canada. The prices for the systemwide passes vary by the season, with significantly higher fares between June 1 and October 15 (adults $969–1,114, seniors, students, and kids 2 and older $872–1,003) than from October 16 through May 31 (adults $606–667, seniors, students, and kids 2 and older $545–627). The Canrailpasses are good for economy-class travel only.

Amtrak

From the United States, American rail carrier Amtrak (800/872-7245, www.amtrak.com) has limited service directly into Ontario, and most routes involve a lengthy layover. The one exception is the train between New York City and Niagara Falls or Toronto, the **Maple Leaf,** which makes the 12.5-hour trip between New York City and Toronto daily, stopping in Niagara Falls along the way.

From Chicago and U.S. points farther west, or from Boston and other northeastern U.S. cities, there's no direct rail service to Toronto or anywhere else in Ontario. Coming from the west, you could take the Amtrak **Wolvervine** train from Chicago to Detroit, where you can cross the border to Windsor to continue your travels or transfer to the Toronto-bound VIA Rail train. Alternatively, you can take the Amtrak **Lake Shore Limited** from Chicago to Buffalo, where you can change to the Maple Leaf or catch a bus on to Toronto.

If you're starting your trip in Boston, you can catch the **Lake Shore Limited** westbound to Buffalo and transfer there, or go first to New York City and change to the Maple Leaf. Unless you're a real rail buff (or you're coming from New York), flying or even taking the bus will be more efficient.

BY BUS
Megabus

Megabus (705/748-6411 or 800/461-7661, www.megabus.com) has some of the best fares and service to Toronto from Montreal and from the eastern United States, including New York City, Syracuse (New York), Washington (D.C.), Baltimore, Philadelphia, and Pittsburgh. They can also take you to Kingston (from Montreal) and Niagara Falls (from New York City). On some routes, they periodically offer one-way sale fares as low as $1.50, so check their website, particularly if you're flexible in your travel dates.

Note that Megabus allows passengers to travel with only one piece of luggage weighing less than 23 kilograms (50 pounds), as well as one small hand baggage item. There's no option to check additional bags; you'll just be turned away.

Greyhound

Greyhound (www.greyhound.ca) can take you to Toronto from many Canadian and U.S. cities, although you'll frequently have to change buses along the way. They run frequent buses between Montreal and Ottawa, though you'll need to change in Ottawa if you're going on to Toronto. If you're traveling to Ontario from Quebec City, Halifax, and points in eastern Canada, you have to transfer in Montreal. Greyhound's long-haul western routes travel to Ontario from Calgary and Winnipeg, stopping in Thunder Bay, Sault Ste. Marie, Sudbury, and Toronto. From Vancouver, you have to change buses in Calgary. From Edmonton, you transfer in either Calgary or Winnipeg.

From the United States, Greyhound runs direct buses to Toronto from New York City (with stops in Syracuse and Buffalo) and Detroit (stopping in Windsor and London). To reach Toronto from Boston, Philadelphia, or Washington, D.C., you need to transfer in New York City. From Chicago, the fastest route has a transfer in Detroit.

Detroit-Windsor Tunnel Bus

If you're crossing the border between Michigan and southwestern Ontario, you can take the Detroit-Windsor Tunnel Bus(www.citywindsor. ca). Assuming no traffic or border delays, the trip takes only 15 minutes. The buses begin running at 5:30 A.M. (8 A.M. on Sundays) and continue until 12:30 or 1 A.M. (midnight on Sundays).

BY CAR
Required Documents for Drivers

If you have a valid driver's license from your home country, that license will be valid in Canada for three months. If you're driving over the border from the United States, bring the car's registration forms and proof of insurance. Either carry the insurance policy itself or get a free Canadian Non-Resident Insurance Card from your insurance agent. You must have a minimum of $200,000 combined liability insurance in Ontario.

If you're planning to rent a car in the United States and drive it across the border, confirm with your car rental company in advance that you're allowed to drive out of the country. Make sure you have a copy of the rental contract handy at the border crossing.

If you're driving a borrowed car across the border, bring a letter of permission signed by the owner, even if the owner is a family member. The border agents may not ask for the letter, but you can save some hassles if you have it on hand.

Ontario Land Border Crossings

You can cross the border between the United States and Canada at a number of Ontario points.

In the Niagara Falls area, four bridges cross the Niagara River, which separates Ontario from New York State: the **Peace Bridge** (www. peacebridge.com), linking Fort Erie, Ontario, with I-190 from the Buffalo area; the **Rainbow Bridge** (www.niagarafallsbridges.com), which directly links Niagara Falls, Ontario, with Niagara Falls, New York; the **Whirlpool Bridge** (www.niagarafallsbridges.com), north of the Rainbow Bridge, available to NEXUS cardholders only; and the **Queenston-Lewiston Bridge** (www.niagarafallsbridges.com) between Queenston, Ontario, and Lewiston, New York.

Between Michigan and southwestern Ontario, you can cross from Detroit to Windsor via the **Ambassador Bridge** or the **Detroit-Windsor Tunnel.** The **Blue Water Bridge** (www.bwba.org) connects Port Huron, Michigan, and Sarnia, Ontario.

The **International Bridge** connects the cities of Sault Ste. Marie, Michigan and Sault Ste. Marie, Ontario.

Three international bridges cross the St. Lawrence River between New York State and eastern Ontario. The **Thousand Islands Bridge** (www.tibridge.com) is a major crossing linking I-81 with Highway 401, the **Ogdensburg-Prescott International Bridge** (www.ogdensport.com) traverses between Ogdensburg (N.Y.) and Prescott (ON), and the **Seaway International Bridge** (www.sibc.ca) links Massena (N.Y.) and Cornwall (ON).

Getting Around

BY AIR

Ontario covers a lot of ground, and when you're traveling from one end to the other, or if your time is limited, you might consider internal flights within the province. On shorter, well-traveled routes, like Toronto to Ottawa (or Montreal), airfares are often priced competitively with the train or bus. On longer routes or in more remote areas, airfares tend to be quite high, so you'll pay for the convenience of flying.

Toronto is the hub for flights within Ontario, although Ottawa has convenient air connections, as well. **Air Canada Jazz** (888/247-2262, www.flyjazz.ca), Air Canada's regional affiliate, flies between Toronto and Ottawa, Kingston, Windsor, North Bay, Sudbury, Timmins, Sault Ste. Marie, and Thunder Bay. Ontario routes on **WestJet** (800/538-5696, www.westjet.com) include Toronto to Ottawa and Toronto to Thunder Bay. Within Ontario, **Porter Airways** (888/619-8622, www.flyporter.com) flies between Toronto and Ottawa, Windsor, Sudbury, Sault Ste. Marie, and Thunder Bay. Porter Airways is based at the City Centre airport, on the Toronto Islands.

Bearskin Airlines (800/465-2327, www.bearskinairlines.com) flies across northern Ontario, including service to Ottawa, Sudbury, Sault Ste. Marie, and Thunder Bay. **Air Creebec** (819/825-8375 or 800/567-6567, www.air-creebec.ca) can take you between Timmins, Moosonee, and points farther north.

BY TRAIN

VIA Rail (888/842-7245, www.viarail.ca) runs trains across Southern Ontario. You can travel between Toronto and Niagara Falls, Stratford, St. Marys, London, Windsor, and Sarnia. In the eastern part of the province, VIA Rail trains connect Ottawa, Brockville, Kingston, Belleville, Cobourg, and Toronto.

Ontario Northland (800/461-8558, www.ontarionorthland.ca) runs trains between Toronto and various points in Northern Ontario, including service to the Muskoka region (Gravenhurst, Bracebridge, Huntsville), North Bay, Temagami, and Cochrane, and continuing north to Hearst. Ontario Northland also operates the *Polar Bear Express Train* from Cochrane north to Moosonee.

GO Transit (416/869-3200 or 888/438-6646, www.gotransit.com) operates a network of commuter trains between Toronto and the surrounding communities, including Oakville, Burlington, Hamilton, Brampton, Barrie, Richmond Hill, and Markham. GO provides seasonal service to Niagara Falls, as well, running weekends and holidays from late May through mid-October, also operating as the Niagara **bike train,** which has a bike rack–equipped baggage car with bike racks.

BY BUS

Buses connect most Ontario cities and smaller communities. When you're comparing the bus to the train on routes that have both options, consider more than just the price. The train is more comfortable, since you have more space and you can walk around. However, the buses on some routes run more frequently, or you may find the schedule more convenient.

Megabus (www.megabus.com) has direct buses and great prices between Toronto and Niagara Falls and between Toronto and Kingston, with one-way sale fares sometimes going as low as $1.50.

Greyhound (www.greyhound.ca) has the most extensive bus service across Ontario. They operate regular buses between Toronto and Kitchener, Waterloo, Stratford, London, Windsor, Owen Sound, Collingwood, Blue Mountain, Barrie, Sudbury, and Sault Ste. Marie. Greyhound also runs most of the bus routes in and out of Ottawa, including service to Toronto, Kingston, North Bay, and Sudbury. You can also take Greyhound buses between Sudbury, Sault Ste. Marie, and Thunder Bay.

To travel between Toronto and the Muskoka Lakes or to Ontario towns farther north, **Ontario Northland** (www.ontarionorthland.ca) has regular bus service. Check their schedules if you're going to Barrie, Gravenhurst, Bracebridge, Huntsville, Parry Sound, Sudbury, North Bay, Temagami, Timmins, or Cochrane.

Look for **Coach Canada** (www.coach-canada.com) routes in the Niagara region, Hamilton, Kitchener-Waterloo, Kingston, and other points in Eastern Ontario. **GO Transit buses** (www.gotransit.com) connect Toronto with surrounding suburbs and towns, including Kitchener, Waterloo, and Hamilton.

BY CAR

If most of your time in Ontario will be in Toronto, Ottawa, or Niagara Falls, you can get around without a car. It's possible to travel to other destinations car-free, and we've detailed car-free options throughout the book. However, for the greatest flexibility in exploring the province, either drive your own vehicle or rent one along the way.

To get information about highway conditions, including winter weather conditions and summer construction status, phone the Ontario Ministry of Transportation's toll-free 24-hour road conditions line (800/268-4686).

Car Rentals

The major North American car rental companies have outlets at Toronto's Pearson airport, at Ottawa International Airport, and at regional airports around the province. A number of smaller car rental agencies also have offices near the Toronto airport; it's worth comparing their rates to other major companies.

Ontario's cities and most small towns also have at least one or two car rental offices in town. **Enterprise** (800/261-7331, www.enterpriserentacar.ca) has an extensive network of rental offices around Ontario; both **National** (877/222-9058, www.nationalcar.ca) and **Discount Car Rentals** (800/263-2355, www.discountcar.com) have offices in many towns, as well.

You can often save money by renting a car at an in-town location rather than at the airport,

Watch out for Mennonite buggies as you drive around rural Ontario.
© CAROLYN B. HELLER

particularly in Toronto. If you're flying into or out of Pearson, however, you'll need to factor in the additional time and cost of getting to/from the airport.

Another strategy that can sometimes save money on car rentals is to take the bus or train from Toronto to your next destination and rent a car from there. Toronto rates are frequently higher than those in nearby cities such as Kitchener or Hamilton.

Most agencies provide discounts for weekly rentals and additional discounts for rentals of a month or more. Some also offer discounts for members of the Canadian Automobile Association (CAA) or American Automobile Association (AAA).

Driving

Ontario law requires adults and children weighing over 18 kilograms (40 pounds) to wear seat belts with both lap and shoulder belts. Toddlers who weigh 9–18 kilograms (20–40 pounds) must ride in a forward-facing child safety seat, and infants weighing up to 9 kilograms (20 pounds) must travel in a rear-facing infant safety seat.

Most Ontario highways have a speed limit of 100 km/h (62 mph). On the Trans-Canada Highway, the speed limit is typically 90 km/h (56 mph), and country roads have a speed limit of 80 km/h (50 mph).

You can make a right turn at a red light in Ontario (as long as you stop and make sure it's clear), unless it's otherwise posted. Hitchhiking is not allowed on major (controlled access) highways, such as Highway 401. Radar detectors are illegal in Ontario. If the police stop you, officers can confiscate a radar device—and fine you—even if the device is turned off.

Emergency Services

Dial 911 to reach the police, ambulance, or other emergency service if you have an automobile accident. Or phone the Ontario Provincial Police emergency line (888/310-1122). If you're involved in a car accident where someone is injured or where the estimated property damage is more than $1,000, Ontario law requires you to contact the police and stay at the scene of the accident until the police officers give you the okay to move on.

BY BOAT
Great Lakes Ferries

The **Owen Sound Transportation Company** (www.ontarioferries.com) operates two ferry services on Ontario's Great Lakes. Between April and mid-December, ferries run to Pelee Island, Ontario's southernmost point, from Leamington or Kingsville in Southwestern Ontario.

To travel from Toronto or other points in Southern Ontario to Manitoulin Island, the quickest route is to take the M.S. *Chi-Cheemaun* Ferry from Tobermory at the tip of the Bruce Peninsula. The ferry runs mid-May to mid-October.

National Park Ferries

Ontario's Georgian Bay Islands National Park is composed entirely of islands, so you can reach the park only by water. Parks Canada (www.pc.gc.ca) runs the *DayTripper* boat service from the town of Honey Harbour to the park's Beausoleil Island from late spring through early fall.

One of only three national marine conservation areas in Canada, Fathom Five National Marine Park (www.pc.gc.ca) includes 22 islands in Georgian Bay off the northern end of the Bruce Peninsula. Access to the park is by boat from the town of Tobermory. Parks Canada has partnered with a private company, **Blue Heron Tours** (www.blueheronco.com), which offers several types of boat trips to the park's Flowerpot Island from mid-May through mid-October.

Visas and Officialdom

ENTERING CANADA

For the most up-to-date requirements for visitors coming to Canada, visit **Citizenship and Immigration Canada** (CIC, www.cic.gc.ca).

Important note: If you have a criminal record, including misdemeanors or Driving While Impaired (DWI), no matter how long ago, you can be prohibited from entering Canada, unless you obtain a special waiver well in advance of your trip. Refer to the "Application forms and guides" section of the CIC website for additional information.

U.S. Citizens

In the past, tourists could cross the border between the United States and Canada simply by providing some proof of citizenship—a birth certificate, a driver's license, or an expired passport. In 2008, when the United States implemented a new law called the Western Hemisphere Travel Initiative (WHTI), the rules changed. The WHTI requires all travelers to present a valid passport or other "approved document" when entering the United States from within the Western Hemisphere, including Canada. So while you technically don't need a passport to enter Canada, without one the United States won't let you back in, which means that Canada won't admit you in the first place. The bottom line: you need a valid passport to enter Canada.

If you are driving over the border, a valid U.S. Passport Card can be used instead of a passport. However, passport cards are not allowed if you're arriving by air. You can get more information about a U.S. Passport Card from the U.S. State Department (www.travel. state.gov).

Several U.S. states and Canadian provinces have begun issuing Enhanced Drivers Licenses that can be used as an alternative to a passport or passport card when you're crossing a land border; they're not valid for air travel. As of this writing, U.S. citizens who are residents of Michigan, New York, Vermont, and Washington can apply for Enhanced Drivers Licenses. The WHTI website (www.getyouhome.gov) has more details about Enhanced Drivers Licenses and other border-crossing documents.

Citizens of the United States do not need a visa to visit Canada for stays of less than six months.

Citizens of Other Countries

All other foreign visitors to Canada must have a valid passport, and depending on your nationality, you may also need a visitor visa. British, Australian, and New Zealand citizens don't require a visa, nor do citizens of many European nations. Check with Citizenship and Immigration Canada (CIC, www.cic.gc.ca) to confirm what documents you require.

CUSTOMS

Visitors to Canada can bring a reasonable amount of "personal baggage," including clothing, camping and sports equipment, cameras, and computers for personal use.

As long as you're at least 19 years old, you can bring in a limited amount of alcoholic beverages duty- and tax-free: up to 1.5 liters of wine or 1.14 liters of other alcohol. Visitors are also allowed to bring in up to 200 cigarettes or 50 cigars.

You can bring gifts for friends or family into Canada duty- and tax-free as long as each gift is valued at $60 or less; if it's worth more, you'll have to pay duty and taxes on the excess amount. Alcohol and tobacco don't count as "gifts." They're subject to the limits above, even if you're bringing them to give as gifts.

Travelers must declare all food, plants, or animals they bring into Canada. In general, you're allowed to bring food for personal use, although there are some restrictions on fresh fruits, vegetables, meats, and dairy products. You can generally bring your pet cat or dog, too, subject to certain restrictions. Get the latest information from the Canadian government's Be Aware and Declare website (www. beaware.gc.ca).

In general, visitors cannot bring weapons into Canada. You're specifically prohibited from bringing automatic weapons, sawed-off rifles or shotguns, most handguns, and semiautomatic weapons into Canada. There are some exceptions for hunters, and all visitors must declare any firearms in writing. Check the detailed requirements with the Canada Border Services Agency (www.cbsa.gc.ca).

Recreation

NATIONAL PARKS

Ontario is home to five of Canada's national parks: Bruce Peninsula National Park, known for its spectacular rock formations, beaches, and wide range of hiking trails; Georgian Bay Islands National Park, comprising 63 islands large and small; Point Pelee National Park, marking the southernmost point on the Canadian mainland; St. Lawrence Islands National Park, in Eastern Ontario; and Pukaskwa National Park on Lake Superior's north shore.

The province also has two national marine conservation areas: Fathom Five National Marine Park and the Lake Superior National Marine Conservation Area.

Parks Canada (888/773-8888, www.pc.gc.ca) is the agency responsible for the country's national parks. You can purchase an annual **Parks Canada Discovery Pass** (adults $67.70, seniors $57.90, kids 6–16 $33.30, family/group $136.40), valid at more than 100 national parks, national marine conservation areas, and national historic sites across the country. The family/group pass is good for up to seven people arriving together at a particular site. If you're going to visit several parks and historic sites during your travels, a Discovery Pass can be a good value.

Tip: If you purchase your Discovery Pass at the beginning of a month, your pass will be valid for 13 months, rather than 12, since the pass expires on the last day of the month in which you bought it. That is, if you purchase your pass on March 1, 2013, it will be valid until March 31, 2014.

You can buy a Discovery Pass online or by phone from Parks Canada or in person at any national park or historic site. If you've already bought a day pass to a park or historic site within the past 30 days, you can credit the price of that ticket toward a Discovery Pass.

When you're spending several days in just one park, you're better off purchasing a **seasonal pass** for that particular park. For example, at the Bruce Peninsula National Park, a day pass is $11.70 per vehicle, and a seasonal pass is $49 per vehicle, so the season pass would save you money if you were staying five days or more.

PROVINCIAL PARKS

Ontario also has more than 300 provincially managed outdoor spaces, run by **Ontario Parks** (www.ontarioparks.com). Among the province's most popular parks are Algonquin Provincial Park in "Cottage Country" near Huntsville, Killarney on Georgian Bay, Lake Superior north of Sault Ste. Marie, Wasaga Beach near Collingwood, and The Pinery, on Lake Huron outside of Grand Bend. It's hard to narrow down more favorite parks, but others worth exploring include Awenda, near Midland on Georgian Bay; Killbear, also on Georgian Bay, north of Parry Sound; Sauble Falls, on the Bruce Peninsula; Bonnechere in the Ottawa Valley; and Sleeping Giant, near Thunder Bay.

Daily park entrance fees vary from $10.75 to $19.25 per vehicle. If you're going to visit several provincial parks, or if you're going to return to the same park over multiple days, consider purchasing a **provincial park pass** (800/668-9938, www.ontarioparks.com). You can buy a seasonal pass good for unlimited park visits during either the summer (Apr.–Nov., $107.50) or the winter (Dec.–Mar., $70), or an annual pass ($150.50) valid for the entire year. Buy park passes online, by phone, or at most provincial parks.

HIKING

Ontario has plenty of opportunities to hit the trail, whether you're looking to tromp around in the woods or along the lake for an afternoon or set off on a multiday hiking adventure. The **Ontario Trails Council** (www.ontariotrails.on.ca) provides information about trails province-wide.

One of Canada's iconic outdoor experiences is a hike along Ontario's **Bruce Trail** (www.bruce-trail.org), an 845-kilometer (525-mile) route that extends from the Niagara region to the tip of the Bruce Peninsula. While some hikers do the entire trail straight through, far more "end to end" hikers complete the trail in a series of shorter excursions over several months or years. And many more hikers use the trail only for day hiking.

The world's longest network of trails, the **Trans-Canada Trail** (www.tctrail.ca) extends—as its name suggests—across the country. Some sections of the trail are urban walks, like parts of Ottawa's **Capital Pathway** (www.canadascapital.gc.ca) or Toronto's **Waterfront Trail** (www.waterfronttrail.org). Others, like the **Voyageur Trail** (www.voyageurtrail.ca) in Northern Ontario, are wilderness routes. Check the Trans-Canada Trail website for more hike ideas.

CYCLING AND MOUNTAIN BIKING

Ontario has an extensive network of trails for both road cycling and mountain biking. Some regions of the province, particularly along the lakeshores, are fairly flat. Inland, it's not the Rockies, but you'll find enough rolling hills to get your heart pumping. The **Welcome Cyclists Network** (www.welcomecyclists.ca) can give you more ideas about where to cycle around the province.

The Niagara region is an excellent spot for cyclists, even if you're a not a hard-core long-distance rider. The **Greater Niagara Circle Route** (www.niagararegion.ca), with more than 140 kilometers (87 miles) of (mostly) paved cycling trails, loops around the Niagara Peninsula. You can bring your bike from Toronto on the seasonal **bike train,** run by GO Transit (www.gotransit.com).

Running nearly 800 kilometers (500 miles), the **Lake Ontario Waterfront Trail** follows the Lake Ontario and St. Lawrence River banks, between the Niagara region and the Quebec border. Another long-distance route, the 450-kilometer (280-mile) mixed-use **Central Ontario Loop Trail** (www.looptrail.com), circles from Port Hope on Lake Ontario, through Peterborough and the Kawarthas region, north to Haliburton and Bancroft. Many sections of the **Trans-Canada Trail** (www.tctrail.ca) are also open to bikers.

Hardwood Ski and Bike (www.hardwoodhills.ca), in the hills northeast of Barrie, ha 80 kilometers (50 miles) of mountain bik trails. Some of Ontario's downhill ski resort become mountain bike meccas in summer, including **Blue Mountain** (www.bluemountain. ca), near Collingwood.

WATER SPORTS

Surrounded by four of the five Great Lakes with over 200,000 inland lakes large and small Ontario is a popular destination for all type of water sports.

You can go **swimming** in most of thes lakes, although the water, particularly in th Great Lakes, can be quite chilly. Pollution o increased bacteria levels can also close beache temporarily. The **Blue Flag** program (www. blueflag.org) assesses the environmental safet of participating beaches, so swim when the blu flag is flying; their website also lists Ontario' approved Blue Flag beaches.

Ontario is a hugely popular destination fo **canoeing** and **kayaking,** whether you want t paddle around a lake for an hour or two or embark on a multiday expedition. The most popula destinations include Algonquin Provincial Park Killarney Provincial Park, and Temagami.

For **whitewater rafting,** head for the Ottaw River region, west of Ottawa. For **scuba diving** the Fathom Five National Marine Conservatio Area, off the Bruce Peninsula, has some of th finest diving in the north.

Ontario may not have oceans or palm trees but yes, you can go **surfing.** Lake Superio routinely sees waves of 3 to 4.5 meters (10 t 15 feet) that bring out hardy surfers and thei boards. Even in midsummer, it's critical to pre pare for the cold, though, with thick wetsuits gloves, hoods, and booties. Thunder Bay is good place to start your surfing adventure.

WINTER SPORTS

Oh, yes, Ontario has plenty of winter weather so if you like to get outdoors, you'll have plent of opportunities for winter sports.

In winter, you can **ice-skate** almost any where in Ontario. Practically every city o town has a rink or a frozen pond where you can strap on your skates. But the best place to skate is on Ottawa's Rideau Canal, which becomes the world's longest rink.

Compared to the snow resorts in the mountains of Western Canada, Ontario's **ski and snowboard** spots are much smaller and more modest. But there are plenty of places where you can schuss down the mountain that are just a short distance from either Toronto or Ottawa. The province's largest ski area is in the Blue Mountain Resort, near Collingwood. Other downhill destinations include Horseshoe Resort near Barrie, or Calabogie Peaks and Mount Pakenham near Ottawa.

While Ontario's rolling hills may seem small for downhill skiing or snowboarding, they offer excellent terrain for **cross-country skiing** or **snowshoeing.** A number of the provincial parks remain open in winter for skiers and snowshoers, including Algonquin, Arrowhead (near Huntsville), Awenda (outside of Midland), Killarney (between Parry Sound and Sudbury), The Pinery (on Lake Huron), and Wasaga Beach (near Collingwood). Gatineau Park, near Ottawa, is also a popular Nordic ski destination.

If you ever wanted to learn about **dogsledding** and lead your own team of dogs, you can give it a try in Ontario. Several outfitters offer dogsledding excursions in and around Algonquin Provincial Park, as does Wolf Within Adventures in Temagami.

Accommodations and Food

Room prices are listed during high season—generally May or June through September or October, except at the ski resorts or other winter destinations, when high season typically runs from late December through February or March. Even within that time period, rates can fluctuate significantly, depending on the lodging's occupancy, nearby special events, and even the weather, so check current rates before making your plans. You'll need to add the 13 percent H.S.T. (harmonized sales tax) to the listed prices.

In Ontario's cities, especially Toronto and Ottawa, accommodation prices tend to be highest midweek when vacationers are competing for lodging space with business travelers. Hotels catering to road warriors will often discount their rates Friday through Sunday. Conversely, in areas that are primarily tourist destinations, including Niagara Falls, the Bruce Peninsula, Georgian Bay, Prince Edward County, and any of the national or provincial parks, weekends are busiest, and you might find lower lodging prices and more availability between Sunday and Thursday.

In most of the province, you'll save money on lodging by visiting in winter. A room for a midwinter weekend in Toronto may cost as much as 50 percent less than that same accommodation in July. However, outside the urban areas, since many attractions close from mid-October through mid-May, accommodations may shut down, as well.

ACCOMMODATIONS
Cottage Rentals and Resorts

Throughout Ontario, going to "the cottage" is a long-established summer ritual. Even if you're not fortunate enough to own a country getaway or have friends or family willing to invite you to their cottage, you can still join the throngs of summer cottagers. Many cottages are available for summer rentals, and cottage resorts—essentially a hotel where you sleep in a cottage but have hotel services like a dining room, watersports, and organized activities for the kids—are also popular. Cottages frequently rent for a minimum of a week, at least in summer, while you can usually book shorter stays at cottage resorts. Weekly rentals most often run Saturday to Saturday.

The Muskoka region north of Toronto is often known simply as "Cottage Country," where Huntsville, Bracebridge, Gravenhurst,

© CAROLYN B. HELLER

Ontario offers a wide range of accommodations.

and the surrounding communities are all magnets for cottagers. You'll also find cottages and cottage resorts around Georgian Bay, along Lake Huron, in the Kawarthas, and pretty much anywhere that there are lakes and woods.

If you're renting a cottage, ask what's included and what's nearby: Do you need to supply your own linens and towels? What appliances—stove, oven, dishwasher, washing machine, clothes dryer—does the cottage have? What types of beds are in each bedroom? Is there a patio or deck? A barbecue? Internet access? A TV? DVD player? Is the cottage on a main road, or at the end of a quiet lane? How far is the nearest beach? Where's the closest grocery store?

Start your hunt for a cottage on the Ontario Tourism website (www.ontariotravel.net), which has a cottage search function where you can search by area, time period, and a range of amenities. Tourism offices and visitors bureaus in most regions can also provide information about cottage rentals in their vicinity.

Bed-and-Breakfasts

Ontario has bed-and-breakfast accommodations in major cities, smaller towns, and out in the country. Some are upscale and modern, with private baths and high-tech amenities like flat-screen TVs, iPod docks, and espresso machines. Others are homey but more modest—like staying with your aunt and uncle, where the bathroom is down the hall and you get a bed and a morning meal but not much else.

If a room has an "en suite" bath, it's "in your suite," that is, it's inside your room, for your own use. A "private" bath can sometimes be en suite, but the term often refers to a bathroom that's outside of your room but reserved for you only; you might have to walk down the hall, but you won't have to share. A "shared" bath is just that: a bathroom used by guests of more than one room. Ask how many guest rooms share each bath; when there are two bathrooms for three guest rooms, you're less likely to have to wait than when six rooms take turns for a single bath.

Wireless Internet access is increasingly common at Ontario B&Bs, and it's generally included in the rates, but always ask if Wi-Fi is important to you. Some B&Bs will have a computer for guest use; again, ask if that's something you need. Outside of major cities, most B&Bs have parking available. In the cities, they may not, or there may be a parking fee.

Remember that in a bed-and-breakfast, you're usually a guest in the owner's home. Many people enjoy staying at B&Bs, where they can chat with the owner and meet other guests over a cup of coffee or breakfast. Most owners will respect your privacy, but they're also your hosts, who can make recommendations about things to see and do nearby.

Hostels

If your vision of a "youth hostel" includes crowded, run-down dormitories filled with unwashed backpackers, it may be time to update your perception. Hostels do still tend to draw younger people, but older travelers and families have discovered the benefits of hostel travel, too.

Some hostels, like Toronto's Planet Traveler, are very modern and very wired—with free Wi-Fi, phone booths where you can make calls via skype or other Internet phone services, even lockers with electrical outlets to plug in your laptop or phone charger. While others may not be as well outfitted, Internet access (usually Wi-Fi) is standard, as are shared kitchens, laundry facilities, and common areas for lounging and meeting other guests. Hostels often organize local activities, from pub crawls to city tours, to acquaint you with the area and with other travelers.

While the standard hostel accommodation is a shared dorm with bunk beds and shared bathrooms, accommodating anywhere from four to 10 (or more) travelers, there are lots of variations. Dorms can be female-only, male-only, or mixed, so ask if you have a preference. Many hostels now offer more "deluxe" rooms that you share with only two or three other people; you're still not getting hotel amenities, but you are getting a little more space. Many have private rooms (with a double bed or two twins) or family rooms (where you share with your family members but no one else), as well. For two or more travelers sharing a room, hostel prices can

sometimes approach those of bed-and-breakfasts or lower-end hotels, so shop around.

Most hostels no longer require you to bring a sleeping bag or provide your own bedding. In fact, to prevent bedbug infestation, the majority now prohibit travelers from bringing in their own linens. Hostels will generally supply sheets, a blanket, and a towel.

Many Canadian hostels are affiliated with **Hostelling International** (www.hihostels.com) and offer discounts to HI members. Not only do you get discounts on hostel stays, but you're also eligible for 25 percent off Greyhound bus travel within Canada. Ontario hostels also provide members with discounts on some tours or museum admissions.

You typically buy a membership from your home country's HI association, which you can do online. For Canadian citizens and residents, **Hostelling International-Canada** (613/237-7884 or 800/663-5777, www.hihostels.ca) sells adult memberships, valid for two years, for $35; junior memberships, for kids under 18, are free. At **Hostelling International-USA** (301/495-1240, www.hiusa.org), memberships are valid for one year for adults (US$28), seniors 55 and older (US$18), and youth (free). Other international hostel organizations include **YHA England and Wales** (www.yha.org.uk), **Fédération Unie des Auberges de Jeunesse** (France; www.fuaj.org), **YHA Australia** (www.yha.com.au), and **Youth Hostels Association of New Zealand** (www.yha.co.nz). Get a complete list of international chapters from Hostelling International (www.hihostels.com).

University Residences

You don't have to be a student or professor to stay in a university residence. Many Ontario universities open their residence halls to visitors during the summer months (generally mid-May through August). Accommodations range from basic dormitory rooms with shared baths down the hall to suites with kitchen facilities that would be comfortable for families. Some residence halls provide breakfast, some give you an option to eat at campus dining facilities, while at others, you're on your own for meals.

Staying in residence is best for independent travelers, since you don't have a hotel staff available to help you out, and you won't get room service or other hotel-style frills. The advantage? The cost can be significantly lower than for nearby hotel accommodations, and the locations are often quite central.

- Hamilton: **McMaster Summer Residences** (http://conference.mcmaster. ca, $56–85.25)

- Kingston: **Queen's University Residence Halls** (613/533-2223, http://eventservices. queensu.ca, $50–60)

- Niagara-on-the-Lake: **Niagara College Residence** (137 Taylor Rd., 905/641-4435 or 877/225-8664, www.stayrcc.com, $70–85)

- Ottawa: **University of Ottawa Residences** (90 University St., 613/562-5771 or 888/564-4545, www.ottawaresidences.com, $42–105); **Carleton University Residences** (Housing and Conference Services, 261 Stormont House, 1125 Colonel By Dr., 613/520-5612, www.carleton.ca, $70–121)

- Toronto: **Massey College Residences** (4 Devonshire Pl., at Hoskin Ave., 416/978-2895, www.masseycollege.ca, $55–90)

- Waterloo: **University of Waterloo Residences** (519/888-4567, www.conferences.uwaterloo.ca, $51–71); **Hotel Laurier** (Wilfred Laurier University, 200 King St. N., 519/884-0710 ext. 2771, www.wlu.ca/ hotel, $45–80)

- London: **Western Bed & Breakfast** (University of Western Ontario, University Dr., 519/661-3476 or 888/661-3545, www. Stayatwestern.com, $48–62)

Camping

In Ontario, you can camp in many of the national and provincial parks, and in private campgrounds. In addition to sites where you can pitch a tent or park your RV, many national and provincial parks have cabins or yurts to rent (the latter are eight-sided tentlike structures modeled after the dwellings of nomads in Mongolia, China, and other regions). You usually have to bring your own sleeping bags and linens, as well as cooking supplies, but you don't have to bring or pitch a tent.

You can camp at four of the five Ontario national parks; there are no individual campgrounds at Point Pelee National Park. At St. Lawrence Islands and Pukaskwa National Parks, campsites are available on a first-come,

LEARN TO CAMP, ONTARIO STYLE

What if you've never been camping, but you've always wanted to give it a try? Or you camped a couple of times as a kid, but don't have the gear you need now?

The **Ontario Parks** agency (www.ontarioparks.com) offers a Learn to Camp program to help get you started on your outdoor adventure. You sign up for a two-day, one-night session, where park staff will teach you the basics, from how to pitch a tent to how to build a campfire. The park provides tents, air mattresses, a camp stove and cooking equipment, firewood, even flashlights; you bring your food, clothes, and other personal items, as well as a sleeping bag or bedding.

The program is offered at certain parks on select dates.

Another get-started-camping option is available at the **Georgian Bay Islands National Park** (705/526-8907, www.pc.gc.ca), which offers an All-Inclusive Camping Experience on select autumn weekends. Park staff provide preassembled tents, with your basic gear, as well as a canoe and kayaks. They'll even cook your dinner on Friday night! You'll need to bring your own sleeping bags and your food for the rest of the weekend, but a park staff person will be on-site to help throughout your stay. Contact the park service for reservations or information.

first-served basis. You can (and should) make campsite reservations if you're planning to camp at the Bruce Peninsula and Georgian Bay Islands National Parks. Book through the **Parks Canada reservation service** (877/737-3783, www.pccamping.ca).

To find a campsite at one of the many campgrounds run by the provincial **Ontario Parks** (888/668-7275, www.ontarioparks.com) agency, search the park reservation website, which not only lists park campgrounds, but also lets you search online for campground availability. For campgrounds that accept reservations, you can book a site up to five months in advance.

For information about Ontario's more than 400 private campgrounds, contact the **Ontario Private Campground Association** (www.campgrounds.org).

FOOD AND DRINK

The "eating local" movement—choosing foods that are grown or produced locally—is sweeping Ontario in a big way. From the biggest cities to many a small town, summer farmers markets have become hugely popular, and many Ontario chefs are sourcing and promoting local products.

The **Ontario Culinary Tourism Alliance** (www.ontarioculinary.com) is a good resource for learning more about the province's foods. **Farmers Market Ontario** (www.farmersmarketsontario.com) lists farmers markets around the province. In the Niagara region, you can get a local food map and information about local products from the **Niagara Culinary Trail** (www.niagaraculinarytrail.com).

While local food is booming, Ontario's long history of immigration has influenced its cuisine, too. Many formerly "foreign" foods are now routine parts of Ontario meals, sometimes adapted to use locally grown ingredients. You'll find the legacy of Italian immigration in many communities, especially in the Niagara region and in Sault Ste. Marie; German and Eastern European fare from Kitchener-Waterloo and St. Jacobs west to Lake Huron and south toward Windsor; and French-Canadian influences in Eastern and Northeastern Ontario and

© CAROLYN B. HELLER

Central and eastern Ontario are maple country.

in the Ottawa region. Multiethnic Toronto has historically Italian, Portuguese, Greek, Indian, and Korean neighborhoods, as well as several "Chinatowns," and across the city you'll find foods from around the globe.

Regional Specialties

Outside of Canada, it's known as "Canadian bacon." Within Canada, the cured pork commonly served for breakfast or in sandwiches is called "back bacon" or **peameal bacon.** Ontario's numerous lakes yield several varieties of fresh fish, including pickerel and perch. It's baked, grilled, or fried up for fish 'n' chips.

Artisanal cheese making is a growing business in Ontario, particularly in Prince Edward County, the Ottawa region, and the region between Kitchener and Lake Huron. Look for Ontario cheeses at farmers markets and specialty cheese shops around the province. One distinctive use of cheese that you'll find both in Ontario's French-Canadian communities and across the country is *poutine,* French fries topped with brown gravy and melted cheese curds. Originally from Quebec, *poutine* may sound unappealing, but its gooey, salty savoriness is surprisingly addicting.

Central and Eastern Ontario is maple country, so you'll find lots of maple products, from syrup to maple butter to taffy. In late winter (usually Mar. and Apr.), you can visit **sugar shacks** that tap the sap from maple trees and produce syrup, although most now are larger commercial operations, rather than little shacks in the woods. Many operate seasonal pancake houses to showcase their maple products. A particular treat is **maple taffy on snow;** hot syrup is poured onto snow, which firms it into a taffy that's rolled on a stick. While late winter is the production season, you can purchase Ontario-made maple syrup at farmers markets and groceries year-round.

In late spring and early summer, you'll find strawberries and rhubarb. As the summer goes on, the markets fill with raspberries, blueberries, and peaches, then grapes, apples, and pears. Look for farms where you can pick your

Artisanal cheesemaking is a growing – and tasty – business in Ontario.

own fruit for the absolute freshest produce (as well as fun for the kids).

Panzarotti are Ontario's version of calzone—think of it as a baked pizza bun. It's a baked dough stuffed with tomato sauce and cheese, often including sausage, peppers, or other toppings typically found on pizza. You'll see plenty of panzarotti in Sault Ste. Marie (which also has excellent pizza) and anywhere there's a large Italian community.

Summer in Ontario is **fruit pie** time, with strawberry, raspberry, blueberry, peach, apple, and other varieties appearing on bakery and farmstand shelves as each fruit comes into season. Year-round, in francophone communities, you might see **tortière,** which is a savory meat pie.

Found in many of Canada's First Nations communities, **bannock** is a biscuit-like bread. It might be baked in an oven or grilled over an open fire.

Beavertails aren't actually the tails of beavers; they're just shaped like them. They're fried slabs of whole-wheat dough topped with cinnamon sugar and a squeeze of lemon (or with all sorts of other ridiculously sweet toppings, like chocolate hazelnut spread or Oreo cookies). They're an Ottawa tradition, but you can now find them in many other parts of Canada and abroad.

If you have only one dessert in Ontario, it should be a **butter tart.** No, it's not a pie shell filled with butter; it's single-serving pastry filled with a gooey mix of brown sugar, butter, and eggs. The dark-sugar custard filling resembles American pecan pie without the nuts, although butter tarts sometimes have pecans or raisins added. You can find butter tarts at bakeries across the province.

Ontario Wines

Ontario is Canada's main wine-producing area, with vineyards and wineries concentrated in several main areas. The largest is the Niagara region, with more than 100 wineries in and around the town of Niagara-on-the-Lake and in the district known as the Twenty Valley, incorporating the towns of Beamsville, Vineland, and Jordan. In Eastern Ontario, Prince Edward County is a growing wine district, and in the southwestern corner of the province is the small wine-producing area known as the Lake Erie North Shore. Most wineries welcome visitors, and you can buy their wines at the winery shops; larger wineries also sell to restaurants and wine stores around the province.

Ontario may be best known for its **ice wine,** a sweet, intense dessert wine that's made from grapes that are allowed to freeze on the vine. The production process is labor-intensive (the frozen grapes must be hand-picked) and very sensitive to temperature variations, which makes ice wine an expensive, if delicious, treat.

The **Wine Council of Ontario** (www.winecountryontario.ca) is a good source of information about Ontario wines and wineries.

Tips for Travelers

OPPORTUNITIES FOR STUDY AND EMPLOYMENT

To go to school or work in Canada, you must apply for and receive a study or work permit *before* you enter the country. The government agency responsible for study and work permits is **Citizenship and Immigration Canada** (www.cic.gc.ca).

For general information about living and working in Canada, refer to **Living Abroad in Canada** (www.livingabroadincanada.com). For specific information about studying and working in Ontario, also see the **Ontario Ministry of Citizenship and Immigration** (www.citizenship.gov.on.ca).

ACCESS FOR TRAVELERS WITH DISABILITIES

Many, but not all, of Ontario's attractions, hotels, restaurants, entertainment venues, and transportation options are accessible to travelers with disabilities. A useful general resource that provides information about accessible travel to and around Canada is the government's **Access to Travel** website (www.accesstotravel.gc.ca). It includes helpful details about transportation between and around Ontario cities and towns, as well as general tips and travel resources.

Persons with Disabilities Online (www.pwd-online.ca) is a Canadian government umbrella website offering resources for people with disabilities. Among other features, it provides the **Persons with Disabilities Accessible Travel Tool,** which lets you search for accessible facilities in particular locations.

Many Ontario provincial parks offer accessible facilities. Most picnic areas, campsites, and park washrooms, as well as some trails, can accommodate wheelchairs and other mobility aids. In many campgrounds, there are larger shower stalls with seats and lower nozzles with hand controls. You can get details on facilities in particular parks from **Ontario Parks** (www.ontarioparks.com).

TRAVELING WITH CHILDREN

Ontario is an extremely family-friendly destination. Not only are there tons of fun things for families to do and lots of special activities and programs for kids, but there are lots of resources to help support traveling families or make travel more affordable.

Many museums and attractions offer free admission for kids under a certain age (often 5 or 6, but sometimes 11 or 12). Many offer discounted family admission rates, which generally include up to two adults and at least two children.

During the summer (late June through August) and during school holiday periods, including Christmas/New Year's (late Dec.–early Jan.) and March break (mid-Mar.), many attractions offer "kids' camps" or other activities for children. Just note that these periods will also be the most crowded times at family-friendly sights.

Kids stay free at some major hotels. Other good lodging options for traveling families, besides the typical chain motels, include suite hotels (in cities) and cottages (in more rural areas), which often provide more space for the money, as well as kitchen facilities where you can prepare your own snacks or meals. Cottage resorts, which offer cottage accommodations as well as the services of a hotel (a dining room, watersports, or other kids' activities), are great fun for families; many specifically target multiple generations traveling together.

Some bed-and-breakfasts don't accept kids, but some do, so always ask. Sometimes innkeepers may allow a family to stay if they don't have other guests or if there's already another family who's booked at the same time. One type of B&B that's typically great for kids is a bed-and-breakfast on a farm. There's usually lots of space for kids to run around, as well as animals to look at; the children may even be able to help with farm chores.

Many Ontario restaurants have "children's menus" with burgers, chicken, sandwiches, or other "nonthreatening" foods. Some will also make smaller portions of regular menu items or prepare a simple pasta dish. Encourage your kids to eat what you're eating, though, since they may surprise you (and themselves!) with a new food that they like.

WOMEN TRAVELING ALONE

Overall, Ontario is a relatively safe destination compared to many spots around the world, and women shouldn't hesitate to travel alone. However, exercise caution wherever you go, and particularly in urban areas, avoid venturing out alone late at night or in the wee hours of the morning. If you are out late on your own, don't walk—take a cab. Take your cues from local women, too; if you don't see other women walking or waiting for the bus, that's a clue that maybe you shouldn't, either.

An excellent resource for women travelers is **Journeywoman** (www.journeywoman.com), a Toronto-based but worldwide website where women travelers can share tips and ask for advice from local women. Another great site for women's travel tips, particularly for solo travelers, is **Wanderlust and Lipstick** (www.wanderlustandlipstick.com).

SENIOR TRAVELERS

The good thing about getting older is that you can often get discounts. Many Ontario attractions, lodgings, and transportation providers offer discounts for seniors. The age of eligibility varies, however; it might be 55, 60, 62, or 65.

For seniors who love the outdoors, Ontario Parks offers discounts at the provincial parks, with reduced rates both for day-use admission and for camping fees.

GAY AND LESBIAN TRAVELERS

Canada is far more welcoming to gay and lesbian travelers than many other destinations. Same-sex marriage is legal in Canada, and Ontario was one of the first provinces to make it permissible, in 2003.

Ontario's largest gay and lesbian community is in Toronto, and the city's annual Pride Week is one of the biggest gay–lesbian pride celebrations in the world. The hub of the community is the Church and Wellesley neighborhood, known as the "Gay Village," although accommodations, restaurants, and other facilities across the city (and indeed across the province) welcome gay travelers. The city also has a newer gay–lesbian neighborhood, dubbed "Queer West," along Ossington Avenue (between Dundas and Queen) and along Queen Street West (between Ossington and Roncesvalles).

Resources for gay and lesbian travel to Ontario include:

- Travel Gay Canada (www.travelgaycanada.com): The country's gay and lesbian tourism association
- TAG Approved (www.tagapproved.com): Gay-friendly hotels and attractions
- Ontario Tourism (www.ontariotravel.net): Search for "LGBT Travel" for information about accommodations, festivals and events, and other travel tips
- Tourism Toronto (www.seetorontonow.com/Visitor/Gay-Community.aspx): Toronto travel tips and resources, including information about same-sex weddings in the city
- The Village Ottawa (www.villageottawa.com): LGBT-friendly businesses and events in the nation's capital.

CONDUCT AND CUSTOMS

Smoking

Smoking is not allowed in any "enclosed public space" in Ontario. That means you can't smoke in restaurants, bars, offices, stores, sports arenas, casinos, theaters, or other entertainment venues. In hotels, you can smoke in your room only if it's a designated smoking room (which

---

ONTARIO HOLIDAYS

Ontario observes all of Canada's national holidays, as well as additional provincial holidays. Banks, post offices, and government offices are typically closed on major holidays; stores may or may not be open. For example, most stores are closed on Christmas Day but reopen for major sales on Boxing Day.

National Holidays

- New Year's Day (Jan. 1)
- Good Friday
- Easter Monday
- Victoria Day (third Monday in May)
- Canada Day (July 1)
- Labour Day (first Monday in September)
- Thanksgiving (second Monday in October)
- Christmas Day (Dec. 25)
- Boxing Day (Dec. 26)

Ontario Provincial Holidays

- Family Day (3rd Monday in February)
- Civic Holiday (1st Monday in August)

are becoming less and less common); smoking is prohibited everywhere else in the hotel.

So where can you smoke? Smoking is permitted on outdoor patios, but only if there's no roof. You can smoke in your car, unless you're traveling with a child who's under 16. And you're still allowed to smoke outdoors on the sidewalk. You must be at least 19 to purchase cigarettes or other tobacco products in Ontario.

Alcohol

The legal drinking age in Ontario is 19. Liquor, wine, and beer are sold in government-run liquor stores. Because the Liquor Control Board of Ontario operates these stores, they're known by the acronym "LCBO." There are separate stores that sell beer called "The Beer Store." Driving under the influence of alcohol or drugs is a criminal offense. The law applies not only to cars, but also to boats, snowmobiles, and all-terrain vehicles. You can immediately lose your driver's license for 90 days if you're found to have a blood-alcohol level of more than 0.8 or if you refuse to take a breathalyzer test.

Tipping

In restaurants, the expected tip is 15 percent, with 18–20 percent for particularly good service. You should also tip around 15 percent in bars and taxis. Give hotel baggage handlers at least a dollar or two for each bag they carry, and tip concierges in proportion to the services they provide; if they've gotten you seats for a sold-out play or reservations at the booked-for-months restaurant, compensate them for their service. Many people also leave tips of at least $5 per night for hotel housekeeping staff.

Etiquette

Canadians have a reputation for being polite, and for the most part, that reputation is well deserved. People generally wait patiently in line to board buses and streetcars and give up their seats on public transit to seniors, pregnant women, and anyone with a disability.

The Canadian Human Rights Act prohibits discrimination on the basis of "race, national or ethnic origin, colour, religion, age, sex, sexual orientation, marital status, family status, disability and conviction for which a pardon has been granted." Discrimination still exists, of course, but most Canadians pride themselves on getting along and try to respect other cultures and customs.

When you enter a Canadian home, you may be expected to remove your shoes. Many bed-and-breakfasts want you to leave your shoes by the front door, as well.

HEALTH AND SAFETY

Travelers should always carry a basic first-aid kit, including bandages, aspirin or other pain reliever, sunscreen, insect repellent, and an antiseptic or antibiotic ointment. You might want to include an ointment or other product to relieve the itching of mosquito bites; if you're prone to allergic reactions, consider packing an antihistamine, as well. If you wear glasses, bring an extra pair. If you take prescription medication, carry a copy of your prescription.

Emergencies

In an emergency, call **911** to reach police, fire, ambulance, or other emergency services. In some remote areas of the province without 911 service, dial 0 and say "This is an emergency" to be transferred to the police. You can also reach the **Ontario Provincial Police emergency line** (888/310-1122).

Healthcare and Insurance

If you become ill or injured while in Ontario, you can go to the nearest hospital emergency room or walk-in health clinic. If you're a resident of another Canadian province, your provincial health plan may not provide health coverage while you're in Ontario. Or if the plan does provide coverage, it may pay only the amount it would pay for the service in your home province, not what you might be billed in Ontario. Either way, before your trip, it's a good idea to purchase supplemental travel health insurance to cover any unexpected medical costs while you're in Ontario.

If you live outside of Canada, make sure that you have health insurance that will cover you and your family in Canada. You will normally have to pay for the service provided in Ontario and then file a claim with your health insurance provider after you return home.

Mosquitoes and Black Flies

Mosquitoes in Ontario may not be a "hazard," but they're surely a major nuisance, particularly from May through August. Try to avoid being outside at dusk or in the early evening when mosquitoes are most active. If you are outside, cover up with long pants and a long-sleeved shirt; don't forget socks, or your feet will be covered with bites. Using an insect repellent is also a good idea; you can get recommendations from a good outdoor store, like Mountain Equipment Corporation.

Black flies are buzzing, biting insects that live in forested areas, particularly in the late spring, and they're a major nuisance. Across much of Ontario, black flies are the worst in May and at least the first half of June; the farther north you go, the later the black fly season. The flies can't bite through clothing, but they can certainly find their way *under* your clothing, especially around your ankles or wrists. Tucking your pants into your socks, while perhaps not the most fashionable solution, will help prevent bites, as will a good insect repellent. Black flies are attracted to darker colors, so wearing lighter hues may help keep them away.

If you're camping, make sure your tent has a screen panel that's not ripped, and *always keep the screen closed*. The kids may whine when you tell them, for the 100th time, to zip the tent fly, but they'll thank you if it keeps the bugs out of the tent! And even if you're staying indoors, make sure the windows have screens. Ceiling fans or window fans that circulate the air around you also make it more difficult for bugs to light.

Information and Services

MONEY

Canada's currency is the dollar, and like its U.S. counterpart, it's divided into 100 cents. Canadian bills include $5, $10, $20, $50, and $100 denominations. Coins include five, 10, and 25 cents, and one and two dollars. The gold-colored one-dollar coin is called the "loonie," for the picture of the loon on its back side. The two-dollar coin is nicknamed the "toonie" (since it's equal to two loonies). Throughout this book, prices are listed in Canadian dollars (unless otherwise specified).

Major credit cards, including Visa, MasterCard, and American Express, are accepted throughout the province, although some smaller establishments may take payment in cash only. You'll find Automated Teller Machines (ATMs)—which Canadian banks call Automated Banking Machines, or ABMs—in almost every town.

Bank of Canada (www.bankofcanada. ca), the Canadian central bank, publishes the official exchange rate between Canadian dollars and other currencies. You can exchange U.S. dollars, Euros, British pounds, Australian dollars, and other major currencies for Canadian dollars at banks across Ontario or at currency exchange dealers in Toronto, Ottawa, and towns near the U.S. border. Most of the Ontario travel information centers around the province can exchange currency. In tourist areas close to the border, like Niagara Falls or the Thousand Islands, some businesses will accept U.S. dollars, although the exchange rate is usually worse than the official rate, and you'll get change back in Canadian funds. You're nearly always better off paying in Canadian currency or using a credit card.

In 2010, Ontario instituted a new 13 percent sales tax, the **H.S.T.**, or harmonized sales tax. Not every purchase a traveler might make is subject to H.S.T., but many are. You don't pay sales tax in Ontario on basic groceries.

COMMUNICATIONS AND MEDIA
Telephone

Across most of Southern and Central Ontario, you must dial the full 10-digit number (the area code plus the seven-digit local number) in order to place a call, even if you're within the same area code. If you're calling from outside Ontario or from a different area code, you must also dial "1" (which is the country code for Canada, the same as in the United States), followed by the 10-digit number.

Toll-free numbers, which you can call for free from a landline and some mobile phones, depending on your plan, begin with the area codes 800, 866, or 877. You must dial "1" before the toll-free number.

If you're going to be making a lot of long-distance phone calls while you're in Ontario, purchasing a pre-paid phone card might save you money. You can also use the cards at the province's dwindling number of public pay phones, which is much easier and cheaper than paying with coins. You can buy phone cards at convenience stores, some drug stores, and many grocery stores.

Cellular phone service is widely available across Ontario, although you may find "dead zones" in more remotes areas.

Internet

Internet access is widely available across Ontario. Ontario's major airports have free Wi-Fi service. VIA Rail offers complimentary Wi-Fi on board most of their trains in the Windsor–Quebec City corridor, which includes service to Windsor, London, Toronto, Kingston, Ottawa, and Montreal. You can access their free Wi-Fi network in major Ontario stations, as well. As of this writing, however, Wi-Fi was not available on the Niagara–Toronto trains.

Most hotels, motels, bed-and-breakfasts, and hostels provide Internet access for guests, and most also have a computer you can use. Larger hotels typically charge a fee for Internet access (either by the hour or by the day), but others include it in the rate; it's always a good idea to ask.

Many coffee shops and cafés have free Wi-Fi, but they expect that you'll purchase at least a cup of coffee or tea before tapping into the network. Some require you to ask for a password.

Some libraries have public Internet access, available free or for a small fee. Tourist information center may also offer free Wi-Fi, or the staff can tell you where you can get online.

As you get out of the cities, you may find it a bit harder to get online, although even in fairly remote areas, many accommodations have Internet access for guests. In rural areas, the signal may be less reliable; sometimes you might be able to get online in the lobby or other public space, but not in your room or cottage.

MAPS AND TOURIST INFORMATION

The best source of information about travel in Ontario (in addition to this book, of course) is **Ontario Travel** (www.ontariotravel.net). Created by the Ontario Tourism Marketing Partnership, an agency of the provincial government, this site provide details about things to see and do all across Ontario, including a calendar of upcoming events.

The **Canadian Tourism Commission** (www.canada.travel) is the government of Canada's official guide to travel across the country and includes information about travel in Ontario.

If you're a member of either the **American Automobile Association** (AAA, www.aaa.com) or the **Canadian Automobile Association** (CAA, www.caa.ca), you can request their free maps of Ontario and its major cities. If you belong to AAA, you can get maps from the CAA, and vice versa.

Ontario Travel Information Centers

The province operates a number of travel information centers that offer travel and tourism information, either by phone or in person. Some are open year-round, while others operate seasonally. The major locations are listed here; you can get a complete list at www.ontariotravel.net.

In Toronto and Central Ontario:

- Toronto (20 Dundas St. W., 416/314-5899, ontariotravel.toronto@ontario.ca)
- Barrie (21 Mapleview Drive East, at Hwy 400, 705/725-7280 or 800/567-1140, ontariotravel.barrie@ontario.ca)

In the Niagara Region:

- Fort Erie (Peace Bridge, 350 Bertie St., 905/871-3505, ontariotravel.forterie@ontario.ca)
- Niagara Falls (Rainbow Bridge, 5355 Stanley Ave., 905/358-3221, ontariotravel.niagarafalls@ontario.ca)
- St. Catharines (Westbound QEW at east end of Garden City Skyway, Niagara-on-the-Lake, 905/684-6354, ontariotravel.stcatharines@ontario.ca)

In Southwestern Ontario:

- Sarnia (Blue Water Bridge, 1455 Venetian Blvd., 519/344-7403, ontariotravel.sarnia@ontario.ca)
- Tilbury (62 Hwy. 401 Eastbound, 519/682-9501, ontariotravel.tilbury@ontario.ca)
- Windsor Park (Detroit/Windsor Tunnel, 110 Park St. E., 519/973-1338, ontariotravel.windsorp@ontario.ca)

In Eastern Ontario:

- Bainsville (22064 North Service Rd., Hwy. 401, at the Ontario/Quebec border, 613/347-3498, ontariotravel.bainsville@ontario.ca)
- Cornwall (Seaway International Bridge, 903 Brookdale Ave., 613/933-2420, ontariotravel.cornwall@ontario.ca)
- Hill Island (700 Hwy. 137, 613/659-2108, ontariotravel.hillisland@ontario.ca, mid-May–Oct.)
- Prescott (1033 Hwy. 16, 613/925-3346, ontariotravel.prescott@ontario.ca, mid-May–Oct.)

In Northwestern Ontario:

- Sault Ste. Marie (Sault Ste. Marie International Bridge, 261 Queen St. W., 705/945-6941, ontariotravel.ssm@ontario.ca)
- Kenora (Hwy. 17, at the Ontario/Manitoba border, 807/468-2495, OntarioTravel.kenora@nlis.ca, mid-May–Oct.)
- Fort Frances (Fort Frances International Bridge, 400 Central Ave., 807/274-7566, ontariotravel.fortfrances@ontario.ca)

Regional Tourism Organizations

Tourism agencies in the regions and major cities around Ontario provide detailed information about their districts:

In Toronto and Central Ontario:

- Tourism Toronto (416/203-2500 or 800/499-2514, www.seetorontonow.com)
- Tourism Hamilton (905/546-2666 or 800/263-8590 www.tourismhamilton.com)

In the Niagara Region:

- Niagara Falls Tourism (905/356-6061 or 800/563-2557, www.niagarafallstourism.com)
- Niagara-on-the-Lake Chamber of Commerce (905/468-1950, www.niagaraonthelake.com)

In Southwestern Ontario:

- Waterloo Regional Tourism Marketing Corporation (519/585-7517 or 877/585-7517, www.explorewaterlooregion.com), including Kitchener-Waterloo, Cambridge, St. Jacobs, and surrounding communities
- Stratford Tourism Alliance (519/271-5140 or 800/561-7926, www.welcometostratford.com)
- Tourism London (519/661-5000 or 800/265-2602, www.londontourism.ca)
- Tourism Windsor, Essex, and Pelee Island (519/255-6530 or 800/265-3633, www.tourismwindsoressex.com)

Around Georgian Bay:

- Bruce Peninsula/County of Bruce Tourism (519/534-5344 or 800/268-3838, www.explorethebruce.com)

- Grey County Tourism (519/376-3265 or 877/733-4739, www.visitgrey.ca), providing information about Owen Sound, Collingwood, and the Blue Mountains
- Muskoka Tourism (800/267-9700, www.discovermuskoka.ca) covering Gravenhurst, Bracebridge, Huntsville, the Muskoka Lakes, and the region surrounding Algonquin Provincial Park
- Georgian Bay Country Tourism (705/746-4213, www.gbcountry.com), providing information about the region from Port Severn to Parry Sound to Killarney
- Rainbow Country Travel Association (705/522-0104 or 800/465-6655, www.rainbowcountry.com), covering Sudbury, Killarney, and other near-north communities

In Eastern Ontario:

- Ottawa Tourism (613/237-5150 or 800/363-4465, www.ottawatourism.ca)
- Prince Edward County Tourism (613/476-2421 or 800/640-4717, www.prince-edward-county.com)
- Tourism Kingston (613/544-2725 or 866/665-3326, www.tourism.kingstoncanada.com)
- 1000 Islands International Tourism Council (800/847-5263, www.visit1000islands.com)

In Northwestern Ontario:

- Algoma Kinniwabi Travel Association (705/254-4293 or 800/263-2546, www.algomacountry.com), including Sault Ste. Marie, Wawa, and Lake Superior's North Shore
- North of Superior Tourism Association (800/265-3951, www.northofsuperior.org), covering Thunder Bay and vicinity

WEIGHTS AND MEASURES

Canada officially uses the metric system. Distances and speed limits are marked in kilometers, gasoline and bottled beverages are sold by the liter, and weights are given in grams or kilograms. Because the country didn't adopt metric units until the 1970s, however, you'll still occasionally see grocery items measured with pounds or ounces, and older folks, who didn't grow up with the metric system, will sometimes use imperial units.

Electrical service in Canada is 120 volts, the same as in the United States, with the same types of plugs.

Ontario has two time zones. Most of the province, including cities as far west as Thunder Bay, is in the Eastern time zone. The westernmost part of the province, on the Manitoba border, is in the Central time zone. Ontario observes daylight savings time. Clocks move forward one hour on the second Sunday in March and turn back one hour on the first Sunday of November.

RESOURCES

Suggested Reading

FICTION

Atwood, Margaret. *Cat's Eye*. Toronto: Mc-Clelland & Stewart, 1988. One of Ontario's most eminent writers, Atwood (www.margaretatwood.ca) has written 13 novels, including this one about a painter who returns to her native Toronto. Atwood has also written numerous works of poetry, short fiction, and nonfiction.

Brand, Dionne. *What We All Long For*. Toronto: A. A. Knopf Canada, 2005. A novel about a young Toronto artist from a Vietnamese immigrant family and several of her friends.

Lansens, Laurie. *Rush Home Road*. Toronto: A. A. Knopf Canada, 2002. Set in the fictional town of Rusholme, an all-black community in southwestern Ontario settled by fugitive slaves, which the author modeled after the village of Buxton, this novel follows descendents of these former slaves in their rural surroundings.

Munro, Alice. *Lives of Girls and Women*. New York: McGraw-Hill, 1973. A collection of linked stories chronicling a young woman's coming-of-age in small-town Ontario.

Shields, Carol. *Unless*. Toronto: Random House Canada, 2002. The eldest daughter of an Ontario novelist becomes a mute panhandler in downtown Toronto. Shields (1935–2003; www.carol-shields.com) wrote several other novels set in Ontario or elsewhere in Canada.

FOOD AND WINE

Ogryzlo, Lynn. *Niagara Cooks: From Farm to Table*. Toronto: Epulum Books, 2008. Part cookbook and part local food guide, this book (www.niagaracooks.ca) features the foods and wines of the Niagara region.

Ogryzlo, Lynn. *Ontario Table: Featuring the Best Food from Across the Province*. Toronto: Epulum Books, 2011. A cookbook and agricultural guide (www.ontariotable.com) that highlights local growers, foods, and wines from around Ontario.

Sanders, Moira, and Elstone, Lori. *The Harrow Fair Cookbook*. Toronto: Whitecap Books, 2011. Recipes, featuring regional produce and products, from southwestern Ontario's Harrow Fair (www.theharrowfaircookbook.com), one of Canada's oldest country fairs.

NONFICTION

Christmas, Jane. *The Pelee Project: One Woman's Escape from Urban Madness*. Toronto: ECW Press, 2002. A Toronto journalist takes a sabbatical on Pelee Island to reevaluate her life and values, learning something about Canadian island life along the way.

Wilkens, Charles. *Walk to New York: A Journey Out of the Wilds of Canada*. Toronto: Viking Canada, 2004. A 50-something author decides to shake up his life by walking 2,200 kilometers (1,300 miles) across Ontario from Thunder Bay to New York City.

TRAVEL

Bogue, Margaret Beattie. *Around the Shores of Lake Superior: A Guide to Historic Sites.* Waterloo, ON: Wilfred Laurier Press, 2007. As the title suggests, this book provides background about historic sites along Lake Superior.

Brown, Ron. *Top 100 Unusual Things to See in Ontario.* Erin, ON: Boston Mills Press, 2005. Author Ron Brown (www.ronbrown.ca) has written more than 20 books about Ontario, including this one about the province's quirkiest attractions. His other recent books include *From Queenston to Kingston: The Hidden Heritage of Lake Ontario's Shoreline* (Toronto: Dundurn Press, 2010) and *The Lake Erie Shore: Ontario's Forgotten South Coast* (Toronto: Dundurn Press, 2009).

Pearen, Shelley. *Exploring Manitoulin.* Toronto: University of Toronto Press, 2001 (3rd edition). Although much of the practical information in this guide to Ontario's Manitoulin Island is dated, it still provides a useful overview of the island's history and culture.

Runtz, Michael. *The Explorer's Guide to Algonquin Park.* Erin, ON: Boston Mills Press, 2008. A detailed guide to Algonquin Provincial Park, one of Ontario's largest protected green spaces.

Internet Resources

GOVERNMENT
Citizenship and Immigration Canada
www.cic.gc.ca
The federal government agency responsible for overseeing visitors and immigrants to Canada, including information about visitor visas, work permits, study permits, and applications for permanent residence.

Government of Ontario
www.ontario.ca
The provincial government website with information for visitors and residents about travel, recreation, money, documents, and more.

ONTARIO
Canada Cool
www.canadacool.com
A website devoted to cool things in Ontario and across Canada, from Toronto-based travel journalist Lucy Izon.

Festival and Events Ontario
www.festivalsandeventsontario.ca
A guide to festivals and special events around the province, including an annual "Top 100 Ontario Festivals" list.

Fun Ontario
www.funontario.com
Publishes a free weekly email about events, festivals, and other activities happening around Ontario during the upcoming weekend.

PARKS
Ontario Parks
www.ontarioparks.com
Information about, and reservations booking service for, Ontario's more than 330 provincial parks.

Parks Canada
www.pc.gc.ca
The federal government agency that manages the country's national parks and national historic sites.

Parks Canada Campground Reservation Service
www.pccamping.ca
Reservations booking service for Canada's national park campgrounds, including those in Ontario.

TRANSPORTATION
Major Airlines
Air Canada
www.aircanada.com

Porter Airlines
www.flyporter.com

Westjet
www.westjet.com

Trains and Buses
Amtrak
www.amtrak.com
U.S. rail carrier that provides train service to Toronto and Niagara Falls from American cities.

Greyhound Bus Lines
www.greyhound.ca
Provides the most extensive network of bus services across Ontario, as well as buses from the eastern United States to Ontario.

Megabus
www.megabus.com
Operates buses between Toronto and Niagara Falls, Kingston, and Montreal, as well as buses between Toronto and the eastern United States, including New York City, Syracuse (N.Y.), Washington (D.C.), Baltimore, Philadelphia, and Pittsburgh.

OC Transpo (Ottawa)
www.octranspo.com
Ottawa's public transit system, including a "Trip Planner" routing feature.

Ontario Northland
www.ontarionorthland.ca
Runs trains and between Toronto and various points in northern Ontario, including service to the Muskoka region and the northeast. Also operates the *Polar Bear Express Train* from Cochrane to Moosonee.

VIA Rail
www.viarail.ca
Canada's national rail system, which operates trains across the country.

Toronto Transit Commission
www.ttc.ca
Toronto's public transit system, including subways, streetcars, and buses. The website includes a "Trip Planner" to help you plan the best route to your destination.

TRAVEL
Canadian Tourism Commission
www.canada.travel
The government of Canada's official guide to travel across the country.

Environment Canada
www.weatheroffice.gc.ca
Provides weather forecasts and historical weather data for more than 150 locations across Ontario (and many more destinations across Canada).

Living Abroad in Canada
www.livingabroadincanada.com
Book and website by author Carolyn B. Heller that provides resources and information about relocating to Canada, including immigration details, work and study permits, housing, education, and jobs.

Ontario Culinary Tourism Alliance
www.ontarioculinary.com
An organization that promotes Ontario's food producers and culinary travel destinations.

Ontario Travel
www.ontariotravel.net
Created by the Ontario Tourism Marketing Partnership, an agency of the provincial government, this website provide details about things to see and do all across Ontario.

Ottawa Tourism
www.ottawatourism.ca
Guide to travel in the nation's capital, Ottawa.

Tourism Niagara
www.tourismniagara.com
Travel information for the Niagara Peninsula, including Niagara Falls, Niagara-on-the-Lake, and the Niagara wine country.

Tourism Toronto
www.seetorontonow.com
A guide to festivals and events, things to see and do, and other travel details in and around the city of Toronto.

Wine Country Ontario
www.winesofontario.org
Annual travel guide to Ontario's wineries, available online and also in print from visitor centers and wineries in the province's main wine-producing regions: the Niagara Peninsula, Prince Edward County, and the North Shore of Lake Erie.

Index

List of Maps

Acknowledgments

I could never have completed a project of this magnitude without the support of many people and organizations across Ontario and beyond.

I'm especially grateful for the assistance of the Canadian Tourism Commission and the Ontario Tourism Marketing Partnership, particularly the ever-helpful Helen Lovekin and Kattrin Sieber.

Thank you to Tourism Toronto, especially former media gal Justine Palinska. Also in Toronto, many thanks to Martha Chapman, Melanie Coates, Tracy Ford, Catherine Kaloutsky, Irene Knight, Jason Kucherawy, Laura Serena, and Dan Young.

Betsy Foster (Tourism Niagara) was a great help in the Niagara region, as were Clark Bernat, Colleen Cone, Holly Goertzen, Lynn Ogryzlo, Anne Robinson, Gloria Simon, Patty Szoldra and Ed Kuiper, Dianne Turner, and Helen Young.

Dana Borcea at Tourism Hamilton was a first-rate guide. I'm also grateful to Tracey Desjardins, Waterloo Regional Tourism Marketing Corporation; Cathy Rehberg, Stratford Tourism; and Marty Rice, Tourism London. More thanks to Katrena Johnston, Anne Lukin, Barrie McAndrews, Kimberley Payne, and Jenny Shantz.

In Southwestern Ontario, the team at Tourism Windsor, Essex, Pelee Island, especially Chris Ryan, Marina Garbutt, Kris Racine, and wine-and-food guru John Parent, were very helpful. Thanks, too, to Shannon Prince, Anna Walls, and Anne Marie Fortner, with bonus points to Sandra Laranja for the delicious breakfast and shelter from the Pelee Island storm.

Special thanks to the top-notch Ottawa Tourism team, especially Jantine Van Kregten and Yael Santo. Also in Ottawa, my gratitude to Caroline Ishii, Dave Loan, Shawn McCarthy, Laura Byrne Paquet, Paola St-Georges, and Shawna Wagman.

Anne Marie Forcier (Rideau Heritage Route Tourism Association) and Marie White (Lanark County Tourism) shared their enthusiasm for the Rideau region. Elsewhere in Eastern Ontario, I appreciated the support of Eileen Lum and the Northumberland Tourism staff, Greg Lister (Peterborough & the Kawarthas Tourism), Deanna Davies and Susan LeClair (St. Lawrence Parks Commission), Kathleen Kennedy and Melissa Larkin (Taste the County), Kathrine Christensen (1000 Islands Tourism), and Connie Markle (Tourism Kingston). Many thanks to Pam Brooks, Michael Burton, Ron Currie, Jackie DeKnock, Paul Fortier, the Irwin family, Jennifer Lyons, Anne Munro, Ben Sämann, and Julia Segal.

On the Bruce Peninsula, Jamie Lee Everatt and her colleagues at Bruce County Tourism offered invaluable assistance, as did innkeeper Ann Bard. Barbara Grison gets the official travel writer's assistant award, and I'm thankful to Dave Peebles and Evan LeBlanc for adopting me into their extended family for Thanksgiving dinner.

Bev Hughes (Georgian Bay Destination Development Partnership) efficiently squeezed scads of activities into one jam-packed week. Elsewhere along Georgian Bay, my thanks to Graham Lamb (Georgian Bay Islands National Park), Donna MacLeod (Rainbow Country Travel Association), Bill Brodeur, Maury and Annabelle East, Liz and Kurt Frost, Patti Kendall, Adele and Paul Malcew, and Keith Saulnier. Thank you to Kathleen Trainor and Pam Bothwright (Tourism Barrie), and in Huntsville, I'm grateful to Doug and Dee Howell.

My appreciation to Gladys King, Great Spirit Circle Trail, Manitoulin Island; Shawna Panas Cole, Sudbury Tourism; Ian McMillan, Tourism Sault Ste. Marie; Mike Morrow, CN/Algoma Central Railway; and to Ontario's Wilderness Region. In Temagami, extra kudos to Caryn Colman, chef Chantelle Mousseau, and guide Kevin Crowhurst (for sharing his regional knowledge and making me French press coffee at 6 A.M.).

A special shout-out to the crew at Ontario Parks, especially Lori Waldbrook, Mike

Armstrong (Awenda), Kenton Otterbein (Killbear), and the staffs at Bon Echo, Frontenac, Lake Superior, Petroglyphs, Presqu'ile, and Sandbanks Provincial Parks. Thanks, too, to Judy Hammond (Clear Communications) for her park advice and connections.

Toasts to my generous media colleagues at the Travel Media Association of Canada, with special cheers to Ron Brown ("Mr. Ontario") for sharing favorite places, Liz Campbell for her gracious hospitality, Evelyn Hannon ("Journeywoman") for wisdom and banana bread, Randall Shirley for tourism contacts, and Nancy Wigston for the parking space.

And for the many others across Ontario who provided timely tips and a warm welcome, you have my gratitude.

Many thanks to the awesome team at Avalon Travel, including Grace Fujimoto, Tabitha Lahr, Kevin McLain, Mike Morgenfeld, Jen Rios, and editor extraordinaire Sabrina Young.

Back home, my appreciation to Anne "Second Mom" Gorsuch and Hal "Second Dad" Siden, to Michaela and Talia for tolerating their rambling mother's messages about Mammoth Cheeses and other oddities, and to Alan, as always, for his love and support.

www.moon.com

DESTINATIONS | ACTIVITIES | BLOGS | MAPS | BOOKS

MOON.COM is ready to help plan your next trip! Filled with fresh trip ideas and strategies, author interviews, informative travel blogs, a detailed map library, and descriptions of all the Moon guidebooks, Moon.com is all you need to get out and explore the world—or even places in your own backyard. While at Moon.com, sign up for our monthly e-newsletter for updates on new releases, travel tips, and expert advice from our on-the-go Moon authors. As always, when you travel with Moon, expect an experience that is uncommon and truly unique.

KEEP UP WITH MOON ON FACEBOOK AND TWITTER
JOIN THE MOON PHOTO GROUP ON FLICKR

MAP SYMBOLS

▦	Expressway	◖	Highlight	✗	Airfield	⚲	Golf Course
	Primary Road	○	City/Town	✈	Airport	ⓟ	Parking Area
	Secondary Road	◉	State Capital	▲	Mountain	▰	Archaeological Site
	Unpaved Road	⊛	National Capital	✛	Unique Natural Feature	⌖	Church
	Trail	★	Point of Interest			⛽	Gas Station
	Ferry	•	Accommodation	≋	Waterfall	⬳	Glacier
	Railroad	▼	Restaurant/Bar	⬥	Park		Mangrove
	Pedestrian Walkway	■	Other Location	⊓	Trailhead		Reef
	Stairs	⋏	Campground	⛷	Skiing Area		Swamp

CONVERSION TABLES

$°C = (°F - 32) / 1.8$

$°F = (°C \times 1.8) + 32$

1 inch = 2.54 centimeters (cm)
1 foot = 0.304 meters (m)
1 yard = 0.914 meters
1 mile = 1.6093 kilometers (km)
1 km = 0.6214 miles
1 fathom = 1.8288 m
1 chain = 20.1168 m
1 furlong = 201.168 m
1 acre = 0.4047 hectares
1 sq km = 100 hectares
1 sq mile = 2.59 square km
1 ounce = 28.35 grams
1 pound = 0.4536 kilograms
1 short ton = 0.90718 metric ton
1 short ton = 2,000 pounds
1 long ton = 1.016 metric tons
1 long ton = 2,240 pounds
1 metric ton = 1,000 kilograms
1 quart = 0.94635 liters
1 US gallon = 3.7854 liters
1 Imperial gallon = 4.5459 liters
1 nautical mile = 1.852 km

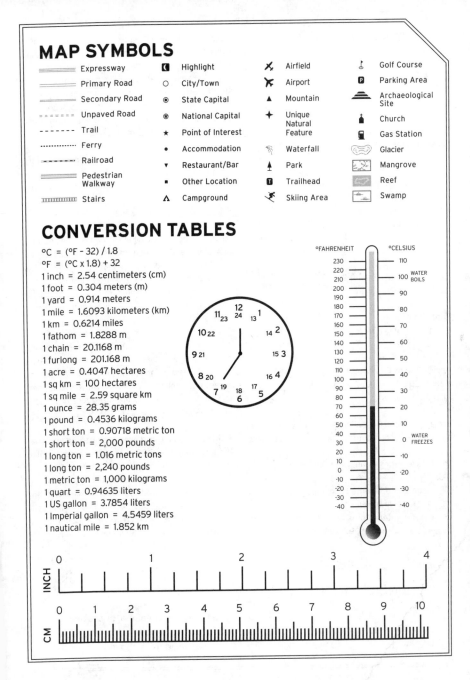

MOON ONTARIO

Avalon Travel
a member of the Perseus Books Group
1700 Fourth Street
Berkeley, CA 94710, USA
www.moon.com

Editor: Sabrina Young
Series Manager: Kathryn Ettinger
Copy Editor: Angela Buckley
Production and Graphics Coordinators: Tabitha Lahr,
    Kathryn Osgood, Christine DeLorenzo
Cover Designer: Tabitha Lahr
Map Editor: Mike Morgenfeld
Cartographers: Chris Henrick, Kaitlin Jaffe, Andrea
    Butkovic
Indexer: Greg Jewett

ISBN-13: 978-1-59880-341-9
ISSN: 2165-4506

Printing History
1st Edition – July 2012
5 4 3 2 1

Front cover photo: Killarney East Lighthouse ©
    Carolyn B. Heller
Title page photo: George Lake, Killarney Provincial
    Park © Carolyn B. Heller
Color frontmatter photos by © Carolyn B. Heller:
page 4, staff dressed as 19th-century soliders at Fort
George, Niagara-on-the-Lake; page 5 (left), sunset
over Lake Huron, Grand Bend; (middle), wine touring
in Niagara's Twenty Valley; (right), Hiking the Bruce
Trail, near Lion's Head; page 6 (icon), Ontario apples at
the St. Jacobs Farmers' Market; (bottom), Kayaks on
Wye Marsh, Midland; page 7 (top right), Royal Botanical
Gardens, Hamilton; (bottom right), Flowerpot Island
on the Bruce Peninsula; Pages 8-20.

Other Color frontmatter photos page 7 (top left),
Niagara Falls © Charles Masters/www.123rf.com;
(bottom left), Toronto city © mark52/www.123rf.com

Printed in Canada by Friesens

KEEPING CURRENT

If you have a favorite gem you'd like to see included in the next edition, or see anything
that needs updating, clarification, or correction, please drop us a line. Send your
comments via email to feedback@moon.com, or use the address above.